Lecture Notes of the Institute
for Computer Sciences, Social Informatics
and Telecommunications Engineering   322

More information about this series at http://www.springer.com/series/8197

Xuyun Zhang · Guanfeng Liu ·
Meikang Qiu · Wei Xiang ·
Tao Huang (Eds.)

Cloud Computing, Smart Grid and Innovative Frontiers in Telecommunications

9th EAI International Conference, CloudComp 2019
and 4th EAI International Conference, SmartGIFT 2019
Beijing, China, December 4–5, 2019, and December 21–22, 2019

Springer

Editors
Xuyun Zhang
Macquarie University
Sydney, NSW, Australia

Guanfeng Liu
Macquarie University
Sydney, NSW, Australia

Meikang Qiu
Pace University
New York, NY, USA

Wei Xiang 🄳
James Cook University
Cairns, QLD, Australia

Tao Huang 🄳
James Cook University
Smithfield, QLD, Australia

ISSN 1867-8211   ISSN 1867-822X (electronic)
Lecture Notes of the Institute for Computer Sciences, Social Informatics
and Telecommunications Engineering
ISBN 978-3-030-48512-2   ISBN 978-3-030-48513-9 (eBook)
https://doi.org/10.1007/978-3-030-48513-9

This Springer imprint is published by the registered company Springer Nature Switzerland AG
The registered company address is: Gewerbestrasse 11, 6330 Cham, Switzerland

Preface

We are delighted to introduce the proceedings the 9th edition of the European Alliance for Innovation (EAI) International Conference on Cloud Computing (CloudComp 2019). This conference brought researchers, developers, and practitioners from around the world together who are leveraging and developing cloud computing related technology for IoT and big data applications.

The technical program of CloudComp 2019 consisted of 48 full papers from several tracks. The conference tracks were: Track 1 – Cloud Architecture and Scheduling; Track 2 – Cloud-based Data Analytics; Track 3 – Cloud Applications; and Track 4 – Cloud Security and Privacy. Aside from the high-quality technical paper presentations, the technical program also featured three keynote speeches and a Distinguished Local Scholar Discussion Panel. The three keynote speeches were delivered by Prof. Michael Sheng from Macquarie University, Australia, Prof. Yew-soon Ong from Nanyang Technological University, Singapore, and Prof. Longbing Cao from University of Technology Sydney, Australia. The scholars who sat on the Distinguished Local Scholar Discussion Panel were Principle Scientist Surya Nepal from CSIRO's Data61, Australia, Prof. Shui Yu from University of Technology Sydney, Australia, Dr. Lina Yao from University of New South Wales, Australia, Dr. Qiang He from Swinburne University of Technology, Australia, Dr. Dong Yuan from The University of Sydney, Australia, and Dr. Jia Wu from Macquarie University, Australia. The panel discussion aimed to gain insights into key challenges and an understanding of the state-of-the-art cloud computing technologies to develop and implement future cloud and edge computing related services and applications.

Coordination with the Steering Committee chairs, Imrich Chlamtac, Victor C. M. Leung, and Kun Yang was essential for the success of the conference. We sincerely appreciate their constant support and guidance. It was also a great pleasure to work with such an excellent Organizing Committee, and we thank them for their hard work in organizing and supporting the conference. In particular, we thank the Technical Program Committee (TPC), led by our TPC co-chairs, Dr. Deepak Puthal, Dr. Chi Yang, and Dr. Zhiyuan Tan, who organized the peer-review process of technical papers and made a high-quality technical program. We are also grateful to the conference manager, Karolina Marcinova, for her support and to all the authors who submitted their papers to the CloudComp 2019 conference.

We strongly believe that the CloudComp 2019 conference provides a good forum for all researchers, developers, and practitioners to discuss all science and technology aspects that are relevant to cloud and edge computing. We also expect that the future CloudComp conferences will be as successful and stimulating, as indicated by the contributions presented in this volume.

April 2020

Xuyun Zhang
Guanfeng Liu
Meikang Qiu

Preface

Preface

We are delighted to introduce the proceedings of the second edition of the European Alliance for Innovation (EAI) International Conference on Smart Grid Inspired Future Technologies (SmartGIFT 2019). This conference brought researchers, developers, and practitioners from around the world together who are leveraging and developing smart grid technology for a smarter and more resilient grid. The theme of SmartGIFT 2019 was "Smart Grid and Innovative Frontiers in Telecommunications".

The technical program of SmartGIFT 2019 consisted of 14 full papers, including 3 invited papers in oral presentation sessions at the main conference track. Aside from the high-quality technical paper presentations, the technical program also featured a keynote speech. The keynote speech was presented by Prof. Zhaocheng Wang from Tsinghua University, Beijing, China. This keynote speech was focused on the technology of AI-based low-power millimeter wave communications.

Coordination with the Steering Committee chairs, Imrich Chlamtac, Victor C. M. Leung, and Kun Yang was essential for the success of the conference. We sincerely appreciate their constant support and guidance. It was also a great pleasure to work with such an excellent Organizing Committee, and we thank them for their hard work in organizing and supporting the conference. In particular, we thank the Technical Program Committee (TPC), led by our TPC chair, Dr Tao Huang, who completed the peer-review process of technical papers and made a high-quality technical program. We are also grateful to the conference manager, Lukas Skolek, for his support and to all the authors who submitted their papers to the SmartGIFT 2019 conference and workshops.

We strongly believe that the SmartGIFT conference provides a good forum for all researcher, developers, and practitioners to discuss all science and technology aspects that are relevant to smart grids. We also expect that the future SmartGIFT conference will be as successful and stimulating, as indicated by the contributions presented in this volume.

April 2020   Wei Xiang

Organization CloudComp 2019

Steering Committee

Imrich Chlamtac   University of Trento, Italy

Organizing Committee

General Chair

Xuyun Zhang   Macquarie University, Australia

General Co-chairs

Xuyun Zhang   Macquarie University, Australia
Meikang Qiu   Pace University, USA

TPC Chair and Co-chair

Deepak Puthal	University of Technology Sydney, Australia
Chi Yang	Huazhong University of Science and Technology, China
Hiyuan Tan	Edinburgh Napier University, UK

Sponsorship and Exhibit Chair

Daniel Sun   CSIRO, Australia

Local Chair

Dong Yuan   The University of Sydney, Australia

Workshops Chair

Lianyong Qi   Qufu Normal University, China

Publicity and Social Media Chairs

Qiang He	Swinburne University of Technology, Australia
Hao Wang	Norwegian University of Science and Technology, Norway

Publications Chairs

Shaohua Wan	Zhongnan University of Economics and Law, China
Xiaolong Xu	Nanjing University of Information Science and Technology, China

Web Chair

Meng Liu	Shandong University, China

Conference Manager

Karolina Marcinova	EAI

Technical Program Committee

Fiza Abdul Rahim	University of the Southern Queensland, Australia
Chaodit Aswakul	Chulalongkorn University, Thailand
Zhifeng Bao	Royal Melbourne Institute of Technology University, Australia
Lili Bo	China University of Mining and Technology, China
Maria Dolores Cano	Universidad Politécnica de Cartagena, Spain
Liqun Chen	Southeast University, China
Lianhua Chi	IBM Research Center
Manuel Fernandez-Veiga	atlanTTic, University of Vigo, Spain
Jidong Ge	Nanjing University, China
Ruili Geng	Spectral MD, USA
Wenwen Gong	China Agriculture University, China
Ying Guo	Qingdao University of Science and Technology, China
Debiao He	Wuhan University, China
Yu-Chen Hu	Providence University, USA
Tao Huang	Silicon Lake University, USA
Md. Kafiul	Islam Independent University, Bangladesh
Juwook Jang	Sogang University, South Korea
Rossi Kamal	Shanto-Mariam University of Creative Technology, Bangladesh
Santanu Koley	Birla Institute of Science and Technology, India
Xin Li	Nanjing University of Aeronautics and Astronautics, China
Zhixu Li	Soochow University, China
Wenmin Lin	Hangzhou Dianzi University, China
An Liu	Soochow University, China
Liangfu Lu	Tianjing University, China
Mahesh Maddumala	University of Missouri, USA
Tamim Al Mahmud	Green University of Bangladesh, Bangladesh
Sofia Meacham	Bournemouth University, UK
Shunmei Meng	Nanjing University of Science and Technology, China
Syeda Naqvi	University of Engineering and Technology, Pakistan
Khine Moe	New University of Computer Studies, Myanmar
Ashish Payal	Guru Gobind Singh Indraprastha University, India
Kai Peng	Huaqiao University, China
Leonard Poon	The Education University of Hong Kong, Hong Kong

Amit Sehgal	G.L. Bajaj Institute of Technology and Management, India
Manik Sharma	DAV University, India
Patrick Siarry	Université Paris Est Créteil, France
Daniel Sun	CSIRO, Australia
Jianyong Sun	Xi'an Jiaotong University, China
Wenda Tang	Lancaster University, UK
Jing Tian	National University of Singapore, Singapore
Shaohua Wan	Zhongnan University of Economics and Law, China
Ding Wang	Peking University, China
Jinwei Wang	Nanjing University of Information Science and Technology, China
Liangmin Wang	Jiangsu University, China
Mingzhong Wang	University of the Sunshine Coast, Australia
Yiping Wen	Hunan University of Science and Technology, China
Yirui Wu	Hohai University, China
Ying Xie	Anhui University, China
Rongbin Xu	Anhui University, China
Tao Xu	Northwestern Polytechnical University, China
Chao Yan	Qufu Normal University, China
Ching-Nung Yang	Taiwan Dong Hwa University, Taiwan
Xiangnan Zhang	China Agriculture University, China
Gaofeng Zhang	Hefei University of Technology, China
Jie Zhang	Nanjing University, China
Xuan Zhao	Nanjing University, China
Chunjie Zhou	Ludong University, China
Yun Zhou	Shaanxi Normal University, China

Organization SmartGIFT 2019

Steering Committee

Imrich Chlamtac   University of Trento, Italy
Victor C. M. Leung   The University of British Columbia, Canada
Kun Yang   University of Essex, UK

Organizing Committee

General Chair

Wei Xiang   James Cook University, Australia

General Co-chair

Lin Cao   Beijing Information Science and Technology
                         University, China

TPC Chair

Tao Huang   James Cook University, Australia

Local Chair

Xuehua Li   Beijing Information Science and Technology
                         University, China

Publicity and Social Media Chair

Xinwei Yue   Beijing Information Science and Technology
                         University, China

Publications Chair

Yuanyuan Yao   Beijing Information Science and Technology
                         University, China

Panels Chair

Yanxiao Zhao   Beijing Information Science and Technology
                         University, China

Posters and PhD Track Chair

Peiran Song   Beijing Information Science and Technology
                         University, China

Web Chair

Eric Wang   James Cook University, Australia

Conference Manager

Lukáš Školek   EAI

Technical Program Committee

Haibin Zhang	Xidian University, China
Mehboob Ul Amin	University of Kashmir, India
Kelvin Anoh	Manchester Metropolitan University, UK
Muhannad Bakir	Georgia Institute of Technology, USA
Xiaoxiong Gu	IBM, USA
Aqdas Naveed Malik	International Islamic University, Pakistan
Minglei You	Durham University, UK
Yinghua Han	Northeastern University at Qinhuangdao, China
Suhong Yang	Northeastern University, USA
Radhakrishna Achanta	IVRL-EPFL, Switzerland
Yves Rozenholc	USPC, France
Xiaoheng Jiang	Zhengzhou University, China
Darui Jin	Beijing University of Aeronautics and Astronautics, China
Xiangzhi Bai	Beihang University, China
Yuan Zhuang	Southeast University, China
Pan Cao	University of Hertfordshire, UK
Yongpeng Wu	Shanghai Jiao Tong University, China
Jiangnan Li	University of Tennessee, USA
Xiangyu Niu	University of Tennessee, USA
Israa Aziz	Huazhong University of Science and Technology, China
Hai Jin	Huazhong University of Science and Technology, China
Dileep K. Verma	Research Center for Information Technology Innovation
Ronald Chang	Research Center for Information Technology Innovation (CITI)
Bing Wang	James Cook University, Australia
Dezhi Li	Harbin Institute of Technology, China
He Yu	Changchun University, China
Tao Huang	James Cook University, Australia
Shushi Gu	Harbin Institute of Technology, China
Jacob Crandall	Brigham Young University, USA
Mihir Laghate	UCLA, USA
Ding Xu	Nanjing University of Posts and Telecommunications, China

Ling Luo	SGCC, China
Ju Ren	Central South University, China
Junying Hu	Central South University, China
Deyu Zhang	Central South University, China
Hui Guo	Central South University, China
Hyungeun Choi	Sogang University, South Korea
Seunghyoung Ryu	Sogang University, South Korea
Hongseok Kim	Missouri University, USA
Ying-Chin Lin	Feng Chia University, Taiwan
Yu-Min Zhang	Feng Chia University, Taiwan
Yen Hung Chen	University of Taipei, Taiwan
Wei-Kuang Wang	Feng Chia University, Taiwan
Liansheng Tan	Central China Normal University, China
Zhaohui Yang	Southeast University, China
Wei Xu	Southeast University, China
Yijin Pan	Southeast University, China
Cunhua Pan	Queen Mary University of London, UK
Ming Chen	National Mobile Communications Research, Laboratory, Southeast University, China
Amritpal Singh	Guru Nanak Dev University, India
Harjit Singh	Guru Nanak Dev University, India
Jurong Bai	University of Posts and Telecommunications, China
Muhammad Asim	National University of Computer and Emerging Sciences, Pakistan
Aswin Raj C.	Amrita Vishwa Vidyapeetham University, India
Qingsi Wang	University of Michigan, USA
Mingyan Liu	University of Michigan, USA
Rahul Jain	University of California, USA
Anwer Al-Dulaimi	EXFO Inc., Canada
Khaled Elbassioni	Khalifa University of Science and Technology, UAE
Trung Thanh Nguyen	Hai Phong University, Vietnam
Mardavij Roozbehani	Massachusetts Institute of Technology, USA
Sofana Reka. S	Vellore Institute of Technology, India
Tomislav Dragicevic	Aalborg University, Denmark
S. R. Sahaya Prabaharan	SRM Institute of Science and Technology, India
Pierluigi Siano	University of Salerno, Italy
Kai Ma	Yanshan University, China
Cailian Chen	Shanghai Jiao Tong University, China
Hao Liang	University of Alberta, Canada
Bing Wang	James Cook University, Australia
Roberto DiCecco	University of Toronto, Canada
Lin Sun	University of Toronto, Canada
Paul Chow	University of Toronto, Canada
Sisi Liu	James Cook University, Australia
Yun Liang	Peking University, China
Liqiang Lu	Peking University, China

Qingcheng Xiao	Peking University, China
Shengen Yan	SenseTime Group, Hong Kong
Hui Tian	Beijing University of Posts and Telecommunications, China
Weipeng Guan	South China University of Technology, China
Hongbin Liu	James Cook University, Australia
Bhalchandra Hardas	Visvesvaraya National Institute of Technology, India
Shengda Tang	Central China Normal University, China
Shailesh Chaudhari	University of California, USA
Danijela Cabric	UCLA, USA
Yunfei Chen	University of Warwick, UK
Hee-Seok Oh	Seoul National University, South Korea
Sixing Yin	Beijing University of Posts and Telecommunications, China
Shufang Li	Beijing University of Posts and Telecommunications, China
Dawei Chen	The Hong Kong University of Science and Technology, Hong Kong
Tong Tong	Imperial Vision, China
Gen Li	Imperial Vision, China
Xiejie Liu	Imperial Vision, China
Qinquan Gao	Imperial Vision, China
Zhaowen Wang	Adobe, USA
Ding Liu	University of Illinois, USA
Jianchao Yang	University of Illinois, USA
Kun Xiao	Guangxi Normal University, China
Xiaole Cui	Peking University ShenZhen Graduate School, China
Xiaoxin Cui	Peking University, China
Paragkumar Thadesar	Georgia Institute of Technology, USA
He Yu	Chang chun University, China
Jeany Son	Seoul National University, South Korea
Kang Han	James Cook University, Australia
Weidang Lu	Zhejiang University of Technology, China
Guangzhe Liu	Zhejiang University of Technology, China
Bo Li	Harbin Institute of Technology, China
Chandresh D. Parekha	Raksha Shakti University, India
Tingting Liu	Beihang University, China
Xiangyang Wang	Southeast University, China
Hiroki Baba	NTT Network Technology Laboratories, Japan
Hucheng Wang	Beijing University of Posts and Telecommunications, China
Shanzhi Chen	Datang Telecom Technology and Industry Group, China
Hongming Yang	Changsha University of Science and Technology, China
Jing Qiu	The University of Newcastle, Australia

A. S. M. Ashraf Mahmud	Heriot Watt University, UK
Bharat J. R. Sahu	Sungkyunkwan University, South Korea
Jing Lei	National University of Defense Technology, China
Dezhi Li	Harbin Engineering University, China
Al-Sakib Khan Pathan	Southeast University, Bangladesh
Lihui Feng	Beijing Institute of Technology, China
Aiying Yang	Beijing Institute of Technology, China
Xiansheng Guo	University of Electronic Science and Technology of China, China
Han Xiao	Ocean University of China, China
Hao Zhang	Ocean University of China, China
Zengfeng Wang	Ludong University, China
Aaron Gulliver	University of Victoria, Canada
Ming-li Lu	NDSC, Zhengzhou University, China
Bruno Carpentieri	University of Bozen-Bolzano, Italy
Kyung Sup Kwak	Inha University, South Korea
Guoqiang Zheng	Henan University of Science and Technology, China
Geng Yang	Royal Institute of Technology (KTH), Sweden
Li Xie	Royal Institute of Technology (KTH), Sweden
Qiang Chen	Royal Institute of Technology (KTH), Sweden
Matti Mantysalo	Tampere University of Technology, Finland
Xiaolin Zhou	Fudan University, China
Zhibo Pang	ABB Corporate Research, Sweden
Sharon Kao-Walter	Blekinge Institute of Technology (BTH), Sweden
Li-Rong Zheng	Royal Institute of Technology (KTH), Sweden
HanSeok Kim	System Design Laboratory, Network Division, Samsung Electronics, South Korea
Tong Zhang	Beijing University of Posts and Telecommunications, China
Shatarupa Dash	Sungkyunkwan University, South Korea
Navrati Saxena	Sungkyunkwan University, South Korea
Abhishek Roy	System Design Laboratory, Network Division, Samsung Electronics, South Korea
Wei Li	National University of Defense Technology, China
Chunlin Xiong	National University of Defense Technology, China
Ji-Bo Wei	National University of Defense Technology, China
Tao Wang	Shanghai University, China
Qi Huang	University of Electronic Science and Technology of China, China
Jian Li	University of Electronic Science and Technology of China, China
Jie Wu	Sichuan Provincial Key Lab of Power System Wide-Area Measurement and Control, China
Wei Zhen	Sichuan Provincial Key Lab of Power System Wide-Area Measurement and Control, China

Jiasheng Liu	Harbin Institute of Technology, China
Zhang Sheng-qing	Southeast University, China
Jian-Chiun Liou	National Kaohsiung University of Applied Sciences, Taiwan
Kang Han	James Cook University, Australia
Lingyu Zhou	University of Electronic Science and Technology of China, China
Yu Han	Harbin Institute of Technology, China
Shi Jing	University of Electronic Science and Technology of China, China
Bing Wang	James Cook University, Australia
Priyanka Mishra	SHUATS, India
Sheraz Alam	National University of Modern Languages, Pakistan
Rana Abbas	The University of Sydney, Australia

Contents

Cloud-Based Data Analytics

Cloud Applications

Cloud Security and Privacy

Smart Grid and Innovative Frontiers in Telecommunications

Cloud Architecture and Scheduling

MCOPS-SPM: Multi-Constrained Optimized Path Selection Based Spatial Pattern Matching in Social Networks

Ying Guo[1(✉)], Lianzhen Zheng[1], Yuhan Zhang[1], and Guanfeng Liu[2]

[1] Qingdao University of Science and Technology, Qingdao 266061, Shandong, China
guoying@qust.edu.cn
[2] Macquarie University, Sydney, Australia

Abstract. In this paper, we study the multi-constrained optimized path selection based spatial pattern matching in Location-Based Social Network (MCOPS-SPM). Given a set D including spatial objects (each with a social identity and a social reputation) and social relationships (e.g., trust degree, social intimacy) between them. We aim at finding all connections (paths) of objects from D that match a user-specified multi-constraints spatial pattern P. A pattern P is a complex network where vertices represent spatial objects, and edges denote social relationships between them. The MCOPS-SPM query returns all the instances that satisfy P. Answering such queries is computationally intractable, and we propose algorithms to solve the multi-constrained optimized path matching problem and guide the join order of the paths in the query results. An extensive empirical study over real-world datasets has demonstrated the effectiveness and efficiency of our approach.

Keywords: Location-Based Social Network · Multiple constraints · Optimized path selection · Spatial Pattern Matching

1 Introduction

The emerging Location-Based Social Network (LBSN) attracts a large number of participants. Foursquare, Twitter and other applications make it easy for people to mark their locations. This has aroused widespread interests among researchers. In LBSN, Multi-Constrained Optimized Path Selection (MCOPS) has become a challenging problem. In this paper, we study a Spatial Pattern Matching (SPM) problem based on MCOPS, that is, in the LBSN, to find all the matches satisfying multi-constrained path pattern P in the space objects set D. The multi-constraints in P include keyword constraint, distance constraint, and social impact factors (trust, intimacy, social reputation) constraints. The related Spatial Keyword Query (SKQ) and Graph Pattern Matching (GPM) have been extensively studied.

In general, a spatial-keyword query (SKQ) [1–4] returns spatial objects that are spatially close to each other and match the keywords. For example, top-k keyword query [5], takes the spatial location and a set of keywords as parameters, returning k spatio-textual

X. Zhang et al. (Eds.): CloudComp 2019/SmartGift 2019, LNICST 322, pp. 3–19, 2020.
https://doi.org/10.1007/978-3-030-48513-9_1

objects that well meet the user's requirements, and the k objects are sorted according to the proximity of the query location and the relevance of the query keywords. Although SKQ plays an important role in geo-location-oriented applications (e.g., Google Maps), however, with the continuous emergence of new application scenarios, the requirements of users are increasingly diversified, which results in the returned query results not meeting the needs of users [6]. Moreover, various relationships between social network participants (e.g., location relationships, social relationships) are not well represented. Suppose that a user wishes to find a supplier, which is close to a bank and is far from a retailer and a whole-seller. SKQ will return objects that are spatially close to each other as shown in the dashed box in Fig. 1(a). However, users generally have restrictions on the spatial objects of the query (e.g., the supplier is at least 10 km away from the retailer in Fig. 1(b)). Therefore, the objects connected by the solid line in Fig. 1(a) are the answer to the query that the user really wants. Second, simply using spatial indexing structures (such as R-tree and their variants) requires dynamically creating an index for each vertex, which results in serious overhead [7]. Therefore, the solution to the SKQ problem cannot be directly applied to the MCOPS-SPM problem.

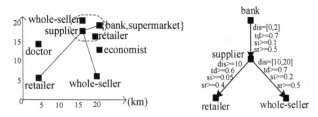

Fig. 1. MCOPS-SPM examples

In general, graph pattern matching (GPM) aims to find all matches of P in data graph G according to a given pattern graph P [8]. However, using GPM algorithms to solve MCOPS-SPM problem is not straightforward because (1) the solution to the GPM problem is primarily designed for the data structure of the graph, rather than spatio-textual objects indexed by an IR-tree index structure, (2) in the pattern graph, only a single constraint (such as hops or distances) among vertices is generally considered. Therefore, if GPM is used to solve the MCOPS-SPM problem, it is necessary to convert the spatial objects into graphs and extend the distance-based constraint to multi-constraints. The experiments in [7] prove that it is not efficient.

There are few studies on Spatial Pattern Matching (SPM). [9] proposed a database query language based on time mode, spatial mode and spatiotemporal mode. In [7], a SPM algorithm is proposed, but only a single constraint (different expression of distance constraint) is considered, which cannot meet the requirements of the user's multiple constraints.

We use an example in [10] to illustrate the importance of specifying multiple constraints for query keywords. In business activities, the pattern graph can be specified to look for keywords about suppliers, retailers, whole-sellers, banks in the social network.

The supplier directly or indirectly provides the retailer, whole-seller with products. Suppliers, retailers, whole-sellers obtain services directly or indirectly from the same bank. As shown in Fig. 1, the user specifies the supplier is at least 10 km from the retailer and the trust value is at least 0.6, the intimacy is at least 0.05, and the social reputation is at least 0.4 in the field. However, SKQ and GPM tend to ignore the distance constraint and social impact factor constraints of these problems, and the results of the query are often not of the most interest to the users.

In order to facilitate users to specify the spatial relationships between the keywords and the social relationships, we propose a multi-constrained optimized path selection based spatial pattern matching query (MCOPS-SPM). As shown in Fig. 1, given a set of spatial objects D (Fig. 1 (a)) and a spatial path pattern P (Fig. 1 (b)), MCOPS-SPM returns all matches about P in D. The pattern P is a complex network in which vertices represent spatial objects associated with keywords, edges represent spatial distance relationships between objects, and social relationships. For example, the distance between the user-specified bank and the supplier is [0, 2] (km), the trust value is at least 0.7, the intimacy is at least 0.1, and the social reputation is at least 0.5. In this example, the four objects connected by solid lines satisfy all constraints in P, which is a match of pattern P.

The main research contents of this paper are as follows:

1. We first proposed Multi-Constrained Optimized Path Matching algorithm (MCOPM). Different from the traditional path selection algorithms, MC-SPM based on MCOPS aims to find the matching of the spatial path pattern P in D. The vertices of the matching results satisfy the query keywords, and satisfy the spatial relationship and social relationship among the spatial objects. This will well support LBSN-based applications.
2. In general, participants and social relationships in social networks are relatively stable for a long period of time. We use IR-tree as an index structure, which is more effective in keyword search and distance pruning. It can effectively reduce search space and improve effectiveness.
3. Based on the IR-tree index structure, we propose an IR-tree based multi-constrained optimized path matching algorithm, namely IR-MCOPM. Matches of the multiple constrained paths of P in D can be found.
4. After mapping all the edges in P to corresponding paths in D, they need to be connected in a certain order to form a complete answer. Therefore, a sampling-based estimation algorithm is proposed to guide the connection order of the paths at the matching result in an efficient way, namely MCPJoin.

The rest of this paper is organized as follows. We first review the related work on SKQ and GPM in Sect. 2. Then we introduce the necessary concepts and formulate the focal problem of this paper in Sect. 3. Section 4 presents our solutions MCOPM, IR-MCOPM, MCPJoin algorithms. We report experimental results in Sect. 5 and conclude in Sect. 6.

2 Related Works

The most related works about spatial pattern matching are spatial keyword query and graph pattern matching. Below we analyze each of them in detail.

2.1 Spatial Keyword Query (SKQ)

In general, researches on SKQ issues can be roughly divided into two types. The first is m-Closest Keywords query [1, 11]. Given spatial data D, the mCK query returns a collection of objects that are spatially close to each other. The objects in the collection satisfy the m keywords specified by the user. [1] proposes an index structure of bR*-tree, and uses distance and keyword constraints to reduce the search space.

The second is the top-k SKQ. Top-k SKQ returns the objects with the highest sorting scores, determined by the sorting function, which takes into account both spatial proximity and text correlation [12]. In order to improve the efficiency of the query, some index structures are proposed, which can be divided into two types of structures depending on the method used. One is an R-Tree based index structure, such as: KR*-Tree [13], Hybrid Spatial-Keyword Indexing (SKI) [14], IR-tree [15], Spatial Inverted Index (S2I) [5], The other is a grid-based index structure, such as: Spatial-Keyword Inverted File (SKIF) [16]. In [17], the author used W-IBR-Tree (using keyword partitioning and inverted bitmaps to organize spatial objects) to solve the joint top-k SKQ problem. Recently, [18] proposed why the answer is why-not (SKQ), returning the result of the smallest modified query containing the expected answer. In [19], in order to improve the query efficiency in space, semantics and text dimensions, the NIQ-tree and LHQ-tree hybrid indexing methods are proposed, and the similarity in these three dimensions is used to prune the search space.

However, our proposed MCOPS-SPM can more clearly reflect users' needs. The MCOPS-SPM problem is also related to the multi-way spatial join [20]. In [21], the vertices in the data graph G are transformed into points in the vector space by the graph embedding method, which converts pattern matching queries into distance-based multi-paths-joining problems on vector space. However, in these solutions, the keyword attributes and multi-constraints between objects are not considered, so they cannot be directly applied to the MCOPS-SPM solution.

2.2 Graph Pattern Matching (GPM)

There are two types of GPM issues in the references. The first one is subgraph isomorphism [10, 22–24]. The subgraph isomorphism is an exact match between the data graph and the pattern graph. It aims to find the subgraph that exactly matches the pattern graph on the nodes and edges properties in the data graph [25]. [25] indicates that the subgraph isomorphism requires too strict conditions and poor scalability, and it is difficult to find a useful matching pattern in the data graph.

The second type of GPM problem is graph simulation. [26–28] pointed out that the graph simulation has more loose constraints, and it is convenient to search the data graph for the subgraph matching the specified pattern P. The returned subgraph can well meet the users' requirements, but it still needs to execute the edge to edge mapping, which is still very harsh for applications that need to meet the specified path length. In order to solve the above problem, a bounded simulation is proposed in [8], in which each node has an attribute, each edge is associated with the path length (hops), and the value of each edge is One of len and *, len indicates that the path length cannot exceed len, and * indicates that there is no constraint on the path length. The bounded simulation maps the edges in pattern P to paths that meet the specified length in the data graph, further reducing the strict constraints, thereby better capturing users' intents.

There are some algorithms that connect the searched edges in a certain order [21]. In [21], an MDJ (Multi-Distance-Join) algorithm is proposed to guide the connection order of edges. In [10], the author proposed an R-join algorithm based on reachability conditions, using the B^+-tree structure as the index method.

However, the solutions above mentioned are based on a single constraint algorithm, and can not meet the requirements of multiple constraints specified by users, so these methods can not be directly applied to the MCOPS-SPM problem.

3 Problem Definition

3.1 Social Impact Factors

Social networks can be modeled as directed graphs, and we use $G = (V, E)$ to express social networks. Where $V = \{v_1, v_2, \ldots, v_n\}$ represents a collection of vertices, each vertex v_i represents a participant in a social network. $E = \{e_1, e_2, \ldots, e_m\}$ is a collection representing edges, each edge e_j represents an interaction or social relationships between two participants. However, the factors that influence social networks are always diverse, and we cannot draw precise conclusions based on a single condition. We propose four factors that influence social networks:

Social Identities. In a social network, each participant has his or her own identities, represented by keywords $k(v_i)$. Each participant may have multiple identities (for example, a digital blogger may be a student at a university), so the social identities help describe the social roles of participants.

Trust Degree. In a social network, trust degree refers to the level of trust that one participant forms in the interaction process with another participant. Let $td(v_i, v_j) \in [0, 1]$ indicate the trust degree that participant v_i evaluates v_j. If $td(v_i, v_j) = 1$, it represents that v_i completely trusts v_j while $td(v_i, v_j) = 0$ represents v_i wholly distrusts v_j.

Social Intimacy. In social networks, intimacy refers to the degree of intimacy formed between participants during the participation of social activities. It reflects the frequency of interaction between the two participants. $si(v_i, v_j) \in [0, 1]$ reflects the degree of intimacy between v_i and v_j. When $si(v_i, v_j) = 1$, it expresses that v_i and v_j are the most intimate. On the contrary, they have the least intimate social relationships.

Social Reputation. In social networks, social reputation refers to the extent to which a participant contributes in the field. It reflects the extent to which all participants rated this participant. Let $sr(v_i) \in [0, 1]$ denote social reputations in the domain. Here $sr(v_i) = 1$ represents that v_i has won the best reputations in the domain. Otherwise, there is no foothold for v_i in this field.

3.2 Social Impact Factor Aggregations

In order to meet the requirements of different conditions of users, the match of an edge in the pattern P may be a path in the data graph G. Then we need to aggregate the social impact factors along this path [29].

Trust Degree Aggregation. The aggregation of trust degree between source participants and target participants can be calculated according to the following formula [29]:

$$td(p) = \prod_{(v_i, v_j) \in p} td(v_i, v_j) \tag{1}$$

Where, p represents a complete path from the source participant to the target participant, (v_i, v_j) represents the path between v_i and v_j.

Social Intimacy Aggregation. The social intimacy aggregation between the source participant and the target participant is calculated according to the following formula [29]:

$$si(p) = \frac{\prod_{(v_i, v_j) \in p} si(v_i, v_j)}{\varepsilon^\sigma} \tag{2}$$

Where, ε denotes the length (hops) of the path from the source participant to the target participant, σ is called the attenuation factor that controls the decay rate.

Social Reputation Aggregation. The social reputation aggregation on the path p is calculated according to the following formula [29]:

$$sr(p) = \frac{\sum_{i=2}^{n-1} sr(v_i)}{n - 2} \tag{3}$$

Here, in addition to the source and target participants, a weighted average of their social reputations is made to express the social reputation about the path p.

3.3 Multi-constrained Path Pattern

The multi-constrained path pattern P is a complex social network (for convenience of description, we will collectively refer to pattern P below). P = (V, E, KV, MCE) obeys the following constraints:

- V and E are the vertex and edge sets in P respectively;
- $KV(V_i)$ is a collection of keywords (social identities) that the user specifies on vertices v_i;
- For $(u, v) \in E$, MCE(u, v) is the multi-constraints that users specified on edge (u, v). MCE(u, v) = {dis(u, v), td(u, v), si(u, v), sr(u, v)}, $\forall \varphi \in$ {td, si, sr}, $\varphi \in [0, 1]$. Where, dis(u, v) denotes their distance limits in real world. We assume the distance metric is Euclidean.

For example, in the pattern P of Fig. 1(b), the limit of distance between bank and supplier is at [0, 2] km, trust degree is no less than 0.7, social intimacy is not less than 0.1, social reputation is no less than 0.5.

3.4 Multi-constraints Path Match

In pattern P, for any two vertices v_i and v_j, for any two spatial objects o_i and o_j in spatial database D, when the following conditions are met:

- $k(o_i) \supseteq k(v_i), k(o_j) \supseteq k(v_j)$;
- $td(o_i, o_j) \geq Q_{td}(v_i, v_j)$, $si(o_i, o_j) \geq Q_{si}(v_i, v_j)$, $sr(o_i, o_j) \geq Q_{sr}(v_i, v_j)$,   where $Q_{td}(v_i, v_j)$, $Q_{si}(v_i, v_j)$, $Q_{sr}(v_i, v_j)$ represent trust degree, social intimacy, social reputation constraints on edge (v_i, v_j) respectively;
- The distance constraint between o_i and o_j holds one of the following conditions:

    1) $dis(o_i, o_j) \geq distL(v_i, v_j)$
    2) $0 \leq dis(o_i, o_j) \leq distU(v_i, v_j)$
    3) $distL(v_i, v_j) \leq dis(o_i, o_j) \leq distU(v_i, v_j)$

Where, $distL(v_i, v_j)$ and $distU(v_i, v_j)$ are the lower distance limit and the upper distance limit on path (v_i, v_j) respectively;

We call o_i and o_j constitute a multi-constraints path match on path (v_i, v_j).

3.5 Match

Given a pattern P and a set O of objects, O is a match of P if: (1) for each path of P, there is a multi-constraints path match in O; (2) all objects in O are elements that match a certain edge in pattern P.

Problem 1 (Multi-Constrained Optimized Path Selection Based Spatial Pattern Matching, MCOPS-SPM). Given a pattern P, MCOPS-SPM returns all the matches of P in D.

In Fig. 1(a), for instance, the four objects connected in solid lines match the pattern in Fig. 1(b), and it is the answer of this MCOPS-SPM query.

Lemma 1 (Hardness). The MCOPS-SPM problem is NP-hard.

Proof. The MCOPS-SPM problem can be reduced to the spatial pattern matching problem. The SPM problem is NP-hard, which can be found in this paper [7].

4 Algorithm Design

4.1 Multi-Constrained Optimized Path Matching Algorithm (MCOPM)

To improve the quality of the solution, the MCOPM algorithm consists of two phases: reverse search (Reverse_Search_Dijkstra, RSD) and forward search (Forward_Search_Dijkstra, FSD). The RSD is executed in the direction from the target node to the source node to determine whether MCOPM exists (ie, from a path of pattern P to a mapping of D that satisfies multiple constraints). If there is a feasible solution, then the FSD is executed in the direction from the source node to the target node to determine whether there are better solutions. The detailed execution flow of the algorithm is as follows:

Step1: Perform RSD. From the target node to the source node, the Dijkstra algorithm is used to find the path with the smallest objective function value and record the aggregated values of each node from the target node to the intermediate node. The objective function [29] is defined as follows:

$$h(p) \triangleq \max \left(\frac{1 - td(p)}{1 - Q_{td}(p)}, \frac{1 - si(p)}{1 - Q_{si}(p)}, \frac{1 - sr(p)}{1 - Q_{sr}(p)} \right) \qquad (4)$$

Where, $td(p)$, $si(p)$, $sr(p)$ respectively represent the trust degree, social intimacy, and social reputation value of the aggregation on the path p. $Q_{td}(p)$, $Q_{si}(p)$, $Q_{sr}(p)$ respectively represent the corresponding constraints specified by users on the path p. It can be seen from Eq. (4) that only the aggregated values on the path all satisfy the constraints, we have $h(p) \leq 1$; if there is an aggregate value that does not satisfy the corresponding constraint, we have $h(p) > 1$.

Step2: If $h(p) \leq 1$, it means that there is a feasible path, that is, there is a match of multiple-constraints-edge, and go to Step 3 to continue execution; if $h(p) > 1$, it means that there is no feasible path, and the algorithm terminates.

Step3: Execute the FSD from the source node to the target node. According to the Dijkstra algorithm, we want to find the path that can maximize the path quality function [29]. The path quality function is defined as follows:

$$U(p) = \alpha \times td(p) + \beta \times si(p) + \gamma \times sr(p) \qquad (5)$$

Here, α, β, γ are the weights of $td(p)$, $si(p)$, $sr(p)$ respectively, $\forall \varphi \in \{\alpha, \beta, \gamma\}$, $0 < \varphi < 1$ and $\alpha + \beta + \gamma = 1$.

MCOPM is basically a two-round execution of the Dijkstra algorithm with particular metric functions. So it consumes twice the execution time of dijkstra. The time complexity of MCOPM is $O(|V|log|V|+|E|)$, where $|V|$ is the number of objects in D, $|E|$ is the number of edges between any two objects.

Algorithm 1: MCOPM

Input: M, sn, tn, Q_{td}, Q_{si}, Q_{sr}

Output: $p_{s \to t}$

1 $P_{t \to s} = \emptyset$, $P_{s \to t} = \emptyset$

2 **Perform Reverse_Search_Dijkstra**(M, sn, tn, Q_{td}, Q_{si}, Q_{sr})

3 **if** $h(P_{t \to s}) \leq 1$ **then**

4   **Perform   Forward_Search_Dijkstra**(M, sn, tn, Q_{td}, Q_{si}, Q_{sr}, Agr_{td}, Agr_{si}, Agr_{sr})

5   **Return** $P_{s \to t}$

6 **else**

7   **Return** no feasible paths that satisfy constraints specified by users

8 **end**

4.2 Multi-Constrained Optimization Path Matching Algorithm Based on IR-Tree (IR-MCOPM)

In order to improve query efficiency and reduce search space in spatial data, we use IR-tree (Inverted File R-tree) [22] to organize spatial objects (social relationships in social networks are stable for a long period of time [30]), inverted files [31] are used for text relevance queries, and R-tree is used for spatial proximity queries. Specifically, each node in the R-tree is associated with a keywords list, and each leaf node is a data entity $<o_i, loc(x_i, y_i), (w_i, score_i)>$. Here, o_i represents an object identifier in a spatial database. $loc(x_i, y_i)$ represents the two-dimensional coordinates of a spatial object o_i. The $score_i$ of w_i can be calculated by the following expression [22]:

$$score = \lambda \times \frac{dis(q.loc, o.loc)}{maxdisD} + (1-\lambda) \times Krel(q.keywords, o.keywords) \quad (6)$$

Where, $dis(q.loc, o.loc)$ denotes the Euclidean distance of query location q.loc and object location o.loc. maxdisD represents the maximum distance between any two objects in the spatial database D. $Krel(q.keywords, o.keywords)$ indicates how similar the query keywords q.keywords is to the keywords of the objects o.keywords in D. $\lambda \in [0, 1]$ is used to weigh the importance of spatial proximity and keywords similarity. Each non-leaf node is an index entity $< id, mbr, IF >$. Here, id denotes the unique identifier of the node, mbr represents the minimum bounding rectangle (MBR) that covers all child nodes, each node points to an inverted file IF. The inverted file of a non-leaf node NF contains the following two parts: (1) list of all the different keywords contained in the sub-tree with NF as the root node, (2) a post list is associated with keywords, including a pointer to the child node and a text relevance in the sub-tree where the child node is the root node. The calculation of text relevance is given by the following formula [31]:

$$w_k = \frac{1 + \ln f_k}{\sqrt{\sum_k (1 + \ln f_k)^2}} \quad (7)$$

Where, f_k indicates the frequency of keyword k, w_k is the text relevance after normalization.

We need to create an IR-tree index for all nodes. The benefits of using IR-tree are as follows: (1) easy searching; (2) the spatial relationships between nodes can be quickly determined by their MBRs. Then we can quickly find the paths that satisfy the multi-constraints pattern according to Algorithm 2. The algorithm is shown in Algorithm 2, and the algorithm execution flow is as follows:

Step 1: Input the root of IR-tree irTree.root, the keywords of the source node and the target node of a edge(path) are respectively k_i and k_j, the trust degree, social intimacy, and social reputation user-specified are Q_{td}, Q_{si}, Q_{sr} respectively. The upper and lower limits of the distance are respectively distU, distL. Output is a set of paths that satisfy the multi-conditions Θ.

Step 2: Join the root node to the path set Ω, and add IR-tree root node to the key of Θ, and the value is the path set Ω.

Step 3: Look for objects x and y that respectively satisfy the keywords k_i and k_j in the IR-tree, and calculate the minimum distance and maximum distance between them based on the MBR of the objects x and y. If maxDist is less than distL, we skip this loop; Otherwise, and (x, y) is a matching pair, then we execute Algorithm 1 to find if there are paths satisfying multi-constraints between the objects x and y. If it exists, then we add it to the path set Ω. The matching objects and the corresponding path set are added into Θ. Finally we return Θ.

Algorithm 2: IR-MCOPM

Input: irTree.root, k_i, k_j, Q_{td}, Q_{si}, Q_{sr}, distL, distU

Output: Θ

1   Ω.add(irTree.root), $\Theta \leftarrow \emptyset$, Θ.add(irTree.root,Ω)

2   **for** $x \in$ irTree.search(k_i) **do**

3          $\Omega \leftarrow \emptyset$

4   **for** $y \in$ irTree.search(k_j) **do**

5   mindist$\leftarrow$min(x.mbr,y.mbr)

6   maxdist$\leftarrow$max(x.mbr,y.mbr)

7   **if** maxdist<distL **then break**

8   **else if** mindist$\leq$distU **then**

9                      $p_{x \to y} \leftarrow$MCOPM$\left(M,x,y,Q_{td}, Q_{si}, Q_{sr}\right)$

10   **if** $p_{x \to y} \neq \emptyset$ **then**

11   Ω.add(y), Θ.add(x,Ω)

12   **Return** Θ

The IR-MCOPM algorithm requires multiple executions of the MCOPM algorithm. So the time complexity of MCOPM is $O(mn|V|log|V|+mn|E|)$. Where, m is the size of tuples satisfying one keyword, and the length of tuples satisfying another keyword is n.

4.3   The Join Order of the Paths in Results (MCPJoin)

In the above algorithm, we can find all the paths that match the multi-constraints pattern P in D. Then we need to connect these paths according to the pattern P, but [7, 24] show that the connection order of different paths has impact effect on the execution of the algorithm.

Example 1. Given a pattern P having vertices (e.g.,$\{v_1, v_2, v_3, v_4\}$) and edges (e.g., $\{v_1 - v_2, v_2 - v_3, v_3 - v_4, v_4 - v_1\}$). Assume that there are 10, 50, 100, 1000 matched paths for these edges respectively. We consider the following two situations:

Situation 1: We run IR-MCOPM for edges $v_1 - v_2, v_2 - v_3, v_3 - v_4$ respectively and get at most 50,000 tuples by linking their respective results to form $v_1 - v_2 - v_3 - v_4$. For $v_4 - v_1$, we do not run IR-MCOPM directly, because we just confirm whether the constraints between the fourth object and the first one is satisfying $v_4 - v_1$ in P.

Situation 2: If we follow the connection order of $v_1 - v_4 - v_3 - v_2$, we will get at most 5,000,000 tuples. Then, we will check whether the constraints between the first and second object match $v_1 - v_2$ in P. In this case, its computational complexity is 100 times that of the above situation.

As can be seen from the above example 1, the computational complexity of Situation 1 is much higher than the computational complexity of Situation 2. Therefore, a good connection order determines the efficiency of linking paths to form an answer to pattern P. In order to improve the efficiency of the algorithm, the number of executions of IR-MCOPM should be minimized, especially for the case where there is a large number of matching pairs about a path in pattern P. The amount of calculation is relatively large, at this time we should try to reduce the execution of IR-MCOPM. Thus, a sampling estimation algorithm is needed to estimate the number of matches for a certain path. We use the estimation method shown in [7].

$$Pr(|Y - E[Y]| \geq \eta E[Y]) \leq \rho \qquad (8)$$

Where, $0 < \eta < 1$, $\rho = e^{\left(\frac{-su^2}{8}\right)}$, $Y = \sum_{i=1}^{s} X_i$ represents the number of samples needed to find s matching pairs. In our experiment, we set $\eta = 0.5$, $\rho = 0.25$. Since the purpose of the estimation is to get the topology connection order of the path, the values of η and ρ are not necessarily large.

In order to improve the integrality of the Algorithm, we present Algorithm 3 to guide the join order of the paths that are returned from Algorithm 2.

Algorithm 3: MCPJoin

Input: irTree.root, P, η, ρ, distL, distU

Output: Υ, the join order of IR-MCOPM

1 $\Upsilon \leftarrow \emptyset, I \leftarrow \emptyset, U \leftarrow \emptyset, Q \leftarrow \emptyset$

2 **for** $(v_i, v_j) \in P$ **do**

3   **if** $dist(v_i, v_j) \geq distL(v_i, v_j)$ **then**

4          $\Theta \leftarrow$ IR-MCOPM(v_i, v_j)

5   I.add$((v_i, v_j), \Theta)$

6 Select u from P, U.add(u)

7 **for** $v \in$ nbr(u) **do**

8   **if** $0 \leq dist(u,v) \leq distU(u,v)$ or $distL(u,v) \leq dist(u,v) \leq distU(u,v)$ **then**

9   Q.add$((u,v),$ sample$(u,v))$

10   **else** Q.add$((u,v),$ I.get(u,v).size$)$

11 **while** Q.size>0 **do**

12     $(v_i, v_j) \leftarrow$ Q.pop()

13   Υ.add(v_i, v_j)

14   **if** $v_i \in U$ and $v_j \in U$ **then** continue

15   select u from P, and $u \notin U$

16   **for** $v \in$ nbr(u) and $v \in U$ **do** Υ.add(u,v)

17   **for** $v \in$ nbr(u) and $v \notin U$ **do**

18   **if** $0 \leq dist(u,v) \leq distU(u,v)$ or $distL(u,v) \leq dist(u,v) \leq distU(u,v)$

19   **then**

20   Q.add$((u,v),$ sample$(u,v))$

21   **else** Q.add$((u,v),$ I.get(u,v).size$)$

22   U.add(u)

23   **Return** Υ

Step 1: Input the IR-tree, multi-constraints pattern P, estimation parameters η, ρ, the lower distance distL, the upper distance distU.

Step 2: For any path (v_i, v_j) in the pattern P, if the distance relationship between two objects satisfies $dist(v_i, v_j) \geq distL(v_i, v_j)$, we need to perform Algorithm 2 and save the match in I(I is a hashmap, key is a paths tuple, value is the matching results).

Step 3: Select a vertex u randomly from P and add it to the set of vertices U that have been accessed. Visit the neighbor nodes of u, if the distance between u and v is $0 \leq dist(u, v) \leq distU(u, v)$ or $distL(u, v) \leq dist(u, v) \leq distU(u, v)$, we do not directly carry out Algorithm 2 on all objects. We perform a sampling function to estimate the number of (u,v). Otherwise, we get the exact number of matched pairs based on the corresponding paths in I and arrange the corresponding paths in ascending order according to the number of matching pairs.

Step 4: We dequeue the fewer pairs of paths and add them to the path join order set Υ. Then we consider another vertex and execute Step 3 until there is no path in the priority queue Q. Finally, we return path join order set Υ.

For satisfying certain distance constraints, we need to perform estimation. The time complexity of it is $O(\mu mn|V|log|V|+\mu mn|E|)$ for each edge in P. μ is the sampling rate and its value is between zero and one. For each while loop, we need perform enqueue and dequeue operations. The time complexity of it is $O(hlogh)$. Where h is the size of priority queue. Thus, the overall complexity of MCPJoin is $O(\mu mn|V|log|V|+\mu mn|E|+hlogh)$.

5 Experiments

5.1 Dataset

We use PoI (Point of Interest) as a dataset, which is obtained from the OpenStreetMap (https://www.openstreetmap.org), including Barcelona, Dubai, Paris, Rome, Tuscany, Trondheim, etc., covering 103,028 spatial objects, about 232,520 keywords. Each record consists of a unique identifier for the object, including geographic coordinates of latitude and longitude, and a set of keywords. The social relationships between the objects are constructed according to the NW small world model, each object is connected with the remaining 3–5 objects, and an edge is added between the randomly selected pair of objects with a probability of 0.3.

The H_OSTP algorithm is the most promising algorithm for solving the optimal path selection problem in social networks [29]. In order to study the performance of our proposed sample-based algorithm, we compare it with the H_OSTP algorithm. The H_OSTP algorithm and the MCPJoin algorithm are implemented using Java IntelliJ IDEA. The operating environment is Intel(R) Core(TM) i5-8265U CPU @ 1.60 GHz 1.80 GHz processor, 8 GB of memory, 512 GB SSD, and operating system is Windows 10.

In our experiments, the trust degree, social intimacy, and social values were randomly generated based on a uniform distribution and ranged from 0–1. The attenuation factor σ is 1.5. The constraints of trust degree, social intimacy, and social reputation are 0.05, 0.001, 0.3 respectively. The estimation parameters η and ρ are respectively 0.5, 0.25. Sampling threshold is set as $0.7 \times |O_i| \times |O_j|$ (In order to avoid unlimited sampling when no match is found, stop sampling when the number of samples reaches the threshold.).

We use 8 different structures (as shown in Fig. 2). The black rectangles in the figure represent spatial objects. The edges between black rectangles represent the constraints and paths of spatial objects. For each structure, we generate 3–6 specific patterns. And there is at least one match in the dataset.

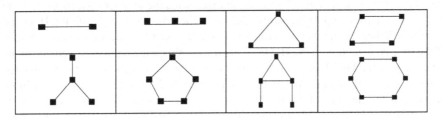

Fig. 2. Structures of path patterns.

We use the IR-tree index, where the fanout is 100, i.e., the maximum number of children of each node. The inverted object list of each keyword is stored in a single file on disk.

5.2 Performance

In order to evaluate the performance of our proposed algorithm, 150, 300, 450, 600, 750, 1050 objects are extracted from the PoI dataset as a subset. The details of the data set are shown in Table 1.

Table 1. The datasets used in experiments.

Datasets	Objects	Edges	Keywords
1	150	788	375
2	300	1,073	3,002
3	450	1,790	4,503
4	600	2,925	6,500
5	750	3,121	7,810
6	1,050	5,456	13,640

In each subset, the eight structures shown in Fig. 2 are independently executed for the MCPJoin algorithm and the H_OSTP algorithm, each of which is executed 3–6 times, and the results are averaged. To enhance comparability, the MCPJoin algorithm and the H_OSTP algorithm perform the same query path pattern each time. The comparison results are shown in Fig. 3.

As can be seen from Fig. 3, when the number of vertices in the pattern P is 2 and the number of objects in the spatial object is small, the H_OSTP algorithm can achieve better performance. There are two reasons for this: (1) The H_OSTP algorithm does not need to establish an IR-tree index for each vertex, thus reducing the building time of the index; (2) When there are only two objects in the pattern P, the H_OSTP algorithm does not involve the connection of the path problem. However, when the number of vertices in the pattern P exceeds 2 and the number of objects in the spatial object increases gradually, the performance of the H_OSTP algorithm decreases sharply. When the number of vertices in the pattern P is 3, the MCPJoin algorithm saves more than the H_OSTP algorithm 57.39% of the time, when the number of vertices in mode P is 4, the MCPJoin algorithm saves 65.28% of the time compared with the H_OSTP algorithm. When the number of vertices in P is 5, the MCPJoin algorithm saves 85.45% of the time compared with the H_OSTP algorithm. When the number of vertices in the pattern P is 6, the MCPJoin algorithm saves an average of 67.12% of the time compared to the H_OSTP algorithm. As can be seen from Table 2, if H_OSTP wants to achieve the same path search result as MCPJoin, it will cost more runtime. The main reasons are as follows: (1) The MCPJoin algorithm creates an IR-tree for spatial objects, which is beneficial to reduce the search space. (2) The MCPJoin algorithm uses a sampling-based estimation algorithm to limit the search time and ensure the efficiency of the path connection process.

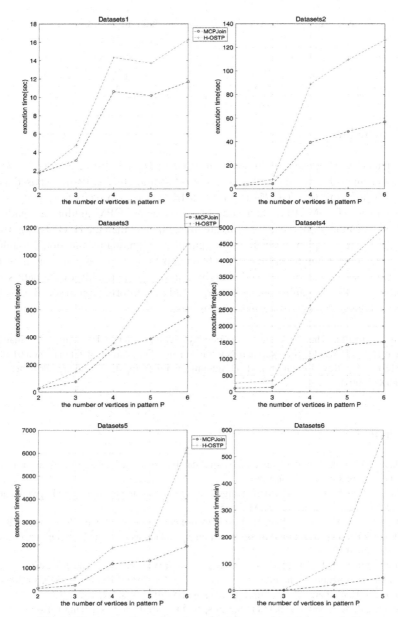

Fig. 3. The comparison of runtime about the number of vertices in P.

Therefore, based on the above analysis, the MCPJoin algorithm is nearly twice as efficient as the H_OSTP algorithm, especially when the number of spatial objects is large, the H_OSTP algorithm is difficult to give a matching result in a reasonable time.

Table 2. The comparison of average runtime about different vertices in P.

Vertices	2	3	4	5	6
MCPJoin	42.6814 (s)	90.0589 (s)	630.4801 (s)	1.0143e + 003 (s)	817.5096 (s)
H_OSTP	74.5253 (s)	211.3464 (s)	1.8159e + 003 (s)	6.9723e + 003 (s)	2.4860e + 003 (s)
Difference	42.73% less	57.39% less	65.28% less	85.45% less	67.12% less

6 Conclusion

In this paper, we propose a multi-constrained path selection problem based on spatial pattern matching. Based on the characteristics of spatial objects, IR-tree is used as the index structure, and IR-MCOPM is based on IR-tree to map paths from pattern P to social network. The MCPJoin algorithm based on IR-MCOPM guiding the path join order show that the proposed algorithms are more efficient than the H_OSTP algorithm.

In the future, we plan to obtain the weight of the path quality function through the machine learning method, and feed the obtained path back to the path search process through the neural network method, thereby improving the quality of the path search algorithm. Another research content is used to add time information to social networks, and extend this problem to time and space issues.

Acknowledgments. The work was supported by Natural Science Foundation of Shandong Province (No. ZR2016FQ10), National Natural Science Foundation of China (No. 6167126, No. 61802217), Key Research and Development Program of Shandong Province (No. 2016GGX101007).

References

1. Zhang, D., et al.: Keyword search in spatial databases: towards searching by document. In: ICDE, pp. 688–699. IEEE (2009)
2. Guo, T., Cao, X., Cong, G.: Efficient algorithms for answering the m-closest keywords query. In: SIGMOD, pp. 405–418. ACM (2015)
3. Deng, K., Li, X., Lu, J., Zhou, X.: Best keyword cover search. TKDE **27**(1), 61–73 (2015)
4. Choi, D., Pei, J., Lin, X.: Finding the minimum spatial keyword cover. In: ICDE, pp. 685–696. IEEE (2016)
5. Rocha-Junior, J.B., Gkorgkas, O., Jonassen, S., Nørvåg, K.: Efficient processing of top-k spatial keyword queries. In: Pfoser, D., et al. (eds.) SSTD 2011. LNCS, vol. 6849, pp. 205–222. Springer, Heidelberg (2011). https://doi.org/10.1007/978-3-642-22922-0_13
6. Pengfei, Z.: Research on related issues of spatial keyword query. Zhejiang University (2018)
7. Fang, Y., Cheng, R., Cong, G., Mamoulis, N., Li, Y.: On spatial pattern matching, pp. 293–304 (2018). https://doi.org/10.1109/icde.2018.00035
8. Fan, W., Li, J., Ma, S., Tang, N., Wu, Y., Wu, Y.: Graph pattern matching: from intractable to polynomial time. In: VLDB 2010, pp. 264–275 (2010)
9. Cheng, T.S., Gadia, S.K.: A Pattern matching language for spatio-temporal databases (1994)
10. Cheng, J., Yu, J.X., Ding, B., Yu, P.S., Wang, H.: Fast graph pattern matching. In: ICDE (2008)
11. Carletti, V., et al.: Challenging the time complexity of exact subgraph isomorphism for huge and dense graphs with VF3. TPAMI (2017)

12. Zhang, P., Lin, H., Yao, B., et al.: Level-aware collective spatial keyword queries. Inf. Sci. **378**, 194–214 (2017)
13. Hariharan, R., Hore, B., Li, C., Mehrotra, S.: Processing spatial-keyword (SK) queries in geographic information retrieval (GIR) systems. In: SSDBM, p. 16 (2007)
14. Cary, A., Wolfson, O., Rishe, N.: Efficient and scalable method for processing top-k spatial Boolean queries. In: Gertz, M., Ludäscher, B. (eds.) SSDBM 2010. LNCS, vol. 6187, pp. 87–95. Springer, Heidelberg (2010). https://doi.org/10.1007/978-3-642-13818-8_8
15. Cong, G., Jensen, C.S., Wu, D.: Efficient retrieval of the top-k most relevant spatial web objects. PVLDB **2**(1), 337–348 (2009)
16. Khodaei, A., Shahabi, C., Li, C.: Hybrid indexing and seamless ranking of spatial and textual features of web documents. In: Bringas, P.G., Hameurlain, A., Quirchmayr, G. (eds.) DEXA 2010. LNCS, vol. 6261, pp. 450–466. Springer, Heidelberg (2010). https://doi.org/10.1007/978-3-642-15364-8_37
17. Wu, D., Yiu, M.L., Cong, G., et al.: Joint top-K spatial keyword query processing. IEEE Trans. Knowl. Data Eng. **24**, 1889–1903 (2012)
18. Zheng, B., Zheng, K., Jensen, C.S., et al.: Answering why-not group spatial keyword queries. IEEE Trans. Knowl. Data Eng. **32**, 26–39 (2018)
19. Qian, Z., Xu, J., Zheng, K., et al.: Semantic-aware top-k spatial keyword queries. World Wide Web Internet Web Inf. Syst. **21**(3), 573–594 (2018)
20. Mamoulis, N., Papadias, D.: Multiway spatial joins. TODS **26**(4), 424–475 (2001)
21. Zou, L., Chen, L., Ozsu, M.T.: Distance-join: pattern match query in a large graph database. PVLDB **2**(1), 886–897 (2009)
22. Chen, L., Cong, G., Jensen, C.S., Wu, D.: Spatial keyword query processing: an experimental evaluation. PVLDB, 217–228 (2013)
23. Tong, H., Faloutsos, C., Gallagher, B., Eliassi-Rad, T.: Fast best-effort pattern matching in large attributed graphs. In: KDD (2007)
24. Zou, L., Chen, L., Ozsu, M.T.: Distance-join: pattern match query in a large graph database. In: VLDB (2009)
25. Jing, Y., Yanbing, L., Zhang, Y., Mengya, L., Jianlong, T., Li, G.: Summary of large-scale graph data matching technology. Comput. Res. Dev. **52**(02), 391–409 (2015)
26. Henzinger, M.R., Henzinger, T., Kopke, P.: Computing simulations on fifinite and infifinite graphs. In: FOCS 1995 (1995)
27. Sokolsky, O., Kannan, S., Lee, I.: Simulation-based graph similarity. In: Tools and Algorithms for the Construction and Analysis of Systems (2006)
28. Liu, G., Zheng, K., Liu, A., et al.: MCS-GPM: multi-constrained simulation based graph pattern matching in contextual social graphs. IEEE Trans. Knowl. Data Eng. **30**, 1050–1064 (2017)
29. Liu, G., Wang, Y., Orgun, M.A., et al.: A heuristic algorithm for trust-oriented service provider selection in complex social networks. In: IEEE International Conference on Services Computing. IEEE Computer Society (2010)
30. Berger, P., Luckmann, T.: The Social Construction of Reality: A Treatise in the Sociology of Knowledge. Anchor Books, New York (1966)
31. Zobel, J., Moffat, A.: Inverted fifiles for text search engines. ACM Comput. Surv. **38**(2), 56 (2006)

A Multi-objective Computation Offloading Method in Multi-cloudlet Environment

Kai Peng[1,2(✉)], Shuaiqi Zhu[1], Lixin Zheng[2], Xiaolong Xu[3],
and Victor C. M. Leung[4]

[1] College of Engineering, Huaqiao University, Quanzhou, China
pkbupt@gmail.com
[2] Fujian Provincial Academic Engineering Research Centre in Industrial Intellectual
Techniques and Systems, Quanzhou, China
[3] Key Laboratory of Intelligent Perception and Systems for High-Dimensional
Information of Ministry of Education, Nanjing University of Science and Technology,
Nanjing 210094, People's Republic of China
[4] Department of Electrical and Computer Engineering, The University of British
Columbia, Vancouver, BC V6T 1Z4, Canada

Abstract. Computation offloading is becoming a promising technology
that can improve quality of service for mobile users in mobile edge computing. However, it becomes much difficult when there are multi-cloudlet
near to the mobile users. The resources of the cloudlet are heterogeneous and finite, and thus it is challenge to choose the best cloudlet for
the multi-user. The issue for multi-user in multi-cloudlet environment
is well-investigated in this study. Firstly, we establish a multi-objective
optimization model with respect to time consumption and energy consumption of mobile devices. Moreover, we devise a multi-objective computation offloading method based on improved fast and elitist genetic
algorithm for selecting the optimal offloading strategies. Finally, compared with other methods, numerous experiments proved that our proposed method have advantages in effectiveness and efficiency.

Keywords: Mobile edge computing · Multi-cloudlet · Energy
consumption · Time consumption

1 Introduction

As the computer network are gaining colossal popularity, Mobile devices (MDs)
are becoming a key role affecting people's lives [1–3]. Nevertheless, differ from
the traditional devices, e.g. desktop computers, MDs are limited by the aspects
with respect to the storage capacity, operational performance, especially for
battery life. Mobile cloud computing (MCC) can provide mobile users with a
variety of extended services. However, an envisioned disadvantage of MCC is

© ICST Institute for Computer Sciences, Social Informatics and Telecommunications Engineering 2020
Published by Springer Nature Switzerland AG 2020. All Rights Reserved
X. Zhang et al. (Eds.): CloudComp 2019/SmartGift 2019, LNICST 322, pp. 20–32, 2020.
https://doi.org/10.1007/978-3-030-48513-9_2

that the centralized cloud is distantly for mobile users to exchange data, which is likely to incur high round-trip delay. A resounding paradigm that emerges recently, namely mobile edge computing (MEC), has been considered the optimal paradigm to solve this issue [4–11]. A cloudlet which is in the vicinity to the mobile users provisions low-latency services for the interactive response. Hence, if the users choose to offload the applications to cloudlet, the time and energy consumption will be decreased.

Suppose the computing resources of cloud in MCC are infinite. In contrast, the computing resources in MEC are finite. A queue latency will arise if a crowd of mobile users are concurrently requesting services from a single cloudlet. In addition, resources in different cloudlets are heterogeneous. Moreover, the difficulty of computing offloading is further increased under the scenarios that there are multi-cloudlet nearby. More specifically, how to choose the best cloudlet for the applications for the multi-user is becoming very important. Additionally, the limited of resources in a single cloudlet needs to be considered. With the increasing of the number of application, the cloudlets may become overload. For executing the applications successfully, the applications need to be taken into consideration to be run locally or offloaded to cloud. In another word, it is essential to balance these three locations, namely, local, multi-cloudlet, as well as cloud.

The issues that computation in single cloudlet have been well investigated [12–14]. Moreover, the computation offloading which is focused on the selection of cloudlet and the allocation of resource in multi-cloudlet MEC has also been well studied in [15–21]. Differ from them, in this study, the energy consumption and time consumption optimization for applications in multi-cloudlet in MEC are taken in to consideration jointly. The main contributions of this study can be concluded as three aspects.

1) We investigated the computation offloading over multi-cloudlet environment in MEC in this study. Both the energy consumption and time consumption are seen as the optimization goals.
2) A multi-objective computation offloading method for multiple applications based on improved Fast and Elitist Multiobjective Genetic Algorithm [22] is proposed.
3) We conduct comprehensive evaluations and analysis to demonstrate the proposed method can provide effective offloading strategies.

The remaining of the paper is arranged as follows. Section 2 firstly introduce the overview of system model and present problem formulation. And then Sect. 3 describe a multi-objective computation offloading algorithm over multi-cloudlet. In Sect. 4, we indicate the experimental evaluation. And Sect. 5 conclude the related work. Section 6, we summarize the paper and describe the future work in the final section.

2   System Model and Problem Formulation

In this section, the network architecture with respect to MEC system is firstly established. After that we introduce the system model and problem formulation with two objectives in terms of decreasing the time consumption and the energy consumption in MEC.

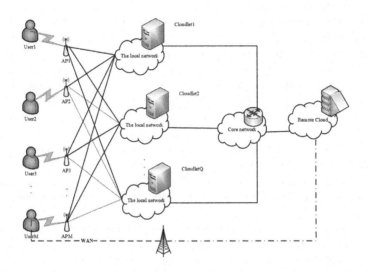

Fig. 1. Multi-cloudlet MEC system

The multi-cloudlet MEC system is shown in Fig. 1. Cloud has infinite resources. Mobile user could be mobile phone or other devices. Every user has a certain number of applications which need to be processed. These applications can be run locally, and also can be offloaded to the remote cloud over Wide Area Network (WAN) or to cloudlets over Local Area Network (LAN). In addition, cloudlet can communicate with cloud directly.

R is a collection of mobile users, which can be modeled as $R = \{r_{1,1}, ..., r_{1,n}, r_{2,n}, ..., r_{i,n}\}$, representing the first application of the first user, the second application of the first user, ..., the n-th application of the o-th user. There are multiple virtual machines in cloudlet which can be used to process multiple applications concurrently. The resource can be expressed as $CL = (L_{LAN}, f_{cl}, U)$, where L_{LAN} is the transmission latency between the cloudlet and MD, f_{cl} denotes the ability of the cloudlet to process the application, and U indicates the total amount of VMs.

$r_{i,n} = (l_{i,n}, o_{i,n})$ is defined as a 2-tuple, where the average instruction length of the application requested by the user is denoted as $l_{i,n}$, and $o_{i,n}$ is the offloading strategy assigned to the f-th request of the i-th user, $o_{i,n} = 0$ indicates that the application request is run locally, $\{o_{i,n} = 1, 2, ..., Q\}$ represent that the application is offloaded to cloudlet for processing, $o_{i,n} = Q + 1$ indicates that the application is offloaded to cloud.

2.1   Time Consumption Model

There are three kinds of time to consider when establishing the time consumption model, e.g., waiting time, processing time and transmission time.

Average Waiting Time. The requests of users' are uncertain, and the resources of cloudlet are limited. That means there is a high possibility that user requests will be queued in the cloudlet. Thus, we need to establish a mathematical model to effectively evaluate this queuing situation. According to the queuing theory [23], we can establish the waiting time mathematical model.

Assuming that the interval of arrival of the application obeys the parameter λ of the negative exponential distribution. Likewise, we assume that the cloudlet has fixed service rate μ. The possibility of the idle state in cloudlet is calculated as

$$P_0 = [\sum_{u=0}^{U-1} \frac{\varphi^U}{U!(1-\varphi_U)}]^{-1} \tag{1}$$

where $\varphi = \frac{\lambda}{\mu}$ shows the intensity of the service. Moreover, the average intensity of the service for U virtual machines in cloudlet is denoted as $\varphi_U = \frac{\varphi}{U}$.

Let p_n be the probability of the cloudlet will reach when it is stable. The probability of waiting for an application is calculated by

$$C_w(U, \varphi) = \sum_{u=U}^{\infty} p_n = \frac{\varphi^U}{U!(1-\varphi_U)} \cdot p_0 \tag{2}$$

The average waiting time of the application can be calculated in the follow

$$W_q = \frac{1}{U \cdot (\mu - \lambda)} \cdot \sum_{u=U}^{\infty} \frac{\varphi^U}{U!(1-\varphi_U)} \cdot p_0 \tag{3}$$

Processing Time and Transmission Time. The processing time of the n-th application from i-th user is given as

$$T_{exe}(r_{i,n}) = \begin{cases} \frac{l_{i,n}}{f_l} & o_{i,n} = 0 \\ W_q + \frac{l_{i,n}}{f_{cl}} + L_{LAN} & o_{i,n} = 1 \text{ or } 2, or \dots or\ Q \\ \frac{l_{i,n}}{f_c} + L_{WAN} & o_{i,f} = Q+1 \end{cases} \tag{4}$$

The application is processed locally when the offloading strategy is 0. The total time consumption is the sum of the processing time, the average waiting time, as well as the transmission time in LAN when the application is offloaded to the cloudlet. The total time consumption includes the transmission time and the processing time in WAN when the application is processed on the cloud.

The transmission time of the $n - th$ application of the i-th user is given as follows

$$T_{trans}(r_{i,n}) = \frac{l_{i,n}}{B} \tag{5}$$

where

$$B = \begin{cases} \infty & o_{i,n} = 0 \\ B_{cl} & o_{i,n} = 1 \, or \, 2, \, or \ldots or \, Q \\ B_c & o_{i,n} = Q+1 \end{cases} \tag{6}$$

In summary, the total time required for the n-th application request execution of the i-th user is

$$T(r_{i,n}) = T_{exe}(r_{i,n}) + T_{trans}(r_{i,n}) \tag{7}$$

2.2   Energy Consumption Model

The transmission energy consumption and processing energy consumption make up the energy consumption of MDs. And the energy consumption for executing the $n-th$ request of $i-th$ user is expressed as $E_{exe}(r_{i,n})$, which is calculated as

$$E_{exe}(r_{i,n}) = \begin{cases} \frac{l_{i,n}}{f_l} \times \delta_A & o_{i,n} = 0 \\ (W_q + \frac{l_{i,n}}{f_{cl}} + L_{LAN}) \times \delta_I & o_{i,n} = 1, \, 2, \ldots \, or \, Q \\ (\frac{l_{i,n}}{f_c} + L_{WAN}) \times \delta_I & o_{i,n} = Q+1 \end{cases} \tag{8}$$

where δ_I and δ_A represent energy consumption of a MD in idle time and active state. The transmission energy consumption is shown as

$$E_{trans}(r_{i,n}) = \frac{l_{i,n}}{B} \cdot \delta_T \tag{9}$$

where δ_T is the energy consumption of the MD during transmission. In summary, it can be concluded that the power consumption required for the n-th application request execution of the i-th user is

$$E(r_{i,n}) = E_{exe}(r_{i,n}) + E_{trans}(r_{i,n}) \tag{10}$$

2.3   Problem Formulation

The objectives of the computational offloading are to achieve the goal of decreasing the energy consumption and time consumption. The multi-objective problem formulation is shown as follows.

$$Min \sum_{i=1}^{I} \sum_{n=1}^{N} T(r_{i,n}); \forall o \in \{1, 2, 3, \ldots, N\} \tag{11}$$

$$Min \sum_{i=1}^{I} \sum_{n=1}^{N} E(r_{i,n}); \forall o \in \{1, 2, 3, \ldots, N\} \tag{12}$$

$$s.t. o_{i,n} \in \{0, 1, 2, ..., Q+1\} \tag{13}$$

3   Multi-objective Computation Offloading Method in Multi-cloudlet

In this section, we present the details of our proposed method: computation offloading method in multi-cloudlet (COMC). In addition, pseudocode of this algorithm are described.

3.1   Method Review

In this study, our objectives are optimizing the consumption of time and energy for all applications. We model the computational migration problem as a multi-objective problem and use the improved NSGA-II to get the best strategies. The details are shown in the following subsection.

3.2   Encoding

Each application is numbered according to this form $\{1, 2, \ldots, n\}$. The gene represents the offloading strategy for each application. Multi-gene forms a full chromosome, and it can be regards as an individual, which represents a solution to our issue.

An example of encoding is shown in Fig. 2. We use integer coding for our issue. More specifically, we have encoded each offloading strategy as $\{0 \ 1, \ 2, \ldots, \ n\}$. Each value in the strategy means the corresponding destination the application offload. For example, number 0 means this application is processed locally, similarly, number 1 means this application is offloaded to the cloudlet1 and number 2 means that this application is executed on the cloudlet2, and so on. Notice that number $\{Q+1\}$ means the application is run on the cloud. Fitness function is used to evaluate individual quality, which is obtained by Eq. (11) and (12). These two fitness functions (11) and (12) indicate the consumption of time and energy. Our goal is finding the best offloading solution which makes these two functions well.

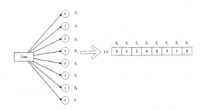

Fig. 2. Encoding.

3.3   Initialization

Randomly generate initialized population P_0, then perform non-dominant sorting on P_0. Moreover, binary tournament selection, crossover, as well as mutation is executed on P_0 to form new population Q_0.

3.4   Selection

To form new group population $R_t = P_t \cup Q_t$, where $t = 0$. In addition, based on non-dominated sort of R_t, we have gotten the non-dominated front-end $\{F_1, F_2, \ldots, F_i\}$ [22] in this step.

3.5   Crossover

In this step, the crossover combines two parental chromosomes and parts of gene fragment between them are exchanged to get better spring chromosomes Q. Some excellent genes are reserved. The fitness is improved by using the similar gene fragments of these chromosomes.

3.6   Mutation

In this step, the mutation slightly modifies certain genes on chromosomes to produce the individuals who are well-fitness while avoiding early convergence. Therefore, an improved mutation is proposed. For example, if cloudlet1 is the best offloading location, the probability of mutating to $o_{i,n} = 1$ should be increased.

3.7   Calculation of Crowding Distance

Based on the crowding distance comparison operation $\prec_n$, we sort all F_i to choose the best N individuals forming a population P_{t+1}. The crowding distance is formulated as:

$$i_d = i_d^T + i_d^E = \sum_{n=1}^{N}(|T_{a,n}^{i+1}(S) - T_{a,n}^{i-1}(S)|)$$
$$+ \sum_{n=1}^{N}(|E_{a,n}^{i+1}(S) - E_{a,n}^{i-1}(S)|) \tag{14}$$

where $1 <= i <= n$ and i_d indicates the crowding distance for the $i - th$ offloading strategy $o_{i,n}$. i_d^T, i_d^E indicate the objective functions (11) and (12), respectively. $T_{a,n}^{i+1}(S)$ is the value for offloading strategy $o_{i+1,n}$ to the objective function $T_{a,n}(S)$. Likewise, $E_{a,n}^{i+1}(S)$ indicates offloading strategy value $o_{i+1,n}$ to the objective function $E_{a,n}(S)$.

3.8   The Algorithm Pseudocode

Based on the above steps, the pseudocode of our method is shown as follows.

Algorithm 1. COMC

Input: Applications, the size of population N, the maximum iterations number G_{max}
Output: Offloading solution S, time consumption as well as energy consumption
1: $G_{cur} = 1, \ell = 1$
2: **while** $G_{cur} \leq G_{max}$ **do**
3:     Initialize P_{cur}
4:     Q_ℓ =selection, crossover and mutation P_ℓ^i
5:     $R_\ell = P_\ell^i + Q_\ell$
6:     $F = fastnondominatesort(R_\ell)$
7:     $P_{\ell+1} = \emptyset$
8:     $s = 0$
9:     **while** $len(P_{\ell+1}) + len(F[s]) < N$ **do**
10:         Using formula (14) to acquire crowding distance $(F[s])$
11:         $P_{\ell+1}+ = F[s]$
12:         $s = s + 1$
13:         $P_{\ell+1}+ = F[s][0 : N - len(P_{\ell+1})]$
14:         $Q_{\ell+1}$=form new generation$(P_{\ell+1})$
15:         $\ell = \ell + 1$
16:         $G_{cur} = G_{cur} + 1$
17:     **end while**
18: **end while**
19: **return** S,energy consumption,time consumption

---

4   Experimental Evaluation

In this section, we present the experimental evaluation of our method. Firstly, the experimental setting is introduced, which includes comparative methods and experimental parameters. Then, the experimental result and discussion is described.

4.1   Experimental Setting

Some other comparative computation offloading methods are proposed and shown as follows.

No offloading (NO): All applications are executed in MDs where no transmission overhead is considered. And it is named as NO.

Full offloading to cloud (FOC): All applications in MDs are offloaded to cloud for processing, named as FOC.

Random full offloading to cloudlet (RFOCL): All applications are offloaded to the multi-cloudlet for processing randomly, named as RFOCL.

The value of parameters are presented in Table 1.

We implement these methods by JAVA and Eclipse over Win10 64 OS with 2 Intel Core i7-7700U 2.80 GHz processors and 16 GB RAM.

Table 1. Experimental parameter.

Parameter description	Value
Power of MDs when CPU is in idle state	0.83 W
Power of MDs when CPU is in active state	0.1 W
Power of MDs when transmitting tasks	0.83 W
Processing capacity of MDs	500 MHZ
Processing capacities of the {cloudlet1-cloudlet3, cloud}	2300 MHZ, 2400 MHZ, 2100 MHZ, 2600 MHZ
The latency of LAN and WAN	0.025 ms, 0.1 ms
The bandwidth of LAN	220/240/230 kb/s
The bandwidth of WAN	110 kb/s
Average waiting time of applications in cloudlet	0.07 s
Crossover probability	0.9
Number of VMs per cloudlet	3

4.2   Experimental Result and Discussion

Different results are received with the different number of applications. We have done 50 experiments under convergence for different user scale and application scale.

Firstly, we describe how COMC makes equilibrium between these two targets, i.e. time consumption and energy consumption of MDs. Figure 3 shows the result of comparison in energy consumption for different number of applications using NO, FOC, RFOCL and COMC. Additionally, the comparison result of the average time consumption with different methods is shown in Fig. 4. We can see that COMC is effective while the number of applications is increasing. Overall, COMC is effective as it makes these two objectives better, not just one best.

Then, we analysis how COMC provides effective offloading strategies to balance multi offloading destinations, i.e. local, cloudlet1, cloudlet2, cloudlet3 and cloud. As shown in Tables 2, 3, 4 and 5, the applications are mainly offloaded to the cloudlet1, cloudlet2, and cloudlet3. That means the cloudlets are the most optimal offloading destinations. When the number of applications increases beyond the processing capacity of cloudlets, parts of applications is migrated into the cloud to avoid the queue latency.

Considering the finite of resource in cloudlet and transmission latency for applications between MDs and cloud. As the applications are increased, the number of them that are executed locally increases at the same time, while the number of applications that are executed on cloud is decreased, that also proves our method can balance every offloading dentation. Above all, our propose method can obtain the best strategy to minimize energy consumption and time consumption for all applications.

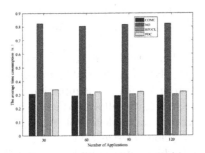

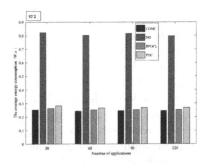

Fig. 3. Comparison of the average time consumption with NO, RFOCL, FOC and COMC

Fig. 4. Comparison of the average energy consumption with NO, RFOCL, FOC and COMC

Table 2. Applications = 30

Location	NO	RFOCL	FOC	COMC
Local	30	0	0	0
Cloudlet1	0	8	0	9
Cloudlet2	0	12	0	10
Cloudlet3	0	10	0	5
Cloud	0	0	30	3

Table 3. Applications = 60

Location	NO	RFOCL	FOC	COMC
Local	60	0	0	7
Cloudlet1	0	18	0	17
Cloudlet2	0	22	0	24
Cloudlet3	0	20	0	7
Cloud	0	0	0	60

Table 4. Applications = 90

Location	NO	RFOCL	FOC	COMC
Local	90	0	0	0
Cloudlet1	0	31	0	24
Cloudlet2	0	30	0	27
Cloudlet3	0	29	0	22
Cloud	0	0	90	4

Table 5. Applications = 120

Location	NO	RFOCL	FOC	COMC
Local	120	0	0	0
Cloudlet1	0	39	0	30
Cloudlet2	0	49	0	33
Cloudlet3	0	32	0	24
Cloud	0	0	120	10

5   Related Work

Computation offloading in single cloudlet scenario has been well investigated in [12–14]. Xu et al. [12] proposed a new method namely MCO to address the challenge that offloading resolvent for workflow applications. Zhang et al. [13] proposed a computation offloading algorithm based on particle swarm optimization to optimize the energy consumption of MDs while meeting time constraints of application. Liu et al. [14] leveraging of Interior Point Method and secularization method to solve the multi-objective problem with respect to average price cost, average execution time and average energy consumption in MEC system.

These methods have provided effective solutions for the computation offloading issue in single cloudlet environment, however they may not used in multi-cloudlet environment directly.

Computation offloading in multi-cloudlet has been studied in [15–21]. Li et al. [15] proposed theoretical model to partition the arbitrarily divisible application in MEC and derive the closed-form expressions to minimize the completion time for application. [16] firstly proposed a two-stage strategy to allocate the resource, and then proposed a mixed integer linear programming model is constructed to optimize computing resources allocation and the cloudlet selection.

An application-aware cloudlet selection method is proposed by Roy et al. [17] with respect to the scenario that multi-cloudlet, which can reduce the execution latency and energy consumption of MDs as well as the load balance of the system. Suppose different types of applications could be processed in different cloudlets, and the coming application type was first checked. Finally, the most suitable cloudlet is chosen according to the verified result. A power and latency aware cloudlet selection method is proposed by Mukherjee et al. [18]. In [19], Dilay Parmar et al. proposed a mechanism included two phases for identifying a cloudlet for computation offloading. Firstly, if the cloudlets that are covered in the WiFi range of the MD did not connect to any cloudlets, they would be identified. And then the second phase, it will accomplish the selection of the ideal offloading cloudlet.

In [20], the objective is to minimize the total energy consumption and they proposed a method to decide which tasks should be offloaded and determine where to offloaded. Mazouzi et al. [21] proposed the optimization problem of joint cloudlet selection and minimizing waiting time in fog environment. The problem is modeled as many-to-one matching game based on game theory and a corresponding algorithm is used to solve this game.

Different from the existing studies, the time consumption and energy consumption of applications in multi-cloudlet environment have been well studied in this study. More specifically, these cloudlets are heterogeneous in the problem we studied. Meanwhile, we will make full use of the resources in local, multi-cloudlet, as well as cloud to provide better services for users.

6   Conclusion

In this paper, we have studied the multi-objective computation offloading problem in multi-cloudlet environment. Aiming at resolving this problem, we proposed a multi-objective method to find the optimal processed destination for all the applications by minimizing time consumption and energy consumption at the same time. Extensive experimental evaluations have shown that our proposed method is efficiency and effectiveness.

In future work, we will explore cloudlet placement for hybrid applications in multi-cloudlet MEC.

Acknowledgment. The authors thank for the Natural Science Foundation of Fujian Province (Grant No. 2018J05106), the National Science Foundation of China (Grant No. 61902133), the Education and Scientific Research Projects of Young and Middle-aged Teachers in Fujian Province (JZ160084), and the Scientific Research Foundation of Huaqiao University under Grant No.14BS316. The Fundamental Research Funds for the Central Universities (No. 30918014108).

References

1. Qi, L., et al.: Finding all you need: web APIs recommendation in web of things through keywords search. IEEE Trans. Comput. Soc. Syst. **6**, 1063–1072 (2019)
2. Zhang, Y., et al.: Covering-based web service quality prediction via neighborhood-aware matrix factorization. IEEE Trans. Serv. Comput. (2019). https://doi.org/10.1109/TSC.2019.2891517
3. Xu, X., Liu, Q., Zhang, X., Zhang, J., Qi, L., Dou, W.: A blockchain-powered crowdsourcing method with privacy preservation in mobile environment. IEEE Trans. Comput. Soc. Syst. (2019). https://doi.org/10.1109/TCSS.2019.2909137
4. Shi, W., Cao, J., Zhang, Q., Li, Y., Xu, L.: Edge computing: vision and challenges. IEEE Internet Things J. **3**(5), 637–646 (2016)
5. Qi, L., Chen, Y., Yuan, Y., Fu, S., Zhang, X., Xu, X.: A QoS-aware virtual machine scheduling method for energy conservation in cloud-based cyber-physical systems. World Wide Web **23**(2), 1275–1297 (2019). https://doi.org/10.1007/s11280-019-00684-y
6. Zhang, Y.W., Zhou, Y.Y., Wang, F.T., Sun, Z., He, Q.: Service recommendation based on quotient space granularity analysis and covering algorithm on Spark. Knowl.-Based Syst. **147**, 25–35 (2018)
7. Raza, S., Wang, S., Ahmed, M., Anwar, M.R.: A survey on vehicular edge computing: architecture, applications, technical issues, and future directions. Wirel. Commun. Mob. Comput. **2019**, 1–19 (2019)
8. Wang, K., Yin, H., Quan, W., Min, G.: Enabling collaborative edge computing for software defined vehicular networks. IEEE Netw. **32**(5), 112–117 (2018)
9. Xu, X., et al.: A computation offloading method over big data for IoT-enabled cloud-edge computing. Future Gener. Comput. Syst. **95**, 522–533 (2019)
10. Xu, X., et al.: An energy-aware computation offloading method for smart edge computing in wireless metropolitan area networks. J. Netw. Comput. Appl. **133**, 75–85 (2019)
11. Peng, K., Leung, V., Xu, X., Zheng, L., Wang, J., Huang, Q.: A survey on mobile edge computing: focusing on service adoption and provision. Wirel. Commun. Mob. Comput. **2018** (2018). Article no. 8267838, 16 pages. https://doi.org/10.1155/2018/8267838
12. Xu, X., et al.: Multi-objective computation offloading for workflow management in cloudlet-based mobile cloud using NSGA-II (2018). https://doi.org/10.1111/coin.12197
13. Zhang, J., et al.: Hybrid computation offloading for smart home automation in mobile cloud computing. Pers. Ubiquit. Comput. **22**(1), 121–134 (2018)
14. Liu, L., Chang, Z., Guo, X., Ristaniemi, T.: Multi-objective optimization for computation offloading in mobile-edge computing. In: 2017 IEEE Symposium on Computers and Communications (ISCC), pp. 832–837. IEEE (2017)

15. Li, B., He, M., Wu, W., Sangaiah, A.K., Jeon, G.: Computation offloading algorithm for arbitrarily divisible applications in mobile edge computing environments: an OCR case. Sustainability **10**(17), 196–210 (2018)
16. Liu, L., Fan, Q.: Resource allocation optimization based on mixed integer linear programming in the multi-cloudlet environment. IEEE Access **6**, 24533–24542 (2018)
17. Roy, D.G., De, D., Mukherjee, A., Buyya, R.: Application-aware cloudlet selection for computation offloading in multi-cloudlet environment. J. Supercomput. **73**(4), 1672–1690 (2016). https://doi.org/10.1007/s11227-016-1872-y
18. Mukherjee, A., De, D., Roy, D.G.: A power and latency aware cloudlet selection strategy for multi-cloudlet environment. IEEE Trans. Cloud Comput. **7**, 141–154 (2016)
19. Parmar, D., Kumar, A.S., Nivangune, A., Joshi, P., Rao, U.P.: Discovery and selection mechanism of cloudlets in a decentralized MCC environment. In: Proceedings of the International Conference on Mobile Software Engineering and Systems, pp. 15–16. ACM (2016)
20. Ali, M., Riaz, N., Ashraf, M.I., Qaisar, S., Naeem, M.: Joint cloudlet selection and latency minimization in fog networks. IEEE Trans. Industr. Inf. **14**(9), 4055–4063 (2018)
21. Mazouzi, H., Boussetta, K., Achir, N.: Maximizing mobiles energy saving through tasks optimal offloading placement in two-tier cloud: a theoretical and an experimental study. Comput. Commun. **144**, 132–148 (2019)
22. Deb, K., Pratap, A., Agarwal, S., Meyarivan, T.A.M.T.: A fast and elitist multi-objective genetic algorithm: NSGA-II. IEEE Trans. Evol. Comput. **6**(2), 182–197 (2002)
23. Vilaplana, J., Solsona, F., Teixidó, I., Mateo, J., Abella, F., Rius, J.: A queuing theory model for cloud computing. J. Supercomput. **69**(1), 492–507 (2014). https://doi.org/10.1007/s11227-014-1177-y

A Survey of QoS Optimization and Energy Saving in Cloud, Edge and IoT

Zhiguo Qu[1,2], Yilin Wang[1,2], Le Sun[1,2(✉)], Zheng Li[1,2], and Dandan Peng[1,2]

[1] Jiangsu Collaborative Innovation Center of Atmospheric Environment and Equipment Technology (CICAEET), Nanjing, China
sunle2009@gmail.com

[2] Nanjing University of Information Science and Technology, Nanjing 210044, China

Abstract. Since the emergence of cloud computing, it has been serving people as an important way of data processing. Later, with the development of computer and people's demand for higher service quality, fog computing, edge computing, mobile edge computing (MEC), Internet of Things (IoTs) and other models gradually appeared. They are developed step by step to bring better service to people. In recent years, IoTs technology has also been developed rapidly. This paper firstly gives a brief overview of cloud computing, fog computing, edge computing, MEC and IoTs. Then, we investigated the important papers related to these technologies, classify and compared the papers, so as to have a deeper understanding of these technologies.

Keywords: Cloud computing · Fog computing · Edge computing · MEC · IoT

1 Introduction

With the development of the Internet and the maturity of various processing and storage technologies, more and more computing resources emerge, and a large amount of data needs to be processed. New computing models emerge when users' requirements on resources increase, which include cloud computing, fog computing, edge computing, mobile edge computing (MEC) and Internet of Things (IoTs).

This paper investigates the important papers related to these computing models, and divides them into five categories based on the problems solved in these papers. On the basis of the problem classification in each section, further division is made according to the model used. For each paper, we point out the problem it aims to solve and introduce the methods it uses to solve the problem. In addition, in each problem category, we compare the methods proposed by the reviewed papers to solve the problem.

Supported by organization CloudComp.

© ICST Institute for Computer Sciences, Social Informatics and Telecommunications Engineering 2020
Published by Springer Nature Switzerland AG 2020. All Rights Reserved
X. Zhang et al. (Eds.): CloudComp 2019/SmartGift 2019, LNICST 322, pp. 33–46, 2020.
https://doi.org/10.1007/978-3-030-48513-9_3

2   Computing Models

2.1   Cloud Computing

With the rapid development of the Internet, more and more computing resources emerge, so a new computing model is needed to manage these resources, and cloud computing comes into being. The National Institute of Standards and Technology defined "cloud computing" as follows: it can provide convenient and quick network access to shared configurable resources, such as networks and servers. In addition, the provisioning and publishing of these resources does not require much administration and interaction of service providers [51].

2.2   Fog Computing

Due to the development of the IoT and the increasing needs of people, the IoT system based on cloud computing faces some limitations, such as the failure of playing a good role in large-scale or heterogeneous conditions [18]. Therefore, a new computing model called "fog computing" is developed on the basis of cloud computing. Compared with cloud computing, the main advantage of fog computing is that it can extend cloud resources to the network edge to facilitate the management of resources and services [26].

2.3   Edge Computing

Edge computing is defined as a technology that allows computing to be performed on the edge of a network [32]. Edge computing refers to all the resources of computing and network from data sources to cloud data centers. In edge computing, the flow of computing is bidirectional, and things in the edge computing can both consume data and produce data. That is, they can not only ask the cloud for services but also carries out computing jobs in the cloud [32].

The most popular embodiment of edge computing is the MEC, which refers to the technology of performing computation-intensive and delay-sensitive tasks for mobile devices by collecting a large amount of free computing power and storage resources located at the edge of a network. The European Telecommunication Standards Institute was the first to define it as a computing model that provides the capabilities of information technology and cloud computing at the network edge closing to mobile customers.

2.4   IoT

The IoT is created by the diffusion of sensors, actuators and other devices in the communication driven network. The development of wireless technologies, such as the wireless sensor network technology and actuator nodes, promotes the development of the IoT technology. With the development of the IoT, its application has gradually expanded to cover increasingly wider domains, but its goal has always been to make computers perceive information [38].

3   Energy Saving Techniques in Different Computing Models

In this section, we introduce the main work of resource allocation and energy saving techniques in the computing models. We categorize these work in terms of the means they use to achieve the objective of energy saving, which are: (1) quality of service (QoS) guaranteeing or service-level agreement (SLA) assurance (2) resource management and allocation, (3) scientific workflow execution, (4) servers optimization, (5) load balancing.

3.1   QoS Guaranteeing or SLA Assurance

Cloud Computing. Mazzucco et al. [24] let cloud service providers get the maximum benefit by reducing power consumption. In addition, they introduced and evaluated the policy of dynamic allocation of powering servers' switches to optimize users' experience while consuming the least amount of power. Mazzucco and Dyachuk [23] were also committed to making cloud service providers obtain the largest profits, and proposed the dynamic distribution strategy of powering server switch, which not only enables users to get good service, but also reduces power consumption. In order to make users have a good experience, this paper further uses a forecasting method to accurately predict the users' needs at different times. Mustafa et al. [25] leveraged the notion of workload consolidation to improve energy efficiency by putting incoming jobs on as few servers as possible. The concept of SLA is also imported to minimize the total SLA violations. Bi et al. [5] established an architecture that can administrate itself in cloud data centers firstly, which is suitable for web application services with several levels and has virtualization mechanism. Then, a mixed queuing model is proposed to decide the number of virtual machines (VMs) in each layer of application service environments. Finally, a problem of misalignment restrained optimization and a heuristic mixed optimization algorithm are proposed to make more revenues and meet different requirements of customers. Singh et al. [34] proposed a technology named "STAR" which can manage resources itself in the cloud computing environment and aims at reducing SLA violations, so that payment efficiency of cloud services can be improved. Beloglazov and Buyya [4] proposed a system to manage energy in cloud data center. By continuously integrating VMs and dynamically redistributing VMs, the system can achieve the goal of saving energy and providing a high QoS level at the same time. Guazzone et al. [14] proposed an automatic management system for resources to provide certain QoS and reduce energy consumption. Different from the traditional static method, this method can not only fit the changing workloads dynamically, but also achieve remarkable results in reducing QoS violations. Sun et al. [36] established a model to simplify the decision of cloud resource allocation and realize the independent allocation of resources. According to the description of advanced application and requirements of QoS and the performance of this method under different loads and resources, the optimal resource configuration can be obtained, so the QoS requirements can be well met. Siddesh and Srinivasa [33] paid close attention to the dynamic resource allocation and risks which meet the SLA and proposed a framework which can deal with workload types that are heterogeneous by dynamically planning capacity and assessing risks. The framework considers not only scheduling methods to reduce SLA, but also risks in resource allocation to maximize revenues on the cloud. Garg et al. [11] proposed a resource allocation strategy for VM dynamic allocation, which can improve resource utilization and increase providers' profits while reducing SLA violation. Jing et al. [6] proposed a new dynamic allocating technique using mixed queue model. Meeting customers' different requirements of performance at different levels by providing virtualized resources to each layer of virtualized application services. All these methods can reasonably configure the resources in the cloud data center, improve the system performance, reduce the additional cost of using resources and meet the required QoS.

Fog Computing. Gu et al. [13] used fog computing to process a large amount of data generated by medical devices and built fog computing supported Medical Cyber-Physical System (FC-MCPS), and in order to reduce the cost of FCMCPS, they did researches on the joint of base station, task assignment and VM layout. In addition, the problem is modeled as a mixed integer linear programming (MILP), and a two-stage heuristic algorithm based on linear programming (LP) is proposed to help solve the problem of large computational amount. Ni et al. [27] proposed a resource allocation approach based on fog computing, which enables users to select resources independently. In addition, this approach takes into account the price and time required to finish the job.

Edge Computing. Wei et al. [43] proposed a unified framework in the sustainable edge computing to save energy, including the energy that is distributed and renewable. And the architecture can combine the system that supply energy and edge computing, which can make full use of renewable energy and provide better QoS.

IoT. Rolik et al. [30] proposed a method to build a framework of IoT infrastructure based on microcloud, which can help use resources rationally, reduce the cost of management infrastructure, and improve the quality of life of consumers. Yao and Ansari [48] proposed an algorithm to determine the number of VMs to be rented and to control the power supply, thus the cost of system can be minimized and the QoS can be improved.

The ultimate goal of these papers is to improve QoS or reduce SLA violations, but the methods used are different and the computing modes are also different. The paper [24] allocates the switch of power servers dynamically to minimize the power cost, so as to solve the contradiction that the high QoS cannot coexist with the low power consumption. The allocation strategy of the paper [23] also manages the opening and closing of the server, and at the same time satisfies a certain QoS and low energy consumption. The paper [4] manages energy and integrates VMs according to the real-time utilization of resources, so as to improve QoS. The method of improving QoS in the paper [27] is making reasonable allocation of resources, but this method allows users to select resources independently. The algorithm in the paper [48] can effectively guarantee QoS in IoT network by controlling VMs and power supply.

The paper [13] introduces fog computing to ensure that Medical Cyber-Physical System (MCPS) provides high QoS and connects medical devices and data centers stably and with short delay at the same time. The framework in the paper [43] can manage energy uniformly, so as to meet the energy demand of equipment and QoS. The paper [30] establishes a framework for the management of IoT infrastructure to make rational use of resources, so as to improve QoS to a certain extent. The system in the paper [14] can self-manage the resources of cloud infrastructures to provide appropriate QoS. The model that can realize the independent allocation of resources established in the paper [36] considers many factors, so it can well meet QoS requirements. The paper [6] introduces a mixed queue model to allocate virtual resources, which can greatly reduce the extra cost of using resources and guarantee QoS.

The paper [25] uses techniques for consolidating workloads to achieve energy savings while reducing SLA violations. The paper [5] minimizes SLA by the reasonable allocation of VMs. The paper [34] takes advantage of technologies that enable self-administration of cloud services to effectively reduce SLA violations. The characteristics of the resource management model in the paper [33] are that it can meet the requirements of heterogeneous load types' resource management and SLA. The measurement and outline of the paper [11] can realize the dynamic allocation of VMs in heterogeneous environment and guarantee the SLA requirement.

3.2 Resource Management and Allocation

Cloud Computing. Wang et al. [40] introduced an allocation method for VM based on distributed multi-agent to allocate VMs to physical machines, which can realize VM consolidation and consider the migration costs simultaneously. In addition, a VM migration mechanism based on local negotiation is proposed to avoid unnecessary VM migration costs. Hassan et al. [15] established a formulation of universal problem and proposed a heuristic algorithm which has optimal parameters. Under this formulation, dynamic resource allocation can be made to meet the QoS requirements of applications, and the cost needed for dynamic resource allocation can be minimized with this algorithm. Wu et al. [44] proposed a scheduling algorithm based on the technology that can scale the voltage frequency dynamically in cloud computing, through which resources can be allocated for performing tasks and low power consumption network infrastructure can be realized. Compared with other schemes, this scheme not only sacrifices the performance of execution operations, but also saves more energy. Sarbazi and Zomaya [31] used two job consolidation heuristic methods to save energy. One is MaxUtil to better utilize resources and the other is Energy-Conscious Task Consolidation to focus on energy consumption which is active and idle. Using these two methods can promote the concurrent execution of multiple tasks and improve the energy efficiency. Hsu et al. [17] proposed a job consolidation technique aiming at energy saving, which can consume the least energy. In addition, the technology will limit the CPU usage and merge tasks in the virtual cluster. Once the task migration happens, the energy cost model will take into account the latency of the network. Hsu et al. [16] proposed a task intergration technology based on the energy perception. According to the characteristics of most cloud systems, the principle of using 70% CPU is proposed to administrate job integration among virtual clusters. This technology is very effective in reducing the amount of energy consumed in cloud systems by merging tasks. Panda and Jana [28] proposed an algorithm with several criteria to combine tasks, which not only considers the time needed for processing jobs, but also considers the utilization rate of VMs. The algorithm is more energy efficient because it takes into account not only the processing time but also the utilization rate of VMs. Wang et al. [42] proposed a resource allocation algorithm to deal with wide range of communication between nodes in cloud environment. This algorithm uses recognition technology to dynamically distribute jobs and nodes according to computing ability and factors of storage. And it can reduce the traffic when allocating resources because it uses dynamic hierarchy. Lin et al. [21] proposed a dynamic auction approach for resource allocation, which can ensure that even if there are many users and resources, the providers will have reasonable profits and the computing resources will be allocated correctly. Yazir et al. [49] proposed a new method to manage resources dynamically and autonomously. Firstly, resource management is split into jobs and each job is executed by autonomous nodes. Second, autonomous nodes use the method called "PROMETHEE" to configure resources. Krishnajyothi [19] proposed a framework which can implement parallel task processing to solve the problem of low efficiency when submitting large tasks. Compared with the static framework, this framework can dynamically allocate VMs, thus reducing costs and reducing the time of processing tasks. Lin et al. [22] proposed a method to allocate resources dynamically by using thresholds. Because this method uses the threshold value, it can optimize the reallocation of resources, improve the usage of resources and reduce the cost.

Fog Computing. Yin et al. [50] established a new model of scheduling jobs, which applies containers. And in order to make sure that jobs can be finished on time, a job scheduling algorithm is developed, which can also optimize the number of tasks that can be performed together on the nodes in fog computing. Moreover according to the specialties of the containers, this paper proposes a redistribution mechanisms to shorten the delay of tasks. These methods are very effective in reducing task delays. Aazam and Huh [1] established a framework to administrate resources effectively in the mode of fog computing. Considering that there are various types of objects and devices, the connection between them may be volatile and they are subject to exit the use of resources. So a method to predict and administrate resources is proposed. The method considers that any objects or devices can quit using resources at anytime, so it can provide effective management. Cuong et al. [9] studied the problem of allocating resources jointly and carbon footprint minimization in fog data center. In addition, a distributed algorithm is proposed to solve the problem of wide range optimization.

Edge Computing. Tung et al. [37] proposed a new framework for resource allocation based on market. The allocated resources come from edge nodes (ENs) with limited heterogeneous capabilities and are allocated to multiple competing services on the edge of the network. The advantages of generating a market equilibrium solution by reasonably pricing ENs is that not only the maximum utilization of marginal computing resources can be obtained, but also the optimal solution can be achieved.

MEC. Chen et al. [8] studied the problem of computing unloading with several users in the environment of mobile edge cloud computing with wireless interference which have many channels. In addition, a distributed algorithm for computing unload is developed, which can perform the unloading well even when there are a large number of users. Gao et al. [10] built a quadratic binary program, which is able to assign tasks in mobile cloud computing environment. Two algorithms are presented to obtain the optimal solution. Both of these heuristic algorithms can effectively solve the task assignment problem.

IoT. Barcelo et al. [3] expressed the problem of service allocation as a mixed flow problem with minimum cost which can be solved effectively by using LP. Solving this service allocation problem can solve the problems of unbalanced network load, delay of end-to-end service and excessive total consumption of electricity brought by the architecture of centralized cloud. Angelakis et al. [2] assigned the requirements of services' resources to heterogeneous network interface of equipment, and a MILP is given, so that more heterogeneous network interfaces of equipment can be used efficiently by a large amount of services. Song et al. [20] proposed a framework for communication used in 5G and the problem of resource allocation is transformed into the problem of power and channel allocation for making the signal data in the channel to be available and make the total energy efficiency of the system maximum.

In order to find better ways to manage computing resources, these papers pay special attention to the allocation of resources. The allocation of VMs or services and so on can make the system more energy efficient and contribute to the realization of green cloud computing. The paper [40] proposes a VM allocation method to efficiently allocate VM resources, and also considers the migration cost of VM migration, so it can consume less energy. The dynamic allocation of resources in the paper [15] is based on QoS requirements of applications, which can effectively reduce the waste of resources. In the paper [10], the tasks under edge computing are assigned scientifically and managed reasonably. The paper [3] studies the distribution of service resources in IoTCloud networks, which can effectively solve the defects of architecture of centralized cloud and bring people better experience. In the paper [2], the allocation strategy of service resource requirements makes the server use network interface efficiently. The method proposed in the paper [19] can effectively improve the efficiency of resource allocation when submitting large tasks by dynamically allocating VMs.

The paper [44] uses scheduling algorithm to allocate resources for executing tasks. The advantages of this scheduling method is to ensure the performance of executing jobs while implementing green computing. The job scheduling algorithm in the paper [50] can realize redistribution, which enables timely response of tasks.

The paper [31] manages resources by integrating tasks to improve resource utilization and reduce energy consumption. The paper [17] also integrates tasks to manage resources, and the methods used limit the use of CPU, which is very helpful for resource saving. The paper [28] also integrates tasks to facilitate efficient management of resources. In particular, this integration method takes into account the time needed to process tasks and the use of VMs.

The paper [1] proposes a framework to administrate resources in fog computing mode, which is characterized by the ability to deal with the phenomenon that objects or devices withdraw from resource utilization at any time. The paper [37] proposes a framework that allocates resources of EN with limited heterogeneous capability. The paper [20] is suitable for 5G communication framework to decompose the problem of resource allocation, promoting the development of 5G.

The paper [8] realizes the effective management of resources by solving the problem of user computing unloading. The paper [16] uses the principle of using 70% CPU to combine tasks, which can also manage resources and improve the utilization of resources. The algorithm in the paper [42] can greatly improve the communication performance in a large range and reduce the communication traffic in allocating resources. The mechanism of the paper [21] can deal with resource allocation in large-scale user and resource situations. The method of resource management in the paper [49] is characterized by its decomposition, and each job is executed by autonomous nodes, which is more flexible and convenient. The paper [22] uses the threshold value to reconfigure the resources, which can optimize the results of the allocation. The paper [9] solves the problem of joint allocation of resources to minimize the footprint of carbon.

3.3 Scientific Workflow Execution

Cloud Computing. Xu et al. [45] proposed a resource allocation method based on energy perception called "EnRealan" to solve the problem of energy consumption caused by the extension of cloud platform, and the dynamic deployment of VMs is generally adopted to obtain executions of scientific workflow. Bousselmi et al. [7] proposed a scheduling method based on energy perception for scientific workflows in cloud computing. Firstly, algorithm of splitting workflow for energy minimization is presented to divide workflow, which can achieve a high parallelism without huge energy consumption. Then a heuristic algorithm used to optimize cat swarm is proposed for the created partitions, which can minimize the total consumption of energy and execution time of workflows. Sonia et al. [35] proposed a workflow scheduling method with several objects and hybrid particle swarm optimization algorithm. In addition, a technology for scaling voltage and frequency dynamically is proposed, which can make the processors work at any voltage level, so as to minimize the energy consumption in the process of work flow scheduling.

The purpose of these papers is to obtain the implementation of scientific workflow, which is also very conducive to the least energy consumption. A scientific workflow can be achieved through resource allocation or scheduling and so on. The paper [45] uses a resource allocation method based on energy perception and dynamic deployment of VMs to obtain executions of scientific workflow. The paper [7] uses scientific workflows' scheduling method based on energy to generate the workflow and partition, so as to get the scientific workflows. The method of obtaining scientific workflows in the paper [35] is to study the scheduling problem of workflows on heterogeneous systems, not only to optimize events and cost constraints, but also to reduce energy consumption as much as possible.

3.4   Servers Optimization

Cloud Computing. Yang et al. [12] proposed a game-theoretic method and transformed the problem of minimizing energy into a congestion game. All the mobile devices in this method are participants in the game, and then it chooses a server to unload the computation, which can optimize the system and save energy. Wang et al. [41] proposed a MapReduce-based multi-task scheduling algorithm to achieve the objective of energy saving. This model is a two-layer model, which not only considers the impact of servers' performance changes on energy consumption, but also considers the limitation of network bandwidth. In addition, a local search operator is designed, and on this basis, a two-layer genetic algorithm is proposed to schedule tens of thousands of tasks in the cloud, so as to achieve large-scale optimization. Yanggratoke et al. [47] proposed a general generic gossip protocol, aiming at allocating resources in cloud environment which is on a large scale. An instantiation of this protocol was developed to enable server consolidation to allocate resources to more servers while meeting changing load patterns.

These papers are all devoted to the optimization of servers. Through the unloading or integration of servers can optimize the number of servers, which can also save the energy. The paper [12] uses a game-theoretic method to unload the server, which can not only optimize the system but also save energy. The task scheduling model and task scheduling method proposed in the paper [41] can effectively improve the energy efficiency of the server and thus reduce the energy consumption of the data center. The protocol proposed in the paper [47] can integrate servers and optimize the number of servers, so that more servers can be allocated to resources and reduce the total energy consumption.

3.5   Load Balancing

Cloud Computing. Paya and Marinescu [29] introduced an operation model that can balance cloud computing load and expand application, which aims at saving energy. The principle of this model is to define an operating system that optimizes its energy, makes as many servers as possible run in the system, and adjusts to sleep when no tasks are being performed or when the server is light, thus saving energy.

Fog Computing. Xu et al. [46] proposed a method that is called "DRAM" to dynamically allocate resources in fog computing environment, which can avoid both too high load and too low load. Through analyzing different kinds of computing nodes' load balance firstly, then allocating resources statically and migrating service dynamically in fog environment to design the relevant resource allocation method, so as to achieve load balance.

IoT. Wang et al. [39] established the architecture of the energy-saving targeted system, which is based on the industrial IoT. And due to its three levels the traffic load can be balanced. In addition, in order to predict sleep intervals, a sleep scheduling as well as a wake protocol are developed, which can save energy better.

All these papers adopt certain methods to achieve load balance, achieve green cloud computing, improve resource utilization and reduce energy consumption. The paper [29] proposes a model to manage the number of servers running in the system and achieve load balance. The approach to make the system's load balance in the paper [46] is to make reasonable allocation of resources in fog environment. The three-tier architecture constructed in the paper [39] can ensure the load balance of traffic.

4   Conclusion

Nowadays, cloud computing, fog computing, edge computing, MEC, IoT and other technologies are developing rapidly, and they are rapidly improving the development of information technology. Although there will be many challenges in this field, their development can greatly change people's lives and bring convenience to people. This paper investigates and classifies the papers related to these five technologies to facilitate people's understanding of them.

Acknowledgement. This work is supported by the National Natural Science Foundation of China (Grants No 61702274) and the Natural Science Foundation of Jiangsu Province (Grants No BK20170958), and PAPD.

References

1. Aazam, M., Huh, E.N.: Dynamic resource provisioning through fog micro datacenter. In: 2015 IEEE International Conference on Pervasive Computing and Communication Workshops (PerCom Workshops), pp. 105–110. IEEE (2015)
2. Angelakis, V., Avgouleas, I., Pappas, N., Yuan, D.: Flexible allocation of heterogeneous resources to services on an IoT device. In: 2015 IEEE Conference on Computer Communications Workshops (INFOCOM WKSHPS), pp. 99–100. IEEE (2015)
3. Barcelo, M., Correa, A., Llorca, J., Tulino, A.M., Vicario, J.L., Morell, A.: IoT-cloud service optimization in next generation smart environments. IEEE J. Sel. Areas. Commun. **34**(12), 4077–4090 (2016)
4. Beloglazov, A., Buyya, R.: Energy efficient resource management in virtualized cloud data centers. In: Proceedings of the 2010 10th IEEE/ACM International Conference on Cluster, Cloud and Grid Computing, pp. 826–831. IEEE Computer Society (2010)
5. Bi, J., Yuan, H., Tie, M., Tan, W.: SLA-based optimisation of virtualised resource for multi-tier web applications in cloud data centres. Enterp. Inf. Syst. **9**(7), 743–767 (2015)
6. Bi, J., Zhu, Z., Yuan, H.: SLA-aware dynamic resource provisioning for profit maximization in shared cloud data centers. In: Wu, Y. (ed.) ICHCC 2011. CCIS, vol. 163, pp. 366–372. Springer, Heidelberg (2011). https://doi.org/10.1007/978-3-642-25002-6_52
7. Bousselmi, K., Brahmi, Z., Gammoudi, M.M.: Energy efficient partitioning and scheduling approach for scientific workflows in the cloud. In: 2016 IEEE International Conference on Services Computing (SCC), pp. 146–154. IEEE (2016)
8. Chen, X., Jiao, L., Li, W., Fu, X.: Efficient multi-user computation offloading for mobile-edge cloud computing. IEEE/ACM Trans. Netw. **24**(5), 2795–2808 (2016)
9. Do, C.T., Tran, N.H., Pham, C., Alam, M.G.R., Son, J.H., Hong, C.S.: A proximal algorithm for joint resource allocation and minimizing carbon footprint in geo-distributed fog computing. In: 2015 International Conference on Information Networking (ICOIN), pp. 324–329. IEEE (2015)
10. Gao, B., He, L., Lu, X., Chang, C., Li, K., Li, K.: Developing energy-aware task allocation schemes in cloud-assisted mobile workflows. In: 2015 IEEE International Conference on Computer and Information Technology; Ubiquitous Computing and Communications; Dependable, Autonomic and Secure Computing; Pervasive Intelligence and Computing, pp. 1266–1273. IEEE (2015)
11. Garg, S.K., Gopalaiyengar, S.K., Buyya, R.: SLA-based resource provisioning for heterogeneous workloads in a virtualized cloud datacenter. In: Xiang, Y., Cuzzocrea, A., Hobbs, M., Zhou, W. (eds.) ICA3PP 2011. LNCS, vol. 7016, pp. 371–384. Springer, Heidelberg (2011). https://doi.org/10.1007/978-3-642-24650-0_32
12. Ge, Y., Zhang, Y., Qiu, Q., Lu, Y.H.: A game theoretic resource allocation for overall energy minimization in mobile cloud computing system. In: Proceedings of the 2012 ACM/IEEE International Symposium on Low Power Electronics and Design, pp. 279–284. ACM (2012)
13. Gu, L., Zeng, D., Guo, S., Barnawi, A., Xiang, Y.: Cost efficient resource management in fog computing supported medical cyber-physical system. IEEE Trans. Emerg. Top. Comput. **5**(1), 108–119 (2015)
14. Guazzone, M., Anglano, C., Canonico, M.: Energy-efficient resource management for cloud computing infrastructures. In: 2011 IEEE Third International Conference on Cloud Computing Technology and Science, pp. 424–431. IEEE (2011)

15. Hassan, M.M., Song, B., Hossain, M.S., Alamri, A.: Efficient resource scheduling for big data processing in cloud platform. In: Fortino, G., Di Fatta, G., Li, W., Ochoa, S., Cuzzocrea, A., Pathan, M. (eds.) IDCS 2014. LNCS, vol. 8729, pp. 51–63. Springer, Cham (2014). https://doi.org/10.1007/978-3-319-11692-1_5

16. Hsu, C.H., et al.: Energy-aware task consolidation technique for cloud computing. In: 2011 IEEE Third International Conference on Cloud Computing Technology and Science, pp. 115–121. IEEE (2011)

17. Hsu, C.H., Slagter, K.D., Chen, S.C., Chung, Y.C.: Optimizing energy consumption with task consolidation in clouds. Inf. Sci. **258**(3), 452–462 (2014)

18. Iorga, M., Feldman, L., Barton, R., Martin, M.J., Goren, N.S., Mahmoudi, C.: Fog computing conceptual model. Technical report, Recommendations of the National Institute of Standards and Technology (2018)

19. Krishnajyothi, K.: Parallel data processing for effective dynamic resource allocation in the cloud. Int. J. Comput. Appl. **70**(22), 1–4 (2013)

20. Li, S., Ni, Q., Sun, Y., Min, G., Al-Rubaye, S.: Energy-efficient resource allocation for industrial cyber-physical IoT systems in 5G era. IEEE Trans. Industr. Inf. **14**(6), 2618–2628 (2018)

21. Lin, W.Y., Lin, G.Y., Wei, H.Y.: Dynamic auction mechanism for cloud resource allocation. In: Proceedings of the 2010 10th IEEE/ACM International Conference on Cluster, Cloud and Grid Computing, pp. 591–592. IEEE Computer Society (2010)

22. Lin, W., Wang, J.Z., Chen, L., Qi, D.: A threshold-based dynamic resource allocation scheme for cloud computing. Procedia. Eng. **23**(5), 695–703 (2011)

23. Mazzucco, M., Dyachuk, D.: Optimizing cloud providers revenues via energy efficient server allocation. Sustain. Comput. Inform. Syst. **2**(1), 1–12 (2012)

24. Mazzucco, M., Dyachuk, D., Deters, R.: Maximizing cloud providers' revenues via energy aware allocation policies. In: 2010 IEEE 3rd International Conference on Cloud Computing, pp. 131–138. IEEE (2010)

25. Mustafa, S., Bilal, K., Malik, S.U.R., Madani, S.A.: SLA-aware energy efficient resource management for cloud environments. IEEE Access. **6**, 15004–15020 (2018)

26. Nebbiolo: Fog vs edge computing. Technical report, Nebbiolo Technologies Inc. (2018)

27. Ni, L., Zhang, J., Jiang, C., Yan, C., Yu, K.: Resource allocation strategy in fog computing based on priced timed petri nets. IEEE Internet Things J. **4**(5), 1216–1228 (2017)

28. Panda, S.K., Jana, P.K.: An efficient task consolidation algorithm for cloud computing systems. In: Bjørner, N., Prasad, S., Parida, L. (eds.) ICDCIT 2016. LNCS, vol. 9581, pp. 61–74. Springer, Cham (2016). https://doi.org/10.1007/978-3-319-28034-9_8

29. Paya, A., Marinescu, D.C.: Energy-aware load balancing and application scaling for the cloud ecosystem. IEEE Trans. Cloud Comput. **5**(1), 15–27 (2015)

30. Rolik, O., Zharikov, E., Telenyk, S.: Microcloud-based architecture of management system for IoT infrastructures. In: 2016 Third International Scientific-Practical Conference Problems of Infocommunications Science and Technology (PIC S&T), pp. 149–151. IEEE (2016)

31. Sarbazi-Azad, H., Zomaya, A.Y.: Energy-efficient resource utilization in cloud computing. In: Large Scale Network-Centric Distributed Systems, pp. 377–408. Wiley-IEEE Press (2014)

32. Shi, W., Jie, C.: Edge computing: vision and challenges. IEEE Internet Things J. **3**(5), 637–646 (2016)

33. Siddesh, G.M., Srinivasa, K.G.: SLA - driven dynamic resource allocation on clouds. In: Thilagam, P.S., Pais, A.R., Chandrasekaran, K., Balakrishnan, N. (eds.) ADCONS 2011. LNCS, vol. 7135, pp. 9–18. Springer, Heidelberg (2012). https://doi.org/10.1007/978-3-642-29280-4_2

34. Singh, S., Chana, I., Buyya, R.: STAR: SLA-aware autonomic management of cloud resources. IEEE Trans. Cloud Comput., 1 (2017)

35. Sonia, Y., Rachid, C., Hubert, K., Bertrand, G.: Multi-objective approach for energy-aware workflow scheduling in cloud computing environments. Sci. World. J. **2013**(3–4), 350934 (2013)

36. Sun, Y., White, J., Eade, S.: A model-based system to automate cloud resource allocation and optimization. In: Dingel, J., Schulte, W., Ramos, I., Abrahão, S., Insfran, E. (eds.) MODELS 2014. LNCS, vol. 8767, pp. 18–34. Springer, Cham (2014). https://doi.org/10.1007/978-3-319-11653-2_2

37. Tung, N.D., Bao, L.L., Vijay, B.: Price-based resource allocation for edge computing: a market equilibrium approach. IEEE Trans. Cloud Comput., 1 (2018)

38. Vashi, S., Ram, J., Modi, J., Verma, S., Prakash, C.: Internet of Things (IoT): a vision, architectural elements, and security issues. In: 2017 International Conference on I-SMAC (IoT in Social, Mobile, Analytics and Cloud) (I-SMAC), pp. 492–496. IEEE (2017)

39. Wang, K., Wang, Y., Sun, Y., Guo, S., Wu, J.: Green industrial internet of things architecture: an energy-efficient perspective. IEEE Commun. Mag. **54**(12), 48–54 (2016)

40. Wang, W., Jiang, Y., Wu, W.: Multiagent-based resource allocation for energy minimization in cloud computing systems. IEEE Trans. Syst. Man Cybern. Syst. **47**(2), 1–16 (2016)

41. Wang, X., Wang, Y., Yue, C.: An energy-aware bi-level optimization model for multi-job scheduling problems under cloud computing. Soft. Comput. **20**(1), 303–317 (2016)

42. Wang, Z., Su, X.: Dynamically hierarchical resource-allocation algorithm in cloud computing environment. J. Supercomput. **71**(7), 2748–2766 (2015)

43. Wei, L., Yang, T., Delicato, F.C., Pires, P.F., Tari, Z., Khan, S.U., Zomaya, A.Y.: On enabling sustainable edge computing with renewable energy resources. IEEE Commun. Mag. **56**(5), 94–101 (2018)

44. Wu, C.M., Chang, R.S., Chan, H.Y.: A green energy-efficient scheduling algorithm using the DVFS technique for cloud datacenters. Future Gener. Comput. Syst. **37**(7), 141–147 (2014)

45. Xu, X., Dou, W., Zhang, X., Chen, J.: EnReal: an energy-aware resource allocation method for scientific workflow executions in cloud environment. IEEE Trans. Cloud Comput. **4**(2), 166–179 (2016)

46. Xu, X., et al.: Dynamic resource allocation for load balancing in fog environment. Wirel. Commun. Mob. Comput. **2018**(2), 1–15 (2018)

47. Yanggratoke, R., Wuhib, F., Stadler, R.: Gossip-based resource allocation for green computing in large clouds. In: 2011 7th International Conference on Network and Service Management, pp. 1–9. IEEE (2011)

48. Yao, J., Ansari, N.: QoS-aware fog resource provisioning and mobile device power control in IoT networks. IEEE Trans. Netw. Serv. Manage. **16**(1), 167–175 (2018)

49. Yazir, Y.O., et al.: Dynamic resource allocation in computing clouds using distributed multiple criteria decision analysis. In: 2010 IEEE 3rd International Conference on Cloud Computing, pp. 91–98. IEEE (2010)

50. Yin, L., Juan, L., Haibo, L.: Tasks scheduling and resource allocation in fog computing based on containers for smart manufacture. IEEE Trans. Industr. Inf. **14**(10), 4712–4721 (2018)
51. Zhang, Q., Cheng, L., Boutaba, R.: Cloud computing: state-of-the-art and research challenges. J. Internet Serv. Appl. **1**(1), 7–18 (2010)

A Multi-objective Computation Offloading Method for Hybrid Workflow Applications in Mobile Edge Computing

Kai Peng[1,2(✉)], Bohai Zhao[1], Xingda Qian[1], Xiaolong Xu[3], Lixin Zheng[2], and Victor C. M. Leung[4]

[1] College of Engineering, Huaqiao University, Quanzhou, China
pkbupt@gmail.com
[2] Fujian Provincial Academic Engineering Research Center in Industrial Intellectual Techniques and Systems, Quanzhou, China
[3] Key Laboratory of Intelligent Perception and Systems for High-Dimensional Information of Ministry of Education, Nanjing University of Science and Technology, Nanjing 210094, People's Republic of China
[4] Department of Electrical and Computer Engineering, The University of British Columbia, Vancouver, BC V6T 1Z4, Canada

Abstract. Computation offloading has become a promising method to overcome intrinsic defects of portable smart devices, such as low operating speed and low battery capacity. However, it is a challenge to design an optimized strategy as the edge server is resource-constrained and the workflow application has timing constraints. In this paper, we investigated the hybrid workflow application computation offloading issue, which further increases the difficulty. According to the analysis of theory and consideration of time consumption and energy consumption, we establish a multi-objective optimization model to solve the issue. Furthermore, we propose a method based on particle swarm optimization algorithm for multi-objective computation offloading to get the optimal strategy for tasks offloading, which is suitable for all the hybrid workflow applications. Finally, extensive experiments have verified the effectiveness and efficiency of our proposed method.

Keywords: Mobile edge computing · Hybrid workflow applications · Multi-objective · Time consumption · Energy consumption

1 Introduction

With the development of cloud computing and big data, mobile devices are becoming an essential part of people's daily life [1,2]. People can obtain all the services they need from cloud computing with the help of mobile devices. Nevertheless, the distance between the remote cloud and users is quite far, which may reduce the quality of service [3,4]. Fortunately, there is another computing platform named mobile edge computing (MEC), which can push computation and

X. Zhang et al. (Eds.): CloudComp 2019/SmartGift 2019, LNICST 322, pp. 47–62, 2020.
https://doi.org/10.1007/978-3-030-48513-9_4

storage closer to mobile users [5,6]. Computation offloading of MEC can solve the resource limitation problem of mobile devices effectively. Namely, offloading some applications from local to the edge servers in MEC may be more energy efficient [7,8].

In this paper, we mainly focus on the computation offloading of workflow applications(WAs) in MEC. Although many studies investigate the computation offloading of WAs in mobile cloud computing (MCC) well [9–13], the solutions in MCC cannot be used for the issue in MEC directly due to the different architectures of MCC and MEC. The MEC has a three-tier architecture, the core of which is the edge server [14]. Besides, we mainly focus on the cloudlet-based MEC in this study [15]. The Edge server can significantly reduce the delay for users to access the remote cloud, but the computing resources of the cloudlet are limited. Therefore, the computation offloading strategy has a significant impact on the completion time of the WA and the energy consumption of the mobile device (MD).

In this paper, the hybrid WAs computation offloading in MEC is well investigated. Hybrid applications consist of several general WAs and several time-constrained WAs. Our primary objective is finding optimization computation offloading strategies to minimize the time consumption and the energy consumption of each WA while meeting the time constraints of each WA that was given in advance. Our primary contributions are summarized as follows.

1) We investigated the hybrid WAs computation offloading issue in MEC.

2) The hybrid WAs computation offloading is molded as a multi-objective optimization problem, both energy consumption and energy consumption are taken into consideration.

3) A multi-objective computation offloading method for hybrid WAs based on improved particle swarm optimization is designed to minimize time consumption and energy consumption for each WA while satisfying the deadline requirements of the WAs.

4) Compared to other methods, the experimental results verify that our proposed method is effective.

The rest of this paper is organized as follows. Section 2 introduces related work. The system model and problem formulation are introduced in Sect. 3. Section 4 gives the multi-objective offloading algorithm for the hybrid WAs method. Section 5 introduces the experimental results and discussion. Section 6 describes the conclusion of this paper and the future work.

2   Related Work

Computation offloading has been well studied in [9–11]. Jia et al. [9] studied the migration of linear topology tasks and parallel topology tasks in the MCC environment and proposed an optimal linear task offloading strategy and heuristic parallel task migration algorithm based on the strategy of load balancing. Deng et al. [10] proposed a computational load offloading strategy for WAs based on a genetic algorithm. Based on their algorithm, some tasks of the WA are offloaded to the remote cloud to execute so as to achieve the optimization of execution time of WA and energy consumption of devices. Zhou et al. [11] consider the delay transmission mechanism and then propose a multi-objective workflow scheduling algorithm. They incorporate the delay transmission mechanism in the WA scheduling process, which can effectively optimize the energy consumption and completion time of WA at the same time.

As a result of the different architecture between MCC and MEC, the computation offloading of WAs in MCC cannot be used for the issue in MEC.

Computation offloading of general applications has been studied in [18]. In terms of using augmented reality applications in the environment of MEC, the authors proposed a corresponding algorithm for computation offloading. Furthermore, they proposed a multi-user computing offloading algorithm for the applications with high latency requirements and multi-user participation. Li et al. [19] try their utmost to minimize the computation latency of each task by proposing a migration algorithm. In this way, the applications are divided into many parts and are migrated to multiple cloudlets. But, they merely consider the latency optimization.

Zhang et al. [20] proposed an offloading strategy which reduced the energy of home automation applications. In order to reduce the WAs' total energy consumption within the constrained deadline, the MDs are made scheduled using the particle swarm optimization. Nevertheless, their method focuses on the optimization of energy consumption.

In this paper, we focus on the multi-objective optimization for hybrid WAs in MEC. Both energy consumption and time consumption are taken into consideration.

3   The System Model and Problem Formulation

In this section, the architecture of MEC is introduced. As shown in Fig. 1, we can see that MEC has a three-tire architecture which consists of mobile users, MEC servers, and remote cloud. In addition, there are some applications like WA in mobile devices that should be executed within given constrained time. In addition, these applications can be processed locally or can be offloaded to the cloud via WAN or cloudlet via LAN according to the strategy to reduce energy consumption or execution time, or both of them.

3.1   Basic Mode

In this section, the referred variable symbols are introduced. N represents computation task. N_f represents the number of the f_{th} WA's computation tasks. The workflow is used to model the mobile application, denoted as $W = \{w_1, w_2, \ldots, w_f\}$. In this paper, the WAs include scheduled and unscheduled WA which are denoted as $W_f(V, \xi)$. The set of computation tasks are represented by $V = \{v_{1,f}, v_{2,f}, \ldots, v_{i,f}\}$ and $\xi = \{r(v_{i,f}, v_{j,f}) | v_{i,f}, v_{j,f} \in V\}$ represents the dependencies between tasks in the certain workflow. S represents the

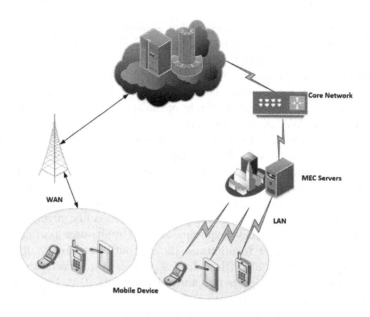

Fig. 1. The architecture of MEC

set of offloading strategies. $S = \{S_{i,f} | i = 1, 2, \ldots, N, f = 1, 2, \ldots, F\}$, where $S_{i,f} \in \{1, 2, 3\}$. $S_{i,f} = 1$ means that the $v_{i,f}$ is executed on the local network, $S_{i,f} = 2$ denotes the task is offloaded and computed by the cloudlet, and $S_{i,f} = 3$ denotes the task is offloaded and computed by the cloud.

3.2 Time Consumption Mode

The time for a single user consumed consists of the waiting time, executing time, and transmitting time. The model of the waiting time in the cloudlet is imitated by the Fig. 2. When the tasks are chosen to be offloaded to the cloudlet, which obeys the rule that first comes will be the first severed. As all tasks arrive randomly and the computing resources in cloudlets are limited, queuing occurs when the number of arriving tasks more than the computing number within capacity.

Average Waiting Time. It is hypothesized that the service time of the cloudlet is subjected to the parameter μ, which presents the negative exponential distribution. And the interval of the time that task arrived at cloudlet from the mobile devices follows the parameter λ, which presents the negative exponential distribution. F indicates the number of virtual machines distributed in the cloudlet, which indicates the computing power of the cloudlet. The waiting time mode is established according to the basis of the queuing theory. The possibility of inactive cloudlet is shown as:

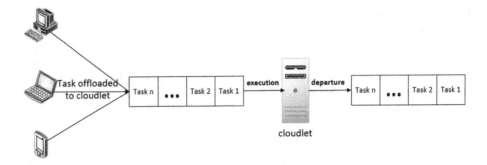

Fig. 2. The task queue in cloudlet

$$P_{idle} = [\sum_{n=0}^{F-1} \frac{\rho^{n_f}}{n_f!} + \frac{\rho^F}{F!(1 - \rho_F)}]^{-1} \tag{1}$$

where $\rho = \frac{\lambda}{\mu}$ denotes the cloudlets utilization and $\rho_F = \frac{\rho}{F}$. n_f represent the f_{th} workflow's queue length. When the cloudlet is working normally, p_{n_f} shows the possibility of the queue size getting to n_f. Then, p_{n_f} is given as:

$$p_{n_f} = \begin{cases} \frac{\rho^{n_f}}{F!F^{n_f-F}} \cdot P_{idle} & n_f \geq F \\ \frac{p^{n_f}}{n_f!} \cdot P_{idle} & n_f < F \end{cases} \tag{2}$$

When $n_f \geq F$, we use C_w to indicate the possibility of the waiting tasks in cloudlet. And it is denoted as

$$C_w(F, \rho) = \sum_{n_f=F}^{\infty} p_{n_f} = \frac{\rho^F}{F!(1 - \rho_F)} \cdot P_{idle} \tag{3}$$

Based on the theory, L_q represents the average waiting length of the queue and L_F represents the waiting length of the current queue and is calculated by

$$L_q = \sum_{n_f=F+1}^{\infty} (n_f - F)p_{n_f} = \frac{P_{idle} \cdot \rho^F}{F!} \cdot \sum_{n_f=F}^{\infty} (n_f - F)\rho_F^{n_f-F} \tag{4}$$

$$L_F = L_q + \rho \tag{5}$$

Generally speaking, the average time of tasks waiting in the cloudlet is given as

$$T_{wait} = \frac{L_F}{\lambda} - \frac{1}{\mu} = \frac{1}{F \cdot \mu - \lambda} C_w(F, \rho) \tag{6}$$

Processing Time and Transmission Time

According to the waiting time model, the execution time of tasks with different strategies $s_{i,f}$, which offload tasks to different locations is exactly computed. w_f represents the f_{th} WA's workload. f_l, f_{cl} and f_c show the computation capacity of the MD, cloudlet and cloud. The latency time of WAN and LAN is denoted as L_{WAN}, L_{LAN}. The execution time model is shown below.

$$T_{exe}^{s_{i,f}}(v_{i,f}) = \begin{cases} \dfrac{w_f}{f_l} & s_{i,f} = 1 \\ T_{wait} + \dfrac{w_f}{f_{cl}} + L_{LAN} & s_{i,f} = 2 \\ \dfrac{w_f}{f_c} + L_{WAN} & s_{i,f} = 3 \end{cases} \tag{7}$$

The time spent during the data transmission among MD, cloud, and cloudlet is computed by

$$T_{tran}^{(s_{i,f}, s_{j,f})}(v_{i,f}, v_{j,f}) = \begin{cases} 0 & S_t = 1 \\ \dfrac{d_{i,f}}{B_{cl}} & S_t = 2 \\ \dfrac{d_{i,f}}{B_c} & S_t = 3 \end{cases} \tag{8}$$

If the tasks $v_{i,f}$ and $v_{j,f}$ are executed in the same locations or they are executed in the cloudlet and the cloud respectively, for instance, $(s_{i,f}, s_{j,f}) \in \{(2,3),(3,2),(1,1),(2,2),(3,3)\}$, the transmission time will be equal to 0, and we define this situation as $S_t = 1$. In addition, when $v_{i,f}$ and $v_{j,f}$ are executed on the different locations, such as $(s_{i,f}, s_{j,f}) \in \{(1,2),(2,1)\}$, the task data is transmitted via the network LAN, where its bandwidth is depicted as B_{cl} and $S_t = 2$. Furthermore, when $(s_{i,f}, s_{j,f}) \in \{(1,3),(3,1)\}$, the task data is transmitted via the network WAN, where its bandwidth is B_c, and $S_t = 3$. The total time consumption is given by

$$T_{total}(S_{i,f}) = \sum_{i=1}^{N_f} T_{exe}^{s_{i,f}}(v_{i,f}) + \sum_{r(v_{i,f}, v_{j,f} \in \xi)} T_{tran}^{(s_{i,f}, s_{j,f})}(v_{i,f}, v_{j,f}) \tag{9}$$

3.3 Energy Consumption Model

The energy consumed for processing and transmission makes up the total energy consumption. The processing energy consumption of the task $v_{i,f}$ is represented by $E_{exe}^{s_{i,f}}(v_{i,f})$ and $E_{trans}(v_{i,f}, v_{j,f})$ denotes the energy consumption which is caused by the data transmission between the task $v_{i,f}$ and the task $v_{j,f}$. The formulation is given as

$$E_{exe}^{s_{i,f}}(v_{i,f}) = \begin{cases} \dfrac{w_{i,f}}{f_l} \cdot p_A & s_{i,f} = 1 \\ (T_{wait} + \dfrac{w_{i,f}}{f_{cl}} + L_{LAN}) \cdot p_I & s_{i,f} = 2 \\ (\dfrac{w_{i,f}}{f_c} + L_{LAN}) \cdot p_I & s_{i,f} = 3 \end{cases} \tag{10}$$

where the consumed power when MD is in the active state is denoted as p_A and p_I denotes the consumed power of inactive MD. The energy consumption caused by transmission between task $v_{i,f}$ and task $v_{j,f}$ is shown as

$$E_{tran}^{(s_{i,f},s_{j,f})}(v_{i,f},v_{j,f}) = \frac{d_{i,j}}{B} \cdot p_T \tag{11}$$

where p_T shows the transmitted power of the MD. Thus, the total energy consumption of the f_{th} workflow is given as

$$E_{total}(S_{i,f}) = \sum_{i=1}^{N} E_{exe}^{s_{i,f}}(v_{i,f}) + \sum_{r(v_{i,f},v_{j,f}\in\xi)} E_{tran}^{(s_{i,f},s_{j,f})}(v_{i,f},v_{j,f}) \tag{12}$$

3.4   Problem Formulation

The objective of the offloading issue is not only to minimize the total consumption of energy, but also optimize the execution time of the WAs while meeting timing constraints of WAs. The objective function is calculated by

$$Min\ E_{total}(S_{i,f}), \forall f \in \{1,2...F\} \tag{13}$$

$$Min\ T_{total}(S_{i,f}), \forall f \in \{1,2...F\} \tag{14}$$

$$s.t. T_{total}(S_{i,f}) \leq T_{ddl}, \forall f \in \{1,2...F\} \tag{15}$$

$$s_i \in \{1,2,3\} \tag{16}$$

where T_{ddl} shows the constrained time of the f_{th} WA.

4   Multi-objective Offloading Algorithm for Hybrid Workflow Applications

In this section, the details of our algorithm are illustrated. Firstly, in order to make PSO algorithm more suitable for solving discrete problem, we redefine some basic parameters. Then, the basic steps of multi-objective offloading algorithm for hybrid WAs(MOHWA) are described. Meanwhile, the structure and the construction method of hybrid WAs are depicted.

4.1   Preliminary

PSO is an effective and efficient algorithm inspired by the foraging behavior of animals where each particle in the group can update its velocity and direction dynamically through continuous learning of the group and its activities so as to improve the collective interests effectively. Originally, PSO algorithm was proposed for solving continuous space problems in 1995 [16]. Later, in 1997, the discrete binary version of the algorithm was presented to operate on discrete binary variables [17].

PSO propose an efficient global search algorithm based on the group intelligence. Firstly, PSO distributes the particles into solution space randomly. Each particle has a position, velocity and other information, and we will record the optimal position of the particle. Then, a fitness function is designed to evaluate the position of particles. Before each movement of particles, it will search the nearby area first, and compare the position of the nearest particle to the target with the best position in its own memory and adjusts its speed and direction according to these, until the particles in the group pass through the target position or reach the upper limit of iteration times.

PSO is often used to solve the continuous problems, but in solving discrete problems, the performance of PSO is not very well. Therefore, we redefine some parameters and attributes in PSO to solve discrete offloading strategy problems. The redefinition is as follows:

Definition 1. The Properties of Particles: As shown in Fig. 3, each task is an individual in the algorithm, also known as a particle, and each WA is a group, also known as population. Every individual in the swarm can search for the best position through his own experience and the experience of the group by vectors adding.

Definition 2. The offloading paths of particles: Defining the location of each particle is its offloading strategy. Each WA consists of many tasks. When tasks are offloaded, they have three paths to choose. We define the offloading path $d \in \{1, 2, 3\}$, and the position of particles $P_i^k(d, n) \in \{0, 1\}$. If $P_i^k(1, n) = 1$, the task will be executed locally. If $P_i^k(2, n) = 1$, the task will be offloaded to cloudlet for execution. Correspondingly, if $P_i^k(3, n) = 1$, the task will be offloaded to the cloud.

Definition 3. The velocity of particles: We define the velocity of each particle as a matrix of $d \times 1$. Correspondingly, the velocity equation $V_i^{k+1}(d, n)$ in discrete case is constructed. Furthermore, the velocity of each WA is a matrix of $d \times n$. In this way, we can easily find out which path the particle offloaded with the fastest speed.

Definition 4. Redefining Decision Parameters: We redefine the determinant parameters of the method. Convert the velocity inertia parameter ω, the impact of the optimal location currently found by individuals c_1 and the impact of the optimal location currently found by groups c_2 from fixed to variable ones. They will change with the need of our offloading strategy. Moreover, the convergence factor α is added to prevent the potential problem of local convergence of the algorithm.

4.2 The Basic Steps of MOHWA

Compared to other algorithms, PSO has a better computing ability, which can achieve convergence in a short time, especially in solving big data issues. However, the diversity of the population in the search space may be lost, which may

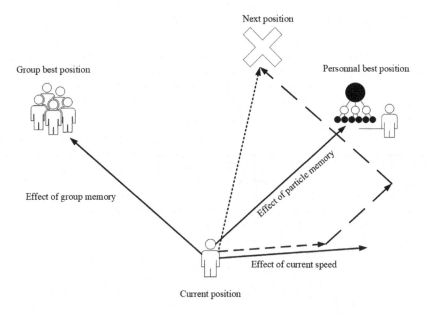

Fig. 3. The graphical representation of PSO

lead to local convergence. In order to solve this problem, we propose an improved optimization method based on PSO algorithm, named MOHWA. Our objective is to find the best offloading strategy to optimize both energy consumption and the time consumption of MDs jointly. In our algorithm, each particle is evaluated by the fitness function and the computation of the fitness value is shown as Eq. (17):

$$Fit(V_{i,j}) = E_{total}(S_i, f) + T_{total}(S_{i,f}), \forall f \in \{1, 2...F\} \tag{17}$$

Equation (17) means the smaller of the fitness, the result is better. The properties of the particle are defined by a $d \times N$ position matrix $P(d, n)$ and a $1 \times N$ velocity matrix $V(d, n)$. The position and the velocity of particles update as the algorithm iterates to find the best position, $P(d, n)$ and $V(d, n)$ is updated by using Eq. (18) and (19):

$$P_i^{k+1}(d, n) = \begin{cases} 1 & if(V_i^{k+1}(d, n) = maxV_i^{k+1}(d, n)) \\ 0 & otherwise \end{cases} \tag{18}$$

$$\begin{aligned} V_i^{k+1}(d, n) = {} & wV_i^k(d, n) \\ & + c_1 r_1((pbest_i(d, n)) - X_i^k(d, n)) \\ & + c_2 r_2((gbest_i(d, n)) - X_i^k(d, n)) \end{aligned} \tag{19}$$

In Eqs. (18) and (19), V_i^k and P_i^k refer to the velocity and position of the task in the k-th iteration. In Eq. (18), the position of particles is updated by comparing their velocities. In Eq. (19), w is inertia weight, which is used to measure the effect of current individual speed, the larger w, the greater the impact of current individual speed vice versa. Similarly, c_1 and c_2 are used to measure the impact of the optimal location currently found by individuals and groups to the next offloading respectively. The greater the values of c_1 and c_2, the greater the impact of the corresponding factors. Finally, the position of the current individual can be updated by adding vectors.

Algorithm 1. PSO-based location updating method

Input: Attributes of Workflow and Deadline $W_f = (V, \xi)$, T_{ddl};
Output: Optimal location $S^* = (s_1^*, s_2^*, \cdots, s_n^*)$, Time, Energy;
1: Predefine the bandwidth of LAN B_c and the bandwidth of WAN B_{cl}
2: Predefine the computation capacity f_c and f_{cl}
3: Set the cloudlet parameters λ, η, and MV
4: Initialize the key parameters w, c_1, c_2, r_1, r_2
5: Initialize the position of particles $P_i = p_1, p_2, \cdots, p_n$, $p_n \in \{1, 2, 3\}$
6: Set the convergence factor $\alpha \in (0, 1)$
7: $gbest_{new} \leftarrow 0, D_p^i \leftarrow 0, D_g^i \leftarrow 0, pbest_{new}^i \leftarrow 0$
8: **for** each $i \in \theta$ **do**
9:     Use (9) and (12) calculate the extremum of two targets $pbest_e^i$, $pbest_t^i$, $gbest_e$ and $gbest_t$
10: **end for**
11: **while** ($k \ll I_{max}$) or ($gbest_{new} \ll I_{stop}$) **do**
12:     $gbest_{new} = Average(gbest_e, gbest_t)$
13:     **for** each $i \in \theta$ **do**
14:         $D_p^i = Abs(pbest_e^i - pbest_t^i)$
15:         $D_g = Abs(gbest_e - gbest_t)$
16:         **if** $D_p^i < D_g$ **then**
17:             $pbest_{new}^i = RandSelect\{pbest_e^i, pbest_t^i\}$
18:         **else if** $D_p^i \gg D_g$ **then**
19:             $pbest_{new}^i = Average\{pbest_e^i, pbest_t^i\}$
20:         **end if**
21:         Bring $pbest_{new}$ and $gbest_{new}$ into (18) and (19) to renewal P and V
22:     **end for**
23:     **for** each $i \in \theta$ **do**
24:         **if** $\alpha = 1$ **then**
25:             $p_i = RandSelect\{1, 2, 3\}$
26:         **end if**
27:     **end for**
28: **end while**

Algorithms 1 describes the basic steps of MOHWA. The input is attribute $W_f = (V, \xi)$ of WAs and the constrained deadline T_{ddl}, the output is the optimal offloading strategy. Firstly, we set B_c, B_{cl}, f_c f_{cl} and some key parameters used in calculation (line 1–4). Next, we need to randomize the initial position $P_i = (p_1, p_2, \cdots, p_n)$. In this experiment, the offloading path is set to three levels: local execution, offloading to cloudlet execution and offloading to cloud execution, which is expressed as $p_n \in \{1,2,3\}$ (line 5). Then we define the scope of α, which is the convergence factor and effectively prevents local convergence and greatly improves the inherent shortcomings of PSO (line 6). Some other characters that need to be predefined are to prepare for iteration (line 7). Next, updating the extremum of the particles (line 8–10). $gbest_{new}$ is a trade-off between the optimal values of a population on two objectives, in which *Average* can be an average or a dynamic selection of a certain proportion (line 11–12). D_p^i and D_g are predefined quantities for the next two-objective optimal solution, and their values change dynamically with the change of iteration (line 13–15). Then, according to the comparison of D_p^i and D_g, the value of $pbest_{new}^i$ can be obtained (line 16–20). Using $gbest_{new}$ and $pbest_{new}^i$ instead of the original $gbest$ and $pbest$ in Eq. (19), which calculate V and P are the result of multi-objective considerations (line 21). Finally, the convergence factor α is used to further modify the results to prevent local convergence of the results (line 22–28).

4.3   The Mechanisms of Hybrid Workflow Applications

When solving hybrid WAs synthetically based on PSO with two objectives of energy consumption and time consumption. The emphasis is on the establishment of WAs model and how to avoid the disadvantage that PSO is easy to converge locally. In order to optimize hybrid WAs, we define a set of ordered WAs and a set of unordered WAs.

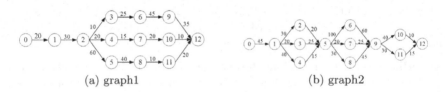

(a) graph1   (b) graph2

Fig. 4. The collection of sequential WAs

As shown in Fig. 4, there are two ordered WAs, each WA has 13 subtasks and each subtask represents a particle in the swarm. There is a certain amount of assignments that need to be transferred between two tasks. Each task may have several precursor tasks and several successor tasks. For each task, it can only be performed if all of its predecessor tasks are finished. For example, for task 5 in Fig. 4.(b), it can only be computed when task 2, task 3 and task 4 have been finished.

Similarly, as shown in Fig. 5, a set of unordered WAs are defined, and the relationship between tasks is more stochastic than the two WAs in Fig. 5. In this way, we can construct three different input situations: two ordered WAs, two ordered WAs and an unordered WA, two ordered WAs, as well as two unordered WAs. Moreover, comparing energy consumption and time consumption of MDs can also test the adaptability of our method efficiency.

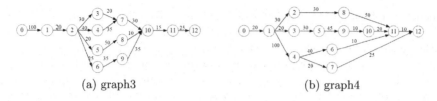

(a) graph3   (b) graph4

Fig. 5. The collection of unordered WAs

5 Experimental Evaluation

In this section, a series of comparative experiments are conducted to evaluate the performance of MOHWA. First, in order to test efficient, we preset a series of relevant parameters. Then, we evaluate the performance of MOHWA by comparing it with the other three traditional task offloading paths, and on this basis, we increase the number of WA to evaluate the performance further.

5.1 Experimental Settings

In order to analyze the effectiveness of the proposed method, we construct some other task offloading methods besides MOHWA. The specific methods are as follows.

No Offloading(NO): All tasks are completed on MDs, which is also the traditional task execution scheme, defined as NO. There is no transmission energy consumption in the execution of tasks, but it may cause a heavy hardware burden on local devices as the limitation of local computing efficiency and resources.

Offloading to Cloudlet Completely (OCCL): All tasks are offloaded to the cloudlet for calculation, defined as OCCL. This is a more efficient strategy, which allows faster computation, but the computing resources on the cloudlet are limited. When the amount of tasks is very large, the task is not suitable for execution on the cloudlet.

Offloading to Cloud Completely (OCC): All tasks are offloaded to could for calculation, defined as OCC. This strategy can reduce the consumption of computing greatly, which has almost infinite computing resources. However, there will be a large transmission delay in task transmission compared with other offloading methods.

MOHWA: One part of tasks are offloaded to the cloudlet, the other part are offloaded to cloud, and the rest of them are completed on MD.

In our experiment, the methods are implemented base on MATLAB language on a physical machine with 2 Intel Core i5-5200U 2.20 GHz processors and 4 GB RAM and the operating system is Win7 64. Specific settings are shown in Table 1.

Table 1. Simulation environment

Parameter	Value
MDs' power when CPU is idle	0.001 W
MDs' power when CPU is busy	0.5 W
Task transfer capabilities of MDs	0.1 W
Task processing capabilities of MDs	500 MHZ
The computing competence of the cloudlet	2000 MHZ
The computing competence of the cloud	3000 MHZ
The latency of LAN	1 ms
The latency of WAN	30 ms
The bandwidth of LAN	100 kb/s
The bandwidth of WAN	50 kb/s

5.2   Performance Evaluation

In this paper, both energy consumption and the time consumption of each WA under the constraint of time are considered, and the benefits are assessed by fitness function. As shown in Fig. 4 and Fig. 5, four WAs are used for experimental evaluation, each WA contains 13 tasks. There are certain constraints and natural attributes between each service. The quantity for each service is set as $\omega = \{5, 14, 20, 5, 16, 13, 68, 55, 23, 53, 10, 22, 5\}$, and the dependence is $\varepsilon_i \in \{1, 2, 3\}$. The relationship between the tasks determines the transmission consumption between them. There are six situations. When $\varepsilon_i = \varepsilon_j$, both tasks are completed at the same location, the transmission consumption $E_{tran} = 0$. When $\varepsilon_i = 1, \varepsilon_j = 2$, we need to use Eq. (12) to calculate the consumption. Similarly, when $\varepsilon_i = 1, \varepsilon_j = 3$ or $\varepsilon_i = 2, \varepsilon_j = 3$ we need to use the corresponding equation to solve its consumption.

As shown in Fig. 6, MOHWA is compared with the other three methods. When WA = 2, the input is a mixture of two ordered WAs. When WA = 3, the input is a mixture of two ordered WAs and one unordered WA. When WA = 4, the input is a mixture of two ordered WAs and two unordered WAs. These

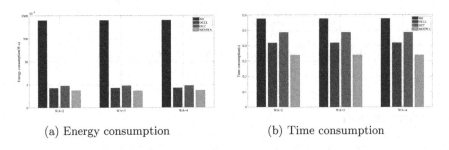

(a) Energy consumption   (b) Time consumption

Fig. 6. Comparison of two objectives with different strategies

three scenarios have included almost all possible scenarios in hybrid WA, greatly simplifying the experimental process. As the number of WAs increases, the consumption of each method also rises, but we can see that MOHWA still has good advantages, and through the analysis of the offloading results, we can get that MOHWA is still feasible although the input is multi-WA.

Then, in order to explore how to optimize the unloading strategy concretely, we analyze the offloading path of tasks. As shown in Fig. 7, we explore the specific offloading paths of the three hybrid WAs we contributed. We can know that most of the tasks will be offloaded to the cloudlet because cloudlet has a high computing speed and a closer distance between the mobile terminal and the cloudlet, which also has a smaller transmission cost. However, there are still a few tasks that have not been offloaded and are still computed locally. This is because it does not generate the cost of task transmission and is suitable for computing with small amount of task. Moreover, a small portion of the rest tasks will be offloaded to the cloud for computation. Although the task offloaded to the cloud will generate a lot of transmission cost, the tasks with a long queue time delay are suitable to be offloaded to cloud due to its strong computing power and nearly infinite computing resources. MOHWA achieves optimization by allocating offloading strategies reasonably.

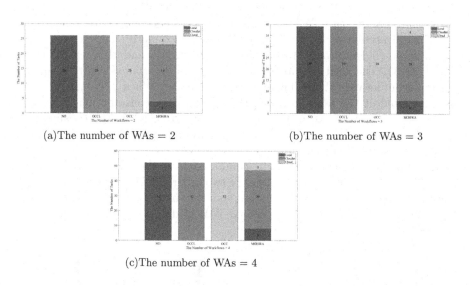

(a)The number of WAs = 2   (b)The number of WAs = 3

(c)The number of WAs = 4

Fig. 7. The number of tasks offloaded to each path

6   Conclusion

In this paper, the multi-objective computation offloading problem for hybrid WAs in MEC environment are investigated. To tackle this problem, we have proposed a multi-objective computation offloading algorithm for hybrid WAs, which generates the optimal application strategy while meeting the constrained deadline of WAs. Extensive experimental evaluations have conducted to show the efficiency and effectiveness of our proposed method.

In the future, we will focus on the computing offloading problem under the dynamic changing circumstance of some key factors such as the queueing waiting time and the power of edge servers. AdditioAccording to the waiting timenally, we will improve the mathematic mode and the efficiency of optimization method further, such as the convergence speed. In addition, the computation offloading for WAs in multi-cloudlet scenario will be studied [21,22].

Acknowledgements. This work is supported by the National Science Foundation of China (Grant No. 61902133), the Natural Science Foundation of Fujian Province (Grant No. 2018 J05106), the Education and Scientific Research Projects of Young and Middle-aged Teachers in Fujian Province (JZ160084), and the Scientific Research Foundation of Huaqiao University under Grant No. 14BS316, Quanzhou Science and Technology Project (No. 2015Z115), the Fundamental Research Funds for the Central Universities (No. 30918014108).

References

1. Qi, L., et al.: Finding all you need: web APIs recommendation in web of things through keywords search. IEEE Trans. Comput. Soc. Syst. (2019)
2. Xu, X., Liu, Q., Zhang, X., Zhang, J., Qi, L., Dou, W.: A blockchain-powered crowdsourcing method with privacy preservation in mobile environment. IEEE Trans. Comput. Soc. Syst. (2019). https://doi.org/10.1109/TCSS.2019.2909137
3. Zhang, Y., et al.: Covering-based web service quality prediction via neighborhood-aware matrix factorization. IEEE Trans. Serv. Comput. (2019). https://doi.org/10.1109/TSC.2019.2891517
4. Qi, L., Chen, Y., Yuan, Y., Fu, S., Zhang, X., Xu, X.: A QoS-aware virtual machine scheduling method for energy conservation in cloud-based cyber-physical systems. World Wide Web J., 1–23 (2019)
5. Shi, W., Cao, J., Zhang, Q., Li, Y., Xu, L.: Edge computing: vision and challenges. IEEE Internet Things J. **3**(5), 637–646 (2016)
6. Zhang, W., Guo, B., Shen, Y., Wang, Y., Xiong, W., Duan, L.: Computation offloading on intelligent mobile terminal. Chinese J. Comput. **39**(5), 1021–1038 (2016)
7. Mach, P., Becvar, Z.: Mobile edge computing: a survey on architecture and computation offloading. IEEE Commun. Surv. Tutorials **19**(3), 1628–1656 (2017)
8. Peng, K., Leung, V., Xu, X., Zheng, L., Wang, J., Huang, Q.: A survey on mobile edge computing: focusing on service adoption and provision. Wireless Commun. Mob. Comput. **2018**, 16 (2018). https://doi.org/10.1155/2018/8267838. Article ID 8267838
9. Jia, M., Cao, J., Yang, L.: Heuristic offloading of concurrent tasks for computation-intensive applications in mobile cloud computing. In: Proceedings of the IEEE Conference on Computer Communications Workshops, INFOCOM Workshops 2014, pp. 352–357 (2014). https://doi.org/10.1109/INFCOMW.2014.6849257

10. Deng, S., Huang, L., Taheri, J., Zomaya, A.Y.: Computation offloading for service workflow in mobile cloud computing. IEEE Trans. Parallel Distrib. Syst. **26**(12), 3317–3329 (2015). https://doi.org/10.1109/TPDS.2014.2381640
11. Zhou, Y., Li., Z., Ge, J., Li, C., Zhou, X., Luo, B.: Multi-objective workflow scheduling algorithm based on delay transmission mechanism in mobile cloud computing environment. J. Softw. **29**(11), 1–20 (2018)
12. Wu, H., Knottenbelt, W., Wolter, K., Sun, Y.: An optimal offloading partitioning algorithm in mobile cloud computing. In: Agha, G., Van Houdt, B. (eds.) QEST 2016. LNCS, vol. 9826, pp. 311–328. Springer, Cham (2016). https://doi.org/10.1007/978-3-319-43425-4_21
13. Xu, X., Dou, W., Zhang, X., Chen, J.: EnReal: an energy-aware resource allocation method for scientific workflow executions in cloud environment. IEEE Trans. Cloud Comput. **4**(2), 166–179 (2015)
14. Wang, S., Zhao, Y., Xu, J., Yuan, J., Hsu, C.: Edge server placement in mobile edge computing. J. Parallel Distrib. Comput., 160–168 (2019)
15. Satyanarayanan, M., Lewis, G., Morris, E., Simanta, S., Boleng, J., Ha, K.: The role of cloudlets in hostile environments. IEEE Pervasive Comput. **12**(4), 40–49 (2013)
16. Kennedy, J., Eberhart, R.: Particle swarm optimization. In: International Conference on Neural Networks, vol. 4, pp. 1942–1948 (1995)
17. Kennedy, J., Eberhart, R.: A discrete binary version of the particle swarm algorithm, pp. 4104–4108 (1997)
18. Jia, M., Liang, W.: Delay-sensitive multiplayer augmented reality game planning in mobile edge computing. In: Proceedings of the 21st ACM International Conference on Modeling, Analysis and Simulation of Wireless and Mobile Systems, pp. 147–154. ACM (2018)
19. Li, B., He, M., Wu, W., Sangaiah, A.K., Jeon, G.: Computation offloading algorithm for arbitrarily divisible applications in mobile edge computing environments: an OCR case. Sustainability **10**(17), 196–210 (2018)
20. Zhang, J., et al.: Hybrid computation offloading for smart home automation in mobile cloud computing. Pers. Ubiquit. Comput. **22**(1), 121–134 (2018)
21. Roy, D., De, D., Mukherjee, A., Buyya, R.: Application-aware cloudlet selection for computation offloading in multi-cloudlet environment. J. Supercomput. **73**(4), 1672–1690 (2017)
22. Liu, L., Fan, Q.: Resource allocation optimization based on mixed integer linear programming in the multi-cloudlet environment. IEEE Access, 1 (2018)

An Introduction and Comparison of the Application of Cloud and Fog in IoT

Zheng Li$^{(\boxtimes)}$ and Yilin Wang

Jiangsu Collaborative Innovation Center of Atmospheric Environment
and Equipment Technology (CICAEET), Nanjing University of Information Science
and Technology, Nanjing 210044, China
`20171344068@nuist.edu.cn`

Abstract. This paper mainly introduces the definitions of cloud computing and fog computing, and expounds their differences. Firstly, the new problems encountered by the Internet of Things (IoTs) are put forward. It also points out the shortcomings of cloud computing in solving these problems. Then it explains the advantages of fog computing over cloud computing in solving these problems, and finally introduces the new challenges fog computing encounters.

Keywords: Cloud computing · Fog computing · IoT

1 Introduction

Over the past few years, cloud computing has gained tremendous popularity from the applications of IoTs. The main reasons are that the cloud computing technology is relatively mature, and it is possible to access and utilize the cloud information and resources at anytime and anywhere. Overall, cloud computing provides users with many advantages, such as low-cost, convenient access to information, rapid deployment, data backup and recovery, and automatic software integration [8]. However, with the emergence of new requirements of the emerging IoTs (such as low latency and high security), the traditional centralized cloud computing is insufficient to support the complex edge network of the interconnection of all things.

At the same time, the number and types of heterogeneous user terminals and IoTs access devices are also increasing sharply: smart headphones, smart phones, mobile computers, smart appliances, on-board networking systems, intelligent traffic control lights and more networking public facilities. In addition, more and more new networking devices are emerging [4]. These billions of devices and heterogeneous data constitute a variety of complex systems. How to effectively manage these systems has become the focus of the cloud and IoT research fields [15].

Supported by National Natural Science Foundation of China (Grants No 61702274) and the Natural Science Foundation of Jiangsu Province (Grants No BK20170958), and PAPD.

X. Zhang et al. (Eds.): CloudComp 2019/SmartGift 2019, LNICST 322, pp. 63–75, 2020.
https://doi.org/10.1007/978-3-030-48513-9_5

In 2012, Cisco proposed an emergency architecture and solution. Instead of using centralized cloud computing servers, the architecture moves the computing servers to data sources and user terminals to overcome the shortcomings of cloud computing, which is the fog computing paradigm [15]. Fog computing has some advantages, such as low latency, low network bandwidth requirements, low performance requirements of terminal devices, stable services and better security and privacy.

However, due to the immaturity of fog computing technology, there are few examples of using fog computing in real life. If we want to truly implement the application and better prospects of fog computing, we must understand fog's complex network system, including complex heterogeneous hardware, software and the process of accessing network [15]. In addition, we have to solve fog's problems, such as a large number of data management, heterogeneous equipment management, the lack of specific processes and technology, and the lack of fog equipment security.

The above issues will be discussed in detail in the following chapters.

2   Cloud Computing

2.1   Definition of Cloud Computing

Cloud is a computing model that supports convenient, ubiquitous and on-demand network access to a shared pool of configurable computing resources like the networks, storage space, servers, applications and services. These resources can be supplied and released with minimal management effort and minimal interaction among service providers [1]. Figure 1 shows an example of a cloud model:

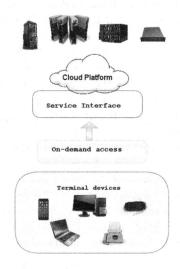

Fig. 1. The cloud model.

2.2 Characteristics of Cloud Computing

Cloud computing is attractive because it has the following four characteristics [10]:

1. Cloud computing does not require pre-investment because it is a pay-on-demand pricing model that allows service providers to benefit from the cost of leasing resources in the cloud without investing in infrastructures.
2. Operating cost is low. Resources in cloud environment can be quickly released based on users' requirements. Service providers can release some idle resources when the service demand is low, instead of providing unnecessary capacities at the peak load.
3. Infrastructure providers can collect a large amount of resources from data centers, and service providers can easily access these data, so as to judge service growth needs according to data trends, and then accurately expand the scale of their services.
4. Cloud services support the access to various devices via the Internet, which is very convenient.

3 Fog Computing

3.1 Definition of Fog Computing

Fog computing is a layered model which supports ubiquitous and convenient access to a shared continuum of extensible computing resources. The model promotes the deployment of distributed and delay-aware applications and services, and consists of fog nodes which are either physical or virtual. Fog nodes reside between intelligent terminal equipments and cloud services. Fog node have context-aware functions and support general data management and communication systems. The organizational form of fog nodes in the cluster is based on the specific working mode. Separation is supported by vertical distribution and association is supported by horizontal distribution. They can also be distributed according to the delay distance to the smart terminal. Fog computing minimizes request response time with applications, provides local computing resources for terminal equipment, and provides network connections to centralized services [2].

Figure 2 shows a fog system, which has three layers: cloud layer, fog layer and IoTs/end user layer. The fog layer can be formed by one or more fog domains and they may be controlled by the same or different service providers. A fog domain covers a number of fog nodes that include the edge routers, gateways, PCs, smart phones, switches and set-top boxes. The IoTs/end-user layer consists of two domains. The first domain includes the end-user devices, and the second domain includes the IoT devices [3].

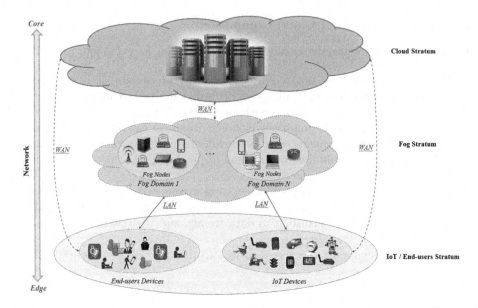

Fig. 2. The fog system [3].

3.2   Characteristics of Fog Computing

Fog computing has several different features from cloud computing [2]. Cloud computing is based on IT operator services and social public clouds. Fog computing is based on the small clouds, such as the personal clouds, the private clouds and the enterprise clouds. Cloud computing emphasizes overall computing power and is usually composed of clusters of high-performance computing devices. Fog computing is composed of more dispersed functional computers, and each computing node needs to play a role. Fog computing extends cloud computing by extending the computing power from the network center to the network edge, and has been widely used in various services.

Location Awareness and Low Latency. Fog nodes are tightly coupled with intelligent terminal devices or access networks and provide computing resources for these devices. And because fog nodes are aware of their logical location in the whole system and the delay cost of communicating with other nodes, fog computing can provide as low a delay as possible by providing services nearby. Because fog nodes usually coexist with smart terminal devices, data generated by these devices can be analyzed and responded much faster than data generated from centralized cloud services or data centers [2].

Geographical Distribution. Fog computing requires a wide deployment of target services and applications which can identify geographic location. Fog nodes provide some form of data management and communication services between the network edge layer where the terminal equipment is located and fog computing services or centralized (cloud) computing resources (if needed) [4]. In order to deploy a given fog computing capability, fog nodes operate in a centralized or decentralized manner and can be configured as separate fog nodes. For example, by locating fog nodes along tracks and highways, fog computing provides high-quality streaming media services to mobile vehicles and achieves a good result [2].

Heterogeneity. In fog computing, fog nodes interact with various types of network terminal devices on the edge of the network, which will generate data of various shape factors [2]. Therefore, fog must have the characteristics of accommodating heterogeneous data and be able to collect, aggregate and process these heterogeneous data.

Scalability and Agility. In nature, fog computing is adaptive. Because contacting with the network edge layer, the amount of data, resource conditions and network environment which fog computing faces may change constantly. Fog computing can support flexible computing, data load change, network condition and resource pool change at the cluster level to list some supporting adaptive functions [2].

Interoperability and Federation. Fog is distributed, and the functions and services provided by each node are not as powerful as those provided by a centralized cloud transport center. A single service provided by fog may require joint support from multiple nodes. Therefore, fog supports cross-domain cooperation among nodes and interoperability of fog computing components. In addition, fog has a unified specification to achieve seamless support for services [2].

Real-Time Interactions. The interaction between fog and data source is real-time, which does not have long waiting and delay. Fog nodes receive data from terminal devices and respond immediately after finishing analysis, rather than sending data as batch processing to the distant cloud center [2].

4   Cloud and Fog Computing

4.1   Comparison of Cloud and Fog Computing

Fog computing is an extension of cloud computing. It has many similarities and differences with cloud computing. We compare cloud and fog from the following aspects, which can intuitively reflect their similarities and differences.

Reaction Time and Latency. The most time-sensitive data will be sent to the nearest fog node for analysis and processing, so as to minimize the reaction time as far as possible. When the fog node closest to the IoT device is used to process data, the recovery time can be reduced to milliseconds or even sub-seconds. Data that is not particularly urgent can wait to be sent to the aggregation area of the fog node for processing, possibly for a few seconds or minutes. But the response time for interacting with the cloud may be a few minutes, days or even weeks [13,14]. So it is not hard to see that fog has more flexible choices and faster responses than clouds. That's why fog has a much lower delay than clouds.

Node Location Distribution. Cloud is in the network while fog nodes are distributed on the edge of the network and interact with IoT devices. Cloud occurs in the form of dense central servers, but fog exists not only in scattered nodes near IoT terminals, but also in dense data centers [14].

Service Scope and Location Perception. Cloud computing has few nodes and can't perceive location, but its service coverage covers the whole world. Unlike cloud computing, the number of fog nodes is very large, and they have the capability of location awareness. In terms of service scope, fog nodes which are very close to the IoT terminal equipment have a generally local service scope, such as a city block. But the service scope of node-intensive area can cover a wider area [13,14].

Vulnerability and Security. In the cloud, the user data is stored in the cloud computing center, and the possibility of damage is very high. Users often worry about the security of their data. Because fog is geographically dispersed, the possibility of damage is very low. Moreover, data processing in fog is closer to users, so users can have control over data security and privacy [8].

4.2 Collaboration Between Cloud and Fog Computing

Cloud is far away from user terminals, and there will be some problems in the application of the emerging IoTs. When we use fog to extend the cloud to terminal devices on the edge of the network, we can fill the new demand. So how can data be processed and analyzed in the collaboration of cloud and fog? Fig. 3 shows an example of a cloud-fog interaction model:

Next, we describe the tasks that cloud and fog nodes need to accomplish in the interaction.

The Things Fog Nodes Need to Do. At the edge of the network, that is, near the data source, the fog nodes at the edge receive data from the terminal devices of IoT in real time. The fog nodes can also receive the heterogeneous dynamic data. Then the real-time control and analysis of the data are carried out by running the application supported by the IoTs to achieve the millisecond

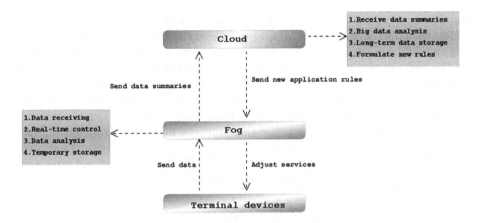

Fig. 3. Interaction model of cloud and fog.

response time. At the same time, fog nodes provide temporary data storage. This storage usually lasts about 1 to 2 h. After processing and analyzing the data, fog nodes should send data summaries to the cloud regularly, and report the overall information of the data [14].

The Things Cloud Needs to Do. When cloud platforms receive data digests sent by various fog nodes, they need to be collected and aggregated by cloud platforms. Then, the cloud platform makes an overall analysis and evaluation of these data to obtain service growth trends and determine the direction of business development. Finally, the cloud platform formulates new application rules based on the results of business evaluation, so as to achieve the goal of adjusting service balance [14].

5   Fog Computing Help on the New Challenges of IoT

Moving computing, control and storage tasks to the cloud has been a trend in the past decade. However, today, with the upgrading of devices and technologies, the emerging IoTs has generated many new demands. Cloud computing faces great challenges in meeting these requirements. At this time, it is a new trend to expand the cloud to the edge of the network. Let us focus on the new challenges of the cloud-based IoTs and the advantages fog has over cloud computing in these new challenges.

5.1   Low Latency Requirements

Nowadays, many industrial systems and life applications require end-to-end communication between devices with low latency, such as, unmanned vehicles, flight control of unmanned aerial vehicles, virtual reality applications and smart home applications, especially those requiring rapid response at high speed and delays of less than tens of milliseconds. It is also necessary to have a low latency processing capability in order to analyze the road conditions and control the duration of the lights according to the changing traffic conditions. In order to eliminate the delay in data transmission, fog deploys nodes on the edge of the network, allowing data to be analyzed, processed and stored near the end user. In [12], the researchers set up a proof-of-concept platform. They tested the face recognition application and reduced the response time from 900 ms to 169 ms by moving the computing program from the cloud to the edge. Fog also supports time-sensitive control functions in local physical systems [4]. This may be ideal and often the only option for meeting low latency requirements.

5.2 Network Bandwidth Constraints

With the advent of the age of interconnection, the speed of data creation is increasing exponentially [5]. For example, networked cars can create tens of megabytes of data per second. This will include a variety of data, including vehicle mobility (e.g. driving routes and speeds), vehicle status (e.g. wear and tear of vehicle components), vehicle surroundings (e.g. road conditions and weather conditions) and videos recorded by vehicle travel recorders. A driverless car will generate more data [6]. The American Smart Grid generate 1,000 gigabytes of data per year. Google trades 1 Gigabyte a month and the Library of Congress generates about 2.4 gigabytes of data each month. In 2010, AT&T's network used up 200 gigabytes [7]. If all the different types of data are sent to the cloud for processing, there will be a very high bandwidth requirement. This will impose a heavy burden on the existing bandwidth, and even lead to congestion, which is obviously not advisable. ABI Research estimates that 90% of the data generated by endpoints will be stored and processed locally, not in the cloud [5].

Fog processes the data between the cloud and the terminal, which can filter out some inappropriate or irrelevant data and prevent them from transmitting over the whole network [8]. Data generated from user terminals can be allocated to the nearest data center for processing without having to transfer all source data to the cloud, because many critical analyses do not require cloud computing processing and storage. Fog's processing method will greatly reduce the amount of data sent to the cloud, greatly reduce the bandwidth pressure and reduce the bandwidth requirements.

5.3 Resource Constraints of Devices

In IoT systems, some devices cannot directly interact with the cloud due to resource constraints (e.g. network, computing and storage resources), so they cannot transfer tasks to the cloud. It is unrealistic to upgrade and update resources for each device at a high cost.

In this case, the cloud will not be able to perform its functions, while fog can replace these devices to perform tasks that require intensive resources [4]. The core components of the fog computing architecture are fog nodes, which are either physical components (such as routers, switches, gateways, and servers) or virtual components (such as virtualized switches and virtual machines). Fog nodes are tightly coupled to intelligent user terminals or access networks and provide these terminal devices with computing resources [2]. Therefore, the complexity of terminal devices and resource requirements are reduced.

5.4 Stability of Service

When the connection to the cloud is not stable and continuous, the cloud can not provide stable and continuous services to users or devices. For example, when a vehicle enters an area that is not covered by the Internet, many necessary applications are unavailable in on-board and personnel equipment, and then the cloud service will be disconnected, so there will be unstable cloud services [4].

But unlike clouds, fog has a dense geographical distribution. Edge networks created by fog computing are located at different points to extend the infrastructure for cloud geographic isolation. Forming a continuous coverage of the service scope helps to process the analysis data more quickly and steadily. And administrators can support mobility requirements which is based on location [8].

5.5 Security and Privacy

Because of the rapid development of the IoTs, more and more data are connected to the network, including a large number of privacy information. For example, people's work and rest rules can be excavated from real-time information generated by intelligent household appliances, and important privacy information such as property can be eavesdropped from chat data. Therefore, both the transmission process and the static state of data in the IoTs need to be well protected, which requires the monitoring and automatic response of malicious attacks in the whole process [11].

In cloud computing, private and corporate data, and even confidential information, are stored in the cloud. Users must rely on cloud service providers to ensure their data security and privacy, which will cause users to worry [8]. For example, a user does not have complete control over his/her data, his/her privacy is maliciously exploited, and cloud computing centers may cause data loss in the process of expansion.

In fog, sensitive data is processed locally rather than sent to the cloud for analysis. Our own administrators can monitor and inspect the devices that collect, analyze, process and store data so that we can control the data by ourselves [11]. In some devices that cannot adequately protect data due to resource constraints, the fog system can act as a proxy for these devices to help manage and update the security credentials and software of these devices to compensate for their security vacancies. Fog system can also use local information to monitor the security status of nearby devices and detect threats immediately to ensure security [4].

6   Problems in Fog Computing

6.1   Data Management

In order to reduce the delay and let users control the data, fog will process and store most of the data locally near the terminal. The Internet Data Center (IDC) points out that by 2020, about 44 zetabytes of data are expected to be generated [18]. How can such a large amount of data generated by heterogeneous devices be managed? Therefore, appropriate data selection and transmission protocols must be considered [14].

In addition, accessing the fog network from the outside is very tedious, and the addition of a new service provider will greatly increase the complexity of the fog network. Therefore, it is pressing to look for the gap as soon as possible, determine the method of data governance and implement it scientifically to achieve data integrity constraints and confidentiality requirements [15].

6.2   Heterogeneous Equipment Management

In the fog, billions of different devices must be distributed. Various heterogeneous devices may produce different faults in many locations. It is a complex task to monitor and track the fault information of hardware and provide software patches for updating and maintenance.

Faced with these possible unknown faults, open fog suggests using machine learning technology to develop a framework with fault comprehensive feature detection and fault tolerance [17,21]; especially in systems involving critical applications of life, such as anomaly detection in the medical field. Only by solving this problem can fog be truly applied to IoT on a wide range of network edges [15].

6.3   Lack of Concrete Processes and Technologies

Fog can be used to support edge network. Fog serves as a local data storage and application server for the edge networks, providing services for end-user devices, and helping these network devices and end-user devices (e.g., vehicles, commercial or industrial intelligent robots, UAVs, smart phones and computers) to form local networks. To help these local devices build trustworthy communications, fog also provides them with temporary security credentials [4].

To achieve this, we have to consider how our fog function connects to the hardware and operating system of the local device. In this context, a lot of research has been done, but the fog-based implementation methods of the IoTS are rarely studied. Most of them focus on embedded devices, protocols, principles, security, QoS and applications [19,20]. The use of D4D to pool idle edge resources is mentioned in [16], but a new protocol stack may also be needed for end-user devices to support fog edge networks. So far, we still lack specific processes and tools to realize the connection between fog computing and IoTs applications [15].

6.4 Security and Privacy

As we mentioned in the section of security challenges of IoT, fog acts as a node for traffic encryption and access control, aggregating and controlling privacy-sensitive data before data leaves the edge. Fog also acts as a proxy for resource-constrained terminal devices, providing them with the choice of security functions to ensure the security of resource-constrained devices [4].

But many studies have also shown that fog devices lack safety [22, 23]. Fog is dispersed, it needs to work in places where the environment is much more fragile than the cloud. Cloud servers are in the cloud center, and many fog devices are in public places, lack of security monitoring, and are very vulnerable to be damaged. Moreover, fog systems do not have the powerful resources to protect themselves like centralized cloud systems, so fog systems are more vulnerable to attacks, such as session riding, session hijacking and SQL injection [15].

In [9], fog security and privacy challenges are divided into the following points: 1) The security and reliability of fog network need a trust model to be ensured. Fog nodes and IoTs devices need to establish mutual authentication trust mechanism. 2) It is difficult for resource-constrained IoTs devices to use traditional certificate and public key infrastructure (PKI) authentication mechanisms. 3) The messages sent by IoTs devices can not be encrypted symmetrically. In addition, asymmetrical encryption technology has great challenges, including resource and environment constraints, overhead constraints and maintenance of the PKI. 4) Privacy protection in fog is challenging, because fog is more likely than cloud to collect location information of user equipment and usage data of facilities, which may lead to the disclosure of important location privacy. The scattered fog nodes may be attacked because of the different security protection intensity. And frequent interaction among the three layers of fog architecture will increase the possibility of privacy disclosure. The last point is that fog is more vulnerable to malicious attacks. The performance of the network may be seriously damaged without proper security measures.

7   Conclusion

In this paper, we first introduced the background of fog generation and the development of fog field. Then we introduced the concept and characteristics of cloud computing based on the cloud computing definition given by NIST, which has the highest recognition at present. We introduced the concept and characteristics of fog computing. We pointed out the difference between cloud computing and fog computing through comparative analysis from different perspectives. The interaction workflow between cloud and fog was also described from two perspectives of fog and cloud. We described the new challenges faced by IoT in today's new application requirements, and briefly described the disadvantages of cloud computing on these issues and the advantages of fog computing in solving this problem. Finally, we introduced the problems that need to be solved in fog computing, and provided some suggestions for future research.

References

1. Mell, P.M., Grance, T.: SP 800–145. The NIST Definition of Cloud Computing. National Institute of Standards & Technology (2011)
2. Iorga, M.: Fog Computing Conceptual Model. Special Publication (NIST SP)- 500–325. https://doi.org/10.6028/NIST.SP.500-325
3. Mouradian, C., Naboulsi, D., Yangui, S., et al.: A comprehensive survey on fog computing: state-of-the-art and research challenges. IEEE Commun. Surv. Tutor. **20**, 416–464 (2017)
4. Chiang, M., Zhang, T.: Fog and IoT: an overview of research opportunities. IEEE Internet Things J. **3**(6), 854–864 (2016)
5. Kelly, R.: Internet of Things Data to Top 1.6 Zettabytes by 2022. https://campustechnology.com/articles/2015/04/15/internet-of-thingsdata-to-top-1-6-zettabytes-by-2020.aspx. Accessed 7 Apr 2016
6. Mearian, L.: Self-driving cars could create 1GB of data a second. http://www.computerworld.com/article/2484219/emergingtechnology/self-driving-cars-could-create-1gb-of-data-a-second.html. Accessed 7 Apr 2016
7. Cochrane, N.: US smart grid to generate 1000 petabytes of data a year, 23 March 2010. http://www.itnews.com.au/news/us-smart-grid-to-generate-1000petabytes-of-data-a-year-170290#ixzz458VaITi6. Accessed 7 Apr 2016
8. Kumar, A., Saharan, K.P., Saharan, K.P., et al.: Fog in comparison to cloud: a survey. Arch. Intern. Med. **141**(13), 1771–1776 (2015)
9. Hong, Y., Liu, W.M., Wang, L.: Privacy preserving smart meter streaming against information leakage of appliance status. IEEE Trans. Inf. Forensics Secur. **12**, 2227–2241 (2017)
10. Zhang, Q., Cheng, L., Boutaba, R.: Cloud computing: state-of-the-art and research challenges. J. Internet Serv. Appl. **1**(1), 7–18 (2010)
11. Pande, V., Marlecha, C., Kayte, S.: A review-fog computing and its role in the Internet of Things. Int. J. Eng. Res. Appl. **6**, 7–11 (2016)
12. Shi, W., et al.: Edge computing: vision and challenges. IEEE Internet Things J. **3**(5), 637–646 (2016)
13. Firdhous, M., Ghazali, O., Hassan, S.: Fog computing: will it be the future of cloud computing? In: Proceedings of the Third International Conference on Informatics & Applications, Kuala Terengganu, Malaysia (2014)
14. Fog Computing and the Internet of Things: Extend the Cloud to Where the Things Are. https://www.innovation4.cn/library/r1490
15. Dasgupta, A., Gill, A.Q.: Fog computing challenges: a systematic review. In: Australasian Conference on Information Systems, Hobart, Australia (2017)
16. Zhang, Z., Zhang, J., Ying, L.: Multimedia streaming in cooperative mobile social networks. Preprint
17. Dastjerdi, A.V., Buyya, R.: Fog computing: helping the Internet of Things realize its potential. Computer **49**(8), 112–116 (2016)
18. MacGillivray, C., et al.: IDC futurescape: worldwide Internet of Things 2017 predictions (2016)
19. Vaquero, L.M., Rodero-Merino, L.: Finding your way in the fog: towards a comprehensive definition of fog computing. SIGCOMM Comput. Commun. Rev. **44**(5), 27–32 (2014)
20. Yi, S., Li, C., Li, Q.: A survey of fog computing: concepts, applications and issues. Paper presented to the proceedings of the 2015 workshop on mobile big data, Hangzhou, China (2015)

21. Consortium, O: Openfog Reference Architecture for Fog Computing (2017). OPFRA001.020817
22. Stojmenovic, I., Wen, S.: The fog computing paradigm: scenarios and security issues. In: 2014 Federated Conference on Computer Science and Information Systems, pp. 1–8 (2014)
23. Li, J., Jin, J., Yuan, D., Palaniswami, M., Moessner, K.: EHOPES: data-centered fog platform for smart living. In: 2015 International Telecommunication Networks and Applications Conference (ITNAC), pp. 308–313. IEEE (2015)

Distributed Cloud Monitoring Platform Based on Log In-Sight

E. Haihong, Yuanxing Chen[(✉)], Meina Song, and Meijie Sun

School of Computer Science,
Beijing University of Posts and Telecommunications, Beijing 100876, China
{ehaihong,mnsong}@bupt.edu.cn, chenyuanxing_bupt@foxmail.com,
sun_magine@163.com

Abstract. Log management plays an essential role in identifying problems and troubleshoot problems in a distributed system. However, when we conducted log analysis on big data cluster, Kubernetes cluster and Ai capability cluster, we found it was difficult to find a Distributed cloud monitoring platform that met our requirements. So, we propose a Distributed cloud monitoring platform based on log insight, which can be used to achieve unified log insight of big data clusters, K8s clusters, and Ai capability clusters. At the same time, through this system, Developers can intuitively monitor and analyze the business system data and cluster operation monitoring data. Once there is a problem in the log, it will immediately alert, locate, display, and track the message. This system is helpful to improve the readability of log information to administrators, In the process of data collection, Filebeat and Metricbeat will be combined to collect data, therefore, the system can not only collect ordinary log data but also support to collect the indicator data of each famous mature system (Such as operating system, Memcached, Mysql, Docker, Kafka, etc.). Besides, the system will monitor and manage the status of cluster nodes through BeatWatcher. Finally, we develop the system and verify its feasibility and performance by simulation.

Keywords: Log insight · Distributed cloud monitoring · Log analysis

1 Introduction

As an essential part of the entire operation and maintenance and even the whole product life cycle, the monitoring system not only needs to be able to feed back the current state of the system in real time. But also promptly detects faults before-hand, and needs to provide sufficient data for fast positioning and tracking after-wards Question, find out the root cause of the problem.

In this paper, we will present a multi-dimensional log insight and analysis system based on Elasticsearch [1]. Most of the monitoring systems using Elasticsearch as data storage and search engine [2] directly use the ELK [3] open source component. In the recent monitoring of a gateway system [4], we have implemented our monitoring function in this way. This way is easy to implement, and its monitoring function is not

X. Zhang et al. (Eds.): CloudComp 2019/SmartGift 2019, LNICST 322, pp. 76–88, 2020.
https://doi.org/10.1007/978-3-030-48513-9_6

weak, but we found that the defects achieved in this way are also obvious. First of all, for many of the same data collection of the cluster, it is necessary to download and start the collector of one server one by one, which brings a vast workload; At the same time, the components of ELK are almost independent of each other, and the entire system cannot be managed uniformly.

Here, we propose a distributed cloud monitoring platform [5] based on log insight that will be able to collect data conveniently from different system clusters. Through the configuration center provided by the insight and analysis system, it can realize the configuration multiplexing of collectors of various categories. And no longer need to deploy each server separately through the command line, We implemented a one-click start for the entire cluster monitoring. The distributed cloud monitoring platform will realize the integration of each component, and the state of the data acquisition node can be synchronized and effectively controlled through the distributed cloud monitoring platform. The insight and analysis platform combines Flink's [6] powerful data processing capabilities to parse and transform various types of log data [7]. The log data will be transformed from unstructured data into structured data [8] for subsequent processing. Finally, the monitoring platform cannot only visualize [9] the log data according to time, label, type, hostname, etc. But also provide multi-dimensional aggregate statistics function and early warning function for analyzing the data. For example, according to the index log data of the system, Analyze whether there is a certain indicator in the current time of each cluster that exceeds the warning line. According to the running log data of the monitored system, you can calculate out whether the log data contains Error, Fail, Warn, etc. And whether the administrator needs to be notified. According to the log data accessed by the user, We can analyze the user's unit time visit amount and regional access heat map [10]. After the design is implemented, the system will perform lots of tests (such as unit test, functional test, and performance test) to verify its feasibility.

The rest of this paper is organized as follows. The second section describes the current work related to monitoring. The third section presents a monitoring system based on Elasticsearch. The fourth part has carried on detailed development to the system. Section five gives the simulation results of operation and performance. Section six is a summary of the entire article.

2   Related Work

We introduce the state of the art for monitoring systems: Splunk [11], Fluentd [12], Loggly [13], Logstash [14], and Graylog [15].

Splunk is a software that provides services such as log-based data search [16], monitoring, and analysis. It can be used for security, management, and applications. Splunk can capture, correlate, collect, monitor, and analyze real-time data from any source. It can also create alerts, dashboards, and identify data patterns. It can be software or cloud services, but the cost of using Splunk in terms of capital and complexity is too high.

Fluentd is an open source data collector designed to handle data flow. It is a bit like syslog, but using JSON as the data format. It features a plug-in architecture with high scalability and high availability, meanwhile also enabling highly reliable message forwarding. As a free data collector, Fluentd is already quite good, But the research data on Fluentd is less than other collectors, and it does not provide any built-in visualization tools.

Loggly is a robust log analysis tool with a very user-friendly interface, with centralized log management and filtering and alerting capabilities, and it is also very easy for developers to customize performance dashboards. But the downside is that after a period of free use, you have to pay to continue using it.

Logstash is part of the ELK stack. With 200 plug-ins, Logstash can access multiple data sources and import data streams to a central analytics system on a large scale. Logstash is designed with scalability in mind, providing APIs for the community to quickly develop plug-ins. The advantage is its freedom and open source and easy integration with other Elastic products. But the disadvantages are more obvious. The filter is difficult to write. And then it is implemented in Java and contains a lot of filtering functions, So if used as a log collector, Logstash takes up a lot of space.

Graylog is an open source solution that claims to be able to do the same thing as Splunk. It is written in Java, and the web interface is written by Ruby on Rails(an open source web application framework written in the Ruby language). The advantage is that it can be easily set up, supports REST APIs [17], and it can be extended with plugins. But the disadvantages are also visible. Graylog only supports system logs and GELF(Graylog Extended Log Format). And Graylog can't read system log files directly. It requires the server to send log messages directly to Graylog, which obviously makes development users more troublesome.

3 System Architecture

This section will show the architectural design of the distributed cloud monitoring platform, which consists of four modules: Monitoring Node Management, Data Collection and Parsing, Data Cleaning and Processing, Data Analysis, and Visualization. The whole system is based on the monitoring of the log data on the monitoring node. The user can monitor and manage the monitoring node according to the visual interface provided by the system (Fig. 1).

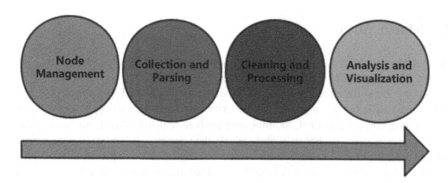

Fig. 1. System architecture diagram

3.1   Monitoring Node Management

The design goal of this system is to make a unified log insight and management platform, which can support access to various servers or systems for management. Therefore, the first need is the management of monitoring nodes. The system uses the self-developed Beatwatcher to manage the monitoring nodes.

The functions of node management mainly include the following parts: one-click download and start, extract monitoring test data, transfer analysis configuration file, Heartbeat Mechanism, Data collector start and stop.

3.2   Data Collection and Parsing

Considering the diversity of monitoring data sources, data collection and simple parsing are done using Filebeat and Metricbeat. Collect and easily parse log type data through Filebeat, Collect metric types and data with standard template types via Metricbeat. The data is then sent to the message queue for subsequent processing.

3.3   Data Cleaning and Processing

The format of the log data is various, so it is necessary to clean and process it before sending it to the log repository. For example, the conversion of the log format, the conversion of the date form, the conversion of the geographical location, the clearing of the invalid data, the processing of various tags, the detection of logs with abnormalities, and subsequent warnings and the like.

3.4   Data Analysis and Visualization

The analysis and visualization of data include two aspects. The first is the analysis of log data. Through various filtering conditions, the log data of each data source that needs to be viewed is displayed through the interface, help users quickly locate the data they need. Secondly, the dashboard visualization part realizes the visualization of the data by implementing the custom creation of the dashboard. It can quickly and conveniently view the required information in the form of a chart and adds data source fusion, multi-field fusion, and other multidimensional display in the visualization process. Data analysis and visualization make the function of the entire system more complete.

4   Implementation

4.1   System Design

The overall module architecture design of the unified log insight analysis platform is as follows (Fig. 2):

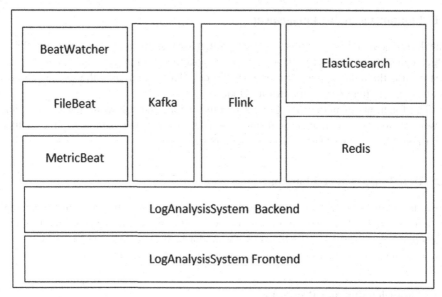

Fig. 2. Distributed cloud monitoring platform overall module architecture diagram

The collectors used by the system to collect data are Filebeat and Metricbeat, and the self-developed BeatWatcher is used to manage and control the collector.

In order to cope with traffic spikes and achieve module decoupling, the system uses Kafka as an external message queue for log data transmission.

Taking into account the real-time requirements of the system, the system uses Flink streaming to process the log data to ensure real-time processing in the case of large log data.

The system uses the Elasticsearch search engine to store and search log data.

At the same time, the system uses Redis as the database of non-log data during system operation, which ensures the high concurrent access requirements of the system.

Finally, the entire cloud monitoring infrastructure platform is built by Spring Boot, and the front and rear ends are separated to achieve real front-end decoupling.

4.2 System Implementation

System implementation includes three dimensions, including monitoring system interface implementation, log monitoring platform layer implementation, data layer implementation. The hardware and software specification of the servers used are shown in Table 1.

Table 1. Development specification

Software/Hardware	Specification
Operating system	Linux/Ubuntu
Number of servers	3
Single server memory	64 GB
Single server storage	1T
Java version	1.8.0_111
Go version	go 1.12
Filebeat version	6.5.4
Metricbeat version	6.5.4
Elasticsearch version	6.5.4
Redis version	4.0.8
Flink version	v1.7.2
Kafka version	Kafka 2.0.0
Browser	Chrome/Firefox/IE/Edge

Monitoring System Visualization

The system adopts the separation of front and rear ends to realize the system separation and data decoupling. On the client side, the interface is realized through the React framework. The user completes a series of functions from machine management, log collection, log processing, log warehouse, log analysis and real-time monitoring through the client interface.

The front end and the back end of the distributed cloud monitoring system interact with each other through the Rest API. The front end and the back end are respectively deployed. The user accesses the client interface by accessing the Http request, and then the client will access the back end of the system according to the user's click request. After receiving the request, the backend will be distributed to different Controllers according to the request parameters. The Controller will call different Services to provide services, and finally, return the request to the client and the user.

In this system, the user can complete the visual configuration of data collection just by using the client, including the configuration of system basic metric data and configuration of common log data. In terms of basic metric data configuration, the system provides a wealth of basic data collection sources to choose from, including Docker's running state, Mysql's running state, Prometheus node's running state, Apache server's running basic indicators, server System's own basic operating indicators, etc. They can be monitored by just clicking and selecting in the visual interface.

The system uses the configuration distribution startup method to start the data collector. Therefore, the collection mode of the startup collector and its configuration can be reused. Data collection of the same type on a cluster can be configured only once and distributed to different nodes via a visual interface to get it up and running.

During the process of log visualization, the user uses the log source, log type, number of displays, and view time to capture data. At the same time, the system designs and provides two filtering options: simple filtering and complex filtering. Simple filtering mode Easy to use. The complex filtering pattern can be continuously combined and nested by the JSON data structure designed in this system. Our system provides users with easy-to-use data filtering options while retaining powerful filtering capabilities (Fig. 3).

Fig. 3. Visualization of log data

In the log data analysis module, the user performs the creation of the Panel through various fields of the log data according to his specific needs and then puts it into a specific Dashboard of a specific folder. In the real-time monitoring module, Users can choose whether to turn on real-time monitoring to update the visual data. As shown in the figure, the system provides a graph fusion technology for different data sources and different filtering conditions. The user can view a comparison graph of the running status of each index of each node in a Panel in the Dashboard, which is convenient for the user to perform data analysis and horizontal and vertical comparisons (Fig. 4).

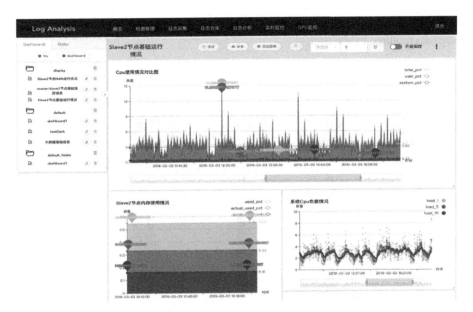

Fig. 4. An example of log analysis dashboard

Log Monitoring Platform Layer Implementation

Node Manager Beatwatcher

Beatwatcher is implemented by the Go language. Its functions mainly include the following parts: one-click script to download and launch, extract monitoring test data, transfer analysis configuration file, the heartbeat mechanism, data collector start and stop.

One-click script download launch: Make it easy to add nodes. The entire process from downloading the complete Shell script to downloading the executable file to start can be completed through a Shell script command containing Key and tags generated by the platform. Greatly simplify the user's operation steps.

Extract monitoring test data: Beatwatcher enables the extraction of test data, ensuring correct configuration when modifying the collector configuration.

Transfer and parse configuration files: Through the interaction with the log management platform, the configuration file is accepted and parsed.

Heartbeat mechanism: The collector sends survival information to the log monitoring platform every 5 s to ensure that the node's survival status can be grasped in the log monitoring management platform.

The data collector starts and stops: the Beatwatcher can be used to start and stop the collector.

Log Monitoring System Center Management Platform

The management platform of the log monitoring system center will be implemented on the basis of the Spring boot framework, receiving the request data of the front end, and calling the corresponding Service according to different Controllers with different parameters. In various such service processing, it will manage the scheduling of Redis,

BeatWatcher, Elasticsearch, Kafka, Flink and other components to complete all the functions required by the user.

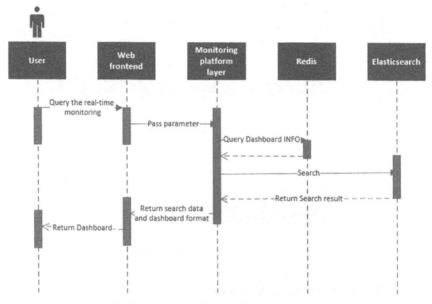

Fig. 5. Query real-time monitoring dashboard

When the user query real-time monitoring dashboard (such as the resource utilization of the big data cluster, the running status of the K8s cluster, the running status of the distributed business system, etc.), the sequence diagram is as shown in Fig. 5. The user will first request the web frontend, the front end will request a specific API, and pass the corresponding parameters. Then, the monitoring center management layer will obtain the attribute information of the Dashboard through the Redis cache, and then initiate an aggregate search request to Elasticsearch according to the Current Para, and obtain the data of each indicator. Finally, the chart style information and indicators data of Dashboard are returned to web frontend uniformly.

The log data in Elasticsearch comes from the big data cluster, K8s cluster, API gateway and other platforms, data collection by Filebeat and Metricbeat managed by BeatWatcher and then processed by Flink, and then imported into Elasticsearch. In Elasticsearch, Indexes are created based on the date and cluster type.

Data Layer Implementation

Data Collector

BeatWatcher is used to manage Filebeat and Metricbeat and to interact with data and command interactions with the monitoring platform (Fig. 6).

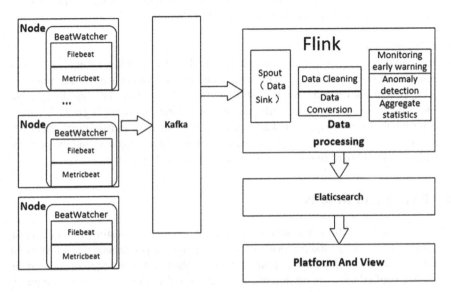

Fig. 6. Data flow graph of data layer

Filebeat is an open source log data collector. When logging data is collected, the log directory or specific log files are monitored with Filebeat. Metricbeat can periodically collect operating system and server operating indicators (CPU, memory, hard disk, IO, read and write speed, processes, etc.), and can also collect running information of many general-purpose systems (such as Kafka, Kubernetes, Memcached, Mysql, etc.).

In our system, they are used to collect multi-source data, and then the collected indicators and data are sent to the specified output (such as Kafka, Elasticsearch, etc.).

Log Message Queue

Apache Kafka is an open source, distributed, partitioned, and replicable publishing-subscription messaging system based on log submissions. It has message persistence, high throughput, distributed, low latency and other features.

In our system, data is sent from the data collector to the corresponding Topic of Kafka, and Flink subscribes to the data from Kafka. It avoids the situation that the server is overwhelmed by the sudden peak value, and can achieve the isolation of data collection and processing well.

Data Processing

Apache Flink is a distributed open source computing framework for data stream processing and bulk data processing. Its core is the distributed stream data flow engine written in Java and Scala, which can support both stream processing and batch processing.

In our system, Flink is used for data processing, and transform the unstructured log data generated by each system (such as the basic data generated by the big data cluster, the operational data generated by the service platform, the basic indicator data of the service platform, etc.) into structured data. In the data processing module, it also includes the operation of deleting useless data, adding tags to the data. The data will be imported into Elasticsearch for data storage and search after Flink processing.

Data Storage and Search

Elasticsearch is an open-source, distributed, RESTful full-text search engine built on Lucene. It can store, search and analyze large amounts of data in a very short time.

Our system uses Elasticsearch to store and search log data. The log data will be divided into different indexes according to the source and date of the log data. Then our monitoring platform will query and aggregate the log data from Elasticsearch according to certain rules. User access The platform can view the filtered log data and the platform provides the Dashboard function for users to analyze the log data.

5 Testing and Results

This section will test this log monitoring system. It includes unit testing, functional testing, integration testing, and performance testing. Only the performance test results are given here. By using JMeter to constantly increase the number of requests and concurrency, We verified the compression resistance and stability of the system by comparing the average response time, accuracy and other indicators of the system.

The system consumes the most performance when performing an aggregate search on all log data. Therefore, what is shown here is the performance of the system in extreme cases where all requests are aggregated search requests (Fig. 7).

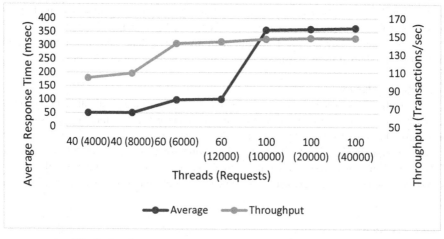

Fig. 7. Load test results (average response time and throughput)

When the system load is 40 threads to access 4000 and 8000 times, the average response time is 51 ms. When the system load is increased to 60 threads to access 6000 and 12000 times, the average response time is 99 ms and 102 ms. When the load is upgraded to 100 threads to access 10000, 20,000, and 40,000 times, the average response time are 345 ms, 360 ms, and 364 ms, respectively.

Figure 8 depicts the amount of data received and transmitted by the system in the above test environment. The resulting curves are almost coincident and similar to throughput. In all of the above tests, the system error rate was 0%.

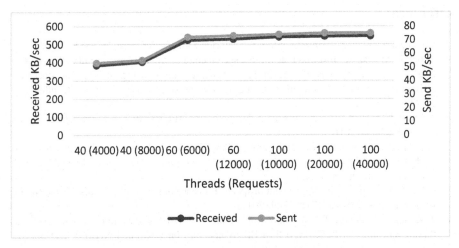

Fig. 8. Load test results (received and sent amount)

6 Conclusions

In this Paper, we provide a solution for log monitoring of distributed systems. Through the distributed cloud monitoring platform based on log insight built on the basis of Spring Boot, We realize functions such as machine management, data collection, data cleaning, log warehouse, data analysis, and real-time monitoring. Users can complete the monitoring and deployment of any server through a unique shell command generated by the distributed cloud monitoring platform.

At the same time, based on the Go language, the Log monitoring analysis platform is implemented to monitor each user cluster node. After the data is collected by Filebeat and Metricbeat managed by BeatWatcher, it will be sent to Kafka for subsequent processing.

The distributed streaming data engine Flink will perform data cleaning and abnormal detection by subscribing to Kafka's corresponding Topic. The functions of Flink module in this system mainly include data deduplication, data enhancement, data conversion, abnormal detection according to rules, unsupervised abnormal detection, etc.

Finally, the data is sent to Elasticsearch for persistent storage. The operator will perform centralized filtering and display and analysis of log data in an effortless way through our system.

In future work, we will intend to add the predictive analysis function of the log data and predict future trends through certain prediction algorithms to assist the operators in making decisions.

Acknowledgment. This work was supported in part by the National Science and Technology Major Project under Grant 2018ZX03001016; Engineering Research Center of Information Networks, Ministry of Education.

References

1. Kononenko, O., et al.: Mining modern repositories with elasticsearch. In: MSR (2014)
2. Zobel, J., Moffat, A.: Inverted files for text search engines. ACM Comput. Surv. **38**, 6 (2006)
3. Prakash, T.R., et al.: Geo-identification of web users through logs using ELK stack. In: 2016 6th International Conference - Cloud System and Big Data Engineering (Confluence), pp. 606–610 (2016)
4. Montesi, F., Weber, J.: Circuit breakers, discovery, and API gateways in microservices. CoRR abs/1609.05830 (2016)
5. Arpitha, P., Kumar, P.V.: Big data computing and clouds: trends and future directions (2018)
6. Carbone, P., et al.: Apache Flink™: stream and batch processing in a single engine. IEEE Data Eng. Bull. **38**, 28–38 (2015)
7. Carbone, P., et al.: State management in apache Flink®: consistent stateful distributed stream processing. PVLDB **10**, 1718–1729 (2017)
8. Tovarňák, D., Pitner, T.: Normalization of unstructured log data into streams of structured event objects. In: 2019 IFIP/IEEE Symposium on Integrated Network and Service Management (IM), pp. 671–676 (2019)
9. Tang, J., et al.: Visualizing large-scale and high-dimensional data. In: WWW (2016)
10. Dumais, S., Jeffries, R., Russell, D.M., Tang, D., Teevan, J.: Understanding user behavior through log data and analysis. In: Olson, J.S., Kellogg, W.A. (eds.) Ways of Knowing in HCI, pp. 349–372. Springer, New York (2014). https://doi.org/10.1007/978-1-4939-0378-8_14
11. Splunk. https://www.splunk.com/
12. Fluentd. https://www.fluentd.org/
13. Loggly. https://www.loggly.com/
14. Logstach. https://www.elastic.co/
15. Graylog. https://www.graylog.org/
16. He, P., et al.: Towards automated log parsing for large-scale log data analysis. IEEE Trans. Dependable Secure Comput. **15**, 931–944 (2018)
17. Surwase, V.: REST API modeling languages - a developer's perspective (2016)

A Self-adaptive PSO-Based Dynamic Scheduling Method on Hierarchical Cloud Computing

Shunmei Meng[1]([✉]), Weijia Huang[1], Xiaolong Xu[2], Qianmu Li[1], Wanchun Dou[3], and Bowen Liu[3]

[1] Department of Computer Science and Engineering, Nanjing University of Science and Technology, Nanjing, China
{mengshunmei,weijia,qianmu}@njust.edu.cn
[2] Key Laboratory of Intelligent Perception and Systems for High-Dimensional Information of Ministry of Education, Nanjing University of Science and Technology, Nanjing, China
xlxu@nuist.edu.cn
[3] State Key Laboratory for Novel Software Technology, Nanjing University, Nanjing, China
douwc@nju.edu.cn, liubw@smail.nju.edu.cn

Abstract. Edge computing has been envisioned as an emerging and prospective computing paradigm for its advantage of low latency, which uses local resources. However, the edge resources are usually limited and could not meet end-users' diversified requirement. Cloud computing paradigm could provide scalable and centralized resources with high computational capabilities, but it has latency issues. Thus it is suggested to combine both computing paradigms together to improve the performance of mobile applications. In this paper, we propose a self-adaptive dynamic scheduling approach based on hierarchical heterogeneous clouds. Our scheduling mechanism considers not only schedule planning but also dynamic scheduling on heterogeneous clouds. Firstly, a self-adaptive scheduling mechanism based on a meta-heuristic optimization algorithm, PSO (Particle Swarm Optimization), is presented for schedule planning. Then a dynamic scheduling mechanism on dynamic partial workflow model is proposed for dynamic optimization during the execution. Finally, external experiments compared with other methods are conducted to demonstrate the effectiveness of our proposal.

Keywords: Dynamic scheduling · PSO · Mobile edge computing · Cloud · Workflow

1 Introduction

Cloud computing has been witnessed to be one of the most promising contemporary technologies, which is a distributed computing paradigm and can provide centralized scalable resources for Internet users [1]. It has been considered to be an effective technique that powers up the implementation of service-oriented computing systems, which drives new levels of performance and productivity in multiple domains [2]. Moreover,

X. Zhang et al. (Eds.): CloudComp 2019/SmartGift 2019, LNICST 322, pp. 89–100, 2020.
https://doi.org/10.1007/978-3-030-48513-9_7

with the development of mobile devices and mobile applications, cloud computing has been proved to be a promising tool for mobile applications where computations/data can be offloaded to these centralized resources [3].

However, migrate workloads of mobile applications to centralized clouds may lead to more time consumption as the conventional centralized cloud resources are usually deployed remotely from mobile users. With the progressive development of wireless communication technology, mobile edge computing (MEC) is conceived as another prospective computing paradigm for its advantage of low latency [4]. MEC could provide local resources for mobile users, which can power up the implementation of delay-sensitive mobile applications. While compared with centralized public cloud resources, the scale and the computing capacity of local edge resources are limited.

Motivated by the different features of the low-latency edge resources and remote scalable cloud instances, heterogeneous cloud are suggested to be jointly scheduled. There have been many researches studying on task or resource provision and scheduling problem in both cloud and MEC systems [5–7]. However, these researches mainly focus the usage of single kind of cloud, i.e., only remote centralized public cloud or only edge cloud. There are few works studying the combination of the heterogeneous cloud. Authors in [8] provide a micro-services provisioning mode for IoT (Internet of Things) applications based on heterogeneous cloud-edge computing paradigm.

In scheduling problem, resource provisioning and scheduling aims to implement the reasonable deployment of cloud resources to satisfy users' requirements. However, most of existing scheduling methods are schedule planning before execution, which ignore the dynamics during the execution. Actually, especially in mobile edge cloud, due to the mobile characteristics and the complicated network environment, there are probably many dynamics and exceptions occurred while executing. Thus reactive dynamic provision is emerged for handling the dynamics and exceptions while executing of mobile applications.

To deal with the issues mentioned above, in this paper, a self-adaptive dynamic scheduling method on hierarchical clouds is proposed to provide effective scheduling mobile applications. It aims to optimize the cost while meeting the deadline. Specifically, a heterogeneous cloud model is designed to apply both centralized and low-latency cloud instances. A self-adaptive PSO-based scheduling approach on heterogeneous clouds is proposed to deploy appropriate resources for the tasks of mobile applications. To react to the dynamics of mobile environment, a dynamic scheduling mechanism is designed on the dynamic partial workflow model. Finally, experiments are conducted to demonstrate the effectiveness of the method proposed in this paper.

The reminder of this paper is organized as follows: Sect. 2 gives the system model of our proposal. In Sect. 3, a self-adaptive PSO-based dynamic scheduling method on heterogeneous clouds is presented. Section 4 presents the empirical performance and effectiveness of the method proposed in this paper. Section 5 reviews some related researches. Finally, Sect. 6 concludes our paper and presents some researches of our future work.

2 System Model

2.1 Overview of the Heterogeneous Cloud Model

In this section, a heterogeneous cloud architecture is proposed to provide both scalable and low-latency cloud resources to meet different requirements of mobile users, which is shown in Fig. 1. It consists of two layers. Layer-1 provides the remote scalable cloud resources providing by public cloud providers. It could apply centralized resources with high availability and scalability. Layer-2 presents the local edge resources provided by local mobile devices, which could provide edge resources with low latency. Mobile users schedule their excessive tasks to low-latency edge devices by the wireless access network. And the mobile edge cloud can be connected to the remote scalable cloud in layer-1 through the Internet. When mobile requests arrive, scheduling decisions are made according to scheduling strategy to determine optimal deployment of resources to each task in the mobile applications so as to meet the requirement of mobile users.

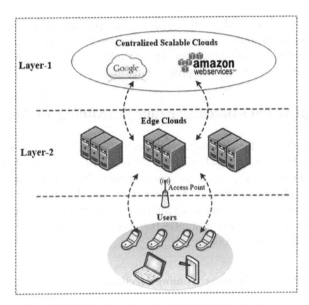

Fig. 1. The heterogeneous cloud architecture.

2.2 PSO Algorithm

The Particle Swarm Optimization (PSO) scheme is a cooperative meta heuristic method, which was proposed by Kennedy and Eberhartin in 1995 [9]. The PSO algorithm is a global search swarm intelligent method based on population mechanism. In initialization of the basic PSO, the initial particles are generated randomly. Every particle in the swarm can be represented as a two-tuple $\{x_i, v_i\}$, where $x_i = \{x_{i1}, x_{i2}, \ldots, x_{iD}\}$ is denoted as the position vector, $v_i = \{v_{i1}, v_{i2}, \ldots, v_{iD}\}$ is denoted as the velocity vector, and D is the dimensional of the search space which corresponds to the number of tasks in the scheduling problem. In PSO, the moving direction of each particle can be determined by Eq. (1).

$$v_{id}^{k+1} = \omega v_{id}^k + c_1 r_1 \left(pbest_{id} - x_{id}^k \right) + c_2 r_2 \left(gbest_{id} - x_{id}^k \right) \tag{1}$$

where $d = 1, 2, \ldots, D (1 \leq d \leq D)$, v_{id}^{k+1} and v_{id}^k are the d-th velocities of particle i at time k and time $k + 1$, respectively. ω is the inertia weight, r_1 and r_2 are random numbers ranging between the interval $[0, 1]$, c_1 and c_2 are acceleration coefficients, $pbest_{id}$ is the personal best position of particle i, $gbest_{id}$ is the global best position of the entire swarm.

Then the individual particle updates its position based on its previous position x_{id}^k and v_{id}^{k+1}, which is shown in Eq. (2):

$$x_{id}^{k+1} = x_{id}^k + v_{id}^{k+1} \tag{2}$$

Then after the iterated advances based on the updating, particles make further searches in the searching space with the new updated velocity and position. The swarm gradually approaches the optimal solution. In our work, we will apply the PSO algorithm into our scheduling problem to find optimal solutions.

3   Self-adaptive PSO-Based Dynamic Scheduling Method

In this work, inspired by the advantages (such as high-precision solutions and fast convergence) of PSO mechanism, a self-adaptive PSO-based dynamic scheduling method is proposed to deal with the scheduling and provisioning problem for mobile users. Specifically, a schedule planning method based on the PSO algorithm is presented firstly. Then to deal with the mobility, a dynamic scheduling method based on the dynamic partial workflow model is presented to minimize the execution cost dynamically during the execution of the application workflow.

3.1   Self-adaptive PSO-Based Scheduling Mechanism

Although PSO has been used in many domains. It is still not easy to get optimal solution based on standard PSO for its robustness, i.e., the ability to track changes in convergence state of the particle swarm. To address this issue, an adaptive PSO algorithm with better search capability is applied to solve the scheduling problem in our proposal. An improved initial population generation strategy and an adaptive parameter setting strategy are designed to improve the search capability and avoid local optimal solution.

(1) Improved Initialization Strategy
     In our PSO-based scheduling method, the critical path (CP) strategy is applied to filter the poor solution and get a better initial population, which consists of two phases:

1) *Determine the CP of the workflow:* The critical path of the workflow must contain the exit task t_{exit}. The CP-finding process starts form the exit task t_{exit} and stop at the entry task t_{entry}. The latest finish time (LFT) of t_{exit} should be no more than the deadline *UD*. In the critical path, each individual task t has a critical predecessor task. And the critical predecessor task t_{cp} is the task which has the latest arrival time to task t. After determining the critical parent t_{cp} of task t in *CP*, t_{cp} will be added to the critical path *CP*. Repeatedly, the overall critical path for the workflow will be found.

2) *CP-based Initialization:* To improve the quality of initial particles, only the random initial particle where the finish time of the critical path is less than the deadline *UD* will be seen as a good initial solution. Otherwise the initial particle will be regenerated until the finish time of the critical path is less than the deadline *UD*. As the number of tasks in the critical path is far less than the number of tasks of the workflow. Thus it will consume little time to filter the bad initial particles.

(2) Adaptive Parameters Settings:

For self-adaptive learning of PSO, an adaptive inertia weight is adopted for velocity and position updating. The inertia weight in the k-th iteration can be determined by Eq. (3).

$$\omega_k = \omega_{max} - \frac{(\omega_{max} - \omega_{min})}{K} * k \tag{3}$$

where ω_{max} and ω_{min} are the maximum and minimum weight factor values, K is the total number of iterations and k is the current number of the iterations.

The acceleration parameters c_1 and c_2 are also adaptively changing, which are varied with the number of iterations and changed asynchronously with the time.

$$c_1 = \frac{k}{K}\left(c_{1f} - c_{1i}\right) + c_{1i}$$
$$c_2 = \frac{k}{K}\left(c_{2f} - c_{2i}\right) + c_{2i} \tag{4}$$

where $c_{1f}, c_{2f}, c_{1i}, c_{2i}$ are constants which are empirically decided, and c_{1i} and c_{2i} are the initial values of c_1 and c_2. Then based on the adaptive inertia weight and the adaptive acceleration parameters described above, the velocity and position of particles of the swarm can be updated based on the Eq. (1) and (2).

(3) Evaluation Function

In PSO-based scheduling problem, an evaluation function is needed to calculate the fitness value of each particle in the swarm. As our goal is to optimize the overall execution cost while meeting the deadline, and the fitness function can be defined as follows.

$$EC = \sum_{i=1}^{n} c_i$$
$$s.t. \sum_{i=1}^{n} ET_i \leq UD \tag{5}$$

where c_i and ET_i represent the execution cost and the execution time of task t_i, respectively. The execution time ET_i of task t_i contains both the output/input data transmission time between task to resource and the execution time on the selected resource.

Calculate the fitness values of each scheduling solution based on the evaluation function. For each particle, if the fitness value of its current position outperforms than the best position of this particle *pbest*, then update *pbest* with current position. And if the fitness value of its current position is better the best position of the swarm *gbest*, then reset *gbest* with the new position of the particle. Then update the velocity and position of all particles based on the updating equations. The search will be iterated until the stop criterion is satisfied.

3.2 Dynamic Scheduling Based on Dynamic Partial Workflow Model

To deal with the influence of mobility of users on scheduling during the execution, a dynamic resource scheduling method is designed. It is based on the adaptive PSO mechanism and a dynamic workflow model to provision appropriate resources for mobile applications dynamically.

(1) Mobility model of mobile users

In this section, a commonly used mobility model named random waypoint [10] is applied to formulate the movement of users in our problem. Based on random waypoint mobility scheme, the movement of users could be modeled as the moving trajectory between different waypoints where mobile users move at pre-set speeds and stop at next waypoint for some time period. More details about the random waypoint model can be referred to reference [10].

Figure 2 gives the moving track of a mobile user, which is designed according to the random waypoint mobility scheme. User starts by choosing its first waypoint p_1 randomly and stop at p_1 for some time period t_r and t_r is within $[PT_{min}, PT_{max}]$. Then the user selects another waypoint, i.e., the second waypoint p_2, and moves to it at a random speed between $[pv_{min}, pv_{max}]$. User will also pause at p_2 for another random time period T_2 which is between $[PT_{min}, PT_{max}]$. This procedure will be repeated for the whole execution process of the mobile application.

(2) Generating dynamic workflows based on the mobility model

Since the local edge resources are constantly changing as the user moves, then the optimized services to each individual task may vary with the movement of mobile users while executing. Thus it is necessary to update the scheduling for the uncompleted tasks dynamically at each waypoint. To address this issue, dynamic partial workflow model is designed for rescheduling, where a dynamic partial workflow will be constructed at each waypoint.

The dynamic partial workflow at a waypoint is a sub workflow cut-off from the original application workflow, which only contains the uncompleted tasks (tasks that are being executed) and unexecuted tasks (tasks that are not yet executed). And each waypoint has a dynamic partial workflow.

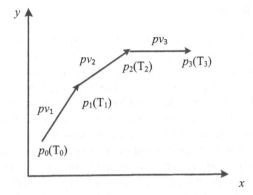

Fig. 2. User moving trajectory based on RWP model.

Different waypoint has different local edge cloud resources, thus re-scheduling should only be conducted for the remaining tasks. At a waypoint p_i, the dynamic workflow has three kinds of tasks: completed tasks, executing tasks and unexecuted tasks. The dynamic partial workflow at each waypoint only contains executing tasks and unexecuted tasks at that time.

(3) Rescheduling based on the dynamic partial workflow
   Due to the local edge resources are changing with the movement of mobile users, real-time optimal scheduling strategy should be applied for the uncompleted tasks. And reactive scheduling strategy should be re-planed on the DPW workflow. In our work, the executing tasks in the DPW workflow will continue to be executed in the original assigned resources. The unexecuted tasks will be re-provisioned with real-time resources according to the above PSO-based scheduling approach at current waypoint.

4   Experiment

Experiments are performed to evaluate the effectiveness of the proposed dynamic scheduling model. Experimental settings are described in the following firstly.

4.1   Experiment Settings

In this paper, to design the hierarchical heterogeneous cloud, Amazon T2 instances are used to simulate remote centralized cloud with scalable resources, and a set of PC nodes are used to simulated as edge resources in Layer-2. It is assumed that the prices of each edge resource and their process capacity are usually positively related.

Two scientific workflows from different areas, i.e., CyberShake and Epigenomics, are applied to model the mobile application workflow with multiple tasks. The details of the five scientific workflows can be referred to reference [11]. In our experiment, the parameters related to c_1 and c_2 (acceleration coefficients in Eq. (6)) are empirical values. Which is set as: $c_{1f} = 0.5, c_{2f} = 2.5, c_{1i} = 2.5, c_{2i} = 0.5$.

4.2 Experimental Result

To validate the performance of our proposal, our method is compared (denoted as SAPDS) with two other comparative methods: IC-PCP [12] and standard PSO [9]. IC-PCP introduced in [12] is designed for deadline-constrained scheduling problem, which also aims to minimize the execution cost and satisfy the deadline.

Figure 3 (a) and Fig. 3 (b) provide the performance of the three methods in the mean execution cost on six different deadlines for Epigenomics and CyberShake, respectively. In our experiment, the deadlines are set between the slowest execution time *se* (all tasks are executed on the slowest resource) and the fastest execution time *fe* (all tasks are executed on the fastest resource), which is similar to the research [13]. The difference between the slowest and fastest runtime *se - fe*, denoted as *D'*, is divided by 4 to obtain an interval size *D'/4*. As shown in Fig. 3, all of the mean execution costs of the three methods decrease with the increase of the deadline in both of the two workflows. And our method, i.e., SAPDS, has lower execution cost than IC-PCP and standard PSO. This is because IC-PCP only executes the scheduling only once, which didn't consider dynamic scheduling during execution. Compared with standard PSO, our method not only adopt critical path to improve the quality of initial particles but also apply adaptive parameter setting strategies.

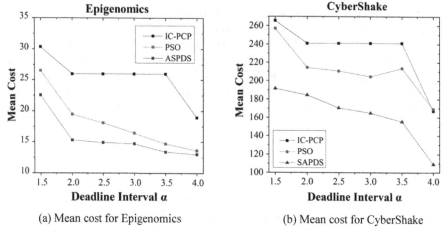

(a) Mean cost for Epigenomics   (b) Mean cost for CyberShake

Fig. 3. Comparison in mean cost under different deadlines for Epigenomics and CyberShake (number of initial particles = 100, number of iterations = 80).

Figure 4 presents the simulation result of the makespan (total execution time) of the three methods under different deadlines where the number of initial particles and the number of iterations are fixed. In Epigenomics, it can be found that our method mostly has less makespan in different deadlines compared with other two methods. While in CyberShake, the performance of our method in makespan under different deadlines is not stable. This is because the CyberShake workflow is more complex than Epigenomics workflow, and the tasks of CyberShake are dependent with each other more closely.

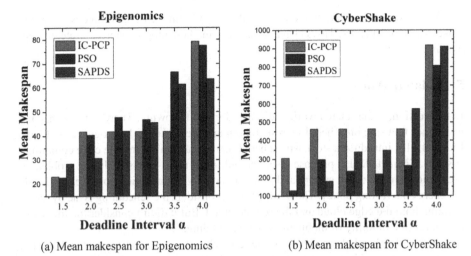

(a) Mean makespan for Epigenomics   (b) Mean makespan for CyberShake

Fig. 4. Comparison in mean makespan under different deadlines for Epigenomics and Cyber-Shake (number of initial particles = 100, number of iterations = 80).

From Fig. 3 and Fig. 4, according to the goal of our proposal, i.e., minimize the overall and satisfy the deadline, we can see that our method could obtain optimized execution cost with fine makespan under different deadlines.

Figure 5(a) and Fig. 5 (b) present the result of PSO and SAPDS in mean cost with the change of the initial particles, respectively. We can see that the execution costs of both of PSO and SAPDS decrease with the increase of initial particles at the beginning and then slowly get steady. Besides, with the change of the number of initial particles, our method constantly consumes less cost than PSO.

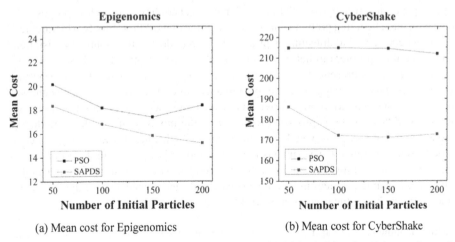

(a) Mean cost for Epigenomics   (b) Mean cost for CyberShake

Fig. 5. Comparison in mean cost with the increase of initial particles for Epigenomics and CyberShake (deadline interval = 2.0, number of iterations = 80).

Overall we can observe that our method can get optimized execution cost with fine makespan in most cases. That is because that our method adopts adaptive strategies and dynamic scheduling.

5   Related Work

In this section, some related work is discussed in the following. There have been some researches focusing on scheduling researching in edge clouds or heterogeneous clouds. Liu et al. [14] introduce a stochastic scheduling mechanism for mobile edge computing systems. Chen et al. [15] propose research multi-user multi-task scheduling problem in green mobile edge cloud system and utilize Lyaponuv optimization approach to decide the energy harvesting policy. The literature [16] considers the scheduling issue by incorporating both the edge cloud and the remote cloud. But it didn't consider the impact of dynamics (the mobility of mobile users) to scheduling.

On the other hand, there are also some researches that have considered the dynamics and uncertainties during the execution of tasks. In our previous work, we have discussed the influence of the uncertainties to scheduling in cloud environment and propose a failure-tolerance scheduling approach to handle the exceptions during the executing of application tasks [17]. The literature [18] and [19] also research uncertainty or failure-aware method for scheduling and task provisioning in both cloud and mobile cloud systems. Sahni et al. [20] provide a dynamic cost-aware heuristic-based scheduling method, which use the VM performance variability and instance acquisition delay to get a just-in-time schedule strategy. Juarez et al. [21] present an energy-aware dynamic scheduling system for parallel task-based applications and aim to minimize both energy consumption and the execution time.

6   Conclusion

In this paper, a self-adaptive PSO-based dynamic scheduling approach is proposed to deal with the scheduling problem during the execution of workflow. Firstly, a hierarchical heterogeneous cloud architecture is proposed. Then to deal with resource provisioning and scheduling problem in heterogeneous clouds, a self-adaptive PSO-based scheduling mechanism is presented to optimize the execution cost and satisfy the deadline, where self-adaptive strategies are adopted to accelerate the convergence speed and get optimized solutions. Moreover, a dynamic scheduling mechanism based on dynamic partial workflow model is proposed to deal with the mobility of mobile users during the execution of workflow, which aims to get an optimal solution with changes in edge cloud resources. Finally, experiments are conducted and demonstrate the efficiency of our dynamic scheduling method. In our future work, we will do further research in multi-objective dynamic problem in heterogeneous clouds and consider more dynamics and uncertainties during the execution of workflows.

Acknowledgment. This paper is supported by the National Science Youth Foundation of China under Grant No. 61702264, the Fundamental Research Funds for the Central Universities No. 30919011282, the Fundamental Research Funds for the Central Universities No. 30918014108.

References

1. Rimal, B.P., Maier, M.: Workflow scheduling in multi-tenant cloud computing environments. IEEE Trans. Parallel Distrib. Syst. **28**(1), 290–304 (2016)
2. Qi, L., et al.: Finding all you need: web APIs recommendation in web of things through keywords search. IEEE Trans. Comput. Soc. Syst. (2019). https://doi.org/10.1109/tcss.2019.2906925
3. Xu, X., Liu, Q., Zhang, X., Zhang, J., Qi, L., Dou, W.: A blockchain-powered crowdsourcing method with privacy preservation in mobile environment. IEEE Trans. Comput. Soc. Syst. (2019). https://doi.org/10.1109/tcss.2019.2909137
4. Abbas, N., Zhang, Y., Taherkordi, A., Skeie, T.: Mobile edge computing: a survey. IEEE Internet Things J. **5**(1), 450–465 (2017)
5. Zhu, Z., Zhang, G., Li, M., Liu, X.: Evolutionary multi-objective workflow scheduling in cloud. IEEE Trans. Parallel Distrib. Syst. **27**(5), 1344–1357 (2015)
6. You, C., Huang, K., Chae, H., Kim, B.H.: Energy-efficient resource allocation for mobile-edge computation offloading. IEEE Trans. Wireless Commun. **16**(3), 1397–1411 (2016)
7. Qi, L., Chen, Y., Yuan, Y., Fu, S., Zhang, X., Xu, X.: A QoS-aware virtual machine scheduling method for energy conservation in cloud-based cyber-physical systems. World Wide Web **23**(2), 1275–1297 (2019). https://doi.org/10.1007/s11280-019-00684-y
8. Filip, I.D., Pop, F., Serbanescu, C., Choi, C.: Microservices scheduling model over heterogeneous cloud-edge environments as support for IoT applications. IEEE Internet Things J. **5**(4), 2672–2681 (2018)
9. Kennedy, J., Eberhart, R.: Particle swarm optimization (PSO). In: Proceedings of the IEEE International Conference on Neural Networks, Perth, Australia, pp. 1942–1948 (1995)
10. Kumar, N., Zeadally, S., Chilamkurti, N., Vinel, A.: Performance analysis of Bayesian coalition game-based energy-aware virtual machine migration in vehicular mobile cloud. IEEE Netw. **29**(2), 62–69 (2015)
11. Bharathi, S., Chervenak, A., Deelman, E., Mehta, G., Su, M.H., Vahi, K.: Characterization of scientific workflows. In: 2008 Third Workshop on Workflows in Support of Large-Scale Science, pp. 1–10 (2008)
12. Abrishami, S., Naghibzadeh, M., Epema, D.H.: Deadline-constrained workflow scheduling algorithms for infrastructure as a service clouds. Future Gener. Comput. Syst. **29**(1), 158–169 (2013)
13. Rodriguez, M.A., Buyya, R.: Deadline based resource provisioning and scheduling algorithm for scientific workflows on clouds. IEEE Trans. Cloud Comput. **2**(2), 222–235 (2014)
14. Liu, J., Mao, Y., Zhang, J., Letaief, K.B.: Delay-optimal computation task scheduling for mobile-edge computing systems. In: 2016 IEEE International Symposium on Information Theory (ISIT), pp. 1451–1455 (2016)
15. Chen, W., Wang, D., Li, K.: Multi-user multi-task computation offloading in green mobile edge cloud computing. IEEE Trans. Serv. Comput. **12**, 726–738 (2018)
16. Zhao, T., Zhou, S., Guo, X., Niu, Z.: Tasks scheduling and resource allocation in heterogeneous cloud for delay-bounded mobile edge computing. In: 2017 IEEE International Conference on Communications (ICC), pp. 1–7 (2017)
17. Meng, S., Li, Q., Wu, T., Huang, W., Zhang, J., Li, W.: A fault-tolerant dynamic scheduling method on hierarchical mobile edge cloud computing. Comput. Intell. (2019). https://doi.org/10.1111/coin.12219
18. Chen, H., Zhu, X., Liu, G., Pedrycz, W.: Uncertainty-aware online scheduling for real-time workflows in cloud service environment. IEEE Trans. Serv. Comput. (2018)
19. Deng, S., Huang, L., Taheri, J., Zomaya, A.Y.: Computation offloading for service workflow in mobile cloud computing. IEEE Trans. Parallel Distrib. Syst. **26**(12), 3317–3329 (2014)

20. Sahni, J., Vidyarthi, D.P.: A cost-effective deadline-constrained dynamic scheduling algorithm for scientific workflows in a cloud environment. IEEE Trans. Cloud Comput. **6**(1), 2–18 (2015)
21. Juarez, F., Ejarque, J., Badia, R.M.: Dynamic energy-aware scheduling for parallel task-based application in cloud computing. Future Gener. Comput. Syst. **78**, 257–271 (2018)

Application of Bluetooth Low Energy Beacons and Fog Computing for Smarter Environments in Emerging Economies

Mingxu Sun[1], Kondwani Michael Kamoto[2]($\boxtimes$) (iD), Qi Liu[3], Xiaodong Liu[4], and Lianyong Qi[5]

[1] School of Electrical Engineering, University of Jinan, Jinan, China
[2] Jiangsu Collaborative Innovation Center of Atmospheric Environment and Equipment Technology (CICAEET), Nanjing University of Information Science and Technology, Nanjing, China
k_kamoto@yahoo.co.uk
[3] Shandong Beiming Medical Technology Ltd., Jinan, China
[4] School of Computing, Edinburgh Napier University, Edinburgh, UK
[5] School of Information Science and Engineering, Qufu Normal University, Qufu, China

Abstract. The Internet of Things (IoT) has already begun to drastically alter the way people operate in various industries across the world, as well as how we interact with our environment. There is a lot of progress being made toward achieving the envisioned goals of IoT, however there are still numerous challenges to be addressed. Bluetooth low energy (BLE) and its beacons protocol have pushed forward innovations in the field of microlocation, which is a key area of IoT. The emergence of fog computing architecture has also lead to reduced dependence on cloud architecture by shifting resources towards users and local applications. Together these two innovations provide ideal conditions for adoption of IoT in emerging economies, which are known to be both financially and technically constrained. In this paper we provide an overview of the key innovations that are suitable for adoption in emerging economies based on BLE and fog computing. We further present three reference models for indoor navigation systems which can help further the research work in the application of BLE and fog computing.

Keywords: Bluetooth low energy · Internet of Things · Emerging economies

1 Introduction

The Internet of Things (IoT) [1] has ushered in a new connected approach to our everyday activities. The promise of connectivity with not just people but 'things' we come across within our respective environments, living or otherwise, opens up a lot of avenues

---

M. Sun and K. M. Kamoto—Both authors are the first author due to equal contribution to this paper.

© ICST Institute for Computer Sciences, Social Informatics and Telecommunications Engineering 2020
Published by Springer Nature Switzerland AG 2020. All Rights Reserved
X. Zhang et al. (Eds.): CloudComp 2019/SmartGift 2019, LNICST 322, pp. 101–110, 2020.
https://doi.org/10.1007/978-3-030-48513-9_8

for smarter world interactions which take into account context (environment and personal preferences). IoT spans across many Cyber-Physical Systems (CPSs) creating an integrated grouping of systems that provide various services to society. Achieving the vision of IoT is a complicated task due to the current state of systems and the amount of work that needs to be done to turn current systems into their connected and autonomous forms. Current challenges span both the technical and non-technical, however experimental and real world implementations of some of the enabling technologies have shown great promise.

When viewing the promise of a smarter environment from the viewpoint of emerging economies, the implementation of IoT can seem to be a challenging task to accomplish. Successful real world implementations of innovations for IoT and its enabling technologies to date have required a considerable amount of resources, both financial and technical, as well as a favorable economic environment. Given the ongoing challenges that emerging economies face, sourcing the necessary financial and technical investment in order to implement IoT-based systems is typically hard to achieve. However, the improvements that such systems can bring to people and activities of daily life (ADLs) are undeniable.

One of most promising enabling technologies for a number of recent IoT innovations is Bluetooth low energy (BLE), which is commonly applied through the use of BLE beacons. BLE is an energy efficient low data rate technology suitable for power constrained IoT applications [2, 3], and the high availability of Bluetooth-enabled devices has resulted in high rate of adoption by both industry and academia. Other known benefits of BLE are that it doesn't interfere with other wireless infrastructure, and beacons are small in size, low in cost, and platform independent. Some of the well-known applications of BLE beacons include improving shopping experiences [4], navigating museums [5], indoor localization and tracking [6], and helping the blind or disabled [7].

The emergence of the fog computing architecture has also helped to overcome challenges faced along the path to the realization of IoT, which include stringent latency requirements, network bandwidth constraints, resource-constrained devices, and the need for uninterrupted services with intermittent connectivity to the cloud. Fog computing is said to distribute computing, control, storage, and networking functions closer to end user devices, and complements the centralized cloud [8]. Such an architecture alleviates the burden on the cloud to handle all IoT functions and more importantly enables the provision of the required services to enable IoT with little or no dependence on the cloud.

BLE and fog computing provide ideal conditions for technological advancements to me be made within emerging economies, mainly owing to the low cost of setup and maintenance of BLE-based applications, and the ability to only consider cloud-based resources if absolutely necessary to a given system's architecture. This means that IoT innovations can be implemented locally, and then expanded into a fully integrated network when conditions are more ideal. Furthermore, people in said economies generally have access to mobile phone services, with Bluetooth 4.0 enabled smartphones prevalent across the population, making the use of BLE-based IoT applications suitable in those places.

The main purpose of this work is to highlight IoT applications that can be adopted within emerging economies taking into consideration the financial and technical constraints in such environments. In Sect. 2 we discuss BLE, and some of the recent IoT innovations based on this technology that can be adopted for emerging economies. Section 3 presents our proposed reference models for indoor navigation systems which blend together BLE beacons, augmented reality, fog computing, and natural language processing according to the required level of system complexity. The final section, Sect. 4, provides a summary of the research work we conducted and de-tails the plans for our future work.

2   Bluetooth Low Energy

The complexity of IoT has motivated the design and provision of low power communication technologies. These demands have resulted in the provisioning of radio-frequency identification (RFID), ZigBee, 6LoPan, amongst others, and now BLE. This section examines the BLE technology and some of its compelling applications with regards to IoT.

2.1   Protocol and Beacons

The BLE protocol operates on the 2.4-GHz ISM spectrum, which it divides into 40 channels, with three channels (channels 37–39) dedicated to advertisement purposes and the rest for data exchange. BLE beacons are devices that are only responsible for advertising. These devices are connectionless and broadcast their signals periodically [9]. These advertising signals contain small data payloads, referred to as advertising protocol data units (PDUs), which typically include a packet header, MAC address, device's unique identifier, and manufacturer-specific data. A device with receiver capabilities typically processing the signals and performs actions based on the received payload. This can range from a simple notification on a smartphone application to more advanced actions such as displaying indoor navigation routes.

2.2   Beacon Protocols

The most well-known beacon protocols are iBeacon [10] developed by Apple, and Eddystone [11] developed by Google. The main difference between these two profiles lies in their definition of the advertising PDU. Eddystone allows developers to switch between URL and TLM frames for the advertising PDU, whereas iBeacon only provides the ability to specify identification information for a beacon. The definitions for each of these profiles is shown in Fig. 1. There are also two open-source alternatives which are AltBeacon [12] by Radius Networks and GeoBeacon [13] by Tecno-World, which are both compatible with any mobile operating platform. AltBeacon provides the same capabilities as iBeacon but is not company specific, and GeoBeacon is geared towards geocaching applications.

(a)

Adv PDU				Payload defined by iBeacon Standard				
1 byte	4 bytes	2 bytes	6 bytes	9 bytes	16 bytes	2 bytes	2 bytes	1 byte
Preamble	Access Address	Header	MAC	iBeacon Prefix	Universally Unique Identifier (UUID)	Major	Minor	Tx Power

(b)

Adv PDU				Payload defined by Eddystone Standard					
1 byte	4 bytes	2 bytes	6 bytes	UID	1 byte	1 byte	16 bytes	2 bytes	
					Frame Type	Ranging	UID	Reserve	
				URL	1 byte	1 byte	18 bytes		
Preamble	Access Address	Header	MAC		Frame Type	Ranging	URL		
				TLM	1 byte	1 byte	2 bytes	2 bytes	4 bytes	4 bytes
					Frame Type	TLM Version	Battery Level	Temperature	ADV_CNT	SEC_CNT

Fig. 1. Definitions for advertising PDU of (a) iBeacon and (b) Eddystone BLE profiles

2.3   Beacon-Based Applications

Since the initial demonstration of the capabilities of BLE beacons via the introduction of iBeacon, there has been much interest in making use of this technology to achieve longstanding problems with regards to localization, proximity detection and interaction, and activity sensing. Jeon et al. [9] who presented a detailed study of BLE beacon technology and its relationship with IoT provided a concise summary of the state-of-the-art research on BLE beacon-based applications. They further enumerated some of the outstanding work to be done with regards to BLE beacons, which include interoperability between different beacon protocols, managing and monitoring battery life, and the need for enhanced security features to better support IoT. Faragher and Harle [12] investigated the feasibility of BLE beacon-based indoor localization systems using given deployment configurations and operation parameters. They set up 19 beacons in an office area, and their findings showed that a beacon-based approach achieved less than 2.6 m error ninety-five percent of the time when beacons were deployed every 30 m², outperforming the 8.5 m error margin of existing Wi-Fi networks. This increased accuracy greatly assists with the task of activity sensing. Proximity detection and interaction up until the introduction of BLE beacons was usually achieved via the use of QR codes and near-field communication (NFC). However, QR codes need to be installed or printed in a large size to reach a large audience, and NPC have very short interaction distance of 10–20 cm, making interactions for large audiences problematic. The use of BLE beacons addresses these shortcomings for such proximity-related tasks.

Three of the most promising applications of BLE beacons which are easily replicated in emerging economies are vehicle-based indoor navigation, building-based indoor navigation, and indoor navigation coupled with mobile augmented reality.

Vehicle-Based Indoor Navigation

Rodriguez et al. [14] presented their work on an indoor positioning and guidance system for drivers which addressed the challenges faced with indoor parking. They made use of a combination of the inertial sensor data of a mobile phone located inside a vehicle, radio signals coming from a network of BLE beacons, an occupancy grid of the car park, and Bayesian estimation in order to identify the position of a vehicle. Their proposed system further incorporated real-time visual, textual, and auditory instructions to the driver. Their experimental evaluation showed that the proposed system reported the correct position of the vehicle 88% of the time on average, and highlighted the feasibility of implementing vehicle-based indoor navigation, with a significant reduction of the resources for set up and maintenance that are typically required for such an endeavor.

As emerging economies continue to develop and people's living standards improve, more people will have access to vehicles and infrastructure will be improved to cater for the increasing demands of the population. The adoption of such a system which embodies the vision of IoT can greatly simplify people's lives and management of parking structures.

Building-Based Indoor Navigation

Building-based indoor navigation includes landmarks [15], museums [5], airports [16], etc. While there have been a number of applications with regards to museums, airports and schools are areas of great interest for providing smart environments which can assist people and guide them through buildings if need be. One of well-known implementations of such a system is that of Gatwick Airport in the UK [17]. The airport installed 2,000 battery-powered beacons across its two terminals in order to guide airline passengers within the building. These beacons were coupled together with an augmented reality wayfinding tool (see Fig. 2) which enabled passenger navigation within a positioning error margin of 3 m. The capabilities of these beacons were made available to airlines which could use the information to send push notifications to warn passengers if they're running late, or even make a decision on whether or not to wait or offload luggage so that an aircraft can take off on time.

The ability to have meaningful interactions with buildings is a key component of IoT, and BLE beacons can greatly simplify the process that makes this possible, regardless of shortage of resources available. As the beacons are typically low cost, an adequate amount can be purchased depending on the required area of coverage. Furthermore as these devices enable indoor positioning and a vast number of services can be built upon knowledge of user location, there is room for growth in innovative solutions.

Indoor Navigation Coupled with Mobile Augmented Reality

Coupling navigation capabilities with augmented reality can greatly aid in contextualizing information, as shown in Fig. 2. Shao et al. [18] investigated whether BLE beacons were capable of enabling provisioning a seamless mobile augmented reality (AR) experience to the users. The authors proposed a self-contained system consisting of a cluster of BLE beacons that are connected to embedded micro-controllers and low-cost stereo cameras. Self-contained here refers to the system being able to function without requiring internet access, external power supply, or other external resources as part of its operations. Unique sets of visual features and a subset of captured 3D point time series data were embedded in the advertising PDUs for each beacon, with a smartphone serving as the receiver for the advertising signals. The received advertising PDUs were merged with a smartphone's inertial data, and the location data and 3D object data were then used to render a 3D object on a smartphone in real-time. The authors modelled two scenarios where they attempted to recognize five basic hand gestures, and two multi-person interactions which were gestures of two people shaking hands, followed by one person waving a hand to another person. Motions were sampled at five different rates 3 Hz, 6 Hz, 9 Hz, 12 Hz and 15 Hz, and their findings showed that 9 Hz sampling frequency is good enough to capture the meaning of a motion that lasts about a second. Low-speed gestures were recognized accurately at 6 Hz with the performance dropping to around 75% for slightly more difficult gestures like two-hand waves.

This work showcased that BLE beacon-based systems which incorporate augmented reality can be designed and implemented with minimal resources. Given the enormous benefits of augmented reality systems from health, to education, and manufacturing, utilizing beacons can greatly enhance the capacity of those different industry sectors within emerging economies. Furthermore with the next generation BLE 5.0 beacons expected to have an increase in broadcasting capacity of up to around 256 bytes, more complex applications utilizing beacons and augmented reality can be put into operation.

Fig. 2. Gatwick Airport wayfinding tool using augmented reality

3 Proposed Reference Models for Indoor Navigation Systems

The research work presented in Sect. 2 shows promising results for BLE beacon-based approaches for indoor navigation. This section introduces our proposed reference models for BLE beacon-based indoor navigation systems.

The typical beacon-based architecture is comprised of beacons and a mobile application that receives advertised PDUs and acts upon them. The mobile application can take action solely using local resources, make use of external resources, or a combination of the two. In general the architecture of BLE beacon-based navigation systems is limited by the complexity brought on by the tasks it needs to fulfil. In this section we discuss three reference models ranging from basic navigation, to enhanced navigation, to the ideal IoT navigation.

3.1 Basic Navigation

Base services of a navigation system include providing current location, route paths, and providing details on nearby points of interest (POI). Two of the commonly used indoor positioning techniques are proximity and fingerprinting, with received signal strength indications (RSSIs) being among the main signal features that are used for localization. Proximity looks at positioning using the closeness relative to a known location based on detected RSSIs. Fingerprinting on the other hand involves a two-step process: 1) record known coordinates and the RSSIs from beacons within close proximity to each coordinate and store them, and then 2) detect RSSIs currently being received by a device and attempt to match these to the stored fingerprints. Proximity at a minimum only requires beacon identification information and additional descriptors if need be, whereas fingerprinting requires storage of the fingerprint vectors. As RSSI measurements tend to fluctuate due to environmental changes, signal processing techniques are usually employed in order to improve accuracy. Commonly used processing techniques include Particle Filter [19] and Kalman Filter [20].

The most basic setup for user location is making use of local resources of the mobile application and either the proximity or fingerprinting approach for positioning. The proximity approach would result in the mobile application receiving broadcast messages, selecting the strongest signal detected, and then comparing the related beacon identification information to the locally stored data. The descriptor tied to the matching beacon would then be presented to the user as their approximate location. The fingerprinting approach would involve a vector of RSSIs received by the mobile application being compared to the locally stored fingerprints. The descriptor tied to the matching fingerprint would then be presented to the user as their approximate location. A more complex version of this form of user location would involve making use of an external service to handle the matching processes.

In order to derive an optimal route from the current location to the chosen destination a weighted graph needs to be modeled and made available (locally or remotely) to the mobile application. The provision of a map of the physical space is usually ideal in this scenario which can be used to present the navigation information on the mobile application in a more meaningful manner. POIs within a building are typically tied to a beacon, whether they are at the actual location of it or in close proximity. The process therefore is to identify the beacon that the mobile application is currently closest to and then determine the shortest path to the POI i.e. the target beacon. Given a weighted graph, Dijkstra's algorithm can be used to determine the shortest path [21] between the two beacons. The path can then be presented in the form of step by step text instructions or visual representations on the map of the physical space. It should be noted that the instructions/map will need to be updated as the mobile application moves towards the destination. This can be achieved by the mobile application actively reacting to the new RSSIs that are received by beacons along the path.

The final basic service is to provide details on nearby POIs. This can be achieved by selecting the closest N POIs nearby, or defining a maximum radius (r) from the current location and selecting the POIs that fall within this radius. These nearby POIs can then be displayed on the mobile application with either textual information or a visualized map.

3.2 Enhanced Navigation

Enhanced navigation provides additional services on top of those described in the previous section. This architecture provides additional context to the user, and this is achieved via augmented reality. Mobile augmented reality based on BLE-beacons is a more complex yet achievable architecture. The main challenges are how best to store the required visual features and how to later reassemble them in an augmented view on the mobile application. As showcased by Shao et al. [18], the required visual features can be distributed across a set of beacons. The mobile application then uses the advertising PDUs for the beacons that are in close proximity to reassemble the visual features, and display the augmented view based on the direction and angle of the mobile device. The bottleneck of this approach lies in how best to store the visual features as the beacons have limited payload size. If the size of the visual features exceeds distribution across a set of beacons with either the payload size of the Blue-tooth 4.0 or 5.0 specifications then an alternative method would be to establish a fog node at the premises to handle storage while minimizing the latency.

3.3 Ideal IoT Navigation

The IoT aims to bring context to our everyday living. In a navigation system this means taking into consideration our preferences or other personal factors and customizing the experience. In our opinion the ideal navigation system would take into consideration each person's culture especially in multi-lingual environments such as airports, universities, or museums, where use of standard languages such as English or French to provide general information is not adequate to all who make use of services within said environment.

Given the tremendous progress in natural language processing techniques in recent years, it has become much easier to develop language models for specific and to some extent general purposes. These language models can be built using various methods and then deployed for use as part of various language services such as translation, part-of-speech tagging, chatbots, etc.

We therefore propose an integrated BLE beacon fog computing architecture. In this architecture BLE beacon can provide services up to those of the Enhanced Navigation approach. However, the language preference set on the mobile application would determine the language in which they view the navigation information. The proposed approach would better contextualize the navigation experience for those with language challenges while still minimizing the infrastructure and computation required.

4 Conclusion

This paper provided a look into Bluetooth low energy and how this technology is helping to bridge gaps along the path to the full realization of IoT. The introduction of BLE beacons and the related protocols has redefined microlocation techniques and also advanced innovations within this subject area.

IoT provides enormous benefits to society, but it and its related systems can be challenging to implement especially in emerging economies which have a considerable number of financial and technical constraints. This research work provided in-sights into what can be achieved by emerging economies with regards to the IoT de-spite these constraints. We additional enumerated three reference models based on increasingly complexity which can be adopted according to the needs of the required indoor navigation system.

Our future work will involve developing a system prototype in order to verify the real world feasibility of the proposed Ideal IoT Navigation reference model. This will give us a better reference point on the capacity of BLE beacons to achieve such a contextualized scenario.

Acknowledgement. This work has received funding from 5150 Spring Specialists (05492018012), the European Union Horizon 2020 research and innovation program under the Marie Sklodowska Curie grant agreement no. 701697, Major Program of the National Social Science Fund of China (Grant No. 17ZDA092), Royal Society of Edinburgh, UK and China Natural Science Foundation Council (RSE Reference: 62967_Liu_2018_2) under their Joint International Projects funding scheme and 333 High-Level Talent Cultivation Project of Jiangsu Province (BRA2018332).

References

1. Ashton, K.: That internet of things' thing. RFID J. **22**(7), 97–114 (2009)
2. Gubbi, J., Buyya, R., Marusic, S., Palaniswami, M.: Internet of Things (IoT): a vision, architectural elements, and future directions. Future Gener. Comput. Syst. **29**(7), 1645–1660 (2013)
3. Miorandi, D., Sicari, S., De Pellegrini, F., Chlamtac, I.: Internet of things: vision, applications and research challenges. Ad Hoc Netw. **10**(7), 1497–1516 (2012)
4. Zaim, D., Bellafkih, M.: Bluetooth low energy (BLE) based geomarketing system. In: Proceedings of 11th International Conference on Intelligent Systems: Theories and Applications (SITA), Mohammedia, Morocco, pp. 1–6. IEEE (2016)
5. Alletto, S., et al.: An indoor location-aware system for an IoT-based smart museum. IEEE Internet Things J. **3**(2), 244–253 (2016)
6. Gast, M.S.: Building Applications with Ibeacon: Proximity and Location Services with Bluetooth Low Energy. O'Reilly Media, Sebastopol (2014)
7. Cheraghi, S.A., Namboodiri, V., Walker, L.: Guidebeacon: beacon-based indoor wayfinding for the blind, visually impaired, and disoriented. In: Proceedings of IEEE International Conference Pervasive Computing Communications (PerCom), Kailua, HI, USA, pp. 121–130. IEEE (2017)
8. Chiang, M., Zhang, T.: Fog and IoT: an overview of research opportunities. IEEE Internet Things J. **3**(6), 854–864 (2016)
9. Jeon, K.E., She, J., Soonsawad, P., Ng, P.C.: BLE beacons for internet of things applications: survey, challenges, and opportunities. IEEE Internet Things J. **5**(2), 811–828 (2018). https://doi.org/10.1109/JIOT.2017.2788449
10. Apple – iBeacon. https://developer.apple.com/ibeacon/. Accessed 21 June 2019
11. Google - Mark up the world using beacons. https://developers.google.com/beacons/. Accessed 21 June 2019
12. AltBeacon. https://github.com/AltBeacon. Accessed 24 June 2019
13. GeoBeacon. https://github.com/Tecno-World/GeoBeacon. Accessed 24 June 2019

14. Faragher, R., Harle, R.: Location fingerprinting with bluetooth low energy beacons. IEEE J. Sel. Areas Commun. **33**(11), 2418–2428 (2015)
15. Rodríguez, G., Canedo-Rodríguez, A., Iglesias, R., Nieto, A.: Indoor positioning and guiding for drivers. IEEE Sens. J. **19**(14), 5923–5935 (2019). https://doi.org/10.1109/JSEN.2019. 2907473
16. Ito, A., et al.: A trial of navigation system using BLE beacon for sightseeing in traditional area of Nikko. In: Proceedings of IEEE International Conference on Vehicular Electronics and Safety (ICVES), Yokohama, Japan, pp. 170–175. IEEE (2015)
17. TechCrunch - Gatwick Airport Now Has 2,000 Beacons for Indoor Navigation. https://techcrunch.com/2017/05/25/gatwick-airport-now-has-2000-beacons-for-indoor-navigation/. Accessed 21 June 2019
18. Shao, C., Islam, B., Nirjon, S.: MARBLE: mobile augmented reality using a distributed BLE beacon infrastructure. In: Proceedings of 2018 IEEE/ACM Third International Conference on Internet-of-Things Design and Implementation, Orlando, FL, USA, pp. 60–71. IEEE (2018)
19. Djuric, P.M., et al.: Particle filtering. IEEE Sign. Process. Mag. **20**(5), 19–38 (2003)
20. Guvenc, I., Abdallah, C., Jordan, R., Dedoglu, O.: Enhancements to RSS based indoor tracking systems using Kalman filters. In: Proceedings of International Signal Processing Conference (ISPC) and Global Signal Processing Expo (GSPx), Dallas, TX, USA (2003)
21. Dijkstra, E.W.: A note on two problems in connexion with graphs. Numer. Math. **1**(1), 269–271 (1959)

Near-Data Prediction Based Speculative Optimization in a Distribution Environment

Mingxu Sun[1], Xueyan Wu[2], Dandan Jin[3(✉)], Xiaolong Xu[3], Qi Liu[4], and Xiaodong Liu[5]

[1] School of Electrical Engineering, University of Jinan, Jinan, China
[2] Jiangsu Collaborative Innovation Center of Atmospheric Environment and Equipment Technology (CICAEET), Nanjing University of Information Science and Technology, Nanjing 210044, China
[3] School of Computer and Software, Nanjing University of Information Science and Technology, Nanjing, China
18751971087@163.com
[4] Shandong Beiming Medical Technology Co., Ltd., Jinan, China
[5] School of Computing Edinburgh, Napier University Edinburgh, Edinburgh, UK

Abstract. Apache Hadoop is an open source software framework that supports data-intensive distributed applications and is distributed under the Apache 2.0 licensing agreement, where consumers will no longer deal with complex configuration of software and hardware but only pay for cloud services on demand. So how to make the performance of the cloud platform become more important in a consumer-centric environment. There exists imbalance between in some distribution of slow tasks, which results in straggling tasks will have a great influence on the Hadoop framework. By monitoring those tasks in real-time progress and copying the potential Stragglers to a different node, the speculative execution (SE) realizes to improve the probability of finishing those backup tasks before the original ones. The Speculative execution (SE) applies this principle and thus proposed a solution to handle the Straggling tasks. At present, the performance of the Hadoop system is unsatisfying because of the erroneous judgement and inappropriate selection for the backup nodes in the current SE policy. This paper proposes an SE optimized strategy which can be used in prediction of near data. In this strategy, the first step is gathering the real-time task execution information and the remaining runtime required for the task is predicted by a local prediction method. Then it chooses a proper backup node according to the near data and actual demand in the second step. On the other side, this model also includes a cost-effective model in order to make the performance of SE to the peak. The results show that using this strategy in Hadoop effectively improves the accuracy of alternative tasks and effects better in heterogeneous Hadoop environments in various situations, which is beneficial to consumers and cloud platform.

Keywords: Distributed systems · Hadoop · Speculative execution · Locally weighted regression · Near data prediction

---

M. Sun and X. Wu—Both authors are the first author due to equal contribution to this paper.

© ICST Institute for Computer Sciences, Social Informatics and Telecommunications Engineering 2020
Published by Springer Nature Switzerland AG 2020. All Rights Reserved
X. Zhang et al. (Eds.): CloudComp 2019/SmartGift 2019, LNICST 322, pp. 111–122, 2020.
https://doi.org/10.1007/978-3-030-48513-9_9

1 Introduction

As the internet has successfully occupied many aspects of people's lives, the amount of data stored in the consumer's private cloud will grow exponentially in the next few years, many consumers need to pay for the cloud service on demand [1]. Whilst cloud computing platforms have evolved such as Apache Storm [2], Spark [3], and Hadoop [4].

Hadoop is widely used in distributed data storage, computing and search functions areas because of the Apache top project and the prevalent cloud computing frameworks [5]. Many strategies have been designed to improve the effectiveness and efficiency of Hadoop clusters and facilitate big data storage and analytics [6], but the inefficient resource allocation in Hadoop job scheduling still bring many difficulties.

Allocation and Coordination of tasks among TaskTrackers has therefore become critical and challenging in a JobTracker due to lack of runtime information of Task-Trackers and difficulty in predicting the completion duration of each tasks [7]. The most effective mechanism to improve Hadoop's fault tolerance is Speculative Execution (SE), which identifies and corrects the inefficient allocation of JobTracker. [8]. Previous research efforts have been conducted to optimize the SE strategy, Although the purpose of these strategies is to identify the remaining time of the task through slow tasks, such self-estimation is often inappropriate due to inaccuracy. [9].

In this paper, we pay attention to real-time task execution and collect the relevant information during a task's run time. A local weighted prediction method called LWR-SE is employed to estimate the running time required for the task. In parallel, the max cost-consumption model and the more appropriate selection strategy of back up task execution nodes are combined. In this way, both cloud platform providers and consumers can take advantage of it. And Sect. 2 lists current user-centric cloud environment research and Hadoop-based fault-tolerant optimization strategies. Section 3 presents the "LWR-SE" we designed, and the reliability of the method was verified by experimental methods in Sect. 4. In Sect. 5, we summarize this article's work and list some key work to be done in the future.

2 Related Work

2.1 Service in User-Centric Cloud

The combination of the consumer electronics industry and cloud computing has led to a growing number of researchers focusing on user-centric cloud services. A new architecture called IDM based on privacy and reputation extensions was put forward to enhance the security of consumers' identity [10]. A new architecture "SuSSo" is designed to deal with the limitation of service continuity when across different consumer electronic devices combined with the cloud computing [11]. Abolfazli et al. gave an overall analysis and compared the different solutions on the mobile cloud computing in the fields of consumer electronics [12]. Fu et al. proposed a new useful multi-keword ranked search strategy towards the encrypted cloud data, which supports synonym queries at the same time [13]. Grzonkowski et al. raised a more secure authentication method for home networks in user-centric cloud environment [14]. Due to the complexity and difference of big data, they propose a cloud computation offloading method, named COM, dynamic schedules of data/control-constrained computing tasks are confirmed [15]. A new and systematic smart home management system, which was deployed in the cloud and acted as the community broker, is presented to provide more electronic information service [16].

2.2 Fault Tolerance in Hadoop

On the other hand, the temporal fault-tolerance aims to automatically detect and restore fault run-time tasks so that it can shorten the execution time, and improve the computing performance and reliability of a cloud system, which involves strategies on MapReduce job and task scheduling, enhancement of speculation execution (SE) strategies, etc. [17].

The original speculative execution was implemented as Hadoop-Naïve in Hadoop [18]. Its primary idea was to recognize a task as a "Straggler" if its progress is below the average level, which can cause misjudged tasks and wasted cluster resources. It goes even worse in a heterogeneous environment. With regard to the average rate used in the LATE to calculate the remaining time of running tasks, which may lead to inaccurate or even incorrect prediction. In 2015, Wu's team improved the accuracy of the prediction by calculating the remaining time of system load situation calculation task [19].

MCP proposal can maximize the startup backup task, which solves the problem that the previous SE strategy is not old, by dividing Map tasks into map and combiner stages, and Reduce tasks into copy, sort and reduce phases [20]. In 2014, an SE optimization algorithm called Ex-MCP was proposed to compare node values with MCP [21]. On top of that, there are some optimization methods put forward. A execution was proposed based on sort nodes out according to the hardware performance of the nodes [22]. Wang et al. proposed a PSE optimization strategy that can ignore the differences between different processors to improve the efficiency of speculative execution [23]. In [24] An effective speculative execution strategy (SECDT) is proposed. The completion time required for the task is calculated by decision tree [25]. Besides, an ATAS strategy can improve the Hadoop's expansive ability by increasing the estimate accuracy on the execution time of backing-up tasks [26]. Adaptive allocation scheduling can also be used for NILM algorithms based on power allocation [27]. Due to the imbalance of cloud platform performance, Edge Computing Nodes (ECNS) has been proposed as an alternative solution for cloud computing in recent years. The team of Xu uses non-dominated sorting genetic algorithm II (NSGA-II) to achieve multiple Target optimization, shortening the unloading time of computing tasks and reducing the energy consumption [28].

In general, the current SE strategy still has great difficulties in quickly backing up and accurately identifying1 potential Straggler tasks in appropriate nodes, and how to balance the overall benefits while maintaining the processing of local universities is also very large challenge.

3 Model and Algorithm

In this section, we introduce a speculative execution method named "LWR-SE". The flow chart of the method is indicated in Fig. 1, with more details discussed in the rest parts of this section.

3.1 The Recognition of Straggler Candidates

Data Collection of Running Tasks. First, confirm Stragglers by collecting detailed information such as the progress and execution time of real-time tasks. To collect features, the raw data is collected from the HDFS (progress, Timestamp) to facilitate prediction. Then convert the progress pair to (progress, execution time) in order to simplify the algorithm. The algorithm for data collection is shown as follows (Table 1).

Table 1. Algorithm for data collection

Algorithm 1: Data Collection
Input: Job Status (*JS*), MapTask Report (*MR*), The running task attempt (*RT*), The id of task attempt (*IT*), A context object for task (*TC*), The progress of a running task (*P*), Execution time (*ET*)
Steps:
Get the *JS* from JobClient
Traverse the JS:
Get the *MR*s from JobId
For each *MR* in the *MR*s
Get the *RT*s from *MR*
Get the collection containing the *IT*
Get *P* from *TC*
If *P* has changed
Write the *P* and *ET* to the file named with *IT*
End If
EndFor
End Data Collection

Figure 1 and Fig. 2 show examples of detailed execution information when running the Wordcount and Sort datasets in the Hadoop cluster. The collected data is shown in the figures.

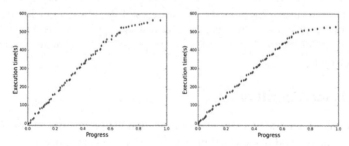

Fig. 1. The execution data collected by running Wordcount

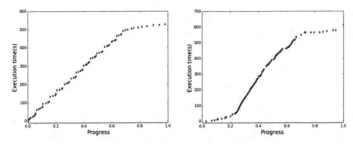

Fig. 2. The execution data collected by running Sort

A Locally Weighted Learning Model. After the running task execution information is collected and Sort datasets, similar tendency can be seen in the figures above. In order to define such non-traditional linear relationship in between, a non-parametric learning algorithm using local weighted regression is designed to establish a linear model on the non-linear datasets. The input dataset $D = \{(p_i, t_i) | i = 1, 2, \ldots, n\}$, and the predicted output as below:

$$\hat{t} = h_\theta(p) = \sum_{i=0}^{n} \theta_i p_i = \theta^T p \tag{1}$$

The number of training set samples is set to n, representing the progress of different tasks. p represents the progress which is an input $n + 1$ dimension. t indicates the execution time of the task. θ is the regression parameter and it should satisfy that the square error Minimize between predicted and true values, which is proposed in Eqs. (2) and (3).

$$E = h_\theta\left(p^i\right) - t^i \tag{2}$$

$$\min_\theta = \sum_{i=0}^{m} \omega_i E^2 = \sum_{i=0}^{m} \omega_i \left[h_\theta\left(p^i\right) - t^i\right]^2 \tag{3}$$

Where E represents the error, (p_i, t_i) is the *ith* training samples, ω_i is the weight in the *ith* local forecasting area, which depends on the local prediction point. To simplify the description, we can transform it into a matrix representation as shown in Eq. (4).

$$\min_\theta = (X\theta - Y)^T W (X\theta - Y) \tag{4}$$

Where X is a matrix, with m rows training dataset $p_0, p_1 \ldots, p_m$ and n being set to 2. W is a matrix as the Eq. (5) shows.

$$W = \begin{pmatrix} \omega_1 & \cdots\cdots & 0 \\ \vdots & \omega_2 & \cdots & \vdots \\ \vdots & \vdots & \ddots & \vdots \\ 0 & \cdots\cdots & \omega_n \end{pmatrix} \tag{5}$$

In addition, θ is also ensure that LWR has the minimum loss function at the predicted q, and the loss function of the LWR algorithm is shown as follows:

$$J(\theta) = \frac{\sum_{i=1}^{n} \omega_i \left[h_\theta(p^i) - t^i \right]^2}{2} = \frac{(X\theta - Y)^T W (X\theta - Y)}{2} \tag{6}$$

Then the regression parameter θ can be calculated using the least square method with a prediction point corresponding to a parameter θ. The final calculated θ is substituted into the Eq. (1) and then the execution time of the corresponding progress is predicted, as shown in Eq. (7) and (8).

$$\frac{\partial J(\theta)}{\partial \theta} = X^T W X \theta - X^T W Y = 0 \tag{7}$$

$$\theta = \left(X^T W X \right)^{-1} X^T W Y \tag{8}$$

The target of LWR is to find θ that minimizes for present prediction, during which the most important process is to compute the weight function, which can be obtained in two steps:

Step 1: Distance Calculation. The local region is firstly determined using Euler distance when predicting the value of the local point, as described in Eq. (9).

$$d = \sqrt{\sum_{i=1}^{n} \left(p^{(q)} - p^{(i)} \right)^2} \tag{9}$$

Step 2: Weight Calculation. The calculation of the weight function depends on the distance d. The greater the distance from the predicted point, the smaller the weight will be assigned. Use the Gaussian kernel function in (10), γ can controls the rate at which the weight decreases with distance. Set to 0.08 in this paper.

$$\omega(d) = \exp\left(-\frac{d^2}{2\gamma^2} \right) = \exp\left(-\frac{\sum_{i=1}^{n} \left(p^{(q)} - p^{(i)} \right)^2}{2\gamma^2} \right) \tag{10}$$

According to the consumption and benefits of launching or non-launching a backup task in the cluster, we can compute the profits of launching or non- launching the backup task to the cluster, the profits of launching speculative execution or not can be obtained as the following Equations.

$$profit_{backup} = \alpha \times \left(t_{rem} - t_{backup} \right) - 2 \times \beta \times t_{backup} \tag{11}$$

$$profit_{not\_backup} = -\beta \times t_{backup} \tag{12}$$

α and β represent the weight of benefit and the cluster cost. When satisfying the following formula, the identified Straggler backup task will be launched so that it can reach the maximum efficiency.

$$profit_{backup} > profit_{not\_backup} \Leftrightarrow \frac{t_{rem}}{t_{backup}} > \frac{\alpha + 2\beta}{\alpha + \beta} \tag{13}$$

Here we let ζ replace β/α, then the above Equation can be simplified as follows.

$$profit_{backup} > profit_{not\_backup} \Leftrightarrow \frac{t_{rem}}{t_{backup}} > \frac{1 + 2\zeta}{1 + \zeta} \tag{14}$$

$$\zeta = load\_factor = \frac{num_{pending\_tasks}}{mum_{free\_slots}} \tag{15}$$

Where t_{backup} is the running time of a backup task, ς is the load factor of the cluster, which is the ratio of the number of pending tasks to the number of the free containers in the cluster.

4   Results and Evaluation

In this section, we first test the performance of our model based on linear predictions and actual values. After that, the LWR-SE strategy is evaluated compared to Hadoop-None, LATE, and MCP in a heterogeneous cloud environment in three different scenarios.

4.1   Experimental Environment Preparation

We use 64-bit Ubuntu Server to be our operating system and our experimental platform is Hadoop-2.6.0. There are eight virtual nodes in the Hadoop cluster and each server is consist of four Intel® Xeon® CPU, 288 GB memory in total and up to 10 TB hard drive. In Table 3, it shows some detail information about each node. In the framework of Hadoop, it is common to use the datasets such as Wordcount and Sort as the experimental workloads. They are available on the Purdue MapReduce Benchmarks Suite (Table 2).

Table 2. The detailed information of each node

NodeID	Memory (GB)	Core processors
Node 1	10	8
Node 2	8	4
Node 3	8	1
Node 4	8	8
Node 5	4	8
Node 6	4	4
Node 7	18	4
Node 8	12	8

4.2 Performance Evaluation of the LWR Model

Data Prediction of LWR. The prediction results using the LWR model in the Word-count and the Sort datasets are depicted in Fig. 3 and Fig. 4 respectively, where the red line represents prediction error rates. It can be depicted that the predictive accuracy of the LWR model much outperforms the linear regression, especially while the progress reaches 80% and over. RMSE is used to evaluate the accuracy of the prediction, and the calculation Equation is as follows.

$$RMSE = \sqrt{\frac{\sum\limits_{i=1}^{n} (p - p_i)^2}{n}} \tag{18}$$

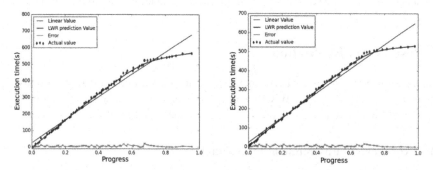

Fig. 3. Comparison of LWR and Linear Regression during running a Wordcount task

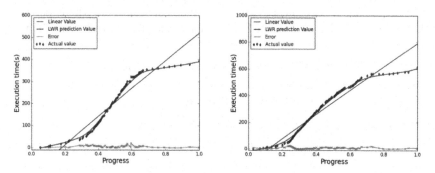

Fig. 4. Comparison of LWR and Linear Regression during running a Sort task

Where p is actual value and p_i represents the prediction value. Table 3 and Table 4 show the RMSE results of fifteen datasets/tasks, which are randomly selected from the Wordcount and Sort tasks. The average prediction RMSE of Wordcount and Sort are 1.56 and 1.75. This happens due to some unusual large values, which are mainly caused by resource contention and the non-data locality in the copy phrase during the Reduce process. If the outliers are ignored, we can find that average prediction RMSE of Wordcount and Sort drops to 0.91 and 0.86.

Table 3. RMSE of LWR for wordcount workloads

	Task 1	Task 2	Task 3	Task 4	Task 5
RMSE(s)	0.89	1.01	0.94	0.48	0.67
	Task 6	Task 7	Task 8	Task 9	Task 10
RMSE(s)	0.77	0.85	0.61	0.84	1.15
	Task 11	Task 12	Task 13	Task 14	Task 15
RMSE(s)	10.55	1.09	1.74	1.1	0.65

Table 4. RMSE of LWR for sort workloads

	Task 1	Task 2	Task 3	Task 4	Task 5
RMSE(s)	0.98	0.97	1.31	1.03	1.13
	Task 6	Task 7	Task 8	Task 9	Task 10
RMSE(s)	0.16	0.63	0.91	14.2	0.05
	Task 11	Task 12	Task 13	Task 14	Task 15
RMSE(s)	0.7	0.96	0.85	1.14	1.34

4.3 Evaluate the Performance of the LWR-SE Strategy in Heterogeneous Situations

Three different kinds of cluster workload scenarios are configured to evaluate the performance of the LWR-SE, they are Normal Load Scenario, Busy Load Scenario, and Busy Load with Data Skew Scenario. In addition, the final results are shown as the best, worse and average outcomes of each strategy.

Performance of the LWR-SE Strategy in a Busy Load Scenario. Abusy load scenario provides the cluster with limited resources to supply additional replication. It therefore is more necessary to ensure the accuracy of speculative execution, since low accuracy can cause the cluster resources to be irrationally occupied and consequently slow down the performance of the whole cluster. The busy load scenario was configured by running other computing-intensive and/or IO-intensive tasks simultaneously. Wordcount and Sort jobs were set up to submit every 150 s (Fig. 5).

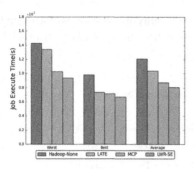
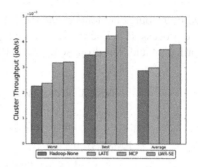

Fig. 5. Performance of strategies in Wordcount jobs in the busy load scenario

As can be seen in Fig. 6, the LWR-SE also fits well when running Sort jobs in the busy load scenario. in terms of the JET, on average cases, LWR-SE completed 9.7% earlier than MCP, 24.9% earlier than LATE and 30.6% earlier than Hadoop-None. When considering CT, the cluster throughput of LWR-SE increased by 9.3% compared with MCP and 36.1% over LATE.

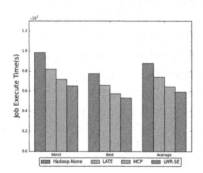
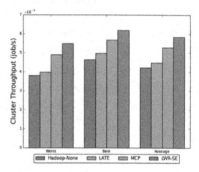

Fig. 6. Performance of strategies in the sorting job in the busy load scenario

5   Conclusion

In this paper, we propose a strategy named LWR-SE based on the relationship between tasks and job execution schedule, which can obtain higher local prediction accuracy and can guarantee the cloud system. Maximize benefits. The experimental results show that it is superior to MCP, LATE and Hadoop-None.

Acknowledgement. This work has received funding from 5150 Spring Specialists (05492018012, 05762018039), Major Program of the National Social Science Fund of China (Grant No. 17ZDA092), 333 High-Level Talent Cultivation Project of Jiangsu Province (BRA2018332), Royal Society of Edinburgh, UK and China Natural Science Foundation Council (RSE Reference: 62967_Liu_2018_2) under their Joint International Projects funding scheme and basic Research Programs (Natural Science Foundation) of Jiangsu Province (BK20191398).

References

1. Vaquero, L.F., Rodero, L., Caceres, J.: A break in the clouds: towards a cloud definition. Acm Sigcomm Comput. Commun. Rev. **39**(1), 50–55 (2008)
2. Iqbal, M.H., Soomro, T.R.: Big data analysis: apache storm perspective. Int. J. Comput. Trends Technol. **19**(1), 9–14 (2015)
3. Zaharia, M., Chowdhury, M., Franklin, M.J.: Spark: cluster computing with working sets. In: Proceedings USENIX Conference on Hot Topics in Cloud Computing, pp. 1765–1773. Springer, Heidelberg (2010)
4. Li, Z., Shen, H., Ligon, W.: An exploration of designing a hybrid scale-up/out hadoop architecture based on performance measurements. IEEE Trans. Parallel Distrib. Syst **28**(2), 386–400 (2017)
5. Gunarathne, T., Wu, T.L., Qiu, J.: MapReduce in the clouds for science. In: Proceedings Second International Conference on Cloud computing, pp. 565–572 (2010)
6. Dean, J., Ghemawa, S.: MapReduce: simplified data processing on large clusters. In: Proceedings OSDI, pp. 107–113 (2004)
7. Liu, Q., Cai, W., Jin, D.: Estimation accuracy on execution time of run-time tasks in a heterogeneous distributed environment. Sensors **16**(9), 1386 (2016)
8. Xu, H., Lau, W.C.: Optimization for speculative execution in big data processing clusters. IEEE Trans. Parallel Distrib. Syst. **28**(2), 530–545 (2017)
9. Xu, H., Lau, W.C.: Optimization for speculative execution in a mapreduce-like cluster. In: Proceedings IEEE Conference on Computer Communications (INFOCOM), pp. 1071–1079 (2015)
10. Sanchez, R., Almenares, F., Arias, P.: Enhancing privacy and dynamic federation in IdM for consumer cloud computing. IEEE Trans. Consum. Electron. **58**(1), 95–103 (2012)
11. Cabarcos, P.A., Mendoza, F.A., Guerrero, R.S.: SuSSo: seamless and ubiquitous single sign-on for cloud service continuity across devices. IEEE Trans. Consum. Electron. **58**(4), 1425–1433 (2012)
12. Abolfazli, S., Sanaei, Z., Alizadeh, M.: An experimental analysis on cloud-based mobile augmentation in mobile cloud computing. IEEE Trans. Consum. Electron. **58**(1), 146–154 (2014)
13. Fu, Z., Sun, X., Linge, N.: Achieving effective cloud search services: multi-keyword ranked search over encrypted cloud data supporting synonym query. IEEE Trans. Consum. Electron. **60**(1), 164–172 (2014)
14. Eom, B., Lee, C., Lee, H.: An adaptive remote display scheme to deliver mobile cloud services. IEEE Trans. Consum. Electron. **60**(3), 540–547 (2014)
15. Xu, X., Xue, Y., Yuan, Y.: An edge computing-enabled computation offloading method with privacy preservation for internet of connected vehicles. Fut. Gener. Comput. Syst. **96**(1), 89–100 (2019)
16. Lee, Y.: An integrated cloud-based smart home management system with community hierarchy. IEEE Trans. Consum. Electron. **62**(1), 1–9 (2016)
17. Liu, Q., Cai, W., Shen, J.: A speculative approach to spatial-temporal efficiency with multi-objective optimization in a heterogeneous cloud environment. Secur. Commun. Netw. **7**(17), 4002–4012 (2016)
18. Liu, Q., Cai, W., Shen, J.: An adaptive approach to better load balancing in a consumer-centric cloud environment. IEEE Trans. Consum. Electron. **62**(3), 243–250 (2016)
19. Huang, X., Zhang, L., Li, R.: Novel heuristic speculative execution strategies in heterogeneous distributed environments. Comput. Electric. Eng. **50**, 166–179 (2015)
20. Chen, Q., Liu, C., Xiao, Z.: Improving MapReduce performance using smart speculative execution strategy. IEEE Trans. Comput. **63**(4), 954–967 (2014)

21. Wu, H., Li, K., Tang, Z.: A Heuristic speculative execution strategy in heterogeneous distributed environments. In: Proceedings Sixth International symposium on Parallel Architectures, Algorithms and Programming (PAAP), pp. 268–273 (2014)
22. Liu, Q., Cai, W., Shen, J.: A smart strategy for speculative execution based on hardware resource in a heterogeneous distributed environment. Int. J. Grid Distrib. Comput. **9**(1), 203–214 (2015)
23. Wang, Y., Lu, W., Lou, R.: Improving MapReduce performance with partial speculative execution. J. Grid Comput. **13**(1), 587–604 (2015)
24. Li, Y., Yang, Q., Lai, S.: A new speculative execution algorithm based on C4.5 decision tree for hadoop. In: Proceedings the International Conference of Young Computer Scientists, Engineers and Educators (ICYCSEE 2015), pp. 284–291 (2015)
25. Tang, S., Lee, B., He, B.: DynamicMR: a dynamic slot allocation optimization framework for MapReduce clusters. IEEE Trans. Cloud Comput. **2**(3), 333–347 (2014)
26. Yang, S., Chen, Y.: Design adaptive task allocation scheduler to improve MapReduce performance in heterogeneous clouds. J. Netw. Comput. Appl. **57**(1), 61–70 (2015)
27. Liu, Q., Chen, F., Chen, F.: Home appliances classification based on multi-feature using ELM. Int. J. Sensor Netw. **28**(1), 34–42 (2018)
28. Xu, X., Li, Y., Huang, T.: An energy-aware computation offloading method for smart edge computing in wireless metropolitan area networks. J. Netw. Comput. Appl. **133**(1), 75–85 (2019)

Rendering of Three-Dimensional Cloud Based on Cloud Computing

Yonghua Xie, Xiaoyong Kou, Ping Li, and Xiaolong Xu$^{(\boxtimes)}$

School of Computer and Software, Nanjing University of Information Science
and Technology, Nanjing, China
xyh_76@nuist.edu.cn, koux_y@qq.com, 724904461@qq.com, xlxu@ieee.org

Abstract. Cloud modeling and real-time render are of great significance
in virtual scene simulation. The lighting model and rendering technology
are image synthesis methods, introduced to computer graphics, aiming
to simplify virtual scene simulation and enhance the fidelity of complex scenes. Currently, the simulation algorithms applied to cloud scene,
inclined to be complicated and computationally intensive. Hence, it is
still a key challenge to implement more efficient algorithms to map higher
quality three-dimensional clouds. In this paper, a computation-reducing
and time-saving method is designed to deal with the above challenge.
Technically, the lighting model and rendering technology for the weather
research and forecasting (WRF) data are proposed to create the cloud
scenes. Then project files are uploaded to the cloud system and directly
for real-time rendering at the same time, which can largely save time
and reduce the cost of rendering. Finally, adequate experimental analyses are conducted to verify the effectiveness and efficiency of the proposed
scheme.

Keywords: Cloud system · Simulation · Three-dimensional · Lighting
model · Rendering

1 Introduction

As one of the most common natural phenomena in nature, clouds have been
simulated in the field of graphics simulation for a long time [1]. There is still
a lot of research on focusing on 3d cloud rendering in that researchers manage
to draw three-dimensional clouds of higher quality through more efficient algorithms [2]. The simulation of three-dimensional clouds has developed rapidly in
recent years, and researchers proposed a series of cloud simulation and rendering
schemes, according to different simulation requirements [3]. Three-dimensional
cloud simulation has a wide range of applications, the weather changes in the
weather simulation research, especially in the case of extreme weather, the three-
dimensional cloud simulation study of meteorology has a very important role;
In the field of military simulation imitation air battle scenario, but have to

© ICST Institute for Computer Sciences, Social Informatics and Telecommunications Engineering 2020
Published by Springer Nature Switzerland AG 2020. All Rights Reserved
X. Zhang et al. (Eds.): CloudComp 2019/SmartGift 2019, LNICST 322, pp. 123–137, 2020.
https://doi.org/10.1007/978-3-030-48513-9_10

consider the cloud simulation; In the field of the game, the simulation of the three-dimensional cloud also plays an important role. It is the cloud that plays such an important role in the field of simulation that makes the research of three-dimensional cloud simulation become a hotspot in graphics [4]. So far, three-dimensional cloud simulation can be divided into two categories [5]. The first is to study the physical factors of natural clouds, in the process of simulation, all physical factors of the natural cloud are calculated as far as possible, including gravity, light, wind, temperature, altitude and other factors. The cloud simulated by this kind of method is relatively close to the real cloud, but each frame requires huge computation, which makes real-time rendering difficult [6,7]. The second approach starts with the appearance of the natural cloud, and only considers whether the cloud looks like the real cloud in the simulation process. This approach is much more efficient than the physical approach, and could even render in real-time on some personal computers [8]. However, there are few researchers using meteorological data to give the simulated clouds real physical information. The effective processing and three-dimensional graphic display of meteorological data could enable weather forecasters to have a more intuitive and in-depth understanding of atmospheric evolution information, so as to make an effective weather forecast. With the development of computer image and graphics technology, scientific computing visualization technology could transform a huge amount of data into static or dynamic images or graphics, providing a powerful means for people to analyze and understand data. With these observations, it continues a challenge to propose a suitable model to endue virtual cloud with real physical significance [9,10]. In view of this challenge, a computation-reducing and time-saving method is proposed. Our main presentations are enumerated as follows:

- Analysis of the meteorological principles of cloud formation and a spherical particle model is built, which constructs the virtual clouds.
- The reflection and projection characteristics of cloud particles are analyzed. Simplify the lighting model and rendering method to improve real-time interaction.
- Cloud computing mode is adopted to complete the rendering task of three-dimensional cloud.
- The validity and effectiveness of the proposed method are verified by sufficient experimental evaluation and comparative analysis.

The rest of this paper is organized as follows. Section 2 gives basic concepts and definitions. Section 3 explains the method we use. Section 4 shows the performance of our method by experiments. Section 5 lists the relevant work. Section 6 summarizes the conclusions.

2   Modeling and Simplification

2.1   Characteristics of Cloud

Clouds are composed of granular ice in the atmosphere and a large number of water droplets. They play an important role in the operation of the water cycle and are an important link in the three-state change of water (gas, liquid and solid). Under the action of sunlight, wind and so on, water in nature, as well as water in animals and plants, will continuously evaporate and be converted into gaseous water vapor and dispersed into the atmosphere.In the atmosphere, temperature decreases with increasing altitude, and gaseous vapor may condense or liquefy as a result of the change in temperature, and then turn into ice particles or water droplets.Impurities in the air play a crucial roe in the formation of ice particles or water droplets. If the impurities are not present, solid or liquid water cannot be condensed together. Even if some ice particles or water droplets are condensed together, they will quickly evaporate into a gas state due to the absence of impurities.The distribution range of these impurities is very wide. When the impurities encounter ice particles or water droplets, they can quickly condense into larger ice particles or water droplets. Under the influence of air flow, wind speed and other factors, these larger water droplets condense with each other again, and the final condensate is the cloud we see in our daily life.The shapes of clouds are caused by the constant movement of ice particles or water droplets in the clouds under the influence of various meteorological factors.At the same time, clouds show a variety of colors because the sunlight is refracted, reflected, and scattered physically as it passes through clouds.

2.2   Meteorological Representation

In this section, The related elements of clouds are represented by means of meteorological study.The movement and formation of clouds are caused by a variety of meteorological elements. In order to show them objectively, the following is a brief introduction of the physics of the relevant elements.In meteorology, the saturation degree of vapor is generally expressed by relative humidity f, as shown in formula (1) :

$$f = \frac{e}{E} \tag{1}$$

where e is the actual vapor pressure and E is the vapor pressure.With the constant change of temperature, the value of saturated vapor pressure will also change with it. The Clausius-Clapeyron Differential Equation mainly represents the relation function between saturated vapor and humidity, which is expressed as. The relative humidity can be calculated by sending a differential equation through calculation (2):

$$\frac{dE}{E} = \frac{L}{AR} \cdot \frac{dT}{T^2} \tag{2}$$

where A represents the heating equivalent, L represents the latent heat of phase change, T is the transformation temperation, and R represents the gas constant of vapor.After differential solution, it can be obtained, as shown in formula (3):

$$\frac{df}{f} = \frac{de}{e} - \frac{dE}{E} = \frac{de}{e} - \frac{1}{E}\left(\frac{dE}{dT}\right)dT = \frac{de}{e} - \frac{L}{EAR} \cdot \frac{dT}{T^2} \tag{3}$$

According to the above equation, the relative humidity will increase with the increase of water vapor. As the temperature decreases, the relative humidity will also decrease, thus reaching saturation.Generally speaking, the decrease of temperature is the main reason for the formation of clouds. The reason is that vapor will keep rising, while the temperature will gradually decrease with the increase of height when the state of humidity changes. When vapor rises to a certain degree, the physical state of vapor will change, leading to the formation of clouds.The condensation of vapor produces different types of clouds at different heights because the height and size of the air mass will cause different physical changes at different times.

2.3   Simplification

On the basis of the above analysis, clouds are thought to be made up of countless tiny particles with different components of their properties (position, color, speed, temperature, etc.). How to model objects with particle is shown in Fig. 1. The region of cloud generation is defined as the xoz plane parallel to the world coordinate system, a circle with center of (x_0, y_0, z_0) and radius of r. After determining the generation region of particles, it is necessary to determine the number of particles that should be produced in each frame. It directly affects the density of the simulated object, and thus affects the fidelity of simulation and the real-time performance of the system. It is one of the most important parameters of the particle system. If the number of particles is too small, it cannot meet the requirement of reality; if the number of particles is too large, it will increase the processing time of the system and reduce the real-time performance of the particle system. So the definition of the number of particles became a key issue in the whole simulation. In traditional particle systems, the generation of particles is controlled by random functions. There are two methods of measuring the average number of new particles and measuring the area of objects. The two methods ignore the important influence of the number of particles on the simulation, which sometimes leads to the waste of the number of particles.

The number of particles required in the system is related to the scale of smoke production and the distance from the viewpoint. When the cloud scale is certain and the viewpoint is far away, due to the low resolution of human eyes, fewer particles can be used to generate clouds that meet the visual requirements. On the contrary, when the viewpoint is closer, more particles are needed to produce detailed details.Based on this, a function $f(r, d)$, which is determined by the scale of the cloud to be plotted and the distance of the cloud from the viewpoint, is proposed to determine the number of generated particles. Where r is the radius of the region where particles are generated, d is the distance between the cloud and the viewpoint, and $n = f(r, d)$ is used to describe clouds of different sizes that meet the visual effect. In this way, the number of particles can be reduced appropriately, the time of computer processing can be reduced, and the rendering efficiency of the system can be improved. When the direct proportionality function is used to describe the relationship between the number of particles and the distance of viewpoint, if the proportionality coefficient is

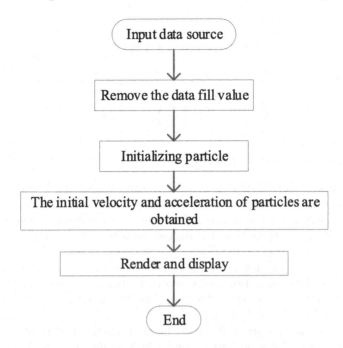

Fig. 1. Particle modeling flow chart

relatively large, the rate of change will change rapidly linearly with the increase of the distance of viewpoint, which makes the number of particles jump too strongly. If the proportionality coefficient is small, the viewpoint distance is far away, but still maintain a more complex state, not to achieve the effect required to simplify the number of particles.

Therefore, as the distance increases, the blurring degree of the object should not change linearly. The number of particles produced by the model increases gradually when the viewpoint is close and the rate of change is large, while the number of particles produced by the model decreases gradually when the viewpoint is far away and the rate of change is small.In order to satisfy the actual situation mentioned above and ensure the sense of reality, take the following non-linear relationship:

$$\alpha = 1 - e^{p/a} \tag{4}$$

where α is the rate of change, $p = -d/d_0$, a is an empirical constant, 280 is appropriate.

Let n_0 be the number of generated particles when the distance of viewpoint is $d_0 = 1$ and $r_0 = 1$, n is the number of particles when the distance of viewpoint is d and radius of cloud is r. At the same time, The rate of change can also be defined as:

$$\alpha = \frac{n_0 - n}{n_0} \times 100\% \tag{5}$$

from Eqs. (1) and (2), it is known that:

$$n = f(r, d) = \left(\frac{r}{r_0}\right)^3 \times n_0 \times e^{p/a} \tag{6}$$

2.4   Illumination and Rendering

The basic task of illumination is to achieve three-dimensional scene rendering and generate realistic images, which is the inevitable development direction of real-time rendering. In rendering, it is necessary to simulate various physical phenomena of light propagation in the scene, such as multiple reflections, refraction, shadow, coloration and causation. It requires an accurate description of geometric features and material properties of various model objects created in the scene, as well as calculation and solution of infinite calculus problems caused by multiple refraction and that reflection. Due to the complexity of calculated lightmass, rendering a realistic image usually takes a long time. Illumination rendering algorithm has always been the focus and hotspot of graphics research. Various researchers focus on how to render high-quality realistic images in less time and achieve real-time rendering requirements.

The light reflection properties of an object surface are usually described by the (bidirectional reflectance distribution function (BRDF). BRDF describes the amount and variation of light reflected, absorbed, and transmitted (refracted) based on the surface properties. Although these reflection distributions are random, they follow certain rules. The reflected energy is concentrated in one direction, and the reflected angle is equal to the incident angle. Diffuse reflection (lambert body) object surface is rough enough, its radiation brightness is constant in 2π space at the center of the object, that is, the radiation brightness does not change with the point of view, also known as isotropic BRDF. The reflection intensity of the non-lamber body is uneven in all directions, also known as anisotropy BRDF.

The rendering equation describes the entire physical process in which light energy is emitted from the light source, reflected and refracted by various material surfaces in the scene, and finally enters the observer's eyes. In fact, the process of solving the rendering equation is the rendering process of the scene.

The classical rendering equation is defined as a point on a plane that radiates in all directions in a hemispheric range. Divide all object surfaces in the scene into small regional surfaces, and convert the rendering equation from the integration of hemispheric direction to the integration of all object surfaces in the scene (Fig. 1). In that sense, the rendering equation is obtained as follows:

$$L(x, x') = L_e(x, x') + \int \Omega/2L(x', x'')f(x, x', x'')G(x, x', x'')dx \tag{7}$$

$$G(x, x', x'') = V(x, x')V(x', x'') \cos \theta \qquad (8)$$

where x, x', x'' represents the position of the scene; $f(x, x', x'')$ is known as BRDF; $G(x, x', x'')$ is the geometry element, dealing with phenomena of attenuation and occlusion ; $V(x, x')$ is visibility function; If x and x' are visible to each other, then $V(x, x')$ equals 1; otherwise, it is 0 due to occlusion. The integral of all the emitting surfaces that can be directly transmitted to the x'. The scenario discussed in this article does not consider the spontaneous light of an object, so ignore the $L_e (x, x')$ term for the time being.

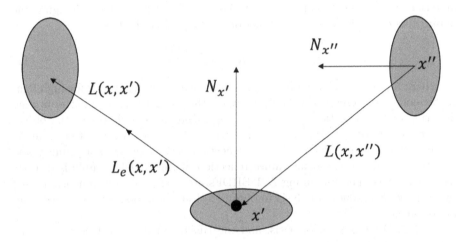

Fig. 2. The integration of all object surfaces in the scene.

Equation (7) shows that light passes through a reflection. If the incident radiation brightness is further distinguished according to different reflection times, then the radiation brightness of the point x' to x, including all radiation brightness that reaches x' through reflection and reaches x through reflection, could be represented as

$$L(x, x') = \sum_{n=1}^{\infty} L_n(x, x') \qquad (9)$$

Let us suppose that the scene is divided into multiple small R_i, rest of another patch material within the same everywhere, with the same reflection properties, the incident radiation intensity according to the different reflection paths to further distinguish, for $n + 1$ times of reflection, different reflection paths to point x' radiation brightness after x' reflection to x radiation brightness could be recursively description for:

$$L_{n+1} = \sum_{P_n} \sum_{R=1}^{N} L'_n(x, x', P_n(R, f_R)) \qquad (10)$$

where, $P_n(R, f_R)$ represents the propagation path of light, that is, the light emitted from the source passes through all the surfaces that x passes through after n times of reflection. L'_n describes the luminance of x' towards position x followed n reflections of the path described by P_n.

The traditional Blinn-Phong illumination model describes the illumination effect of the scene from the different reflection characteristics of the object surface to diffuse, specular and ambient light, as well as the attenuation of the light along the propagation path. The algorithm in this paper assumes that the path of light is transformed only when it touches the surface the of object, regardless of refraction and ambient light, and uses Blinn-Phong's BRDF to represent the material of the object. Different materials will be described by changing the parameters of the function. The function could be described as

$$f_{BP} = \frac{K_d}{\pi} + K_s \cdot \frac{n_s + 2}{2\pi} cos^{n_s} \gamma \tag{11}$$

where K_d stands for the diffuse reflection coefficient; K_s stands for high light coefficient; γ represents the angle between the incident, exit and the normal direction of the reflection position; N_s represents the roughness of the object surface. N_s uniformly sampled n_s times within the selected range to obtain N_s linearly independent BRDFs. Diffuse reflection usually presents a primary and sensitive visual effect, so the diffuse reflection of the BRDF sample is directly used as a basis. The remaining $N_s 1$ BRDFs are extracted and dimensionalized by principal component analysis to obtain $N_b 1$ eigenvectors, a total of N_b bases are obtained.

The BRDF has a set of basis, and the BRDF function on face R could be expressed with them

$$f_R(x, x', x'') = \sum_{i=1}^{N_b} c_i f_i(x, x', x'') \tag{12}$$

where f_i represents the ith basis of BRDF on surface R; c_i is the coefficient corresponding to the i basis; N_b is the number of bases. Substitute Eq. (11) into Eq. (9), and recurse to n to get

$$L_n(x, x') = \sum_{\{R_i\}=1}^{N} \sum_{\{f_i\}=1}^{N_b} (L'(x, x', p(R, f_i))) \prod_{i=1}^{n} c_i \tag{13}$$

The above is the result of n reflections, just two reflections, where n equals 2, and take the point of view x_e at x.

After obtaining BRDF bases, all faces in the scene are select BRDF from these bases, and calculate the corresponding illumination effect of various distribution combinations of these bases by using ray projection, so that $L'(x_e, x', P_1(R, f'))$ and $L'(x_e, x', P_2(R, f')$ in Eq. (12) could be obtained. Assuming that there are n facets in the scene, all n facets are introduced into Eq. (12) to get

$$L_n(x, x') = \sum_{f' \in B(R')} c'_i \sum_{\{R_i\}=1}^{N} \sum_{\{f_i\} \in B(R')} (L'(x, x', P_n, f')) \prod_{i=1}^{n} c_i) \qquad (14)$$

where R' represents the face where x' is; f' is the corresponding BRDF. Take two reflections into account and take x as the viewpoint x_e, then the first reflection is

$$L_1(x, x') = \sum_{f' \in B(R')} c'_i L'(x_e, x', P_1, f') \qquad (15)$$

The second reflection is

$$L_2(x, x') = \sum_{f' \in B(R')} c'_i \sum_{\{R_i\}=1}^{N} \sum_{\{f_i\} \in B(R')} (L'(x_e, x', P_2, f')c_i) \qquad (16)$$

2.5   Algorithm Structure

(1) The light source is represented by illumination function $I(x, y, z, \theta, \varphi, \lambda)$ with 6 properties, where (x, y, z) represents the position coordinate of the light source; (θ, φ) said the direction of the light in the three-dimensional space; λ is the energy intensity of the light source. (2) The direct illumination and radiation luminance I_d of each plane is an attribute of the plane, which can be directly accessed when calculating the first reflection or the second reflection.(3) The algorithm in this paper only calculates two reflections to satisfy the user's requirements. The first reflection mainly provides direct illumination, which is provided by all the direct visible light sources in the scene. The second reflection provides indirect light, which is contributed by the light provided by other surfaces through the second reflection, and the light energy is preserved in the surface property I_i.

3   Experiment and Evaluation

This paper puts a large number of scenario component location calculations into the cloud computing platform and transfers them to the cloud server using dynamic component processing. After the implementation of cloud computing services, different task forms are assigned according to the quantity and demand detection in the overall environment. Service cost must be calculated for some large service forms. Segmentation of service modes can effectively promote the efficiency of pattern execution and strategy formulation. The frame data to represent the contrast result, contrast experiment result is shown in Fig. 3.

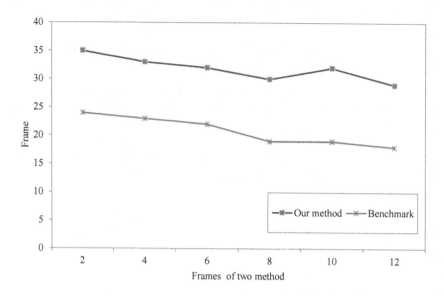

Fig. 3. Frames of two methods.

From Fig. 3, when the game thread is serialized with the rendering thread, the Frame floats around 30, while when the game thread is parallel with the rendering thread, the Frame floats around 20, which reduces the time spent on a Frame by about 40. Figure 4 shows the rendering results of our method and Fig. 5 shows Benchmark's, obviously, the former has more details.

Fig. 4. An example of cumulus cloud.

When the cloud cluster is 20 and the number of particles is within the range of [5,000, 8000], the frame number of Benchmark rendering is between 27 and 50. The frame number of dynamic cloud rendering with time variable is between 43 and 65. The rendering effect is shown in Fig. 2. The test results show that this algorithm greatly improves the rendering efficiency and Fig. 7 is the result (Fig 6).

Fig. 5. An example of cloud.

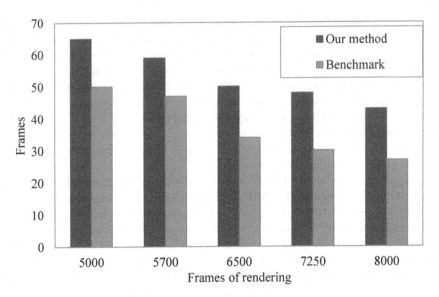

Fig. 6. Frames of rendering.

Fig. 7. An example of stratus cloud.

4   Related Work

In recent years, researchers at home and abroad have proposed a series of cloud simulation and rendering methods to achieve better simulated performance, according to different simulation requirements. In terms of ways of modeling, it can be divided into individual growth-based model and physics-based model [11].

The modeling method based on individual growth can obtain the visual shape of cloud by using the visual morphological features, without simulating the real physical process of cloud formation. Meanwhile, the density distribution of cloud is generated by fractal theory and the effect of cloud is simulated by texture generation [12]. This method has a small amount of cloud computing and is easy to implement. When the viewpoint is far away from the cloud, it has a good effect. However, when the viewpoint is very close to the cloud, and even requires the effect of penetrating the cloud, this method cannot meet such requirements [13]. Currently, the commonly used methods include body process method, fractal method and particle system method.

The volume process method adopts noise (such as Perlin noise) function to simulate the complexity of the cloud, and applies the same rendering technology to every element in the scene [14], which requires a large amount of computation and is difficult to generate real-time animation. Fractal method adopts iterative or recursive method combined with deformation ball to calculate individual growth, which is suitable for generating static fine graphics [15]. Relative to the front two methods, the method of particle system direct simulation of particles in the clouds, and give the particle size, position and color attributes, such as through texture mapping, mapping eight side ring, the formation of different types of cloud, and realized the real-time simulation of large-scale three-dimensional cloud, but the method from the angle of the nonphysical to describe, not well reflect the cloud physics authenticity. Direct concept, easy to control the shape of clouds, suitable for real-time flight visual simulation. However, the physics-based modeling method is to build the cloud model by simulating the meteorological generation process of cloud, which requires too much computation and cannot meet the current needs of image simulation. On the basis of Harris and according to the laws of atmospheric physics, Li et al. derived a new net buoyancy formula and simulated the formation of cumulus clouds in a more real way [16]. However, this method was realized by increasing cloud sources when simulating a large number of clouds, which was not suitable for large-scale cloud simulation.

According to the existing work, we have learned that particle system and view-based multi-level detail model are beneficial to the simulation of large-scale cloud shape; Body element algorithm, program noise algorithm and texture mapping algorithm were used to simulate the shape of cloud with higher detail level [17]. On the basis of voxel grid [18], the algorithm for solving partial differential equations can be used to simulate the dynamic effect of cloud to get better results. Using spherical harmonic function method, finite element integration method, Monte Carlo method and other methods to accurately solve the multiple scattering is beneficial to the illumination calculation of clouds with higher trueness [19]. Mining Linear integration method and linear interpolation method are beneficial to the real-time rendering of cloud in large-scale scene [20]. Different algorithms should be developed to simulate different characteristics of the cloud. From the initial drawing a cloud in the smaller scope, then draw a certain scale of cloud, the cloud rendering technology has made great progress, but the technology is still far can not meet the demand of the simulation of flight simulator in flight simulator, the scene big wide scope of speed, real-time generate all kinds of different requirements of clouds is very challenging.

5   Conclusion

In this paper, simulation methods and graphic algorism have been studied, which applies to irregular fuzzy objects , such as clouds, smoke and fog. Specifically, simplification of particle system and rendering method of three-dimensional cloud has been established based on cloud computing. We simplify the lighting model and rendering method to improve real-time interaction. Cloud computing mode is adopted to complete the rendering task of the three-dimensional cloud. At last, the experimental results show that the proposed method has achieved that the cloud generated has meteorological significance, using real meteorological data. While effectively reducing the number of particles, the realistic visual effect is guaranteed and the rendering efficiency is improved. Lots of meteorological factors have influence on the cloud formation , and it is difficult to build a model taking all factors into consideration. In the future, more effective methods with better performance will be proposed.

Acknowledgment. This research is supported by the National Natural Science Foundation of China under grant no. 41675155.

References

1. Grabner, A., Roth, P.M., Lepetit,V.: 3d pose estimation and 3d model retrieval for objects in the wild. In Proceedings of the IEEE Conference on Computer Vision and Pattern Recognition, pp. 3022–3031 (2018)
2. Xu, X., Liu, Q., Zhang, X., Zhang, J., Qi, L., Dou, W.: A blockchain-powered crowdsourcing method with privacy preservation in mobile environment. IEEE Trans. Comput. Soc. Syst. **6**(6), 1407–1419 (2019)
3. Berger, M., Li, J., Levine, J.A.: A generative model for volume rendering. IEEE Trans. Vis. Comput. Graph. **25**(4), 1636–1650 (2018)
4. Kniss, J., Premoze, S., Hansen, C., Shirley, P., McPherson, A.: A model for volume lighting and modeling. IEEE Trans. Vis. Comput. Graph. **9**(2), 150–162 (2003)
5. Qi, L., Chen, Y., Yuan, Y., Fu, S., Zhang, X., Xu, X. A qos-aware virtual machine scheduling method for energy conservation in cloud-based cyber-physical systems. In: World Wide Web, pp. 1–23 (2019)
6. Chawla, I., Osuri, K.K., Mujumdar, P.P., Niyogi, D.: Assessment of the weather research and forecasting (wrf) model for simulation of extreme rainfall events in the upper ganga basin. Hydrol. Earth Syst. Sci. **22**(2) (2018)
7. Choi, T., Ghan, S., Chin, S.: Biological property-based artificial scar synthesis using inverse lighting. Multimedia Syst. **24**(4), 407–418 (2017). https://doi.org/10.1007/s00530-017-0564-7
8. Bae, S.Y., Hong, S.Y., Lim, K.S.S.: Coupling wrf double-moment 6-class microphysics schemes to rrtmg radiation scheme in weather research forecasting model. In: Advances in Meteorology, 2016 (2016)
9. Xu, X., Dou, W., Zhang, X., Chen, J.: Enreal: an energy-aware resource allocation method for scientific workflow executions in cloud environment. IEEE Trans. Cloud Comput. **4**(2), 166–179 (2015)
10. Qi, L., He, Q., Chen, F., Dou, W., Wan, S., Zhang, X., Xu, X.: Finding all you need: web APIs recommendation in web of things through keywords search. IEEE Trans. Comput. Soc. Syst. **6**(5), 1063–1072 (2019)
11. Ahasan, M.N., Debsarma, S.K.: Impact of data assimilation in simulation of thunderstorm (squall line) event over bangladesh using wrf model, during saarc-storm pilot field experiment 2011. Nat. Hazards **75**(2), 1009–1022 (2015)
12. Li, Z., Shafiei, M., Ramamoorthi, R., Sunkavalli, K., Chandraker, M.: Inverse rendering for complex indoor scenes: Shape, spatially-varying lighting and svbrdf from a single image (2019). arXiv preprint arXiv:1905.02722
13. Smirnova, T.G., Brown, J.M., Benjamin, S.G., Kenyon, J.S.: Modifications to the rapid update cycle land surface model (ruc lsm) available in the weather research and forecasting (wrf) model. Mon. Weather Rev. **144**(5), 1851–1865 (2016)
14. She, J., Tan, X., Guo, X., Tan, J., Liu, J.: Rendering 2d lines on 3d terrain model with optimization in visual quality and running performance. Trans. GIS **21**(1), 169–185 (2017)
15. Xu, X., Yuan, C., Liang, X., Shen, X.: Rendering and modeling of stratus cloud using weather forecast data. In: 2015 International Conference on Virtual Reality and Visualization (ICVRV), pp. 246–252. IEEE (2015)
16. Sur, F., Blaysat, B., Grediac, M.: Rendering deformed speckle images with a boolean model. J. Math. Imaging Vis. **60**(5), 634–650 (2018)
17. Qi, L., et al.: Structural balance theory-based e-commerce recommendation over big rating data. IEEE Trans. Big Data **4**(3), 301–312 (2016)

18. Drăgan, I., Selea, T., Fortiş, T.-F.: Towards the integration of a HPC build system in the cloud ecosystem. In: Barolli, L., Terzo, O. (eds.) CISIS 2017. AISC, vol. 611, pp. 916–925. Springer, Cham (2018). https://doi.org/10.1007/978-3-319-61566-0_87

19. Yáñez-Morroni, G., Gironás, J., Caneo, M., Delgado, R., Garreaud, R.: Using the weather research and forecasting (wrf) model for precipitation forecasting in an andean region with complex topography. Atmosphere 9(8), 304 (2018)

20. Rautenhaus, M., et al.: Visualization in meteorologya survey of techniques and tools for data analysis tasks. IEEE Trans. Vis. Comput. Graph. 24(12), 3268–3296 (2017)

Cloud-Based Data Analytics

Distributed Stochastic Alternating Direction Method of Multipliers for Big Data Classification

Huihui Wang[1], Xinwen Li[2], Xingguo Chen[2], Lianyong Qi[3],
and Xiaolong Xu[1(✉)]

[1] Key Laboratory of Intelligent Perception and Systems for High-Dimensional Information of Ministry of Education, Nanjing University of Science and Technology, Nanjing, China
huihuiwang@njust.edu.cn, xlxu@nuist.edu.cn
[2] School of Computer Science and Technology, School of Software, Nanjing University of Posts and Telecommunications, Nanjing, China
lxinwen31@gmail.com, chenxg@njupt.edu.cn
[3] School of Information Science and Engineering, Qufu Normal University, Jining, China
lianyongqi@gmail.com

Abstract. In recent years, classification with big data sets has become one of the latest research topic in machine learning. Distributed classification have received much attention from industry and academia. Recently, the Alternating Direction Method of Multipliers (ADMM) is a widely-used method to solve learning problems in a distributed manner due to its simplicity and scalability. However, distributed ADMM usually converges slowly and thus suffers from expensive time cost in practice. To overcome this limitation, we propose a novel distributed stochastic ADMM (DS-ADMM) algorithm for big data classification based on the MPI framework. By formulating the original problem as a series of sub-problems through a cluster of multiple computers (nodes). In particular, we exploit a stochastic method for sub-problem optimization in parallel to further improve time efficiency. The experimental results show that our proposed distributed algorithm is suitable to enhance the performance of ADMM, and can be effectively applied for big data classification.

Keywords: Big data · ADMM · Stochastic ADMM · Distributed classification

1 Introduction

Linear classification has been widely applied in machine learning, such as medical diagnosis, pattern recognition, and credit scoring [1]. Under the explosive increase of global data, extreme-scale data requiring classification is a very challenging task. Formally, the size of big data challenges standard machine learning

X. Zhang et al. (Eds.): CloudComp 2019/SmartGift 2019, LNICST 322, pp. 141–153, 2020.
https://doi.org/10.1007/978-3-030-48513-9_11

algorithms those are not usually able to deal with huge data on a single machine which the amount of data exceeds the capabilities of its system to process the data [2]. Moreover, the data in many applications are usually generated and collected in decentralized different machines. This is particularly natural for processing the large data on a computer cluster. Nowadays, big data is attracting much attention both from industry and academia in a wide variety of fields. This is because of the availability of distributed optimization can deal with a huge amount of data. Distributed classification is developed to take advantage of the computational power of multi-machines to solve the original classification problem in a decentralized environment. In these algorithms, the global classification problem is decomposed into as a series of small classification problems (sub-problems), and then the computing nodes (different machines) solve sub-problems in parallel, and then local results of sub-problems are aggregated to obtain a global result [3].

Recently, distributed classification algorithms can be roughly divided into two categories: (i) *primal optimization* [4], in these algorithms, stochastic gradient descent (SGD) is an efficient method, which only computes the gradient of one sample instead of all gradients of the whole samples in each iteration [5]. Because of the variance in stochastic optimization, initial SGD suffers from a slow convergence rate. Recently, some many accelerated versions of SGD are proposed to efficiently solve large-scale learning problems, and obtain some better convergence rate [6]. (ii) *dual optimization* [7], which introduces dual variables and designs the dual problem of the primal problem, and then obtain the final result by solving it. Specifically, alternating direction method of multipliers (ADMM) is an efficient and widely-used optimization method in many application fields [8]. Batch ADMM need to compute the empirical risk loss on all training samples in each iteration, which makes it unsuitable for the large-scale learning problem. Thus, various versions of ADMM have been developed to improve the convergence [9]. In recent years, ADMM has been widely-used for distributed optimization because of its high decomposability property [3]. The main idea of distributed ADMM is global consensus, it means that all the local models on each machine need to be in consensus with the global model when finding the global solution.

Distributed ADMM is an iterative method which includes the computation of sub-problem optimization that happens locally on each node, and the communication of information in each iteration. A lot of distributed ADMM algorithms have been proposed for solving large-scale optimization problems [10,11]. In particularly, a distributed classification algorithms based on the ADMM framework had been proposed to solve linear SVM problems in [12]. Moreover, distributed ADMM was applied for specific tasks in [13]. Nevertheless, distributed ADMM always converges slowly, and it needs much more iterations to obtain the final solution, and thus it is always time-consuming [14]. Therefore, the development of efficient distributed ADMM algorithms improve the convergence distributed ADMM for big data classification is an important problem. However, this issue has not been well studied in the previous works.

In this work, we focus on ADMM-based distributed classification problems, and propose a novel distributed stochastic ADMM algorithms (DS-ADMM) for big data classification that can improve the efficiency of local computation and communication. In particular, we integrate a stochastic gradient descent method, Pegasos [15], into ADMM for the sub-problem optimization in the distributed ADMM framework compared with traditional distributed ADMM, and then we utilize a symmetric dual update to further reduce the time cost. Finally, we investigate the performance of our proposed algorithm. Experiments on various datasets empirically validate that DS-ADMM outperforms distributed ADMM-based classification algorithms. The main contributions of our work are briefly outlined as follows:

- An efficient classification algorithm integrated with stochastic ADMM is proposed for big data classification. Specifically, the accelerated strategy can reduce local computation cost to improve efficiency.
- We implement our proposed DS-ADMM under message passing interface (MPI), which can run on clusters with many different machines (nodes). Moreover, stochastic ADMM can efficiently solve the sub-problems in parallel. Hence, DS-ADMM can be efficiently used to handle big data classification.
- Experiments on several binary classification datasets show that DS-ADMM outperforms other distributed ADMM-based algorithms, and converges faster to reduce time cost. Therefore, it could be an effective algorithm for big data classification.

The rest of this paper is organized as follows. The background of this work is presented in Sect. 2, followed by the details of our proposed algorithms in Sect. 3. And then, the experimental results are analyzed in Sect. 4. Finally, we present the conclusion in Sect. 5.

2   Background

In this section, we briefly introduce the related background of our work, which includes linear classification, ADMM and distributed ADMM.

2.1   Linear Classification

It has shown that the performance of linear classification is close to that of non-linear classification when handling large-scale data, but with much less training time [1]. Support Vector Machine (SVM) is an widely-used tool for solving data classification [16]. Moreover, The task of learning a support vector machine can be transformed as a constrained quadratic programming problem. Formally, given a dataset $\{(\mathbf{x}_i, y_i)\}_{i=1}^{l}$, where $\mathbf{x}_i \in \mathbb{R}^n$ and $y_j \in \{-1, +1\}$. We use SVM as the classification model, and the minimization problem can be reformed as:

$$\min_{\mathbf{w}} \quad \frac{1}{2}\|\mathbf{w}\|^2 + C \sum_{i=1}^{l} \xi(\mathbf{w}, \mathbf{x}_j, y_j), \tag{1}$$

where $C>0$ is the penalty parameter, and ξ is the misclassification loss function usually with two common forms:

$$\max\{0, 1 - y_j \mathbf{w}^T \mathbf{x}_j\}, \max\{0, 1 - y_j \mathbf{w}^T \mathbf{x}_j\}^2$$

Furthermore, the optimization method has been proved that it can obtain an ϵ-accurate solution $\mathbf{w}^*$, if it satisfies $f(\mathbf{w}^*) \leq f(\mathbf{w}) + \epsilon$ [15,17].

2.2 ADMM

ADMM is a powerful optimization algorithm and has recently get a lot of attention in many applications [9,12]. ADMM minimizes the sum of two local problems, and alternately solves them. Specifically, ADMM solves the optimization problem in the following form:

$$\min_{\mathbf{x},\mathbf{z}} \quad f(\mathbf{x}) + g(\mathbf{z}), \tag{2}$$
$$s.t. \quad \mathbf{Ax} + \mathbf{Bz} = \mathbf{C},$$

where $\mathbf{x} \in \mathbb{R}^{N_x}$ and $\mathbf{z} \in \mathbb{R}^{N_z}$ are the optimization variables, functions $f(\mathbf{x})$ and $g(\mathbf{z})$ are convex. $\mathbf{A} \in \mathbb{R}^{N_c \times N_x}$, $\mathbf{B} \in \mathbb{R}^{N_c \times N_z}$ and $\mathbf{C} \in \mathbb{R}^{N_c}$ are the linear constraints in the problem. Given a penalty parameter $\rho > 0$, the optimization problem (2) can be efficiently solved by minimizing the augmented Lagrangian as:

$$L_\rho(\mathbf{x}, \mathbf{z}, \boldsymbol{\lambda}) = f(\mathbf{x}) + g(\mathbf{z}) + \boldsymbol{\lambda}^T (\mathbf{Ax} + \mathbf{Bz} - \mathbf{C}) \\ + \frac{\rho}{2} \|\mathbf{Ax} + \mathbf{Bz} - \mathbf{C}\|^2, \tag{3}$$

where $\boldsymbol{\lambda}$ is the Lagrangian multipliers. Furthermore, we can combine the linear and quadratic terms in (3) into a slightly scaled form [3] as follows:

$$L_\rho(\mathbf{x}, \mathbf{z}, \mathbf{u}) = f(\mathbf{x}) + g(\mathbf{z}) + \frac{\rho}{2} \|\mathbf{Ax} + \mathbf{Bz} - \mathbf{C} + \mathbf{u}\|^2, \tag{4}$$

where $\mathbf{u} = \frac{1}{\rho} \boldsymbol{\lambda}$. We can find that the problem in (4) is clearly equivalent to the problem in (3), but it is more convenient to solve. Hence, alternating minimization steps of $\mathbf{x}$ and $\mathbf{z}$ can be performed as follows:

$$\mathbf{x}^{k+1} = \arg\min_{\mathbf{x}} f(\mathbf{x}) + \frac{\rho}{2} \|\mathbf{Ax} + \mathbf{Bz}^k - \mathbf{C} + \mathbf{u}^k\|^2, \tag{5}$$

$$\mathbf{z}^{k+1} = \arg\min_{\mathbf{z}} g(\mathbf{z}) + \frac{\rho}{2} \|\mathbf{Ax}^{k+1} + \mathbf{Bz} - \mathbf{C} + \mathbf{u}^k\|^2, \tag{6}$$

$$\mathbf{u}^{k+1} = \mathbf{u}^k + (\mathbf{Ax}^{k+1} + \mathbf{Bz}^{k+1} - \mathbf{C}). \tag{7}$$

ADMM is an iterative method and its objective is separable across the variables. The known theoretical study on ADMM has shown that it has a sublinear convergence rate [3,18]. In recent years, ADMM has been applied to solve large-scale machine learning problems. Moreover, many stochastic or online variants of ADMM have been proposed to further improve the time efficiency [19,20].

2.3   Distributed ADMM

Recently, distributed ADMM has been widely-used for machine learning tasks due to its simplicity and flexibility towards distributed computation [21]. Unlike the method of multipliers, ADMM minimizes $L_\rho(\mathbf{x}, \mathbf{z}, \boldsymbol{\lambda})$ in terms of $\mathbf{x}$ and $\mathbf{z}$ alternatively and then updates $\boldsymbol{\lambda}$, which enables the problem to be easily decomposed for distributed optimization. Assume that the data are stored on N nodes respectively, and the loss function $f(\mathbf{x})$ can be decomposed into N components with respect to $\mathbf{x}$. Hence, the general optimization problem can be defined as:

$$f(\mathbf{x}) = \sum_{i=1}^{N} f_i(\mathbf{x}_i),$$

where $\mathbf{x} = (\mathbf{x}_1, \ldots, \mathbf{x}_N)$ and each f_i the local function which involves only the samples on node i. By formulating the original problem as a global optimization problem, we reforms the minimization of (2) in the ADMM form as follow:

$$\min_{\mathbf{x}_i, \ldots, \mathbf{x}_n, \mathbf{z}} \sum_{i=1}^{n} f_i(\mathbf{x}_i) + g(\mathbf{z}), \tag{8}$$
$$s.t. \quad \mathbf{A}\mathbf{x}_i + \mathbf{B}\mathbf{z} = \mathbf{C}, i = 1, 2, \ldots, n.$$

In the problem (8), $\mathbf{x}_i$ and $\mathbf{z}$ can be called ad the local and global variables, respectively. Given the global consensus problem, the original optimization problem is decomposed into N sub-problems, and $f_i(\mathbf{x}_i)$ is the local objective of sub-problem i. We want to find the global optimal variable $\mathbf{z}$ that minimizes the sum of objective functions, and the constraint $\mathbf{x}_i = \mathbf{z}$ is used to force all the local variables to reach a global result. In a distributed computing environment, the global formulation is suitable for solving distributed optimization in machine learning and computer vision areas [3,22]. Moreover, the global consensus problem can be solved equally by optimizing its augmented Lagrangian which can be mathematically formulated in a scaled form as follow:

$$\mathcal{L}_\rho(\mathbf{x}, \mathbf{z}, \mathbf{u}) = \sum_{i=1}^{N} f_i(\mathbf{x}_i) + g(\mathbf{z}) + \frac{\rho}{2} \sum_{i=1}^{N} \|\mathbf{A}\mathbf{x}_i + \mathbf{B}\mathbf{z} - \mathbf{C} + \mathbf{u}_i\|^2, \tag{9}$$

where $\mathbf{u} = \frac{\boldsymbol{\lambda}}{\rho}$ and $\mathbf{u}_i$ is the dual variable. As mentioned in the introduction, although distributed ADMM and its convergence rate have been studied in recent years, it usually converges slowly.

3   Distributed Stochastic ADMM for Big Data Classification

In this section, we introduce our distributed stochastic ADMM (DS-ADMM) in detail. We first present the proposed distributed ADMM framework to solve sub-problems optimization in parallel. Then, we propose a stochastic learning algorithm to speed up the convergence speed. Moreover, a symmetric dual update is used to reduce the difference between local and global variables.

3.1 Framework of DS-ADMM

Based on the framework of ADMM over a computer cluster with a star topology which has a master node and N slave nodes, the classification problem can be formulated as a global optimization problem:

$$\min_{\mathbf{w}_i,\dots,\mathbf{w}_N,\mathbf{z}} \quad \sum_{i=1}^{N}\sum_{j=1}^{l_i} C * \xi(\mathbf{w}_i,\mathbf{x}_j,y_j) + g(\mathbf{z}), \tag{10}$$

$$s.t. \quad \mathbf{w}_i = \mathbf{z}, i = 1,2,\dots,N,$$

where $g(\mathbf{z}) = \frac{1}{2}\|\mathbf{z}\|^2$, $\sum_{j=1}^{l_i} C * \xi(\mathbf{w}_i,\mathbf{x}_j,y_j)$ is the loss function in slave node i, and l_i is the number of samples on slave node i. For simplicity, we denote $\mathbf{w} = \{\mathbf{w}_1,\dots,\mathbf{w}_N\}$, and $\boldsymbol{\lambda} = \{\boldsymbol{\lambda}_1,\dots,\boldsymbol{\lambda}_N\}$. Basically, The augmented Lagrangian function for distributed classification in (10) can be rewritten as:

$$L_\rho(\mathbf{w},\mathbf{z},\boldsymbol{\lambda}) = g(\mathbf{z}) + \sum_{i=1}^{N}\sum_{j=1}^{l_i} C * \xi(\mathbf{w}_i,\mathbf{x}_j,y_j)$$
$$+ \sum_{i=1}^{N}(\boldsymbol{\lambda}_i(\mathbf{w}_i - \mathbf{z}) + \frac{\rho}{2}\|\mathbf{w}_i - \mathbf{z}\|^2). \tag{11}$$

where $\rho > 0$ is a penalty parameter, and $\boldsymbol{\lambda} > 0$ is the dual variable. By scaling $\boldsymbol{\lambda}$ with $\mathbf{u} = \frac{\boldsymbol{\lambda}}{\rho}$ in (11), the distributed classification problem in (10) is formulated as follows:

$$L_\rho(\mathbf{w},\mathbf{z},\mathbf{u}) = \frac{1}{2}\|\mathbf{z}\|^2 + \sum_{i=1}^{N} f_i(\mathbf{w}_i) + \frac{\rho}{2}\sum_{i=1}^{N}\|\mathbf{w}_i - \mathbf{z} + \mathbf{u}_i\|^2. \tag{12}$$

where $f_i(\mathbf{w}_i) = \sum_{j=1}^{l_i} C * \xi(\mathbf{w}_i,\mathbf{x}_j,y_j)$. Therefore, the problem in (10) can be solved by the minimization in terms of $\mathbf{w}_i$ and $\mathbf{z}$ alternately:

$$\mathbf{w}_i^{k+1} = \arg\min_{\mathbf{w}_i} L_\rho(\mathbf{w},\mathbf{z}^k,\mathbf{u}^k), \tag{13}$$

$$\mathbf{z}^{k+1} = \arg\min_{\mathbf{z}} L_\rho(\mathbf{w}^{k+1},\mathbf{z},\mathbf{u}^k), \tag{14}$$

$$\mathbf{u}_i^{k+1} = \mathbf{u}_i^k + \mathbf{w}_i^{k+1} - \mathbf{z}^{k+1}. \tag{15}$$

Note that distributed ADMM updates $\mathbf{w}_i$s and $\mathbf{u}_i$s locally on different nodes. Because distributed classification on big data can be decomposed into N sub-problems solved in parallel. Actually, our proposed DS-ADMM is a distributed ADMM framework. In the problem (10), each slave node optimizes its local variable $\mathbf{w}_i$ by oneself, and then sends $\mathbf{w}_i$ to generate the global variable $\mathbf{z}$ on the master node. Finally, the latest $\mathbf{z}$ is broadcasted to each slave node for $\mathbf{u}_i$-updating in each ADMM iteration until the train process obtain the consensus global variable.

3.2   Stochastic Learning for Sub-problem Optimization

In sub-problem optimization. it easy to find that $L_\rho(\mathbf{w}, \mathbf{z}, \mathbf{u})$ is separable with respect to $\mathbf{w}_i$. Consider a particular worker i, the sub-problem optimization problem can be formulated in a readable way:

$$\min_{\mathbf{w}_i} F_i(\mathbf{w}_i) = f_i(\mathbf{w}_i) + \frac{\rho}{2}\|\mathbf{w}_i - \mathbf{v}\|^2, \tag{16}$$

where $\mathbf{v} = \mathbf{z}^k - \mathbf{u}_i^k$ at the k_{th} ADMM iteration. Although the sub-problem is different from traditional machine learning problems in its regularization term, $\frac{\rho}{2}\|\mathbf{w}_i - \mathbf{v}\|^2$ also is a $L2$ regularization function in the $\mathbf{w}_i$-update of sub-problem i. Therefore, the sub-problem can be solved efficiently by widely used optimization methods such as gradient descent method, dual coordinate descent method and trust region Newton method [6,17,23]

In this paper, we utilize Pegasos in [15], a stochastic method, to solve $L2$-regularized $L1$-loss SVM with the objective function as follows:

$$\min_{\mathbf{w}} F_i(\mathbf{w}, A^k) = \frac{\lambda}{2}\|\mathbf{w}\|^2 + \frac{1}{m} \sum_{(\mathbf{x},y)\in A^k} \max\{0, 1 - y\mathbf{w}^T\mathbf{x}\}, \tag{17}$$

where subset A^k is the subset of size m chosen at iteration k. Pegasos is selected owing to the following reasons: (i) Pegasos performs SGD on the primal objective (16), which can be used to accelerate the convergence. (ii) A projection step is incorporated in Pegasos, and it has been proved that Pegasos has an ϵ-accurate solution after $O(1/(\epsilon))$ iterations [1]. Hence, Pegasos can obtain a fast convergence result. Given a training subset D^k of size m at each iteration, Pegasos approximately solves the objective in Eq. (16) replaced as follows:

$$\min_{\mathbf{w}_i} F_i(\mathbf{w}_i, D) = \frac{\rho\lambda}{2}\|\mathbf{w}_i - \mathbf{v}\|^2 + \frac{C}{m} \sum_{(\mathbf{x}_j,y_j)\in D^k} \max\{0, 1 - y_j\mathbf{w}_i^T\mathbf{x}_j\}, \tag{18}$$

Here, if D is the whole training set, Pegasos is a batch method with the deterministic setting. Pegasos can take the subgradient direction of $F_i(\mathbf{w}_i, D)$ because that $L1$-loss is not differentiable:

$$\nabla F_i(\mathbf{w}_i^k, D^k) = \rho\lambda(\mathbf{w}_i^k - \mathbf{v}^k) - \frac{C}{m} \sum_{j\in D_+^k} y_j\mathbf{x}_j, \tag{19}$$

where $D_+^k = \{\mathbf{x}_j | 1 - y_j\mathbf{w}_i^T\mathbf{x}_j > 0\}$, and update $\mathbf{w}_i$ by

$$\mathbf{w}_i^{k+\frac{1}{2}} \leftarrow \mathbf{w}_i^k - \eta\nabla F_i(\mathbf{w}_i^k, D^k), \tag{20}$$

where $\eta^k = C/\rho\lambda k$ is the learning rate and k is the iteration number. Compared with subgradient descent, Pegasos obtains $\mathbf{w}_i^{k+\frac{1}{2}}$, and then projects it onto the ball set where $\{\mathbf{w}_i \| \|\mathbf{w}_i\| \le 1/\sqrt{\frac{\rho\lambda}{C}}\}$. Therefore, the procedure of Pegasos can be summarized in Algorithm 1.

Algorithm 1. Pegasos for sub-problem optimization

Input: Choose $\mathbf{w}_i^1$ such that $\|\mathbf{w}_i^1\| \leq 1/\sqrt{\frac{\rho\lambda}{C}}\}$.

1: **for** $k = 1, 2, 3, \ldots, T$ **do**

2:    Choose training subset D^k, where $|D^k| = m$, uniformly at random.

3:    Compute the learning rate $\eta = C/\rho\lambda k$.

4:    Compute the subgradient of $F_i(\mathbf{w}_i^k, D^k)$ by (19).

5:    Update the latest $\mathbf{w}_i^{k+\frac{1}{2}} \leftarrow \mathbf{w}_i^k - \eta\nabla F_i(\mathbf{w}_i^k, D^k)$.

6:    Project $\mathbf{w}_i^{k+1} \leftarrow \min\{1, \frac{1/\sqrt{\frac{\rho\lambda}{C}}}{\|\mathbf{w}_i^{k+\frac{1}{2}}\|}\}\mathbf{w}_i^{k+\frac{1}{2}}$.

7: **end for**

Output: The local result $\mathbf{w}_i^{k+1}$

3.3   Update Procedures of Global and Dual Variables

Firstly, before y-update, a symmetric dual update similar as that in [24] is used to update the dual variable $\mathbf{u}_i^{k+\frac{1}{2}}$ as

$$\mathbf{u}_i^{k+\frac{1}{2}} \leftarrow \mathbf{u}_i^k + \mathbf{w}_i^{k+1} - \mathbf{z}^k. \tag{21}$$

The update process in (21) can reduce the difference between $\mathbf{w}_i$ and $\mathbf{z}$, and pull $\mathbf{w}_i$ into global consensus when solving sub-problems. Then, the new $\mathbf{w}_i^{k+1}$, together with $\mathbf{u}_i^{k+\frac{1}{2}}$, are sent to the master for $\mathbf{z}$-update which can be mathematically formulated as

$$\mathbf{z}^{k+1} = \frac{1}{2}\|\mathbf{z}\|^2 + \frac{\rho}{2}\sum_{i=1}^N \|\mathbf{w}_i - \mathbf{z} + \mathbf{u}_i\|^2. \tag{22}$$

Because of the right term in (22) is differentiable, thus the global variable $\mathbf{z}^{k+1}$ can be updated by the weighted average of $\mathbf{x}_i^{k+1}$s and $\mathbf{u}_i^{k+\frac{1}{2}}$s which are showed as follows:

$$\mathbf{z}^{k+1} = \frac{\rho}{1 + N\rho}\sum_{i=1}^N (\mathbf{w}_i^{k+1} + \mathbf{u}_i^{k+\frac{1}{2}}). \tag{23}$$

Finally, each worker waits for the new $\mathbf{z}^{k+1}$ which is broadcasted from the master for the dual update which is same as that in distributed ADMM

$$\mathbf{u}_i^{k+1} \leftarrow \mathbf{u}_i^{k+\frac{1}{2}} + \mathbf{w}_i^{k+1} - \mathbf{z}^{k+1}. \tag{24}$$

Hence, the update for $\mathbf{z}$ usually can be efficiently solved in many optimization problems. Moreover, each worker can send $\mathbf{w}_i^{k+1}$ and $\mathbf{u}_i^{k+\frac{1}{2}}$ to the master for $\mathbf{z}$-update, and can reduce the communication at each iteration. In summary, the overall procedure of our proposed DS-ADMM is showed in Algorithm 2.

Algorithm 2. DS-ADMM for Big Data Classification

Input: $\mathbf{w}_i^0$, $\mathbf{u}_i^0$ and $\mathbf{z}^0$, parameters $(\mathbf{r}^0, \mathbf{s}^0)$, tolerances (ϵ^p, ϵ^d)

1: **while** $\|\mathbf{r}^k\|_2 > \epsilon^p$ or $\|\mathbf{s}^k\|_2 > \epsilon^d$ **do**

2:     $\mathbf{w}_i^{k+1} = \min_{\mathbf{w}_i} f_i(\mathbf{w}_i) + \frac{\rho}{2}\|\mathbf{w}_i - \mathbf{v}\|^2$ solved by Pegasos in parallel.

3:     $\mathbf{u}_i^{k+\frac{1}{2}} \leftarrow \mathbf{u}_i^k + \mathbf{w}_i^{k+1} - \mathbf{z}^k$.

4:     $\mathbf{z}^{k+1} = \frac{\rho}{1+N\rho} \sum_{i=1}^{N}(\mathbf{w}_i^{k+1} + \mathbf{u}_i^{k+\frac{1}{2}})$.

5:     $\mathbf{u}_i^{k+1} \leftarrow \mathbf{u}_i^{k+\frac{1}{2}} + \mathbf{w}_i^{k+1} - \mathbf{z}^{k+1}$.

6:     $\mathbf{r}^{k+1} \leftarrow \sum_{i=1}^{N}(\mathbf{w}_i^{k+1} - \mathbf{z}^{k+1})$

7:     $\mathbf{s}^{k+1} \leftarrow \rho(\mathbf{z}^{k+1} - \mathbf{z}^k)$

8:     $k \leftarrow k + 1$

9: **end while**

Output: The global variable $\mathbf{z}^{k+1}$

---

4 Experiments

4.1 Experimental Datasets and Settings

In this paper, we perform binary classification tasks on three benchmark datasets: *webspam*, *rcv1* and *epsilon* whose detailed information can be found from LibSVM website[1] for performance evaluation. Furthermore, The details of experimental datasets are showed in Table 1. For parameter settings, we choose the hyperparameter C is consistent with distributed ADMM in [12] for fair comparison. Also, it has been studied that its relaxation form of local variable $\mathbf{w}_i^{k+1}$ can facilitate the solution, which is defined as followes:

$$\mathbf{w}_i^{k+1} \leftarrow \alpha \mathbf{w}_i^{k+1} + (1-\alpha)\mathbf{z}_i^k,$$

where $\alpha \in (0,2)$ is a relaxation parameter, and it had been analyzed and suggested that $\alpha \in (1.5, 1.8)$ can improve the convergence in [3]. In this paper, we define M as the number of inner iterations of sub-problem optimization in each ADMM iteration. For ρ, α and M, we set them as 1, 1.6, 50 which is same with [12] for comparative tests. Moreover, we empirically choose the parameter in Pegasos which is guided by [15] for sub-problem optimization. All the algorithms are implemented under an MPI-cluster with ten nodes, each of which has a 2.6 GHz Intel(R) Xeon(R) processor and 64 GB RAM.

4.2 Comparison with Other Distributed ADMM-Based Algorithms

To validate the effectiveness of our proposed algorithm, CS-ADMM is compared with distributed ADMM-based algorithms. In sub-problem optimization, we use DCD [17] and a trust region newton method (TRN) [23] as the baseline for sub-problem optimization, and Pegasos as acceleration to evaluate the local computation. To evaluate the performance, we use the number of outer iterations

---

[1] The datasets are available at http://www.csie.ntu.edu.tw/~cjlin/libsvmtools/datasets/binary.html.

Table 1. Experimental datasets. d and l are the dimension and the number of examples respectively, C is the hyperparameter.

Dataset	l	d	C
Webspam	350,000	16,609,143	32
Epsilon	500,000	2,000	1
rcv1	6,797,641	7,236	1

((Iter), total time (Ttime), communication time (Ctime), running time (Rtime) and accuracy (Acc(%)) as evaluation metrics. The details of comparison algorithms are described as follows:

- **D-ADMM.D**: D-ADMM is distributed ADMM based the original framework of ADMM [12], and DCD is used for sub-problem optimization.
- **D-ADMM.N** : In the distributed ADMM framework, TRN is used to solve the SVM model with $L2$-regularized squared hinge loss.
- **DS-ADMM**: Ttis based on the framework of distributed ADMM. Pegasos is utilized to solve sub-problems, and a symmetric dual update is used to update dual variables before z-update.

Table 2. Performance comparisons on dataset *webspam*

	Iter	Ttime(s)	Ctime(s)	Rtime(s)	Acc(%)
DS-ADMM	8.9	**565.4**	**498.1**	**67.3**	98.83
D-ADMM.D	25.2	872.4	704.2	168.2	99.26
D-ADMM.N	**7.8**	1405.3	789.6	615.7	**99.34**

Table 3. Performance comparisons on dataset *epsilon*

	Iter	Ttime(s)	Ctime(s)	Rtime(s)	Acc(%)
DS-ADMM	**56.3**	**45.7**	**6.5**	**39.2**	89.08
D-ADMM.D	76.4	86.4	10.6	75.8	89.81
D-ADMM.N	65.4	164.5	72.2	92.3	**89.86**

Time Cost of Local Computation. We study the performance of our proposed algorithm with stochastic optimization. Table 2, 3 and 4 show that distributed stochastic ADMM integrated with Pegasos converges faster and improves time efficiency than these algorithms only with DCD and TRN methods, respectively. In the experimental results, we can find that Pegasos significantly reduces the running time of local computation with the acceptable accuracy loss on all datasets. In particular, compared with D-ADMM.D, DS-ADMM

Table 4. Performance comparisons on dataset *rcv1*

	Iter	Ttime(s)	Ctime(s)	Rtime(s)	Acc(%)
DS-ADMM	34.5	**6.2**	**3.4**	**2.8**	97.48
D-ADMM.D	53.2	12.6	3.8	8.8	**97.82**
DS-ADMM.N	**30.4**	18.9	4.3	14.6	97.80

can save up about 2 times of the total time with about 0.4% accuracy loss on dataset *rcv1*. The main possible reason may be that in large-scale data, the number of training samples are very huge, and the local models would be well trained in inner iterations. Therefore, stochastic ADMM can improve the convergence speed of sub-problem optimization.

Accuracy and Efficiency. We find that DS-ADMM integrated with Pegasos can obviously save up the training time with acceptive accuracy loss, which is less than 0.8%, on all datasets in Table 2, 3 and 4. The main reason is that DCD is a batch optimization method, in which all examples should be trained to learn the classification model in each inner iteration. TRN uses a conjugate gradient method to find the Newton-like direction and use the trust region Newton method to iterate. While Pegasos is a min-batch method, which will may introduce the noise in the learning process. Hence, stochastic ADMM with Pegasos reduces the time cost with a little accuracy loss. Moreover, we can find that TRN is more time-consuming compared with DCD and Pegasos when dealing with high-dimensional data, such as *webspam* and *rcv1* datasets. To sum up, DS-ADMM converges faster, and can obviously reduce the time cost with the competitive accuracy compared with D-ADMM.D and D-ADMM.N. Hence, DS-ADMM is can be applied for large-scale machine learning, could be an effective algorithm for big data classification.

5 Conclusion

In this paper, we propose a novel distributed stochastic ADMM algorithm called as DS-ADMM, for big data classification. Specifically, we explore a distributed framework based on ADMM, and divide the global problem into small sub-problems. And then, we integrate a stochastic method, Pegasos with ADMM in the distributed framework for sub-problem optimization. Furthermore, we utilize a symmetric dual update to reduce the difference between local variables and the global variable, which can force to reach global consensus. Finally, experiments on binary classification datasets show that DS-ADMM outperforms distributed ADMM-based classification algorithms. Therefore, it could be used for big data classification.

Acknowledgement. This work is partially supported by the Fundamental Research Funds for the Central Universities, No. 30918014108, and the National Science Foundation of China No. 61806096.

References

1. Yuan, G.-X., Ho, C.-H., Lin, C.-J.: Recent advances of large-scale linear classification. Proc. IEEE **100**(9), 2584–2603 (2012)
2. Zaharia, M., et al.: Apache spark: a unified engine for big data processing. Commun. ACM **59**(11), 56–65 (2016)
3. Boyd, S., Parikh, N., Chu, E., Peleato, B., Eckstein, J.: Distributed optimization and statistical learning via the alternating direction method of multipliers. Found. Trends ® Mach. Learn. **3**(1), 1–122 (2011)
4. Agarwal, N., Suresh, A.T., Yu, F.X.X., Kumar, S., McMahan, B.: cpSGD: Communication-efficient and differentially-private distributed SGD. In: Advances in Neural Information Processing Systems, pp. 7564–7575 (2018)
5. Haddadpour F., Kamani, M.M., Mahdavi M., Cadambe V.: Trading redundancy for communication: speeding up distributed SGD for non-convex optimization. In: International Conference on Machine Learning, pp. 2545–2554 (2019)
6. Reddi, S.J., Hefny, A., Sra, S., Poczos, B., Smola, A.J.: On variance reduction in stochastic gradient descent and its asynchronous variants. In: Advances in Neural Information Processing Systems, pp. 2647–2655 (2015)
7. Suzuki, T.: Stochastic dual coordinate ascent with alternating direction method of multipliers. In: Proceedings of the 31st International Conference on Machine Learning, pp. 736–744 (2014)
8. Wang, H., Gao, Y., Shi, Y., Wang, R.: Group-based alternating direction method of multipliers for distributed linear classification. IEEE Trans. Cybern. **47**(11), 3568–3582 (2017)
9. Zheng, S., Kwok, J.T.: Stochastic variance-reduced admm. arXiv preprint arXiv:1604.07070 (2016)
10. Dajun, D., Xue, L., Wenting, L., Rui, C., Minrui, F., Lei, W.: Admm-based distributed state estimation of smart grid under data deception and denial of service attacks. IEEE Trans. Syst. Man Cybern. Syst. **49**(8), 1698–1711 (2019)
11. Forero, P.A., Cano, A., Giannakis, G.B.: Consensus-based distributed support vector machines. J. Mach. Learn. Res. **11**, 1663–1707 (2010)
12. Zhang, C., Lee, H., Shin, K.: Efficient distributed linear classification algorithms via the alternating direction method of multipliers. In: Artificial Intelligence and Statistics, pages 1398–1406 (2012)
13. Lee, C.P., Chang, K.W., Upadhyay, S., Roth, D.: Distributed training of structured SVM. arXiv preprint arXiv:1506.02620 (2015)
14. Lee, C.P., Roth, D.: Distributed box-constrained quadratic optimization for dual linear SVM. In: International Conference on Machine Learning, pp. 987–996 (2015)
15. Shai, S.-S., Yoram, S., Nathan, S., Andrew, C.: Pegasos: primal estimated sub-gradient solver for SVM. Math. Program. **127**(1), 3–30 (2011). https://doi.org/10.1007/s10107-010-0420-4
16. Xiaohe, W., Wangmeng, Z., Liang, L., Wei, J., Zhang, D.: F-SVM: Combination of feature transformation and SVM learning via convex relaxation. IEEE Trans. Neural Netw. Learn. Syst. **29**(11), 5185–5199 (2018)
17. Hsieh, C.J., Chang, K.W., Lin, C.J., Keerthi, S.S., Sundararajan, S.: A dual coordinate descent method for large-scale linear SVM. In: Proceedings of the 25th international conference on Machine learning, pp. 408–415 (2008)
18. He, B., Yuan, X.: On the o(1/n) convergence rate of the douglas-rachford alternating direction method. SIAM J. Numer. Anal. **50**(2), 700–709 (2012)

19. Liu Y., Shang F., Cheng J.: Accelerated variance reduced stochastic ADMM. In: Proceedings of the Thirty-First AAAI Conference on Artificial Intelligence, pp. 2287–2293 (2017)
20. Yu Y., Huang L.: Fast stochastic variance reduced ADMM for stochastic composition optimization. In: Proceedings of International Joint Conferences on Artifical Intelligence, pp. 3364–3370 (2017)
21. Shi, W., Ling, Q., Yuan, K., Gang, W., Yin, W.: On the linear convergence of the ADMM in decentralized consensus optimization. IEEE Trans. Signal Process. **62**(7), 1750–1761 (2014)
22. Chen, C., He, B., Ye, Y., Yuan, X.: The direct extension of admm for multi-block convex minimization problems is not necessarily convergent. Math. Program. **155**(1–2), 57–79 (2016)
23. Lin, C.J., Weng, R.C., Keerthi, S.S.: Trust region newton method for logistic regression. J. Mach. Learn. Res. **9**, 627–650 (2008)
24. He, B., Ma, F., Yuan, X.: On the step size of symmetric alternating directions method of multipliers (2015). http://www.optimization-online.org

Personalized Recommendation Algorithm Considering Time Sensitivity

Fuzhen Sun[1], Haiyan Zhuang[2], Jin Zhang[1], Zhen Wang[1], and Kai Zheng[1(✉)]

[1] School of Computer Science and Technology, Shandong University of Technology,
Zibo 255049, China
zhengkai@uestc.edu.cn
[2] Image and Network Investigation Department, Railway Police College,
Zhengzhou 450053, China

Abstract. Aiming to solve the problem of goods popularity bias, this paper introduces the prevalence of items into user interest modeling, and proposes an item popularity model based on user interest feature. Usually, traditional model that does not take into account the stability of user's interests, which leads to the difficulty in capturing their interest. To cope with this limitation, we propose a time-sensitive and stabilized interest similarity model that involves a process of calculating the similarity of user interest. Moreover, by combining those two kinds of similarity model based on weight factors, we develop a novel algorithm for calculation, which is named as IPSTS (IPSTS). To evaluate the proposed approach, experiments are performed and results indicate that Mean Absolute Difference (MAE) and root mean square error (RMSE) could be significantly reduced, when compared with those of traditional collaborative filtering Algorithms.

Keywords: Time sensitivity · Stability of interest · Prevalence of item · Personalized recommendation · Popularity bias

1 Introduction

Collaborative Filtering Recommendation Algorithms are mainly divided into two categories: user-based and item-based. The idea of Item Based Collaborative Filtering Algorithm is that, basing on the user historical behavior, making data analysis and calculation, to get a user's behavior preferences and make recommendations for users basing on their preferences. However, the prerequisite of this algorithm should be that, users can not change the interest within a period of time. The idea of Item-Based Collaborative Filtering Recommendation Algorithms is that, basing on the behavior data of the user A, calculating the neighbor users who have similar preferences with user A, and then recommend the items - which are of interest to the neighboring users but user A has not yet found. Therefore, no matter which collaborative filtering recommendation algorithm, the core is the calculation of similarity.

© ICST Institute for Computer Sciences, Social Informatics and Telecommunications Engineering 2020
Published by Springer Nature Switzerland AG 2020. All Rights Reserved
X. Zhang et al. (Eds.): CloudComp 2019/SmartGift 2019, LNICST 322, pp. 154–162, 2020.
https://doi.org/10.1007/978-3-030-48513-9_12

As for the dynamics problem in collaborative filtering technology, a recommendation algorithm is proposed in literature [3], which adapt to user interest to evaluate the time weight and Data weight of resource similarity. Literature [4] proposed a dynamic recommendation technique. As the mobile device flourishesa SUCM model is proposed in [5], which learn fine-grained user preferences to make recommendations to users.

As for the dynamics problem in collaborative filtering technology, a recommendation algorithm, which adapt to user interest, is proposed in literature [3] where the time weight and Data weight of resource similarity are weighted. Literature [4] proposed a dynamic recommendation technique. As the mobile device flourishesa SUCM model is proposed in [5], which learn fine-grained user preferences to make recommendations to users.

Generally, there are two traditional solutions to the problem of scalability in collaborative filtering technology. The first is based on clustering. In literature [6], it proposes to set up a representative user for each cluster, and select the neighbor user set by calculating and representing the similarity of the user. There is a method basing on deep learning to solve the problem of scalability as proposed in [7]. In [8], a hierarchical Bayesian network with cooperative deep learning is proposed to solve the problem of data researchers even propose to use of principal component analysis techniques in statistics to achieve the scale matrix dimensionality reduction [10]. For the problem of cold-starting, the literature [11] proposed the use of proximity, impact and popularity to comprehensively consider the influence of user rating on the similarity between users. In [12], a new heuristic similarity calculation model is proposed, which can alleviate the cold-starting problem and improve the similarity between users. Literature [13] solve the cold-starting problem with self-coding, and improve the quality of top-N recommendation. In [14], the social network is utilized to analyze the strong and weak relationships in the social community, and an EM algorithm is proposed to improve the recommendation quality. In [15], deep learning technique is adopted to generate a learning function between the content and the user interaction, and to transform the user preference into a ranking list that will be recommended to users.

On the issue of popularity bias of item, literature [16] alleviates the problem by changing the popularity distribution of recommended result. This study tries to "box" all items popularity, and then maps the "box" according to the user's actual score. After mapping, a three-dimensional vector will be generated, standing for object popularity basing on the user interest feature - "vectorization". Finally, calculate the similarity between users.

Generally, the higher popularity of the item, the more interest of the user, that is, user interest is related to the popularity of items. Regarding the popularity of items as user interest feature to build a model, this paper proposes a user interest similarity model basing on the popularity of items. This article holds that the user's short-term interest is not necessarily constant, which needs to be determined according to the stability of the user's interest. If the user's interest is stable, thus the user's interest will not change with the past of time. If the user's interest is unstable, the interest varies. This paper, from the perspective of popularity and stability of interest, proposes a time-aware, user interest stable, hybrid recommendation algorithm.

2 Methodology

2.1 User Interest Feature Similarity Model Basing on Item Popularity

Definition 1 (The popularity of Item i): The ratio of the number of evaluation to the total number of items. The formula is as follows:

$$popularity_i = \frac{count_i}{count_I} \tag{1}$$

Where $count_i$ represents the number of user who had evaluated item I, $count_i$ represents the total number of items.

Algorithm Description

(1) Take 3 intervals of items popularity $[a_1, a_2), [b_1, b_2), [c_1, c_2)$
(2) Use formula $popularity_i$ to calculate all items popularity which had been evaluated by user u.
(3) Box all the item popularity derived in step (2), and then map to step (1). pseudo boxing code are as following:

Algorithm 1. Popularity packing algorithm

Input: Training data: $X = \{x_1, ..., x_n\}$; Binary bits: M
Output: Bitwise weights functions: $U = \{\mu_1, \cdots, \mu_M\}$; Hash functions: $V = \{v_1, \cdots, v_M\}$
1: **for** $p_i \to p_n$ by 1 **do**
2:    **if** $p_i \in [a_1, a_2)$ **then**
3:       boolean flagfirst=true
4:    **else if** $p_i \in [b_1, b_2)$ **then**
5:       boolean flagse=true
6:    **else if** $p_i \in [c_1, c_2)$ **then**
7:       boolean flaghird=true
8:    **end if**
9: **end for**

Notes: $a_1, a_2, b_1, b_2, c_1, c_2$ are threshold data derived from the experiment. The pseudo mapping code is shown in Algorithm 2 .

(4) Calculate interest feature similarity of user A and user B basing on item popularity with User Feature Vector derived from step (3), using cosine similarity formula. The formula is as following:

$$Item\_pop\_sim = cos<A, B> \frac{A \cdot B}{\|A\| \cdot \|B\|} \tag{2}$$

The above Model called Item_pop_sim Model (Item Popularity Similarity Model), simply put as IPS Model.

Algorithm 2. Mapping feature vector algorithm

Input: Training data: $X = \{x_1, ..., x_n\}$; Binary bits: M
Output: Bitwise weights functions: $U = \{\mu_1, \cdots, \mu_M\}$; Hash functions: $V = \{v_1, \cdots, v_M\}$
1: **if** flagfirst&&!flagse&&!flagthird **then**
2:    featurevector:=(a,b,b)
3: **else if** flagfirst&&!flagse&&flagthird **then**
4:    featurevector:=(a,b,a)
5: **else if** flagfirst&&flagse&&!flagthird **then**
6:    featurevector:=(a,a,b)
7: **else if** flagfirst&&flagse&&flagthird **then**
8:    featurevector:=(a,a,a)
9: **else if** !flagfirst&&!flagse&&!flagthird **then**
10:    featurevector:=(b,b,a)
11: **else if** !flagfirst&&flagse&&!flagthird **then**
12:    featurevector:=(b,a,b)
13: **else if** flagfirst&&flagse&&flagthird **then**
14:    featurevector:=(b,a,a)
15: **else**
16:    featurevector:=(b,b,b)
17: **end if**

2.2   Time-Aware Similarity Model with Stability of Interest

In the actual application process, the user's interest is usually volatile, related not only with the item score value given by the user, but also with the popularity of items, and combining the two makes the user interest, which is defined as follows:

Definition 2 (The Interest of User u). The interest vector set made by user u for Items $P_u = (p_{u1}, p_{u2}, p_{u3} \cdots p_{ui})$.

Definition 3 (The Interest Vector of User u to item i). The weighted sum of the ratio of the actual Score of user u for item i to Full Score, and plus the popularity degree of this item. Formula are as following:

$$P_{ui} = \alpha \times \frac{R_{ui}}{R_{max}} + \beta \times popularity_i \tag{3}$$

$$popularity_i = \frac{popularity_i - popularity_{min}}{popularity_{max} - popularity_{min}} \tag{4}$$

where p_{ui} represents The Popularity of user u to item i, R_w is the rating of user u to item, R_{max} represents the full score, indicates the maximum score to the item. $popularity_i$ is the Popularity of item i in formula (1). $popularity_{min}$ is the Minimum Popularity for all items, while $popularity_{max}$ is the Maximum Popularity. α, β are parameters which can be verified through experiments, and $\alpha + \beta = 1$. Calculate the Interest Similarity for users by using Cosine Similarity, formula is as following:

$$sim_p(u, v) = \frac{P_u \cdot P_v}{\|P_u\| \cdot \|P_v\|} \tag{5}$$

The model can effectively alleviate the problem of deviations of user by introducing the weighted popularity of items.

Definition 4 (Stability of Interest to User u). The variance of score for user u to all item.

$$s_{interest(u)} = \frac{\sum_{i=1}^{n}(u_i - E(u))^2}{n} \tag{6}$$

where u_i represents the ratings to item u, n is total number of item evaluated by user u, u is the average value for all items given by the user.

Actually, the variance is to measure the stability of the user's interest, in other words, the smaller the variance, the more stable the user's interest.

Factors influencing the user interest: personal factor, time and environment. In reality, the user's interest is actually volatile, may be affected by their own factors, the surrounding environment, friends and family, interest will silently transform over time, previous interest may fade or disappear, gradually. But, If the user's interest is relatively stable, the paper does deem that user interest will not have much change as time go by. Therefore, from the factors that affect the user's interest, the time-sensitive will be put forward.

Definition 5 (time-sensitive). On the basis of the stability of the two users' interest, the closer of evaluation time of the user's score to the item is, the higher the similarity between the users, that is, the user's interest similarity is time-sensitive.

Overall, this paper presents a time-sensitive similarity calculation model with user interest stability.

$$stability\_Time\_sim_p = \frac{\delta|\sigma_u - \sigma_v| \frac{\sum X^2}{\sum Y^2} \sum_{i \in I_u \cap I_v} e^{-\varphi|t_{ui} - t_{vi}|} \vec{P}_u \cdot \vec{P}_v}{\|P_u\| \cdot \|P_v\|} \tag{7}$$

where, $\sigma_u = \sigma_u - \sigma_{med}$, $\sigma_v = \sigma_v - \sigma_{med}$, σ_u and σ_v represent the decentralized variance, for user u and user v reviews, σ_{med} is the median of variance, respectively. The model in the above formula (7) called the Stability_Time_Sim model, STS in brief.

2.3   The Fusion of Two Similarity Models

In the above, we introduced two similarity models, and each has its own advantages, among which the user interest similarity model basing on item popularity can effectively alleviate the problem of item bias, while the similarity model introducing time-sensitive stability of user interest in real-time, digs long tail items, improves the novelty of recommendation system. So, in order to make the recommendation system better, we linear weight the two models and put forward the function Item_Pop_Stability_Time_sim model:

$$Item\_Pop\_Stability\_Time\_Sim = \lambda \times IPS + (1 - \lambda) \times STS \qquad (8)$$

This is IPSTS Model, which comprehensively puts the stability of users, time-sensitive, and item popularity factor etc. into consideration. We synthesize these factors to build a model, and the experiment shows that, the weighted similarity model has a marked improvement in the quality of recommendation.

3   Experiment Design and Result Analysis

3.1   Data

The data set in this experiment is provided by the MovieLens site and developed by the GroupLens team at the University of Minnesota. MovieLens was founded in 1997, a web-based recommendation system. Currently, the site offers three different levels of data sets: 100,000 records of 943 users to 1682 movies; 6040 users to 3900 films ratings of 1 million data; 71567 users to 10,681 films ratings of 10 million data.

This Experiment adopts the first data sets above, in which each user evaluated 20 films at least. The sparsity for this data sets is $1 - 1000000/(943 \times 1682) = 0.937$. In this paper, the data set is divided into training set and test set, among which 80% are the training set, and 20% are test set.

The Evaluation for quality of recommender in this paper is, Mean Absolute Error (MAE) and Root Mean Squared Error (RMSE), respectively [16].

3.2   Experimental Results

Experiment in this paper makes a comparison among the IPSTS model, the Pearson model and the Euclidean model.

IPSTS Model Result. Figure 1 (abscissa is the number of selected neighborsordinate is RMSE) shows the effect of each similarity model on RMSE when selecting different neighbors. The number of neighbors is 10, 20, 30, 40, 50, 60, 70, 80 and 90 respectively. The results showed that the RMSE of IPSTS Model is less than Euclidean Model and Pearson Model (e.g. When the number of neighbors is 20, the RMSE of Model about 6% lower than Pearson Model,

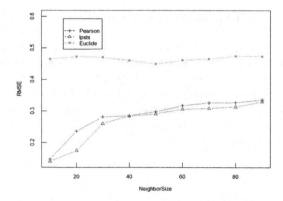

Fig. 1. IPSTS model, pearson model and euclidean model in RMSE comparison

and approximately 30% lower than the Euclide Model). Therefore, the error is reduced and the recommender quality is improved.

Figure 2 (abscissa is the number of selected neighborsordinate is MAE) shows the effect of each similarity model on MAE when selecting different neighbors. The number of neighbors is 55, 60, 65, 70, 75, 80, 85 and 90 respectively. The results showed that the MAE of IPSTS Model is less than Euclidean Model and Pearson Model (e.g. When the number of neighbors is 80, The MAE of IPSTS Model about 1% lower than Pearson Model, and approximately 8% lower than the Euclidean Model). Therefore, the recommender quality is improved, too.

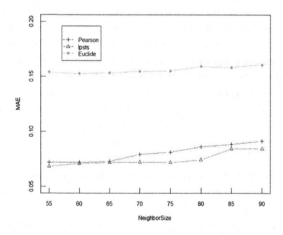

Fig. 2. IPSTS model, pearson model and euclidean model in MAE comparison

The Impact of *IPSTS* Model on Long Tail Items. Figure 3 indicates that these items exhibit long tail phenomenon. Among which the higher the rank of the item ID, the more prevalent and vice versa, Item ID after 1000 are the long tail items. To test the long tail items mining ability of the model, the experiment is as follows: randomly select 3 users (user ID are 80, 800, 888) and make top-5 recommendation for them respectively. Encode for the user ID that needs to be recommended, the recommended list size is 5, and the number of Neighbor is 90. In the Pearson model, the RMSE is 0.33560, and the RMSE is 0.32965 in IPSTS model.

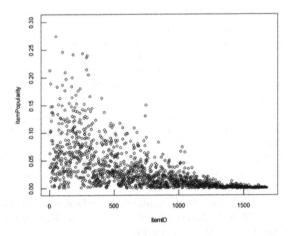

Fig. 3. Diagram for item ID and item popularity

4 Conclusion

Recommendation system is to help user to find useful information that they are interested in big data, then display and recommend to user by appropriate ways, in the situation that they do not have clear requirements. This paper focuses on reducing ratings error and excavating long tail items, alleviating bias of popularity of item and importing stability of interest, at the same time, which also draws the attention of time-sensitive factor thereby, to construct a time-sensitive similarity fusion model of importing interest stability. Experimental data indicates that the model put forward in this paper can dynamically recommend item to users in real-time and improve the recommendation quality simultaneously.

However, user interest can be affected by external factors. With the development of mobile devices and positioning system, which can also be imported into the hybrid model proposed in this paper. Secondly, the fusion model is weighted linearly, and the follow-up study could consider building a non-linear model for recommendation.

Acknowledgements. This research is partially supported by the Chinese National Natural Science Fund (No. 61841602), the Natural Science Foundation of Shandong

Provice (No. ZR2018PF005) and Shandong Province International Cooperation Tri-aning Project for University Teacher. We express our thanks to Dr. Rongju Li who checked our manuscript.

References

1. Anonymous: statistical report on internet development in China. Internet Commun. (7), 54–59 (2015)
2. Resnick, P., Iacovou, N., Suchak, M., et al.: GroupLens: an open architecture for collaborative filtering of netnews. In: Working Paper Series, pp. 175–186 (2015)
3. Liang, X.: Research on key technologies of dynamic recommendation system. Institute of Automation, Chinese Academy of Science, Beijing (2011)
4. Liu, B., Wu, Y., Gong, N.Z., et al.: Structural Analysis of User Choices for Mobile App Recommendation. ACM Transactions on Knowledge Discovery from Data 11(2) (2016). Article No. 17
5. Rashid, A.M., Lam, S.K., Karypis, G., et al.: ClustKNN: a highly scalable hybrid model- memory-based CF algorithm. In: The Workshop on in Proceeding of WebKDD (2006)
6. Elkahky, A.M., Song, Y., He, X.: A multi-view deep learning approach for cross domain user modeling in recommendation systems. In: The International Conference, pp. 278–288 (2015)
7. Wang, H., Wang, N., Yeung, D.Y.: Collaborative deep learning for recommender systems. In: ACM SIGKDD International Conference on Knowledge Discovery and Data Mining, pp. 1235–1244. ACM (2014)
8. Koren, Y.: Factorization meets the neighborhood: a multifaceted collaborative filtering model. In: ACM SIGKDD International Conference on Knowledge Discovery and Data Mining, Las Vegas, Nevada, USA, pp. 426–434 (2008)
9. Kim, D., Yum, B.J.: Collaborative filtering based on iterative principal component analysis. Expert Syst. Appl. Int. J. 28(4), 823–830 (2005)
10. Ahn, H.J.: A new similarity measure for collaborative filtering to alleviate the new user cold-starting problem. Inf. Sci. 178(1), 37–51 (2008)
11. Liu, H., Hu, Z., Mian, A., et al.: A new user similarity model to improve the accuracy of collaborative filtering. Knowl.-Based Syst. 56(3), 156–166 (2014)
12. Li, S., Kawale, J., Fu, Y.: Deep collaborative filtering via marginalized denoising auto-encoder. In: The ACM International, pp. 811–820 (2015)
13. Wu, Y., Dubois, C., Zheng, A.X., et al.: Collaborative denoising auto-encoders for Top-N recommender systems. In: ACM International Conference on Web Search and Data Mining, pp. 153–162. ACM (2016)
14. Vuurens, J.B.P., Larson, M., De Vries, A.P.: Exploring deep space: learning personalized ranking in a semantic space. In: Workshop on Deep Learning for Recommender Systems, pp. 23–28 (2016)
15. Adomavicius, G., Kwon, Y.O.: Improving aggregate recommendation diversity using ranking-based techniques. IEEE Trans. Know. Data Eng. 24(5), 896–911 (2012)
16. Herlocker, J.L.: Evaluating collaborative filtering recommender systems. ACM Trans. Inf. Syst. 22(1), 5–53 (2004)

Cloud-Based Master Data Platform for Smart Manufacturing Process

Lei Ren[1,2(✉)], Ziqiao Zhang[1], Chun Zhao[3], and Guojun Zhang[1]

[1] School of Automation Science and Electrical Engineering, Beihang University, Beijing, China
renlei@buaa.edu.cn
[2] Beijing Advanced Innovation Center for Big Data-Based Precision Medicine,
Beihang University, Beijing, China
[3] School of Computer, Beijing Information Science and Technology University, Beijing, China

Abstract. With the development of technology and application of industrial internet of things, a large amount of data is generated in the research and development (R&D) processes in manufacturing domain, including manufacturing procedures, enterprise management, and product transactions. However, these data usually maintained in different departments, which result in information isolation and data with relations cannot be synchronized. This issue leads to the waste of storage space for redundant data and human resources for coordinating essential information. Aiming these problems, we proposed a cloud-based data management platform architecture to collect and maintain the data from isolated domains and distributed departments. A graph database is employed to store the data emphasizing the relations between entities and Master Data Management is deployed to link the entities cross standalone databases. The efficiency of inspecting, managing and updating information across databases shall be improved by the features of the proposed platform.

Keywords: Cloud manufacturing · Master data management · Graph database

1 Introduction

The appliance of smart manufacturing is rapidly increasing with the development of cyber technology. Concepts such as Industrial Internet of Things, Industry 4.0, Cloud Manufacturing were proposed in the progress of manufacturing industry cyberization. The Cloud manufacturing stressed that resources and capabilities in manufacturing should be transformed into services, which means sharing and communicating between enterprises [1]. Domain ontologies in distributed department should be accumulated to knowledge which is a key role in supporting the cloud manufacturing system. Scheduling and optimizing the production procedure requires the directions of the knowledge which indicates the detail of services in the system.

While cloud platforms were establishing widely in the industry to manage the process of productions and the supply chains, they collect and generate an enormous amount of data then analyze them to optimize the work process separately. Isolations between

© ICST Institute for Computer Sciences, Social Informatics and Telecommunications Engineering 2020
Published by Springer Nature Switzerland AG 2020. All Rights Reserved
X. Zhang et al. (Eds.): CloudComp 2019/SmartGift 2019, LNICST 322, pp. 163–170, 2020.
https://doi.org/10.1007/978-3-030-48513-9_13

systems were widely found within and across enterprises. Therefore, the data sharing and synchronization is a complicated and repeated task. The Master Data Management was proposed to effectively manage the data in the distributed systems. The MDM (Master Data Management) extracts information from existing systems and timely processes them automatically [2]. Data service is provided that integrating information from the standalone databases across the whole enterprise and knowledge can be mined utilizing this service. Furthermore, master data can be expressed by ontologies, and the linkage between master data from different enterprises is exploited by analyzing the extracted ontologies. The manufacturing process can be optimized by the guidance from every segment data in the supply chain.

The graph database is developing and gaining attentions rapidly with the growing scale and complexity of big data. A graph database stores data in the form of nodes, edges, and properties using the graph structure which represents the relations between the data [3]. Therefore, a graph database is suitable for maintaining strongly related data and have major advantages in searching information according to relationships between nodes. In the platform we proposed, a graph database is used in storing descriptions and references of data, for instance, the header of tables, the name of tables and the known relations between tables. The establishment procedure and the evaluation results of the master data model often require efforts of experts. With the data descriptions visualized by the function of the graph database, the master data shall be intuitively operated and evaluated. The items in graph database with relations and references can created a dataset for algorithms to establishing and evaluating the master data automatically.

The platform we proposed integrates a graph database and master data management features. The demanding functions, for example, demonstrating the relations of items, coordinating the changes across systems and removing redundant information is also provided.

2   Related Work

The solutions we presented is designed to resolve the data management issues in manufacturing process. The key components and technologies involved in our solutions were continuously studied and developed in recent years.

2.1   Cloud Manufacturing

Cloud manufacturing paradigm utilized technologies to provide manufacturing services with the support of knowledge containing the information to integrate the whole life cycle of products [1]. The knowledge base and data management function are essential parts of cloud manufacturing systems accordingly. Domain experts were often acquired for knowledge editing and knowledge could be generated by data mining as well [4]. A knowledge cloud architecture was presented [5] using big data collected in the manufacturing process to provide support for enterprise manufacturing cloud.

2.2 Master Data Management

The researches on MDM is growing for the actual need created by the developing of big data in varies of fields. A knowledge-based machine scheduling is proposed considering the uncertainties in master data [6]. This approach used a knowledge-based system to provide previously actual data and scheduling parameters is provisioned accordingly. A master data exchange service architecture is presented [7]. An API to manage the messages of master data and algorithms to measure the data quality is also presented in this paper. A data cleaning system which can identifies incorrect data and generates possible repairs were proposed [8]. This system utilizes the knowledge-base and crowdsourcing to identify the data.

2.3 Graph Database

Graph database is tented to be more efficient when storing and processing data with complex relationships. Considering ontology as a large graph, a graph database-oriented approach is proposed [9]. The storing and querying operations on ontologies is claimed to be more efficient and scalable. Data generated by wireless multimedia sensor network can also be stored on the graph database [10]. The experiment showed graph database performs better than relational database in querying the big data related to internet of things. A common information model-oriented graph database was also proposed [11]. Graph database was outperformed relational database again in the multiple test case.

2.4 Summary

These studies indicated that graph database is an effective approach for managing big data with complex relationships, and MDM provides valid method to manage related data in different systems. The approach we proposed utilized these two technologies and aim to provide support in data and knowledge management process in the cloud manufacturing system.

3 Architecture

The functions of cloud-based master data platform are collecting and managing data from distributed database. The data in varies of forms collected were preprocessed and stored in graph database establishing the relations according to the origin data relations. Master data of distinguished departments is generated by the descriptions in the graph database. The master data of different source can be described in ontology form, which enables further analyses and integration. The integrated master data represent the knowledge in this field which included multiple distributed enterprises. Relations between entities in this procedure can be created in the graph database accordingly. The data management can be performed across the isolated databases and coordination of data modification will be an automated and immediate operation.

To realize the functions in the platform, the architecture is depicted in Fig. 1. The cloud-based master data platform can be divided into 4 layers as the data is processed

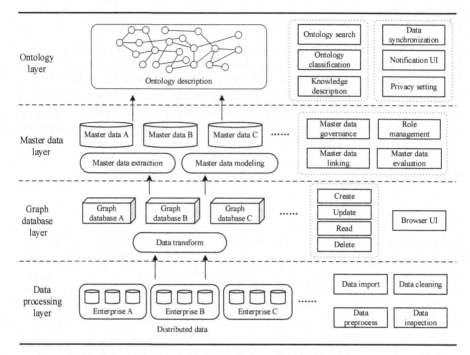

Fig. 1. Architecture of master data platform

and transformed, which are data processing, graph database, master data and ontology description.

The data processing layer collects and preprocesses the data in the disturbed source of original data. The information is described by different form and standard in the systems. A uniformed description of information is generated in this layer from relational databases, tables or raw string files.

A graph database platform is included in the platform. The uniformed data provided by the data processing layer is imported and maintained in the graph databases where data in different enterprises are still stored separately. Typical CURD functions of database are provided as well as the APIs tent to export data to the master data layer and receive update request when data need to be changed in multiple related data source.

The master data layer establishes multiple master database for each graph database which corresponding to the data source. MDM functions are provided to maintain the collected manufacturing data, and the key information are provided to the ontology layer.

The relations between data from different enterprises were established in the ontology layer. Ontologies are constructed by the key information by domain experts or algorithms. Connections revealed in the ontologies are provided for the graph database to update the data relations between isolated databases.

4 Key Techniques

The function of master data platform is to manage the data distributed in different systems. The data is collected, processed and their relations are analyzed in the platform, the procedure can be divided into 4 parts according to the 4 layers described in Sect. 3. Each layer has configuration panels for operators and users to manage the data processing procedures and interfaces are also provided for the data managing.

4.1 Data Processing Layer

In data processing layer, data from different enterprises were accumulated. These data have different sources thus they have diverse formats as well.

Data import functions are provided for users to configure which data were to submitted and what type of data they are submitting. Relational databases from manufacturing systems, information tables from internal management software as well as the raw data files generated by the production equipment is supported to be contained in the platform. The key data describe the structure of data is only needed to be stored in the platform for analyzing and managing. Data processed by the platform also maintained in the platform to insure the accessibility.

The data in different forms are collected, thus the data preprocess techniques is required to uniform the data in more flexible method rather than simple storing. The raw data generated in the equipment is varied and complicated, thus this function is required in this layer. For example, features should be extracted from time sequence data and items with wrong or missing features should be excluded from normal data. Standards like metrics and date forms should be unified in tables or databases.

Data inspection and rectification function are essential in this layer. Users can view the data that imported in the platform and check if there are mistakes in the import and preprocess procedures. The change of items in graph database is simple when the rectification is only performed to data items, while the modification for the structure of databases needs every layer to reconstruct the data involved.

4.2 Graph Database Layer

A graph database platform is maintained in the platform, and the key data processed and provided in the data processing layer were reorganized by their relations to support further analyses.

The key function of the graph database layer is importing and transforming the data from the data processing layer. The data stored in relational database can be described as table which is the most common form. These structural data can be described by the relations between each item using the header of table. The key or the major item of a row in the table can be described in nodes and the other items can be the attribute or another node with relations depend on its value.

Basic CURD function is provided by the graph database. The graph database performs better in search items according to the relations between nodes. Thus, the proper relations in the graph database is vital for the platform to operate correctly. In conversion, simple rules are applied for the automation process. The corrections of errors can be fixed by the manual updates. Update function is also required when the original data were modified.

A browser UI demonstrating the data in graph database is intuitive and simple method to inspect and rectify the items in the database. The CURD functions are integrated in the web UI and the items in database is presented by figures. Relations between nodes can be easily read by users through lines between entities and filtering irrelevant nodes.

4.3   Master Data Layer

In the master data layer, master data in each graph database is extracted and identified, and the master data management technique is available for users. The master data are marked and stored in graph database rather than a standalone database.

Master database establish function is essential for data management using master data. Key entities like customers, equipment ID or products is commonly selected to be the master data [2]. The data in the graph database is collected from multiple systems in one enterprise, so the same entity as master data may be showed up multiple times. Thus, though rule-based filter can be deployed in the platform, domain experts are often needed to extract master data and build master data models. Master database is established for each enterprise and maintained separately.

Master data management functions is supported in the master database layer. Operators in enterprise can utilize the benefit provided by the master data. Data reference is built between master data and items in the graph database which is another reference to the original data in disturbed systems. The graph database in the middle provide a unified and efficient tool to conduct the manage process to the data. MDM can match the information in multiple databases and merge them to provide detailed information. The modification of master data can be applied to all sources and applications across the databases. Historical records of audition trail data are also supported in the platform.

4.4   Ontology Layer

After master data is extracted and identified in the master data layer, each enterprise can manage their data more efficiently. While the master data across the enterprises still need to be identified and integrated, ontology is constructed to analyze the relations of master data. Interfaces are provided to manage the knowledge from the ontology and coordinate the change of data.

Ontology construction from the master data is a necessitate function for analyzing the relations between data from different enterprises. Domain experts are usually required to participate in the establishment procedures, because identifying and integrating master data in distributed enterprises needs practical experiences. Semi-automatic acquisition methods can be adopted to assist the construction procedure with template-based, rule-based ontology generation methods or machine learning algorithms if adequate amount of data is collected and validated.

The constructed ontology describes knowledge and provides support for building semantics, which means the data in distributed enterprises is linked and described in form of knowledge. The domain knowledges described by ontologies make data management, knowledge search, entity match, ontology fusion and other services is available for users. Integrating data across various sources and inspecting information related to the key data from other sources can significantly improve the quality of data and usability of data management.

With the linkages between nodes in all graph database are established by the knowledges described in ontology, the coordination of data changes between different enterprises is an addition function when users manage their own data. The request of changing data in other database of different enterprises can be pushed, and operators for corresponding database will get the notification and inspect the relevant data. This function is suitable for manufacturing enterprises exchanging their information.

5   Conclusion

By the establishment of the cloud-based master data platform, the manufacturing enterprises can manage their data efficiently for the benefits of exploiting the data relations between distributed databases. With the applications of graph database, master data management, and ontology analyses, the knowledge of the manufacturing domain is extracted and expressed. On this basis, several services are provided to support information integrating, exchanging and updating process in the cloud manufacturing systems.

In the future, researches will be focused on the algorithms to process data automatically. The procedure of extracting and evaluating master data, constructing ontology relies on domain experts to operate. With enough concrete data collected, a machine learning model can be trained and applied on the procedures to reduce consumption of manpower. Besides, the method to effectively utilize knowledge of linkage between data in the smart manufacturing system is another topic need further studies.

Acknowledgment. The research is supported by The National Key Research and Development Program of China No. 2018YFB1004001, and the NSFC (National Science Foundation of China) project No. 61572057 and 61836001.

References

1. Zhang, L.: A new manufacturing paradigm. Enterp. Inf. Syst. **8**(2), 167–187 (2014)
2. Loshin, D.: Master Data Management. Morgan Kaufmann, Burlington (2010)
3. Ron, H.: Combining computational models, semantic annotations and simulation experiments in a graph database. Database **2015** (2015). Article ID BAU130
4. Ren, L.: Cloud manufacturing: from concept to practice. Enterp. Inf. Syst. **9**(2), 186–209 (2015)
5. Chun, Z., Ren, L.: Study on a knowledge-based master data management method for manufacturing big data. In: CIE48, vol. 353, pp. 1–6 (2018)
6. Geiger, F.: Knowledge-based machine scheduling under consideration of uncertainties in master data. Prod. Eng. Res. Devel. **10**(2), 197–207 (2016)
7. Rivas, B.: Towards a service architecture for master data exchange based on ISO 8000 with support to process large datasets. Comput. Stand. Interfaces **54**, 94–104 (2017)

8. Chu, X., Morcos, J.: Katara: a data cleaning system powered by knowledge bases and crowdsourcing. In: Proceedings of the 2015 ACM SIGMOD International Conference on Management of Data. ACM, pp. 1247–1261(2015)
9. Elbattah, M., Roushdy, M.: Large-scale ontology storage and query using graph database-oriented approach: the case of freebase. In: 2015 IEEE Seventh International Conference on Intelligent Computing and Information Systems (ICICIS), pp. 39–43. IEEE (2015)
10. Küçükkeçeci, C.: Big data model simulation on a graph database for surveillance in wireless multimedia sensor networks. Big Data Res. **11**, 33–43 (2018)
11. Ravikumar, G., Khaparde, S.A.: CIM oriented graph database for network topology processing and applications integration. In: 2015 50th International Universities Power Engineering Conference (UPEC), pp. 1–7. IEEE (2015)

A Semi-supervised Classification Method for Hyperspectral Images by Triple Classifiers with Data Editing and Deep Learning

Guoming Zhang[1,2], Junshu Wang[3,4], Ge Shi[3,4], Jie Zhang[1], and Wanchun Dou[1(✉)]

[1] State Key Laboratory for Novel Software Technology, Nanjing University, Nanjing, China
kelvinzhang@smail.nju.edu.cn, njujiezhang@gmail.com,
douwc@nju.edu.cn
[2] Health Statistics and Information Center of Jiangsu Province, Nanjing, China
[3] Key Laboratory for Virtual Geographic Environment, Ministry of Education,
Nanjing Normal University, Nanjing, China
jlsdwjs@126.com
[4] Jiangsu Center for Collaborative Innovation in Geographical Information Resource
Development and Application, Nanjing, China

Abstract. A semi-supervised classification method for hyperspectral remote sensing images based on convolutional neural network (CNN) and modified tri-training is proposed. The abstract features are captured by training a CNN model with the pixels' vectors as inputs. Based on the extracted high-level features, different classifiers will perform different outputs under the same training set, due to the different types of classifiers take on diverse characteristics. Thus, taking multiple classifiers' results into consideration can integrate different prediction labels synthetically from a high level and can perform more credible results. At the meantime, the number of training samples of hyperspectral images is limited, which will hinder the classification effect. Illuminated by tri-training algorithm, we utilize triple different classifiers to classify the hyperspectral images based on the extracted high-level features in the semi-supervised mode. By utilizing triple classifiers jointly to train and update the training samples set when the number of labeled samples is limited. At the meantime, we pick the confident samples via randomize and majority vote into the training set for data editing during the iterative updating process. Experiments performed on two real hyperspectral images reveal that our method performs very well in terms of classification accuracy and effect.

Keywords: Deep learning · Hyperspectral images (HSI) classification · Tri-training · Data editing

1 Introduction

With the development of imaging spectrometry technology, hyperspectral remote sensing application achieves more and more attention, due to the enormous ability of describing the detailed land covers, such as precision agriculture, anomaly detection, mineral

X. Zhang et al. (Eds.): CloudComp 2019/SmartGift 2019, LNICST 322, pp. 171–183, 2020.
https://doi.org/10.1007/978-3-030-48513-9_14

resources, etc. For the hyperspectral remote sensing images, the goal of classification is to assign each pixel with a unique type of land cover label.

Actually, the high dimensional hyperspectral data always lead to some challenging problems, such as Hughes phenomenon. The unbalance between the number of labeled samples and the spectral dimensionality always decades the classification. Feature extraction (FE) is an effect way to tackle this ill-posed problem. Before 2013, the available FE [1, 2] and diversifying methods were generally designed for the shallow models. Lots of popular shallow learning models and algorithms have been developed in hyperspectral images area and achieved great success, such as Bayes [3], SVM [4], conditional random fields [5] and multinomial logistic regression [6]. The shallow expression method needs to rely on the prior knowledge of remote sensing professionals and mainly relies on the manual design features, which is sensitive to parameters and only a few parameters are usually allowed. Meanwhile, affected by external conditions such as the imaging process, the image quality will be greatly different, so the rules of feature extraction/selection should be formulated according to the image's characteristics. Therefore, most feature extraction/selection methods have the problem of poor generalization. Usually, the shallow models is effective to the linear data, but their ability to deal with the nonlinear data, take the hyperspectral images for example, is limited.

High-level representation and classification by deep learning can avoid the complexity of manual design features and automatically learn high-level representation of data through increasing network layers, which brings new development opportunities for hyperspectral image classification. In this work, we propose a semi-supervised classification framework based on abstract features extracted by CNN. The key idea of the semi-supervised model integrates the modified tri-training algorithm and the data editing strategy, to explore the information gain and positive effect among classifiers on the classification task. Since the performance of different classifiers on the same feature is various, our proposed approach, could improve the final classification results by integrating their predicted results.

The rest of this paper is arranged as follows. Section 2 reviews the previous related work. Section 3 depicts the preliminary, and develops the proposed method named DMTri-training, which modified Tri-training with data editing, based on the features extracted by CNN. Section 4 evaluates the proposed method over two real-world hyperspectral images. Finally, Sect. 5 summarizes our study.

2 Related Work

In hyperspectral images application, deep learning methods plays an important role. Stack autoencoder [7] and sparse-constrained autoencoder [8] and deep belief network [9] have been applied to the processing of hyperspectral images. In order to solve the problem that automatic encoders and deep belief networks cannot directly extract spatial features, the advantages of convolutional neural network in extracting image features are utilized to extract spectral features through 1-dimensional CNN and 2-dimensional CNN to extract spatial features [10]. The combination of CNN and other shallow models, such as CRF [5], sparse dictionary learning [11], transfer strategy [12] have been successfully used to provide more comprehensive spectral and spatial information for classification to obtain better classification results.

Semi-supervised sparse expression [13], semi-supervised logistic regression [14], semi-supervised support vector machine (SVM) [15], graph-based method [16], generative model [17], EM [18] and divergence-based method [19] have been well applied in hyperspectral images. Divergence-based methods utilize multiple learners to predict samples and select unlabeled samples from the predicted results of multiple classifiers to assist the classification process. When the number of learners is single, it is self-training learning [20]. When the number of classifiers is two, it is the classic co-training algorithm [21]. When the number of learners is 3, it is the famous tri-training learner [22]. In this work, we take 1-dimensional CNN for consideration and treat each pixel as a spectral vector to extract abstract features. We modified the tri-training algorithm to adjust the hyperspectral data, and introduce data editing and majority voting at the process of adding new samples into the training set at each iteration, which improves the classification results compared with other methods.

3 Methods

3.1 Preliminary

Hyperspectral remote sensing image integrates the spectrum standing for the radiance of the land cover with images on behalf of the spatial and geometric relationships. Usually, a hyperspectral image can be taken as a data cube, $X \in \mathbb{R}^{m \times n \times L}$, where m, n and L denote the number of samples (width), lines (height) and bands (depth) of the HSI respectively. Generally, there are hundreds of bands in the hyperspectral images, that is, the spectral resolution of is very high, which make it possible to describe the land cover in detail. In order to facilitate the following processing for HSI images, the image cubes are often transformed into 2D matrices, $X \in \mathbb{R}^{mn \times L}$. The column L denotes the number of samples in total of the image, and the row mn represents the radiance of each pixel. Feature extraction or representation can remove the redundant data and perform a better representation, at the meantime, reduce the data dimension. In this work, we take a CNN model to learn the high-level feature representation of HSI. Thus, the 2D data, $X \in \mathbb{R}^{mn \times L}$ can be simplified into another formula, $X \in \mathbb{R}^{mn \times d}, d < T$. In a HSI classification task, given the training data set $T \in \mathbb{R}^{mn \times d}$ and the corresponding labels set $y \in \{y_1, \ldots, y_m\}, m \in (1, \ldots, C)$, C is the number of categories. The goal of classification is to assign a class label to each sample in the hyperspectral image.

3.2 Feature Extraction Based on CNN

CNN is a kind of feedforward neural networks, it includes input layer, convolution layer, pooling layer and full connection layer. The CNN structure is shown in Fig. 1.

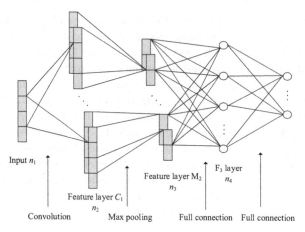

Input n_1

Feature layer M_2
n_3

F_3 layer
n_4

Feature layer C_1
n_2

Convolution   Max pooling   Full connection   Full connection

Fig. 1. CNN network structure.

As for hyperspectral images, each pixel can be regarded as a two-dimensional image with the size of $1 \times n_1$, which serves as input layer of the network, and n_1 is the number of spectral bands. The size of the input layer is $(n_1,1)$. Suppose the convolution layer C_1 contains twenty kernels with size of $k_1 \times 1$. After the convolution operation on the input data by layer C_1, we can obtain $20 \times n_2 \times 1$ nodes, where $n_2 = n_1\text{-}k_1 + 1$. The kernel size of the maximum pool layer M_2 is $(k_2,1)$, and the M_2 layer contains $20 \times n_3 \times 1$ nodes, where $n_3 = n_2/k_2$. Full link layer F_3 has n_4 nodes, which is the number of extracted features. The output layer has n_5 nodes, which is the number of categories of data to be classified. In this work, we only utilize the training samples to construct CNN feature extraction model. Each hidden layer h_i is multiplied by the input node V and the weight W, and the neuron nodes in each layer share the weight W, which reduces the complexity of network parameter number and parameter selection. In most cases, training samples are randomly selected, and it is generally assumed that training samples have the same feature distribution as test samples. In our work, we take the *relu* function as the activation function of CNN model, and some neurons are randomly discarded by Dropout to prevent overfitting.

3.3 DMTri-Training Algorithm

During the iterative learning process, the semi-supervised classification algorithm usually needs to evaluate the predicted confidence of unlabeled samples, which is always time consuming. Whereas tri-training omits this process, which eliminates the computational complexity to some extent and gives the final prediction via majority voting from the classifiers. Based on the characteristics of hyperspectral image data, we proposes the DMTri-training algorithm, which improves the tri-training algorithm as follows:

1) Tri-training utilizes a single supervised learning algorithm, and the diversity of the initial three classifiers is obtained by training the labeled data via bootstrap sampling from the pool of original labeled samples set. Whereas, DMTri-training trains three

different supervised learning algorithms based on the same data sets generated via randomized sampling from the original labeled samples set.

2) DMTri-training takes the predicted results of labeled and unlabeled samples into account synthetically. Then computes the classification error rate of labeled samples err_1 and the inconsistent predicted results between two classifiers to the total sample in unlabeled sample set err_2. The total error rate err is calculated as follows: $err = $ ERR_WEIGHT$*err_1 + $ (1-ERR_WEIGHT)$*err_2$.

3) l_i' is the number of new labeled samples added into training set at i-th iteration. In tri-training algorithm, l_i' is very small, that is, the new added training samples are limited at the first time. The predicted error rate of labeled samples maybe do not meet the condition $e_i < e_i'$, which will result in the semi-supervised process cannot continue and a low classification accuracy result. Our algorithm verified the initial value of l_i' to $(|L_i| * e_i)/e_i' + 1$, in order to satisfy the iterative condition and increase more samples at each iteration.

4) When adding new samples into training set, we utilize randomization and data editing strategy, and integrate the samples predicted by the three classifiers to filtrate the misclassified ones. The rules are as follows: first, we adopt random sampling strategy to pick some labeled samples into training set, which can reduce the quantity of training samples and speed up the learning process. Meanwhile, the random sampling ensure more information gain. Second, these samples are filtrated by data editing. According to the rules of neighborhood consistency, if the two classifiers, take h_1 and h_2 as example, do not consider the sample i need to be filtrated, which means i is a high confident sample. Then sample i should be put into the classifier h_3, otherwise the sample i will be removed as a noisy example.

5) If one sample's labels predicted by the three classifiers are not consistent with each other, this sample always brings high information gain, and should be added into training set after manual correction.

6) Furthermore, we take secondary data editing during the training process. After each iteration, rectify the mislabeled samples automatically by nearest neighbor voting rule, then execute data editing to obtain high confident samples, and put them into the training set for next iteration and prediction.

L denotes the initial training set. In each iteration, the classifiers h_1 and h_2 select some samples and predict their labels, then put them into the training set of classifier h_3. L^{t-1} and L^t represent the new added labeled samples into classifier h_3 at the $(t-1)$-th and t-th iteration respectively, the corresponding training set of h_3 is $L \cup L^{t-1}$ and $L \cup L^t$. η_L denotes the classification error rate of the training set L, and the number of misclassified samples is $\eta_L |L|$. e_1^t represents the upper bound of classification error rate at t-th iteration. Suppose that the number of consistent samples predicted by h_1 and h_2 is z, in which the number of samples with correct predicted labels is z', then we can infer $e_1^t = (z - z')/z$. The number of mislabeled samples in set L^t is $e_1^t |L^t|$. At the t-th iteration, the error classification rate is:

$$\eta^t = \frac{\eta_L |L| + e_1^t |L^t|}{|L \cup L^t|} \tag{1}$$

4   Experimental Results and Comparisons

4.1   Data Set

a. Indian Pines

Indian Pines located in northwest Indiana, the data was acquired by an airborne visible/infrared imaging spectrometer (AVIRIS) in 1992. The wavelength range from 0.4–2.5 μm, 220 bands in total, each pixel (with 145 × 145 pixels) has 30 m spatial resolution. After removing bad bands and water absorption band, 200 bands were available for experiment. Figure 2 (a) shows the RGB image of the Indian Pines, with red, green and blue bands of 70, 45 and 9 respectively. Figure 2 (b) is the corresponding ground truth map, with 10,249 samples from 16 different categories of land cover.

b. Pavia University

Pavia University located in Pavia, Italy, the data was acquired by ROSIS sensor. The spectral range from 0.43 to 0.86 μm, and 115 bands in total, each pixel (with 610 × 340 pixels) has 1.3 m spatial resolution. After removing 12 bad bands, 103 bands were

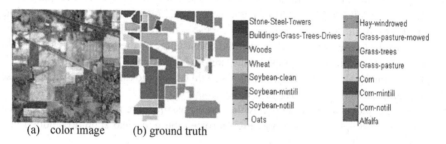

(a)   color image   (b) ground truth

Fig. 2. Indian Pines data and ground truth.

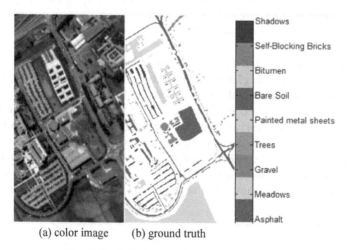

(a) color image   (b) ground truth

Fig. 3. Pavia University data and ground truth.

available. Figure 3(a) shows the RGB image of Pavia University, with red, green and blue bands of 170, 95 and 9 respectively. Figure 3(b) is the corresponding ground truth map, with a total of 42776 samples from 9 different categories of land cover.

4.2 Experimental Analysis for Feature Extraction Based on CNN

In the feature extraction experiment, the size of input samples is $1 \times n_1$, where n_1 is the number of bands. The CNN architecture consists of five layers, as listed in Sect. 3.

From the experimental results in Table 1 and Table 2, we can see that the classification accuracy based on CNN with only 20 features performs best compared with PCA, LDA feature extraction methods and raw data. At the meantime, the classification accuracy generally presents a linear increase trend with the increase of the number of features, as shown in Fig. 4. Feature extraction based on deep network is more consistent with the characteristics of hierarchical abstraction and layer-by-layer cognition of human vision, and performs better class discrimination. Experimental results in this section demonstrate that the features extracted by CNN can be used for the classification task, and the obtained classification results are competitive with other shallow models.

Table 1. Overall classification accuracy based on different FE methods of Indian Pines

OA (%)	SVM	GBM	RF
PCA/(30 D)	72.34	71.71	70.65
LDA/(15 D)	83.6	76.45	76.74
Raw/(200 D)	78.12	74.28	75.35
CNN/(20 D)	82.54	73.16	80.00
CNN/(30 D)	**83.73**	**79.97**	**81.95**

Table 2. Overall classification accuracy based on different FE methods of Pavia University

OA (%)	SVM	GBM	RF
PCA/(30 D)	85.21	82.82	79.38
LDA/(8 D)	86.95	87.36	87.36
Raw/(103 D)	89.77	81.89	82.21
CNN/(20 D)	89.91	86.89	89.12
CNN/(30 D)	**90.19**	**87.76**	**89.17**

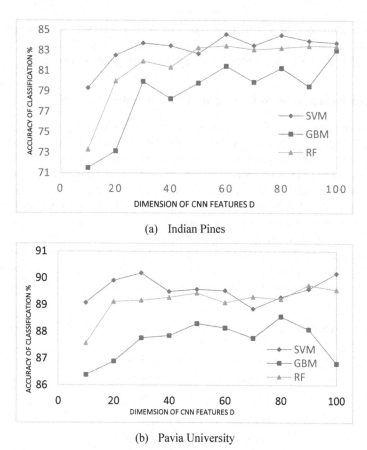

(a)　Indian Pines

(b)　Pavia University

Fig. 4. The relationship between the classification accuracy of CNN feature extraction and the feature dimension (D) for Indian Pines and Pavia University data

4.3　DMTri-Trainning Experimental Results

In order to verify the classification accuracy of the proposed method, we compared and analyzed the results of three classifiers, SVM, GBM and RF, which are taken as initial three classification models in DMTri-training algorithm. As for Indian pines data, we select randomly 1000 samples as training set, the rest of samples as test set. As for Pavia University data, we select randomly 500 samples as training samples and the remaining 42276 samples as test set.

Table 3. The classification accuracy of different classifiers of Indian Pines data

Category	SVM	GBM	RF	DMTri-training
Alfalfa	76.09	52.17	47.83	42.50
Corn-notill	80.46	81.79	82.98	90.27
Corn-mintill	78.31	70.48	72.89	93.72
Corn	65.40	46.84	46.41	97.86
Grass-pasture	88.82	87.58	87.78	98.96
Grass-trees	97.67	96.44	98.08	100.00
Grass-pasture-mowed	89.29	67.86	50.00	100.00
Hay-windrowed	98.95	98.33	99.79	100.00
Oats	55.00	15.00	25.00	30.77
Soybean-notill	79.12	72.12	74.07	89.44
Soybean-mintill	82.97	84.81	83.75	98.61
Soybean-clean	80.61	78.75	80.78	100.00
Wheat	96.10	85.37	90.24	100.00
Woods	95.34	95.49	96.68	100.00
Buildings-Grass-Trees-Drives	62.18	60.88	63.21	83.38
Stone-Steel-Towers	93.55	97.85	97.85	100.00
OA(%)	84.44	82.60	83.48	**95.79**
κ	0.82	**0.80**	0.81	0.94

In Table 3 and Table 4, we list the overall classification accuracy and class-specific classification accuracy corresponding to different algorithms based on CNN features for the two data sets. As for Indian Pines data, the overall accuracy is 84.44%, 82.60% and

Table 4. The classification accuracy of different classifiers of Pavia University data

Category	SVM	GBM	RF	DMTri-training
Asphalt	88.10	91.39	92.50	90.09
Meadows	95.57	96.44	96.37	99.68
Gravel	75.04	67.46	70.75	83.09
Trees	88.87	93.93	93.60	97.88
Painted metal sheet	99.18	99.33	99.26	100.00
Bare Soil	89.56	86.90	88.27	98.13
Bitumen	80.83	71.13	75.11	99.62
Self-Blocking Bricks	84.90	85.36	86.56	97.85
Shadows	99.79	99.58	99.89	100.00
OA(%)	91.05	91.36	92.03	**96.93**
κ	0.89	0.90	0.91	**0.97**

83.48% based on SVM, GBM and RF classifier. The corresponding kappa coefficient is 0.82, 0.80 and 0.81. The overall accuracy and kappa coefficient of DMTri-training is 95.79% and 0.94 respectively, improve 11.35% and 12.2% respectively compared to SVM classification, the best results among the three classifiers. Four classification maps are illustrated in Fig. 5. As for Pavia University data set, we can see that RF classification accuracy is the highest one. The overall classification accuracy is 91.05%, 91.36% and 92.03% based on SVM, GBM and RF respectively, and the corresponding kappa coefficients are 0.89, 0.90 and 0.91. The classification accuracy of DMTri-training algorithm is 96.93%, and the kappa coefficient is 0.97. Compared with the best RF classification result, the overall accuracy is improved by 4.9%, and the kappa coefficient is improved by 6.38%. The classification maps of different classification methods are listed in Fig. 6.

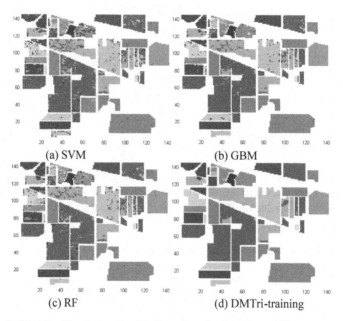

(a) SVM   (b) GBM

(c) RF   (d) DMTri-training

Fig. 5. The classification maps of Indian pines data based on different classifiers.

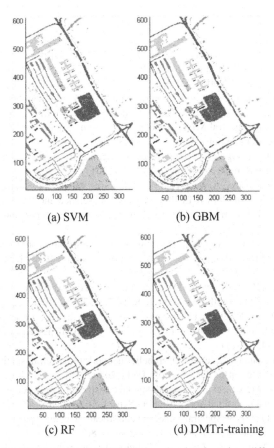

(a) SVM   (b) GBM

(c) RF   (d) DMTri-training

Fig. 6. The classification maps of Pavia University data based on different classifiers

5 Conclusion

In this paper, we proposed a semi-supervised classification method named DMTri-training for hyperspectral images classification. The proposed framework is composed of two parts, the abstracted feature exaction are based on CNN model and DMTri-training classification is based on modified tri-training algorithm and data editing. The experimental results show that our method can perform better classification results.

Acknowledgement. This work is supported in part by the National Science Foundation of China under Grant No. 61672276, the National Key Research and Development Program of China under Grant No. 2017YFB1400600, Jiangsu Natural Science Foundation of China under Grant No. BK20171037, the Program of Natural Science Research of Jiangsu colleges and universities under Grant No.17KJB170010, and the Collaborative Innovation Center of Novel Software Technology and Industrialization, Nanjing University.

References

1. Ji, S., Ye, J.: Generalized linear discriminant analysis: a unified framework and efficient model selection. IEEE Trans. Neural Networks **19**(10), 1768–1782 (2008)
2. Fejjari, A., Ettabaa, K.S., Korbaa, O.: Fast spatial spectral Schroedinger Eigenmaps algorithm for hyperspectral feature extraction. Procedia Comput. Sci. **126**, 656–664 (2018)
3. Fang, Y., Xu, L., Peng, J., et al.: Unsupervised Bayesian Classification of a Hyperspectral Image Based on the Spectral Mixture Model and Markov Random Field. IEEE J. Sel. Top. Appl. Earth Obs. Remote Sens. **11**(9), 3325–3337 (2018)
4. Mountrakis, G., Im, J., Ogole, C.: Support vector machines in remote sensing: a review. ISPRS J. Photogrammetry Remote Sens. **66**(3), 247–259 (2011)
5. Alam, F.I., Zhou, J., Liew, A.W.C., et al.: CRF learning with CNN features for hyperspectral image segmentation. In: 36th IEEE International Geoscience and Remote Sensing Symposium, pp. 6890–6893. Institute of Electrical and Electronics Engineers Inc, Piscataway, USA (2016)
6. Qian, Y., Ye, M., Zhou, J.: Hyperspectral image classification based on structured sparse logistic regression and three-dimensional wavelet texture features. IEEE Trans. Geosci. Remote Sens. **51**(4), 2276–2291 (2013)
7. Chen, Y., Lin, Z., Zhao, X., et al.: Deep learning-based classification of hyperspectral data. IEEE J. Sel. Top. Appl. Earth Obs. Remote Sens. **7**(6), 2094–2107 (2014)
8. Tao, C., Pan, H., Li, Y., et al.: Unsupervised spectral–spatial feature learning with stacked sparse autoencoder for hyperspectral imagery classification. IEEE Geosci. Remote Sens. Lett. **12**(12), 2438–2442 (2015)
9. Li, C., Wang, Y., Zhang, X., et al.: Deep belief network for spectral–spatial classification of hyperspectral remote sensor data. Sensors **19**(1), 204 (2019)
10. Yue, J., Zhao, W., Mao, S., et al.: Spectral–spatial classification of hyperspectral images using deep convolutional neural networks. Remote Sens. Lett. **6**(6), 468–477 (2015)
11. Liang, H., Li, Q.: Hyperspectral imagery classification using sparse representations of convolutional neural network features. Remote Sens. **8**(2), 99 (2016)
12. Yang, J., Zhao, Y.Q., Chan, J.C.W.: Learning and transferring deep joint spectral–spatial features for hyperspectral classification. IEEE Trans. Geosci. Remote Sens. **55**(8), 4729–4742 (2017)
13. Li, J., Huang, X., Zhang, L.: Semi-supervised sparse relearning representation classification for high-resolution remote sensing imagery. In: 36th IEEE International Geoscience and Remote Sensing Symposium, pp. 2618–2621. Institute of Electrical and Electronics Engineers Inc, Piscataway, USA (2016)
14. Erkan, A.N., Camps-Valls, G., Altun, Y.: Semi-supervised remote sensing image classification via maximum entropy. In: IEEE International Workshop on Machine Learning for Signal Processing pp. 313–318. IEEE Computer Society, Washington DC, USA. (2010)
15. Yang, L., Yang, S., Jin, P., et al.: Semi-supervised hyperspectral image classification using spatio-spectral Laplacian support vector machine. IEEE Geosci. Remote Sens. Lett. **11**(3), 651–655 (2014)
16. Camps-Valls, G., Marsheva, T.V.B., Zhou, D.: Semi-supervised graph-based hyperspectral image classification. IEEE Trans. Geosci. Remote Sens. **45**(10), 3044–3054 (2007)
17. Ren, G., Zhang, J., Ma, Y., et al.: Generative model based semi-supervised learning method of remote sensing image classification. J. Remote Sens. **6**, 1090–1104 (2010)
18. Prabukumar, M., Shrutika, S.: Band clustering using expectation–maximization algorithm and weighted average fusion-based feature extraction for hyperspectral image classification. J. Appl. Remote Sens. **12**(4), 046015 (2018)

19. Zhou, Z.: Disagreement-based semi-supervised learning. ACTA AUTOMATICA SINICA **39**(11), 1871–1878 (2013)
20. Aydav, P.S.S., Minz, S.: Granulation-based self-training for the semi-supervised classification of remote-sensing images. Granul. Comput. 1–19(2019)
21. Samiappan, S., Moorhead, R.J.: Semi-supervised co-training and active learning framework for hyperspectral image classification. In: 35th IEEE International Geoscience and Remote Sensing Symposium, pp. 401–404. Institute of Electrical and Electronics Engineers Inc, Milan, Italy (2015)
22. Ou, D., Tan, K., Du, Q., et al.: A novel tri-training technique for the semi-supervised classification of hyperspectral images based on regularized local discriminant embedding feature extraction. Remote Sens. **11**(6), 654 (2019)

A Survey of Image Super Resolution Based on CNN

Qianxiong Xu and Yu Zheng[✉]

School of Computer and Software, Jiangsu Engineering Center of Network Monitoring, Nanjing University of Information Science and Technology, Nanjing 210044, Jiangsu, China
yzheng@nuist.edu.cn

Abstract. With the advent of the information age in contemporary society, images are everywhere, no matter in military use or in daily life. Therefore, as a medium for people to obtain information, images have become more and more important. With the fast development of deep convolution neural networks (DCNNs), Single-Image Super-Resolution (SISR) becomes one of the techniques that have made great breakthroughs in recent years. In this paper, we give a brief survey on the task of SISR. In general, we introduce the SR problem, some recent SR methods, public benchmark datasets and evaluation metrics. Finally, we conclude by denoting some points that could be further improved in the future.

Keywords: Single-image · Super-resolution · Deep learning · DCNNs

1 Introduction

As vital image processing class of image processing techniques in image processing and computer vision, Single-Image Super-Resolution (SISR), whose basic goal is to recover high-resolution (HR) images from low-resolution (LR) images, plays an important role in our daily lives. It could be applied to various types of applications, for example, surveillance and security [1–3], video noise removing, medical [4–6] and etc. Besides, it could provide help to other computer vision tasks, because we could make a better dataset with higher quality images. Generally speaking, SISR is quite challenging for there is a one-to-many mapping between the LR images and HR images.

As deep convolution neural networks (DCNNs) appear to be able to handle tasks related to images well, super-resolution (SR) models that based on deep network architectures have been explored and often result in the state-of-the-art (sota) performance on various benchmarks. Date back to 2014, Dong et al. [7, 8] first introduced their model of SRCNN which combined Convolutional Neural Networks (CNN) with the task of SISR and made a huge breakthrough at that time. And as Goodfellow et al. [10] propose the Generative Adversarial Networks (GAN) which contains a theory of adversarial, some great methods, like SRGAN [9] introduce GAN into the field of SR and get satisfying results. In general, different SR algorithms differ from each other mainly in the following major aspects: different types of network architectures [11–13], loss functions [14–16], learning strategies [14, 17, 18], etc.

X. Zhang et al. (Eds.): CloudComp 2019/SmartGift 2019, LNICST 322, pp. 184–199, 2020.
https://doi.org/10.1007/978-3-030-48513-9_15

In this paper, a brief overview of recent methods of SISR with deep learning is presented. While most of the existing surveys focus on traditional methods, our survey will mainly focus on deep learning methods.

Our survey has the following contributions:

1) We give a brief review of SISR techniques based on deep learning, including problem definitions, benchmark datasets, evaluation metrics, etc.
2) We provide a general overview of recent methods with techniques that are based on deep learning hierarchically and explore the pros and cons of each component for an effective SR method.
3) We analyze the challenges and future directions to provide an insightful guidance.

In the following sections, we will cover various aspects of recent advances in SISR with deep learning. Section 2 gives the problem definition, reviews the benchmark datasets and introduce some common evaluation metrics. Section 3 analyzes main components of supervised SR. Section 4 gives an introduction to our experiments and Sect. 5 expresses conclusions and discusses future directions.

2 Problem, Datasets and Evaluation Metrics

2.1 Problem Definitions

Single-Image Super-Resolution problem aims at recovering a high-resolution (HR) image from a single low-resolution (LR) image effectively. We could model the process of the acquisition of LR image I_{LR} with the degradation process as follows:

$$I_{LR} = \mathcal{D}(I_{HR}; \theta_{\mathcal{D}}) \tag{1}$$

Where I_{LR} represents the LR image, $\mathcal{D}$ is a degradation mapping function, I_{HR} denotes the corresponding ground-truth HR image and $\theta_{\mathcal{D}}$ corresponds to the parameters of the degradation process, like some noise factors or scaling factors. The degradation process is quite simple, however, in most situations, the details of the degradation process is unknown and only LR images are provided. Therefore, a requirement of recovering a HR image $\hat{I}_{HR}$ from the provided LR image I_{LR} is raised up, so that $\hat{I}_{HR}$ should be identical to the ground-truth HR image I_{HR} by the following formula:

$$\hat{I}_{HR} = \mathcal{F}(I_{LR}; \theta_{\mathcal{F}}) \tag{2}$$

Where $\mathcal{F}$ is the SR model and $\theta_{\mathcal{F}}$ denotes the parameters of the model.

Most works directly model the degradation as a single downsampling operation as follows:

$$\mathcal{D}(I_{HR}; \theta_{\mathcal{D}}) = (I_{HR}) \downarrow_s, s \in \theta_{\mathcal{D}} \tag{3}$$

Where $\downarrow_s$ is a downsampling operation with the scaling factor s and bicubic interpolation with antialiasing is the most commonly used downsampling operation.

Finally, the objective of SR is given as follow:

$$\hat{\theta} = \arg\min_\theta \, \mathcal{L}\left(\hat{I}_{HR}, I_{HR}\right) + \lambda\phi(\theta) \tag{4}$$

Where $\mathcal{L}\left(\hat{I}_{HR}, I_{HR}\right)$ represents the loss function between the generated HR image $\hat{I}_{HR}$ and the ground-truth image I_{HR}, $\phi(\theta)$ is the regularization term and λ is a trade-off parameter.

2.2   Datasets

Currently, there are some popular used benchmarks for testing the performance of SR models including Set5 [19], Set14 [20], BSD100 [21], Urban100 [22], DIV2K [23] and Manga109 [24]. More details of these datasets are presented in Table 1 and some images from these datasets are shown in Fig. 1.

Table 1. Public image datasets for SR benchmarks

Dataset	Amount	Format	Categories
Set5 [19]	5	PNG	Baby, bird, butterfly, head, woman
Set14 [20]	14	PNG	Humans, animals, insects, flowers, vegetables, comic, slides, etc.
BSD100 [21]	100	JPG	Animal, building, food, landscape, people, plant, etc.
Urban100 [22]	100	PNG	Architecture, city, structure, urban, etc.
Manga109 [23]	109	PNG	Manga volume
DIV2K [24]	1000	PNG	Environment, flora, fauna, handmade object, scenery, etc.

Fig. 1. Image samples from benchmark datasets

Set5 [19] is a classical dataset and only contains five test images of a baby, bird, butterfly, head, and a woman. Set14 [20] consists of more categories compared to Set5. However, the number of images are still low, with only 14 test images. BSD100 [21] is another classical dataset having 100 test images proposed by Martin et al. The dataset is composed of a large variety of images ranging from natural images to object-specific such as plants, people, food etc. Urban100 [22] is a relatively more recent dataset introduced by Huang et al. The number of images is the same as BSD100. However, the composition is entirely different. The focus of the photographs is on human-made structures, such as urban scenes. Manga109 [23] is the latest addition for evaluating super-resolution algorithms. The dataset is a collection of 109 test images of a manga volume. The manga was professionally drawn by Japanese artists and were available only for commercial use between the 1970s and 2010s. DIV2K [24] is a dataset used for NITRE challenge. The image quality is of 2K resolution and is composed of 800 images for training while 100 images each for testing and validation. As the test set is not publicly available, the results are only reported on validation images for all the algorithms.

2.3 Evaluation Metrics

In the task of SR, evaluation metrics are used to assess the quality of the recovered HR image, not only refers to the differences between the recovered pixel and the corresponded pixel in the ground-truth HR image, but also focus on the perceptual assessments of human viewers. In this section, we'll introduce two types of the most commonly used Evaluation metrics, Peak Signal-to-Noise Ratio (PSNR) and Structural Similarity (SSIM).

2.3.1 Peak Signal-to-Noise Ratio

Peak Signal-to-Noise Ratio (PSNR) is one of the most commonly used evaluation metrics in SR. Its main goal is to measure the reconstruction quality of lossy transformation. The MSE and the PSNR between the ground-truth image I and the generated image $\hat{I}$ are defined as follows:

$$\text{MSE} = \frac{1}{HWC} \sum_i^W \sum_j^H \sum_k^C \left(I^{i,j,k} - \hat{I}^{i,j,k} \right)^2 \tag{5}$$

$$\text{PSNR} = 10 * log_{10}\left(\frac{L^2}{MSE}\right) \tag{6}$$

Where H, W, C denote the height, width and channels of the image, respectively, $I^{i,j,k}$ denotes the pixel in the ground-truth HR image with the coordinates of (i, j, k) in the dimensions of width, height and channels, respectively, $\hat{I}^{i,j,k}$ is defined similarly, L is the maximum possible pixel value(usually 255 for 8-bit image). As L is always fixed, MSE becomes the only factor influencing PSNR, only caring about the differences between the pixel values at the same positions instead of human visual perception. In this way, the generated image might be much better in the perspective of pixel values, but can't be considered as good by human visual systems (HVS). However, due to the necessity to compare performance with literature works and the lack of completely accurate perceptual metrics, PSNR is currently the most widely used evaluation metric for SR models.

2.3.2 Structural Similarity

HVS is more likely to extract the structural information from the viewing field [25], therefore, an evaluation metric named structural similarity index (SSIM) [26] is proposed to measure the structural similarity between images, and there are three relatively independent comparisons: luminance, contrast, and structure comparisons. For an image I with the shape $H * W * C$, its mean and the standard deviation value are given as follows:

$$\mu_I = \frac{1}{HWC} \sum_i^W \sum_j^H \sum_k^C I^{i,j,k} \tag{7}$$

$$\sigma_I = (\frac{1}{HWC - 1} \sum_i^W \sum_j^H \sum_k^C (I^{i,j,k} - \mu_I)^2)^{\frac{1}{2}} \tag{8}$$

Where μ_I indicates the mean value of image I, σ_I denotes the standard deviation of the image intensity. And the comparison functions on luminance and contrast, denoted as $C_l(I, \hat{I})$ and $C_c(I, \hat{I})$, respectively, are given as follows:

$$C_l(I, \hat{I}) = \frac{2\mu_I\mu_{\hat{I}} + C_1}{\mu_I^2 + \mu_{\hat{I}}^2 + C_1} \tag{9}$$

$$C_c(I, \hat{I}) = \frac{2\sigma_I\sigma_{\hat{I}} + C_2}{\sigma_I^2 + \sigma_{\hat{I}}^2 + C_2} \tag{10}$$

Where $C_1 = (k_1 L)^2$ and $C_2 = (k_2 L)^2$ are constants for avoiding instability, in which $k_1 \ll 1$ and $k_2 \ll 1$ are small constants.

The image structure is represented by the normalized pixel values (i.e., $\frac{I - \mu_I}{\sigma_I}$), whose correlations (i.e., inner product) measure the structural similarity. Then, the structure comparison function $C_s(I, \hat{I})$ is defined as follows:

$$\sigma_{I\hat{I}} = \frac{1}{HWC - 1} \sum_i^W \sum_j^H \sum_k^C (I^{i,j,k} - \mu_I)(\hat{I}^{i,j,k} - \mu_{\hat{I}}) \tag{11}$$

$$C_s(I, \hat{I}) = \frac{\sigma_{I\hat{I}} + C_3}{\sigma_I\sigma_{\hat{I}} + C_3} \tag{12}$$

Where $\sigma_{I\hat{I}}$ is the covariance between I and $\hat{I}$, C_3 is a constant to assure stability.

At last, the formula of calculating SSIM is given by:

$$\text{SSIM}(I, \hat{I}) = [C_l(I, \hat{I})]^\alpha [C_c(I, \hat{I})]^\beta [C_s(I, \hat{I})]^\gamma \tag{13}$$

Where α, β, γ are constants for adjusting the relative importance. In practice, researcher often set $\alpha = \beta = \gamma = 1$ and $C_3 = \frac{C_2}{2}$, then SSIM is calculated as:

$$\text{SSIM}(I, \hat{I}) = \frac{(2\mu_I\mu_{\hat{I}} + C_1)(\sigma_{I\hat{I}} + C_2)}{(\mu_I^2 + \mu_{\hat{I}}^2 + C_1)(\sigma_I^2 + \sigma_{\hat{I}}^2 + C_2)} \tag{14}$$

As its aim shows, the SSIM evaluates the quality of the generated images from the perspective of the HVS, it better meets the requirements of perceptual assessment [27, 28] compared to PSNR. Therefore, it is also widely used by researchers.

3 Supervised Super-Resolution

Supervised SR models are trained with both LR images and the corresponding ground-truth HR images. The essential components of SR models include: model frameworks, upsampling methods, network architecture and strategies for learning. Therefore, although these models differ from each other greatly, they are all exactly a combination of the components above. In this section, we will focus on the basic components of SR models, analyze their pros and cons, and in Sect. 4, we will choose some classical models to do the experiments.

3.1 Super-Resolution Frameworks

A key problem of SISR is the way of performing upsampling. Although the network architectures of SR models vary greatly, they can be corresponded to four categories: pre-upsampling SR, post-upsampling SR, progressive upsampling SR and iterative up-and-down sampling SR, as Fig. 2 shows.

3.1.1 Pre-upsampling Super-Resolution

As Dong et al. [7, 8] show in their work SRCNN, they first introduce a straightforward method that upsamples the LR images using a traditional method, then refine them using DCNNs in an end-to-end way. This framework (Fig. 2a) is considered the pre-upsampling SR framework. More specifically, the network first uses traditional upsampling method, like bicubic interpolation, to upsample the LR images to coarse HR images, then DCNNs are applied to construct concrete details.

Since this framework does the upsampling with traditional algorithms first, CNNs only need to refine the coarse HR images, therefore, one of the advantages is that the learning difficulty is reduced. Then, this framework appears to be more flexible because it could take arbitrary images and scale factors as input and gives output with the same model [11]. The main differences between models with this framework are the design of the network model and the learning strategies. However, there are also some drawbacks. Firstly, the traditional upsampling methods like bicubic interpolation, would often cause something like noise, blurring, etc. Further, compared with models using other frameworks, the temporal and spatial cost is always much higher [29, 30].

3.1.2 Post-upsampling Super-Resolution

As using pre-upsampling framework would result in much efficiency cost, the post-upsampling framework is then proposed by researchers. Similar to the pre-upsampling framework and just as its name illustrates, the post-framework does the complex mappings in the low-dimensional space and after that, it performs a learnable upsampling at the end (Fig. 2b).

It's obvious that this framework cost less because the operations of convolutions are performed in the low-dimensional space and this could also provide with faster speed. As a result, this framework also occupies one position in the SR field [9, 16]. However, there are also some shortcomings. The first one is that the upsampling is only performed in one

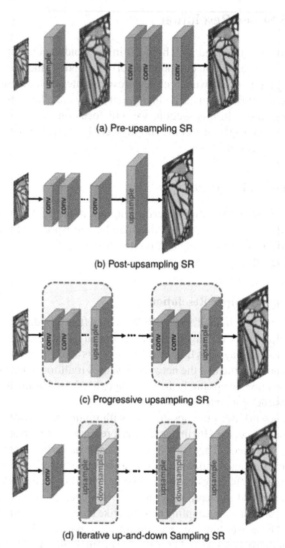

(a) Pre-upsampling SR

(b) Post-upsampling SR

(c) Progressive upsampling SR

(d) Iterative up-and-down Sampling SR

Fig. 2. SR model frameworks based on deep learning. The blue boxes indicate convolutional layers, the gray boxes represent predefined upsampling operations, the green and yellow boxes denote learnable upsampling and downsampling layers, respectively. (Color figure online)

step and this might fail to learn when the scale factors are large. Another disadvantage is that it lacks some flexibility, for it can't handle the work using a single model well when the scale factors vary.

Generally speaking, models using this type of framework differ to each other mainly in aspects of network design, learnable upsample layers and strategies for learning.

3.1.3   Progressive Upsampling Super-Resolution

To address the drawbacks of post-upsampling framework, a progressive upsampling SR framework is come into use (Fig. 2c). A typical example of this framework is the Laplacian pyramid SR network (LapSRN) [12]. It is based on a cascade of CNNs and progressively reconstruct the HR images. At each stage, the images are upsampled to higher resolution and refined by CNNs.

The main feature of progress upsampling framework is that it decomposes a difficult task into several simple tasks, models with this framework could both become much easier to learn to obtain better performance and could handle the conditions of different scale factors well without much extra cost. Furthermore, this kind of framework requires a multi-stage design, so, some strategies for learning can be further considered to reduce the learning difficulty to enhance the performance. However, one problem is that the network designing task is quite difficult and therefore, we need more guidance and instructions.

3.1.4   Iterative Up-and-Down Sampling Super-Resolution

Iterative up-and-down sampling framework is proposed to make the relationship between the LR and HR images pairs become more tightly. Back-projection is a new efficient iterative procedure within this framework, it is used to better refine the relationship between the LR and HR images [31]. Haris et al. [26] propose a deep back-projection network (DBPN) using blocks of connected upsampling and downsampling layers and reconstruct the final HR image by using the concatenation of all the reconstructed HR feature maps during the process of forward propagation. Combine with other techniques, like dense connections [32], DBPN became the champion algorithm in the competition of NTIRE 2018 [33].

The models under this framework can better mine the deep relationships between LR-HR image pairs and thus provide higher-quality reconstruction results. Nevertheless, the design criteria of the back-projection modules are still unclear. In fact, the back-projection units used in DBPN have a very complicated structure and require heavy manual design. Since this mechanism has just been introduced into super-resolution based on deep learning, the framework has great potential and needs further exploration.

3.2   Upsampling Methods

As the above section shows, there are mainly four frameworks to deal with the upsampling layers. Besides, it's also important to know how to implement the upsampling operations. Although there has already been various of traditional upsampling algorithms, like nearest-neighbor interpolation, bilinear interpolation, bicubic interpolation, etc. Using CNNs to learn upsampling operators has become more and more popular. In this section, we'll discuss about some classical interpolation-based algorithms and upsampling layers that are based on deep learning.

3.2.1 Interpolation-Based Upsampling

Traditional interpolation methods include nearest-neighbor, bilinear, bicubic interpolation and etc. Although upsampling layers that are based on deep learning perform quite well, some of the traditional interpolation-based upsampling methods are still in use in some networks.

Nearest-Neighbor Interpolation. The nearest-neighbor interpolation is simple. Its basic idea is to select the value of the nearest pixel for each interpolating position. On the one hand, this method is very fast to execute. On the other hand, it would usually produce blocky results.

Bilinear Interpolation. Just as the name denotes, bilinear interpolation would first do linear interpolation once on one axis, after that, it would do it again on another axis. Compared with nearest-neighbor interpolation, bilinear interpolation not only results in better performance, but also run fast.

Bicubic Interpolation. Similar to bilinear interpolation, the bicubic interpolation does cubic interpolation once on each of the two dimensions of the image. The bicubic interpolation could generate smoother results with fewer interpolation artefacts and lower speed compared to bilinear interpolation. As a matter of fact, the bicubic interpolation with anti-aliasing is now widely used to degrade the HR image to generate the corresponding LR image to make a dataset and is also widely accepted by researchers to use a pre-upsampling framework.

The interpolation-based upsampling methods don't provide any new information, just focus on its content and as a result, there would always be some side effects.

3.2.2 Learning-Based Upsampling

CNNs could handle the task of "understanding" the images well and therefore, researchers tried to use CNNs to force the network to understand the image and do a better upsampling. Two popular methods of learning-based upsampling are transposed convolution layer and sub-pixel layer.

Transposed Convolution Layer. While a normal convolutional operator with a stride greater than one, the output of the operation would result in smaller width and height, a transposed convolution layer, also known as deconvolution layer [34], behaves just as the opposite, it tries to get bigger width and height, so they could be used to do the upsampling task [26, 35]. More concretely, it could enlarge the resolution of images by inserting zero values and then doing convolution.

Although transposed convolution layer can be used in the field of SR to perform learnable upsampling, it could also cause "uneven overlapping" on each axis [36] and would easily generate chessboard-like patterns to reduce the SR performance.

Sub-pixel Layer. Another learnable upsampling layer is the sub-pixel layer [30], it performs upsampling by generating feature maps with the shape of $H * W * s^2C$ by convolution and then reshaping them into a shape of $sH * sW * C$, where s is the upscale factor.

One of the advantages of using sub-pixel layer is that we could obtain larger receptive field, which could provide more contextual information to generate better HR images. However, blocky regions actually share the same receptive field and therefore it may result in some artefacts near the boundaries of different blocks.

These two learnable upsampling layers are widely used in post-upsampling framework and are always set in the final upsampling stage.

3.3 Network Architecture

The network design is currently one of the most important part in deep learning, researchers would always use some technologies, like residual learning, dense connection, etc. to improve their design.

3.3.1 Residual Learning

He et al. [37] propose a kind of DCNN named ResNet in 2016 and from then on, residual blocks are widely used in the design of networks. But before the proposal of ResNet, in the field of SR, researchers have already employed the technique of residual learning to their SR models. The residual learning can be roughly divided into two types: global residual learning and local residual learning.

Global Residual Learning. First of all, global residual learning is widely used especially in the pre-upsampling framework, because it only learns the residuals between the coarse HR image and the ground-truth HR image. Instead of learning the complicate information an image need, global residual learning only learns a residual map to restore the missing high-frequency details, and therefore reduce the learning difficulty and complexity.

Local Residual Learning. Both of the local residual learning and residual blocks in ResNet are used to improve the problem of degradation and gradient vanishing due to the learning difficulty caused by the network depths.

With the structure of shortcut connection and element-wise addition operations, global residual learning directly connects the input and output images, while local residual learning usually sets several this kind of structure between the layers.

3.3.2 Dense Connection

Huang et al. [32] come up with a network named DenseNet in CVPR 2017, the main components of this network are dense blocks, then more and more people use dense blocks to design their networks. Inside the dense blocks, the inputs consist of all former layers, which results in C_l^2 connections in a dense block with l layers. Similar to residual learning, the dense connections could effectively help avoid gradient vanishing, enhance signal propagation and encourage feature reuse. Besides it could also substantially reduce the number of parameters by reducing the number of channels in dense blocks and squeezing channels after concatenation.

Dense connections are widely used, some famous networks like, ESRGAN [38] and DBPN [26], adopt dense connections and get good results.

3.4 Strategies for Learning

There are various of strategies that are useful to promote the performance, like running time, the quality of the generated HR images, etc. The most commonly used strategies can be roughly divided into three categories: the loss functions, batch normalization and others.

3.4.1 Loss Functions

In the area of SR, loss functions are used to measure the difference between ground-truth HR images and the generated HR images it could help to optimize the model greatly. In the early stage of this task, researchers usually used pixel-wise L2 loss for optimization, but found it couldn't measure the reconstruction quality well. Since then, many other loss functions showed up for solving the problem. Despite of the loss functions combined with GAN, e.g., adversarial loss, cycle consistency loss, etc., there are four commonly used loss functions: Pixel Loss, Content Loss, Texture Loss and Total Variation Loss. The formulas are shown in Table 2.

Table 2. Common loss functions

Loss function	Formula
Pixel loss	$\mathcal{L}_{pixel\_l1}\left(I, \hat{I}\right) = \frac{1}{HWC} \sum_{i}^{W} \sum_{j}^{H} \sum_{k}^{C} \left| \hat{I}^{i,j,k} - I^{i,j,k} \right|$ $\mathcal{L}_{pixel_{l2}}\left(I, \hat{I}\right) = \frac{1}{HWC} \sum_{i}^{W} \sum_{j}^{H} \sum_{k}^{C} \left(\hat{I}^{i,j,k} - I^{i,j,k} \right)^2$
Content loss	$\mathcal{L}_{content}\left(I, \hat{I}; \phi, l\right) = \frac{1}{H_l W_l C_l} \left\{ \sum_{i}^{W_l} \sum_{j}^{H_l} \sum_{k}^{C_l} \left[\phi_{(l)}^{i,j,k}\left(\hat{I}\right) - \phi_{(l)}^{i,j,k}(I) \right]^2 \right\}^{\frac{1}{2}}$
Texture loss	$G_{(l)}^{ij}(I) = vec\left(\phi_{(l)}^{i}(I) \right) \cdot vec\left(\phi_{(l)}^{j}(I) \right)$ $\mathcal{L}_{texture}\left(I, \hat{I}; \phi, l\right) = \frac{1}{c_l^2} \left\{ \sum_{i}^{W} \sum_{j}^{H} \left[G_{(l)}^{i,j}\left(\hat{I}\right) - G_{(l)}^{i,j}(I) \right]^2 \right\}^{\frac{1}{2}}$
Total variation loss	$\mathcal{L}_{TV}\left(\hat{I}\right) =$ $\frac{1}{HWC} \sum_{i}^{W} \sum_{j}^{H} \sum_{k}^{C} \left[\left(\hat{I}^{i,j+1,k} - \hat{I}^{i,j,k} \right)^2 + \left(\hat{I}^{i+1,j,k} - \hat{I}^{i,j,k} \right)^2 \right]^{\frac{1}{2}}$

Pixel Loss. Pixel loss is used to measure the pixel-wise difference between I and $\hat{I}$ which includes L1 loss (mean absolute error) and L2 loss (mean square error). By using pixel loss as the loss function, it could guide the network to generate $\hat{I}$ to be close to the ground-truth I. L1 loss tends to have better performance and convergence compared to L2 loss [13, 17]. As the definition of PSNR illustrates, it is highly correlated with pixel-wise difference and minimizing pixel loss could directly maximize PSNR, the pixel loss appears to be the most popular choice. But the generated image would often lack high-frequency details and result in perceptually unpleasant results with over smooth textures [9, 15].

Content Loss. In order to solve the perceptual problem in pixel loss, the content loss is then introduced into SR [15]. By extracting feature maps by using a pre-trained image classification network, it could measure the semantic differences between images. Denote this pre-trained network as ϕ and the extracted feature maps on l^{th} layer as $\phi_{(l)}(I)$, the content loss is the Euclidean distance between high-level representations between two images. Content loss encourages the output image $\hat{I}$ to be perceptually similar to the ground-truth image I instead of forcing them to match pixels exactly.

Texture Loss. Inspired by Gatys et al. [39], the style of an image is considered to be an important factor influencing the quality of the generated image, Gram matrix $G_{(l)} \in \mathcal{R}^{c_l * c_l}$ is then introduced into SR, where $G_{(l)}^{ij}$ is the inner product between the vectorized feature maps i and j on layer l.

Total Variation Loss. The total variation loss is introduced into the SR field by Aly et al. [40] to suppress the noise. The sum of the absolute differences between neighboring pixels consists of the total variation loss and it could measure the amount of noise is in the image.

3.4.2 Batch Normalization

Batch normalization (BN) is proposed by Sergey et al. [41] to reduce internal covariate shift of networks. BN enables us to use much higher learning rates and initialization is not a big problem any more. BN results in accelerating the speed of convergence and improve the accuracy, therefore, it is widely adopted by researchers. However, Lim et al. [17] argue that using BN would lose the scale information of each image and the range flexibility. There is a trade-off whether using BN or not.

4 The Experiment Result and Performance Analysis

In this section, we mainly focus on the experiments, we select some of the classical models and some of the benchmark datasets, then apply PSNR and SSIM on them to make some comparisons. For SR models, we choose bicubic, SRCNN, EDSR, SRGAN and ESRGAN to recover HR images with a scale factor of 4. And use all benchmark datasets above to evaluate the PSNR and SSIM values of these models.

We evaluate each SR algorithm selected on the peak signal-to-noise ratio (PSNR) and the structural similarity index (SSIM) on the benchmark datasets in Sect. 2.2. Table 3 presents the results for 4x for the SR algorithms. In Fig. 3, we present the visual comparison between the selected SR algorithms and Fig. 4 shows a detailed comparison between a pair of images of the ground truth image and an image recovered by ESRGAN.

Table 3. Evaluation on PSNR and SSIM on recovered images with a upscale factor of 4

Methods	Set5		Set14		BSD100		Urban100		Manga109		DIV2K	
	PSNR	SSIM	PSNR	SSIM	PSNR	SSIM	PSNR	SSIM	PSNR	SSIM	PSNR	SSIM
Bicubic	28.43	0.8109	26.00	0.7023	25.96	0.6678	23.14	0.6574	25.15	0.789	28.11	0.775
SRCNN	30.48	0.8628	27.50	0.7513	26.90	0.7103	24.52	0.7226	27.66	0.858	29.33	0.809
EDSR	32.46	0.8968	28.80	0.7876	27.71	0.7420	26.64	0.8033	31.02	0.914	29.25	0.9017
SRGAN	32.05	0.8910	28.53	0.7804	27.57	0.7351	26.07	0.7839	–	–	28.92	0.896
ESRGAN	32.73	0.9011	28.99	0.7917	27.85	0.7455	27.03	0.8153	31.66	0.9196	–	–

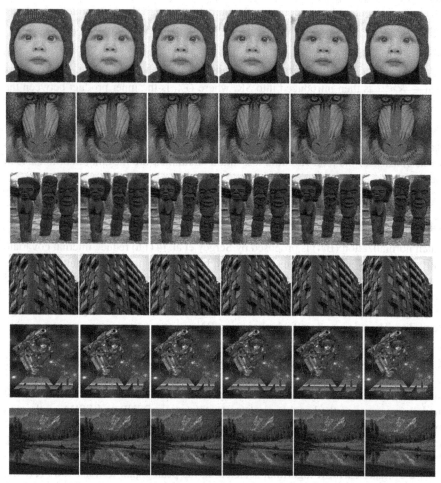

Fig. 3. Comparison between images, the images of each column are the ground-truth image, image recovered by bicubic, image recovered by SRCNN, image recovered by EDSR, image recovered by SRGAN and image recovered by ESRGAN, respectively.

Fig. 4. 0002.jpg of DIV2K, the left one is the ground-truth image and the right one is the image recovered by ESRGAN.

5   Conclusion

SISR methods based on deep learning have achieved great success recently. In this paper, we give a brief survey on recent SISR methods and mainly discussed the improvement of supervised SR methods. However, there still exists something that we could improve to get a better result and, in this section, we will talk about this.

Network Design. Current sota SR methods tend to mainly focus on the final results of the recovered HR images while ignoring the complexity of their models and result in low inference speed. With a high-performance GPU, i.e. Titan GTX, current SR methods would take over 10 s for 4x SR per image of DIV2K, which is unacceptable in daily usage, therefore, we need to come up with some lightweight architectures to improve this problem. In addition, an important component of SR is the upsampling layers, the current upsampling methods, i.e. interpolation-based methods would result in expensive computation and couldn't be end-to-end learned, the transposed convolution would probably cause checkerboard artefacts. So, improving the upsampling methods could probably improve the recovering effects and inference time.

Learning Strategies. Loss function plays a critical part in the training of SR models which would build up constraints among LR and HR images and guide the network to optimize. In practice, some loss functions like L1 loss, L2 loss, perceptual loss are widely used. However, if there is any better loss function for SR is still unclear. Another factor is normalization, current sota SR methods prefer not to use normalization for some side effects, so other effective normalization techniques should be studied.

References

1. Lin, F., Fookes, C., Chandran, V., Sridharan, S.: Super-resolved faces for improved face recognition from surveillance video. In: Lee, S.-W., Li, Stan Z. (eds.) ICB 2007. LNCS, vol. 4642, pp. 1–10. Springer, Heidelberg (2007). https://doi.org/10.1007/978-3-540-74549-5_1

2. Zhang, L., Zhang, H., Shen, H., Li, P.: A super-resolution reconstruction algorithm for surveillance images. Sig. Process. **90**, 848–859 (2010)

3. Rasti, P., Uiboupin, T., Escalera, S., Anbarjafari, G.: Convolutional neural network super resolution for face recognition in surveillance monitoring. In: Perales, F.J.J., Kittler, J. (eds.) AMDO 2016. LNCS, vol. 9756, pp. 175–184. Springer, Cham (2016). https://doi.org/10.1007/978-3-319-41778-3_18

4. Greenspan, H.: Super-resolution in medical imaging. Comput. J. **52**, 43–63 (2008)

5. Isaac, J.S., Kulkarni, R.: Super resolution techniques for medical image processing. In: ICTSD (2015)

6. Huang, Y., Shao, L., Frangi, A.F.: Simultaneous super-resolution and cross-modality synthesis of 3D medical images using weakly-supervised joint convolutional sparse coding. In: CVPR (2017)

7. Dong, C., Loy, C.C., He, K., Tang, X.: Learning a deep convolutional network for image super-resolution. In: Fleet, D., Pajdla, T., Schiele, B., Tuytelaars, T. (eds.) ECCV 2014. LNCS, vol. 8692, pp. 184–199. Springer, Cham (2014). https://doi.org/10.1007/978-3-319-10593-2_13

8. Dong, C., Loy, C.C., He, K., Tang, X.: Image super-resolution using deep convolutional networks. TPAMI **38**, 295–307 (2016)

9. Ledig, C., et al.: Photo-realistic single image super-resolution using a generative adversarial network. In: CVPR (2017)

10. Goodfellow, I., et al.: Generative adversarial nets. In: NIPS (2014)

11. Kim, J., Kwon Lee, J., Mu Lee, K.: Accurate image super-resolution using very deep convolutional networks. In: CVPR (2016)

12. Lai, W.-S., Huang, J.-B., Ahuja, N., Yang, M.-H.: Deep Laplacian pyramid networks for fast and accurate superresolution. In: CVPR (2017)

13. Ahn, N., Kang, B., Sohn, K.-A.: Fast, accurate, and lightweight super-resolution with cascading residual network. In: Ferrari, V., Hebert, M., Sminchisescu, C., Weiss, Y. (eds.) ECCV 2018. LNCS, vol. 11214, pp. 256–272. Springer, Cham (2018). https://doi.org/10.1007/978-3-030-01249-6_16

14. Sajjadi, M.S., Schölkopf, B., Hirsch, M.: EnhanceNet: single image super-resolution through automated texture synthesis. In: ICCV (2017)

15. Johnson, J., Alahi, A., Fei-Fei, L.: Perceptual losses for real-time style transfer and super-resolution. In: Leibe, B., Matas, J., Sebe, N., Welling, M. (eds.) ECCV 2016. LNCS, vol. 9906, pp. 694–711. Springer, Cham (2016). https://doi.org/10.1007/978-3-319-46475-6_43

16. Bulat, A., Tzimiropoulos, G.: Super-FAN: integrated facial landmark localization and super-resolution of real-world low resolution faces in arbitrary poses with GANs. In: CVPR (2018)

17. Lim, B., Son, S., Kim, H., Nah, S., Lee, K.M.: Enhanced deep residual networks for single image super-resolution. In: CVPRW (2017)

18. Wang, Y., Perazzi, F., McWilliams, B., Sorkine-Hornung, A., Sorkine-Hornung, O., Schroers, C.: A fully progressive approach to single-image super-resolution. In: CVPRW (2018)

19. Bevilacqua, M., Roumy, A., Guillemot, C., Alberi-Morel, M.L.: Low-complexity single-image super-resolution based on nonnegative neighbor embedding (2012)

20. Zeyde, R., Elad, M., Protter, M.: On single image scale-up using sparse-representations. In: Boissonnat, J.-D., et al. (eds.) Curves and Surfaces 2010. LNCS, vol. 6920, pp. 711–730. Springer, Heidelberg (2012). https://doi.org/10.1007/978-3-642-27413-8_47

21. Martin, D., Fowlkes, C., Tal, D., Malik, J.: A database of human segmented natural images and its application to evaluating segmentation algorithms and measuring ecological statistics. In: ICCV (2001)

22. Huang, J.-B., Singh, A., Ahuja, N.: Single image super-resolution from transformed self-exemplars. In: CVPR (2015)

23. Fujimoto, A., Ogawa, T., Yamamoto, K., Matsui, Y., Yamasaki, T., Aizawa, K.: Manga109 dataset and creation of metadata. In: International Workshop on coMics ANalysis, Processing and Understanding (2016)
24. Timofte, R., et al.: NTIRE 2017 challenge on single image super-resolution: methods and results. In: CVPRW (2017)
25. Wang, Z., Bovik, A.C., Sheikh, H.R., Simoncelli, E.P.: Image quality assessment: from error visibility to structural similarity. IEEE Trans. Image Process. **13**, 600–612 (2004)
26. Haris, M., Shakhnarovich, G., Ukita, N.: Deep back-projection networks for super-resolution. In: CVPR (2018)
27. Sheikh, H.R., Sabir, M.F., Bovik, A.C.: A statistical evaluation of recent full reference image quality assessment algorithms. IEEE Trans. Image Process. **15**, 3440–3451 (2006)
28. Wang, Z., Bovik, A.C.: Mean squared error: love it or leave it? A new look at signal fidelity measures. IEEE Sig. Process. Mag. **26**, 98–117 (2009)
29. Dong, C., Loy, C.C., Tang, X.: Accelerating the super-resolution convolutional neural network. In: Leibe, B., Matas, J., Sebe, N., Welling, M. (eds.) ECCV 2016. LNCS, vol. 9906, pp. 391–407. Springer, Cham (2016). https://doi.org/10.1007/978-3-319-46475-6_25
30. Shi, W., et al.: Real-time single image and video super-resolution using an efficient sub-pixel convolutional neural network. In: CVPR (2016)
31. Timofte, R., Rothe, R., Van Gool, L.: Seven ways to improve example-based single image super resolution. In: CVPR (2016)
32. Huang, G., Liu, Z., Van Der Maaten, L., Weinberger, K.Q.: Densely connected convolutional networks. In: CVPR (2017)
33. Ancuti, C., et al.: NTIRE 2018 challenge on image dehazing: methods and results. In: CVPRW (2018)
34. Zeiler, M.D., Fergus, R.: Visualizing and understanding convolutional networks. In: Fleet, D., Pajdla, T., Schiele, B., Tuytelaars, T. (eds.) ECCV 2014. LNCS, vol. 8689, pp. 818–833. Springer, Cham (2014). https://doi.org/10.1007/978-3-319-10590-1_53
35. Mao, X., Shen, C., Yang, Y.-B.: Image restoration using very deep convolutional encoder-decoder networks with symmetric skip connections. In: NIPS (2016)
36. Odena, A., Dumoulin, V., Olah, C.: Deconvolution and checkerboard artifacts. Distill (2016)
37. He, K., Zhang, X., Ren, S., Sun, J.: Deep residual learning for image recognition. In: CVPR (2016)
38. Wang, X., et al.: ESRGAN: enhanced super-resolution generative adversarial networks. In: Leal-Taixé, L., Roth, S. (eds.) ECCV 2018. LNCS, vol. 11133, pp. 63–79. Springer, Cham (2019). https://doi.org/10.1007/978-3-030-11021-5_5
39. Gatys, L.A., Ecker, A.S., Bethge, M.: Image style transfer using convolutional neural networks. In: CVPR (2016)
40. Aly, H.A., Dubois, E.: Image up-sampling using total-variation regularization with a new observation model. IEEE Trans. Image Process. **14**, 1647–1659 (2005)
41. Sergey, I., Christian, S.: Batch normalization: accelerating deep network training by reducing internal covariate shift. In: ICML (2015)

Design and Development of an Intelligent Semantic Recommendation System for Websites

Zhiqiang Zhang[1](✉), Heping Yang[1], Di Yang[1], Xiaowei Jiang[1], Nan Chen[1], Mingnong Feng[1], and Ming Yang[2]

[1] National Meteorological Information Center, Beijing 100081, China
zhangzhiqiang@cma.gov.cn
[2] Zhejiang Meteorological Information Network Center, Hangzhou 310001, China

Abstract. When searching for the interesting content within a specific website, how to describe the initial need by selecting proper keywords is a critical problem. The character-matching search functions of website can hardly meet users' requirements. Furthermore, building the content of webpages of a specific website and the associated rules is uneconomical. This paper, based on the framework of the Lucene engine, applied a semantic ontology, the calculation of the relevance of word entries, and the semantics of keywords to design an intelligent semantic recommendation system with the Jena secondary semantic analysis technique. Subsequently, the expanded keywords were semantically ranked based on the term frequency analysis technique. Meanwhile, the ontology algorithm and their relevance were introduced as the dynamic weight values. Finally, in the text content retrieval process, the search results were ranked based on the previous relevance weights. The experimental results show that the system designed in this paper is not only easy to develop but also capable of expanding users queries and recommending relevant content. Further, the system can improve the precision and recall for website search results.

Keywords: Ontology · Vertical search engine · Semantic expansion · System design

1 Introduction

With the development of computer and network, the conventional character-matching search technology need to be improved because appropriate keywords can not be confirmed to meet users' requirements. To improve the search accuracy and semantic relevance, VSEs (vertical search engines) with a relatively deep background in domain knowledge have been gradually applied in various industries [1]. VSEs are characterized by providing professional search results and carry the marks of the industries, such as Google Scholar, China National Knowledge Infrastructure Search Engine, Wan-Fang Data, Book Search Engines [2], Education Resource Search Engines [3] and Geographic Information Search Engines [4]. A pure VSE filter can screen, reindex and store web crawler data based on a certain domain knowledge format for the users' retrieval [5].

X. Zhang et al. (Eds.): CloudComp 2019/SmartGift 2019, LNICST 322, pp. 200–209, 2020.
https://doi.org/10.1007/978-3-030-48513-9_16

Semantics reasoning based on VSEs was introduced to expand the implicit information from users' queries with the logical relationships in an ontology [6]. The previous ontologies, such as Cyc (http://www.cyc.com/) [7] and WordNet (a lexical database; http://wordnet.princeton.edu/) [8], can augment the content of different characters based on the semantics. Therefore, ontologies introduced into VSEs had significantly improved the precision and recall of the search results. Ontology-based VSEs are extensively used in various fields, including agriculture [9], industry [10] and text mining [11]. This technology has become an effective method and development trend for knowledge summarization and query sharing in various fields.

Currently, building an ontology requires a generalized or specialized thesaurus and clear logical relationships between the descriptors. Furthermore, the query is expanded through reasoning based on the semantic logical relationships in the ontology [12]. To ensure high precision and recall in the retrievals, it is necessary to set up higher standards for both the integrity of the thesaurus and the logical relationships between the objects in the ontology (the terms in the thesaurus).

Focused on the above analyses, the paper presented a simple ontology for a data website based on the structure of its navigation directory, which could apply vertical searching with the development framework of the search engine. Indexes and semantics expanded the word segmentation results after query segmentation, and then the relevance of each expanded keyword was applied to the query as the dynamic weight in the subsequent calculation of the relevance ranking from the search results. For realizing relevance ranking, it is critical to improve the precision of search results and permit users to rapidly and accurately search for the target data and relevant information from the website. This intelligent semantic recommendation simplified the process of building an ontology-based VSE for a website, which is suitable for building ontology-based vertical search systems for the specific websites of varying sizes (large, medium and small).

2   Structural Framework and Flow of the System

The technical contents of the system were divided into three modules: analyze the relevant contents of the website and build an index database in the background; establish an ontology and an ontology index database based on the map and navigation directory of the website; segment, expand and index the content based on the users' queries and rank of the recommended results. Figure 1 shows the main design flow.

2.1   Webpage Index Database

An index database for previous webpage contents can be built by the following steps:

Step 1: store the relevant links (e.g., the homepage) in the URL (Uniform Resource Locator) list in a web crawler;
Step 2: traverse the URL list to obtain the webpage contents;
Step 3: analyze webpage contents, store the text, extract the relevant URL links, store them in the URL list, and then go to Step 2;

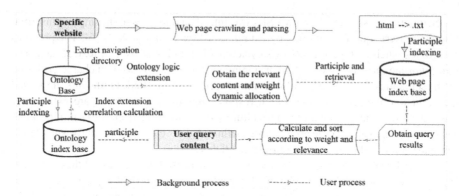

Fig. 1. Design framework for an ontology-based vertical search system.

Step 4: divide text contents into various fields, segment the words in each field, and build a webpage index database.

For information added to the website at later stage, Step 4 can be directly executed to improve the webpage index database.

2.2 Ontology and Ontology Index Database

From a prototype development point of view, this system established a simple ontology based on the navigation directory of website.

Step 1: list the column headings as ontology objects;
Step 2: define the relationship attributes between the ontology objects based on the column levels;
Step 3: build an ontology for the website;
Step 4: build indexes for objects name in an ontology and build an ontology index database.

2.3 Webpage Index Database

Step 1: segment the words in a query input by the user (original query);
Step 2: perform an index search in the ontology index database (Step 4 in Sect. 2.2), rank the search results based on the relevance, and take the relevance scores as the weight of the keywords for later-stage analysis:

$$RESULT\{(K1, Score\_1), (K2, Score\_2), \ldots\ldots, (Kn, Score\_n),$$

where K represents a record in the ontology index database related to the query, and Score represents the corresponding relevance score;

Step 3: perform reasoning on each object in RESULT within the ontology obtained in same type objects:
RESULT{{(K1, Score_1), (K1_k1, Score_1), (K1_k2, Score_1) , ontology to obtain n Sect. 2.2), rank the search results based on the relevance a website.si, where, Kn_km represents the mth object of the same type determined by reasoning based on the nth content, and Score represents the weight inherited from Step 2;
Step 4: segment and deduplicate the words in each object in RESULT (the segmented keywords inherit the previous weight (for duplicate keywords, the highest weight is inherited)) and perform an index search;
Step 5: set the weight of each field in the webpage index database, rank the search results based on the weights dynamically assigned to the keywords, and list the results.

3   Key Technologies

Focused on the intelligent semantic recommendation system framework, the related technologies and their implementation were introduced in this section.

3.1   Web Crawler

Heritrix, an open-source web crawler written with Java language, can be customized, modified and encapsulated as flexible web crawling tool [13]. Heritrix was applied to crawl and import a data website into the Html parser package to analyze and design webpage contents, and then a patterned data extraction framework was developed. Currently, two types of webpage data website are dataset information webpage and dynamic news information webpages, respectively. The relative webpage analysis and extraction framework are developed for these two types of webpage, which were used to screen the effective information.

3.2   Index Building and Retrieval

Webpage information was processed and stored as a new text file, and Lucene was used to build a search engine. Lucene is an open-source full-text search library in the Java development environment. For creating indexes between files, Lucene can also create indexes within a file to improve the retrieval efficiency. Moreover, Lucene can also perform Boolean operations and fuzzy and group searches [14]. Meteorological data website was selected in the research, and the text files were introduced to creating indexes. Meanwhile, intra-text file indexes were created with 10 components of the data composition, including data name, keyword and spatial range. During the search process, Lucene was used to perform a multi-field search for the keywords (Multi-Field Query Parser) and allocate the corresponding weight to facilitate the calculation and rank the relevance of the results.

3.3 Chinese Word Segmentation

Building a search engine (including creating indexes and realizing user retrieval) with Lucene, it is necessary to perform word segmentation on the metadata and to index for users' queries. The IKAnalyzer, fine-grained segmentation algorithm for forward iteration, was designed to segment word in the system with processing capacity of 600,000 words per second. Chinese word segmentation toolkit was developed with Java language and supported industry-specific and users' customized dictionaries [15]. The system applied IKAnalyzer 5.0 jar toolkit and configures industry-specific and user's dictionaries through the designment.

3.4 Ontology Establishment

Ontology was built based on Protégé [16] for the CMDSC (China Meteorological Data Service Center) website. The main concepts in this ontology include data technology and service processes. The data technology include ground, upper-air and maritime data. The ground data include basic meteorological element data observed at Chinese ground meteorological stations, climate data collected at Chinese ground international exchange stations and standard value of ground climate in China. The main relationships between the concepts are part-of and instance-of relationships (the system considers only part-of relationships).

3.5 Query Expansion

The system expanded a query and dynamically assigns a weight to the relevant contents by the method described in Sect. 2.3. This section focuses mainly on the sematic expansion of ontology. Jena is primarily used to expand the ontology for queries with logical reasoning and a parser for files in the RDF (Resource Description Framework)/Extensible Markup Language and OWL formats. The SPARQL Protocol and RDF Query Language in Jena can be used to retrieve relevant semantics in the ontology. The Jena application programming interface can be used to determine the position of an object in the ontology as well as the class/subclass above and below and at the same the position of the object [17].

3.6 Result Ranking

Result ranking is a key part for users' experience. The higher relevance of the content keywords had in users' queries, the higher rank the content located. Using the TF-IDF (Term Frequency–Inverse Document Frequency) algorithm [18], the system calculates the relevance of the search results by setting the field weight and dynamically assigning weight to the segmented words based on Eq. (1):

$$SCORES = TF \times IDF \times BOOST \times fieldNorm \tag{1}$$

where TF is the square root of the number of appearances of the searched word in the file, IDF is the inverse document frequency, which is the number of files appeared by retrieved content, *BOOST* is the boost factor, whose value can be set using both field and doc (the values set using field and doc will take effect at the same time), *fieldNorm* is calculated in advance (when the TF and IDF remain unchanged, the less content a file contains, the higher value the fieldNorm has):

$$IDF = log(numDocs/(docFreq + 1)) + 1 \qquad (2)$$

where *numDocs* is total number of files, *docFreq* is the number of files contained the word.

$$fieldNorm = 1/\sqrt{(wordsNum - 1)} \qquad (3)$$

where *wordsNum* is file length.

4   Experiment and Analysis

4.1   Data Preparation

Total 1,640 dataset webpages and 159 pieces of published dynamic and popular science information were crawled from a meteorological data website from CMDSC with the Heritrix web crawler. Fields were designed and indexed for the relevant file information (Table 1). TextField showed that indexes were created for segmentic words and supports users' queries. StringField showed that indexes were not created for the segmented words. Weight showed the BOOST (boost factor) of results ranking after users' searches in each field.

Table 1. Building index information for dataset file fields.

Field name	Explanation	Field type	Weight
Title	Data name	TextField	1.0f
Description	Data description	TextField	1.2f
Keyword	Keyword	TextField	1.2f
s_date	Start time of the data	StringField	–
e_date	End time of the data	StringField	–
Range	Spatial range	TextField	1.0f
Source	Data source	TextField	1.0f
q_description	Data quality description	TextField	1.1f
m_time	Time of creation	StringField	–
Freq	Update frequency	TextField	1.0f
Url	Website	StringField	–

4.2 Chinese Word Segmentation

The accuracy of segmenting the words in a file and a user's query directly affects the precision of the search results. To improve the word segmentation accuracy, 15,456 specialized meteorological terms were imported into IKAnalyzer as a customized lexicon. Table 2 summarizes the comparison of the segmentation of 10 common meteorological terms selected from the main types of data on the CMDSC website. Apparently, the intelligent word segmentation accuracy of IKAnalyzer increased significantly after importing the specialized terms. Further, specialized terms need to segment the words in a file at a finer granularity level during the indexing process. The system uses the fine-granularity mode of IKAnalyzer to segment sentences to ensure the comprehensiveness of the index building.

Table 2. Search results obtained based on keyword matching and ontology matching.

Number	Word content	Search results obtained based on character matching	Search results obtained based on ontology matching
1	Vertical cumulative liquid water content	86(15)	1084(105)
2	Multi-year ten-day upper-air level value	1092(219)	1416(151)
3	Dew point temperature of air	486(32)	486(32)
4	Single-station Doppler radar base data	287(23)	287(23)
5	Chinese FengYun polar-orbiting meteorological satellite	992(69)	1414(148)
6	Historical atmospheric dust fall	433(46)	1092(131)
7	Agricultural meteorological data	1176(131)	1362(141)
8	Tropical cyclone data	1355(129)	1360 (138)
9	Numerical weather forecast model	571(53)	902(135)
10	Integrated grid precipitation data	1347(142)	1351(149)

5   Result and Discussion

The precision (hit rate) and the recall of the retrieval results are the standard measures for determining the quality of a search engine. Searches were performed using the terms listed in Table 2. Table 2 shows the search results obtained by pure character-matching searching and by searching after query expansion in the ontology. Clearly, the recall was significantly higher than that performed based on ontology-matching. The two approaches yielded the same numbers of search results for "dew point temperature of air" and "single-station Doppler radar base data". For "dew point temperature of air", and the object names in the ontology did not contain the information without expanded words. For "single-station Doppler radar base data" within the ontology, "Doppler radar base data" was expanded, and the expanded keywords were included after segmenting the original word. Therefore, the two approaches yielded the same number of search results.

The accuracy of the first N number of search results (TopN) (i.e., the proportion of the first relevant N records) was used to examine the precision (hit rate). Research data obtained showed that the user views of the first page of the search results account for 47% of the total user views [19]. Searches were performed using the terms listed in Table 2. The accuracy of the top 20 search results was calculated and found to be at 100%. This finding occurs mainly because there was a hit on the names of some of the datasets, the datasets of 31 provinces of the same type could be obtained (i.e., the dataset headings have the same characters except for only the name of the province), which affected the determination of the overall accuracy. During the statistical analysis, datasets for 31 provinces of the same type were treated as one record. For example, the Standard value of 31 provinces were treated as only one record. The numbers in the brackets in Table 2 are the statistical values obtained after this treatment.

Figure 2 shows the search accuracy determined after the abovementioned treatment. As shown in Fig. 2, the accuracy of the search results obtained after the expansion of the ontology was significantly higher than that of the search results obtained by character matching. This finding occurs mainly because weights were assigned to the keywords obtained by semantic expansion when scoring and ranking the relevance of the search results, which improved the hit rate (precision) for the query. There were relatively few search results for "dew point temperature of air" and "single-station Doppler radar base data", which basically appeared in the first 20 records. So, the accuracy was same. The accuracy of the search results for "tropical cyclone data" was low in both cases, which is mainly due to the relatively small amount of relevant information on the website.

A comparison between the pure character-matching searching approach and ontology-matching shows that this system has higher recall and precision. This system is suitable for rapidly locating requisite information within the enormous volumes of meteorological data on the CMDSC website and then it was proved to be an effective means for realizing meteorological data sharing.

(1) Indexing and query segmentation. In the process of building the index database for the system and segmenting a user's query, a specialized lexicon and a stop word library were introduced to segment the indexes at a coarse granularity level and intelligently segment the query. The aim to segment and filter the specialized terms and improve the relevance of the search results to the special field had been achieved.

(2) Ontology building and expansion. An ontology was built for a website based on the functional requirement of the system and the structure of the navigation directory of

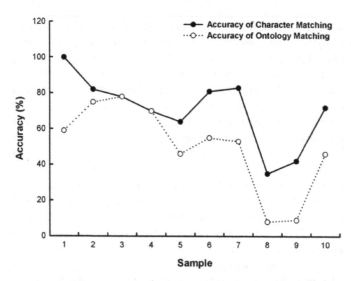

Fig. 2. Accuracy of the top 20 search results for the 10 query contents.

the website. In addition, the ontology index searching and analysis techniques were applied to expand a user's query, which increases the number of records relevant to the queries retrieved with higher recall.

(3) Dynamic assignment of weight to terms. The system not only assigned weights to the indexed contents of a webpage in various fields but also dynamically assigns weight to the keywords in a query. In other words, the relevance of a user's query for expanding the ontology object index database was used as the weight of each keyword when calculating the relevance rank of the search results. This approach optimizes the ranking results and significantly improves the precision (hit rate) of the search engine.

6 Conclusions

The intelligent semantic recommendation system established an ontology based on the navigation directory of a website. In the query expansion process, the ontology object index database and semantic reasoning had been combined. A comprehensive investigation and experiment were performed on an ontology-matching search engine. The design process of this method can serve as a reference for building simple ontology-based VSEs for other websites. The ontology-based semantic vertical searching function can be further improved later by expanding the ontology of the relevant specialized terms. Further, some other objects could be introduced into the ontology and the better searching results could be obtained.

Acknowledgments. This work was supported partially from Chinese National Natural Science Foundation "Development of Data Sharing Platform of Tibetan Plateau's Multi-Source Land-Atmosphere System Information" under grant number 91637313; the Special Scientific Research

Fund (Major Special Project) for Public Welfare Professions (Meteorology) under the grant number GYHY(QX) 20150600-7.

References

1. Aizawa, A.: An information-theoretic perspective of TF-IDF measures. Inf. Process. Manag. **39**, 45–65 (2003)
2. Chang, P.C., Galley, M., Manning, C.D.: Optimizing Chinese word segmentation for machine translation performance. Presented at The Workshop on Statistical Machine Translation, pp. 224–232. Association for Computational Linguistics (2008)
3. Cong, Y., Chan, Y., Ragan, M.A.: A novel alignment-free method for detection of lateral genetic transfer based on TF-IDF. Sci. Rep. **6**, 1–13 (2016)
4. Corby, O., Dieng-Kuntz, R., Faron-Zucker, C.: Querying the semantic web with corese search engine. Presented at European Conference on Artificial Intelligence, pp. 705–709 (2017)
5. Fu, Q.: Lucene research and implementation on the vertical search engine application to university library books. J. Taiyuan Normal Univ. **10**, 104–107 (2011)
6. Hendler, J., Lenat, D., Lenat, D., et al.: Very large knowledge bases-architecture vs engineering. Presented at International Joint Conference on Artificial Intelligence, pp. 2033–2036. Morgan Kaufmann Publishers Inc. (1995)
7. Hsu, Y.Y., Chen, H.Y., Kao, H.Y.: Using a search engine-based mutually reinforcing approach to assess the semantic relatedness of biomedical terms. Plos One **8** (2013). https://doi.org/10. 1371/journal.pone.0077868
8. Kara, S., Alan, O., Sabuncu, O., et al.: An ontology-based retrieval system using semantic indexing. Presented at the IEEE International Conference on Data Engineering Workshops, pp. 197–202 (2012)
9. Liu, D.F., Fan, X.S.: Study and application of web crawler algorithm based on heritrix. In: Advanced Materials Research, vol. 220, pp. 1069–1072 (2011)
10. Lombardo, V., Piana, F., Mimmo, D.: Semantics–informed geological maps: conceptual modeling and knowledge encoding. Comput. Geosci. **116**, 12–22 (2018)
11. Mcbride, B.: A semantic web toolkit. IEEE Internet Comput. **6**, 55–59 (2002)
12. Noy, N.F., Sintek, M., Decker, S., et al.: Creating semantic web contents with Protégé-2000. IEEE Intell. Syst. **16**, 60–71 (2005)
13. Yao, Y.: Library resource vertical search engine based on ontology. Presented at International Conference on Smart Grid and Electrical Automation, pp. 672–675. IEEE Computer Society (2017)
14. Huntley, R., Dimmer, E., Barrell, D., et al.: The gene ontology annotation (GOA) database. Nat. Preceding **10**, 429–438 (2009)
15. Pirro, G., Talia, D.: An approach to ontology mapping based on the Lucene search engine library. Presented at IEEE International Workshop on Database and Expert Systems Applications, pp. 407–411 (2007)
16. Wang, C., Li, S., Xiao, H.: Research on Ontology-based arid areas agriculture search engine. J. Agric. Mech. Res. **8**, 184–191 (2013)
17. Reviewer-Lin, D.: Review of WordNet: An Electronic Lexical Database. MIT Press, Ch. 25, pp. 292–296 (1999)
18. Sun, J., Li, Y., Wan, J.: Design and implementation of the search engine for earthquake based on Heritrix and Lucene. Seismol. Geomagnetic Obs. Res. **37**(5), 172–178 (2016)
19. Ding, Y.H., Yi, K., Xiang, R.H.: Design of paper duplicate detection system based on Lucene. Presented at IEEE Wearable Computing Systems, pp. 36–39 (2010)

A Lightweight Neural Network Combining Dilated Convolution and Depthwise Separable Convolution

Wei Sun[1,2], Xijie Zhou[1(✉)], Xiaorui Zhang[2,3], and Xiaozheng He[4]

[1] School of Automation,
Nanjing University of Information Science and Technology, Nanjing 210044, China
sunw0125@163.com, cfcfwyjd@163.com
[2] Jiangsu Collaborative Innovation Center of Atmospheric Environment and Equipment Technology, Nanjing 210044, China
[3] Jiangsu Engineering Center of Network Monitoring,
Nanjing University of Information Science and Technology, Nanjing 210044, China
[4] Department of Civil and Environmental Engineering, Rensselaer Polytechnic Institute, Troy, NY, USA

Abstract. Aimed to reduce the excessive cost of neural network, this paper proposes a lightweight neural network combining dilated convolution and depthwise separable convolution. Firstly, the dilated convolution is used to expand the receptive field during the convolution process while maintaining the number of convolution parameters, which can extract more high-level global semantic features and improve the classification accuracy of the network. Second, the use of the depthwise separable convolution reduces the network parameters and computational complexity in convolution operations. The experimental results on the CIFAR-10 dataset show that the proposed method improves the classification accuracy of the network while effectively compressing the network size.

Keywords: Lightweight neural network · Dilated convolution · Depthwise separable convolution · Classification accuracy · Cloud computing

1 Introduction

In recent years, convolutional neural networks have been used as an effective model in deep learning with significant progress in many fields, such as image processing, object detection and semantic segmentation. In 2012, Krizhevsky, et al. [1] first adopted deep learning algorithm and the AlexNet and won the champion of ImageNet Large Scale Visual Recognition Challenge. Since then, various convolutional neural network models have been proposed in the computer vision competition. In 2014, the Visual Geometry Group at the University of Oxford proposed the VGGNet [2], Google researchers proposed the GoogLeNet [3], and He et al. proposed the ResNet [4, 5] in 2015. These networks improve the performance of the AlexNet [6] at the cost of deeper and more complex networks to achieve higher accuracy. With the higher and higher precision for computer

X. Zhang et al. (Eds.): CloudComp 2019/SmartGift 2019, LNICST 322, pp. 210–220, 2020.
https://doi.org/10.1007/978-3-030-48513-9_17

vision tasks, the model depth and parameters are also exponentially increasing, making these models only run on GPUs with high computing power [3]. As a consequence, existing deep neural network models cannot be deployed on these resource-constrained devices [10, 18], such as mobile phones and in-vehicle embedded devices, due to their limitations in computing power and storage capacity. The emerging cloud computing has the potential to solve this challenge.

Cloud computing technology, which combines the characteristics of distributed computing, parallel computing, and grid computing, provides users with scalable computing resources and storage space by using massive computing clusters built by ordinary servers and storage clusters built by a large number of low-cost devices. However, the currently-existing high-performance cloud computing servers are too expensive to afford for individuals and small companies.

To enhance the affordability of cloud computing, many studies propose various lightweight neural networks. Some of them aim at reducing the size of neural network through compressing model. For example, Landola et al. [3] proposed the SqueezeNet that applies a convolution kernel to convolve and dimension the upper features and a feature convolution to perform feature stacking, which greatly reduces the number of parameters of convolution layers. Zhang et al. [14] proposed the ShuffleNet, which groups multi-channel feature lines and performs convolution to avoid unsmooth information flow. Howard et al. [15] proposed the depthwise separable convolution model, named MobileNet, which convolves the features of each channel separately and uses 1×1 convolution to splice all features of different channels. These light-weight models greatly reduce the number of network parameters and computational cost. However, the classification accuracy of the compression process cannot be guaranteed because the compression implementation only uses local information of the image.

In order to address these issues, this paper proposes a lightweight neural network combining dilated convolution and depthwise separable convolution. The proposed model divides the convolution process into two processes: expansion convolution and depthwise separable convolution. Depthwise separable convolution is used to reduce network computation. However, the use of the depthwise separation convolution cannot guarantee the classification accuracy of the model [11]. To solve this problem, we introduce dilated convolution to the depthwise separable convolution architecture. The dilated convolution can increase the receptive field of the network in the convolution process without increasing the number of convolution parameters, which help extract more global features and higher-level semantic features, thus improving the classification accuracy.

2 Approach

This paper uses dilated convolution as a filter to extract the feature of the image. Compared with the traditional filters, the dilated convolution yields more full-image information without increasing the number of network parameters, where the dilated rate δ controls the size of each convolution dilation. Then, we apply depthwise separable convolution to reduce the computational complexity and size of the model. This section first presents the idea of building a joint module for dilated convolution and depthwise separable convolution, which is used to build the deep convolution network.

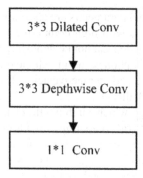

Fig. 1. Joint module

2.1 Joint Module

The joint module is the core of the proposed neural network. As shown in Fig. 1, the proposed model dilates each filter to obtain more image information without increasing the amount of calculation. The dilated filter is then used to convolve each input channel, and the final filter combines the output of different convolution channels.

Figure 2 illustrates the dilation process of 3×3 filter for the dilated convolution process in Fig. 1. The position of the dot mark in Fig. 2 indicates that there is a non-zero weight, and the node without the dot mark represents zero weight to that position. In Fig. 2(a), (b), and (c) represent filters with different dilated rates, respectively. The parameters of the convolution layer remain the same, and the amount of convolution process is the same too. The receptive fields of the filters (a), (b), and (c) are defined as $3 \times 3 = 9, 7 \times 7 = 49$ and $11 \times 11 = 121$, respectively. The increase of the receptive field means that each node contains higher semantic features, which can improve the classification accuracy. To factor the influence of different dilated convolution on model accuracy, we apply hyperparameter δ to control the size of each dilated convolution. As illustrated by Fig. 2, the relationship between the receptive field and the original filter size can be represented as:

$$C = \{(S + 1)\delta + S\} \tag{1}$$

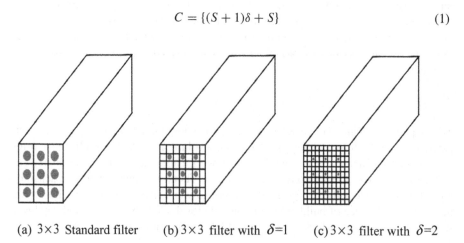

(a) 3×3 Standard filter   (b) 3×3 filter with δ=1   (c) 3×3 filter with δ=2

Fig. 2. Dilated convolution process

where C denotes the size of the receptive field, S the size of the initial filter, and δ the expansion rate.

Separable convolution operation is carried out on the obtained dilated convolution filter. The size of the dilation filter is $L_k \times L_k$ with $L_k = \sqrt{C}$. Figure 3 shows the process of constructing a $L_i \times L_i \times H$ feature map and a $L_i \times L_i \times N$ feature map. This process clearly shows how to reduce the number of parameters in the model.

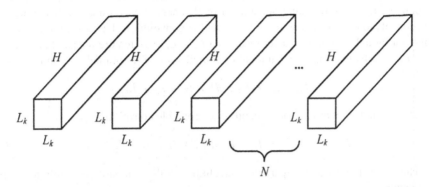

(a) Traditional convolution filters

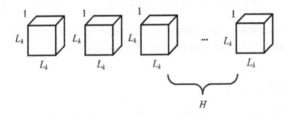

(b) Depthwise convolution filters

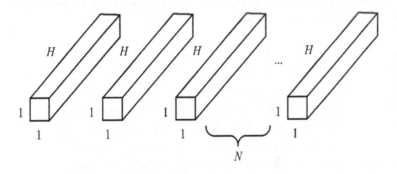

(c) Pointwise convolution filters

Fig. 3. Depthwise separable convolution process for dilated filters

Figure 3(a), (b) and (c) represent the traditional convolution filter, depthwise convolution filter, and pointwise convolution filter, respectively. Figure 3(b) and (c) together represent a separable convolution process, where $L_i \times L_i$ is the width and height of the input feature map, N is the number of filters, $L_k \times L_k$ is the width and height of the dilated filter, and H is the number of channels. For example, a single dilated filter of $L_k \times L_k$ is firstly used to carry out convolution operations on each channel. If the number of the feature map channels is H, there are H filters with the same size to participate in the convolution operation, and the number of channels of each filter is 1. The image is then convolved by N filters with 1×1 size and H convolution channels. Figure 3 shows that a traditional convolution layer receives a $L_i \times L_i \times H$ feature map and produces a $L_i \times L_i \times N$ feature map. The amount of computation of traditional convolution is:

$$G = L_k \times L_k \times H \times N \times L_i \times L_i \tag{2}$$

The amount of computation of depthwise separable convolution is:

$$G = L_k \times L_k \times H \times L_i \times L_i + H \times N \times L_i \times L_i \tag{3}$$

Therefore, the ratio of separable convolution to the standard convolution can be represented by:

$$\frac{L_k \times L_k \times H \times L_i \times L_i + H \times N \times L_i \times L_i}{L_k \times L_k \times H \times N \times L_i \times L_i} = \frac{1}{N} + \frac{1}{L_k^2} \tag{4}$$

Equation (4) quantifies the computational reduction of separable convolution as $\frac{1}{N} + \frac{1}{L_k^2}$ compared to the conventional convolution process.

2.2 Network Architecture

To avoid the vanishing gradient problem and accelerate the network training, we apply the BN layer (Batch Normalization) and the ReLU layer to make the gradient larger [16, 17] after the joint module introduced in Sect. 2.1. This paper labels the process presented in Fig. 4 as a basic network structure.

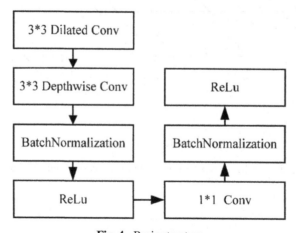

Fig. 4. Basic structure

Using only one basic structure is often not enough to form a usable neural network. Because the network is too shallow, we won't get the deep information of the image. Therefore, applying the basic structure repetitively to construct a lightweight neural network can improve the neural network performance, as shown in Fig. 5. This lightweight neural network complements the joint module to form the basic structure. Several basic network structures are combined with the average pooling layer, the full connection layer, and the Softmax layer to form the overall neural network structure. In total, the model consists of 30 layers, including one average pooling layer and one fully connected layer, 9 dilated convolution layers, 9 depthwise separable convolution layers, 9 BN layers, and one Softmax layer.

2.3 Loss Function and Optimization

We adopt cross-entropy as the loss function of neural network, using Adam as the network optimizer. The formula for cross-entropy is as follows:

$$W(p, q) = \sum_i p(i) * \log(\frac{1}{q(i)}) \tag{5}$$

where $W(p, q)$ represents cross-entropy of the distribution of the true mark, q is the predicted mark distribution of the trained model, and cross-entropy loss function measures the similarity between p and q.

Adam is considered to be robust in selecting hyperparameters. Therefore, this paper adopts adaptive Adam learning rate to optimize the proposed model.

3 Experiments

In order to verify the effectiveness of the proposed model, we constructed an experimental platform and selected a typical dataset. Then, the proposed network model was compared with other models to verify the effectiveness of the proposed model. Furthermore, we investigated the influence of the dilated convolution size on the classification accuracy of the model and verified that the classification accuracy of the proposed model.

All experiments were carried out on a computer with Intel Core i7-7700k CPU, 4.20 GHz × 8 frequency, and GTX 1080Ti graphics card. CUDA version 9.0 and cuDNN version 7.3.1 were installed. To configure the environment required for the training model. The proposed model and algorithms were compiled and operated on TensorFlow 1.12.2.

3.1 Comparison of the Proposed Network with Other Networks

To demonstrate the performance of the proposed model in network compression while ensuring accuracy of classification, we compare the proposed network with other mainstream networks and illustrate their classification accuracy based on the dataset CIFAR − 10. The comparisons are shown in Table 1.

Table 1 shows that, compared with some mainstream networks, the proposed network model achieves high accuracy on CIFAR-10 dataset. The proposed network provides

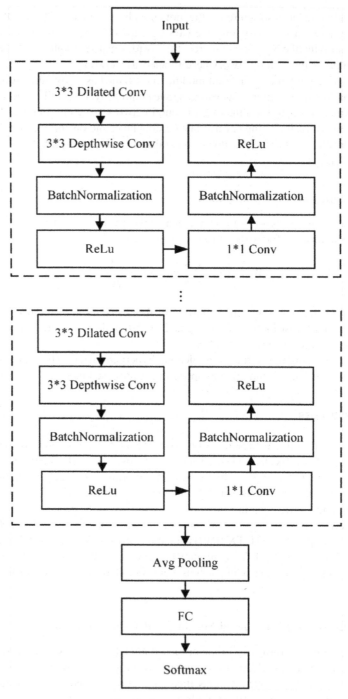

Fig. 5. Structural flow chart

Table 1. The proposed network vs popular networks

Model	CIFAR-10 accuracy	Million parameters
This paper	84.25%	3.1
1.0 MobileNet 224	83.91%	4.2
GoogleNet	83.84%	6.8
SqueezeNet	69.83%	1.25
VGG 16	86.17%	138

accurate results while greatly reducing the number of network parameters compared with MobileNet and GoogleNet. The SqueezeNet typically acquires fewer parameters, however, at the cost of low accuracy. Although the proposed network requires more parameters than SqueezeNet, it is much better in terms of classification accuracy. Because SqueezeNet sacrifices classification accuracy, it cannot meet the high-accuracy need in practical applications. Therefore, the proposed network is superior to SqueezeNet. In addition, although the VGG16 network has slightly higher accuracy in classification results than the proposed network, its model size is dozens more than the proposed model, resulting in computational difficulty when computing power is limited. Due to much fewer network parameters, the proposed network can be easily implemented on mobile devices with less storage capacity while having good classification accuracy.

3.2 Different Dilated Rate

This study applies the dilated rate to control the size of the dilated convolution, which affects the size of the receptive field, leading to the change of classification accuracy. Therefore, we compare the network classification accuracy under different dilated rates to verify the effect of the dilation rate, as summarized in Table 2.

Table 2. Classification accuracy of different dilated rates

Dilated rate	CIFAR-10 accuracy
0	82.04%
1	83.32%
2	84.25%
3	83.56%

Applying different dilated rates to the dilated convolution using the CIFAR-10 dataset, Table 2 shows that the joint dilated convolution and the depthwise separable convolution improve classification accuracy by two percent compared to those networks without joint dilated convolution. It also shows that the maximum classification accuracy is achieved when the dilated rate is 2. As the dilated rate continues to increase, the classification accuracy decreases slightly. This is because the dilated rate increases the receptive field, while the larger the receptive field, which means it may contain more global and semantic features. This observation warns us that blindly expanding the receptive field can lose a lot of local and detailed information during the convolution process, affecting the classification accuracy of small targets and distant objects.

3.3 Generalization Capability

The results in previous sections show that the proposed network performs well on the CIFAR-10 dataset. To investigate the proposed model's performance stability on other datasets, we conducted training and testing on Tiny ImageNet. The result is as follows.

Table 3. This paper network in Tiny ImageNet

Model	Tiny ImageNet accuracy
This paper	85.01%
1.0 MobileNet 224	83.81%
GoogleNet	82.94%

Table 3 shows that the proposed network has good accuracy on Tiny ImageNet. Compared with the MobileNet of Width Multiplier = 1 and Resolution Multiplier = 224, the proposed network improves the accuracy on both datasets. Compared with GoogleNet, the proposed network enhances the accuracy rate on Tiny ImageNet from 82.94% to 85.01%. Based on these comparisons, we can conclude that the proposed network can consistently improve classification accuracy, indicating a good generalization ability. The proposed model also reduces the size under the premise of ensuring accuracy, which makes it possible to achieve better classification accuracy on mobile devices.

Although the proposed network is a classification network, the proposed network can be used as the basic network of SSD or YOLO models, or transplanted to different devices, to realize real-time pedestrian detection. However, the model of pedestrian detection requires higher computational cost, which will affect the accuracy of pedestrian detection on the equipment.

4   Conclusion

This paper proposes a lightweight neural network model for joint dilated convolution and depthwise separable convolution. The joint model can reduce the computational burden with depthwise separable convolution, making it possible to apply the network to computationally-constrained devices. Meanwhile, the dilated convolution is used to increase the receptive field in the process of convolution without increasing the number of convolution parameters. It supplies global features, and higher semantic-level features can be extracted in the process of convolution. The joint model can also improve classification accuracy. Experimental results demonstrate that the proposed model makes a good compromise between the classification accuracy and the model size, while the classification accuracy of the network is guaranteed when the network is compressed. Article puts forward the lightweight of neural network can reduce the cost of cloud computing. In addition, the proposed network can be combined with Internet-of-things. For example, the depth network can be further optimized and transplanted in Android mobile devices, embedded devices such as MCU or FPGA. Such applications will convey significant impacts on human life, work, health, and many other areas of our society [21, 22].

Acknowledgement. This work is supported in part by the National Nature Science Foundation of China (No. 61304205, 61502240), Natural Science Foundation of Jiangsu Province (BK20191401), and Innovation and Entrepreneurship Training Project of College Students (201910300050Z, 201910300222).

References

1. Krizhevsky, A., Sutskever, I., Geoffrey, E.H.: ImageNet classification with deep convolutional neural networks (2012). http://papers.nips.cc/paper/4824-imagenet-classification-with-deep-convolutional-neural-networks.pdf
2. Simonyan, K., Zisserman, A.: Very deep convolutional networks for large-scale image recognition. Comput. Sci. (2014)
3. Szegedy, C., et al.: Going deeper with convolutions. In: Proceedings of the IEEE Conference on Computer Vision and Pattern Recognition, pp. 1–9 (2015)
4. He, K., Zhang, X., Ren, S., Sun, J.: Identity mappings in deep residual networks. In: Leibe, B., Matas, J., Sebe, N., Welling, M. (eds.) ECCV 2016. LNCS, vol. 9908, pp. 630–645. Springer, Cham (2016). https://doi.org/10.1007/978-3-319-46493-0_38
5. Xie, S., Girshick, R., Dollar, P., Tu, Z., He, K.: Aggregated residual transformations for deep neural networks, pp. 1–6. arXiv preprint arXiv:1611.05431 (2016)
6. Iandola, F.N., Han, S., Moskewicz, M.W., Ashraf, K., Dally, W.J., Keutzer, K.: SqueezeNet: AlexNet-level accuracy with 50x fewer parameters and <0.5 MB model size, pp. 1–8. arXiv preprint arXiv:1602.07360 (2016)
7. Ghemawat, S., Gobioff, H., Leung, S.T.: The Google file system. ACM SIGOPS Oper. Syst. Rev. **37**(5), 29–43 (2003)
8. Chang, F., Dean, J., Ghemawat, S., et al.: Bigtable: a distributed storage system for structured data. ACM Trans. Comput. Syst. (TOCS). **26**(2), 4–5 (2008)
9. Dean, J., Ghemawat, S.: MapReduce: simplified data processing on large clusters. Commun. ACM **51**(1), 107–113 (2008)
10. Chollet, F.: Xception: deep learning with depthwise separable convolutions, p. 1. arXiv preprint arXiv:1610.02357v2 (2016)
11. Hu, J., Shen, L., Sun, G.: Squeeze-and-excitation networks, pp. 1–7. arXiv preprint arXiv:1709.01507 (2017)
12. Zhang, X., Zhou, X., Lin, M., Sun, J.: ShuffleNet: an extremely efficient convolutional neural network for mobile devices. arXiv preprint arXiv:1707.01083 (2017)
13. Howard, A.G., et al.: MobileNets: efficient convolutional neural networks for mobile vision applications. arXiv preprint arXiv:1704.04861 (2017)

14. Han, S., Mao, H., Dally, W.J.: Deep compression: compressing deep neural networks with pruning quantization and Huffman coding. arXiv preprint arXiv:1510.00149v5 (2016)
15. Ioffe, S., Szegedy, C.: Batch normalization: accelerating deep network training by reducing internal covariate shift, pp. 3–5. arXiv preprint arXiv:1502.03167 (2015)
16. Krizhevsky, A., Sutskever, I., Geoffrey, E.H.: ImageNet classification with deep convolutional neural networks. In: NIPS (2012)
17. Hu, H., Peng, R., Tai, Y.W., et al.: Network trimming: a data-driven neuron pruning approach towards efficient deep architectures. In: Proceedings of the International Conference on Learning and Representation (ICLR), pp. 214–222. IEEE (2017)
18. Qiu, J., et al.: Going deeper with embedded FPGA platform for convolutional neural network. In: ACM International Symposium on FPGA (2016)
19. Wu, J., Leng, C., Wang, Y., Hu, Q., Cheng, J.: Quantized convolutional neural networks for mobile devices, pp. 1–2. arXiv preprint arXiv:1512.06473 (2015)

Resource Allocation Algorithms of Vehicle Networks with Stackelberg Game

Ying Zhang[1] , Guang-Shun Li[1,2] , Jun-Hua Wu[1(✉)] , Jia-He Yan[1] ,
and Xiao-Fei Sheng[1]

[1] School of Information Science and Engineering, Qufu Normal University,
Rizhao 276800, China
shdwjh@163.com
[2] Department of Computer, The Hong Kong Polytechnic University, Hung Hom, Hong Kong

Abstract. With the emergence and development of the Internet of Vehicles (IoV), higher demands are placed on the response speed and ultra-low delay of the vehicle. Cloud computing services are not friendly to reducing latency and response time. Mobile Edge Computing (MEC) is a promising solution to this problem. In this paper, we introduce MEC into the IoV to propose a specific vehicle edge resource management framework, which consists of fog nodes (FN), data service agents (DSA), and cars. We proposed a dynamic service area partitioning algorithm that enables the DSA to adjust the service area and provide a more efficient service for the vehicle. A resource allocation framework based on Stackelberg game model is proposed to analyze the pricing problem of FN and data resource strategy of DSA. We use the distributed iterative algorithm to solve the problem of game equilibrium. Our proposed resource management framework is finally verified by numerical results, which show that the allocation efficiency of FN resources among the cars is ensured, and we also get a subgame perfect nash equilibrium.

Keywords: Internet of Vehicles · Edge computing · Stackelberg game · Wireless resource allocation · Nash equilibrium

1 Introduction

The Internet of Vehicles technology has gradually come into people's field of vision. Many applications in this field, such as safe driving analysis, camera image processing, and optimal route planning, etc., have high requirements for low latency and high throughput [1]. In cloud computing, data service agents aggregate resources into a shared pool, and data service subscribers who need these services can get data services based on demand [2, 3]. However, the geographically long distance between the cloud server and the terminal may cause large network delays and increase costs, which is a great disadvantage for applications that require fast response time and high mobility requirements [4, 5]. Therefore, it is very important to bring resources closer to the end user. In this case, a new architecture and technology called MEC emerged [6]. Therefore, FN is slowly entering people's sight. FNs are lower in the network topology, have a smaller

X. Zhang et al. (Eds.): CloudComp 2019/SmartGift 2019, LNICST 322, pp. 221–230, 2020.
https://doi.org/10.1007/978-3-030-48513-9_18

network delay, and have a wide geographical distribution. These characteristics can meet the small delay and location-aware services of the car as an terminal user requirements for data services [7, 8].

In this paper, MEC technology is introduced into IoV to form vehicular edge computing (VEC). Vehicles cannot directly interface with FNs, so it is important to add a layer of DSA between them. DSA can serve as an intermediary to provide FN data services to the vehicle. When service requests are received from all cars, each DSA can aggregate resources from the FN and sell data services to the car. In this way, cars can use the computing resource services provided by FN through DSA. Each car is a data service subscriber and needs to apply for data services from DSA. We focus on the service radius of each DSA and the benefits of each layer, proposing an efficient data resource management framework.

2 Related Work

In some literatures, fog computing has been proposed as an extension of cloud computing to make up for shortcomings in cloud computing. Ahlgren et al. [9] studied that fog can make up for the shortcomings of the cloud, and cooperate with the cloud to work together. Yannuzzi et al. [10] started from the application scenario of the Internet of Things. The resource limitation of the terminal device talked about the demand for the cloud, and the limitation caused by the position of the cloud in the network talked about the fog. The contrast of clouds and fog, the combination of clouds and fog, the advantages of fog, the application of fog, and the challenges of fog are discussed. Taleb et al. [11] have studied the application of combining edge computing network and cloud computing network. The overview of MEC architecture, typical technologies and main application scenarios are described. In the previous work of our team, we have also studied the resource scheduling in edge computing. Li et al. [12] aimed at the difficulties of resource scheduling in current edge computing, and obtained a new resource scheduling method using improved clustering methods. And in [13], fuzzy clustering and particle swarm optimization are combined to generate a resource scheduling algorithm, which improves the service level and average response time.

Kumar et al. [14] have discussed the advantages of edge computing in building a low-latency, lightweight, high-performance, and highly reliable smart grid platform. It introduces various application scenarios and corresponding edge computing solutions in smart grid. Hou et al. [15] have presented to mine a large number of unused vehicle resources and reduce communication costs. Zhang et al. considered the shortcomings in cloud computing and the massive amount of data, combined with the demand for services in the Internet of Vehicles, transferred some services to the edge computing layer, and proposed a smart vehicle network based on collaborative fog computing in [16]. Li et al. [17] added a service intermediary between the cloud layer and the user, and leased the cloud service to the user. And improved the traditional pricing strategy and realized higher benefits. In [18], a Stackelberg game theory model for bandwidth allocation was established to maximize the benefits of both players through a defined pricing mechanism. Wang et al. [19] analyzed two customer scenarios, these two scenarios are homogeneous and heterogeneous, and built a Stackelberg game based on customer scenarios to improve profits.

3 System Framework

The car needs data service during the driving process, each car can deliver it to the FN at the edge of the network. Each DSA selects a FN to provide cars with the required data services, as shown in Fig. 1. Such a three-layer edge network is the main core framework of this paper. DSA is located in the middle layer, which serves the lower car and manages the upper FN through connecting car and FN. We set the unit of computing resources of each FN to CRB and provide services at a speed of u. Cars rent FN's computing resources through DSA.

The system architecture is shown in Fig. 1. FN stands for fog server, DSA is multi-data agent, and car stands for data service subscribers.

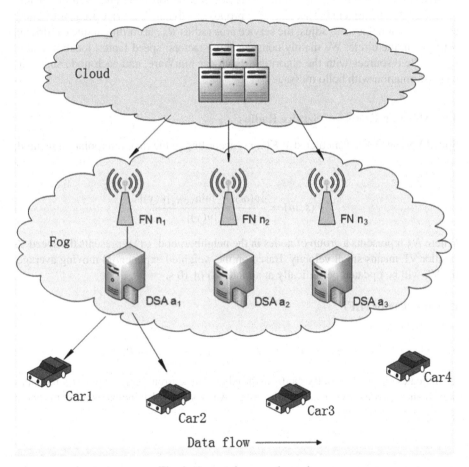

Fig. 1. System framework graph

4 Service Area Partitioning Algorithm

In order to enable the car to apply for services at any time and reduce the service response time, it is necessary to divide the service area of each DSA. The service area of DSA is a circle with a radius of R_{ref}. By default, all cars in this circle are served by the corresponding DSA. Each car can communicate with FN through DSA, or with vehicles in different service areas through mmWare or other networks. One FN is responsible for one DSA, and each DSA can communicate directly with the corresponding FN. Because the traffic conditions on different roads are different and the driving of vehicles is random, the density of vehicles in the service area of each DSA is different, which leads to the unbalanced load of DSA. If there are too many cars requesting data services within a DSA service area, the response time of service will be too long, and even the quality of service will be affected. Therefore, we proposed a dynamic service area partitioning algorithm that helps us to adjust the service area radius R_{ref} according to the car driving behavior in the circle. We mainly consider three factors: speed factor, location factor, server idle resources with the algorithm. Each car mmWare, and each node shares its own information with hello messages.

4.1 Affecting Factors of Service Radius

Speed Factor (VF). Calculated $VF(s, m)$ according to the time interpolation method:

$$VF(s, m) = \frac{|v(m)| - \min_{y \in N_S} |v(y)|}{|v(y)|} \tag{1}$$

Where N_S represents a group of nodes in the neighborhood, $v()$ represents the speed. A smaller VF means small velocity. Based on the weighted exponential moving average, the VF will be updated periodically at an interval of 10 s.

Location Factor (LF)

$$LF(s, i) = |tv_{si} - 2(R_{ref\,1} + R_{ref\,2} + \cdots + R_{ref\,i})| \tag{2}$$

LF indicates the position of the car from the edge of the current service area, tv_{si} indicates the distance traveled by the car s in the area i. And a smaller LF indicates the car is about to leave the service area.

Server Idle Resources

$$(1 - \delta_i) \leq \delta_\Delta$$
$$s.t$$
$$\sum_{i=1}^{R} 2(R_{ref\,i})\pi \geq M. \tag{3}$$
$$\exists i, \forall R$$
$$(1 - \delta_i) \geq \delta_{min}$$

δ_i represents the resource occupancy of the server. All service areas add up to exceed M, and idle resources should be greater than the minimum value. Only by guaranteeing these two conditions can the server provide data resource services.

5 Stackelberg Game Decision

5.1 Stackelberg Game Analysis for Two-Layer Interaction

Assume that in a particular edge computing network, there are multiple FNs, set to set $M = \{1, 2, \ldots, m\}$. The set of DSAs covered in this range is $N = \{1, 2, \ldots, n\}$, and FN competes for all DSAs. The price strategy of the FN_j node is p_j, exist $j \in M$, and the price strategy of all FNs is $p = (p_1, p_2, \ldots, p_m)$ [20]. The CRB requirement strategy of DSA_i is x_{ij}, exist $i \in N$ which means the quantity of CRB purchased by DSA_i at FN_j. We define $x_i = (x_{ij}, x_{-ij})$ as the CRB requirement strategy vector of DSA_i, where x_{-ij} represents the strategy of DSA_i at other FN except FN_j, and $q = (q_1, q_2, \ldots, q_n)$ denotes the set of data requirement strategies for all DSAs.

The game between FN and DSA consists of two phases. In the first phase, different FNs first declare their own price strategy p and broadcast the strategy to all DSAs. In the second phase, the DSA makes its own data resource strategy q based on the received price strategy vector p. The strategic combination of DSA and FN (p, q) is a solution to the Stackelberg game. Next, we formulate the utility of DSA and FN.

The Utility of DSA. The utility function of DSA is composed of two parts: the benefits and costs of providing data services for car. The utility of DSA can be expressed by the following formula:

$$U_{Ni} = U_i \left(\sum_{j=1}^{m} x_{ij} \right) - \sum_{j=1}^{m} P_j(p_j x_{ij}) - \sum_{j=1}^{m} D_j(x_{ij}) \tag{4}$$

Where $U_i \left(\sum_{j=1}^{m} x_{ij} \right)$ is the total revenue earned by DSA when car is served by DSA, p_j is the price set by FN, $P_j(p_j x_{ij})$ is the price paid by DSA to FN, and $D_j(x_{ij})$ represents the delay cost of DSA's service to cars.

We set that the workload of each DSA follows the Poisson arrival process. If the total load $Q_j \geq C_j$ of all DSAs in an FN, the network will be congested. Only when the load of all DSAs in FN satisfies $Q_j < C_j$, the effective transmission of data can be guaranteed. Specifically, the load of FN is Q_j, and the delay cost function of DSA_i in FN_j can be expressed as:

$$D_j(q) = \begin{cases} \frac{\beta_j}{C_j - Q_j}, & \text{if } Q_j < C_j \\ \infty, & \text{if } Q_j \geq C_j \end{cases} \tag{5}$$

Where β_j is a constant related to data transfer technology.

The Utility of FN. For FN, the total utility is total income minus total expenses. We set c_{ij} to the transmission cost per unit CRB, and DSA_i is the service price per unit for FN. Therefore, the utility of FN can be expressed by the following formula:

$$U_{Mj} = \sum_{i=1}^{n} (p_j - c_{ij}) x_{ij} \tag{6}$$

Where $\sum_{i=1}^{n} p_j x_{ij}$ is the total revenue received by the FN from the DSA, and $\sum_{i=1}^{n} c_{ij} x_{ij}$ is the total transmission cost estimated by the FN.

To get data services from FN, DSA should buy less CRB from FN to get satisfactory service, which comes at a price. How much resources does car need to apply for to complete its own tasks, but also to ensure the quality of service without wasting resources. FN provides data computing services to DSA and needs to give a price that will bring benefits to itself. But if given a higher price, DSA will reduce the number of CRB purchases or chooses another FN, so it is necessary to predict the response of DSA to determine the service price in order to maximize utility. Therefore, how FN price its own resources to protect its own revenue without losing user satisfaction is a key.

Aiming at the characteristics of local sharing of decision information among players in Stackelberg game model mentioned above, we solve the perfect Nash equilibrium (x^*, p^*) of the sub-game with the distributed iteration algorithm proposed in [21].

6   Simulation Experiments

The scene we simulated was in a 3,000-m road. All the cars were running in one direction. The initial DSA service area was 500 m. In this 3,000-m area, we allocated 3 FNs and DSAs. We assume that each car's sensor is in the same location on the car, the rate of data transmission is 50 km/ms, and the delay tolerance of car is 60 ms. In the experiment of iterative algorithm, we only use two service areas covered by different FNs. There are three kinds of DSAs in this area, which are $\alpha = 0.5$, $\alpha = 0.9$ and $\alpha = 2$. Assume that under the initial conditions, the price strategies of both FNs are both 0.1, the value of β is 1, and the initial data resource strategy of the DSA at both FNs is 0.

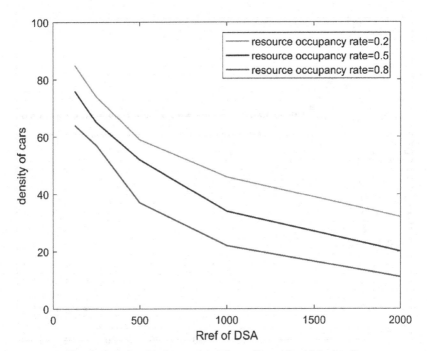

Fig. 2. Relationship between service radius and vehicle density

As shown in the above figure, as the density of vehicles in the area continues to increase, the service area of the DSA will also increase. When the density of car is fixed, we find that the DSA has a higher resource occupancy rate, that is, when the server is busy, the service area of the DSA is smaller. As can be seen from the Fig. 2, the greater the density of car, the less resources available to the server and the smaller the service area.

Figure 3 shows the curve changes of three different utility functions of DSA in the iteration process. The users of curve $\alpha = 2$ are cars which is the least sensitive to data service delay, so the corresponding price paid by car is relatively low. The resource in FN is preferentially contested by DSA which is sensitive to delay and applies for more resources, so the effect is relatively low. The curve of $\alpha = 0.5$ is car is the most sensitive to data service delay, so DSA needs to buy more data resources from FN, price strategy of FN will be more friendly, so the utility of DSA is higher, but as the equilibrium point of game is reached, the resource of FN is effectively utilized, and the utility of DSA decreases accordingly. Car in the DSA service area of $\alpha = 0.9$ is moderately sensitive to service delay, and the curve increases gradually at first, and then gradually becomes stable. All three curves tend to stabilize after reaching that equilibrium point.

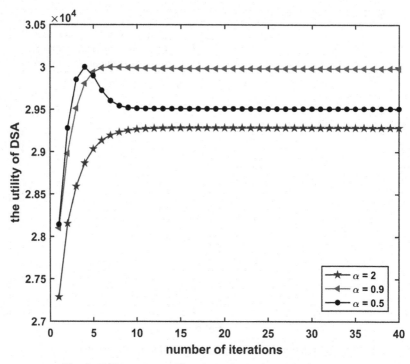

Fig. 3. Different user utility changes with the iterative process

From Fig. 4, we obtain the subgame perfect Nash equilibrium of the Stackelberg game of heterogeneous wireless networks. The two curves in the figure are the optimal price curve of the first FN and the optimal price curve of the second FN. The intersection of the two curves is the Nash equilibrium point p^*. The intersection of two curves corresponds to the optimal price strategy of two FNs. At this point, both the FN layer and the DSA layer have reached the Nash equilibrium, and the subgame perfect Nash equilibrium is obtained for the Stackelberg game.

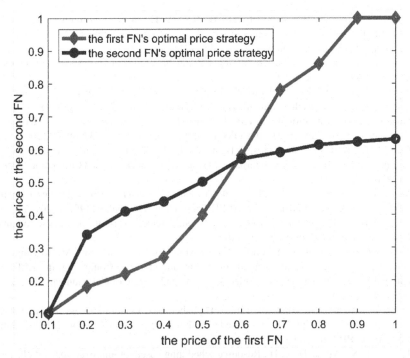

Fig. 4. Nash equilibrium of game between FNs

7 Conclusion

In this paper, we propose a framework for FN, DSA and car scenarios for VEC. Under this framework, we first judge the service area of the DSA according to the characteristics of the car movement. On this basis, a Stackelberg game model is established to study the pricing of FN and the optimal purchase amount of DSA resources. At each stage, it is necessary to meet the best results of the participants, and no one in this framework can unilaterally change their behavior to achieve better utility. Through simulation results, it is proved that both sides of the game, FN and DSA, have reached the highest effectiveness, and the proposed framework achieves high-performance services. For future work, we can consider the contact between the cars of lowest layer, and whether some data services can be obtained in the neighborhood vehicles. If data services can be provided between cars, how to choose neighbor vehicles to provide services to achieve lower latency services.

References

1. Hu, Q., Wu, C., Zhao, X., Chen, X., Yoshinaga, T.: Vehicular multi-access edge computing with licensed Sub-6 GHz, IEEE 802.11p and mmWave. IEEE Access **6**, 1 (2017)
2. Gubbi, J., Buyya, R., Marusic, S., Palaniswami, M.: Internet of Things (IoT): a vision, architectural elements, and future directions. Future Gener. Comput. Syst. **29**(7), 1645–1660 (2013)

3. Zhang, H., Yong, X., Bu, S., Niyato, D., Yu, R., Zhu, H.: Computing in resource allocation three-tier IoT fog networks: a joint optimization approach combining stackelberg game and matching. IEEE Internet Things J. **4**(5), 1204–1215 (2017)
4. Dastjerdi, A.V., Buyya, R.: Fog computing: helping the Internet of Things realize its potential. Computer **49**, 112–116 (2016)
5. Ning, Z., Kong, X., Xia, F., Hou, W., Wang, X.: Green and sustainable cloud of things: enabling collaborative edge computing. IEEE Commun. Mag. **57**, 72–78 (2019)
6. Greenberg, A.G., Hamilton, J.R., Maltz, D.A., Patel, P.: The cost of a cloud: research problems in data center networks. ACM SIGCOMM Comput. Commun. Rev. **39**, 68–73 (2008)
7. Goiri, I., Le, K., Guitart, J., Torres, J., Bianchini, R.: Intelligent placement of datacenters for internet services. In: 2011 31st International Conference on Distributed Computing Systems, pp. 131–142 (2011)
8. Yu, L., Chen, L., Cai, Z., Shen, H., Liang, Y., Pan, Y.: Stochastic load balancing for virtual resource management in datacenters. IEEE Trans. Cloud Comput. **PP**(99), 1 (2016)
9. Ahlgren, B., et al.: Content, connectivity, and cloud: ingredients for the network of the future. Commun. Mag. IEEE **49**(7), 62–70 (2011)
10. Yannuzzi, M., Milito, R.A., Serral-Gracià, R., Montero, D., Nemirovsky, M.: Keyingredient sinan iotrecipe: fog computing, cloud computing, and more fog Computing. In: IEEE International Workshop on Computer Aided Modeling and Design of Communication Links and Networks (2015)
11. Taleb, T., Samdanis, K., Mada, B., Flinck, H., Sabella, D.: On multi-access edge computing: a survey of the emerging 5G network edge architecture and orchestration. IEEE Commun. Surv. Tutor. **PP**(99), 1 (2017)
12. Li, G., Xu, S., Wu, J., Ding, H.: Resource scheduling based on improved spectral clustering algorithm in edge computing. Sci. Program. **2018**(5), 1–13 (2018)
13. Li, G., Liu, Y., Wu, J., Lin, D., Zhao, S.: Methods of resource scheduling based on optimized fuzzy clustering in fog computing. Sensors **19**(2), 2122 (2019)
14. Kumar, N., Zeadally, S., Rodrigues, J.J.P.C.: Vehicular delay-tolerant networks for smart grid data management using mobile edge computing. IEEE Commun. Mag. **54**(10), 60–66 (2016)
15. Hou, X., Yong, L., Min, C., Di, W., Jin, D., Sheng, C.: Vehicular fog computing: a viewpoint of vehicles as the infrastructures. IEEE Trans. Veh. Technol. **65**(6), 3860–3873 (2016)
16. Zhang, W., Zhang, Z., Chao, H.C.: Cooperative fog computing for dealing with big data in the internet of vehicles: architecture and hierarchical resource management. IEEE Commun. Mag. **55**(12), 60–67 (2017)
17. He, L., Dong, M., Ota, K., Guo, M.: Pricing and repurchasing for big data processing in multi-clouds. IEEE Trans. Emerg. Top. Comput. **4**(2), 1 (2016)
18. Cong, W., Ying, Y., Wang, C., Xi, H., Zheng, C.: Virtual bandwidth allocation game in data centers. In: IEEE International Conference on Information Science and Technology (2012)
19. Hao, W., Zhao, Y., Guan, H.: On pricing schemes in data center network with game theoretic approach. In: International Conference on Computer Communication and Networks (2014)
20. Pu-yan, N., Pei-ai, Z.: A note on Stackelberg games. In: 2008 Chinese Control and Decision Conference, pp. 1201–1203 (2008)
21. Jiang, Y., Chen, S.Z., Hu, B.: Stackelberg games-based distributed algorithm of pricing and resource allocation in heterogeneous wireless networks. J. Commun. **1**, 61–68 (2013)

Research on Coordination Control Theory of Greenhouse Cluster Based on Cloud Computing

Xiangnan Zhang, Wenwen Gong, Yifei Chen$^{(\boxtimes)}$, Dan Li, and Yawei Wang

College of Information and Electrical Engineering, China Agricultural University, Beijing, China
glfei_cau@126.com

Abstract. With the development of modern agriculture, the clustering phenomenon of greenhouses is prominent. The traditional single greenhouse management is oriented to farmers. It is difficult for upper management to obtain the information of greenhouses conveniently. The real-time transmission of monitoring results and the real-time regulation of the internal environment of greenhouse clusters are difficult. And the scope of management of large-scale agricultural companies is also growing, and an integrated management platform is urgently needed. The emergence of cloud computing technology has made this management model possible. On the other hand, the greenhouse cluster is a non-linear complex large system, which not only needs to improve the capacity of the greenhouse cluster, but also take into account the utilization of regional resources. The traditional control methods are insufficient in the efficient use of regional resources, and the existing control theory can't meet the above requirements. Target requirements. The computing power of local equipment can't meet the needs of massive data processing. Therefore, based on the cloud computing platform, this paper draws on the theory of complex systems to carry out coordinated control theory research on greenhouse clusters, establishes a cloud computing-based greenhouse cluster management system, and designs greenhouse clusters. The control system description model is coordinated; on this basis, the greenhouse cluster coordination control structure model is designed. This study provides a reference for the control of modern greenhouse clusters, and has certain theoretical significance and application value for the development of greenhouse cluster coordinated control theory.

Keywords: Cloud computing · Greenhouse cluster · Coordinated control

1 Introduction

Greenhouses are facilities that provide a production environment and increase production for off-season cash crops. The regulation of the greenhouse environment is one of the important factors affecting crop yields in the greenhouse [1]. Control in the greenhouse (the influence of the two control methods) greenhouse atmospheric environment,

© ICST Institute for Computer Sciences, Social Informatics and Telecommunications Engineering 2020
Published by Springer Nature Switzerland AG 2020. All Rights Reserved
X. Zhang et al. (Eds.): CloudComp 2019/SmartGift 2019, LNICST 322, pp. 231–239, 2020.
https://doi.org/10.1007/978-3-030-48513-9_19

greenhouse plant growth environment, is two common single greenhouse environmental control methods. However, under the large-scale greenhouse planting mode, the construction of a control system for greenhouse clusters can greatly enhance the core competitiveness of the regional economy [2].

The coordinated control of greenhouse clusters is significantly different from the previous single greenhouse control, and it also faces more problems: 1. Effectively use and manage resources under the constraints of regional resources [3, 4]; 2. Effectively control the fruiting period [5, 6], linkage Regulate the parameters in each greenhouse; 3. Monitor the growth of crops in each greenhouse and make regional-level warnings and forecasts [7]. Therefore, research on the regulation of such large-scale greenhouse cluster systems is not only very important, but also challenges existing greenhouse research methods and greenhouse control theories.

At present, the research on smart agriculture has seen the issue of intelligent regulation of agricultural systems from a more macro perspective. Mainly manifested in: the agricultural system is a complex large system with many specialities, such as: the ambiguity of the system dynamics characteristics and the uncertainty and uncertainty of the object feature model with different objects and environments [8] etc. Therefore, it is difficult to control by traditional control methods, so there are still many difficulties in the study of the overall intelligent control of agricultural systems.

Based on the cloud computing architecture, this paper studies the coordinated control theory model for greenhouse clusters based on the theory of large-scale agricultural systems. With the help of complex large-system theory, this paper studies the construction of greenhouse system hierarchical control system and establishes greenhouse from the perspective of large-scale system control. The cluster coordination control system description model and the control structure model have theoretical significance and application value for improving the accuracy of greenhouse cluster control. In addition, the analysis of the greenhouse cluster coordination control process from the perspective of large-scale hierarchical control has undoubtedly expanded a new research field and enriched the theoretical research in the field of greenhouse control.

2 Related Work

For greenhouse cluster systems, the direct target is a single greenhouse. The greenhouse cluster system based on tens of thousands of greenhouses is a typical MIMO nonlinear system. If the controlled parameters of each greenhouse are 5 typical parameters of temperature, light, ventilation, irrigation and fertilization, the control parameters of the greenhouse will reach 50,000. Based on the foregoing analysis, if the specific parameters of each greenhouse are directly controlled by this large system, it is obvious that the system is a high-dimensional complex system. In order to reduce the dimension and reduce the complexity of the control system, according to the control architecture of the complex system, the design is a hierarchical control mode, and the micro-, medium-, and macro-architecture is adopted from the bottom to construct the greenhouse cluster system [9].

In the description model of the greenhouse cluster coordinated control system, the traditional modeling method is to treat the greenhouse system as a simple and independent environmental system for analysis and modeling, which has some drawbacks. Considering the greenhouse system as a greenhouse-crop system, that is, dividing the greenhouse system into an environmental system and a crop growth system is currently the accepted greenhouse system analysis and modeling method in Europe [10]. Figure 1 shows a general description of the greenhouse system.

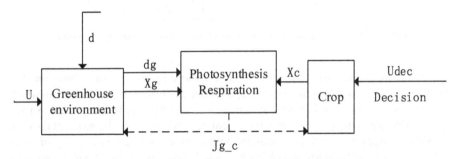

Fig. 1. Greenhouse cluster coordinated control system description model diagram

In Fig. 2: j_{g_c} represents the exchange of greenhouse environmental systems with crop systems, such as reduction of CO2 by photosynthesis, increase of CO2 caused by various exhalation of crops, and transpiration of water and gas [11].

In terms of the control structure model of the greenhouse system, the state space model of the traditional single-unit greenhouse system can be expressed by the following formula:

$$\dot{x}(t) = f(x(t), u(t), d(t), t)$$
$$y(t) = g(x(t), u(t), d(t), t)$$
$$x \in \mathfrak{R}^{n_x}, u \in \mathfrak{R}^{n_u}, d \in \mathfrak{R}^{n_d}, y \in \mathfrak{R}^{n_y}$$

Where: $x(t)$ is the n_x dimensional system state vector, such as greenhouse air temperature, air humidity, air CO2 concentration, crop physiological carbon content, fruit weight, etc.; $u(t)$ is the n_u dimensional control input vector, such as: heat input or mixing valve position, window opening, CO2 application Quantity, shading net position, etc.; $d(t)$ is the n_d external disturbance vector, such as solar radiation, outside air temperature, external light, wind speed, etc.; but $y(t)$ is the n_y dimensional output vector, such as: air temperature, relative humidity, crop dry matter [12]. The greenhouse system control structure is shown in Fig. 3.

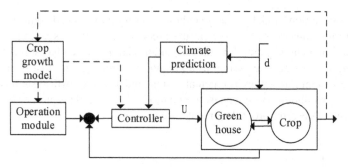

Fig. 2. Structure diagram of greenhouse cluster coordination control system

Monolithic greenhouse systems are often regulated by single crop cultivation. The above system is currently recognized as a greenhouse control system structure in which crop models are introduced into the system as a given reference for the system. Such a control system can indirectly control the greenhouse according to the needs of the crop at different stages of growth [13]. Planting in greenhouse clusters is a variety of crops with different growth cycles, which poses great difficulties for coordinated control of greenhouse clusters.

3   Greenhouse Cluster Theory Model

According to the characteristics of the nonlinearity of greenhouse clusters and the basic requirements for the regulation of plant growth environment, based on the theoretical basis of complex large-scale systems, the application of multi-level hierarchical nonlinear decoupling adaptive control is practical, efficient and robust. The theory of greenhouse cluster control solves the bottleneck problem that plagues greenhouse cluster control to wide-area intelligent expansion from a theoretical level, and makes breakthroughs in the theory of nonlinear control such as greenhouse cluster.

The research scheme of the greenhouse system hierarchical large-scale system architecture control theory is as follows: Based on the actual application status, the conditions can be assumed here: according to the coordinators A, B, C, D, and $\cdots$, each greenhouse under the control of the coordinated controller is to be planted. The same crop, including the same plant and the same variety. For example, the greenhouse A_i $|_{i=1,2...,n}$ is planted with the same crop (others). The level of the coordinator A, B, C, D, $\cdots$ is the micro level of the large system, the z coordinate level of the regional coordinator is the middle level of the large system, and the level above the Ethernet is the macro level coordinator H. The crop model W acts on the microlevel coordinator. Figure 3 shows the block diagram of the system control.

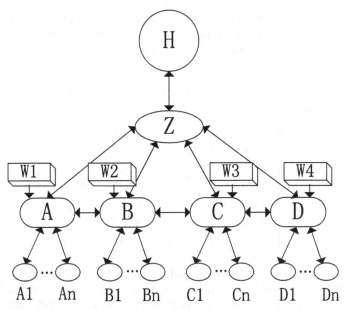

Fig. 3. Greenhouse cluster large system control structure diagram (taking 4 micro-coordinators as an example)

The characteristics of the control structure are:

(1) the crop model expert description acts as a constraint on each micro-coordination controller;
(2) each bottom-level greenhouse system within the micro-level: $(A_1 - A_n)$, $(B_1 - B_n)$, $(C_1 - C_n)$, $(D_1 - D_n)$, D Control recommendations are ON. OFF feedback control mode;
(3) micro-level coordination controllers A, B, C and D can establish a coordination relationship with each other;
(4) from macro coordinator H to meso-level coordinator Z, then to micro-level coordinator A, B, C and D both optimize and design three optimal indicators as constraints, while the underlying control of each greenhouse system is set according to actual needs;
(5) the coordinator not only has network communication and router capabilities, It also features advanced control computing capabilities and a common standard I/O interface.

In this large system control structure, how to design a greenhouse description model based on three constraint parameters is the basis of the control system. Here, the micro-level coordination controller takes the humidity, temperature, and illuminance as the necessary binding amount for the three crops, and the three constraints of the middle-level coordination controller are: water consumption, electricity consumption, output, and macro-level coordination. The three constraints of the device are: output, electricity consumption, and labor. And the generalized space modeling method of large system cybernetics is used to construct the mapping relationship of models in three-dimensional space of granularity, format and intelligent form. There is also a space vector matrix: $\overline{A} = \left[\overline{A}_1, \overline{A}_2, \overline{A}_3\right]$, to establish the following greenhouse cluster object description model:

$$Z_1 = \begin{bmatrix} \overline{A}_1 & 0 & 0 \\ 0 & \overline{A}_2 & 0 \\ 0 & 0 & \overline{A}_3 \end{bmatrix} \cdot \begin{bmatrix} S(x,y)_{z_1} & 0 & 0 \\ 0 & S(x,z)_{z_1} & 0 \\ 0 & 0 & S(y,z)_{z_1} \end{bmatrix}$$

$$Z_2 = \begin{bmatrix} \overline{A}_1 & 0 & 0 \\ 0 & \overline{A}_2 & 0 \\ 0 & 0 & \overline{A}_3 \end{bmatrix} \cdot \begin{bmatrix} S(x,y)_{z_2} & 0 & 0 \\ 0 & S(x,z)_{z_2} & 0 \\ 0 & 0 & S(y,z)_{z_2} \end{bmatrix}$$

$$Z_3 = \begin{bmatrix} \overline{A}_1 & 0 & 0 \\ 0 & \overline{A}_2 & 0 \\ 0 & 0 & \overline{A}_3 \end{bmatrix} \cdot \begin{bmatrix} S(x,y)_{z_3} & 0 & 0 \\ 0 & S(x,z)_{z_3} & 0 \\ 0 & 0 & S(y,z)_{z_3} \end{bmatrix}$$

In the formula: three spatial vectors $\overline{A}_1, \overline{A}_2, \overline{A}_3$, respectively, can represent the spatial hierarchy in the generalized model, that is, the microscopic level, the intermediate level and the macro level, and can also represent the mapping level of a single complex model in different spatial coordinates: Z the granularity direction Fine-grained Z_1, medium-grained Z_2, and coarse-grained Z_3, Math X_1, knowledge X_2, and relationship X_3 in the format X direction, Form self-learning Y_1 in the direction Y, adaptive Y_2, and self-organizing Y_3. And $S(x,y)$, $S(x,z)$, $S(y,z)$ is the object description of a certain layer in the hierarchical structure of the system after dimension reduction. For example, the three most concerned indicators x, y, and z in the greenhouse cluster system represent water consumption, electricity consumption, and output, then: $\overline{A} \cdot S(x,y) \,|\, z_1$ represents the microscopic level, that is, the fine-grained relationship between water consumption and electricity consumption in the bottom greenhouse group. However, $\overline{A} \cdot S(x,y) \,|\, z_2$ indicates the medium-grain relationship between the water consumption and the output of the greenhouse cluster at the meso level. These descriptions relate to the particularity of the agricultural system, boundary fuzzy, coupled associations, non-zero starting points, etc., which can be obtained by fuzzy cluster analysis. Based on this description model, a cloud computing-based greenhouse cluster management system can be built.

4   Greenhouse Cluster Coordinated Control System Model Algorithm

In the hierarchical intelligent control architecture of the greenhouse cluster, the adaptive layer is added to introduce the feedback information of the controlled object, so as to study the robust problem of the objective slow disturbance in the greenhouse, and derive the effective and convergent based on the Lyapunov function. Control rate and adaptive rate; 2. According to the coupling phenomenon of greenhouse cluster control parameters, solve the problem of primitive event sequence organic conversion between the dispatcher and each coordinator in the coordination layer, and use Petri net to solve the conversion operation language combination problem; 3. In the execution layer, according to the objective requirement that the intelligence of the hierarchical system is higher and higher and the control precision is lower and lower, an effective entropy function is designed to find the optimal control instruction sent by the coordinator. (Language), and use this to assess the performance of the greenhouse multi-level hierarchical intelligent control system. The specific design is as follows:

The coordinator designed in this paper consists of four functional modules, which are attached to the cloud server to implement the operation of the four internal modules. Its architecture is shown in Fig. 4. The information is processed, delivered to the task processor and the learning processor, the output of the learning processor is then constrained to the processing of the task, and finally the result is output through the distributor. The key research here is: for the data processor, for determining information, such as: feedback information of on-site detection, processing of sub-controller state feedback information, and given information for uncertain information such as crop yield target and energy consumption target processing method.

For the task processor, the cognitive model should be studied, that is, the cognitive modeling method should be used to establish a knowledge representation; for the learning processor: the cognitive reasoning and optimization algorithm should be studied, and the comprehensively calculated information should be constrained to the task processor. Work so that the task assignments made during each time period are optimal; For the allocator: To study a membership function assignment method, and the algorithm that the distributor generates the output according to the requirements of the task processor output. After four modules, the control output of the greenhouse environmental controller and the crop growth controller is extracted at the output of the coordinator through the distributor. The calculation of the entire module is run on the cloud server. After the control parameters are calculated, they are sent to the controller in the specified greenhouse. The controller controls the actions of the actuator according to the command parameters to realize coordinated control of the greenhouse cluster.

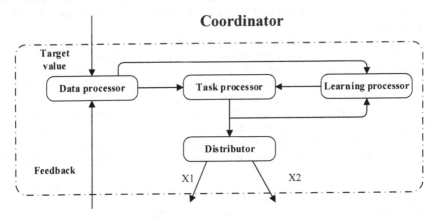

Fig. 4. Coordinator architecture

5   Conclusion

Aiming at the problems in the current greenhouse cluster control system, an information management platform was built based on cloud computing, which realized the distributed collection and unified management of greenhouse cluster information. On this basis, the theoretical research on coordinated control of greenhouse clusters was carried out. On the one hand, the research scheme of the greenhouse system hierarchical large-scale system architecture control theory is proposed. Based on this description model, the cloud computing-based greenhouse cluster management and control system can be built. On the other hand, the greenhouse cluster coordinated control system model algorithm research scheme is designed. A reasonable code framework. In order to study the theoretical model of greenhouse cluster coordinated control, construct a large-scale system of greenhouse cluster hierarchical control, and provide a reference for establishing a greenhouse cluster coordinated control system, it lays a foundation for solving the key model construction and control theory innovation in the greenhouse cluster coordinated control system. It is of theoretical significance and application value to reveal the essential characteristics of hierarchical control in greenhouse clusters, to establish a greenhouse cluster coordination description model, and to establish a greenhouse system control structure model based on large system theory.

Acknowledgements. This paper was funded by the international training and improvement project of graduate students of China agricultural university; the Ministry of Education of China and Chinese Academy of Sciences (Grant: 4444-10099609).

References

1. Rogge, E., Dessein, J., Gulinck, H.: Stakeholders perception of attitudes towards major landscape changes held by the public. The case of greenhouse clusters in Flanders. Land Use Policy **28**(1), 334–342 (2011)
2. Salazar, R., Rojano, A., et al.: A model for the combine description of the temperature and relative humidity regime in the greenhouse. In: 9th Mexican International Conference on Artificial Intelligence, vol. 12, pp. 113–117. IEEE Computer Society (2010)
3. Xu, X., et al.: A computation offloading method over big data for IoT-enabled cloud-edge computing. Future Gener. Comput. Syst. **95**, 522–533 (2019)
4. Zhang, J., et al.: Hybrid computation offloading for smart home automation in mobile cloud computing. Pers. Ubiquitous Comput. **22**(1), 121–134 (2018)
5. Qi, L., Xiang, H., Dou, W., Yang, C., Qin, Y., Zhang, X.: Privacy-preserving distributed service recommendation based on locality-sensitive hashing. In: 2017 IEEE International Conference on Web Services (ICWS), pp. 49–56 (2017)
6. Xu, X., et al.: An IoT-oriented data placement method with privacy preservation in cloud environment. J. Netw. Comput. Appl. **124**, 148–157 (2018)
7. Qi, L., Dai, P., Yu, J., Zhou, Z., Xu, Y.: "Time–Location–Frequency"–aware Internet of things service selection based on historical records. Int. J. Distrib. Sensor Netw. **13**(1) (2017). paper ID: 1550147716688696
8. Qi, L., Dou, W., Wang, W., Li, G., Yu, H., Wan, S.: Dynamic mobile crowdsourcing selection for electricity load forecasting. IEEE Access **6**, 46926–46937 (2018)

9. Xu, X., et al.: An energy-aware computation offloading method for smart edge computing in wireless metropolitan area networks. J. Netw. Comput. Appl. **133**, 75–85 (2019)
10. Qi, L., Dou, W, Ni, J, Xia, X., Ma, C, Liu, J.: A trust evaluation method for cloud service with fluctuant QoS and flexible SLA. In: 2014 IEEE International Conference on Web Services, pp. 345–352 (2014)
11. Qi, L., Zhou, Z., Yu, J., Liu, Q.: Data-sparsity tolerant web service recommendation approach based on improved collaborative filtering. IEICE Trans. Inf. Syst. **100**(9), 2092–2099 (2017)
12. Xu, X., et al.: An edge computing-enabled computation offloading method with privacy preservation for internet of connected vehicles. Future Gener. Comput. Syst. **96**, 89–100 (2019)
13. Chen, R., Imani, F., Reutzel, E., et al.: From design complexity to build quality in additive manufacturing—a sensor-based perspective. IEEE Sens. Lett. **3**(1), 1–4 (2019)

Anomalous Taxi Route Detection System Based on Cloud Services

Yu Zi[1], Yun Luo[2(✉)], Zihao Guang[1], Lianyong Qi[3], Taoran Wu[4], and Xuyun Zhang[1]

[1] Department of Electrical, Computer and Software Engineering,
University of Auckland, Auckland, New Zealand
{zgua779,zyu539}@aucklanduni.ac.nz, xuyun.zhang@auckland.ac.nz
[2] Faculty of Engineering and IT, University of Technology Sydney, Ultimo, Australia
Yun.Luo@student.uts.edu.au
[3] Qufu Normal University, Jining, China
liangyongqi@gmail.com
[4] Guizhou University of Finance and Economics, Guiyang, China
taoran.wu@mail.gufe.edu.cn

Abstract. Machine learning is very popular right now. We can apply the knowledge of machine learning to deal with some problems in our daily life. Taxi service provides a convenient way of transportation, especially for those who travel to an unfamiliar place. But there can be a risk that the passenger gets overcharged on the unnecessary mileages. To help the passenger to determine whether the taxi driver has made a detour, we propose a solution which is a cloud-based system and applies machine learning algorithms to detect anomaly taxi trajectory for the passenger. This paper briefly describes the research on several state-of-art detection methods. It also demonstrates the system architecture design in detail and gives the reader a big picture on what parts of the application have been implemented.

Keywords: Anomaly detection · Taxi route · Cloud service · Machine learning

1 Introduction

In the recent years, more and more organizations store, process, and extract value from data of all forms and sizes. With a certain amount of information available, it is inevitable that the big data will be continuously integrated into and influence our daily life. For example, researchers can use mobile phone data to analyze how people's location and traffic pattern influence the urban planning. This can help those urban planners to determine the best practices for stoplights, construction and parking. This is also a good example of applying machine learning methods. With the use of machine learning algorithm, we can learn patterns from given information and make predictions on data using the trained model.

© ICST Institute for Computer Sciences, Social Informatics and Telecommunications Engineering 2020
Published by Springer Nature Switzerland AG 2020. All Rights Reserved
X. Zhang et al. (Eds.): CloudComp 2019/SmartGift 2019, LNICST 322, pp. 240–254, 2020.
https://doi.org/10.1007/978-3-030-48513-9_20

In our daily life, taxi service plays a uniquely important role. It provides a convenient door-to-door way of transportation. That makes it very helpful to people who travel to an unfamiliar place. The taxi service usually charges passengers based on the time or mileages they have taken. However, taxi passengers can suffer from the risk of being overcharged on the unnecessary mileages incurred by taxi drivers intentionally or unintentionally. Due to the lack of background about the cities, most passengers cannot notice the subtle differences between the normal route and the altered one.

Smart phones equipped with GPS can be viewed as sensors which track the taxi trajectory. The advances in location-acquisition and mobile computing techniques has generated massive taxi trajectory data from GPS devices on taxis and mobile devices carried by the passengers. In this paper, we focus on constructing a system which can collect the trajectory data of the taxi trips, extract the temporal and spatial information, and analyse them using machine learning methods. This anomaly analysis can help the passengers know if the taxi has taken a normal route. It can also contribute to traffic management which is one of the most important aspects of smart cities. For example, if the travel distance of an anomalous trajectory is shorter than that of the normal routes, this route can be considered as one of the recommended routes for missioncritical drivers in emergency cases.

The rest of the paper is organised as follows. We review the related work in the next section. Section 3 states and analyse the targeted problem and our goal. We describe the system overview in Sect. 4 and the details of implementing the system in Sect. 5, including development tools and frameworks involved, data preprocessing, and anomalous taxi trajectory detection algorithm. In Sect. 6, we conduct a suite of experiments on real-life data to evaluate the proposed system. Finally, Sect. 7 concludes our research work and points out the future work.

2   Related Work

2.1   Existing Solutions

We tried to find out mobile apps with the functionality of anomaly route detection, from the app store. Unfortunately, by now there does not exist such an app in the market that provides the functionality we concern.

A map application like Google Maps can predict the directions to the destination for the user. The passenger may compare this predicted route with the taxi route tracked by the GPS on the mobile device. However, the routes recommended by the map application are quite limited. For example, even the route taken by the taxi driver is not shown as one of the recommended directions provided by Google Maps, this route may still be normal due to current traffic condition. Another case is that if the road network on the digital map is not up-to-date, the directions provided by the map application cannot be considered as accurate. Hence this method is not strong enough for the passenger to determine if the taxi has taken an anomaly route or not.

2.2   Trajectory Outlier Detection Methods

Some researchers have published papers which propose methods for anomalous trajectories detection. iBoat is a real-time detection method and can also identify which parts of the trajectory are responsible for its anomalousness [3]. The project team claims that the method has an excellent accuracy and overcomes many shortcomings of other state-of-the-art methods. iBoat compares a test trajectory against a set of sampled historical trajectories with the same SourceDestination pair, rather than using time and distance to directly judge whether it is anomalous or not. We also found another paper on anomaly taxi trajectory detection. The method is named as iBAT [10]. iBAT exploits anomalous trajectories intrinsic properties of being few and different, and applied the isolation mechanism to detect anomalous trajectories. Another research group developed a taxi driving fraud detection system [4]. They mainly considered two aspects of evidence:travel route evidence and driving distance evidence. Based on the Dempster-Shafer theory, those two aspects of evidence are combined to perform the detection. Besides, on Fisher's paper [9], they demonstrated a novel human assisted learning/classification framework for identifying anomalous behaviour on the basis of motion trajectories.

3   Problem Statement

Taxi passengers can suffer from the risk of being overcharged on unnecessary detours. To ensure the quality of taxi services, it is crucial to detect such cases and penalize the corresponding driver. Currently, the detection process is often done by experienced staff via manually checking the geolocation trajectory of a taxi trip. But this is costly and not effective because sometimes the passengers cannot even notice the subtle differences between a normal route and the altered one. And also the accuracy of manual detection is not quite reliable.

In this paper, we aim to develop an anomalous taxi route detection system that helps the end user to know if the route the taxi driver has taken is normal or not. The anomalous trajectories detection process should be done automatically rather than manually. Thus, we need to apply a smart state-of-the-art machine learning methods to achieve this purpose. In addition, the system should be deployed on the cloud so that it can be easily scaled on demand. As the potential end users of the system are the taxi passengers, a mobile application needs to be developed as the interface between the users and the system, so that the users can access the detection system remotely. As well, the mobile devices are responsible for collecting geolocation points of each taxi ride.

4   System Overview

To achieve the goal mentioned above, we need to implement a client-server architecture which consists of a front end mobile application and a back end server. The mobile application should provide functionality of recording and storing the location information during the taxi trip. A tunnel needs to be built up as well so that the client and the server can communicate with each other. Mover, a anomaly detection algorithm for trajectory data should be implemented using machine learning methods. This algorithm will be integrated into the architecture and can return meaningful results with a given route dataset. The back end server will be deployed onto the cloud to achieve high scalability.

The system overview of our solution is shown in Fig. 1. The back-end server, MapReduce data processing module and the database are deployed on the cloud. To detect anomalous routes, we utilize a machine learning method. Thus a huge amount of raw taxi traffic data is required as the training dataset. As the original raw data does not meet the requirement for the detection algorithm, the raw data firstly gets pre-processed by MapReduce module and then stored in the database. The mobile application is responsible for route data collecting and acts as the bridge connecting the end-users and the back-end detection system. Once the taxi arrives at the destination, the application will send the recorded trajectories data to the back-end servers. The anomalous detection algorithm runs on the server will then take samples from database and use them to analyze the received test trajectory. At last, the resulted score will be returned.

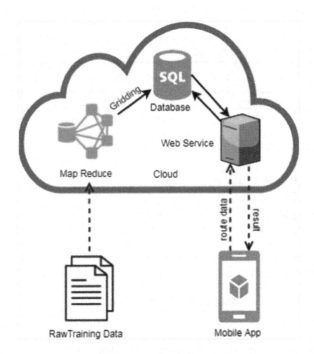

Fig. 1. System overview.

In general, the application is developed as a client-server architecture as shown in Fig. 2. As MapReduce data processing module only relates to the functionality of raw training data processing, it is not considered as one of the primary modules hence we omit it when we discuss the architecture.

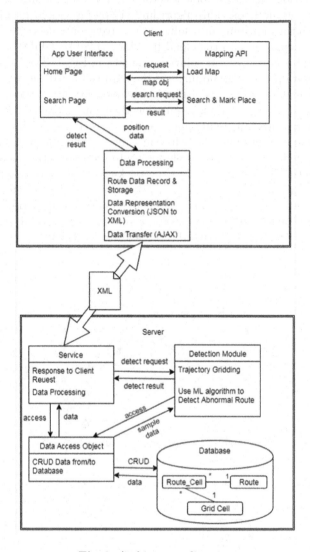

Fig. 2. Architecture diagram.

The client side is split into three modules. App User Interface (UI) module consists of two pages whose structures and styles are described by corresponding HTML and CSS files. The Mapping API module should provide functionality related to mapping service. It passes a map object to the App UI module when the application loads the home page for the first time. This module can also predict the location based on the text entered by user, and return the geographical location back to the UI. Data Processing module is the core logic part of the front end. It is responsible for route data recording, data transforming and interacting with the back end side. The current position data is obtained from the UI module using HTML Geolocation API and stored in Data Processing module. Once the user reaches the destination, Data Processing module stops recording the current position, and then transform the dataset into XML form before sending it to the server. When the detected result is received, it will be passed to the UI and shown to the user.

The server side is split into three modules as shown in the diagram. Service module can deal with the request from the client and reformat the received raw data. Anomalous route detection methods and the trajectory gridding algorithm are packed into the Detection Module. It can process the data by map gridding and then analyze the given test trajectory. The map gridded taxi trajectory will be stored in the database as well. Every time a module tries to access the database, a data access object will be used to perform create, read, update and delete (CRUD) operations.

5   System Implementation

5.1   Implementation Environment

We develop the server side of the app using Java Enterprise Edition (Java EE) [8]. Java EE is the industry standard for developing portable, robust, scalable and secure server-side Java applications. To support the web application development, it provides web services, component model, management, and communications APIs. Thanks to the flexibility of Java, our solution can be deployed across platforms. We implement web services on back end side following REST style [7]. REST refers to Representational State Transfer which is an architectural style that specifies constraints, such as the uniform interface. It promotes scalability, modifiability and good performance. In our implementation, HTTP is used as the protocol and it provides API for the web service. The processed taxi trajectory data for machine learning algorithms is stored in a MySQL database [6].

The mobile application is developed using HTML, CSS and TypeScript, as we build the application with the hybrid mobile application approach. The mobile application of our solution is designed to be run on not only a specific mobile operation systems as the popular mobile OS like iOS and Android have certain portions of market share. A good way is to develop mobile apps for different mobile platform, which is a hybrid application. It is basically a web application which is developed using HTML, CSS and JavaScript, and then wrapped in a native application using platforms like Cordova, also known as write once and run everywhere approach. Ionic Framework [1] which is an open source project with a licence under MIT is used for front end development. It provides over 120 native plugins to utilize the native device features.

On the front end side, Google Maps JavaScript API [5] are integrated into the mobile application. With the use of mapping API, the trajectory data can be visualized by displaying location points on a map so that the user knows the route the taxi goes through. Google Maps API provides auto-complete predictions service which allows the text box to retrieve auto-complete results based on the user input for the trip destination. It provides place service as well which can retrieve the precise geographical location information of the destination set by the user. It also meets all requirements related to map visualization of our solution.

Raw taxi traffic data is required to be pre-processed before getting stored in the database. However, due to the computing speed and memory size issues, it is very time-consuming to process the data if the size of the data expands to a certain amount. To overcome this computational bottleneck, We implement the data pre-processing module with the use of Hadoop MapReduce [2]. MapReduce is a framework that allows programmers write applications to process a huge amount of data on large clusters of commodity hardware in parallel. It mainly contains two tasks called Map and Reduce. Map task takes a set of data as input, and converts it into another set of data. As the result, the individual elements are broken down into tuples of key-value pairs. Reduce task takes the output from a Map as an input and then combines those tuples into a smaller set of tuples. The major advantage of MapReduce is the scalability. It is easy to scale the data processing over multiple computing nodes. Once the data-processing module is implemented in the MapReduce form, we can just make a configuration change to scale the module to run on over hundreds, or even thousands of machines in a cluster. Besides, we do not need to care about how the data-passing works during a MapReduce job, as the framework can manage all the details of data-passing around the cluster. The detail of MapReduce version of data pre-processing module will be discussed subsequently.

5.2   Data Pre-processing

1) Trajectory Sorting and Splitting: A taxi trip trajectory record consists of taxi id, a geolocation point represented by latitude-longitude pairs, generated by the GPS device on that taxi, time stamp and the service status associated with that time stamp. A complete taxi trajectory can be obtained by connecting those geolocation points in the order of time stamp. As the taxi overcharging problems only occur when the taxi is in service, i.e. carrying the passenger, we need to split those taxi trajectories corresponding to the taxi trips from the raw dataset. However, the order of the raw taxi trajectory dataset cannot be guaranteed. That means the dataset needs to be sorted before splitting. Since the anomalous trajectory detection algorithm utilizes a machine learning method, a huge amount of taxi trajectories data are needed for the better performance of detection. During the earlier development of data pre-processing module, we encountered an issue related to memory bottleneck, as the whole dataset needs to be loaded into memory in order to sort the trajectory points for a taxi. Instead, in the current solution, Hadoop MapReduce is used to achieve the trajectory sorting and splitting tasks as mentioned in the Decision Making on Tool Selection sub-section.

As shown in Fig. 2, at the first step, the raw taxi trajectory dataset is fed into mappers, which will form keyvalue pairs from single geolocation points. In our case, the taxi id is defined as key and all other information is defined as value so that the whole dataset can be effectively separated into small pieces. Then the shuffler will group pairs with the same key (i.e. same taxi id) together and send them to the reducer. The next step is to extract taxi routes from the set with specific taxi id. As mappers and reducers do not interfere with each other as shown in Fig. 3, the map and reduce tasks could be parallelized easily. That means it will take much shorter time to extract routes from the raw dataset than using the earlier implementation theoretically.

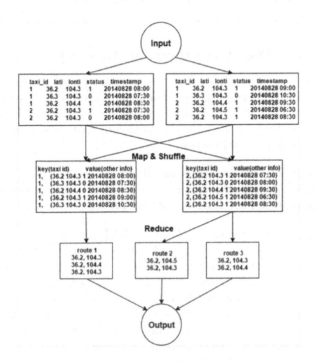

Fig. 3. The work flow of MapReduce program.

2) Map Gridding and Trajectory Augmenting: As a preparation of anomalous trajectory analysis, the city map is split into grid-cell with equal size. Then each taxi trajectory is mapped to grid cells and can be represented by a sequence of traversed cells. However, the GPS devices on taxi record a geolocation at a low frequency in practice. Therefore a map-gridded taxi trajectory may consist of some sequences of geolocation points which are not adjacent to each other, i.e. there exists a gap between some of the GPS points. Thus, we need to fill up those gaps by inserting pseudo cells to ensure that the same taxi trajectories can be represented equally in the system. This operation is called trajectory augmenting. Once the route information is extracted from

the raw dataset and gets map-gridded, it can then be stored in the back-end database.

During the map gridding process, the size of the grid cell is an important parameter we need to care about. It affects the performance of the anomalous trajectory detection algorithm. If the size is too small, the city map will be separated into a huge number of grid cells. This results in a sparse sample set when sampling from the training data. This makes it difficult to perform evaluation and testing. Also, routes with similar shapes and location points may be considered as different which is not what we expect. If the size is too large, the sequence of gridded points cannot reflect the shape and trend information of the original trajectory.

5.3   Anomalous Trajectories Detection Algorithm

In our research work, we address the problem of anomalous trajectory detection by using iBAT (isolation based anomalous trajectories detection) method which is described in [10]. Instead of comparing trajectories based on distance or density measure, iBAT method detects anomalous route based on the following properties of anomalous trajectories:

- anomalous trajectories are few in number;
- they are different from the majority, in particular, they pass different locations, or pass similar locations in different orders.

Here we briefly describe the workflow of iBAT method. It is a lazy learning algorithm, which does not train a model until a test sample is given. iBAT method tries to separate the given test trajectory from the rest of trajectories with the same source and destination, by randomly picking cells solely from the test trajectory. For example, if t is a test route and the rest form the sample set, we randomly select one cell from t and remove the trajectories that do not pass the selected cell from the sample set. This process is repeated until no trajectory is left or all the trajectories left contain all the cell t has. Since anomalous trajectories are few and different, most grids contained by anomalous trajectories are not contained by normal ones. Therefore, the anomalous routes can be easier to be isolated, i.e. the expected number of used grid cells to isolate an anomalous route should be much smaller.

5.4   Back End Web Service

On back end side, a runnable web service is implemented. It provides an API so that the front end client can get the time interval parameter from the server and send the route dataset for a taxi ride to the server. Once received the raw route data, this service re-formats the trajectory first. The Detection module performs map gridding and trajectory augmenting on this test trajectory and then retrieves those routes with the same source and destination grid as the test trajectory, from the database. And these route information will then be used to analyze the test trajectory by iBAT method. Currently, the back end web service is deployed and being tested on the cloud computing platform provided by Unitec Institute of Technology.

5.5   Mobile Application

On front end side, the mobile application has been implemented. The application basically has a simple user interface with two pages, map page and search page as shown in Fig. 4. Here we briefly describe the work flow of the mobile application. When the mobile application is launched, the map page will show up, and mark the user's current location as shown on the left screen in Fig. 4. To set up the taxi trip destination, the user needs to navigate to the search page by pressing the round floating button at the bottom right corner first then pressing the pop-up button with a search icon to navigate to the search page. Initially, the search page only shows a header bar and a text box which allows the user to enter the address of the destination. A result list will show up and display predicted locations based on the text entered. Once the user pressed one of the location, it will navigate back to the home page. Then a marker is pinned at the centre of the map showing the selected destination on the map. If the user is satisfied with the set destination and wants to start to record the taxi ride trajectory, the user needs to press the start button to trigger the geolocation record logic. Before reaching the destination, the route points are recorded at a pre-set interval which is 2 s by default. The system manager can change this interval by setting the corresponding parameter at the back-end server.

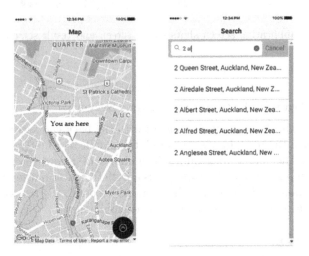

Fig. 4. Mobile application screen shots-initial screen and search page.

Meanwhile, the map page displays the route the taxi has passed, the current speed of the taxi and the accumulated duration of the taxi ride as shown in Fig. 5. Once the taxi gets close enough to the pre-set destination point, a dialog will pop up to inform the user. The user can then confirm to stop the record logic or press "keep going" button to keep record the taxi trajectory until the user presses the stop button. Once record logic is stopped, the complete trajectory will be sent to the back-end server for anomaly analysis. The result of the detection will be returned in the form of a score scaled from 0 to 1. The higher the score, the more abnormal the taxi trajectory. The route will be marked by a specific color based on the resulted score. As shown in Fig. 5, we assume that the resulted score is at a high rank, thus the route and the status are marked as red.

Fig. 5. Mobile application screen shots-status screen and result screen. (Color figure online)

5.6   Data Transfer Between Client and Server

The mobile application can communicate with the back end server using HTTP protocol. When the recording is triggered, the mobile app firstly sends a request with GET to the server to acquire the number of record interval. Once the recording is stopped, the mobile app sends a POST request to the server with the location information dataset in XML form. As respond, the resulted anomalous score will then be returned to the front end mobile app.

6   Evaluation

6.1   Experimental Setup

For evaluation purpose, we use a real-world taxi geolocation dataset, which is collected from taxis served in Chengdu, China for about half a month. The total number of records is over 1.4 billion. Each record consists of the taxi id, service status, geolocation point and the corresponding time stamp. This is consistent with the format requirement for data pre-processing. For the sake of simplicity in computation and visualization, we restrict our interest within the city center of Chengdu with longitude [103.9E, 104.2E] and latitude [30.5N, 30.8N]. The size of each grid cell is set to be 250 m × 250 m and the map is split into 75 × 75 grid cells. To ensure the accuracy and stability of the anomalous route detection algorithm, two parameters (the number of trial m and sub-sample size) need to be adjusted properly. We use m = 40 and s = 250 in our experiments which is quite reasonable based on a 10-fold evaluation.

6.2 Trajectory Visualization

With the assist of visualization, we can compare the sample trajectories with the corresponding anomalous score to check if the resulted score is reasonable. To visualize a gridded trajectory, we calculate the geolocation of the center of each grid cell and connect the geolocation points in a proper order to reshape the trajectory. Then the processed trajectories set will be transformed into a file in GPX format in order to be displayed on Google Maps. During the experiment, we found that there are some cases where a part of the trajectory keeps looping in a region consists of a few grid cells. This can be caused by the unstable GPS signal during the taxi ride. Thus, we mesh such geolocation point sequences before visualizing the trajectories.

Here we show an example of trajectory visualization on a relatively small dataset. As shown in Fig. 6, it is quite obvious that route A and route B behave differently from the others. We checked the corresponding results and found that the anomalous score of route A is 0.874 and route B is 0.732, while the scores for 85% of the rest trajectories are below 0.5. We can say that route A and B can be successfully marked out as anomalous routes by the implemented detection algorithm. But we don not have enough evidence to say that all of the anomalous routes can be successfully classified as abnormal.

6.3 Anomalous Statistics

We conducted another 5 groups of experiments on the Chengdu taxi trajectory dataset. Specifically, we tried 5 differents pairs of origin and destination, labelled from A to E. Here we show five of the visualization results from Figs. 7, 8, 9, 10 and 11. Since it is impossible for us to mark all the anomalous routes and compare with the corresponding score, we only calculate the ratio of anomalous trajectories based on the resulted scores. The corresponding ratio is shown in Table 1.

6.4 Abnormality Rank

After visualizing the sampled trajectories, following are the findings determining the abnormality rank of trajectories based on our observation:

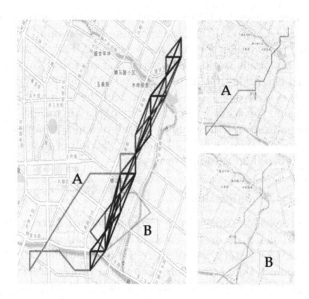

Fig. 6. An example of trajectory visualization on a relatively small dataset.

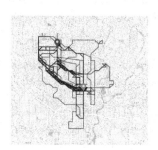
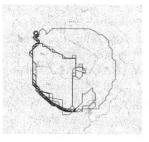
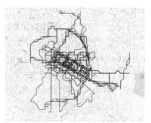

Fig. 7. Trajectory visualization A.

Fig. 8. Trajectory visualization B.

Fig. 9. Trajectory visualization C.

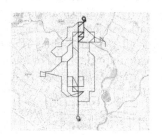
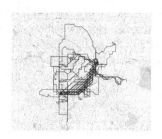

Fig. 10. Trajectory visualization D.

Fig. 11. Trajectory visualization E.

Table 1. Anomalous statistics.

	Routes	Anomalous	Ratio
A	567	42	7.4%
B	327	43	13.15%
C	1596	73	4.57%
D	150	18	12%
E	631	68	10.8%

- 0–0.5: normal. This means many taxi drivers take the similar route.
- 0.5–0.7: possibly anomalous. They are usually similar to normal routes in most segments while only a few are different.
- 0.7–1: anomalous. They have few identical segments with the normal.

7   Conclusions and Future Work

In this paper, we have implemented an anomaly route detection system which can help users, the passengers who take a taxi, to know if the taxi has taken an anomaly route or not. The core part of the system have been implemented based on an anomalous route detection algorithm named iBAT. The backend server has been deployed and validated on a cloud computing platform. The implemented detection algorithm has been evaluated on a real-life taxi trajectory dataset collected from Chengdu, China. In the future, we will consider working on real time data transfer and detection and implementing the MapReduce version of anomalous route detection algorithm.

Acknowledgement. This work was supported in part by the New Zealand Marsden Fund under Grant No. 17-UOA-248, and the UoA FRDF fund under Grant No. 3714668.

References

1. Build amazing native apps and progressive web apps with ionic
2. Welcome to apache hadoop. https://hadoop.apache.org/old/
3. Chen, C., et al.: iBOAT: isolation-based online anomalous trajectory detection. IEEE Trans. Intell. Transp. Syst. **14**(2), 806–818 (2013)
4. Ge, Y., Xiong, H., Liu, C., Zhou, Z.H.: A taxi driving fraud detection system. In: IEEE 11th International Conference on Data Mining, pp. 181–190 (2011)
5. Google: [9] google maps APIs - google developers. https://developers.google.com/maps/documentation/
6. MySQL: Why MySQL? https://www.mysql.com/why-mysql/
7. Oracle: The Java EE 6 tutorial. https://docs.oracle.com/javaee/6/tutorial/doc/
8. Oracle: Java EE at a glance. https://www.oracle.com/technetwork/java/javaee/overview/javaee-135128.html

9. Sillito, R.R., Fisher, R.B.: Semi-supervised learning for anomalous trajectory detection. In: BMVC, vol. 1, pp. 035–1 (2008)
10. Zhang, D., Li, N., Zhou, Z.H., Chen, C., Sun, L., Li, S.: iBAT: detecting anomalous taxi trajectories from GPS traces. In: ACM 13th International Conference on Ubiquitous Computing, pp. 99–108 (2011)

Collaborative Recommendation Method Based on Knowledge Graph for Cloud Services

Weijia Huang[1], Qianmu Li[1], Xiaoqian Liu[2], and Shunmei Meng[1(✉)]

[1] School of Computer Science and Technology, Nanjing University of Science and Technology, Nanjing, China
{weijia,qianmu,mengshunmei}@njust.edu.cn
[2] Jiangsu Police Institute, Nanjing, China
liuxiaoqian@jspi.edu.cn

Abstract. As the number of cloud services and user interest data soars, it's hard for users to find suitable could services within a short time. A suitable cloud service automatic recommendation system can effectively solve this problem. In this work, we propose KGCF, a novel method to recommend users cloud services that meet their needs. We model user-item and item-item bipartite relations in a knowledge graph, and study property-specific user-item relation features from it, which are fed to a collaborative filtering algorithm for Top-N item recommendation. We evaluate the proposed method in terms of Top-N recommendation on the MovieLens 1M dataset, and prove it outperforms numbers of state-of-the-art recommendation systems. In addition, we prove it has well performance in term of long tail recommendation, which means that more kinds cloud services can be recommended to users instead of only hot items.

Keywords: Cloud services · Recommendation systems · Knowledge graph · Collaborative filtering

1 Introduction

In recent years, the number of cloud services and user interest data have exploded. Users often don't know which one to choose when facing a large number of cloud service instances, and even many cloud service resources are not known to users. To solve this problem, recommendation system was proposed and has been springing up in the last years. Not only the general public benefit from it, but also service providers do. Greg Linden, Former Amazonian scientist, once said in his blog that at least 20% of Amazon's sales come from recommendation algorithms when he leaves Amazon. Netflix's recommendation algorithm has been well received, and the company has claimed that about 60% of its members customize the rental order based on the recommended list.

Recommendation systems can be classified into two main approaches: collaborative filtering methods and content-based methods. Filtering methods recommend a user items based on the human experience that similar people have similar preferences. Another method provides a user with items that have the similar features with those preferred

X. Zhang et al. (Eds.): CloudComp 2019/SmartGift 2019, LNICST 322, pp. 255–265, 2020.
https://doi.org/10.1007/978-3-030-48513-9_21

by this user. These methods also can be merged into a hybrid system [1]. Furthermore, many works [2–5] focus on making use of semantics when face content-based methods.

Although the usage of semantic information can improve the performance of the recommendation systems, the cost of manually tagging semantic information is very large. Knowledge graph, which represents a wealth of freely available multi-domain ontological knowledge [15], can provide semantic information of items. And we can make use of it to handle the large cost problem.

In this work, we automatically apply semantic analysis into the collaborative filtering approach. Consider the assumption that the semantic information, such as stars, subjects or feedback, extracted from items can represent users' preferences better than items can, and the same kind of semantic information can cover more items, which means collaborative filtering methods making use of it will perform better in the term of long tail. For example, compared with films, its semantic information, such as subjects or stars, may represent a user's taste better. However, the cost of manually tagging semantic information is very large and this information is usually not comprehensive. Therefore, we proposed an approach that using knowledge graph to automatically extract semantic information from items and representing users' preferences through it. Our work consists that: a) use knowledge graph to extract and expand items' semantic information. b) use semantic information that extracted from items to represent a user's preference. We have verified that this method can improve the performance of recommendation, and have the ability to recommend long tail items.

The reminder of this paper is organized as follows: Sect. 2 introduces the UserCF and knowledge graph. In Sect. 3, a collaborative recommendation method based on knowledge graph for cloud services is presented. Section 4 empirically studies the empirical performance and accuracy of our method. Section 5 reviews some related researches. Finally, Sect. 6 concludes this paper and provides some future work.

2 Preliminary Knowledge

2.1 User-Based Collaborative Filtering

User-based Collaborative Filtering (UserCF) is the most popular algorithm in Recommendation System Field, which was proposed for E-mail Filtering System in 1992, and applied to News Filtering by GroupLens two years later.

UserCF is based on the experience that birds of a feather flock together. For example, if you like "Batman", "Mission in the Dish", "Interstellar", "Source Code" and other movies, and some people like these movies, and he also likes "Iron Man", it is very likely that you also like the movie "Iron Man". Therefore, when the system recommends for a user A, it will first find a user group G similar to his interest, and then recommend an item that G likes and A has not heard of to A, which is UserCF.

Based on the above basic principles, we can split the user-based collaborative filtering recommendation algorithm into two steps: First, find a collection of users with similar interests to the target user. Then, find items in the collection that the user likes and that the target user has not heard of are recommended to the target user.

Discover Users with Similar Interests. The proximity between two users is usually measured by the Jaccard formula or cosine similarity. Here, $N(u)$ represents the collection of items which user u likes, and $N(v)$ represents the collection of items that user v likes, so the similarity between u and v is:

Jaccard formula:

$$w_{uv} = \frac{|N(u) \cap N(v)|}{|N(u) \cup N(v)|} \qquad (1)$$

Cosine similarity:

$$w_{uv} = \frac{|N(u) \cap N(v)|}{\sqrt{|N(u)| \cdot |N(v)|}} \qquad (2)$$

Suppose there are currently 4 users: A, B, C, D, and there are 5 items: a, b, c, d, e. A likes a, b and c, B likes a and c, C likes b and e, D likes c, d and e. Taking cosine similarity as an example, the user-similarity matrix is represented as Fig. 1.

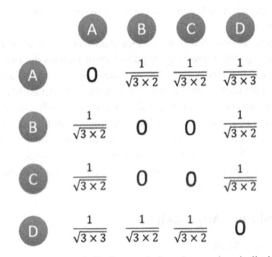

Fig. 1. The user-similarity matrix based on cosine similarity

Recommend. First, we need to find the K users most similar to the target user u from the matrix, which can be represented as the set $S(u, K)$. Then, we extract all items that users in S like, and remove the items that u already likes. For each candidate item i, the degree of which user u is interested in it is calculated by the following formula:

$$p(u, i) = \sum_{v \in S(u,K) \cap N(i)} w_{uv} \times r_{vi} \qquad (3)$$

Where r_{vi} is the degree of which user v likes i.

For example, suppose that we need to recommend user A items, and select $K = 3$ similar users, so similar users are B, C, D. They liked and A did not like the items are c and e. Then respectively calculate $p(A, c)$ and $p(A, e)$:

$$p(A, c) = w_{AB} + w_{AD} = \frac{1}{\sqrt{6}} + \frac{1}{\sqrt{9}} = 0.7416 \tag{4}$$

$$p(A, e) = w_{AC} + w_{AD} = \frac{1}{\sqrt{6}} + \frac{1}{\sqrt{9}} = 0.7416 \tag{5}$$

It seems that user A may have the same level of preference for c and e. In a real recommendation system, just sort by score and take the first few items.

2.2 Knowledge Graph Based on Ontology

Essentially, the knowledge graph is a network with semantics. It is a graphic data structure which consists of Points and Edges. In the knowledge graph, each edge represents a Relationship between two entities, and each node is an Entity existing in the real world. Knowledge graphs are the most effective representation of relationships. In general, a knowledge graph is a network of relationships that connects all the different kinds of information together. Knowledge graphs can help us analyze problems in terms of the relationship perspective.

When knowledge is obtained from various data sources, it is necessary to provide a unified term to merge the knowledge acquired from various data sources into a large knowledge base. The structure or data that provides unified term is called ontology. The ontology not only provides a unified term dictionary, but also builds relationships and restrictions between terms. The ontology allows users to easily create and modify data models based on their own business. The data mapping technology is used to establish the mapping relationship between the terms in the ontology and the vocabulary in different data sources, and then the data of different data sources are merged together.

The knowledge graph based on ontology can help us to add more semantics to the items' description in our approach.

3   Recommendation Approach

3.1   Overview of Our Model

Usually, in our overall model, collaborative filtering is used to predict users' preferences, where user similarity is calculated by user-semantic information relatedness, which are obtained from knowledge maps. As can be seen from Fig. 2, the operations in our model can be broken down into two main phases.

1) Property-specific user-item relations: User-feedback are linked to DBpedia resources to create a new knowledge graph. Then extract user preferences vectors from the graph, which is introduced in Sect. 3.2.
2) Recommend algorithm: Fed preferences vectors into collaborative filtering. Here, we make use of user-semantic information, instead of user-items, to calculate user similarity matrix. We will introduce its details in Sect. 3.3.

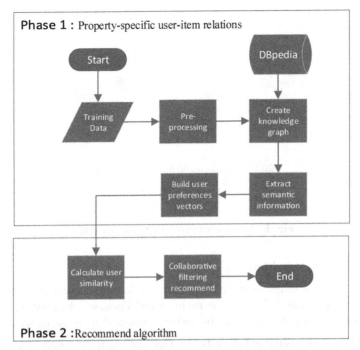

Fig. 2. Framework of our proposed model

3.2 Property-Specific User-Item Relations

As shown in Fig. 3, users have feedback relation with items, and items have property-specific relations with semantic information. We can learn it from the knowledge graph. For example, we can create vector $\rho_{subject}(u)$ which represents subjects that user u prefers. The dimension of $\rho_{subject}(u)$ is the number of nodes in knowledge map with the incoming edge as subjects. The initial values of all the dimensions are 0. On the graph, the traversal starts from user u, and stops at another user. If a dimension in the vector is traversed to the corresponding node on the graph, the value is incremented by 1. In Fig. 3, $\rho_{subject}(Emma) = (2, 1)$, the nodes corresponding to each dimension are Buddy_films and 1941_films.

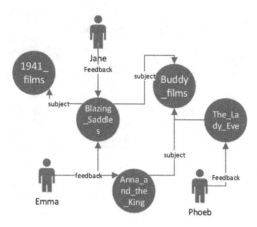

Fig. 3. A sample example for knowledge graph

3.3 Recommend Algorithm

There are two steps in this section: First, find a collection of users who have similar interests to the target user. Then, find items in the collection, which the similar user likes and that the target user has not heard of, and recommend them to the target user.

Discover Users with Similar Interests. In Our approach, we have improved the UserCF algorithm. When measure the proximity of user u and v, instead of using user-item relations, we make use of the property-specific vector in Sect. 3.1. We take cosine similarity of two vectors as users' similarity. The equation is:

$$\text{similarity}(u, v) = \frac{\rho u \cdot \rho v}{||\rho u|| \cdot ||\rho v||} \qquad (6)$$

For the graph shown in Fig. 3, the user-similarity matrix is represented as Fig. 4.

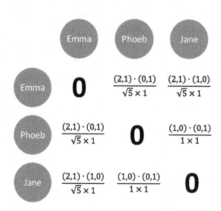

Fig. 4. The user-similarity matrix

Then the steps of finding the K most similar users of user u and generating the Top-N recommendation list of user u are the same as UserCF mentioned in Sect. 2.

Recommend. First, we need to find the K users most similar to the target user u, which can be represented as the set $S(u, K)$. Then, we extract all items that users in S like, and remove the items that u already likes. For each candidate item i, the degree of which user u is interested in it is calculated by the following formula:

$$p(u, i) = \sum_{v \in S(u,K) \cap N(i)} w_{uv} \times r_{vi} \tag{7}$$

Where r_{vi} is the degree of which user v likes i.

Then sort candidate items and recommend u top N items.

4 Experiment

4.1 Experimental Setup

Dataset: In this work, we use MovieLens 1M [10] to evaluate the proposed approach. It is a prevalent dataset in the field of RS evaluation, with 1,000,209 anonymous ratings made by 6,040 MovieLens users on approximately 3,900 movies. Items in Movie 1M have been mapped to the corresponding DBpedia entities in [11], and make use of these publicly available mappings to build knowledge graph.

4.2 Performance Metrics

Evaluation of recommendation is important, especially facing the problem that obtaining users' feedback on recommendations is difficult for researchers, and RS researchers need quality measures to evaluate the quality of algorithms in terms of predictions and recommendations. Many works [6–9] focus on quality measures and propose diverse evaluations. Considering this work is Top-N recommendation, we take classification accuracy measures, including precision, recall and F1. For a user u, in the list of recommended lengths of N, the Precision and Recall of u are:

$$Precision_u = \frac{|R(u) \cap T(u)|}{|R(u)|} \tag{8}$$

$$Recall_u = \frac{|R(u) \cap T(u)|}{|T(u)|} \tag{9}$$

where, $R(u)$ is the set of items that recommended for user u, and $T(u)$ represents the set of items that u likes in the test dataset.

The average Precision, average Recall and F1 of the system can be defined as follows:

$$Precision = \frac{\sum_u Precision_u}{N} \tag{10}$$

$$Recall = \frac{\sum_u Recall_u}{N} \tag{11}$$

$$F1 = \frac{2 \times Precision \times Recall}{Precision + Recall} \tag{12}$$

The Ref. [8] proposes several methods measuring the ability of leveraging long tail. In this experiment, we take Coverage which can be defined as follow:

$$Coverage = \frac{|\bigcup_u R(u)|}{|T|} \tag{13}$$

where T is the set of items in test dataset.

4.3 Performance Evaluation

Figures 5, 6, 7 and 8 report the performance of different approaches on the MovieLens 1M. It is clear that our method significantly outperforms the other methods in terms of recall, precision, F1 and coverage. Figures 5, 6 and 7 show the accuracy results in terms of recommended items number N. where it can obtain 0.345 in terms of precision at $N = 5$, 0.065 in terms of recall at $N = 5$, and 0.109 in terms of F1 at $N = 5$. The result shows that our approach has a good Top-N recommendation accuracy. As far as its own results are concerned, the precision decreases with the increase of N, and the recall increases with the increase of N, which is in line with our expectations. Within a certain interval, as N increases, $|R(u) \cap T(u)|$ increases, but $|R(u)|$ increases more, which makes Precision decrease. And with $|T(u)|$ unchanged, Recall increases.

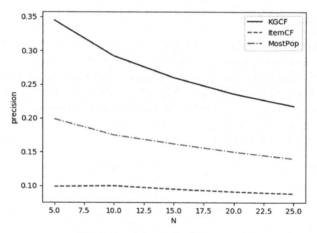

Fig. 5. Precision under different N

Figure 8 shows the coverage result in terms of recommended items number N. We can see that KGCF has well performance in term of long tail recommendation, where it can obtain 0.1320 in terms of coverage.

Obviously, our approach is able to improve the performance of personalized recommendation, and can explore long tail items.

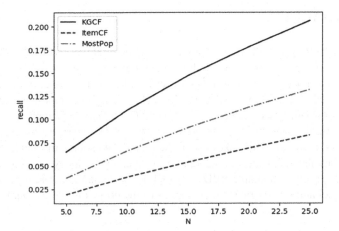

Fig. 6. Recall under different N

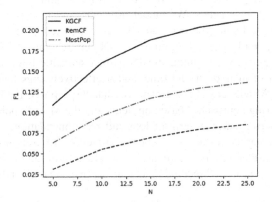

Fig. 7. F1 under different N

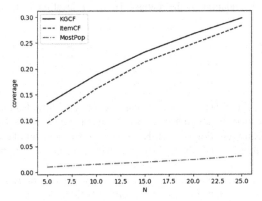

Fig. 8. Coverage under different N

5   Related Work

Recommendation systems based on ontology and semantics have been proposed in many of the past work. [16] proposes an ontology recommendation system that calculates collaborative recommendations by semantic user profiles, thereby improving recommendation accuracy and reducing cold start. [17, 18] use a hybrid graph-based data model to extract meta-path-based features using Linked Open Data, which were used to learn the ranking framework. In [19], entity2rec is proposed to learn user-item correlation from knowledge graph. [20] makes use of the linked data source to calculate the top N recommendations. [21] uses link data and user diversity for an event recommendation system. [22] proposes SemanticSVD++, which is the semantic-aware extension of the SVD++ model and incorporates the semantics of the project into the model.

6   Conclusion

In this work, we propose KGCF, a novel method to recommend users cloud service instances that meet their needs. We model user-item and item-item relatedness in a knowledge graph, and study property-specific user-item relations from it, which are fed to a collaborative filtering algorithm for Top-N item recommendation. This method has two major benefits: it can automatically extract semantic information from items which saves a lot of manpower and time, and it effectively digs long tail items. The experiment on the MovieLens 1M dataset proves that the proposed approach outperforms collaborative filtering approaches based on items and the Most Popular items strategy, and it has well performance in term of long tail recommendation, which means that more kinds cloud service instances can be recommended to users instead of only hot items. We will consider a more comprehensive evaluation in future work, and improve the feasibility of the proposed method in a cloud services recommendation scenario.

Acknowledgment. This paper is supported by the National Science Youth Foundation of China under Grant No. 61702264, the Fundamental Research Funds for the Central Universities No. 30919011282, the Fundamental Research Funds for the Central Universities No. 30918014108, the Natural Science Foundation of the Jiangsu Higher Education Institutions of China No. 19KJB510022.

References

1. John, K., Niu, Z., Kalui, D.: A hybrid recommender system for e-learning based on context awareness and sequential pattern mining. Soft. Comput. **22**(8), 2449–2461 (2018)
2. Nilashi, M., Ibrahim, O., Bagherifard, K.: A recommender system based on collaborative filtering using ontology and dimensionality reduction techniques. Expert Syst. Appl. **92**, 507–520 (2018)
3. Ahmad, N., Ghauth, K.I., Chua, F.-F.: Utilizing learners' negative ratings in semantic content-based recommender system for e-learning forum. J. Educ. Technol. Soc. **21**(1), 112–125 (2018)

4. Cai, G., Lee, K., Lee, I.: Itinerary recommender system with semantic trajectory pattern mining from geo-tagged photos. Expert Syst. Appl. **94**, 32–40 (2018)

5. John, K., Niu, Z., Mustafa, G.: Knowledge-based recommendation: a review of ontology-based recommender systems for e-learning. Artif. Intell. Rev. **50**(1), 21–48 (2018)

6. Shani, G., Gunawardana, A.: Evaluating Recommendation Systems. In: Ricci, F., Rokach, L., Shapira, B., Kantor, Paul B. (eds.) Recommender Systems Handbook, pp. 257–297. Springer, Boston, MA (2011). https://doi.org/10.1007/978-0-387-85820-3_8

7. Sarwar, B., Karypis, G., Konstan, J., Riedl, J.: Analysis of recommendation algorithms for e-commerce. In: ACM Conference on Electronic Commerce, pp. 158–167 (2000)

8. Park, Y.J., Tuzhilin, A.: The long tail of recommender systems and how to leverage it. In: Proceedings of the 2008 ACM Conference on Recommender Systems, pp. 11–18 (2008)

9. Hurley, N., Zhang, M.: Novelty and diversity in top-N recommendations analysis and evaluation. ACM Trans. Internet Technol. **10**, 1–29 (2011)

10. Harper, F.M., Konstan, J.A.: The MovieLens datasets: history and context. ACM Trans. Interact. Intell. Syst. (TiiS) **5**(4) (2015). Article 19, 19 pages

11. Ostuni, V.C., Noia, T.D., Sciascio, E.D., Mirizzi, R.: Top-n recommendations from implicit feedback leveraging linked open data. In: Proceedings of the 7th ACM conference on Recommender systems, pp. 85–92. ACM (2013)

12. Xu, X., Liu, Q., Zhang, X., Zhang, J., Qi, L., Dou, W.: A blockchain-powered crowdsourcing method with privacy preservation in mobile environment. IEEE Trans. Comput. Soc. Syst. **6**, 1407–1419 (2019)

13. Qi, L., Chen, Y., Yuan, Y., Fu, S., Zhang, X., Xu, X.: A QoS-aware virtual machine scheduling method for energy conservation in cloud-based cyber-physical systems. World Wide Web J. **23**, 1275–1297 (2019)

14. Qi, L., et al.: Finding all you need: web apis recommendation in web of things through keywords search. IEEE Trans. Comput. Soc. Syst. **6**, 1063–1072 (2019)

15. Bizer, C., Heath, T., Berners-Lee, T.: Linked data-the story so far. In: Semantic Services, Interoperability and Web Applications: Emerging Concepts, pp. 205–227 (2009)

16. Middleton, Stuart E., Roure, D.D., Shadbolt, Nigel R.: Ontology-based recommender systems. In: Staab, S., Studer, R. (eds.) Handbook on Ontologies. IHIS, pp. 779–796. Springer, Heidelberg (2009). https://doi.org/10.1007/978-3-540-92673-3_35

17. Di Noia, T., Ostuni, V.C., Tomeo, P., Di Sciascio, E.: SPrank: semantic path-based ranking for top-n recommendations using linked open data. ACM Trans. Intell. Syst. Technol. (TIST) **8**(1), 9 (2016)

18. Ostuni, V.C., Di Noia, T., Di Sciascio, E., Mirizzi, R.: Top-n recommendations from implicit feedback leveraging linked open data. In: Proceedings of the 7th ACM Conference on Recommender Systems, pp. 85–92. ACM (2013)

19. Palumbo, E., Rizzo, G., Troncy, R: entity2rec: learning user-item relatedness from knowledge graphs for top-N item recommendation, pp. 32–36 (2017)

20. Ostuni, V.C., Di Noia, T., Di Sciascio, E., Mirizzi, R.: Top-N recommendations from implicit feedback leveraging linked open data. In: Proceedings of the 7th ACM Conference on Recommender Systems, pp. 85–92. ACM, New York (2013)

21. Khrouf, H., Troncy, R.: Hybrid event recommendation using linked data and user diversity. In Proceedings of the 7th ACM Conference on Recommender Systems, pp. 185–192. ACM, New York (2013)

22. Rowe, M.: SemanticSVD++: incorporating semantic taste evolution for predicting ratings. In: 2014 IEEE/WIC/ACM International Conferences on Web Intelligence, WI (2014)

Efficient Multi-user Computation Scheduling Strategy Based on Clustering for Mobile-Edge Computing

Qing-Yan Lin[ID], Guang-Shun Li[ID], Jun-Hua Wu[(✉)][ID], Ying Zhang[ID], and JiaHe Yan[ID]

School of Information Science and Engineering, Qufu Normal University, Rizhao 276800, China
shdwjh@163.com

Abstract. The Mobile Edge Computing (MEC) is a new paradigm that can meet the growing computing needs of mobile applications. Terminal devices can transfer tasks to MEC servers nearby to improve the quality of computing. In this paper, we investigate the multi-user computation offloading problem for mobile-edge computing. We study two different computation models, local computing and edge computing. First, we drive the expressions for time delay and energy consumption for local and edge computing. Then, we propose a server partitioning algorithm based on clustering. We propose a task scheduling and offloading algorithm in a multi-users MEC system. We formulate the tasks offloading decision problem as a multi-user game, which always has a Nash equilibrium. Our proposed algorithms are finally verified by numerical results, which show that the scheduling strategy based on clustering can significantly reduce the energy consumption and overhead.

Keywords: Mobile edge computing · Offloading decision · Node clustering · Optimal strategy · Nash equilibrium

1 Introduction

The growing popularity of mobile devices has revolutionized mobile applications [1]. As function of cloud computing increasingly move to the edge of the network, a new trend of computing has emerged. It is estimated that many edge computing devices will be deployed on the edge of the network [2, 3]. The network edge has enough capacity to support mission-critical and latency-critical tasks on mobile devices [4]. This mode is called Mobile Edge Computing (MEC). This MEC paradigm can provide low latency, high bandwidth and computing agility in the computation offloading process [5]. It can support applications and services with reduced latency and improved QoS [6, 7]. This article is organized as follows. In Sect. 2, we introduce the related work. In Sect. 3, we describe the system model of MEC. In Sect. 4, we proposed a clustering algorithm

© ICST Institute for Computer Sciences, Social Informatics and Telecommunications Engineering 2020
Published by Springer Nature Switzerland AG 2020. All Rights Reserved
X. Zhang et al. (Eds.): CloudComp 2019/SmartGift 2019, LNICST 322, pp. 266–274, 2020.
https://doi.org/10.1007/978-3-030-48513-9_22

for mobile device. Section 5 introduces the task scheduling and offloading algorithm based on game theory. Section 6 shows the experiment evaluation. Finally, we will draw conclusions in Sect. 7.

2 Related Work

Wang and Yuan et al. [8] described the placement problem of energy-aware edge server as a multi-objective optimization problem, and designed a placement algorithm based on particle swarm optimization for energy-aware edge servers to find the optimal solution. Zeng et al. [9] expressed the task scheduling problem as a mixed integer nonlinear programming problem and solved its high computational complexity, and proposed a computationally effective solution. Song and Gao et al. [10] used cloud atomization technology to transform physical nodes into virtual machine nodes. Adila Mebrek et al. [11] used energy and quality of service (QoS) as two important indicators of fog performance. Chen et al. [12] describe multi-user multi-task unloading as NP-hard problem, and use the separable semi-deterministic relaxation problem to obtain the lower bound of the system overhead, and obtain the optimal performance of the system under multi-parameter conditions. Qi et al. [13] consider the user's job size, service invocation time, and service quality level, a set of experiments are designed, deployed, and tested to validate the feasibility of our proposal in terms of cost optimization. Chen and Liang et al. [14] consider a general multi-user mobile cloud computing system, the mobile users share the communication resource while offloading tasks to the cloud. Zhu et al. [15] formulated a minimum energy consumption problem in deadline-aware MEC system.

3 The Description of MEC

Mobile Edge Computing (MEC) can be defined as an implementation of edge computing that introduces compute and storage capacity to the edge of the radio access network, reducing latency by dropping the cloud and service platform to the edge of the network [16]. In the mobile edge computing system, the edge server is connected to the core network through a wired link, and the edge server can directly be a mobile device [17]. Most of the computing tasks can be processed at the edge node without entering the cloud core network, so the computing and communication load of the cloud core network can be significantly reduced. Redundant computing resources at the edge of the network can also be fully utilized, and mobile devices and IoT devices can achieve lower computational task completion delays [18] (Fig. 1).

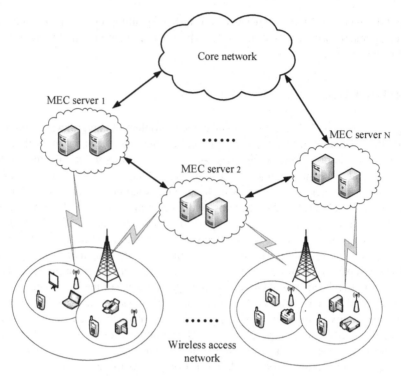

Fig. 1. MEC deployment architecture diagram

4 Graph-Based Energy-Clustering Algorithm

Now, we introduce the system model of mobile edge computing system. We assume that there are some mobile devices, in which each device has a task to complete. Each device can connect directly to its neighbors.

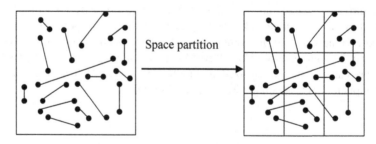

Fig. 2. The graph of nodes in the area

In this paper, the network topology diagram composed of the physical nodes of the edge computing is abstracted into an undirected weighted connected graph From a network system standpoint we consider a mobile device deployment as presented in

Fig. 2. The first graph represents the region where the node is located, the second graph represents the discretized distribution of nodes after space partition. Now, we will use the node set as the starting point for node partitioning.

The Fig. 3 represents the interactions between the nodes the area.

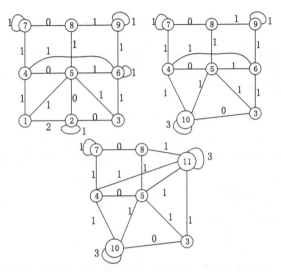

Fig. 3. The interaction graph $G_{int} = (C, E_{int})$

- (1) First, we look for the edge with the highest weight and get the amount of resources for each node, and the highest weight between node i and node j is lower than the cluster maximum weight M_{max}, the sum of resource of node i and node j is also lower than the cluster maximum resource res_{max}.
- (2) Then, we cluster node i and node j, updating the graphs G_a and G_{int}. The weight of the link between the new node and its neighbor is determined by the sum of the link weights between the former node i and its neighbors and the former node j and its neighbors.

5   System Model and Problem Describe

5.1   System Model

Local Computing Model

The communication delay mainly consists of transmission delay T_m^n of tasks transmitted through wireless network and execution time T_i^m of computing tasks at nodes. When task is executed at local layer, the execution time T_i^m is expressed as

$$T_i^m = \frac{K_i}{F_i} \tag{1}$$

The energy consumption of task i at the local device is

$$E_i^m = c_n T_i^m \tag{2}$$

c_n is the CPU power of local mobile device, So the transmission delay can expressed as

$$T_m^n = \frac{K_i}{w \log(1 + \frac{P_m g_{mn}}{\omega_0})} \tag{3}$$

When the task want to be transmitted to other device for execution, the device chooses a channel, and the energy consumption during transmission is as follows $E_{trans}^{mn} = r_m^n \times K_i$, the total energy consumption is

$$E_i^{mn} = E_{trans} + E_i^n \tag{4}$$

Among them, E_{trans} is the energy consumed by the transmission process, and E_i^n is the energy consumed by other device to execute the task. Therefore, the total overhead is

$$\min \sum_{i=1}^{n} \left[\sum_{j=1}^{n} \alpha_l \left[E_i^m x_{ij} + E_i^{mn} (1 - x_{ij}) \right] + \lambda_l \left[T_i^m x_{ij} + T_i^n (1 - x_{ij}) \right] \right]$$
$$s.t \quad i \in (1, n), \, j \in (1, n) \tag{5}$$
$$T_i^m + T_i^n \le L_i$$

α_l, λ_l are two weighting factors which indicate the weights of time consumption and consumption in the decision-making process respectively.

MEC Computing Model

$$\varphi_{ij} = \begin{cases} 0 \text{ Task excute at local mobile device} \\ 1 \text{ Task excute at MEC device} \end{cases} \tag{6}$$

When $\varphi_{ij} = 1$, tasks needs to be uninstalled to the MEC device for execution, energy consumption E_n^{edge} can be divided into transmission energy consumption $E_{n,trans}^c$ and calculation energy consumption $E_{n,com}^c$.

$$E_n^{edge} = E_{n,trans}^{edge} + E_{n,com}^{edge} \tag{7}$$

$$E_{n,trans}^{edge} = P_i \cdot T_{i,trans}^e, \, \forall i \in N \tag{8}$$

P is the unit energy consumption when the mobile device accesses the channel, $E_{n,com}^c$ is the energy consumed by task execution at the MEC layer.

$$E_{n,com}^{edge} = T_{i,com}^e \cdot \varepsilon_e \tag{9}$$

The communication delay mainly consists of transmission delay $T_{i,trans}^e$ and execution time $T_{i,com}^e$ of computing tasks.

$$T_{i,trans}^e = \frac{K_i}{r_n} \tag{10}$$

$$T_{i,com}^e = \frac{K_i}{F_c} \qquad (11)$$

Therefore, the total overhead of MEC is

$$\min \sum_{i=1}^{n} \alpha_c \left[E_{n,trans}^{edge} + E_{n,com}^{edge} \right] + \lambda_c \left[T_{n,trans}^e + T_{n,com}^e \right] \qquad (12)$$

6 Evaluation and Analysis

In this section, we use the MATLAB software simulation method to evaluate the performance of the proposed unloading strategy. In this simulation, the parameters of the task are set as, The calculated value of the task is, the time delay constraint; The computing power of mobile devices is. The computing power of MEC devices is. The parameters of the Wi-Fi wireless channel are set as (Fig. 4):

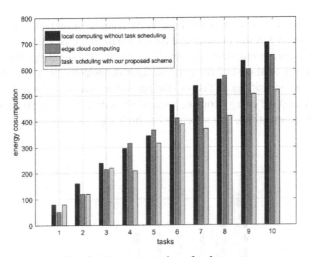

Fig. 4. The consumption of task owner

The experimental results show that when the amount of tasks increases, the local computing task scheduling of our proposed scheme has less energy consumption than local computing without task scheduling and all tasks to edge cloud computing. We can see that when $I \leq 3$ h, the energy consumption between our proposed solution and all tasks of the edge layer calculation is not much different. When $I > 3$, due to the increased workload, all transmission to the edge layer will consume a large amount of transmission energy, while the local device is idle. At this time, the game theory-based scheduling scheme is better.

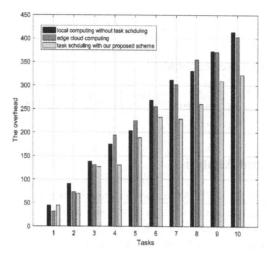

Fig. 5. The overhead for mobile device

From Fig. 5, we can see that the local computing without task scheduling has the largest overhead. When the number of tasks is small, there is a little difference of the total overhead between our schemes and the edge cloud computing. When the number of tasks is low, the total cost of the two solutions is basically the same. As the number of tasks increases, unloading all tasks to the edge cloud creates a large delay. This leads to high latency, and the energy consumption of uploading tasks to the edge layer is also increasing at the same time. Our schemes has higher performance.

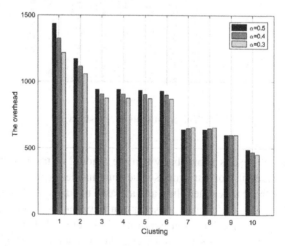

Fig. 6. The overhead of cluster

We select different values for the weight parameters α. The Fig. 6 shows that when α is gradually larger, the proportion of energy consumption in total overhead increases, and in our method, it is more suitable for calculating tasks with low delay requirements.

7 Conclusion

This paper analyzes the task scheduling problem based on self-organized edge computing, and proposes a graph-based server region clustering algorithm. The game scheduling based task scheduling mechanism mainly considers energy consumption and aims to minimize mobile devices. In this paper, the communication model and the computational model are proposed firstly. The graph-based server clustering algorithm is proposed, and the algorithm is applied to the edge computing. Then the task unloading problem is analyzed, which effectively reduces the edge computing task scheduling energy consumption.

References

1. Mao, Y., Zhang, J., Letaief, K.B.: Dynamic computation offloading for mobile-edge computing with energy harvesting devices. IEEE J. Sel. Areas Commun. **34**, 3590–3605 (2016)
2. Wang, S., et al.: A survey on mobile edge networks: convergence of computing, caching and communications. IEEE Access **5**, 6757–6779 (2017)
3. Jin, L., Li, S., Yu, J.G., He, J.B.: Robot manipulator control using neural networks: a survey. Neurocomputing **285**, 23–34 (2018)
4. Shahzadi, S., Iqbal, M., Dagiuklas, T., Qayyum, Z.U.: Multi-access edge computing: open issues, challenges and future perspective. J. Cloud Comput. **6**(1), 30 (2017)
5. Zhang, K., et al.: Energy-efficient offloading for mobile edge computing in 5G heterogeneous networks. IEEE Access **4**, 5896–5907 (2016)
6. Corcoran, P., Datta, S.K.: Mobile-edge computing and the internet of things for consumers: extending cloud computing and services to the edge of the network. IEEE Consum. Electron. Mag. **5**(4), 73–74 (2016)
7. Qi, L.Y., et al.: A two-stage locality-sensitive hashing based approach for privacy-preserving mobile service recommendation in cross-platform edge environment. Futur. Gener. Comp. Syst. **88**, 636–643 (2018)
8. Li, Y., Wang, S.: An energy-aware edge server placement algorithm in mobile edge computing. In: 2018 IEEE International Conference on Edge Computing (EDGE), San Francisco, pp. 66–73 (2018)
9. Zeng, D., Gu, L., Guo, S., Cheng, Z., Yu, S.: Joint optimization of task scheduling and image placement in fog computing supported software-defined embedded system. IEEE Trans. Comput. **65**(12), 3702–3712 (2016)
10. Song, N., Gong, C., Xingshuo, A.N., Zhan, Q.: Fog computing dynamic load balancing mechanism based on graph repartitioning. China Commun. **13**(3), 156–164 (2016)
11. Mebrek, A., Merghem-Boulahia, L., Esseghir, M.: Efficient green solution for a balanced energy consumption and delay in the IoT-Fog-Cloud computing. In: IEEE International Symposium on Network Computing and Applications, pp. 1–4 (2017)
12. Chen, X., Jiao, L., Li, W., Fu, X.: Efficient multi-user computation offloading for mobile-edge cloud computing. IEEE/ACM Trans. Networking **24**(5), 2795–2808 (2016)

13. Qi, L.Y., Yu, J.G., Zhou, Z.L.: An invocation cost optimization method for web services in cloud environment. Sci. Program. **2017**, 9 (2017)
14. Chen, M.H., Liang, B., Min, D.: Joint offloading decision and resource allocation for multi-user multi-task mobile cloud. In: IEEE International Conference on Communications, Kuala Lumpur, pp. 1–6 (2016)
15. Zhu, T., Shi, T., Li, J., Cai, Z., Zhou, X.: Task scheduling in deadline-aware mobile edge computing systems. IEEE Internet Things J. **6**(3), 4854–4866 (2019)
16. Deng, R., Lu, R., Lai, C., Luan, T.H., Liang, H.: Optimal workload allocation in fog-cloud computing toward balanced delay and power consumption. IEEE Internet Things J. **3**(6), 1171–1181 (2016)
17. Pham, Q.V., Leanh, T., Tran, N.H., Hong, C.S.: Decentralized computation offloading and resource allocation in heterogeneous networks with mobile edge computing (2018)
18. Zheng, J., Cai, Y., Yuan, W., Shen, X.S.: Stochastic computation offloading game for mobile cloud computing. In: IEEE/CIC International Conference on Communications in China, Chengdu, pp. 1–6 (2016)

Grazing Trajectory Statistics and Visualization Platform Based on Cloud GIS

Dong Li[1,2,3], Chuanjian Wang[1,2,3(✉)], Qilei Wang[1], Tianying Yan[1], Ju Wang[1], and Wanlong Bing[1]

[1] College of Information Science and Technology, Shihezi University, Shihezi 832000, China
wcj_inf@shzu.edu.cn
[2] Geospatial Information Engineering Research Center, Xinjiang Production and Construction Corps, Shihezi 832000, China
[3] Geospatial Information Engineering Laboratory, Xinjiang Production and Construction Corps, Shihezi 832000, China

Abstract. In order to meet the needs of ranchers and grassland livestock management departments for the visualization of grazing behavior, this study develops a statistical and visual platform for herd trajectory. The Web AppBuilder for ArcGIS and ArcGIS Online were used to implement statistics and visualization of herd trajectories. The walking speed, walking trajectory and feed intake of the herd were calculated by the GP service on the server. The calculation results were published to the ArcGIS online platform. The relevant information was analyzed and displayed by Web AppBuilder for ArcGIS calling the data on ArcGIS Online. This platform achieved the visualization function of walking speed, walking trajectory and feed intake of the herd. It can provide technical support and data support for relevant management departments to monitor grazing information and study the living habits of herds.

Keywords: ArcGIS · Trajectory · Statistics · Grazing

1 Introduction

Animal husbandry is an important part of agriculture. It has very important impact on socioeconomic development and people's production and life [1]. Grassland is an extremely important natural resource in the development of animal husbandry [2]. Rational use of grassland resources is related to the sustainable development of animal husbandry. However, most grassland has different degrees of grassland degradation [3], and overfeeding of herds on grassland is one of the causes of grassland degradation [4, 5]. In a period of time, the feed intake of the herd exceeds the tolerance limit of the grassland in the region [6]. It breaks the ecological balance of grassland and leads to the failure of regeneration of grassland resources. Therefore, it is necessary to analyze the grazing behavior of herds in time and accurately. It is of great significance to adjust grazing strategies, improve grassland productivity and protect grassland ecosystems [7, 8].

X. Zhang et al. (Eds.): CloudComp 2019/SmartGift 2019, LNICST 322, pp. 275–282, 2020.
https://doi.org/10.1007/978-3-030-48513-9_23

Traditionally, the feeding behavior was mainly studied by observation methods. Devices such as counters, stopwatches, and telescopes were used to track the feeding behavior of the herd [9–11]. But there are some limitations due to the number of people, devices capabilities and study area. The traditional methods waste time and energy. The information collected by traditional methods is small and the timeliness is poor. It is difficult to describe the spatiotemporal information of herd feeding behavior accurately [12].

In recent years, GPS (Global Positioning System) technology, GIS (Geographic Information System) technology, modern communication and computer technology have gradually matured. Domestic and foreign scholars have applied the above technologies into the grassland and animal husbandry [13, 14]. These methods are not limited by conditions such as time and terrain. It can record the grazing trajectory of the herd and generate spatiotemporal trajectory data containing the movement information of the herd. The habits of the herd can be studied through trajectory data [15, 16].

Arnon et al. conducted his experiment at a study site in the semi-arid region of the Negev, northern Israel. They used GPS devices to record the trajectory of the herd. They analyzed the herd's walking speed by the factors of the pasture (slope, aspect, and distance between the herd and the corral). The speed of flock movement is greatly affected by the distance of the corral. The flock walks fastest when the distance between the flock and the corral is the largest or the smallest. As the slope increases, the walking speed of the flock decreases. The walking speed of the flock is also affected by the aspect [17].

Henkin et al. studied the effects of topographical factors on cattle foraging behavior in hilly areas. In this study, they used the LOTEK 2200 series GPS collar (Lotek Engineering, Newmarket, ON, Canada) to record the trajectory of the herd at intervals of 5 min. They analyzed the grazing trajectory under different grazing intensities and different seasons. They found that the herd likes to eat in flat terrain. Only when the grazing intensity tends to be saturated or the forage biomass is low will it eat in areas with steep terrain [18].

Manuel Lomillos Pérez et al. used global positioning system and general packet radio technology (GPS-GPRS) to track and monitor free-range cow. The circadian rhythm map of the walking distance of cattle in a few hours was obtained. It was concluded that the average daily walking distance of cattle is 3.15 km [19].

Wang, Akasbi, Kawamura et al. used GPS devices to obtain temporal and spatial trajectory data of herd grazing. The feed intake distribution of herds was obtained by grid method [12, 20, 21].

According to the current literature, there are very few studies on the visualization platforms that provide ranchers and grassland livestock management departments with attribute information such as herd movement trajectory, walking speed, feed intake distribution and their relationship with grassland environment. The purpose of this study is to develop a statistical and visual platform for herd trajectory. The specific objectives are to 1) to calculate herd's walking speed, walking trajectories and feed intake, 2) to publish the results to ArcGIS Online, and 3) to show the relationship among trajectory points, grazing time and environment intuitively.

2 Data and Methods

2.1 Grazing Track Data Acquisition

In this study, the GT03C positioning tracker of Shenzhen Gumi was used to locate the geographical position of sheep. The positioning error of the device is less than 10 m. The overall quality of the device is 202 g. The specification is 91.5 mm × 57.0 mm × 37.5 mm (length × width × height). Hulbert et al. showed that when the ratio of the quality of the device and the quality of the sheep is less than 2.2%, it will not affect the physiological behavior and feeding speed of sheep [18]. In this experiment, the sampling time interval of GPS device was 3 min.

The trajectory data was collected from April to September 2016 and April to August 2017. During the sampling period, GPS data was uploaded to Exlive (Location Service Platform) and stored in Microsoft SQL Server 2008 database. The main information of trajectory data included GPS device ID, longitude and latitude information, sending time, etc. The trajectory data of this study were derived from the Ziniquan ranch, No. 151st regiment of the 8th division of Xinjiang production and Construction Corps. Its geographical location is 85°46′15. 06″ E, 44°00′13. 23″ N.

2.2 Grazing Track and Speed

Grazing Trajectory: $T = \{T_{1,1} \ldots, T_{i,j}, \ldots, T_{n,m}\}$ represents the trajectory unit set. It is a collection of herd trajectory over a period of time. $T_{i,j} = \{P_1, P_2, \ldots, P_n\}$ $(0 \leq i \leq n, 0 \leq j \leq m)$ represents the trajectory unit. It is the set of trajectory points of the j-th monitored sheep on the i-th day and the set of spatial points with time series. $P_k (0 \leq k \leq n)$ is the k-th trajectory point in the set of trajectory points, including longitude, latitude, positioning time t_i and other information.

Trajectory segment: Several trajectories $L_i (0 \leq i \leq n)$ were obtained by segmenting the trajectory elements. The segmentation method is based on the GPS points contained in the trajectory segment and GPS points are not less than 2. The smaller the number of trajectory points contained in the trajectory segment, the closer the fitted grazing trajectory is to the real grazing trajectory. Therefore, L_i represents the trajectory between two trajectory points P_i and P_{i+1}.

Grazing speed: The trajectory segment is a sequential trajectory segment connected by two trajectory points (Fig. 1). Therefore, grazing speed is the ratio of trajectory segment $\overrightarrow{P_i P_{i+1}}$ and the time difference $t_{i+1} - t_i$ (Eq. 1):

$$\overrightarrow{v_i} = \frac{\overrightarrow{P_i P_{i+1}}}{t_{i+1} - t_i} \tag{1}$$

The study used the TrackIntervalsToLine_ta() function to calculate the trajectory speed and plot the trajectory of the herd. The trajectory of a sheep could be got by inputting device ID and using the MakeQueryTable_management() function.

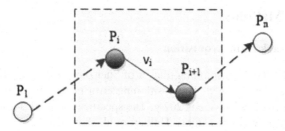

Fig. 1. The speed of grazing trajectory point in continuous time

2.3 Feed Intake Distribution

The feed intake distribution is a grid consisting of cells containing feed intake values and spatial information. Assuming that there is no significant difference between the total daily herd feed intake and daily herd speed of eating [12], the daily feed intake of the herd was calculated as:

$$D_{FID} = F(S, t_{start}, t_{end}, I_{DHFI}) = \sum_{i=0}^{k} \sum_{j=0}^{l} f(T_{i,j}, I_{DHFI}) \qquad (2)$$

Where S is the given spatial region; t_{start}, t_{end} is the given start and end time. I_{DHFI} is the total daily feed intake. It is composed of the feed intake I_i of each trajectory segment. $T_{i,j}$ is the herd trajectory unit of the jth monitored sheep on the ith day. $f(T_{i,j}, I_{DHFI})$ is the daily feed intake distribution generated by the corresponding trajectory unit $T_{i,j}$. The first summation is the distribution of feed intake for all herds in a day. The second summation is the distribution of feed intake for all herds over several days. The feed intake I_i was calculated as:

$$I_i = \frac{t_i \cdot v_{DHSE}}{S_i} = \frac{t_i}{S_i} \cdot \frac{I_{DHFI}}{t_{ADFT}} \ (0 < i < n) \qquad (3)$$

Where t_i is the effective feeding time extracted from the time attribute of the trajectory segment L_i. v_{DHSE} is the average eating speed of the herd daily. S_i is the buffer area of each trajectory segment, and t_{ADFT} is the total daily feed time.

The study used the GenerateNearTable_analysis() function, the Buffer_analysis() function and the CalculateField_management() function to calculate the daily feed intake distribution of the herd. For the multi-day feed intake distribution of the herd, it was necessary to add up the daily feed intake of the herd.

3   Results

The architecture of the platform consisted of the presentation layer, the business logic Layer and the data layer (Fig. 2). The Web AppBuilder for ArcGIS framework was used by the Presentation Layer to provide a user-friendly display interface. It implemented some functions such as statistical analysis, spatial query, spatial analysis, map navigation operations and so on. The cloud computing-based GIS mapping platform (ArcGIS Online) was used by the business logic layer to create a basic map service. The platform built some models for calculating speed, trajectory and feed intake through ArcGIS. The models were packed as GP services. They were uploaded to the server for trajectory data processing. The Data Layer provided the system with the data of pasture boundary and trajectory points of herd.

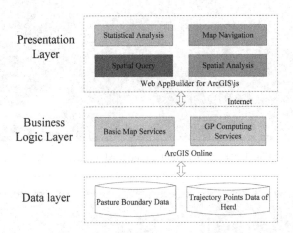

Fig. 2. Platform architecture diagram

The platform could calculate the speed, altitude and slope of the trajectory points of the herd. It also could display information such as the herd trajectory and the proportion of the number of trajectory collected by various devices. Meanwhile, the relationship between walking speed and grazing time could be analyzed.

In this study, Ziniquan pasture, No. 151st regiment of the 8th division of Xinjiang production and Construction Corps was taken as an example. The trajectory relation diagram of the herd was obtained by collecting the trajectory information of the herd on June 16, 2017 (Fig. 3). Figure 3 shows that there were 5 GPS devices to monitor the grazing behavior of the herd on that day. The number of effective trajectory points recorded was 745. The herd was about to leave the sheepfold for feed at 6:40 a.m.

The trajectory route and the feed intake of sheep with sheepID 9339081 on June 23, 2017 was calculated (Fig. 4). From the heat map of feed intake, it could be seen that the feeding area of this sheep is in the east and southeast of the pasture. According to the chart of feed intake changing with grazing time, we can know that the sheep left the sheepfold at about 8:00 a.m. The sheep arrived at the feeding area around 8:30 and began to eat freely. This sheep walked basically in the valley. This hills and slopes may be steep, which was not conducive to feed for sheep. The terrain of the valley area may be flat. The feeding along the valley may be consistent with the feeding and grazing habits of sheep.

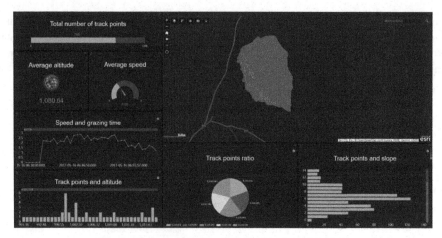

Fig. 3. Trajectory graph of the herd on June 16, 2017

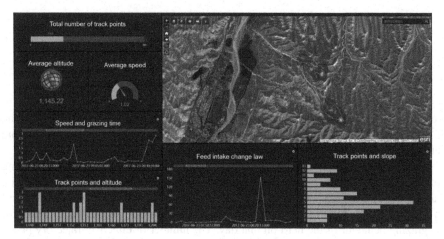

Fig. 4. Feed intake graph of sheepID 9339081 on June 23, 2017

4 Discussion

The platform achieved the visual display of the walking speed, the walking trajectory, the feed intake and other data of the herd. It was developed by Web AppBuilder for ArcGIS framework. The platform uses the ArcGIS model builder to build models. The models were published as GP service to calculate walking speed, walking trajectory, feed intake of herd and other attribute information on the server. The GIS mapping platform (ArcGIS online server) was used to publish map services. It is beneficial to make a reasonable grazing strategy and promote the sustainable development of animal husbandry. However, the grazing behavior of the herd can't be monitored in real time. For example, the walking speed and direction of the herd can't be measured in real time. In addition, the platform mainly relies on ArcGIS online platform so that the display of results is slightly delayed. Therefore, we will add the functions of grazing trajectory prediction, real-time monitoring of walking speed, and improve the loading speed of data in the future study.

5 Conclusions

The trajectory statistics and visualization platform based on cloud GIS achieved the visual display of the walking speed, the walking trajectory and the feed intake of the herd. It also could show the relationship among trajectory points, grazing time and environment intuitively. It can make ranchers, grassland livestock management departments and related researchers intuitively understand the feed state and habits of the herd.

Acknowledgments. We highly appreciate the Yang Yonglin of the Xinjiang Academy of Agricultural Reclamation and the pastoralists of Ziniquan farm, who participated in the GPS trajectory data collection and shared their knowledge on herd. We are thankful to all the professional GIS technicians, graduate students and undergraduates who contributed to the development of this system. We are grateful for the thoughtful and constructive comments of the reviewers that improved this manuscript in major ways.

Funding. This work was supported by the National Key R&D Program of China (Grant No. 2017YFB0504203), the National Natural Science Foundation of China (Grant No. 41461088, and the XJCC XPCC Innovation Team of Geospatial Information Technology (Grant No. 2016AB001).

Conflicts of Interest. The authors declare no conflict of interest.

References

1. Zhao, Q., Hou, X., Duan, J., et al.: Production benefit trend analysis of grazing regime by sunite wether on mixed artificial pasture. Chin. J. Grassl. **41**(3), 130–135 (2019)
2. Voormansik, K.: Observations of cutting practices in agricultural grasslands using polarimetric SAR. IEEE J. Sel. Top. Appl. Earth Obs. Remote Sens. **9**(4), 1382–1396 (2016)
3. Chen, Y.X., Lee, G., Lee, P., et al.: Model analysis of grazing effect on above-ground biomass and above-ground net primary production of a Mongolian grassland ecosystem. J. Hydrol. **333**(1), 155–164 (2007)
4. Marquart, A., Eldridge, D.J., Travers, S.K., et al.: Large shrubs partly compensate negative effects of grazing on hydrological function in a semi-arid Savanna. Basic Appl. Ecol. **38**, 58–68 (2019)
5. Yu, L., Chen, Y., Sun, W., et al.: Effects of grazing exclusion on soil carbon dynamics in alpine grasslands of the Tibetan Plateau. Geoderma **353**, 133–143 (2019)
6. Shen, H., Zhu, Y., Zhao, X., et al.: Analysis on the current situation of grassland resources in China. Sci. Bull. **61**(02), 139–154 (2016)
7. Liu, J., Wang, Z., Hao, D., et al.: Effect of heavy grazing on the organization ability of main plant species and functional groups in a desert steppe. Chin. J. Grassl. **40**(5), 85–92 (2018)
8. Yin, G., Qian, H., Wei, Z., et al.: Comparison of grazing sheep foraging behavior at different environment. Acta Agric. Bor. Sin. **24**(4), 205–208 (2009)
9. Guo, Q., Yin, G., Zhao, H., et al.: Study on grazing behavior and feed intake of grazing sheep. J. Chin. Acad. Grassl. **33**(4), 95–98 (2011)

10. Wang, S., Li, Y.: A study on behavior ecology of grazing sheep III influence of grazing time on grazing behavior. Acta Prataculturae Sin. **06**(02), 7–13 (1997)

11. Wang, H., Ding, X., Lang, X., et al.: Foraging behavior of Oula sheep in summer pastures of Maqu Gannan. Acta Agrestia Sin. **20**(03), 583–588 (2012)

12. Wang, C., Wang, W., Lu, W., et al.: Distribution model of herd feed intake based on grazing time-space trajectory data. Trans. Chin. Society Agr. Eng. **32**(13), 125–130 (2016)

13. Benke, K.K., Sheth, F., Betteridge, K., et al.: Application of geovisual analytics to modelling the movements of ruminants in the rural landscape using satellite tracking data. Int. J. Digit Earth **8**(7), 579–593 (2015)

14. Wu, Q., Yang, B.: 3S-based grassland information system for Western China. Trans. Chin. Soc. Agr. Eng. **17**(5), 142–145 (2001)

15. Du, Y., He, P., Li, B., et al.: Research on regional attribute mining based on herd trajectory in massive pastoral areas. Appl. Res. Comput. **35**(04), 1033–1036 (2018)

16. Wang, X.: The effects of different grazing management system on livestock behavior. Inner Mongolia University (2017)

17. Arnon, A., Svoray, T., Ungar, E.D.: The spatial dimension of pastoral herding: a case study from the Northern Negev. Isr. J. Ecol. Evol. **57**(1–2), 129–149 (2011)

18. Henkin, Z., Ungar, E.D., Dolev, A.: Foraging behaviour of beef cattle in the hilly terrain of a Mediterranean grassland. Rangeland J. **34**(2), 163 (2012)

19. Pérez, J., Varga, M., García, J., et al.: Monitoring lidia cattle with GPS-GPRS technology: a study on grazing behaviour and spatial distribution. Vet. Mex. **4**(4), 1–17 (2017)

20. Akasbi, Z., Oldeland, J., Dengler, J., Finckh, M.: Social and ecological constraints on decision making by transhumant pastoralists: a case study from the Moroccan Atlas Mountains. J. Mt. Sci. **9**(3), 307–321 (2012). https://doi.org/10.1007/s11629-009-2320-8

21. Kawamura, K., Akiyama, T., Yokota, H.O., et al.: Quantifying grazing intensities using geographic information systems and satellite remote sensing in the Xilingol steppe region, Inner Mongolia, China. Agr. Ecosyst. Environ. **107**(1), 83–93 (2005)

Cloud-Based AGV Control System

Xiangnan Zhang[1], Wenwen Gong[1], Haolong Xiang[2], Yifei Chen[1(✉)], Dan Li[1], and Yawei Wang[1]

[1] College of Information and Electrical Engineering,
China Agricultural University, Beijing, China
glfei_cau@126.com
[2] University of Auckland, Auckland, New Zealand

Abstract. With the development of artificial intelligence technology, the application of mobile robots is more and more extensive. How to solve the control problem of mobile robots in complex network environment is one of the core problems that plague the promotion and application of AGV clusters. In view of the above problems, this paper studies the control technology in the cloud big data environment, and realizes the decision, planning and control of AGV in the cloud environment. Firstly, cloud-side data sharing and cross-domain collaboration are used to realize intelligent adaptive association of heterogeneous data, then establish a collaborative hierarchical information cloud processing model, and design a new AGV sensing structure based on various devices such as laser radar and ultrasonic sensors. Finally, a set of AGV motion control methods in cloud environment is proposed. The experimental results show that the efficient coordination among network nodes in the heterogeneous AGV system in the cloud environment is stable overall and has a lower delay rate, which will greatly promote the application of AGV in various complex network environments.

Keywords: Cloud environment · AGV · Control system

1 Introduction

Automated guided transport vehicle (AGV) is a transport vehicle equipped with an automatic guiding device such as electromagnetic or optical, which can travel along a prescribed guiding path, with security protection and various transfer functions. Kiva in Amazon Smart Warehouse The handling robot is one of the typical representatives. The AGV has become one of the important transportation equipments in modern logistics systems with its unique advantages. The core of the AGV transport vehicle lies in the control and navigation system. However, for the research of the AGV navigation system, the combination of the encoder and the gyroscope is mainly used in the early stage [1, 2], but it cannot be avoided due to the inherent characteristics of the inertial navigation elements such as the gyroscope. The influence of traditional hardware defects such as zero drift and temperature drift will cause cumulative error when it is used as the core component of the navigation system. In the traditional way, the absolute position method is adopted to calibrate the AGV position. As in the literature [3, 4], GPS is used as the

© ICST Institute for Computer Sciences, Social Informatics and Telecommunications Engineering 2020
Published by Springer Nature Switzerland AG 2020. All Rights Reserved
X. Zhang et al. (Eds.): CloudComp 2019/SmartGift 2019, LNICST 322, pp. 283–293, 2020.
https://doi.org/10.1007/978-3-030-48513-9_24

absolute position to calibrate, in addition to the multi-source data fusion calibration scheme using GPS and machine vision images [5], and the multi-source fusion scheme has become a mainstream solution for navigation systems. With the popularization and application of laser radar in the unmanned field, it is possible to integrate AGV and laser radar. The robot level uses different guiding methods, such as laser guidance, to control the robot to move autonomously on the free path or the fixed path, and the guiding and expanding of the robot becomes simple and easy.

The emergence of a variety of high-precision sensors such as laser radar has greatly increased the amount of data processing. It is difficult for ordinary computers to meet the timeliness requirements. Adding a server not only increases the cost of AGV but also compresses the space of other components. Due to the complexity of the AGV operating environment, a single LAN is difficult to meet the needs of AGV control, especially in complex environments where communication node loss, signal delay, and data loss are common.

Cloud computing is one of the hotspots of current research and application. It is based on grid computing [6], parallel computing and distributed computing. It has the characteristics of high reliability and versatility. It uses data multi-copy fault tolerance and computational node isomorphism. Interchangeable measures to ensure high reliability of services [7, 8], using cloud computing is more reliable than using local computers. Cloud computing is not targeted at specific applications. Under the support of "cloud", it can be constructed for a variety of applications. The same "cloud" can support different application operations at the same time [9, 10], which is very suitable for AGV control in complex environments. In order to solve the above phenomenon, the heterogeneous AGV control system in the specially designed cloud environment has a large amount of computation in the AGV environment, and the communication nodes are easily lost in a complex environment. Ordinary equipment is difficult to meet the current calculation requirements, so a heterogeneous AGV computing environment is designed. Simple data preprocessing is performed by running Ubuntu 14.04 industrial computer, and then the final mission planning result is given by the cloud computing environment.

2 System Logic Architecture

The common architecture is difficult to support the calculation of the AGV in operation in this design. Therefore, the cloud environment AGV system architecture for big data is designed to virtualize large-scale resources and distributed resources, and finally realize the parallel of lidar data and sensor data. deal with. The system realizes the control and management of AGV by constructing the "application layer - logic layer - cloud computing layer" three-tier architecture (Fig. 1). The application layer is mainly responsible for the collection of environmental data and the execution of AGV actions. The logic layer is mainly a module that manages the basic ROS node, and is responsible for the transmission, parsing, preprocessing, and execution of control instructions of the sensor acquisition data. The cloud computing layer is mainly responsible for the fusion analysis of multi-source data, the assignment of tasks, and the storage of location information, attribute information, and status information of the AGV.

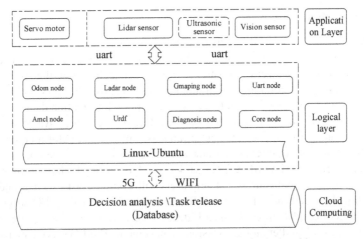

Fig. 1. Cloud environment based AGV system logical architecture

2.1 Application Layer

The application layer provides data acquisition and AGV action execution functions, including laser radar sensors, ultrasonic sensors, vision sensors, and servo motors. Laser lightning sensor is an important part of AGV environment sensing. It provides basic data for positioning navigation for AGV. Single-line laser radar is used in this system. The ultrasonic sensor is an important collision avoidance device, which can effectively avoid the collision of the AGV with the wall and other obstacles while driving, and maintain a safe distance. Vision sensors are used to identify two-dimensional codes on the ground and at specific locations to aid in precise positioning.

The servo motor is the component used in the AGV control system to convert the electrical signal into a corner or speed on the shaft to control the motion of the AGV.

2.2 Logical Layer

The logic layer is the core of AGV control and is responsible for receiving, parsing, storing, and managing sensor upload data. The core carrier of the logic layer is the industrial computer with Ubuntu14.04 installed. The basic ROS node module is run on the carrier to realize the basic functions of AGV operation, such as uploading and downloading of data, control command release, etc., wherein the Urdf node is responsible for AGV. The description of the action description; the Amcl node is responsible for the probabilistic positioning of the AGV two-dimensional motion, using the particle filter to track the attitude of the AGV to the known map; the Gmapping node creates a two-dimensional grid map from the lidar data and the pose data acquired by the AGV; Diagnostics The diagnostic node is responsible for collecting, publishing, analyzing, and viewing data.

2.3 Cloud Computing Layer

The cloud computing layer is the decision basis of the AGV control system. It is responsible for the analysis and integration of the AGV multi-source data. The data server in the cloud computing layer establishes a TCP/IP connection with the AGV through WIFI, GPRS and other communication methods, and receives the AGV environmental data and the AGV ontology. Attribute data and exception information data.

The cloud server uses the Java SE Runtime Environment, the Java SDK, and the Tomcat technology to build a data server, and uses the MINA (Multipurpose Infrastructure for Network Applications) framework to process large-scale concurrent data from the AGV cluster. The MINA framework is used to develop high performance. And highly available web applications that help users with complex tasks such as underlying I/O and thread concurrency. The MINA framework is dominated by I/O service management (IoService), I/O filter chain (IoFilterChain), and I/O processing. It consists of modules such as IoHandler and I/O session management. The I/O service management interacts directly with the operating system I/O interface to handle the actual I/O operation protocol read and write operations. Its two implementation classes IoAcceptor and IoConnector correspond to the server-side and client-side service management classes respectively; then, IoFilterChain receives the events passed by IoService, and the IoProcessor thread is responsible for handling the filters (IoFilter) contained in the call chain; finally, IoFilter Processed events are sent to the IoHandler and implement specific business logic. Sending a message to the client by calling the IoSession write method will be passed in the exact opposite order of receiving the data until the IoService finishes sending the data to the cloud server.

The Socket port listener running in the data processing server listens to the specified port dynamics at all times. When there is a data packet access, the protocol parsing program is called to parse the data in the data packet into environment location data and attribute data, and finally use the DBMS to write the data classification. In the MySQL database, the storage of AGV data is completed.

3   The Design of AGV

For humans, we get the environmental information around us through the integration of hearing, vision and touch. By combining data from multiple sensors to take advantage of the strengths of each sensor while avoiding its disadvantages, the central control computer can obtain more reliable external environmental information, make optimal decisions efficiently, and cope with more complex and diverse road conditions.. For example, ultrasonic sensors are the most indispensable sensors for robots due to their small size and low price. However, ultrasonic sensors can only be used in applications where the accuracy of environmental sensing is not high. They are generally used in combination with other sensors, such as monocular vision sensors, etc. [8]. Infrared ranging also detects the distance of an object by emitting infrared rays and receiving the reflected light back by the photodetector. It is greatly affected by the environment. The color of the object and the surrounding light can cause measurement errors, and the measurement range is very short. It is only suitable for short distance ranging. It is generally not used alone, such as the detection of obstacles combined with ultrasonic sensors [5], so in the overall structural design of the AGV, the position of each sensor should be scientific and reasonable, so that the sensors are closely matched.

The structural design of the AGV body is closely related to the construction of the operational control algorithm. The common wheeled AGV structure is mainly composed of three-wheeled AGV and four-wheeled AGV. This design is a four-wheeled AGV. The four-wheel AGV is suitable for large-sized car bodies. This type of car body has the characteristics of negative weight and stable operation. It is suitable for structured space such as large workshops. Steering ability puts higher demands.

At present, the mainstream four-wheel AGV car adopts the front wheel drive and the rear wheel slave mode. In this driving mode, the AGV can adopt the differential control method to realize the steering motion of the vehicle body. In the four-wheel AGV design, the laser radar is often placed in the center of the structure, but the laser radar is located in the middle of the vehicle body, which reduces the bearing space of the vehicle body and is not suitable for the weight bearing. Therefore, in this design, the laser radar is embedded in the head of the vehicle body, assisting the attitude correction algorithm, taking into account the AGV weight bearing problem and the motion control accuracy problem. The specific design diagram is shown below. Two-wheel drive. The lidar AGV requires high load capacity, drive performance and volume, and a limited spatial range, thus requiring a small turning radius (Fig. 2).

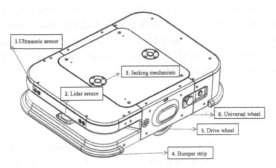

Fig. 2. AGV sensor distribution

1. It is an ultrasonic sensor used to detect nearby obstacle information and emergency obstacle avoidance, in addition to the navigation algorithm to detect obstacles of about 30 cm, cone-shaped, 15° angle cone; 2. Lidar, Fan-shaped distribution, detecting the angular range of 270°, detecting the surrounding environment and distance; 3. Lifting mechanism, scissors differential mechanism, capable of lifting 1 ton of weight; 4. Anti-collision strip, triple protection, 1 cow's force touch It can stop; 5. The driving wheel plays the role of the whole vehicle driving, adopts DC brushless servo motor, the precision can reach 2 mm; 6. The universal wheel can assist the steering of the car body under the driving of the driving wheel, and bear part of the weight.

The AGV system consists of a main control module, a power supply module, a boot module, a drive module, a safety detection module, and a communication module. The AGV uses the Advantech development board as the main control unit. The main control module issues straight, in-situ rotation and turning commands to the car based on the feedback signals of the laser radar, ultrasonic sensors and collision sensors.

The drive module coordinates the operation of the two wheel drive motors through the motor controller to realize the forward, reverse and steering of the AGV. The controller uses the PWM or DA speed regulation method to adjust the motor speed, and different speeds are required at different stages of the AGV operation. Such as starting, stopping, turning, and the transition between the stages at a smooth speed, which puts higher requirements on the performance of the drive module. After receiving the instruction, the industrial computer drive module executes the corresponding code, changes the AGV running status, and monitors. The motor running status uploads the motor running information to the main control module.

The function of the auxiliary safety module is to prevent the AGV body from colliding with obstacles. Because the single-line lidar is embedded in the AGV head, the laser radar blind zone is inevitable during the driving process of the car. The auxiliary safety module is composed of ultrasonic radar and collision sensor. When the laser radar fails to detect the blind obstacle, the ultrasonic radar assists the detection. When the obstacles are not detected at present, the collision sensors arranged on the front and rear casings of the AGV are used as the last protection means. When the collision sensor has contacted the obstacle, the system gives priority to the event and issues an emergency brake. Command and alarm.

The function of the communication module is responsible for the communication of the various functional modules within the AGV. On the other hand, it is responsible for connecting the AGV and the control background server. When multiple AGVs are running at the same time, the working paths of other AGVs are coordinated to avoid mutual interference between the AGVs.

4   AGV Motion Control

The AGV system consists of two parts: the hardware body and the control system. During the operation, the car body and the control system will affect the motion process of the AGV. In order to achieve the precise control of the AGV motion process, the AGV motion is studied on the basis of rational design of the car body. The relationship between learning and dynamics ultimately led to the construction of a kinematic algorithm that achieves precise control of AGV.

The AGV adopts the PID control method, and the PID control method is mainly applied to the system whose basic linearity and dynamic characteristics do not change with time. The controller is composed of the proportional unit P, the integral unit I and the differential unit D. Set the three parameters of Kp, Ki and Kd. The chassis PID controller is an important feedback loop component of the chassis control system. The controller compares the collected data with a reference value and then uses this difference to calculate a new input value. The purpose of this new input value is to allow the system data to be reached or maintained at the reference value. Unlike other simple control operations, the PID controller in the AGV can adjust the input value according to the historical data and the occurrence rate of the difference, which can make the system more accurate and more stable.

A PID feedback loop can keep the system stable while other control methods cause the system to have stable errors or process iterations. In a PID loop, this correction has three algorithms that eliminate the current error, the average past error, and the change in the error to predict future errors. For example, in the chassis system, if you want to control the trolley to go straight, when the speed of the two wheels of the car is given, the car starts to walk. At this time, the speed value will be fed back to the chassis control system. If there is a slip, etc., it will lead to two rounds. The speed of the car is different, the car will deviate from the original track, then the PID controller will adjust the given speed according to the speed deviation according to the error value.

There are two control modes for the chassis servo electric wheel, and the position control mode and the speed control mode are combined.

Position Control: Determine the rotation speed by the frequency of the externally input pulse, determine the angle of rotation by the number of pulses, or directly assign speed and displacement by communication. Since the position mode has strict control over speed and position, it is generally applied to positioning devices. For the ribbon navigation mode, if the displacement is specified, the AGV will follow the command to move to the relevant position and then stop.

Speed Mode: The rotation speed can be controlled by the analog input or the frequency of the pulse. The speed mode can also be positioned when the outer ring PID of the position control device is controlled, but the position signal of the motor or the position signal of the direct load must be used. Give feedback to the upper level for calculation. The position mode also supports the direct load outer loop detection position signal. At this time, the encoder at the motor shaft end only detects the motor speed, and the position signal is provided by the detection device of the final load end. This has the advantage of reducing the error in the intermediate transmission process. increasing the positioning accuracy of the entire system. For the laser autonomous navigation mode, the speed is specified for the car, and the car will drive at this speed (Fig. 3).

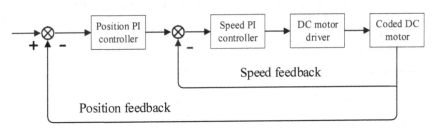

Fig. 3. PID control flow chart

AGV PID Control Algorithm Design

The PID controller consists of a proportional unit (P), an integral unit (I), and a differential unit (D). The relationship between the input e(t) and the output u(t) is:

$$u(t) = kp[e(t) + 1/TI \int e(t)dt + TD * de(t)/dt$$

The upper and lower limits of the integral are 0 and t.

So its transfer function is:

$$G(s) = U(s)/E(s) = kp[1 + 1/(TI * S) + TD * s]$$

Where kp is the proportionality factor; TI is the integral time constant; TD is the differential time constant.

Two types of PID algorithms:

(1) Position control

$$u(n) = K_P \left\{ e(n) + \frac{T}{T_I} \sum_0^n e(i) + \frac{T_D}{T}[e(n) - e(n-1)] \right\} + u_0$$

Pseudo code of positional PID algorithm:

Algorithm: *Cloud environment Location PID*

Inputs: *SetValue, ActulaValue, PID, E_n, E_{n1}, E_{n2}*
Outputs: *Result: PID_Loc*

```
1   for i=1 to n do
2       PID_En = SetValue- ActulaValue;
3   If
4   PID_En1=PID_En ;
5   then
6   PID_LocSum+=PID_En
7   PID_Loc=( PID_Kp*PID_ En)+(PID_Ki*PID_ LocSum)+ PID_Kd*
        (PID_ En1-PID_ En2);
8   Return
9   PID_Loc
```

---

(2) Incremental control

$$\Delta u(n) = u(n) - u(n-1)$$

$$= K_P[e(n) - e(n-1)] + K_P \frac{T}{T_I} e(n) + K_P \frac{T_D}{T}[e(n) - 2e(n-1) + e(n-2)]$$

Pseudo code of incremental PID algorithm:

Algorithm: *Cloud environment Incremental PID*

Inputs: *SetValue, ActulaValue, PID, E_n, E_{n1}, E_{n2}*
Outputs: *Result*: *PID_Inc*

1	**for** *i=1 to n* **do**
2	$PID\_E_n = SetValue- ActulaValue;$
3	**If**
4	$PID\_En2=PID\_En1$;
5	$PID\_En1=PID\_En$;
6	**then**
7	$PID\_Inc=(PID\_Kp*PID\_ En)-(PID\_Ki*PID\_ En1)+(PID\_kd*PID\_ En2);$
8	**Return**
9	PID_Inc

---

5 Experiment Analysis

Experimental design: Three methods were tested in the contrast experiment. The first method is the cloud environment-based AGV control method designed in this paper; the second method is the same computing server placed on the AGV, the wired connection method; the third method is all the calculations are all on the cloud, and the AGV ontology does not do preprocessing.

Positioning analysis: The system uses a variety of distance sensors. For indoor applications, the system uses a 270° laser scanner to build a map of its environment. The laser system measures the shape, size, and distance from the laser source through the energy return mode and signal return time. In the mapping mode, the laser system describes the characteristics of the workspace by combining the scan results at multiple different locations within the work area. This produces a map of the object's position, size, and shape as a reference for runtime scanning. The laser scanner function provides accurate positional information when used in conjunction with mapping information. All three methods can achieve the centimeter-level precise positioning requirements, and can't distinguish the superiority of the method, so the response time is introduced as a new evaluation index. The positioning accuracy is the best indicator.

Corresponding time analysis: The AGV response time is defined as the time from when the system issues an instruction to when the AGV moves to the specified position. By comparison, it can be known that the method used in Method 2 is similar in time, but compared with Method 2, the AGV local space and cost are saved, and Method 1 takes much less time than Method 3. The method in this paper is more advantageous on the basis of accomplishing the same task (Fig. 4).

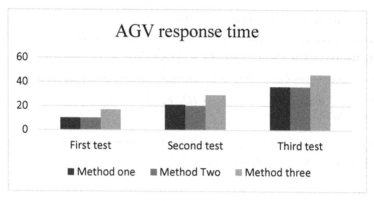

Fig. 4. AGV response time

6 Conclusion

The system is supported by cloud computing technology, combined with the characteristics of AGV control, designed and implemented a heterogeneous AGV control system in the cloud environment. The system makes full use of the high reliability and scalability of the cloud environment, builds the AGV control architecture, establishes a stable information transmission channel, unifies the service data, and solves the poor environmental adaptability of the AGV system in complex environments. In response to the delay, the AGV control system cloud platform was constructed, which has the characteristics of high integration, wide coverage and regulatory integration. The application of cloud computing optimizes the task scheduling power, which will further promote the development of collaborative control of AGV clusters, provide data support for distributed collaborative management and decision making of heterogeneous robot clusters in complex environments, and coordinate for robot clusters in the cloud environment. Aggregation mechanisms and intelligent dynamic evolution theory provide the basis for verification.

Acknowledgements. This paper was funded by the international training and improvement project of graduate students of China agricultural university; the Ministry of Education of China and Chinese Academy of Sciences (Grant: 4444-10099609).

References

1. Zhong, X., Feng, M., Huang, W., Wang, Z., Satoh, S.: Poses guide spatiotemporal model for vehicle re-identification. In: 25th International Conference, MMM 2019, Thessaloniki, Greece, 8–11 January, Proceedings, Part II, MultiMedia Modeling (2019)
2. Zhang, J., et al.: Hybrid computation offloading for smart home automation in mobile cloud computing. Pers. Ubiquitous Comput. **22**(1), 121–134 (2018). https://doi.org/10.1007/s00779-017-1095-0
3. Xu, X., et al.: An IoT-Oriented data placement method with privacy preservation in cloud environment. J. Netw. Comput. Appl. **124**(2), 148–157 (2018)

4. Nguyen, D.A., Huynh, M.K.: A research on locating AGV via RSS signals. Appl. Mech. Mater. **889**, 418–424 (2019)
5. Xu, X., Liu, X., Qi, L., Chen, Y., Ding, Z., Shi, J.: Energy-efficient virtual machine scheduling across cloudlets in wireless metropolitan area networks. Mob. Netw. Appl. (2019). https://doi.org/10.1007/s11036-019-01242-6
6. Yoshitake, H., Kamoshida, R., Nagashima, Y.: New automated guided vehicle system using real-time holonic scheduling for warehouse picking. IEEE Robot. Autom. Lett. **4**(2), 1–1 (2019)
7. Xu, X., et al.: A computation offloading method over big data for IoT-enabled cloud-edge computing. Future Gener. Comput. Syst. **95**, 522–533 (2019)
8. Xu, X., et al.: An edge computing-enabled computation offloading method with privacy preservation for internet of connected vehicles. Future Gener. Comput. Syst. **96**, 89–100 (2019)
9. Kim, C.Y., Kim, Y.H., Ra, W.-S.: Modified 1D virtual force field approach to moving obstacle avoidance for autonomous ground vehicles. J. Electr. Eng. Technol. **14**, 1367–1374 (2019)
10. Xu, X., et al.: An energy-aware computation offloading method for smart edge computing in wireless metropolitan area networks. J. Netw. Comput. Appl. **133**, 75–85 (2019)

Cloud Applications

A Parallel Drone Image Mosaic Method Based on Apache Spark

Yirui Wu, Lanbo Ge, Yuchi Luo, Deqiang Teng, and Jun Feng$^{(\boxtimes)}$

College of Computer and Information, Hohai University, Nanjing, China
{wuyirui,junfeng}@hhu.edu.cn, lanbo_cs@163.com, hhu_lyc@126.com,
3247592726@qq.com

Abstract. MapReduce has been widely used to process large-scale data in the past decade. Among the quantity of such cloud computing applications, we pay special attention to distributed mosaic methods based on numerous drone images, which suffers from costly processing time. In this paper, a novel computing framework called Apache Spark is introduced to pursue instant responses for the quantity of drone image mosaic requests. To assure high performance of Spark-based algorithms in a complex cloud computing environment, we specially design a distributed and parallel drone image mosaic method. By modifying to be fit for fast and parallel running, all steps of the proposed mosaic method can be executed in an efficient and parallel manner. We implement the proposed method on Apache Spark platform and apply it to a few self-collected datasets. Experiments indicate that our Spark-based parallel algorithm is of great efficiency and is robust to process low-quality drone aerial images.

Keywords: Distributed mosaic method · Parallel processing · Apache Spark · Big data · Drone aerial image

1 Introduction

In recent years, drones have shown significant potential to satisfy the demands of outdoor aerial exploration in different fields, such as aerial photography, agricultural, disaster observation and military purposes [7]. During a variety of applications, one of the key problems is to provide a high-resolution image with an aerial view for large areas, which could offer sufficient and abundant information for further analysis.

Generating a large and high-resolution aerial image with a traditional and single-threaded mosaicking method is essentially low in running speed since it requires two key and time-consuming steps, i.e., image registration and image stitching, for quantity of high-resolution drone images. The former step is designed to register the image in the same coordinate system to discover the correspondence relationships among images with varying degrees of overlap, meanwhile, the latter step is to generate a high-resolution image by stitching

© ICST Institute for Computer Sciences, Social Informatics and Telecommunications Engineering 2020
Published by Springer Nature Switzerland AG 2020. All Rights Reserved
X. Zhang et al. (Eds.): CloudComp 2019/SmartGift 2019, LNICST 322, pp. 297–311, 2020.
https://doi.org/10.1007/978-3-030-48513-9_25

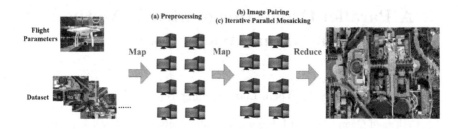

Fig. 1. Framework of the proposed method to mosaic drone aerial images.

the registered images. Image stitching algorithms take alignment estimates produced by such registration algorithms as input. Afterwards, they are responsible to blend the images seamlessly.

With the significant development of cloud computing for big data processing, we try to utilize distributed computing idea and appropriate framework to save computing time and efforts for drone image mosaicking. More precisely, we proposed to accelerate the efficiency of the traditional mosaicking method by modifying its structure with parallel and distributed computing idea, and utilize Spark framework to implement drone image mosaic processing for instant running speed. Supposing hundreds of drones have uploaded different sequences of aerial images to the proposed mosaicking system, we show the framework of the proposed system in Fig. 1, including steps of (a) preprocessing, (b) roughly drone image pairing and (c) iterative parallel mosaicking with PCA-SIFT features.

Specifically, corrections of perspective distortions and extraction of PCA-SIFT features are performed during step (a). During step (b), we roughly pair images based on image similarity before mosaicking, since it not only saves time-consuming mosaicking trials but also helps improve traditional mosaicking method to fit for distributed and parallel computing with such a light-weight pre-processing part. Finally, a novel and distributed mosaicking algorithm based on PCA-SIFT feature is carried out on Spark framework during step (c). It's noted that mosaicking process of step (c) is performed iteratively until all input drone images are integrated to generate a single and final aerial image. Moreover, we utilize two operations of Map and one operation of Reduce to construct the proposed "MapReduce" system. The reason that we could design two separate Map operations lies in the fact that steps of preprocessing and rough pairing could be executed without interactions among different input drone images.

The main contribution of this paper is to propose a parallel and distributed drone images mosaicking method, which has been successfully implemented on Spark platform. Essentially, how to design task-specified and cloud-based systems to perform image processing tasks with high efficiency is a major concern in the domain of cloud computing for big data processing. We try to complete such tasks by design a novel drone images mosaicking method based on the traditional mosaic method, which is further improved with thoughts of parallel and distributed running. After implementation on Spark with in-memory representation, results on several self-collected datasets with relatively cheap drones have proved that the proposed system is of great efficiency and accuracy for drone image mosaicking tasks.

2   Related Work

The existing methods related to our work can be categorized into image mosaicking methods and the development of cloud computing.

Mosaicking Methods. Essentially, mosaicking is well-developed in the domain of image processing. Generally speaking, it consists of five steps [13]: 1) image pre-processing, including operations of image denoising, creating image matching templates and so on; 2) image matching, which is the key step to find the exact position of feature points between the original and reference image; 3) calculate transformation parameters of two images in the geometric model based on matching feature points; 4) uniform coordinate transformation, which converts the image to be stitched into the coordinate system of the reference image; 5) fusion reconstruction, where the overlapping regions of both images are fused to reconstruct a large image. It's noted that the second and third steps refer to image registration procedure, meanwhile, the fourth and fifth steps represent the procedure of image mosaicking.

With similar structure explained above, quantity of mosaicking methods is proposed to deal with different situations in a variety of applications. For example, Wang et al. [20] convert a surveillance video clip into one abstraction image with SIFT-based image aligning and integrating. Zhang et al. [23] propose an image mosaic method based on Speed Up Robust Feature (SURF) to achieve rapid image splicing in UAV low-altitude remote sensing field. To obtain the morphology of the whole microstructure, Wang et al. [18] proposes a SIFT-based mosaic algorithm by using multiple images from a microgroove structure processed by femtosecond laser. Afterwards, a stitched image of the whole groove structure could be studied experimentally and realized.

Based on former successful implements of image mosaicking methods, we can notice it's useful to adopt the classic SIFT algorithm for step 2, i.e., image matching. To solve problems of translation, rotation and scale variances between original and reference images, the SIFT algorithm realizes the matching of the extracted feature points and forms a high quality panoramic image by matching several feature points [2]. However, directly utilizing SIFT for large-scale mosaicking is impossible, due to the large amount of computation brought by quantity trials of image matching between each pair of input images. Therefore, drone image data with the huge volume feature cannot be directly mosaicked by a single computing node with a traditional mosaicking algorithm.

Development of Cloud Computing. Faced with "big data" challenge [10], adopting a parallel computing architecture such as MapReduce [4] is a proper choice to mosaic quantity of drone images. MapReduce is carefully designed to store and parallel process large volumes of data in a distributed network. By separating available disk, computing resource and scheduling jobs, its successor platforms, such as Hadoop Standalone and Hadoop YARN [17], have become popular for big data operating. Recently, Apache Spark (Spark), an innovative framework for real-time processing, has been proposed by the University of California, Berkeley to perform in-memory computing and big data analysis [22]. In Spark, Berkeley proposed to utilize internal memory rather than disk to process in MapReduce, considering the fact that internal memory channels have higher bandwidth than disks and other PCI devices. Based on the Spark platform, Amazon.com constructed a general-purpose and scalable in-memory computing framework to process large-scale data at extremely high speed (reported 100-TB data sort in 23 min on 207 nodes) [21]. It's great potential to use the Spark framework on Hadoop platform to mosaic large-scale drone images. However, How to design a task-specified mosaic algorithm to fit parallel programming and utilize features of drone images, and what the performance gain is remain to be explored.

Most related to our project, Huang et al. [5] propose a strip-oriented parallel programming model to facilitate the design of generic remote-sensing (RS) algorithms using an Apache Spark on Hadoop YARN. They report a multitasking algorithm took less than 4 h to process more than half a terabyte of RS data on a small YARN cluster, which proved their proposed algorithms are of great efficiency. However, they pay special attention to generic parallel RS algorithms other than a complicated and task-specified algorithm, such as mosaic, detection, classification and so on. Plaza et al. [14] introduce an open-source segmentation framework that runs efficiently on large electron microscopy (EM) image datasets. Their proposed framework is implemented in Apache Spark and laid over DVID [1], a volume data-service for accessing and versioning volume data. It's reported that ingestion and segmentation with the proposed system on 453 GB EM data only took 1 h, which demonstrates the scalability and efficiency by applying image processing algorithms on the Spark platform.

3 Methodology

In this section, we describe the proposed system by preprocessing, Drone Images Pairing based on Similarity and Iterative Parallel Mosaicking with PCA-SIFT features.

3.1 Preprocessing

In this subsection, we first utilize flight parameters as input to correct perspective distortions and then extract PCA-SIFT features for further mosaicking.

Essentially, adopting a cheap consumer drone to collect data would bring several matters to quality of the inputting images. Among these matters, perspective distortion caused by unsteady flight would harm visual effect of the final mosaicking image without preprocessing. Therefore, the core of the preprocessing step is to design suitable Correlation filters (CF), which acts as a measure of similarity

Fig. 2. Illustration of perspective distortion model. (a) Perspective distortion is caused by the angle between the camera of drone and land planes, (b) input image with perspective distortion, and (c) the image after correction of perspective distortion.

between two functions. Many CF designs can be interpreted as optimizing a distance metric between an ideal desired correlation output for an input image and the correlation output of the training images with the filter template [15].

We model the discussed problem as shown in Fig. 2. As a result, the projections from land plane to the imaging plane, i.e., drone plane should be a group of divergent trapezoid shapes. Therefore, perspective distortion correction for the drone is actually a reverse trapezoid-based compensation problem. According to the above analysis, we use trapezoid-based reverse transformations for perspective distortion correction. Suppose (x, y) is a pixel from a captured aerial image, while (x', y') is its corresponding corrected point, then (x, y) and (x', y') obey the following linear transformation model:

$$\begin{bmatrix} x' \\ y' \\ \omega' \end{bmatrix} = \begin{bmatrix} S_u & 0 & 0 \\ 0 & S_v & 0 \\ 0 & 0 & 1 \end{bmatrix} \begin{bmatrix} x \\ y \\ \omega \end{bmatrix} \tag{1}$$

where (ω, ω') are Homogeneous coordinates and S_u , S_v are flight parameters in X-axis and Y-axis achieved directly from the drone we use in the experiments. We show an example result in Fig. 2, where (b) and (c) represent the image with perspective distortion and after correction, respectively.

Due to camera auto exposure and white balance affected by ambient light, there exists a difference in brightness and color between the images. This is contrary to the brightness constancy, so we should adjust the brightness of the images. We can use the sample point to adjust image brightness. The three image channels RGB are handled separately, and the difference in brightness and color can be approximated by the following linear equation:

$$\begin{bmatrix} R' \\ G' \\ B' \end{bmatrix} = \begin{bmatrix} a_r & 0 & 0 \\ 0 & a_g & 0 \\ 0 & 0 & g_b \end{bmatrix} \cdot \begin{bmatrix} R_1 \\ G_1 \\ B_1 \end{bmatrix} + \begin{bmatrix} b_r \\ b_g \\ b_b \end{bmatrix} \tag{2}$$

where a and b are linear transformation parameters. The sample points are chosen from the SIFT match previous step and its neighbor points. MSAC [3] was used to refine the sample points. Regression analysis is used to fetch the linear transform parameters of the three channels.

After correction, we extract PCA-SIFT features to prepare for further mosaicking. SIFT is proved to be a robust and stable descriptor in image matching or content analysis [8,9]. However, the extracted 128-dimension SIFT feature makes matching quite inefficient, especially for instant drone image mosaic. We thus utilize PCA-SIFT [6], a PCA (Principal Components Analysis) version of original SIFT features, to decrease the dimensions of feature space and fasten the process of image mosaic. Besides, for images containing a large number of straight lines (such as buildings, etc.), the different angles' collection of the same object by the drone will make the contour not parallel. To increase the quality of image mosaic, we made some small rotation transformation.

3.2 Drone Images Pairing Based on Similarity

In this subsection, we mainly describe the proposed algorithm to roughly pair drone images based on the similarity between two images.

Calculating the similarity between two images is a hot topic in computer vision [19,25]. Former methods adopt elementary image processing to calculate, such as histogram, Average Hash and Perceptual Hash [24]. These methods are not only fast in speed, but also simple and straightforward in implementation. However, they are not effective in calculating category-level image similarity [16]. Inspired by the significant power of deep learning architectures, researchers propose a deep ranking model to calculate and sort similarity among category-level images. For example, Wang et al. [19] integrate deep learning techniques and fine-grained ranking model to learn the image similarity ranking model directly from images.

For the proposed method, we aim to utilize a paring algorithm to avoid time-consuming mosaicking trials and convert the following parallel mosaic algorithm to fit for parallel running. Considering the feature of suitability for small computation tasks of the Spark-based system, we adopt histogram, a light-level but highly effective for resemble images similarity calculating algorithm, to be the pairing algorithm. In fact, we utilize histogram to search and pair two aerial images by calculating the similarity between the subareas of two images captured in a disorderly flying video sequence, which could be written as following:

$$Sim(G, S) = \max_{k=1,2} \sum_{i=1}^{N} \sum_{i=1}^{255} (1 - \frac{|g_{i,j,k} - s_{i,j,k}|}{\max(g_{i,j,k}, s_{i,j,k})}) \tag{3}$$

where g and s refer to the histograms of G and S respectively, N represents the blocks we split for each subarea and k represents the number of subareas. Note that k is settled with 2, which represents we utilize the left and right parts of aerial images with preset areas to calculate. In that way, we aim to search horizontal neighboring images and pair them up. Splitting blocks are used to improve the robustness of the histogram method, preventing similar color of

G, S results in high similarity. After calculating similarity, we roughly pair two images by

$$P(I_i) = \arg\max_j Sim(I_i, I_j), where\ I_i, I_j \in \psi \tag{4}$$

where ψ refers to the set of unpaired images. We show two successful mosaicked samples in Fig. 3 to illustrate the calculation of similarities, where we can notice the right part of (a),(e) and the left part of (b),(f) are similar in both appearance and corresponding histograms.

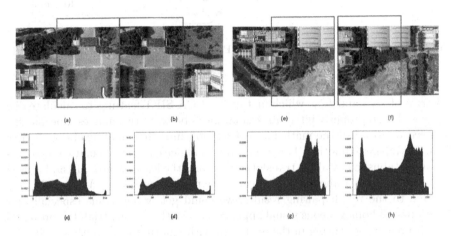

Fig. 3. Sampling images and their corresponding histograms.

The importance of such roughly pairing operation lies in the fact that we cannot achieve a parallel workflow without pre-arrangement. More precisely, the collected images are often disordered and will not succeed if mosaicked directly because they share few same features. We need to do similarity matching to adjust these images to a sequence that can be mosaicked correctly, that is, two images that can be mosaicked put together. Specifically, for an image, another image that is most likely to be mosaicked with it is selected through similarity comparison. Thus, the image sequence that can be mosaicked correctly can be generated through multiple operations.

3.3   Iterative Parallel Mosaicking with PCA-SIFT

In this subsection, we describe the proposed iterative parallel mosaicking algorithm.

We show the workflow of the proposed mosaic algorithm in Fig. 4 . We can observe the input is a pair of drone images $P_{m,t,r} = \{I_{i,t,r}, I_{j_t,r}\}$ computed by former subsection, where t and r represents the index of turn and iteration, respectively. We firstly judge whether $t < \eta$ to prevent cycle running, where η equals 4 in experiments. Then, we follow [20] to try mosaicking between paired

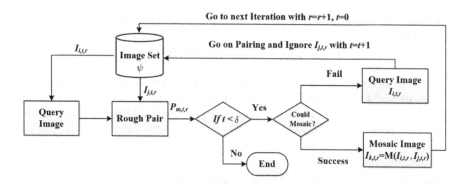

Fig. 4. Workflow of the proposed Iterative Parallel Mosaicking algorithm for disorderly fly model.

subareas of $I_{i,t,r}$ and $I_{j_t,r}$, which first utilize PCA-SIFT features to calculate distance and then properly integrate similar parts between two images. Specifically, we need to establish the mathematical relationships that map pixel coordinates from one image to another. For standard lens images, the mathematical model is usually established by affine transformation, and the least squares method is used to optimize the parameters, which can be expressed as $I_{k,t,r} = M(I_{i,t,r}, I_{j_t,r})$.

Due to the rough pairing results, we could get wrong trials especially for location with homogeneous visual appearances. With a wrong trial, the proposed algorithm goes on pairing in the next turn with ignoring $I_{j_t,r}$. With a successful mosaic trial, the proposed algorithm outputs the mosaic image $I_{k,t,r}$ and puts it in dataset ψ for next iteration of computation by setting $r = r + 1$ and $t = 0$.

Essentially, the proposed iterative mosaicking algorithm could be parallel performed. We could utilize spark nodes to execute the workflow presented in Fig. 4 at the same time, where the number of the nodes could be defined as half of the size of ψ for each iteration and we only need a lock scheme on acquiring permissions of the image set to guarantee the successfully parallel running. The highly parallel performance of the proposed mosaicking algorithm is actually ensured by a simple but effective pair algorithm and a short pipeline length, *i.e.*, the maximal turn number η. It's noted that several corner images may result in unpaired images with $t \geq \eta$, which will be regarded as images in ψ for the next iteration.

3.4   Implementation Details

We adopt spark to be the implementation framework and believe Spark to be an ideal framework for several reasons:

- An in-memory representation for large label data will empower future algorithms to use high-level, global context to improve mosaic quality.
- Spark expands the widely-used MapReduce model by supporting many computational models, such as interactive query and stream processing, and supporting to work with other famous big data tools, such as Hadoop clusters.

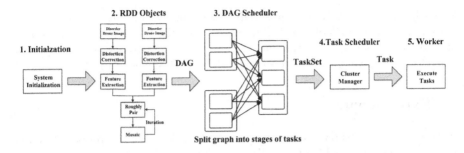

Fig. 5. Execution workflow of the proposed mosaic algorithm implemented on Spark.

- The core component of Spark is fast and versatile so that it supports to be designed for a variety of application scenarios, such as machine learning and image processing.

The implementation is built on the core component of Spark since it supports fast response for requests. The Core component consists of different modules, such as task scheduling, memory management, error recovery, interaction with the storage system and so on. It also includes definitions of APIs for Resilient Distributed Datasets (RDDs), which can be operated parallel on multiple compute nodes. As shown in Fig. 5, we describe detailed steps as below:

1. Read dataset of drone images and set initial parameters based on data size and node configuration. We specially define a reasonable partition scale parameter to maximize the usage of cluster resources by guidance of [5]. Apply for Executor resource to Hadoop Standalone and start the Standalone Executor.
2. According to the total workflow of the proposed mosaicking algorithm, perform MAP operation to define the corresponding RDD objects, which further construct a directed acyclic graph (DAG). From Fig. 5, we can notice steps of distortion correction and feature extraction could be parallel executed, since such RDD objects for each image is irrelevant with other images. Meanwhile, steps of pair and mosaic could be parallel performed for every two images if designing the proper lock scheme.
3. Through the operation of Reduce, DAG is translated into a physical execution plan by splitting DAG into stages of tasks and tracking parent nodes.
4. With the physical execution plan, the Spark task scheduler would submit a job to perform these operations. Note that each job contains one or more procedures, which consist of a series of parallel computing tasks.
5. Every procedure, corresponding to one or more steps in the DAG, would be performed with multiple parallel pipelines inside one worker.

The experiment environment consists of six nodes. We used 2 Amax PSC-HB1X servers. Both of them have 24 cores, 12 GB main memory and 2 TB disk. We employ a VMware Workstation Pro 12.1.0 to create 4 more virtual nodes and all of them hosted on Amax PSC-HB1X servers. Therefore, each node owns 4 cores and 2 GB in total. All nodes adapt as OS 14.04.2 LTS. The Spark version is Spark 2.1.3. The JDK version is JDK 1.8.0. The python interpreter version is python 3.5.2. Daemons of the Hadoop master and the Spark master are running on the same nodes, with other nodes being used for storage and computing. Therefore, we have one spark master and five spark slaves in total.

4   Experiments

In this section, we show the effectiveness and efficiency of the proposed system for drone image mosaicking tasks. We first introduce dataset and measurements, and then describe performance analysis on both time and quality.

4.1   Dataset and Measurement

We apply the proposed drone image mosaic method on a self-collected dataset, which contains 5840 images with 31.38 GB size. All these data are captured at six locations named Campus, GeneralMount, CowheadMount, XiaolongBridge, JinzhiFactory, BaijiaLake, and the corresponding captured image numbers are 540, 810, 620, 1000, 1540 and 1330. We use a DJI Phantom 3 drone to collect data. Samples of data and the drone are shown in Fig. 2. Note that we achieve aerial images by firstly taking videos and then equally sampling videos. For the video captured at Campus, we fly the drone at 140 m to get aerial images at 4700 * 3200 resolution. For other videos, we fly the drone at 90 m to get images at 4000 * 3000 resolution. In fact, DJI Phantom 3 drone is developed for consumer utilization, so that it's cheap in cost, *i.e.*, only around 600 dollars. Therefore, the proposed method could be further developed as an online service to instantly offer mosaicking aerial images, even if users upload low quality sequences with consumer level drones.

To evaluate the performance of the proposed system for mosaicking, we utilize two popular methods, i.e., NIQE [12] and BRISQUE [11], to measure the quality of generated aerial image, where both measurements are image quality estimation algorithm without reference, NIQE refers to Natural Image Quality Evaluator, and BRISQUE represents Blind/Referenceless Image Spatial Quality Evaluator. The detail of these two measurements can be found in [12] and [11].

4.2   Performance Analysis

To evaluate the proposed mosaic method on Spark, we compare it on six sets of collected drone images with the single process (not using Spark on a single node) and using Spark Local mode. Spark Local mode refers to local operating mode with the single node, which simulates Spark distributed computing environment with multiple threads of a single node. Note that methods running on the single process and Spark Local mode are the same as that on P[2] and P[5]. Table 1 gives the time comparison, where number in "Campus(540)" refers to the drone image number, L[N] represents Spark Local Mode, N means that N threads are used and each thread occupies a core, P[M] and P[M]' refers to the proposed

Table 1. Comparison of running time on collected dataset with the proposed method, Spark Local mode and single process.

Sequence	Order fly mode(s)				Disorder fly mode(s)				
	P[2]	P[5]	Local[4]	Single	P[2]	P[5]	P[5]'	Local[4]	Single
Campus(540)	5248.0	**3913.3**	7195.3	9496.4	5401.7	**3845.2**	5441.0	7392.2	9855.9
GMount(810)	4534.7	**2766.2**	5895.2	7841.2	4718.0	**2810.1**	11042.1	6128.7	8263.0
CMount(620)	3943.2	**2029.4**	4832.1	6185.5	4094.2	**2058.9**	6444.1	5022.7	6514.3
XBridge(1000)	5294.8	**2536.2**	7140.8	9923.3	5544.4	**2617.9**	16723.1	7456.8	10485.7
JFactory(1540)	7812.9	**3554.7**	10694.1	15017.3	8305.2	**3803.4**	39249.8	11309.8	16041.7
BLake (1330)	6762.9	**3017.7**	8735.0	12927.3	7130.4	**3210.7**	29523.0	9197.6	13717.8
Average	5599.4	**2969.6**	7415.4	10231.8	5865.7	**3057.7**	20817.7	7751.3	10813.1

method running with M computation nodes with and without parallel design, respectively. Moreover, we utilize brute force to try matching drone images with either left or right parts, which is the same as the proposed pair algorithm. The reason to set N and M as 4 and 5 lies in the fact that each node owns 4 cores and the spark cluster has 5 nodes, respectively. We also design two modes for flying, i.e., orderly fly and disorderly fly. The former implies upload drones offer images in consist orders, while the latter means drones have flown in a free way. By comparing these two modes, we can notice how Spark platform and parallel mosaicking algorithm help perform tasks with higher efficiency. To offer a more intuitive sense on how Spark-based mosaic method help, we show a comparison graph with ratio values on disorder fly mode in Fig. 6.

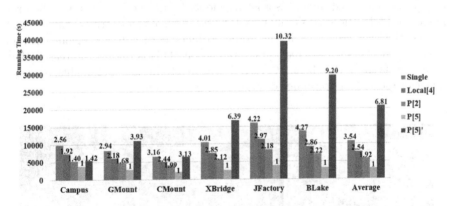

Fig. 6. Comparison graph and ratio values of running time on collected dataset under disorder fly mode. Note that numbers above refer to ratio values and the basis number is running time achieved by P[5].

As shown in Table 1, P[5] achieves the lowest running time in all 6 drone image sets. This is reasonable since P[5] utilizes the larger amount of computation resources than other comparative methods. By introducing parallel modifications, i.e., roughly pair and iterative parallel mosaicking, we could notice the large amount of computation time is saved by comparing running time of P[5] and P[5]' under disorder fly mode. It's noted the times of saving time are unstable, since brute force adopted by P[5]' is not stable in performance and running time of P[5] is highly related to visual layout of scene. Moreover, we could find consuming time in disorder fly and order fly modes are nearly same with parallel modifications in all datasets. All these facts prove that parallel modifications are robust, efficient and fit for parallel executing.

We pay special interest to running time values under disorder fly mode, since it's more suitable than order fly mode for situations of how users use consumer drones. As shown in Fig. 6, we could notice that the running time of P[2] is nearly twice as large as that of P[5]. However, the computation resources of P[5] is 2.5 times larger than that of P[2], which proves that there is a loss in computation resources with more nodes. Drawing a map to analyze trends of computation loss with nodes requires more computation resource and is included in our future work. By comparing Local[4] and P[2], we could find a decrease in running time. However, it's not linearly related to the computation resource, which is due to the computation loss as well. But the extendibility of P[2] is far larger than Spark local mode, since we can easily involve more distributed computation nodes in the Spark cluster. With Spark system to MapReduce tasks, we can observe a quite large decrease in running time between Local[4] and Single using the same computation resource, which proves that the Spark system is much more appropriate for fast and parallel computation than multithread scheme.

Sample qualitative results of the proposed method are shown in Fig. 7, where original images of (a) are captured under order fly mode, and images of (b) and (c) are captured under disorder fly mode. From Fig. 7, we can see the proposed method could successfully mosaic whole aerial images with desirable visual effects. However, we can still view some artifacts, especially for regions with no obvious objects, such as trees, grass and so on. This is due to the reason that such objects are lack robust PCA-SIFT features to mosaic and quality of aerial images captured by consumer drones is not good enough.

(a)   (b)   (c)

Fig. 7. Mosaic Results of Drone aerial images with the proposed method on (a) Campus, (b) CowheadMount and (c) GeneralMount dataset.

Finally, we use two measurements, i.e., NIQE and BRISQUE, to evaluate quality of generated aerial image, where we show exact results on three sets of self-collected data in Table 2. From the table, we can notice the decrease in calculation values before and after mosaic processing, which helps to verify the accuracy and robustness of the proposed mosaicking algorithm for drone images.

Table 2. The quality measures before and after the mosaic.

Data	Metric	Before process	After process
Campus	BRISQUE	42.86	41.51
	NIQE	16.38	15.85
GMount	BRISQUE	42.75	42.20
	NIQE	16.37	15.13
CMount	BRISQUE	43.24	42.77
	NIQE	16.62	16.18

5   Conclusions

In this paper, we propose a parallel drone image mosaic method to assure its high performance in a Spark-based cloud computing environment. The proposed method makes its steps to be fit for fast and parallel running to run efficiently on Spark-based system. The proposed method is implemented and tested on six self-collected dataset. Comparative results show that the proposed method is of great efficiency and could achieve visual desirable images even with low-quality input images. Our future work includes applying the proposed mosaic method on a large spark-based cluster to offer instant on-line mosaicking service and improve traditional image processing methods by transforming them to be fit for the Spark-based system.

References

1. Distributed, versioned, image-oriented dataservice (dvid). http://github.com/janelia-flyem/dvid
2. Brown, M., Lowe, D.G.: Automatic panoramic image stitching using invariant features. Int. J. Comput. Vision **74**(1), 59–73 (2007). https://doi.org/10.1007/s11263-006-0002-3
3. Capel, D.: Image mosaicing and super resolution. Ph.D. thesis, University of Oxford (2004)
4. Dean, J., Ghemawat, S.: Mapreduce: a flexible data processing tool. Commun. ACM **53**(1), 72–77 (2010)

5. Huang, W., Meng, L., Zhang, D., Zhang, W.: In-memory parallel processing of massive remotely sensed data using an Apache Spark on Hadoop YARN model. IEEE J. Sel. Top. Appl. Earth Obs. Remote Sens. **10**(1), 3–19 (2017)
6. Ke, Y., Sukthankar, R.: PCA-SIFT: a more distinctive representation for local image descriptors. In: Proceedings of Computer Vision and Pattern Recognition, vol. 2, p. II. IEEE (2004)
7. Lee, J.N., Kwak, K.C.: A trends analysis of image processing in unmanned aerial vehicle. Int. J. Comput. Inf. Sci. Eng. **8**(2), 2–5 (2014)
8. Lowe, D.G.: Distinctive image features from scale-invariant keypoints. Int. J. Comput. Vision **60**(2), 91–110 (2004). https://doi.org/10.1023/B:VISI.0000029664.99615.94
9. Lyu, M.R., Song, J., Cai, M.: A comprehensive method for multilingual video text detection, localization, and extraction. IEEE Trans. Circuits Syst. Video Techn. **15**(2), 243–255 (2005)
10. Ma, Y., et al.: Remote sensing big data computing: challenges and opportunities. Future Gener. Comput. Syst. **51**, 47–60 (2015)
11. Mittal, A., Moorthy, A.K., Bovik, A.C.: No-reference image quality assessment in the spatial domain. IEEE Trans. Image Process. **21**(12), 4695–4708 (2012)
12. Mittal, A., Soundararajan, R., Bovik, A.C.: Making a "completely blind" image quality analyzer. IEEE Signal Process. Lett. **20**(3), 209–212 (2013)
13. Moravec, H.P.: Rover visual obstacle avoidance. In: Proceedings of the 7th International Joint Conference on Artificial Intelligence, pp. 785–790 (1981)
14. Plaza, S.M., Berg, S.E.: Large-scale electron microscopy image segmentation in spark. arXiv preprint arXiv:1604.00385 (2016)
15. Rodriguez, A., Boddeti, V.N., Kumar, B.V.K.V., Mahalanobis, A.: Maximum margin correlation filter: a new approach for localization and classification. IEEE Trans. Image Process. **22**(2), 631–643 (2013)
16. Taylor, G.W., Spiro, I., Bregler, C., Fergus, R.: Learning invariance through imitation. In: Proceedings of Conference on Computer Vision and Pattern Recognition, pp. 2729–2736 (2011)
17. Vavilapalli, V.K., et al.: Apache Hadoop YARN: yet another resource negotiator. In: Proceedings of ACM Symposium on Cloud Computing, pp. 5:1–5:16 (2013)
18. Wang, F.B., Tu, P., Wu, C., Chen, L., Feng, D.: Multi-image mosaic with SIFT and vision measurement for microscale structures processed by femtosecond laser. Opt. Lasers Eng. **100**, 124–130 (2018)
19. Wang, J., et al.: Learning fine-grained image similarity with deep ranking. In: Proceedings of Conference on Computer Vision and Pattern Recognition, pp. 1386–1393 (2014)
20. Wang, L.M., Wu, Y., Tian, Z., Sun, Z., Lu, T.: A novel approach for robust surveillance video content abstraction. In: Qiu, G., Lam, K.M., Kiya, H., Xue, X.-Y., Kuo, C.-C.J., Lew, M.S. (eds.) PCM 2010. LNCS, vol. 6298, pp. 660–671. Springer, Heidelberg (2010). https://doi.org/10.1007/978-3-642-15696-0_61
21. Xin, R., Deyhim, P., Ghodsi, A., Meng, X., Zaharia, M.: Graysort on apache spark by databricks. GraySort Competition (2014)
22. Zaharia, M., Chowdhury, M., Franklin, M.J., Shenker, S., Stoica, I.: Spark: cluster computing with working sets. In: Proceedings of 2nd USENIX Workshop on Hot Topics in Cloud Computing (2010)
23. Zhang, W., Li, X., Yu, J., Kumar, M., Mao, Y.: Remote sensing image mosaic technology based on SURF algorithm in agriculture. EURASIP J. Image Video Process. **2018**(1), 1–9 (2018). https://doi.org/10.1186/s13640-018-0323-5

24. Zhou, G., et al.: Paper infrared image retrieval of power equipment based on perceptual hash and surf. In: Proceedings of International Conference on Advanced Infocomm Technology (ICAIT), pp. 387–392. IEEE (2017)
25. Zhou, Z., Wang, Y., Wu, Q.J., Yang, C.N., Sun, X.: Effective and efficient global context verification for image copy detection. IEEE Trans. Inf. Forensics Secur. **12**(1), 48–63 (2017)

CycleSafe: Safe Route Planning for Urban Cyclists

Mehdi Shah[1], Tianqi Liu[2], Sahil Chauhan[1], Lianyong Qi[3],
and Xuyun Zhang[1(✉)]

[1] Department of Electrical, Computer and Software Engineering,
University of Auckland, Auckland, New Zealand
{msha563,scha676}@aucklanduni.ac.nz, xuyun.zhang@auckland.ac.nz
[2] Northeastern University, Boston, USA
liu.tianq@husky.neu.edu
[3] Qufu Normal University, Jining, China
liangyongqi@gmail.com

Abstract. Cyclist numbers in major cities are constantly increasing whilst traffic conditions continue to worsen. This poses a major issue for cyclists who attempt to share congested roads with motor vehicles. This paper shows that there is not enough work being done to improve the safety of cyclists on the road, and proposes a solution to this problem in the form of a route planning application. Current cyclist route planning applications do not take safety factors like traffic, rain or visibility into account when providing cycle routes. We use Auckland city as a case study to explore our solution. The traffic and weather data in Auckland are acquired by using Google, Bing and Wunderground APIs. An evaluation of our solution shows that our system successfully implements a route planning application that routes users away from unsafe traffic conditions, thus improving cyclist safety.

Keywords: Traffic data fusion and analytics · Mobile computing · Cloud services

1 Introduction

With the increase in popularity of cycling, cyclist safety is becoming a much more important concern to society. For example, Auckland Transport statistics show that there has been a 62% increase in all day cycle trips in the city center compared to 2013 [4]. There are many awareness campaigns to warn drivers that they must safely share the road with cyclists, however, research shows there is not enough work done to ensure the safety of cyclists on the road. We believe that awareness campaigns alone are not enough to improve cyclist safety. Whilst cycling has become much more common, with more cyclists on the road than ever before, traffic congestion has also increased. This poses a much higher risk for cyclists as there are more of them on the road but there are also more cars,

© ICST Institute for Computer Sciences, Social Informatics and Telecommunications Engineering 2020
Published by Springer Nature Switzerland AG 2020. All Rights Reserved
X. Zhang et al. (Eds.): CloudComp 2019/SmartGift 2019, LNICST 322, pp. 312–327, 2020.
https://doi.org/10.1007/978-3-030-48513-9_26

the risk of injury is very high for cyclists who share the road with motor vehicles. This problem of cyclist safety will be addressed in this paper and a viable route planning solution will be presented. This solution takes traffic conditions into account when planning routes and will adjust the route accordingly to ensure that cyclists are on the safest route possible.

2   Problem Background

The major problem that is examined is the lack of any applications or systems that directly improve cyclist safety. Statistics show that cyclist numbers are increasing over time, however, there is not an increased effort put into improving the safety of these cyclists. Awareness campaigns are put into place to educate the public in terms of sharing the road with cyclists, however, they are simply not enough as most people do not pay them any heed. Whilst infrastructure is finally being put into place to accommodate for cyclists, it cannot be implemented fast enough to compensate for the increasing number of cyclists. In order for us to find a comprehensive solution to this issue, we must first look at the root cause of the problem and figure out what it is that makes cyclists unsafe on the roads. It was clear that sharing the road with motorists was the primary cause of injury or death on the roads. Because cyclists have to share the road with motor vehicles there is an ever-present danger of injury or death. In 2016, 6% of the total number of casualties from police reported crashes were from cyclists [6]. This statistic only looks at police reported crashes too, there are likely numerous unreported crashes that occur. There are several factors which apply to cyclists, that increase their risk on the road, but do not apply to the vehicles around them. Firstly, they have less protection in the event of any kind of accident, as well as no protection against weather conditions. In a city like Auckland, which has worsening traffic and can undergo many weather changes in a single day, it is very important to ensure that cyclists do not travel in unsafe traffic and weather conditions. The cycling increase statistics do not take into account the bike-sharing increase in recent times. In late 2017, the bike-sharing application ONZO was launched in New Zealand. These ONZO bikes are placed all around Auckland city. Users are able to go to one and using the application, unlock it and rent it for a short or long trip. The rise of bike sharing poses new problems for cyclist safety. It not only increases the amount of cyclists in general but it also allows for less experienced cyclists to share the road with vehicles, these inexperienced cyclists are at an even greater risk as they have not been cycling in traffic conditions and may not the best ways to do so safely. ONZO users also do not always wear helmets whilst riding the bikes. This obviously increases the risk to their lives drastically as helmets, whilst offering little protection compared to vehicles, can still save lives in a crash. Sharing the road with cars during high levels of congestion is a huge problem for cyclists as it reduces the space between cyclists and vehicles, thus, increasing the risk of accidents. This is one of the two major risks in sharing the road with vehicles, with the other being the speed of the vehicles. Vehicles travelling faster are obviously more dangerous for cyclists. A thorough analysis of the Auckland Traffic Count data spreadsheet shows that traffic trends continuously worsened from July 2012 to February 2018 [5]. Because traffic conditions are only worsening as time goes on, cyclists need a way to travel that can allow them to avoid unsafe traffic congestion. Our proposed solution to this issue is to give cyclists a way to travel safely and circumvent congested roads which increase road usage risks.

3   Related Work

Because we are looking into a route planning application that can be used by cyclists to improve their safety, the main area of research covered in this paper is cycle route applications. The biggest issue with existing cycle route applications is that they do not focus on cyclist safety. They do not take traffic congestion into account when planning routes for these cyclists so the routes often prove to be unsafe.

3.1   Cyclist Route Planning Applications

Whilst there are many route planning applications, from research conducted we found that there are not many which cater primarily for cyclists. Also, after an in-depth analysis, we found that there are no route planning applications which are designed to improve cyclist safety. Several applications were examined thoroughly and then narrowed down to the best 3 applications. A summary of the notable features of these 3 applications can be found in the Table 1 below.

Table 1. Comparing existing applications.

Existing solution	Shortest path	Support cycleways	Elevation tracking	Traffic data	Weather checks
Google Maps	Yes	Yes	Yes	No	No
Flattest Route	No	No	Yes	No	No
Open Cycle	No	Yes	No	No	No
Proposed	Yes	Yes	Yes	Yes	Yes

Out of the 3 applications that were examined, the very best one was Google Maps. Open Cycle Map simply provides a map which shows users the locations of cycle paths [8], it does not have any route planning aspect. Flattest Route is a route planning application that is aimed at finding the flattest route between two points [7]. These two applications are overshadowed by Google Maps which can outperform them in every aspect, thus we will be comparing our application to Google Maps in our results and evaluations.

The main focus for Google Maps is to determine the fastest route to a destination [3]. This application contains many cyclist friendly features such as elevation information and cycle path support for routes and is very efficient at finding the shortest path. It does not, however, take traffic congestion into account when plotting these routes. Thus, the safety of cyclists is not a consideration, this further proves the need for our research and application. There is also no consideration for weather conditions.

All these existing route planning applications contain a concerning lack of focus on the safety of their users. Even Google Maps, which is the best route planning application on the market, does not take traffic or weather conditions into account. These are the most important factors in determining cyclist safety and must be considered in order to ensure that cyclists have the safest route possible.

3.2   Data Collection Techniques

This section covers the research done to look into traffic data collection techniques. For this paper we required real-time traffic data as that can be used in our route planning application to improve cyclist safety by avoiding areas which show unsafe traffic congestion.

Traditional methods of traffic data collection utilize static sensors such as roadside cameras with image recognition [2] and underground & radar sensors. Whilst, these sensors are effective in the long term they lack redundancy, have a limited sample size and are fairly expensive to implement. They also sometimes require specific installation which can result in road closure and thus an increase in traffic congestion in that area. These systems require a vast amount of static sensors to ensure accurate readings and provide an accurate representation of traffic congestion.

For this paper, time constraints meant that we could not implement static sensors and collect historical data manually. We also wanted to use real-time data to ensure that traffic is updated in our application in real-time. We felt that this would ensure the safest possible travel for our users. After further research, we found that the most accurate method of real-time data collection is through the use of floating car data. This method utilizes the phones of road users to provide an easily obtainable, accurate source of real-time data [9]. We obtained this data through the use of Google and Bing REST APIs as these sources were found to be the most accurate and easiest to use.

The weather data that was used in the application was sourced using Weather Undergrounds REST API. After careful study into this part of the paper, we found it most beneficial to provide our users with warnings if they intend on cycling in unsafe weather conditions. We also looked into weather prediction data, however, found that this can be very inaccurate and is difficult to use in our application. By using real-time data, we can provide users with accurate warnings as they plan their route. Perhaps, once weather prediction becomes more accurate and available this can be implemented in our paper, but for now real-time data proved to be the most appropriate.

4   Development Methodology

The goal of this paper is to implement an application that can be used by cyclists to plan routes which will improve their safety. After several ideas, it became clear that the easiest way to implement this is through the use of a phone application. We aim to ensure that the safety of our users is a priority by taking traffic data into account when providing routes. The application also takes weather information into account and provides the user with warnings if conditions are unsafe. We want this application to also provide users with other cyclist specific features that can increase their quality of life as well as add more depth to the application.

4.1   Commute Mode

Because the main focus of this paper was the safety applications for cyclists, this was the core functionality that was implemented first. This part of the application was called commute mode. The route planning was implemented using Google & Bing APIs. The information taken from these APIs was plugged into our own algorithm which found the safest route between two points. Once this part of the application was implemented, it could serve as a base to the extra features that we wanted to add and any future work can be built off of this.

4.2   Weather Warnings

Next, we focused on getting the weather warnings to be functional as we felt that this is another aspect of cyclist safety that can be improved. Weather data is taken from the Weather Underground Wunderground REST API. This API was chosen as it provides accurate easy to use data that is also readily available. We realized that all we can do in terms of the weather is provide warnings during unsafe travel periods. We cannot physically route cyclists away from unsafe weather if it is raining throughout Auckland, we can only provide users with information and warnings.

4.3   Exercise Mode

The next part of the application was implemented as the exercise mode. This mode allows users to plan exercise routes based off of a distance that they input. This mode is based off of the previously developed algorithm. Thus, the route provided will be the safest possible route and take traffic conditions into account. This mode was added to ensure that our application can provide tangible benefits and an increased quality of life for not only those who use cycling to commute but those who use it as an exercise form too.

4.4   Machine Learning

We also decided to add a prediction feature to our application. This would allow the traffic levels on common routes to be predicted and shown to our users. The information can be viewed in the application in the form of a graph, it plots the level of congestion against time of day. This feature is useful for cyclists as they can see in advance if their route will be safe to travel or not (Fig. 1).

5   System Architecture

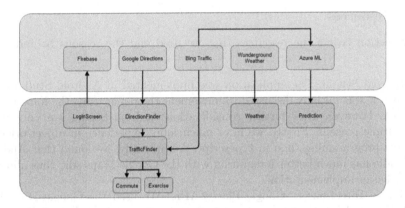

Fig. 1. System architecture. (Color figure online)

Our system is split into two main areas, the cloud end and the front end mobile part. The route planning is done locally on the user's mobile device, whilst the cloud is used to pull all the data that we are using. For the following sections, please refer to the above system architecture diagram. The back end (cloud) services are in the large blue box with the front end modules in the large red box. The system is comprised of several modules, with each one having a specific purpose. Our modular system allows for easy expansion and easy integration of more data sources. The Direction Finder module is used to call the Google Directions API and process the JSON data that it receives from Google. The processed data is then fed into our Traffic Finder module. The Traffic Finder module receives its data from Direction-Finder. It calls the Bing Traffic API and finds the traffic along the routes that it receives from Direction Finder. Traffic Finder passes data into the Azure Machine Learning studio to train it and allow for prediction, it is also used to find the safest route. The Weather module is called after a route has been found. It calls the Wunderground API and processes the data that is received. The Prediction Module acquires data from the Azure Machine Learning studio which trains our prediction model. The login Screen module handles logins and was intended to communicate with Google

Firebase to store information. However, the login section of this application was not necessary to ensure functionality and we had to focus on the safety aspect of the paper. Thus, the login database has been added to future work.

6 Implementation

Before starting the implementation of this paper there was much planning that had to be done. After conducting sufficient background research, we began to formulate our own solution which would address the problem and its lack of current solutions.

6.1 Resources

This section covers the resources that we used and the reasons behind using them.

1) Android Studio: The application was implemented in Android Studio using Java. It was initially discussed to implement the paper using the Ionic framework, however, after further consideration Android Studio was chosen for multiple reasons. Firstly, we have much more experience in object-oriented Java programming than in typescript. Additionally, we found that Android Studio has much better integration with the Google Maps sdk, thus allowing for easier implementation.

2) Google Directions & Google Places APIs: We used the Google Directions API in order to acquire route data between two points. This API takes a start and end location then returns multiple possible routes between the two points. The directions API is the best of its kind and can be very easily integrated with our application. The places API is used in our autocomplete text view to ensure that user experience is of a high quality. This API allows users search for locations more easily.

3) Bing Traffic API: The bing traffic API looks at a segment of road and returns the amount of congestion on it. This API uses traffic data to provide congestion information, from a comparison with other traffic APIs this was found to be the best and easiest to use.

4) Azure Machine Learning Studio: We use the Azure Machine Learning (ML) studio to implement a prediction algorithm and predict traffic along commonly travelled routes. A specified date and time can be passed in and a prediction for traffic congestion is returned. The Azure ML studio was used as it was relatively easy to use and allowed for easy integration with our application.

During this paper, due to time constraints and the fact that we could not get many users to use the application, it was not possible to input the user's common routes into the machine learning algorithm. Instead we ran a python script that called the Google and Bing APIs to find traffic data for specific routes, this data was stored and plugged into the machine learning algorithm. Our prediction model uses this data to make predictions rather than data taken from users who use the application. Thus, our prediction model was more of a proof of concept for now and will need to be worked on in the future to incorporate data from the users themselves.

6.2 Modules

The following section covers the modules that were implemented and provide insights into their functionality. 1) Direction Finder: This module uses the Google Directions API to find all the possible routes between two points. It takes the origin and destination coordinates and then calls the Google API. After processing the results, it obtains a list of all the possible routes. From here, it needs to check which route is the safest for our users. This is done by splitting each route into steps and then checking the traffic conditions along each step of the route. The traffic checking is done by the Traffic Finder module. After the Traffic Finder module is run, each route is assigned a total congestion score based on our algorithm. Direction Finder then chooses the route with the lowest congestion score and takes this as the safest route. This route is then sent to the fragment for our current mode (commute or exercise) and plotted onto the map. This module also provides information to our Weather Finder module. It provides the weather module with two sets of coordinates which can allow it to find weather data in that specific area. 2) Traffic Finder: This module is used to find traffic congestion levels. It is given a segment of a route and uses the Bing API to find the current traffic conditions on that segment. This module uses our safety algorithm in order to give each segment of road, thus each route, an overall traffic congestion score. Safety Algorithm: Our algorithm takes specific safety factors into account when looking at traffic conditions. A complete lack of traffic is obviously the safest way to travel for cyclists, so we give this a congestion score of 0. Next, light congestion is assigned a congestion score of 1 with medium being a higher congestion score of 3. High traffic levels are considered the most unsafe and thus have a congestion score of 4, however, very high/standstill traffic is considered to be safer as the vehicles are essentially not moving whereas cyclists can go between cars and be quite safe. Thus, this has a congestion score of 3. This can be easily seen in the Table 2 below:

Table 2. Safety algorithm.

Traffic conditions	Safety
No traffic	High
Low congestion	Medium
High congestion (Slow moving)	Low
Very high congestion (Standstill)	Medium

3) Weather Finder: This module handles all the weather information in our application. It takes two sets of coordinates as an input, which are provided by Direction Finder, and uses this area to call the Wunderground API and acquire weather information. It displays rain info, wind conditions and visibility conditions using a dialog pop up box after finding the safest route.

7   Evaluation

The main goal of this paper was to improve cyclist safety. This was done by providing cyclists with a novel route planning application that takes their safety into account whilst still planning efficient routes. The first method of evaluation that was carried out is a direct route comparison with Google Maps. We felt that Google Maps is currently the best route planning application that cyclists have at their disposal. We evaluate against Google Maps to assess the efficiency and improved safety of the routes that our application provides. The next evaluation method is an evaluation of our application itself and its usability. This was done by providing surveys to users of our app. The following section will discuss the evaluation of our results in detail.

7.1   Google Maps Comparison

For each of the following results, a route was calculated using cycling mode on Google Maps and using our application on the same day at the exact same time. The traffic conditions along the routes are also shown in images which follow each route. This was done by manually plotting the routes on Google Maps using driving mode, as this is the only way to see traffic along the route, so the safety of our routes can be assessed. For each of these routes we are looking at an efficiency comparison between our route and the Google route. We also want to judge our algorithm to see if we are successfully avoiding unsafe traffic conditions and providing safer routes than Google Maps. This was repeated for different routes on different days at various times to provide a wide range of results.

1) Grange Rd - Bassett Rd: In the following figure (Fig. 2) we can see a route from Grange Road in Mount Eden to Bassett Road in Remuera. Our application is displayed on the left with Google Maps on the right as a comparison.

Our route is vastly different from the one provided by Google Maps. In terms of efficiency, ours is 5.3 km long while the Google route is 4.4 km it also takes five extra minutes of travel time. So our route is slightly less efficient than the one Google recommends.

Safety Comparison: Fig. 3 utilises Google Maps' driving mode to show the traffic congestion along our route and the Google Maps cycling route.

As can be seen in Fig. 3 above, our route (left) avoids a lot of the unsafe congestion that is present (circled) on the Google route. There is slight congestion along our route (red arrows), however, we feel that this is negligible compared to the amount that we avoid in comparing with the Google route. It should also be

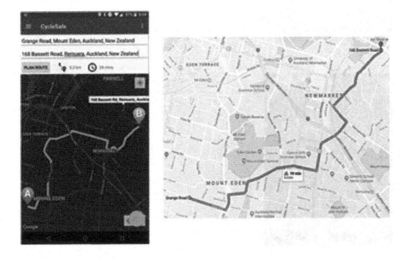

Fig. 2. Grange Rd. - Bassett Rd. route comparison

Fig. 3. Grange - Bassett: traffic comparison. (Color figure online)

noted that the red circle in our route shows the driving mode differing from our actual route. This is because our cycling route goes through a park at this point which cannot be done in the driving route, this is taken as being safe as there cannot be any traffic congestion in the park. From this result, it appears that our initial assessment of Google Maps was correct. Google does not take traffic conditions into account when planning routes for cyclists, instead the application just plots the shortest path between two points. The results which follow will further prove this assessment.

2) Paice Ave - OGGB (UOA): Fig. 4 below shows the cycling route from Paice Avenue in Sandringham to the Owen Glenn building in the University of Auckland as given by our application (left) compared to Google Maps (right).

Both these routes are very similar, they both end up taking the Northwestern & Grafton Gully cycle paths. Because the routes are so similar they are almost identical in length, with ours being 200 m longer and taking 2 min longer in

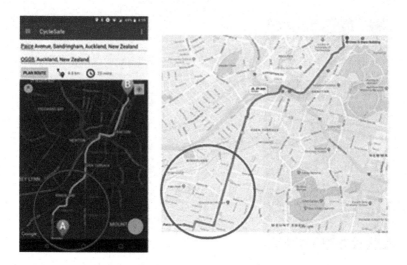

Fig. 4. Paice Ave - OGGB: route comparison

travel time. The main difference between the two routes has been circled and will be assessed in terms of safety.

Safety Comparison: Fig. 5 shows the traffic conditions along the parts of the routes that differ (circled in the previous images).

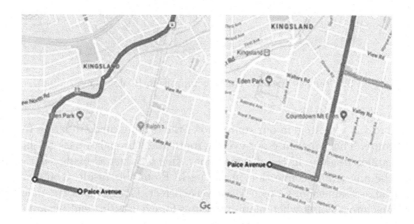

Fig. 5. Paige - OGGB traffic comparison

The very start of the two routes is the only point of difference. Our route avoids slight congestion on dominion road and has almost the same time and distance as the Google Maps route. This shows that our algorithm is working as intended as it routes our cyclists away from unsafe congestion conditions.

Whereas, Google Maps' route only acts as the shortest path and routes cyclists through Dominion road which contains some unsafe traffic congestion conditions.

3) Larchwood Ave - George Street: Figs. 6 shows the cycling route from Larchwood Avenue in Westmere to George Street in Mount Eden.

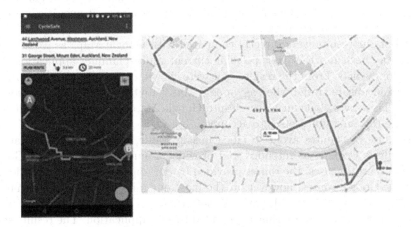

Fig. 6. Larchwood Ave - George street route comparison

In this scenario, our route once again differs quite a lot compared to the Google route. This time, however, our route is 300 m shorter than the Google route but takes 2 extra minutes to travel. The main difference is that our route takes a cycle path while the Google route is more of a direct route to the destination.

Safety Comparison: Fig. 7 shows the traffic conditions along our route and the Google Maps route for the time at which these screen shots were taken.

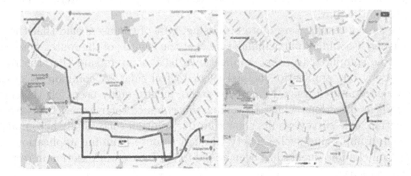

Fig. 7. Larchwood - George traffic comparison (Color figure online)

From Fig. 7, we can see unsafe congestion all along the Google Maps route (red and orange parts), our route avoids this congestion and takes the cycle path.

Resulting in an overall shorter & safer path, with a 2 min increase in travel time. The red box shows where this route differs from our actual cycling route. This is because our route takes the cycle path at this point and then cuts across a park which cannot be done in driving mode. This part of the route is considered very safe as there can be no unsafe traffic conditions on cycle paths or in parks. Our route can be seen to be much safer than Google's route as it avoids congestion and prioritizes the cycle path.

All of our results were directly compared with Google Maps as we felt that this is the best and the most popular current route planning application that exists for cyclists. From the results that were shown, our application plots routes that avoid unsafe traffic whereas Google Maps' routes are simply the shortest path. This proves that our research into Google Maps was accurate and it does not take the safety of users into account.

Because our routes avoid so much unsafe traffic, we can conclude that our algorithm is working as intended and provides a much safer path than Google Maps. In certain cases, the routes provided by our application are slightly longer than the Google routes, however, at the most our routes were no more than an extra five minutes of travel time. We feel that this tradeoff is worth it when looking at the extra safety that is provided by our application. The results show that our application takes traffic conditions into account and provides users with safer routes than any other current application.

7.2 User Surveys

In order to assess the functionality and user friendliness of our application we decided to carry our several user surveys. We wanted to see if cyclists who used our application felt that their safety was improved whilst travelling. The survey asked specific questions about the length of the routes and impact on their safety. It also inquired about the app in general such as its ease of use and any suggestions that they wanted to make about it. The surveys were handed out after exhibition day.

The survey results were quite promising. 80% of the users said that the app was easy to use and all participants said that the lengths of the routes were quite reasonable compared to other applications. 94% of users said that the routes provided by our application helped them to feel safer. A common suggestion that we encountered was a request for audio queues, many users felt that being able to hear directions whilst travelling will enhance their experience with the application. The survey results show that our solution successfully accomplishes our goal of improving cyclist safety through a route planning application. The suggestion of audio queues has been added to the future work section in response to the user survey.

8   Future Work

8.1   Algorithm Improvements

Whilst, the results and evaluation show that our algorithm can successfully route our users away from unsafe traffic conditions, we would like to work more on this algorithm in the future and improve it in any way we can.

The first way that we'd like to improve our algorithm is by integrating more data sources. HERE map data can be easily integrated with our current system as another data source. HERE maps provides another accurate real-time data source that we can use [1]. They are also a proven source of data and are widely used in conjunction with Garmin technologies. Integrating this with our current application can increase the accuracy of our results as it will provide us with more information about current traffic conditions. In the future we would also like to integrate Taxi GPS data with our application. Taxi data can provide us with more valuable traffic information. Also, if we acquired a big data set then we would be able to improve our prediction algorithm as our machine learning model will have much more data to work with.

Finally, we need to work further on our algorithm for exercise mode and on our prediction model. Both of these modes were not worked on as much as the commute mode and the weather functionality as we felt that these were the core parts of this paper. The implementation of exercise mode is entirely based on the algorithm for commute mode with minor tweaks, this can be changed in the future to have its own specific algorithm. We feel that having its own algorithm would significantly improve our exercise mode algorithm.

Our prediction model also needs to be changed to incorporate data from the cyclists who use the application. This could not be done earlier as the core safety aspects of the application had to be mostly complete as we did not want cyclists using an unfinished and unproven safety application. We only gave our application our for use to cyclists after exhibition day so users could respond to the surveys.

8.2   Quality of Life Changes

We would like to implement multiple quality of life upgrades to our application to improve usability and user experience. These changes will not affect our safety algorithm, instead they will just enhance the application and make it more appealing for cyclists to use.

Firstly, we would like add GPS tracking and audio direction queues for users whilst they travel the route. The GPS tracking will allow the application to know the users current location on the route. This tracking can then be used to provide helpful audio queues to the users. This way the user can just listen to the queues and understand which direction they need to go next instead of having to memorize the route beforehand or put their phone on a mount.

We feel it could potentially be useful for users if they had the option to look at a list of directions that they must follow on their route. This way, they can just look at a handy list of instructions and memorize them instead of trying to discern them from looking at the plotted route on the map.

Another quality of life change that we would like to implement in the future is stat tracking for users. In order to implement this we must first implement our login database. We intended on having a database for logins, but instead had to move that to future work as other parts of the application required more immediate attention. This database can be used to store exercise statistics and provide the user with useful information such as distances travelled, speeds travelled and calories burnt. It can also remember common trips that users take and suggest these trips to them when the app is opened.

9   Conclusions

In this paper, we proposed to develop a mobile route planning application that can improve cyclist safety. We used Google and Bing APIs to acquire route and traffic data for Auckland, New Zealand. Using this data, we provided a route planning application that can take traffic conditions into account to ensure that cyclists are not routed through unsafe areas. We also implemented an exercise mode so the users of our application can be routed safely when planning workout routines. Our machine learning algorithm can be used by users to plan their future trips and ensure they are travelling during safe times.

The results show that our application provides a vast improvement in safety compared to current cyclist route planning applications. We compared our application against Google Maps as we felt that this is the best application that cyclists have at the moment. The results show that our application takes unsafe traffic conditions into account and successfully routes users away from these unsafe areas whilst still providing an efficient route. Google Maps does not do this and only looks at the shortest path for users. Thus, our application has successfully addressed the problem and can be seen to improve cyclist safety.

In the future, we would like to firstly improve our algorithm by adding more data sources to improve accuracy. We also need to look further into our exercise mode and prediction algorithms as there is some room for improvement there. Finally we would like to add several quality of life improvements for our users in order to increase the usability of our application.

Acknowledgement. This work was supported in part by the New Zealand Marsden Fund under Grant No. 17-UOA-248, and the UoA FRDF fund under Grant No. 3714668.

References

1. HERE: Here map data. https://www.here.com/en/products-services/map-content/here-map-data
2. Jain, V., Sharma, A., Subramanian, L.: Road traffic congestion in the developing world. In: Proceedings of the 2nd ACM Symposium on Computing for Development, p. 11. ACM (2012)

3. Machay, J.: How does google detect traffic congestion?. http://smallbusiness.chron. com/google-detect-traffic-congestion-49523.html
4. Auckland Transport: The auckland cycling account. https://at.govt.nz/cycling-walking/research-monitoring/
5. Auckland Transport: Traffic counts 2012 to 2018. https://at.govt.nz/about-us/reports-publications/traffic-counts/
6. Ministry of Transport: Ministry of transport - cyclist crash facts 2017. https://www. transport.govt.nz/resources/road-safety-resources/crashfacts/cyclistcrashfacts/
7. Weinstock, Z.: Flattest route. https://www.flattestroute.com/
8. OpenStreetMap Wiki: Open cycle map. https://wiki.openstreetmap.org/wiki/OpenCycleMap
9. Xu, L., Yue, Y., Li, Q.: Identifying urban traffic congestion pattern from historical floating car data. Procedia Soc. Behav. Sci. **96**, 2084–2095 (2013)

Prediction of Future Appearances via Convolutional Recurrent Neural Networks Based on Image Time Series in Cloud Computing

Zao Zhang[✉] and Xiaohua Li

State University of New York at Binghamton, Binghamton, NY 13902, USA
zhangzao1003@163.com, xli@binghamton.edu

Abstract. In recent years, cloud computing has become a prevalent platform to run artificial intelligence (AI) and deep learning applications. With cloud services, AI models can be deployed easily for the convenience of users. However, although cloud service providers such as Amazon Web Services (AWS) have provided various services to support AI applications, the design of AI models is still the key in many specific applications such as forecasting or prediction. For example, how to forecast the future appearance of ornamental plants or pets? To deal with this problem, in this paper we develop a convolutional recurrent neural network (CRNN) model to forecast the future appearance according to their past appearance images. Specifically, we study the problem of using the pine tree's past appearance images to forecast its future appearance images. We use a plant simulation software to generate pine tree's growing images to train the model. As a result, our model can generate the future appearance image of the pine tree, and the generated images are very similar to the true images. This means our model can work well to forecast the future appearance based on the image series.

Keywords: Cloud computing · CRNN · Image series · Forecasting

1 Introduction

In today's computer science field, cloud computing and artificial intelligence are the two most potential research directions. Cloud computing is an important innovation in the information area. The core idea of cloud computing is to coordinate many computer resources together so as to allow users to obtain unlimited resources through the network without the limitation of time and space. Cloud computing is a kind of services related to information technology, software, and the Internet. Cloud computing brings together many computing resources and implements automatic management through software. Computing platforms such as Amazon web service (AWS) can provide this type of on-demand cloud computing services to individuals or companies, and users can build their project conveniently.

© ICST Institute for Computer Sciences, Social Informatics and Telecommunications Engineering 2020
Published by Springer Nature Switzerland AG 2020. All Rights Reserved
X. Zhang et al. (Eds.): CloudComp 2019/SmartGift 2019, LNICST 322, pp. 328–340, 2020.
https://doi.org/10.1007/978-3-030-48513-9_27

To build a project for a specific task, artificial intelligence is a popular choice, because artificial intelligence always leads to low human resource cost and high working speed. There are many subclasses in artificial intelligence. Among them, deep learning has become increasingly popular due to its wide applications in many areas such as computer vision, speech recognition, natural language processing, text processing, etc. Although the specific name of "deep learning" was coined just several years ago, deep learning has achieved profound progress and played important roles in the living and working of human beings. The quick and dramatic success of deep learning has motivated many more people to conduct further research in deep learning. Due to the importance of cloud computing and deep learning, it is not difficult to see that a combination of them has great potential.

A lot of artificial intelligence or deep learning models have been developed. Many of them have been applied successfully in practice to meet user's requirement, and the applications usually rely on cloud computing because of the high computing resource and data resource requirement.

However, for many specific applications, existing artificial intelligence models are still unable to meet people's requirements. For instance, with the continuous improvement of social productivity, people's living standards are also constantly improving, and people naturally begin to pursue more spiritual enjoyment. Raising ornamental plants and keeping pets have become very popular entertainment. However, when people buy ornamental plants or pets, they can't know if flowers or pets grow into their favorite appearance in the future. At this time, a scientific and accurate prediction method is needed to help buyers choose their flowers and pets.

As to future appearance forecasting, there are existing image-based aging models for human face aging forecasting. Although face aging has very interesting market applications, the models rely on special face patterns and can hardly extended directly to other forecasting applications. Existing face aging methods can be roughly categorized into prototype-based approaches and physical model-based approaches. Prototype-based approaches transfer feature of age according to the difference of face images in different age groups [1, 2]. Physical model-based approaches focus on the block physical details of the human face [3, 4]. But neither of them can be well promoted to the field of image aging outside the face aging because both of them focus on the unique structure of human face to improve their forecasting accuracy. For other applications that are different from human face forecasting, such as forecasting the future appearance of plants or animals, new deep learning models need to be developed.

For this purpose, this paper develops a new convolutional recurrent neural networks (CRNN) model [5, 6], which can effectively forecast the plants' or pets' future appearance according to the image series of their past appearance. The CRNN neural network model developed in this paper is a multi-level neural network model consisting of a convolutional neural network (CNN) portion and a recurrent neural network (RNN) portion. The CNN portion is used to extract features in each image, while the RNN portion is used to process the time correlation among images and generate simulated forecasting images. The desired training data of this CRNN model is time-series images, which means a sequence of images of one individual under different ages. For example, a sequence of images of a tree of one-year old, two-year old, three-year old, and so on.

The output of the model is also a sequence of images of the same individual with older age labels. For example, a sequence of images of the same tree of four-year old, five-year old, six-year old and so on. Our experiments show that our model can successfully generate future images that are pretty similar to the label images.

There are two contributions in this paper. The first and the most important contribution is that we find a good model to forecast the future appearance of one object according to its past appearance. Plants and animals always look similar when they are young. But when they grow up, they will have significant differences. At this time, if we can accurately forecast their future appearance through our neural network model, the buyers will be able to choose satisfied plants or pets. This model can be applied in shops to help customers purchase plants and pets. The application is not limited to such an example, though. For example, it can be helpful to plant breeding. Existing plant breeding techniques, whether genetic techniques, chromosome techniques or molecular techniques, all need to select desired characteristics by long-time observation of the plants. If we can forecast plants' appearance features by our model, we can save a lot of time and costs.

The second contribution of this paper is that we demonstrate the CRNN structure can work very well in image series generation and forecasting. There are two main popular image generation methods: conditional generative adversarial networks (CGAN) [13] and conditional adversarial autoencoder (CAAE) [11]. This paper gives a new alternative method. In addition, we also show that the CRNN can learn time dependency among images well. The majority of existing researches use CRNN structure to learn the spatial dependency of an image, while we use the CRNN differently.

The rest of this paper is organized as follows. In Sect. 2, a brief review of related work will be given, including several existing forecasting methods and some application cases of CRNN. Then our CRNN structure will be described in Sect. 3. In Sect. 4, results of our experiments and evaluation will be given. Finally, a conclusion of our work and a discussion about some possible future research directions will be given.

2   Related Work

2.1   Image Forecasting Networks Model

Some effective imaging forecasting and face aging generative networks model include Variational Autoencoder (VAE), Adversarial Autoencoder (AAE), Conditional Adversarial Autoencoder (CAAE) and Conditional Generative Adversarial Networks (CGAN), which will be reviewed below.

Variational Autoencoder is a useful approach to unsupervised learning of complicated distributions, VAE is appealing because they are built on top of standard function approximates (neural networks), and can be trained with stochastic gradient descent [7]. There have been a lot of improvements based on the original VAE defined in 2013 by Kingma and Rezende. For instance, in 2016, Y. Pu et al. developed a new Variational Autoencoder setup to analyze images, this VAE uses Deep Generative Deconvolutional Networks (DGDN) as the decoder and uses a Convolutional Neural Networks (CNN) based encoder for the distribution of DGDN parameters [8]. The main advantage of VAE is that we can compare the pixel values of generated images and input images more easily because VAE uses encoding-decoding. The main disadvantage of VAE is that the generated images are always blurry, which means VAE may not be suitable in some situations with high precision requirements.

Adversarial Autoencoder is a probabilistic autoencoder that uses the recently proposed GAN to perform variational inference by matching the aggregated posterior of the hidden code vector of the autoencoder with an arbitrary prior distribution [9]. AAE combines the strengths of VAE and GAN. AAE discarded KL-divergence loss and choose to use adversarial networks. But AAE can still extract and learn the feature of images by the encoder part, which replaces the random noise-based generative networks of GAN and leads to more precise generative networks. These characteristics make AAE works well in generative networks and semi-classification problem.

In the structure of CAAE, a convolutional neural network is adopted as the encoder. The convolution is employed instead of pooling and allows the network to learn its spatial downsampling [10]. Two discriminator networks are imposed and this makes CAAE can generate more photo-realistic images. Compared to AAE, the main difference is that the CAAE uses discriminator in both the encoder and the generator. This structure guarantees a smooth transition in the latent space, and the discriminator on generator assists to generate photo-realistic images [11].

Conditional Generative Adversarial Networks (CGAN) is developed from the traditional Generative Adversarial Network (GAN). CGAN adds a condition in both the generator and the discriminator, and such condition could be added based on the label or some part of data [12]. The condition is feeding with input noise together, and will combine into joint hidden representation. The adversarial training framework allows for considerable flexibility in how this hidden representation is composed [13]. As a result, CGAN can generate images with specific attributes more conveniently.

2.2 Applications of CRNN

Convolutional Neural Networks (CNN) and Recurrent Neural Networks (RNN) are two widely used neural network structures. Convolutional neural networks are special neural network architectures that are especially suitable for processing image data. Besides their superior performance in image processing, they can also be used to process other types of data, such as text, speech, audio, etc. Convolutional neural network architectures are usually built with the following layers: convolution layer, activation function layer, pooling layer, fully connected layer and loss layer [14]. Recurrent neural networks (RNN) are developed specifically for processing sequential data with correlations among data samples. They have the nice capability of processing sequential data, and can be designed to model both long and short term data correlations. By combining the CNN and RNN, the CRNN not only utilizes the representation power of CNN, but also employs the context modeling ability of RNN. The CNN layers can learn good middle-level features, and help the RNN layer to learn effective spatial dependencies between image region features. Meanwhile, the context information encoded by RNN can lead to better image representation, and transmit more accurate supervisions to CNN layers during backpropagation (BP) [15].

In a single image, the distribution of features always relies on each other, and CRNN can work very well in this task. Because CNN can extract the embedded features and RNN can process their spatial dependency, CRNN has been used in single-image distribution learning tasks [15]. Another task, i.e., learning spatial dependency of the image, is more complicated. For example, if images are highly occluded, the recover the original image including the occluded portion is very difficult. Some researchers are still working in this area. But if the occluded images are image series with some inherent context information, this problem can be processed with the CRNN model. In the paper [16], the CRNN structure works very well and gets good performance.

CRNN structure has also been applied to the text recognition problems, where CNN can be used to recognize a single character while RNN can be used to extract text dependency according to the context. Especially, if the edge feature of the text is strong, then a Max-Feature-Map (MFM) layer can be added into the CRNN model to enhance the contrast [17].

CRNN also shows pretty good performance in music classification tasks, where CNN can be used to extract local feature and RNN can be used to extract temporal summarization of the extracted features [18].

3   CRNN Model for Prediction of Future Appearances

This section focuses on developing our CRNN model to forecast the future appearance of plants. The illustration of the convolutional recurrent neural network model is shown in Fig. 1.

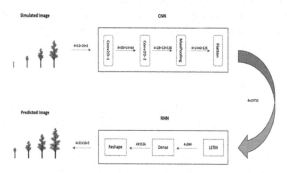

Fig. 1. Outline of CRNN model

As shown clearly in Fig. 1, our training data are pine tree image series with series length 4, which includes images of a pine tree at 10, 15, 20 and 25 years old. Then we apply a CNN to process each image. The CNN mainly consists of four layers: two convolution layers, one pooling layer and one flatten layer. After the CNN, there is an RNN with LSTM structure, which mainly consists of two layers: an LSTM layer and a Dense layer. The output will be a generated image series of length 4. This will be compared with the label, which is a real image series with series length 4 as well. The label is the images of this pine tree at ages 15, 20, 25 and 30 years. We focus on analyzing the performance of predicting the pine tree at 30 years of age from this pine tree's images at 10, 15, 20 and 25 years of age. After training, this CRNN model can be used to predict the future appearance of pine trees from their past appearances.

3.1 CRNN Forecasting Model

As shown in Fig. 1. Our input data is an image series $x_{i,t}$ with size T × H × W × D, which i denotes the index number of images sequence and t donates the time step label in time-series images sequence. H means the height of each image, W means the width of each image and D means the dimensions of each image. Input data is sent into our CNN portion and the output of CNN portion is a tensor $z_{i,t}$, which equals to:

$$z_{i,t} = f(x_{i,t}; \{w_x\}) \tag{1}$$

where w_x denotes the weighting coefficients in our CNN portion. Two CNN layer extracts the spatial feature in each image and adds one max-pooling layer and one flatten layer. Our CNN model can learn spatial dependency in each image individually. The CNN portion can map our input data $x_{i,t}$ to tensor $z_{i,t}$, and $z_{i,t}$ is the input of the RNN portion.

In our RNN portion, the LSTM layer is the core structure to learn time dependence in time series images sequence, and the LSTM layer maps the tensor $z_{i,t}$ to a representation series $h_{i,t}$ which equals to:

$$h_{i,t} = f(h_{i,t-1}, z_{i,t}; \{w_z\}) \tag{2}$$

where w_z denotes the weighting coefficients in the LSTM layer. Then the output of the LSTM layer H_i is sent to a dense layer. Actually, the dense layer is a classifier to classify the pixel value of every pixel, the value internal is [0, 255], which means the classification class is 256. The number of pixels is equal to our input time-series images sequence which is T × H × W × D. The output of the dense layer equals to:

$$\hat{y}_i = f(H_i; \{w_h\}) \tag{3}$$

In the last, a reshape layer is added to transfer our prediction value to generated forecasting images. Our model can generate forecasting future images according to the past time-series images of the same individual.

3.2 Data Processing in CRNN Model

In order to understand our CRNN model better, it is helpful to describe the procedure of data processing in detail, including the dimensions and values of important parameters and tensors. The values of the CRNN parameters are also selected carefully with many repeated experiments.

From Fig. 1, we can see that the dimension of the input tensor is 4 × 32 × 16 × 3, which means the input data is a series of color images with series length 4 and the size of each image is 32 rows and 16 columns. Because the kernel size of the first convolution layer is 3 × 3 and the number of filters is 64, the output of the first convolution layer is a tensor of dimension 4 × 30 × 14 × 64.

The output of the first convolution layer becomes the input of the second convolution layer. In the second convolution layer, the number of filters is 128 and the kernel size is still 3 × 3. Therefore, the dimension of the output tensor of the second convolution layer is 4 × 28 × 12 × 128. After the two convolution layers, a pooling layer is applied, which reduces the dimension of the data tensor to $4 \times 14 \times 6 \times 128$ with a stride (or decimation ratio) 2.

Then, a Flatten layer is used in order to connect the CNN with the RNN. As the layer name suggests, the function of this layer is to flatten each $4 \times 14 \times 6 \times 128$ data tensor into a two-dimensional data array with size $4 \times (14 \times 6 \times 128) = 4 \times 10752$. This finishes the CNN portion of the CRNN model.

Note that the CNN portion processes each image individually. Next, we apply RNN to learn the information embedded in the image series. The first layer of the RNN portion is an LSTM layer. The LSTM layer has 4 time steps, which consists of 4 LSTM cells. We set the dimensions of both the LSTM states and outputs to be 384. Therefore, the output of the LSTM layer is a data array with dimension 4×384.

To generate the predicted images, we use a Dense layer to generate output data tensors with the same dimension as the targeting pine tree image series. Specifically, the dimension is 4×1536. Note that 1536 equals to $32 \times 16 \times 3$, the size of a color image. We apply a reshape step at the end to obtain 4 predicted images with size $32 \times 16 \times 3$. This will be compared to the label image series for loss function calculation during training.

4   Experiments

4.1   Data Collection

We apply the software tool L-studio to generate images of pine trees. L-studio is a standard software that has been used widely in the botanical research community to create plant simulation models [19]. With L-studio we can conveniently generate various plant images with desired labels. The generated time-series images of a kind of pine tree can be shown in Fig. 2.

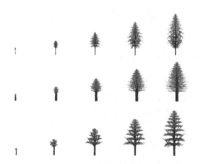

Fig. 2. Time-series images of pine tree generated by L-Studio

We chose this kind of pine because there are many variable parameters to guarantee the diversity of simulated images. As shown in Fig. 1. We choose years of pine to be 10, 15, 20, 25, and 30, which means to model pine that is 10 years old, 15 years old, 20 years old, 25 years old, and 30 years old, respectively. Each image of each pine tree thus forms an image series. Each series consists of 5 images, which are images of a pine tree at 10, 15, 20, 25 and 30 years old.

Besides the parameter of the age of the tree, there are many other parameters that can be adjusted in order to model different pine trees and to generate different images. Some important parameters include the growth rate of tree's height, the growth rate of tree's diameter, the shrinkage rate of tree's growth, the slope of needle leaf of pine, the angle between branch, the slope of branch, the shrinkage rate of tree's height growth, the shrinkage rate of tree's diameter growth, the shrinkage rate of branch, the shrinkage rate of second-level branch, the diameter of branch, the diameter of crown. There are about fourteen parameters that can be used to generate different trees. Each of these parameters is adjustable within a certain interval, such as [0, 1] or [0, 180] degree. Therefore, L-studio is very powerful for generating pine tree images with great differences in appearance. We can be confident our training data is fully diverse.

We use such simulated image series as training data to train our CRNN model. We use the 3463 series (about nine-tenths of the total data) as training data and 384 series (about one-tenth of the total data) as test data. Our CRNN is expected to predict the fifth image, which means the image of the 30 years-old pine tree, based on the first four images. This means we predict the future appearance images of the pine tree after several years of growth. We will compare the real fifth image with the predicted image to analyze the prediction performance.

4.2 Parameter Optimization

Several parameters in the CNN portion need to be set after test, such as the number of filters, size of the kernel, stride value, padding method, dilation rate, activation functions, etc. The difference in the activation function brings the biggest difference in results. The learning curves of different activation functions is shown in Fig. 3.

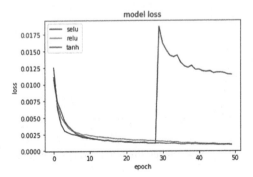

Fig. 3. Learning curves of different activation functions.

From the learning curves of these activation functions shown in Fig. 3, we can see that *tanh* and *relu* has better performance than *selu*. The performances of *tanh* and *relu* are almost similar. However, because of the instability issue we encountered with the

Table 1. Adopted parameters value in CNN portion.

Parameter	Value
Number of filters	61/128
Size of kernel	3×3
Stride	1
Padding method	Valid padding
Pooling size	(2, 2)

relu function, we adopt *tanh* as the activation function in the convolution layers of our CRNN model. The rest parameter values used in CNN portion can be shown in Table 1.

A long short-term memory (LSTM) structure is used in the RNN portion of our model to solve the vanishing gradient problem [20]. The cause of this problem is that gradients used in learning the weighting parameters are obtained by multiplying the error gradients of each time step. Because the time step of RNN may be big, if the error gradients of each time step are mostly smaller than one, the overall multiplication results will approach zero. On the other hand, if the error gradients are mostly bigger than one, then the overall gradients may explode to infinity. And this vanishing gradients will prevent the convergence of training. Although some other structures such as Gate Recurrent Unit (GRU) can achieve similar performance in many tasks with a simpler structure and lower computational complexity [21]. Our task is an image series problem, LSTM can achieve better performance in image processing are. As a result, one LSTM layer is added into the RNN portion.

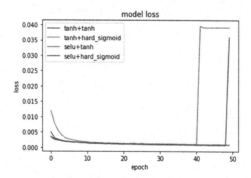

Fig. 4. Learning curves under different activation functions in LSTM.

Some other parameters also affect the difference of results, such as the number of LSTM neurons, the initialize method of the recurrent kernel, dropout value, implementation mode, activation function, etc. The main difference also comes from the different choices of activation functions. In LSTM, there are two activation functions, one for initializing the LSTM and the other for the recurrent steps in the LSTM. Considering that the *relu* function may lead to too big outputs in RNN [22] and *tanh* or hard *sigmoid* is an improvement over *sigmoid*, we try to choose the initializing activation function from *tanh* and *selu*, and to choose the recurrent activation function from *tanh* and *hard-sigmoid*. Therefore, we need to compare four combinations in total. The result is shown in Fig. 4.

From Fig. 4, we can see that the *selu* activation function will saturate much earlier than *tanh*, and the hard *sigmoid* has better performance in the recurrent step. Therefore, we choose *tanh* as the initial activation function and hard *sigmoid* function as the recurrent step activation function. The rest parameter used in RNN portion is shown in Table 2.

Table 2. Adopted parameters values in RNN portion.

Parameter	Value
Number of LSTM neurons	384
Initializer of recurrent kernel	Orthogonal recurrent kernel
Dropout value	0.3/0.3
Implementation mode	Products of a large number of small dots

During training, we need to choose appropriate loss function, optimizer, batch size and number of epochs. Because the training data and predict results are all images, mean squared error (MSE) can be a good choice of the loss function. The result of the different optimizer is shown in Fig. 5. And the result of the different number of batch size and epoch is shown in Fig. 6.

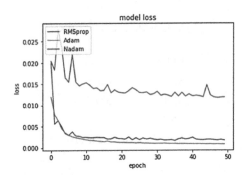

Fig. 5. Learning curves with different optimizers.

From Fig. 5, we can see that the loss of *Nadam* is not stable and not smooth. This means that *Nadam* may lead to learning too fast and finally lead to over-fitting. In contrast, the performance of *Adam* is stable and outstanding. Therefore, we use *Adam* as the optimizer in our CRNN training.

From the experiment results shown in Fig. 6, we can find that higher batch sizes will lead to over-fitting earlier. However, when the batch size decreases to 8, the loss suffers from a higher error floor compared with batch size 16. This might be due to gradient

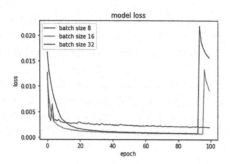

Fig. 6. The learning curve with different batch sizes.

vanishing. As a result, we set batch size as 16 and set the number of epochs to 95 because this gives the lowest loss in Fig. 6. All parameter optimization work has been displayed.

5   Result and Evaluation

The performance of our CRNN for pine tree image prediction is listed in Table 3. The result is evaluated according to four criterions: Mean Squared Error (MSE), Mean Average Error (MSE), Signal to Noise Ratio (SNR) and minimum validation loss. All results are calculated between the predicted image and real image. Some typical examples of the real pine tree images (which are generated by L-studio) and predicted pine tree images (which are the output of CRNN) are shown in Fig. 7. As can be seen, our CRNN model can successfully predict the pine tree images.

Table 3. Performance of CRNN.

Criterion	Value
MAE	8.57
MSE	377.35
SNR	322.55
Min Val-Loss	6.24e−04

From Fig. 7, we can see from the perspective of human eyes that the predicted image is very close to the original real image. From Table 3, all four criterion values are very low, which means that our predictions are also successful from a data perspective.

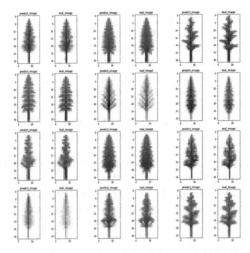

Fig. 7. Comparison between real pine tree images and predicted pine tree images.

6 Conclusion and Future Work

In this paper, we have developed a deep learning model that uses the convolutional recurrent neural network (CRNN) for image prediction. Specifically, we train the CRNN model with a pine tree image data set generated by L-studio and demonstrate that this model can successfully predict the future appearance of pine trees according to their past appearances. The predicted result of the developed CRNN is very good.

There are some issues that can be addressed to further improve performance. First, the data set is generated by the simulation software L-studio, which is still far away from real pine tree photos. Although L-studio has many adjustable parameters for us to generate many different images, it still cannot be fully compared with the diversity of natural images. As future work, we should try to collect enough images of natural pine trees or other objects and use them to test the prediction capability of the proposed CRNN model.

Second, we will try to extend the model developed in this paper to more application scenarios, such as medical image processing. Organs of the same disease usually have a similar development process. If the disease process of the diseased organ is regularly recorded as training data, we can train a suitable model to predict the development of the disease in other patients, to prevent it with some advance treatments. Of course, how to collect enough training data is still a core issue.

References

1. Fu, Y., Guo, G., Huang, T.S.: Age synthesis and estimation via faces: a survey. IEEE Trans. Pattern Anal. Mach. Intell. **32**(11), 1955–1976 (2010)
2. Kemelmacher-Shlizerman, I., Suwajanakorn, S., Seitz, S.M.: Illumination-aware age progression. In: Proceedings of the IEEE Conference on Computer Vision and Pattern Recognition, Columbus, OH, USA, pp. 3334–3341. IEEE (2014)

3. Suo, J., Zhu, S.-C., Shan, S., Chen, X.: A compositional and dynamic model for face aging. IEEE Trans. Pattern Anal. Mach. Intell. **32**(3), 385–401 (2010)
4. Tazoe, Y., Gohara, H., Maejima, A., Morishima, S.: Facial aging simulator considering geometry and patch-tiled texture. In: ACM Special Interest Group on Computer Graphics and Interactive Techniques Conference, Los Angeles, CA, USA, p. 90 (2012)
5. Pinheiro, P.H.O., Collobert, R.: Recurrent convolutional neural networks for scene labeling. ICML **4**, 82–90 (2014)
6. Zihlmann, M., Perekrestenko, D., Tschannen, M.: Convolutional recurrent neural networks for electrocardiogram classification. In: Computing in Cardiology (CinC), Rennes, France. IEEE (2017)
7. Doersch, C.: Tutorial on variational autoencoders. Carnegie Mellon/UC, Berkeley. https://arxiv.org/abs/1606.05908. Accessed 13 Jul 2019
8. Pu, Y., et al.: Variational autoencoder for deep learning of images, labels and captions. In: 30th Conference on Neural Information Processing Systems, Barcelona, Spain, vol. 29. NIPS (2016)
9. Makhzani, A., Shlen, J., Jaitly, N., Goodfellow, I., Frey, B.: Adversarial autoencoders. In: International Conference on Learning Representations (2016)
10. Radford, A., Metz, L., Chintala, S.: Unsupervised representation learning with deep convolutional generative adversarial networks. In: International Conference on Learning Representations (2016)
11. Zhang, Z., Song, Y., Qi, H.: Age progression/regression by conditional adversarial autoencoder. In: IEEE Conference on Computer Vision and Pattern Recognition. IEEE, Honolulu, HI, USA (2017)
12. Goodfellow, I., Mirza, M., Courville, A., Bengio, Y.: Multi-prediction deep Boltzmann machines. In: Advances in Neural Information Processing Systems, pp. 548–556. NIPS (2013)
13. Mirza, M., Osindero, S.: Conditional generative adversarial nets. https://arxiv.org/. Accessed 24 June 2019
14. Gers, F.A., Schmidhuber, J.: LSTM recurrent networks learn simple context free and context sensitive languages. IEEE Trans. Neural Networks **12**(6), 1333–1340 (2001)
15. Zuo, Z., et al.: Convolutional recurrent neural networks: learning spatial dependencies for image representation. In: IEEE Conference on Computer Vision and Pattern Recognition Workshops, Boston, MA, USA, pp. 18–26. IEEE (2015)
16. Zheng, J., Wang, Y., Zhang, X., Li, X.: Classification of severely occluded image sequences via convolutional recurrent neural networks. In: IEEE Global Conference on Signal and Information Processing, Anaheim, CA, USA (2018)
17. Chen, L., Li, S.: Improvement research and application of text recognition algorithm based on CRNN. In: 2018 International Conference on Signal Processing and Machine Learning, New York, NY, USA, pp. 166–170. IEEE (2018)
18. Choi, K., Fazekas, G., Sandler, M., Cho, K.: Convolutional recurrent neural networks for music classification. In: IEEE International Conference on Acoustics, Speech and Signal Processing, New Orleans, LA, USA. IEEE (2017)
19. L-studio 4.0 User's Guide. http://algorithmicbotany.org/lstudio/
20. Glorot, X., Bengio, Y.: Understanding the difficulty of training deep forward neural networks. In: Proceedings of the Thirteenth International Conference on Artificial Intelligence and Statistics, vol. 9, pp. 249–256 (2010)
21. Cho, K., et al.: Learning phrase representations using RNN encoder-decoder for statistical machine translation. In: Proceeding of the 2014 Conference on Empirical Methods in Natural Language Processing, pp. 1724–1734 (2014)
22. Bengio, Y., Simard, P., Frasconi, P.: Learning long-term dependencies with gradient descent is difficult. IEEE Trans. Neural Networks **5**(2), 157–166 (2014)

Video Knowledge Discovery Based on Convolutional Neural Network

JinJiao Lin[1,4], ChunFang Liu[1], LiZhen Cui[2,5(✉)], WeiYuan Huang[3], Rui Song[4], and YanZe Zhao[1]

[1] School of Management Science and Engineering,
Shandong University of Finance and Economics, Jinan 10456CN, CO, China
[2] School of Software, Shandong University, Jinan, China
clz@sdu.edu.cn
[3] School of Marxism, Shandong University of Finance and Economics, Jinan 10456CN,
CO, China
[4] School of Control Science and Engineering, Shandong University, Jinan 10422CN, CO, China
[5] Joint SDU-NTU Centre for Artificial Intelligence Research (C-FAIR), Shandong University,
Jinan, China

Abstract. Under the background of Internet+education, video course resources are becoming more and more abundant, at the same time, the Internet has a large number of not named or named non-standard courses video. It is increasingly important to identify courses name in these abundant video course teaching resources to improve learner efficiency. This study utilizes a deep neural network framework that incorporates a simple to implement transformation-invariant pooling operator (TI-pooling), after the audio and image information in course video is processed by the convolution layer and pooling layer of the model, the TI-pooling operator will further extract the features, so as to extract the most important information of course video, and we will identify the course name from the extracted course video information. The experimental results show that the accuracy of course name recognition obtained by taking image and audio as the input of CNN model is higher than that obtained by only image, only audio and only image and audio without ti-pooling operation.

Keywords: Knowledge discovery · TI-pooling · Convolutional nerve

1 Introduction

Online education platforms, forums, personal homepages, Weibo, various training groups, live broadcast platforms, etc. are all scattered with a large number of course video resources. Some of the course resources are normative, with course names, course knowledge points, and course evaluations. However, there are many video resources that are not standardized and are uploaded spontaneously by individuals on the Internet. Therefore, when searching for learning resources, the search may be incomplete due to the irregular description of the video resources, the irregularity or lack of naming, so it is

© ICST Institute for Computer Sciences, Social Informatics and Telecommunications Engineering 2020
Published by Springer Nature Switzerland AG 2020. All Rights Reserved
X. Zhang et al. (Eds.): CloudComp 2019/SmartGift 2019, LNICST 322, pp. 341–348, 2020.
https://doi.org/10.1007/978-3-030-48513-9_28

increasingly important to identify the courses name from the video for us to effectively use the Internet learning resources.

Identifying course names from video is a category of knowledge discovery, and knowledge discovery is the process of identifying effective, novel, potentially useful, and ultimately understandable knowledge from the data [1]. At present, most researches on knowledge discovery focus on text documents. For example, Wang et al. [2] proposed a convolutional neural network event mining model using distributed features, which uses word embedding, triggering word types, part of speech characteristics and multiple features of topic model to conduct event mining in text. Li et al. [3] used gated recurrent neural network (GRU) with attention mechanism to identify events in texts. However, few people study video, audio and other multimedia files. Video and audio generally contain rich knowledge, especially courses video, which is not only rich in content but also related to knowledge. At present, there are a large number of courses video on the Internet, and these course resources have the phenomenon that the course name does not correspond to the content or lacks the course name. Research on how to identify the course name in video will help learners make better use of learning resources. In recent years, deep neural networks have made remarkable achievements in many machine learning problems, such as image recognition [4], image classification [5] and video classification. However, identifying course names from courses video is still a challenge.

Based on the above analysis, this study uses a deep neural network model to collect video fragments of different courses from MOOC of China University and input the pictures and audio of course video into the model for training. After the completion of convolution and pooling, a TI-pooling operation is added. The TI-pooling operation can automatically find the best "standard" instance for training input, reduce the redundancy of learning features, and reduce the parameters and training time of the model. Ti-pooling operation will be introduced in detail in Sect. 3.2. In terms of the selection of activation function, we choose FReLU activation function. Compared with traditional ReLU function, FReLU function has the advantages of rapid convergence, higher performance, low calculation cost and strong adaptability. To verify the effectiveness of the method we used, we compared it with only images, only audio, and with images and audio but no TI-pooling model. Experimental results show that the performance of our method is better than the other three methods. Generally, this study offers at least three contributions as follows.

1. The CNN is applied to the course name recognition of course video.
2. The images and audio of course video are used as the input of the model to identify the name of course video.
3. The course name is automatically recognized from the course video.

2 Related Work

Massive data and poor knowledge lead to the emergence of data mining and knowledge discovery research. Knowledge discovery originates from artificial intelligence and machine learning. It is a new interdisciplinary subject with strong adaptability formed by the integration of machine learning, artificial intelligence, database and knowledge base. There are two main branches of knowledge discovery research at present, namely knowledge discovery based on database (KDD) and knowledge discovery based on literature (KDT).

Knowledge discovery based on database (KDD) can be defined as using data mining methods to identify valid, potentially useful, and ultimately understandable patterns from the database [7]. Knowledge discovery technology based on database is very mature and has been applied in many industries. For example, Wu Dan [8] used database knowledge discovery technology to predict employee turnover based on the basic information database of employees, and identified important factors that affect employee turnover, including the company's equity ownership, monthly salary, work environment satisfaction, work participation and so on. Xu et al. [9] developed the PhenoPredict system, which can infer the therapeutic effects of therapeutic drugs for diseases with similar phenotypes on schizophrenia from the knowledge base. Li Xiaoqing [10] studied bank data mining and knowledge discovery, and pointed out that data mining and knowledge discovery provide a basis for bank decision-making and customer relationship management. Knowledge discovery based on database has its limitation that it can only deal with structured data.

However, in the real world, knowledge does not all appear in the form of structured data in traditional databases, and quite a lot of knowledge is stored and presented in various forms, such as books, journals, newspapers, research papers, radio and television news, WEB pages, E-mail and so on. There is also a large amount of valuable information in these unstructured data sources. Therefore, data mining from these unstructured data sources to extract useful knowledge for users has become a new research hotspot in data mining, which is knowledge discovery based on text. For example, Kerzendorf [11] has developed a tool that can find similar articles based entirely on the text content of the input paper. By mining Web server logs, Novanto Yudistira et al. [12] found the correlation knowledge in the indicators of e-learning Web logs. Strong typed genetic programming (STGP) is used as a cutting edge technique to find precise rules and summarize them to achieve goals. The knowledge displayed may be useful to teachers or scholars, and strategies can be improved according to course activities to improve the use quality of e-learning. Enrique Alfonseca et al. [13] describes a combination of adaptive hypermedia and natural language processing techniques to create online information systems based on linear text in electronic formats, such as textbooks. Online information systems can recommend information that users may want based on their interests and background. Text-based knowledge discovery can process a variety of unstructured data. However, the current social data volume is growing exponentially. Traditional knowledge discovery technology based on database and opportunity text has been difficult to process massive data.

In recent years, deep learning technology has achieved good results in image recognition, image classification and audio processing, and promoted the application of knowledge discovery in video and audio. We use a two-channel convolutional neural network model to process the pictures and audio in the course video, and realize the automatic recognition of the course names without naming or non-standard naming of video from a large number of course video.

3   Methodology

3.1   The Network Architecture

For video knowledge discovery, CNN-related technology usually adopts multi-channel network structure, and has the following three main characteristics: first, weight sharing, second, local reception field (LRF), and third, pooling operation. CNN generally uses local information rather than global information.

The CNN model we use consists of two channels, picture and audio, which share parameters, The model consists of five convolution layers, each of which is followed by a maximum pooling layer after convolution. After the five convolution layers, a TI-pooling operation is conducted, and then the full connection layer is connected. The CNN model is shown in Fig. 1:

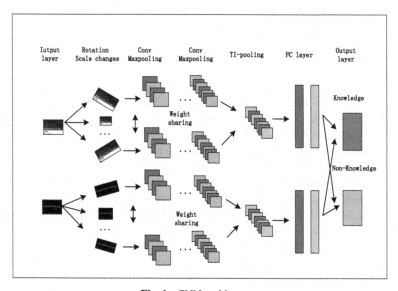

Fig. 1. CNN architecture

3.2   TI-Pooling Operation

In this study we represent features in a convolutional neural network as invariant transformations, which means that the machine learning algorithm only processes inputs that have not changed for some transformations. The most famous examples of general-purpose transformation-invariant features are SIFT (scale-invariant feature transform) [14] and its rotation-invariant modification RIFT (rotation-invariant feature transform) [15].

Because we did some processing on the sample before entering the data into the model, such as rotation, scaling and other changes to enhance the richness of the sample. The goal of TI-pooling is to carry out exhaustive search on the transformed samples to obtain the instance corresponding to the current response of the feature, and then only improve the performance of the feature with this instance.

As shown in Fig. 1, in the CNN model, the original sample and the transformed sample are input together. Instead of considering all the inputs as independent samples, but all the responses of the original sample and the transformed sample are accumulated and the maximum response is taken. Compared with data expansion, TI-pooling operation can learn fewer parameters without the disadvantage of losing relevant information after sample conversion, because it uses the most representative strength for learning.

Assume that, given a set of possible transformations Φ, we want to construct new features g_k (x) in such a way that their output is independent from the known in advance nuisance variations of the image x. We propose to formulate these features in the following manner:

$$g_k(x) = \max_{\phi \in \Phi} f_k(\phi(x)) \qquad (1)$$

Where $\phi(x)$ is the input sample x according to a set of transform Φ transform after get the sample, $f_k \phi(x)$ is the input sample characteristics of the model, and TI-pooling ensures that we use the best instance $\phi(x)$ for learning.

3.3 Activation Function

ReLU is an activation function widely used in CNN, but due to the zero-hard rectification, it cannot obtain the benefits of negative values. ReLU simply restrains the negative value to hard-zero, which provides sparsity but results negative missing. The variants of ReLU, including leaky ReLU (LReLU) [16], parametric ReLU (PReLU) [17], and randomized ReLU (RReLU) [18], enable non-zero slope to the negative part. It is proven that the negative parts are helpful for network learning. In this paper we use a new activation function called flexible rectified linear unit (FReLU), FRELU extends the output state of the activation function, adjusts the output of the ReLU function by adjusting the rectifying point, captures negative information and provides 0 features. It has the advantages of fast convergence, high performance, low calculation cost and strong adaptability [19].

As shown in Fig. 2(a), the input is x and the ReLU function is:

$$relu(x) = \begin{cases} x \ if \ x > 0 \\ 0 \ if \ x < 0 \end{cases} \qquad (2)$$

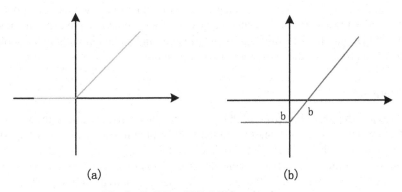

(a)   (b)

Fig. 2. ReLU and FReLU function images

The FReLU activation function we use is shown in Fig. 2(b). The function is:

$$frelu(x) = \begin{cases} x + b_l & if \ x > 0 \\ b_l & if \ x < 0 \end{cases} \tag{3}$$

where b_l is the l_{th} layer-wise learnable parameter, which controls the output range of FReLU. Note that FReLU naturaly generates ReLU when $b_l = 0$.

3.4 Loss Function

We choose the cross entropy function as the loss function of the training network. The specific function is:

$$C = \frac{1}{n} \sum_x [yln a + (1 - y)\ln(1 - a)] \tag{4}$$

Where x is the input to the training, y is the output of the training, a is the actual output of each neuron, and n is the entire number of samples trained.

3.5 Back Propagation

Let $\nabla f_k(x)$ be the gradient of the feature $f_k(x)$ defined in Eq. 1 with respect to the outputs $O(\cdot, \theta_j^{l-1})$ of the previous layer. This gradient is standard for convolutional neural networks and we do not discuss in details how to compute it [20]. From this gradient we can easily formulate the gradient $\frac{dg_k(x)}{df_k(x)}$ of the transformation-invariant feature $g_k(x)$ in the following manner:

$$\frac{dg_k(x)}{df_k(x)} = \nabla f_k(\phi(x)) \tag{5}$$

$$\phi = arg \max_{\phi \in \Phi} f_k(\phi(x)) \tag{6}$$

4 Experiments

The method we used is to input the images and audio of course video into the model. In order to verify the accuracy of the model, we conducted a comparative experiment with the model that only images, only audio, only images and audio but without TI-pooling. The detailed process of the experiment is shown below.

4.1 Data Set

We collected 15 video clips from MOOC of China University, processed the video into 324 pictures and 62 pieces of audio, and marked the picture and audio according to the course name. In order to increase the richness of the sample, we will make the picture and audio. After the rotation and scaling changes, 1296 pictures and 248 pieces of audio were obtained, and then 70% of the samples were selected into the training set, and 30% of the samples entered the test set.

4.2 Parameter Settings

The optimizer of the whole model uses the stochastic gradient descent method. The initial learning rate of the stochastic gradient descent method is set to 0.005, and the learning rate is attenuated by 1×10^{-6} after each update. The batch size of the data set read by the neural network during training is 16. The training data is transmitted to the neural network we use in the form of "sample-tag" for training the network model. The number of iterations is 10^3.

4.3 Experimental Result

To evaluate the effectiveness of the method we used, we compared the model using only images, using only audio, and using images and audio without increasing the TI-pooling operation. The experimental results show that the model we used is identified. Course names are more accurate than other methods. As shown in Table 1:

Table 1. Experimental result

Methods	Accuracy
Image only	61.3%
Audio only	57.7%
Image and Audio(without TI-pooling)	71.6%
Image and Audio(with TI-pooling)	77.4%

5   Conclusion

Identifying course names from a large number of non-naming or naming non-standard course videos can help learners improve the efficiency of resource retrieval and thus improve learning efficiency. In this paper we use a two-channel convolutional neural network model to process the image and audio signals of the course video. The framework adds a TI-pooling operation after all convolutional pooling layers. TI-pooling can Extract the most important features from the course video. The experimental results show that the CNN framework we use can better identify the course name from the course video, thus helping learners to better utilize the video learning resources on the Internet.

Acknowledgement. This work was financially supported by the Teaching Reform Research Project of Undergraduate Colleges and Universities of Shandong Province (Z2016Z036), the Teaching Reform Research Project of Shandong University of Finance and Economics (jy2018062891470, jy201830, jy201810), Shandong Provincial Social Science Planning Research Project (18CHLJ08), Scientific Research Projects of Universities in Shandong Province (J18RA136).

References

1. Fayyad, U, Shapiro, G.P., Smyth, P.: From data mining to knowledge discovery in databases [EB/OL]. http://www.kdnuggets.com/gpspubs/imag-kdd-overview-1996-Fayyad.Pdf. Accessed 22 Jun 2003
2. Wang, A., Wang, J., Lin, H., et al.: A multiple distributed representation method based on neural network for biomedical event extraction. BMC Med. Inform. Decis. Mak. **17**(S3), 171 (2017)
3. Lishuang, L., Yang, L., Meiyue, Q.: Extracting biomedical events with parallel multi-pooling convolutional neural networks. IEEE/ACM Trans. Comput. Biol. Bioinf. 1–1 (2018)
4. LeCunand, Y. Bengio, Y.: Convolutional networks for images, speech, and time series. In: The Handbook of Brain Theory and Neural Networks, vol. 3361, no. 10, p. 1 (1995)
5. Schmidhuber J. Multi-column deep neural networks for image classification. In: Computer Vision & Pattern Recognition (2012)
6. Karpathy, A., Toderici, G., Shetty, S., et al.: Large-scale video classification with convolutional neural networks. In: Computer Vision & Pattern Recognition (2014)
7. Peng, S.: Application of knowledge discovery in subject service. Northeast Normal University
8. Wu, D.: Prediction of employee turnover based on database knowledge discovery. Sci. Technol. Innov. 14 (2019)
9. Xu, R., Wang, Q.Q.: PhenoPredict: a disease phenome-wide drug repositioning approach towards schizophrenia drug discovery. J. Biomed. Inform. **56**(C), 348–355 (2015)
10. Li, X.: Decision analysis of banks based on data mining and knowledge discovery. Fintech Times 1, 56–59 (2014)
11. Kerzendorf, W.E. Knowledge discovery through text-based similarity searches for astronomy literature (2017)
12. Yudistira, N., Akbar, S.R., Arwan, A.: Using strongly typed genetic programming for knowledge discovery of course quality from e-Learning's web log. In: 2013 5th International Conference on Knowledge and Smart Technology (KST) (2013)
13. Alfonseca, E., Rodríguez, P., Pérez, D.: An approach for automatic generation of adaptive hypermedia in education with multilingual knowledge discovery techniques. Comput. Educ. **49**(2), 0–513 (2007)
14. Lowe, D.G.: Object recognition from local scale-invariant features. In: The proceedings of the seventh IEEE international conference on Computer Vision 1999, vol. 2, pp. 1150–1157. IEEE (1999)
15. Lazebnik, S., Schmid, C., Ponce, J., et al.: Semi-local affine parts for object recognition. In: British Machine Vision Conference (BMVC 2004), vol. 2, pp. 779–788 (2004)
16. Maas, A.L., Hannun, A.Y., Ng, A.Y.: Rectifier nonlinearities improve neural network acoustic models. In: Proceedings of ICML, vol. 30, no. 1 (2013)
17. He, K., Zhang, X., Ren, S., Sun, J.: Delving deep into rectifiers: surpassing human-level performance on imagenet classification. In: Proceedings of the IEEE International Conference on Computer Vision, pp. 1026–1034 (2015)
18. Xu, B., Wang, N., Chen, T., Li, M.: Empirical evaluation of rectified activations in convolutional network. arXiv preprint arXiv:1505.00853 (2015)
19. Qiu, S, Xu, X, Cai, B.: FReLU: flexible rectified linear units for improving convolutional neural networks (2017)
20. Laptev, D., Savinov, N., Buhmann, J.M., et al.: TI-POOLING: transformation-invariant pooling for feature learning in convolutional neural networks (2016)

Time-Varying Water Quality Analysis with Semantical Mining Technology

Jun Feng, Qinghan Yu$^{(\boxtimes)}$, and Yirui Wu

College of Computer and Information, Hohai University, Nanjing, China
{fengjun,qinghanyu,wuyirui}@hhu.edu.cn

Abstract. Water resources is one of the most important natural resources. With the development of industry, water resource is harmed by various types of pollution. However, water pollution process is affected by many factors with high complexity and uncertainty. How to accurately predict water quality and generate scheduling plan in time is an urgent problem to be solved. In this paper, we propose a novel method with semantical mining technology to discover knowledge contained in historical water quality data, which can be further used to improve forecast accuracy and achieve early pollution warning, thus effectively avoiding unnecessary economic losses. Specifically, the proposed semantical mining method consists of two stages, namely frequent sequence extraction and association rule mining. During the first stage, we propose FOFM (Fast One-Off Mining) mining algorithm to extract frequently occurred sequences from quantity of water quality data, which can be further considered as input of the second stage. During the process of association rule mining, we propose PB-ITM (Prefix-projected Based-InterTransaction Mining) algorithm to find relationship between frequently occurred water pollution events, which can be regarded as knowledge to explain water pollution process. Through experimental comparisons, we can conclude the proposed method can result in flexible, accurate and diverse patterns of water quality events.

Keywords: Pattern mining · Sequence patterns · Association rules · Water quality forecasting

1 Introduction

Single-sequence pattern mining can be defined as technology of discovering patterns that occurs frequently in a single sequence. Considering that there is a fixed time interval between each event of time-varying water quality sequence, we can conclude a significant relationship between water pollution events. With discovering knowledge of relationship among water pollution events, researchers can be aware of changes of water quality in a few weeks. Therefore, it is necessary to adopt a semantical mining method to mine knowledge inside the time-varying water quality sequence.

© ICST Institute for Computer Sciences, Social Informatics and Telecommunications Engineering 2020
Published by Springer Nature Switzerland AG 2020. All Rights Reserved
X. Zhang et al. (Eds.): CloudComp 2019/SmartGift 2019, LNICST 322, pp. 349–362, 2020.
https://doi.org/10.1007/978-3-030-48513-9_29

Since we can gain quantity of water quality data with help of sensor technology, it's necessary to first extract frequent sequence of water quality events as input to be analyzed. We thus develop the semantical mining method with two stages, where the first stage is used to extract frequent sequence and the second stage is applied to discover association rules among frequent sequences of water quality events.

During the **first stage**, we adopt interval constraint to help discover more useful patters from time-varying water quality sequence, where interval constraint refers to that each event in the mode needs to meet the interval condition. To better explain such property, we take sequence $S = abcabcdefgabbbadacbabc$ and pattern $ababc$ as an example. If we examine the exact pattern inside the sequence, we can't find such pattern. Once we define a constraint as the minimum interval is 0 and the maximum interval is 2, we can find that the pattern $ababc$ appears twice, where the positions of such pattern sequences are $\{0, 1, 3, 4, 5\}$ and $\{16, 18, 19, 20, 21\}$. From such example, we can see that interval constraint makes the single-sequence pattern mining more complicated and more flexible to dig useful patterns.

Based on the property of time-varying water quality sequence, we further define One-Off condition [4] to calculate uncertainty, where the position sequence of any two same patterns shouldn't share the same position under One-Off condition. Considering sequence as $S = abacc$, pattern as $P = abac$ and interval constraint as $[0, 1]$, the positions of such pattern P can be solves as $\{0, 1, 2, 3\}$, $\{0, 1, 2, 4\}$ without One-Off condition. Once we adopt One-Off Condition, pattern P can be only solved with positions $\{0, 1, 2, 3\}$, since the three identical positions $0, 1, 2$ are shared in above two occurrences of pattern P. In the water quality time sequence, it is obviously unreasonable to think that this pattern P occurs twice.

Although quantity of fast single-sequence pattern extraction algorithms have been proposed, they own high potential to lose patterns and may decrease efficiency under interval constraint and One-Off condition. In order to solve the problem of extracting frequent sequence of water quality events, we thus propose FOFM (Fast One-Off Mining) algorithm with interval constraints and One-Off condition, which can improve efficiency and accuracy during the process of mining water quality time sequence.

During the **second stage**, traditional association rule mining algorithms can only be applied on transaction database, which are not suitable to mine association rules from water quality sequences due to their high complexity and diversity. Moreover, water quality events are often occurred with time delay, since water pollution event happened in area A cannot immediately affect the area B. Therefore, mined association rules should own the property of temporal characteristics, where we use "Water quality deteriorates in area A this week, water quality of area B deteriorates in the second week $\Longrightarrow$ Water quality of area C deteriorates in the third week" as an example. In order to mine such rules with temporal characteristics, we proposes the PB-ITM algorithm (Prefix-projected Based-InterTransaction Mining), which not only considers association items, but also pay special attention on time relationship between transactions items.

The rest of the paper is organized as follows. Section 2 reviews the related work. Section 3 presents the details of the proposed FOFM algorithm to extract frequent sequences. The proposed PB-ITM algorithm to discover traditional association rules is discussed in Sect. 4. Section 5 presents the experimental results and discussions. Finally, Sect. 6 concludes the paper.

2   Related Work

With the rapid development of network and information technology, how to effectively use the gradually accumulated data is a hot research topic. As one of the core contents of data mining, pattern mining can obtain the implicit association between things, thus helping people to achieve prediction and recommendation. Pattern mining is a process of discovering high-frequency item sets, sub-sequences or sub-structures from a large amount of data, and is divided into three types of classical mining algorithms.

Association rule mining is one of the most basic methods, search for frequent item sets in the form of traversal trees. The most popular method of this type is the breadth-first search Apriori algorithm [1] and depth-first search FP-growth algorithm. Agrawal et al. proposed three test mining algorithms based on Apriori properties: AprioriAll, AprioriSome, DynamicSome [2], and then GSP [21]. The above algorithms are based on horizontal format algorithms. Zaki [23] proposed a sequence pattern algorithm SPADE based on the vertical format, which converts the sequence database into a vertical format database that records the location of the item set, and then dynamically joins the mining frequent sequence pattern. The algorithm only needs to scan the database three times, reducing the I/O overhead.

The pattern mining problem of the sequence was first proposed by Agrawal and Srikant in 1995, and introduced many related algorithms, including FreeSpan [10], PrefixSpan [20], and some improved algorithms have been proposed [3,5], Zou Xiang et al. studied the sequential pattern mining algorithm in distributed environment [26]. The traditional sequential pattern mining algorithm is to mine frequent occurrence patterns from sequence databases, without defining wildcard constraints. Ji et al. [14] and Li et al. [17] studied the problem of pattern mining with wildcards in the sequence database. The concept of minimum distinction mode with wildcards is proposed in article [13]. Another focus of sequential pattern mining research is to mine frequent patterns from a single sequence, which is usually quite long, for example. NA sequences and protein sequences, etc. Zhang et al. studied the pattern mining problem with wildcards in a single sequence, and proposed the MPP algorithm [24]. He et al. [11] studied the problem of sequential pattern mining in a single sequence, and the pattern satisfies the One-Off condition. Zhu et al. [25] proposed the MCPaS algorithm to mine frequent patterns from multiple sequences.

Graph pattern mining is the process of identifying high-frequency substructures from a set of graphs or a single large graph. Most of the current algorithms are for atlas, including SUBDUE based on greedy strategy [6], gSpan

[22] using depth-first search, GASTON [19], and AGM using breadth-first search [12], PATH [13], FGS [15]. The SUBDUE algorithm is also applicable to single pictures.

Mining interesting patterns from different types of data is quite important in many real-life applications [7,16]. Sequential pattern mining (SPM) [9] has been extensively studied a novel utility mining framework, called utility-oriented pattern mining (UPM) or high-utility pattern mining, which considers the relative importance of items, has become an emerging research topic in recent years. Affinitive utility [18] is proposed to address the special task of correlated UPM, but not used for the general task of UPM. The utility occupancy [8] is more suitable than the utility concept and average utility for discovering the high-utility patterns which have high utility contribution.

3   Fast One-Off Mining Algorithm

The proposed FOFM algorithm is used to extract frequent sequences from quantity of water quality data. We present steps of FOFM by first defining related conceptions and then presenting its detail.

3.1   Related Definition

This section mainly describes the related definitions and theorems involved in the single-sequence pattern of water quality time sequence.

Given a sequence $S = \{s_1, s_2, s_3, \ldots s_{n-1}, s_n\}$ with n characters, its length can be defined as n, where the set of all the different characters in the sequence can be denoted as $\sum$. The interval constraint consists of a minimum interval and a maximum interval, which can be denoted as N and M. Moreover, size $(M - N)$ is defined as the interval constraint length.

Given patterns $P = \{p_1, p_2, p_3, \ldots p_{m-1}, p_m\}$ and $Q = \{q_1, q_2, q_3, \ldots q_{t-1}, q_t\}$, for any k with $1 \leq k \leq t$, if existing a sequence with positions $1 \leq i_1 \leq i_2 \leq \cdots \leq i_t \leq m$ which satisfy $p_{i_k} = q_k$, Q can be regarded as a sub-pattern of P. Meanwhile, P can be regarded as the parent pattern of Q. For any j with $2 \leq j \leq t$, if existing a sequence with positions which satisfy $i_j - i_{j-1} = 1$, Q can be regarded as a continuous sub-pattern of P. Moreover, Q can be defined as the prefix pattern of P, only if Q is a continuous sub-pattern of P and $i_1 = 1$. For any k with $2 \leq k \leq m$, if existing $p_k = q_{k-1}$, pattern P and Q can be connected to generate a new pattern, which can be represented as $p_1 q_1 q_2 q_3 \cdots q_{m-1} q_m$.

Once the appearing frequency of the pattern P in the sequence S satisfies the given interval constraint and One-Off condition, i.e., P's support is bigger than minimum support as settled, pattern P can be regarded as the frequent pattern. Under One-Off conditions, single-sequence pattern mining satisfies Apriori properties: all non-empty sub-pattern of frequent patterns must be frequent, while the parent patterns of infrequent patterns must be infrequent.

3.2   Algorithm Steps

Before describing steps of the proposed FOFM algorithm, we describe the how to calculate support value of pattern in Algorithm 1. Afterwards, the proposed FOFM algorithm can be described as four steps. During the first step, the proposed method scans the original sequence to obtain all patterns with length one and records their positions, which forms the set of to-be-connected patterns. In the second step, the proposed method tries to connect two patterns in the set of to-be-connected patterns by firstly traversing the pre-sequence, and then judging whether the position in the pre-sequence and post-sequence satisfy the interval constraint. If satisfied, position of the current post-sequence is saved as the new pattern. If not satisfied, the proposed method would continue to perform traversing and judging steps. After generating patterns, the proposed method would clear the set of to-be-connected pattern and calculate support values of generated patterns with steps described in Algorithm 1. The proposed method would save pattern as frequent pattern by judging whether its support value is larger than minimum support value requirement. If not, The proposed method would save these patters into the set of to-be-connected patterns and repeat step 2 until all sequences are used.

Algorithm 1. Calculating supporting value.

1: $sup = 0$ //Initialize the supporting value;
2: **for** each $i = vec.size$ **do**
3:     **if** The position $vec[i]$ is already used, the next position is matched. **then**
4:         continue;
5:     **end if**
6:     initialize list //Initialize a list of locations to record the occurrence of patterns that satisfy the condition
7:     $list.add(vec[i])$
8:     $prevval = vec[i]$
9:     $TP = P.max_prefix$ // Get the pattern's maximum prefix pattern
10:     **while** $TP! = ""$ **do**
11:         $pvec = TP.list$ // Get the tail sequence of the largest prefix pattern
12:         Check if there is a position that meets the interval constraint requirements;
13:         if meets,add this location to your location list $TP.list$
14:         $TP = TP.max_prefix$ //Use TP as the reference pattern to obtain the maximum prefix pattern of TP
15:     **end while**
16: **end for**

---

4   Prefix-Projected Based-InterTransaction Mining Algorithm

The PB-ITM algorithm first perform preprocessing based on the characteristics of frequent water quality sequence, which is the output of the proposed FOFM algorithm. After preprocessing, the proposed algorithm generates frequent item set by considering time characteristics of water quality data. Finally, the proposed algorithm generate association rules, which can be regarded as knowledge on relationship between water quality events.

4.1 Data Preprocessing

Data preprocessing consists of three steps, namely frequency sequence transactionalization, sliding window for processing, and data reduction.

Frequency Sequence Transactionalization. The main purpose of frequency sequence transactionization is to transform multiple water quality time sequence into transactional data, which can be easily processed by latter steps.

Water quality can be classified into six categories based on surface water quality standards of China, i.e., I, II, III, IV, V and bad V class. In order to mine association rules of water quality sequence, it is necessary to use characters to represent water quality sequence, where we show the transformation rule in Table 1.

Table 1. Water quality characterization based on categories

Water quality categories	The corresponding representing character
I class	1
II class	2
III class	3
IV class	4
V class	5
Bad V class	6

Given a frequency water quality sequence $S = \{s_1, s_2, s_3, \ldots s_{n-1}, s_n\}$, we define its corresponding variation sequence as $S' = \{e_1 = s_2 - s_1, e_2 = s_3 - s_2, \ldots, e_{n-2} = s_{n-1} - s_{n-2}, e_{n-1} = s_n - s_{n-1}\}$. In sequence S', $e > 0$, $e < 0$ and $e = 0$ implies water quality is decreasing, improving and remains constant, respectively. With multiple variant values to represent water quality, we can represent $S' = \{e_{i,j} | i = 1, ..., n; j = 1, ..., m\}$, where i implies time and j refers to the category of multiple variants. In fact, multiple dimensions variants describe attributes associated with water quality events, such as when the event occurred or where the event occurred. Above all, frequency water quality sequence transactionization converts time-varying sequence into multiple variation sequence.

Sliding Window for Pre-processing. In reality, relevant researchers generally only care about the changing association in water quality over time. When mining water quality time sequence data with time attributes, it is necessary to consider the time interval between events. In order to avoid mining unnecessary patterns that do not meet the time requirements, the proposed method uses a sliding window method to process the transaction database. The size of the sliding window W is w, W is composed of multiple transactions in the transaction database, the interval of the dimension attributes of these transactions is less than w from the beginning to the end. Where $W[i](0 \leq i \leq w-1)$ is called the child window of W.

After drawing multiple windows by the method of sliding the window, each of them can generate a new set. The number of events in the transaction database is u, then merge set $M = \{e_i(j)|e_i \in W[j], 1 \leq i \leq u, 0 \leq j \leq w-1\}$. The Expanded event, also known as expanded item, is shaped as $e_i(j)$, which is an event in the merge set that has expanded information, and call the set of all expanded events as $\sum'$. A transaction database consisting of multiple merge sets is called a cross-transaction database.

The original transaction database is transformed into multiple merge sets by sliding window method. These merge sets are separated from each other, avoiding mining the patterns that are not interested. The expanded events in the merged set retain the relative dimensional information, so that the mining process retains the relevant characteristics which the researcher is interested in. Figure 1 illustrates the processing of the transaction database sliding window, where the size of sliding window is 4.

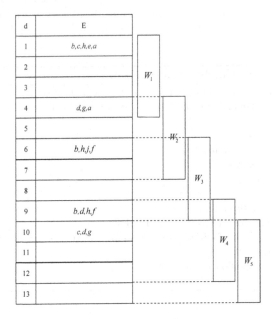

Fig. 1. Sliding window of the transaction database.

Data Reduction. The data reduction method is used to deal with the cross-transaction database formed by the water quality time sequence. The specific strategy is: in the process of generating the expansion item in the sliding window, determining whether the current event is a constant event, and if the event is a constant event, the event is not added to the appropriate window.

4.2 The Generation of Frequent Item Set

The part is to generate frequent pattern from the cross-transaction database that get by data preprocessing. It accelerates the mining efficiency of frequent patterns by expanding only from the item, whose sliding window index is 0. In the process of obtaining the suffix from the prefix projection database, the PB-ITM algorithm uses pseudo-projection technology, it only save the items that can be expanded and their position information. The specific steps of generating frequent pattern are as follows:

4.3 The Generation of Association Rules

The generation of association rules is the last step of mining association rules. The goal is to generate corresponding association rules based on the frequent patterns.

The cross-transaction association rule is shaped like $X \Longrightarrow Y$, where X and Y are both subsets of the expansion item set $\sum'$, and $X \cap Y = \emptyset$. $T(X)$ is the supporting value of the item set X in the cross-transaction database, and $T(XY)$ is the supporting value of the item set $X \cup Y$, and the confidence level for the association rule pattern of cross-transactional databases is $T(X)/T(XY)$.

The main steps of generating the association rule are as follows:

Algorithm 2. Generating frequent item set.

$freitem1 = getfreitem1(db);$ //Initialize frequent item sets
$time0item = gettime0item(freitem1);$ //Obtain an extension with time information of 0
for each s in db **do**
  if s is not frequent **then**
    Delete s from db;
  end if
end for
for each s in $time0item$ **do**
  Create a prefix for the projection database;
  Build an initial list of extended location information for each item with a sliding window value of 0;
  Start mode expansion Recursively;
end for

Algorithm 3. Generating association rules.

for each lk in *itemsets* do
    initialize list //Initialize the list of items that meet the minimum confidence;
    for each j in lk do
        Stop association rule generation if time information is unreasonable
        Calculate the confidence of the association rule $(lk - item) \Longrightarrow item$
        Store the item if the rule meets the minimum support requirement
    end for
end for

5 Experiments

5.1 Dataset

This paper experiments on water quality time single sequence mode and water quality time sequence association rules. For the experiment of water quality time single sequence mode, we choose the water quality time sequence data of Nanjing Tuqiao 2007–2016. The water quality time sequence of the three water quality sites, Tuqiao, Liangyi and Xinyanggang, were selected. The length of the water quality time sequence of the Tuqiao in Nanjing is 521, the length of the water

Table 2. Partial mining results of Tuqiao water quality time sequence from 2007 to 2016.

Serial number	Pattern	Support	Weeks of occurrence
1	443333	10	81~88, 130~141, 146~171, 188~196, 252~261, 392~399, 465~475, 503~510
2	466664	10	15~30, 40~46, 95~132, 176~184, 227~237, 330~336, 365~374
3	666666	10	21~27, 45~51, 97~104, 108~115, 116~123, 124~129, 177~182, 218~224, 225~234, 367~372
4	22433	10	248~258, 304~317, 407~415, 424~430, 436~445, 459~470, 500~509, 515~521
5	6634	10	4~11, 77~83, 103~107, 181~184, 233~237, 272~279, 284~290, 334~339, 360~365, 478~484
6	5434	10	7~15, 36~40, 78~83, 90~95, 102~107, 131~135, 151~158, 259~264, 375~389
7	6434	12	27~35, 80~89, 104~107, 129~135, 182~189, 233~242, 253~260, 335~339, 372~377, 390~398, 478~484
8	3464	10	14~18, 39~46, 94~100, 106~113, 258~264, 287~290, 314~319, 328~336, 387~393, 475~479

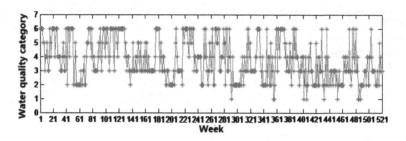

Fig. 2. Changes in water quality of Nanjing Tuqiao from 2007 to 2016.

quality time sequence of Liangyi in Dongtai is 511, and the length of the water quality time sequence of Xinyang Port in Yancheng is 509. The water quality time sequences are arranged weekly. The weekly water quality category is based on the relevant surface water environmental quality standards. The results are comprehensively evaluated by pH, dissolved oxygen, permanganate index and ammonia nitrogen. The experimental data of the water quality time sequence association rules are from 8 water quality monitoring sites in the Taihu Basin. The eight water quality monitoring stations are Lanshanzui, Dapu Port, Baiyu Port, Wujin Port, Zhihu Port, Shazhu, Wangting and Niaozuiqiao.

5.2   Result

The water quality are divided into six categories. In order to better mine the water quality time sequence, different characters are used here to represent different water quality categories, and the corresponding relationship is shown in Table 1:

This section selects the water quality time sequence data of Nanjing Tuqiao from 2007 to 2016. The minimum interval is 0, the maximum interval is 2, and the minimum support is 10. The experiment uses the FOFM algorithm for mining. The results of some mining are shown in Table 2:

The water quality change of Nanjing Tuqiao from 2007 to 2016 is shown in Fig. 2.

In order to compare the relevant algorithms, the water quality time sequence of the three water quality sites, Tuqiao, Liangyi and Xinyanggang, in 2007–2016 were selected. In the experiment, the control variable method was used to test the running time of the FOFM algorithm, OFMI algorithm, I-OFMI algorithm and the number of mining patterns under different interval constraint lengths or different minimum support. The minimum support is set to 6, 8, 10, 12, 14, 16, 18, and the interval constraint is set to $[0, 2]$.

By mining the pattern of the water quality time sequence from the three locations, it can be seen from the Fig. 3 that as the minimum support set increases, the fewer the number of models mined, the less time it takes to run. For the mining of water quality time sequence in the same place, if given the same minimum supporting value, the number of patterns mined by the method proposed

Table 3. Partial mining results of Tuqiao water quality time series from 2007 to 2016.

Serial number	Association rule	Support	Confidence level
1	Baidu Port's water quality deterioration(0), Wujin Port's water quality deterioration(1) $\Longrightarrow$ Wangting's water quality deterioration(3)	8	0.57
2	Lanshanzui's water quality improvement(0), Wujin Port's water quality improvement(0), Wangting's water quality improvement(2) $\Longrightarrow$ Niaozuiqiao's water quality improvement(3)	6	0.75
3	Baidu Port's water quality improvement(0), Lanshanzui's water quality improvement(1) $\Longrightarrow$ Niaozuiqiao's water quality improvement(3)	8	0.57
4	Shazhu's water quality improvement(0), Lanshanzui's water quality improvement(1) $\Longrightarrow$ Niaozuiqiao's water quality improvement(3)	7	0.5
5	Baidu Port's water quality improvement(0), Zhihu Port's water quality improvement(0) $\Longrightarrow$ Niaozuiqiao's water quality improvement(3)	7	0.64
6	Zhihu Port's water quality deterioration(0), Wujin Port's water quality deterioration(1) $\Longrightarrow$ Wangting's water quality deterioration(3)	10	0.59
7	Shazhu's water quality deterioration(0), Dapu Port's water quality deterioration(2) $\Longrightarrow$ Lanshanzui's water quality deterioration(3)	7	0.54

in this paper is basically the same as the I-OFMI algorithm, but far more than the OFMI. In terms of running time, the time used in the proposed method is the least among the three methods. In summary, the water quality sequence pattern mining method proposed in this paper has higher efficiency than other algorithms, while ensuring the high completeness of the patterns.

In the association rule mining experiment, the parameter sliding window size is 4, the minimum support is 5, and the minimum confidence is 0.5. The experimental results are shown in Table 3.

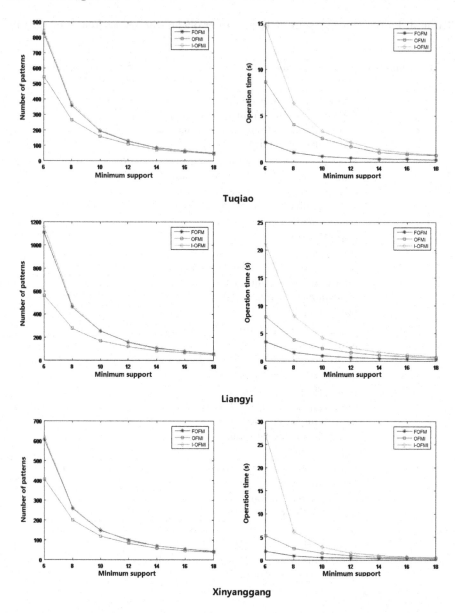

Fig. 3. Comparison of different methods.

Through the mining of the association rules between the water quality time sequence of the eight sites, we can see from the above table, in the requirements of higher minimum support and minimum confidence, the method proposed in this paper can accurately mine the association rules with time characteristics in the water quality time sequence, it fully consider the relationship between events and events, and solve the main problem: the water quality time series has high complexity and the association rules are difficult to mine.

6 Conclusion

This paper proposes two time-varying water quality analysis methods based on pattern mining, sequence pattern mining and association rule mining for water quality data. Through theoretical and experimental analysis, first, the sequence pattern mining method FOFM has high efficiency while ensuring the completeness of pattern mining. Then, the association rule mining method PB-ITM considers the relationship and time characteristics of the transaction, so that the reliability of the prediction result is higher. In the next work, we will increase the experiment. Based on, to further improve the model and improve model performance.

References

1. Agrawal, R., Srikant, R., et al.: Fast algorithms for mining association rules. In: Proceedings of 20th International Conference Very Large Data Bases, VLDB, vol. 1215, pp. 487–499 (1994)
2. Agrawal, R., Srikant, R., et al.: Mining sequential patterns. In: ICDE, vol. 95, pp. 3–14 (1995)
3. Ayres, J., Flannick, J., Gehrke, J., Yiu, T.: Sequential pattern mining using a bitmap representation. In: Proceedings of the Eighth ACM SIGKDD International Conference on Knowledge Discovery and Data Mining, pp. 429–435. ACM (2002)
4. Chen, G., Wu, X., Zhu, X., Arslan, A.N., He, Y.: Efficient string matching with wildcards and length constraints. Knowl. Inf. Syst. **10**(4), 399–419 (2006)
5. Chiu, D.Y., Wu, Y.H., Chen, A.L.: An efficient algorithm for mining frequent sequences by a new strategy without support counting. In: Proceedings of 20th International Conference on Data Engineering, pp. 375–386. IEEE (2004)
6. Cook, D.J., Holder, L.B.: Substructure discovery using minimum description length and background knowledge. J. Artif. Intell. Res. **1**, 231–255 (1993)
7. Fournier-Viger, P., Lin, J.C.W., Kiran, R.U., Koh, Y.S., Thomas, R.: A survey of sequential pattern mining. Data Sci. Pattern Recogn. **1**(1), 54–77 (2017)
8. Gan, W., Lin, J.C.W., Fournier-Viger, P., Chao, H.C., Philip, S.Y.: HUOPM: high-utility occupancy pattern mining. IEEE Trans. Cybern. **99**, 1–14 (2019)
9. Gan, W., Lin, J.C.W., Fournier-Viger, P., Chao, H.C., Yu, P.S.: A survey of parallel sequential pattern mining. arXiv preprint arXiv:1805.10515 (2018)
10. Han, J., Pei, J., Yin, Y.: Mining frequent patterns without candidate generation. ACM SIGMOD Rec. **29**, 1–12 (2000)
11. He, Y., Wu, X., Zhu, X., Arslan, A.N.: Mining frequent patterns with wildcards from biological sequences. In: 2007 IEEE International Conference on Information Reuse and Integration, pp. 329–334. IEEE (2007)
12. Inokuchi, A., Washio, T., Motoda, H.: An Apriori-based algorithm for mining frequent substructures from graph data. In: Zighed, D.A., Komorowski, J., Żytkow, J. (eds.) PKDD 2000. LNCS (LNAI), vol. 1910, pp. 13–23. Springer, Heidelberg (2000). https://doi.org/10.1007/3-540-45372-5_2

13. Inokuchi, A., Washio, T., Motoda, H.: Complete mining of frequent patterns from graphs: mining graph data. Mach. Learn. **50**(3), 321–354 (2003)

14. Ji, X., Bailey, J., Dong, G.: Mining minimal distinguishing subsequence patterns with gap constraints. Knowl. Inf. Syst. **11**(3), 259–286 (2007)

15. Kuramochi, M., Karypis, G.: Frequent subgraph discovery. In: Proceedings 2001 IEEE International Conference on Data Mining, pp. 313–320. IEEE (2001)

16. Lepping, J.: Wiley Interdisciplinary Reviews: Data Mining and Knowledge Discovery (2018)

17. Li, C., Wang, J.: Efficiently mining closed subsequences with gap constraints. In: Proceedings of the 2008 SIAM International Conference on Data Mining, pp. 313–322. SIAM (2008)

18. Lin, J.C.W., Gan, W., Fournier-Viger, P., Hong, T.P., Chao, H.C.: FDHUP: fast algorithm for mining discriminative high utility patterns. Knowl. Inf. Syst. **51**(3), 873–909 (2017)

19. Nijssen, S., Kok, J.N.: A quickstart in frequent structure mining can make a difference. In: Proceedings of the Tenth ACM SIGKDD International Conference on Knowledge Discovery and Data Mining, pp. 647–652. ACM (2004)

20. Pei, J., et al.: PrefixSpan: mining sequential patterns efficiently by prefix-projected pattern growth. In: Proceedings 17th International Conference on Data Engineering, pp. 215–224. IEEE (2001)

21. Srikant, R., Agrawal, R.: Mining sequential patterns: generalizations and performance improvements. In: Apers, P., Bouzeghoub, M., Gardarin, G. (eds.) EDBT 1996. LNCS, vol. 1057, pp. 1–17. Springer, Heidelberg (1996). https://doi.org/10.1007/BFb0014140

22. Yan, X., Gspan, J.: Graph-based substructure pattern mining. In: Proceedings of 2002 International Conference Data Mining (ICDM 2002), pp. 721–724 (2001)

23. Zaki, M.J.: SPADE: An efficient algorithm for mining frequent sequences. Mach. Learn. **42**(1–2), 31–60 (2001)

24. Zhang, M., Kao, B., Cheung, D.W., Yip, K.Y.: Mining periodic patterns with gap requirement from sequences. ACM Trans. Knowl. Discovery Data (TKDD) **1**(2), 7 (2007)

25. Zhu, X., Wu, X.: Mining complex patterns across sequences with gap requirements. A... A 1(S2), S3 (2007)

26. Zou, X., Zhang, W., Liu, Y., Cai, Q.: Study on distributed sequential pattern discovery algorithm. J. Softw. **16**(7), 1262–1269 (2005)

Data-Driven Fast Real-Time Flood Forecasting Model for Processing Concept Drift

Le Yan[1(✉)], Jun Feng[1], Yirui Wu[1,2], and Tingting Hang[1,3]

[1] Computer and Information College, Hohai University, Nanjing 211100, China
{yanle,fengjun,wuyirui,httsf}@hhu.edu.cn
[2] National Key Lab for Novel Software Technology,
Nanjing University, Nanjing, China
[3] Key Laboratory of Unmanned Aerial Vehicle Development & Data
Application of Anhui Higher Education Institutes,
Wanjiang University of Technology, Maanshan 243031, China

Abstract. The hydrological data of small and medium watershed develops with the passage of time. The rainfall-runoff patterns in these data often develop over time, and the models established for the analysis of such data will soon not be applicable. In view of the problem that adaptability and accuracy of the existing data-driven flood real-time forecasting model in medium and small watershed with concept drift. We update the data-driven model using incremental training based on support vector machine (SVM) and gated recurrent unit (GRU) model respectively. According to the rapid real-time flood forecasting test results of the Tunxi watershed, Anhui Province, China, the fast real-time flood forecast data-driven model with incremental update can more accurately predict the moment when the flood begins to rise and the highest point of flood stream-flow, and it is an effective tool for real-time flood forecasting in small and medium watersheds.

Keywords: Medium and small watershed · Concept drift · Data-driven model · Fast real-time flood forecasting

1 Introduction

The floods in small and medium watershed are characterized by sudden bursts, shorter concentration of flow time and shorter foresight period. Timely and effective flood warning and forecasting of small and medium watershed can help humans effectively prevent floods and reduce flood damage. It is one of the important non-engineering measures for disaster prevention and mitigation [1]. Flood prediction models are important for disaster assessment and extreme event management. Robust and accurate predictions contribute significantly to water management strategies, policy advice and analysis, and further evacuation modeling [2]. Therefore, the importance of forecasting systems for rapid real-time

© ICST Institute for Computer Sciences, Social Informatics and Telecommunications Engineering 2020
Published by Springer Nature Switzerland AG 2020. All Rights Reserved
X. Zhang et al. (Eds.): CloudComp 2019/SmartGift 2019, LNICST 322, pp. 363–374, 2020.
https://doi.org/10.1007/978-3-030-48513-9_30

and short-term prediction of floods and other hydrological events is emphasized. At present, flood forecasting generally adopts a hydrological model based on runoff process and a data driven model considering historical data input and output. Moreover, due to the dynamic nature of climatic conditions, the prediction of flood front time and location is basically complicated. Therefore, to simulate the complex mathematical expressions of physical processes and watershed behavior, data-driven modeling basically does not consider the physical mechanism of hydrological processes and aims to establish an optimal mathematical relationship between input and output data is more popular [3].

The classic black box hydrological time series data-driven forecasting model has a long tradition in flood models, which prediction methods assimilate measured climate and hydrometeorological parameters to provide better insights, including Auto-Regressive (AR) [4], Auto-Regressive and Moving Average (ARMA) [5], Auto-Regressive Integrated Moving Average (ARIMA) [6], Linear Regression (LR) [7], and Multiple Linear Regression (MLR) [8]. Compared with the physical model considering the computational cost and the large parameters the above models have certain advantages. However, it cannot deal well with the problems of non-stationarity and nonlinearity in the hydrological process.

In the past two decades, forecasting models using data-driven technology have made great progress in predicting and simulating the application of nonlinear hydrology and capturing noise in complex data sets. Classical data-driven modeling methods mainly include Artificial Neural Networks (ANN) [9–11], Support Vector Machines (SVM) [12–14], Adaptive Neuro-Fuzzy Inference Systems (ANFIS) [15,16], Wavelet Neural Networks (WNN) [17–19], Decision Tree (DT) [20,21], and Ensemble Prediction System (EPS) [22–25].

In recent years, hydrologists have been trying to use the artificial learning method based on deep learning to deal with this hydrological time series prediction task, and [26–28] have better performance. Among these deep learning-based methods, Long and short term memory (LSTM) Neural network can be used as data-driven models for describing the rainfall-runoff relationship and the performance is better than some commonly used conventional prediction models. The Gated Recurrent Unit (GRU) structure [29] was proposed in 2014. Analysis of the work of chung2014empirical, trofimovich2016comparison shows that GRU performance is comparable to LSTM, but its advantages are more computationally efficient and fewer parameters.

In this paper, based on the SVM and GRU models, we propose an incremental update method to forecast floods in small and medium watershed with data drift.

2   The Method of Prediction Model

2.1   Concept Drifts

In machine learning, the unexpected changes in data mining and predictive analysis of basic data over time are called concept drifts [35–38]. Concept drifts of Medium and small watershed due to changing of watercourse, new reservoir, human activities or they can be attributed to a complex nature of the environment. Usually, when the research data has a conceptual drift, there are several ways to deal with it. The first is based on resampling and adaptive sliding window selection samples, [38] uses a fixed-size sliding window for sample selection, which only retains the current trusted data window to solve the concept drift in the data stream, but This led to another problem, the sample selection of model training completely abandoned the old samples outside the time window. [39] proposed a "Adwin" method, which constructs a sliding window of different sizes to select the appropriate amount of training data to learn new concepts. Second, build by updating the weights of the submodels, such as [40] learning The key idea is to automatically adjust the window size, sample selection, and example weighting separately to minimize the estimated generalization error; third, recently, the dynamic classifier set, [41] proposes a new dynamic clustering forest to handle Concept drift in the emergence of time series, this new collection method aims to classify "new and old" data by combining multiple cluster trees.

2.2   Support Vector Machine Model

Support vector machine (SVM) models based on statistical learning theory can be used for pattern classification and nonlinear regression [42–45]. Literature [14] uses SVM to predict the groundwater level, the results show that the SVM water level prediction model is more accurate than the artificial neural network model. Moreover, [12] demonstrates that the SVM model works better in terms of uncertainty and is more predictive of extreme hydrological events. [46] Under the uncertainty of climate change scenarios, the SVR model estimates regional floods more accurately than the ANN model. [47] Processing real-time flood forecasting Using support vector machine to do single output, multi-output forecasting, and multi-step iteration strategy forecasting and other experimental schemes, the results show that the single-output scheme has the highest forecasting accuracy, and the multi-step iterative forecasting accuracy is the worst.

Based on the principle of structural risk minimization, SVM maps hydrological historical sample data from nonlinear regression in low-dimensional space to high-dimensional space by solving the flood forecasting problem that belongs to nonlinear regression. Then, the linear regression of high-dimensional space is further realized to correspond to the nonlinear regression of low-dimensional space. Given a historical flood sample datasets $D = \{(x_1, y_1), (x_2, y_2), \cdots, (x_l, y_l)\}$, where l denote sample number. The principle of flood forecasting is to find the mapping between input and output by training the sample datasets: $y = f(x)$. The basic idea of the SVM prediction is to learn a regression model so that $f(x)$ and y are as close as possible. The regression model is as follows:

$$f(x) = \omega\phi(x) + b \tag{1}$$

where $\phi(\cdot)$ denote the nonlinear mapping, ω is the wights, b is the bias. Suppose the support vector regression can allow a maximum deviation of ε between $f(x)$ and y, so the loss is calculated when the absolute value of the deviation between

$f(x)$ and y is greater than ε. As shown in Fig. 1, a strip of width 2ε is constructed on both sides of $f(x)$. When the training sample is within this space, the sample is predicted correctly.

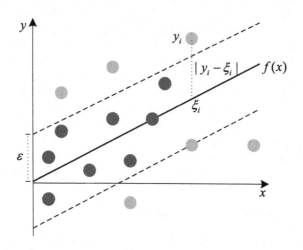

Fig. 1. Illustration of support vector machine.

2.3   Gated Recurrent Unit Model

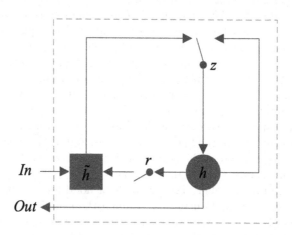

Fig. 2. Illustration of gated recurrent unit.

Recently, LSTM and GRU Recurrent Neural Networks (RNN) have proven to achieve the most advanced results in many time series applications (e.g., machine translation, and speech recognition). Their powerful predictive performance, ability to capture long-term time-dependent and variable-length observations are also advantageous in processing predictions in hydrological time series data. We use a GRU-based rapid flood forecasting model because it has higher computational efficiency and fewer parameters than LSTM. The structure of GRU is shown in Fig. 2. For a hidden unit, GRU has a update gate z and a reset gate r, z_t determine how much the previous state of the unit is updated to the current state at time t, r_t is used to forget the state of the previous calculation. z_t and r_t are calculated as follows

$$z_t = \sigma(W_z \mathrm{x}_t + U_z h_{t-1}) \tag{2}$$

$$r_t = \sigma(W_r \mathrm{x}_t + U_r h_{t-1}) \tag{3}$$

The activation h_t and candidate activation $\widetilde{h}_t$ of the GRU at time t are computed as follow

$$\widetilde{h}_t = tanh(W_h \mathrm{x}_t + U_h(r_t \odot h_{t-1})) \tag{4}$$

$$h_t = (1 - z_t)h_{t-1} + z_t \widetilde{h}_t \tag{5}$$

where matrices W_z, W_h, W_r, U_z, U_h, and U_r are model parameters.

3   Experiment

3.1   Datasets

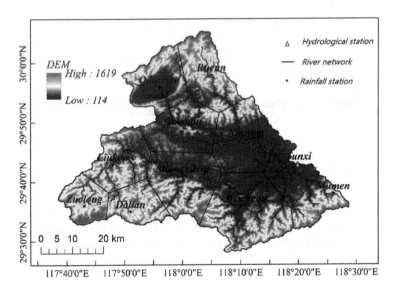

Fig. 3. Map of the study Tunxi watershed.

In this paper, our study used a datasets from 1981–2003 in Tunxi watershed, Anhui Province, China. As shown in Fig. 3, Tunxi hydrological station is located in the river outflow location of Tunxi watershed, and it monitors the flow and rainfall values. In addition, there are another 10 rainfall stations in the Tunxi watershed.

3.2 Model Forecasting Method

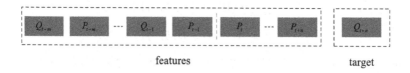

features   target

Fig. 4. Features and target of the forecasting model.

In order to improve the flood forecasting and early warning period in small and medium watershed, we use rainfall forecast information that is known in advance. As shown in Fig. 4, Our forecast target stream-flow Q_{t+n} is contributed by creatures previous rainfall $[P_{t-m} \cdots P_{t-1}]$, previous stream-flow $[Q_{t-m} \cdots Q_{t-1}]$, and forecast rainfall $[P_t \cdots P_{t+n}]$. Where Q_{t-m} denote actual measured stream-flow at time $t-m$, P_{t-m} denote actual measured area rainfall at time $t-m$, Q_{t+n} denote forecasted stream-flow at time $t+n$, P_{t+n} denote future area rainfall at time $t+n$, m denote m hours before the start of the forecast time t, n denote model forecast n hours.

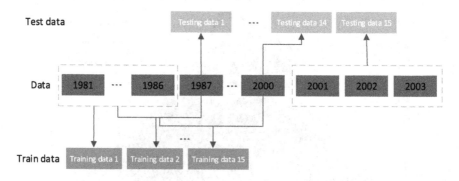

Fig. 5. Distribution of data training sets and test sets in Tunxi watershed. Data from the Tunxi watershed from 1981 to 2003, where the data from 1981 to 1986 was used as the first batch training data, and each subsequent year's data is added to the training set in batches. The data from 2001 to 2003 was used as the final batch testing data.

The training data and test data distribution method of adding our model is shown in Fig. 5. We first use the data from 1981–1986 as the training data for the initial model, We first use the data from 1981–1986 as the training data of the initial model, and then the data of each year was added to the training data. Testing data was also added in a similar way. The training model was updated as shown in Fig. 6. We feed the assigned training data to the corresponding training model, and then the training model is updated by the test error of the testing data. The training models 2–15 are updated in the same way. Finally, the prediction model performance is evaluated by the testing data 15.

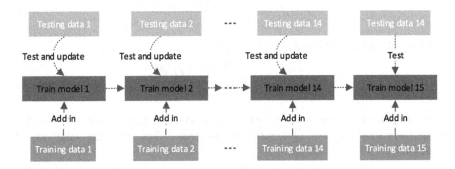

Fig. 6. The incremental update method of training model. First, the training data 1 was added to the training model 1, and then the training model 1 was tested by the testing data 1, and finally the training model 1 was updated to the training model 2 based on the error between the test result and the real value.

In this paper, we trained two types of data-driven models with incremental update capabilities using experimental data with conceptual drift. As a comparative experiment, we also trained two types of without using incremental update data driven models. The model is classified as follows

- **SVM:** The support vector machine model that does not use incremental updates.
- **SVM-IU:** The support vector machine model that use incremental updates.
- **GRU:** The gated recurrent unit model that does not use incremental updates..
- **GRU-IU:** The gated recurrent unit model that use incremental updates.

3.3   Model Performance Criteria

The average deviation between the flood forecast value and the actual value in the experiment is to be measured by the following four evaluation criteria. forecast error of the maximum flow value of a flood is calculated as

$$E_{Q,max} = \left| \frac{Q'_{max} - Q_{max}}{Q_{max}} \right| \times 100\% \qquad (6)$$

where Q'_{max} denote the peak value of a flood forecasting stream-flow, Q_{max} denote the recording peak value of a flood stream-flow.

Forecast error of the time when the peak of the flood occurs is calculated as

$$t_{max} = |t'_{max} - t_{max}| \tag{7}$$

where t'_{max} denote the moment of the predicted flow maximum, t_{max} denote the moment of the recording flow maximum.

Root mean square error is calculated as

$$RMSE = \sqrt{\frac{\sum_{i=1}^{N}(P_i - Q_i)^2}{N}} \tag{8}$$

Determination coefficient is calculated as

$$D_y = 1 - \frac{\sum_{i=1}^{N}(P_i - Q_i)^2}{\sum_{i=1}^{N}(P_i - \overline{Q})^2} \tag{9}$$

where P_i denote stream-flow recording value at time i, Q_i denote stream-flow prediction value at time i, $\overline{Q}$ denote average stream-flow recording value, and N is the number of test samples.

3.4 Results and Analysis

Table 1. Average performance criteria of the models.

Model	$E_{Q,max}(\%)$	$t_{max}(s)$	$RMSE$	$D_y(\%)$
SVM	25.21	2.88	421	71.32
SVM-IU	**15.38**	**1.58**	**255**	**81.65**
GRU	16.51	1.61	262	82.35
GRU-IU	**10.81**	**0.63**	**114**	**87.98**

In this section, we compare data-driven models under different training methods. To be fair, we present the best performance for each type of method under different parameter settings in Table 1. Moreover, the same kinds of model uses the same parameters for different update methods.

In terms of fast real-time flood stream-flow prediction, we propose four indicators to evaluate model performance. The predicted flood peak error $E_{Q,max}$ and the error at the moment of occurrence t_{max} are the most important indicators for hydrologists. SVM-IU shows 9.83% and 1.3 s improvements beyond SVM on $E_{Q,max}$ and t_{max}. GRU-IU shows 5.7% and 0.98 s improvements beyond GRU on $E_{Q,max}$ and t_{max}. In addition, $RMSE$ and D_y are the fitting performance of the evaluation prediction model. SVM-IU shows 166 and 10.33% improvements beyond SVM on $RMSE$ and D_y. GRU-IU shows 148 and 5.63% improvements beyond GRU on $RMSE$ and D_y. We conclude that the SVM improvement is higher than the GRU improvement after using incremental update training method.

A more clear illustrate of the real-time prediction performance of the models is shown in Fig. 7. The model using incremental training can more accurately predict the moment when the flood begins to rise and the highest point of flood stream-flow occurs.

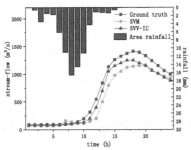
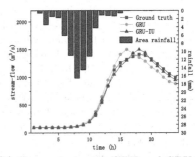

(a) Comparison with SVM and SVM-IU   (b) Comparison with GRU and GRU-IU

Fig. 7. Comparison with the ground truth stream-flow and predicted stream-flow computed by SVM and GRU model, where (a) shows a comparison of SVM models using incremental update and no using incremental update, (b) shows a comparison of GRU models using incremental update and no using incremental update.

4   Conclusion

In this paper, we propose a incremental update method based on SVM and GRU flood predict model in the Tunxi watershed with drift concept. In the proposed data-driven forecasting model with incremental updates, we construct training data and testing data in batches through the hydrological characteristics of small and medium watersheds. During training, we update the model based on the error of the small batch of test data on the initial model. Experiment results on the Tunxi dataset show the proposed method outperforms initially comparative methods and the effectiveness of the proposed incremental update model. In the future, our work includes the exploration on other hydrology purposes with the proposed method, such as flood submergence area warning and urban storm flooding.

References

1. Danso-Amoako, E., Scholz, M., Kalimeris, N., Yang, Q., Shao, J.: Predicting dam failure risk for sustainable flood retention basins: a generic case study for the wider greater manchester area. Comput. Environ. Urban Syst. **36**(5), 423–433 (2012)
2. Xie, K., Ozbay, K., Zhu, Y., Yang, H.: Evacuation zone modeling under climate change: a data-driven method. J. Infrastruct. Syst. **23**(4), 04017013 (2017)
3. Mosavi, A., Bathla, Y., Varkonyi-Koczy, A.: Predicting the future using web knowledge: state of the art survey. In: Luca, D., Sirghi, L., Costin, C. (eds.) INTER-ACADEMIA 2017. AISC, vol. 660, pp. 341–349. Springer, Cham (2018). https://doi.org/10.1007/978-3-319-67459-9_42

4. Salas, J.D.: Applied Modeling of Hydrologic Time Series. Water Resources Publication, Littleton (1980)

5. Valipour, M., Banihabib, M.E., Behbahani, S.M.R.: Parameters estimate of autoregressive moving average and autoregressive integrated moving average models and compare their ability for inflow forecasting. J. Math. Stat. **8**(3), 330–338 (2012)

6. Valipour, M., Banihabib, M.E., Behbahani, S.M.R.: Comparison of the ARMA, ARIMA, and the autoregressive artificial neural network models in forecasting the monthly inflow of Dez dam reservoir. J. Hydrol. **476**, 433–441 (2013)

7. Xinying, Y., Liong, S.-Y.: Forecasting of hydrologic time series with ridge regression in feature space. J. Hydrol. **332**(3–4), 290–302 (2007)

8. Adamowski, J., Chan, H.F., Prasher, S.O., Ozga-Zielinski, B., Sliusarieva, A.: Comparison of multiple linear and nonlinear regression, autoregressive integrated moving average, artificial neural network, and wavelet artificial neural network methods for urban water demand forecasting in Montreal, Canada. Water Resour. Res. **48**(1) (2012)

9. Tanty, R., Desmukh, T.S.: Application of artificial neural network in hydrology-a review. Int. J. Eng. Technol. Res **4**, 184–188 (2015)

10. Taormina, R., Chau, K.-W., Sethi, R.: Artificial neural network simulation of hourly groundwater levels in a coastal aquifer system of the Venice lagoon. Eng. Appl. Artif. Intell. **25**(8), 1670–1676 (2012)

11. Sulaiman, J., Wahab, S.H.: Heavy rainfall forecasting model using artificial neural network for flood prone area. In: Kim, K.J., Kim, H., Baek, N. (eds.) ICITS 2017. LNEE, vol. 449, pp. 68–76. Springer, Singapore (2018). https://doi.org/10.1007/978-981-10-6451-7_9

12. Nayak, M.A., Ghosh, S.: Prediction of extreme rainfall event using weather pattern recognition and support vector machine classifier. Theor. Appl. Climatol. **114**(3), 583–603 (2013). https://doi.org/10.1007/s00704-013-0867-3

13. Granata, F., Gargano, R., de Marinis, G.: Support vector regression for rainfall-runoff modeling in urban drainage: a comparison with the EPA's storm water management model. Water **8**(3), 69 (2016)

14. Gong, Y., Zhang, Y., Lan, S., Wang, H.: A comparative study of artificial neural networks, support vector machines and adaptive neuro fuzzy inference system for forecasting groundwater levels near Lake Okeechobee, Florida. Water Resour. Manage. **30**(1), 375–391 (2015). https://doi.org/10.1007/s11269-015-1167-8

15. Shu, C., Ouarda, T.B.M.J.: Regional flood frequency analysis at ungauged sites using the adaptive neuro-fuzzy inference system. J. Hydrol. **349**(1–2), 31–43 (2008)

16. Sharma, S., Srivastava, P., Fang, X., Kalin, L.: Performance comparison of adoptive neuro fuzzy inference system (ANFIS) with loading simulation program C++ (LSPC) model for streamflow simulation in El Niño Southern Oscillation (ENSO)-affected watershed. Expert Syst. Appl. **42**(4), 2213–2223 (2015)

17. Tiwari, M.K., Chatterjee, C.: Development of an accurate and reliable hourly flood forecasting model using wavelet-bootstrap-ANN (WBANN) hybrid approach. J. Hydrol. **394**(3–4), 458–470 (2010)

18. Augusto, C., Santos, G., Barbosa, G., da Silva, L.: Daily streamflow forecasting using a wavelet transform and artificial neural network hybrid models. Hydrol. Sci. J. **59**(2), 312–324 (2014)

19. Partal, T.: Wavelet regression and wavelet neural network models for forecasting monthly streamflow. J. Water Clim. Change **8**(1), 48–61 (2017)

20. Dehghani, M., Saghafian, B., Rivaz, F., Khodadadi, A.: Evaluation of dynamic regression and artificial neural networks models for real-time hydrological drought forecasting. Arab. J. Geosci. **10**(12), 1–13 (2017). https://doi.org/10.1007/s12517-017-2990-4

21. Choubin, B., Zehtabian, G., Azareh, A., Rafiei-Sardooi, E., Sajedi-Hosseini, F., Kişi, Ö.: Precipitation forecasting using classification and regression trees (CART) model: a comparative study of different approaches. Environ. Earth Sci. **77**(8), 1–13 (2018). https://doi.org/10.1007/s12665-018-7498-z

22. Sajedi-Hosseini, F., Malekian, A., Choubin, B., Rahmati, O., Cipullo, S., Coulon, F., Pradhan, B.: A novel machine learning-based approach for the risk assessment of nitrate groundwater contamination. Sci. Total Environ. **644**, 954–962 (2018)

23. Moore, K.J., Kurt, M., Eriten, M., McFarland, D.M., Bergman, L.A., Vakakis, A.F.: Wavelet-bounded empirical mode decomposition for measured time series analysis. Mech. Syst. Signal Process. **99**, 14–29 (2018)

24. Wang, W., Chau, K., Xu, D., Chen, X.-Y.: Improving forecasting accuracy of annual runoff time series using ARIMA Based on EEMD decomposition. Water Resour. Manage. **29**(8), 2655–2675 (2015). https://doi.org/10.1007/s11269-015-0962-6

25. Al-Musaylh, M.S., Deo, R.C., Li, Y., Adamowski, J.F.: Two-phase particle swarm optimized-support vector regression hybrid model integrated with improved empirical mode decomposition with adaptive noise for multiple-horizon electricity demand forecasting. Appl. Energy **217**, 422–439 (2018)

26. Bai, Y., Chen, Z., Xie, J., Li, C.: Daily reservoir inflow forecasting using multiscale deep feature learning with hybrid models. J. Hydrol. **532**, 193–206 (2016)

27. Liu, F., Xu, F., Yang, S.: A flood forecasting model based on deep learning algorithm via integrating stacked autoencoders with BP neural network. In: IEEE Third International Conference on Multimedia Big Data (BigMM), pp. 58–61. IEEE (2017)

28. Klotz, D., Kratzert, F., Herrnegger, M., Hochreiter, S., Klambauer, G.: Towards the quantification of uncertainty for deep learning based rainfall-runoff models (2019)

29. Cho, K., Van Merriënboer, B., Bahdanau, D., Bengio, Y.: On the properties of neural machine translation: encoder-decoder approaches. arXiv preprint arXiv:1409.1259 (2014)

30. Anderson, M.G.: Encyclopedia of Hydrological Sciences. Wiley, New York (2005)

31. Beven, K.J.: Rainfall-Runoff Modelling the Primer. Wiley, New York (2012)

32. Todini, E.: Rainfall-runoff models for real-time forecasting. In: Encyclopedia of Hydrological Sciences (2006)

33. Butts, M.P., Hoest Madsen, J., Refsgaard, J.C.: Hydrologic forecasting. In: Encyclopedia of Physical Science and Technology, pp. 547–566 (2003)

34. Sene, K.: Flash Floods: Forecasting and Warning. Springer, Dordrecht (2012). https://doi.org/10.1007/978-94-007-5164-4

35. Gama, J., Žliobaitė, I., Bifet, A., Pechenizkiy, M., Bouchachia, A.: A survey on concept drift adaptation. ACM Comput. Surv. (CSUR) **46**(4), 44 (2014)

36. Moreno-Torres, J.G., Raeder, T., Alaiz-RodríGuez, R., Chawla, N.V., Herrera, F.: A unifying view on dataset shift in classification. Pattern Recognit. **45**(1), 521–530 (2012)

37. Tsymbal, A.: The problem of concept drift: definitions and related work. Comput. Sci. Dept. Trinity Coll. Dublin **106**(2), 58 (2004)

38. Widmer, G., Kubat, M.: Learning in the presence of concept drift and hidden contexts. Mach. Learn. **23**(1), 69–101 (1996). https://doi.org/10.1023/A:1018046501280

39. Bifet, A., Gavalda, R.: Learning from time-changing data with adaptive windowing. In: Proceedings of the 2007 SIAM International Conference on Data Mining, pp. 443–448. SIAM (2007)

40. Klinkenberg, R.: Learning drifting concepts: example selection vs. example weighting. Intell. Data Anal. **8**(3), 281–300 (2004)

41. Song, G., Ye, Y., Zhang, H., Xu, X., Lau, R.Y.K., Liu, F.: Dynamic clustering forest: an ensemble framework to efficiently classify textual data stream with concept drift. Inform. Sci. **357**, 125–143 (2016)

42. Cortes, C., Vapnik, V.: Support-vector networks. Mach. Learn. **20**(3), 273–297 (1995). https://doi.org/10.1007/BF00994018

43. Collobert, R., Bengio, S.: SVMTorch: support vector machines for large-scale regression problems. J. Mach. Learn. Res. **1**, 143–160 (2001)

44. Tay, F.E.H., Cao, L.: Application of support vector machines in financial time series forecasting. Omega **29**(4), 309–317 (2001)

45. Pontil, M., Mukherjee, S., Girosi, F.: On the noise model of support vector machines regression. In: Arimura, H., Jain, S., Sharma, A. (eds.) ALT 2000. LNCS (LNAI), vol. 1968, pp. 316–324. Springer, Heidelberg (2000). https://doi.org/10.1007/3-540-40992-0_24

46. Dehghani, M., Saghafian, B., Nasiri Saleh, F., Farokhnia, A., Noori, R.: Uncertainty analysis of streamflow drought forecast using artificial neural networks and Monte-Carlo simulation. Int. J. Climatol. **34**(4), 1169–1180 (2014)

47. Bao, Y., Xiong, T., Zhongyi, H.: Multi-step-ahead time series prediction using multiple-output support vector regression. Neurocomputing **129**, 482–493 (2014)

A Survey on Dimension Reduction Algorithms in Big Data Visualization

Zheng Sun[1], Weiqing Xing[2], Wenjun Guo[1], Seungwook Kim[1], Hongze Li[1], Wenye Li[1], Jianru Wu[2], Yiwen Zhang[3], Bin Cheng[2(✉)], and Shenghui Cheng[1(✉)]

[1] Shenzhen Research Institute of Big Data and the Chinese University
of Hong Kong, Shenzhen, China
chengshenghui@cuhk.edu.cn
[2] Shenzhen Institute of Pharmacovigilance and Risk Management, Shenzhen, China
[3] Anhui University, Hefei, China

Abstract. In practical applications, the data set we deal with is typically high dimensional, which not only affects training speed but also makes it difficult for people to analyze and understand. It is known as "the curse of dimensionality". Therefore, dimensionality reduction plays a key role in the multidimensional data analysis. It can improve the performance of the model and assist people in understanding the structure of data. These methods are widely used in financial field, medical field e.g. adverse drug reactions and so on. In this paper, we present a number of dimension reduction algorithms and compare their strengths and shortcomings. For more details about these algorithms, please visit our Dagoo platform via www.dagoovis.com.

Keywords: High dimension · Dimension reduction · Radar map · Data visualization

1 Introduction

With the rapid development of society, the large amount of data is produced in various field daily and the big data sets with a few attributes are really hard for people to recognize its structure and important information, difficult to analyze and visualize as well, so the requirement of advanced technology in big data analysis is urgent since dimension reduction problem is a big concern [1]. The complexity and vastness of big data lead to the need for various dimensionality reduction algorithms [2] in the analysis process, and these methods are used to improve the performance of the operators of data analytics process [3], so choosing an appropriate dimensionality reduction method is crucial to analysis the big data set. As years' accumulation of data and analysis technologies, big data analysis and applications have entered into a new period. To visualize and analyze the big data set, reduce the dimension of data set and meanwhile preserve characteristics of original data as much as possible, a variety of algorithms is used to reduce dimensions

---

Z. Sun and W. Xing—Co-first author.

© ICST Institute for Computer Sciences, Social Informatics and Telecommunications Engineering 2020
Published by Springer Nature Switzerland AG 2020. All Rights Reserved
X. Zhang et al. (Eds.): CloudComp 2019/SmartGift 2019, LNICST 322, pp. 375–395, 2020.
https://doi.org/10.1007/978-3-030-48513-9_31

of big data set [4]. After applying the dimensionality reduction methods, the results are always much easier to analyze and get the relevant information.

Nowadays, no matter in which area, the data we deal with are always complex, which have a large volume of information with multiple attributes, and no longer simple to understand. That is why dimension reduction algorithms are so important since these algorithms are exactly used to reduce features when facing high dimensional data sets. So far, many dimension reduction methods have been proposed, like principle component analysis [5], local linear embedding and so on. In this paper, we are going to introduce several dimension reduction algorithms and apply a bunch of dimension reduction methods including Principle Component Analysis this kind of very common algorithm, and visualize the results of different methods with radar maps, which makes results easier to understand. We will analyze the performance of these algorithms, and then make a comparison of the performances of different algorithms applied, which is shown as in the Fig. 1.

Radar map, which is usually used in the financial field, it is also known as the spider map or the network map. We combine the visualization of different algorithms with the radar map, which is used as user portrait, it is a graphical method to display multivariable data in the form of a 2D map, which corresponds to parallel coordinate diagrams, helps us get to know the general information of any points after dimension reduction. The relative positions and angles of the axes in the maps are usually with no information.

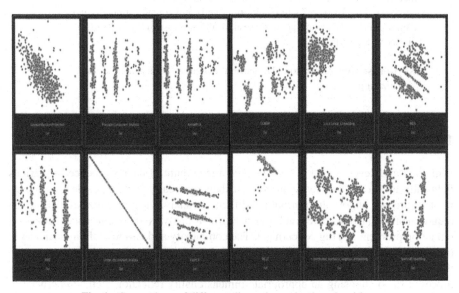

Fig. 1. Comparison of different dimension reduction algorithms

1.1 Problem Statement

The typical high dimensional data is represented as the data matrix X, with m data points and n dimensions.

$$X = \begin{bmatrix} x_{11} & x_{12} & \dots x_{1,n-1} & x_n \\ x_{21} & x_{22} & \dots x_{2,n-1} & x_{2n} \\ \dots & \dots & \dots & x_{3n} \\ x_{m-1,1} & x_{m-1,2} \dots & \dots & x_{m-1,n} \\ x_{m,1} & x_{m,2} & \dots & \dots & x_{mn} \end{bmatrix},$$

where x_{ij} is the value of i-th data point on j-th dimension.

$$X_i = [x_{i1}, x_{i2}, \dots, x_{in}] \text{ is a data point.}$$

The purpose of dimension reduction is to seek the lower dimensional data matrix $X'_{\{m \times p\}}$, where

$$\left\| X_i - X_j \right\| \approx \left\| X'_i - X'_j \right\|$$

Here, $p < n$ ensures the dimensions reduction. Typical p = 2.

1.2 Data Encoding

The most important function of the computer is to process information. The first problem needs to be solved is how to express, store and transfer information in the computer. Obviously, information in the computer can only be expressed, stored and transferred after being digitally encoded. There are various types of data, like numerical data, categorical data, image data, text data etc. These types of data are quite common, especially in medical field.

Taking Adverse Drug Reaction (ADR) as an example. ADR is caused by taking medication which is bad for people's health. ADRs may occur by a single or combined drugs. It is a typically "side effect" for our body, and the effects can be beneficial. It uses text data to show the levels like "good", "bad" or some feelings after medicine. The data they typically got are text data. Some text data can also be categorical data. Dimensional reduction can recover the correlations and co-existence among the drugs. During the dimensional reduction, the data should be numbers. For the text, if data is the serial text, it is easy to be encoded as a number. For example, if the text are "low", "middle", "high", we can encode them as 1, 2, 3 or some other numbers by the domain experts. For the texts which are not serial, we can use word2tec, Latent Semantic Analysis methods to encode them as numbers. After that, the text can be processed as numbers.

2 Typical Dimension Reduction Algorithms

First of all, a brief introduction of dimensionality reduction algorithms we use is given necessarily as the following: Random Projection is a powerful dimensionality method known for its simplicity and less erroneous output, including Gaussian Random Projection and Sparse Random Projection. Linear Discriminant Analysis (LDA) is similar to Principle Component Analysis (PCA), the difference is that the result of LDA is to project the data to different classifications, while PCA is to project the data to the highest similarity group. PCA, which synthesizes multiple indexes into a few independent comprehensive indexes, simplifies the problem to obtain more effective data information. PCA can maintain the maximum variance of the sample and greatly preserve the information of the original data set. Local Linear Embedding is the process of the dimension reduction of manifolds from high dimension to low dimension, consisting of Hessian LLE and Modified LLE. The LLE algorithm keeps the local linear embedding structure. Local Tangent Space Alignment (LTSA) is a kind of new manifold learning algorithm, which can effectively learn low-dimensional embedding coordinates from high-dimensional sampling data. Multidimensional Scaling (MDS) is a mean of the intuitive spatial map using points in multidimensional space to represent the perceptual and psychometric relationship. MDS method keeps the distances between sample points. Isometric Feature Mapping (ISOMAP) is similar to MDS, while the difference lies in the calculation of the distance matrix in the original space. It is a popular dimensionality reduction method for nonlinear data. ISOMAP method can keep the same geodesic distance approximately. Non-negative Matrix Factorization (NMF) makes all components of the decomposed matrix non-negative and realizing the non-linear dimensionality reduction. The NMF method preserves the information under non-negative constraints. Fast Independent Component Analysis is to extract original independent signals from mixed data. T-Distributed Stochastic Neighbor Embedding (t-SNE) is a non-linear method to reduce the dimension of high-dimensional data and can be visualized through points. Spectral Clustering uses the eigenvalues of the data similarity matrix to reduce dimensions. Figure 1 is the comparison of different dimension reduction algorithms which we are going to introduce in this paper, we can vividly see the differences between various methods from visualization graphs.

2.1 Gaussian Random Projection Algorithm

Gaussian random projection is a powerful method for dimensionality reduction. The general idea of Gaussian random projection is, for high dimension data X, Y, with dimension n, we can first produce a random matrix R, and then use these data to multiply the random matrix R to get a lower-dimensional data. The data from a mixture of k Gaussians can be projected into log k dimensions while maintaining the approximate level of separation between clusters. Controlling the dimension and distribution of the random projection matrix so as to retain the paired distance between any two samples of the data set, therefore, random projection is a suitable approximation technique for solving the distance-based problems, and also random projection makes original clusters more spherical although the original clusters are highly eccentric.

As shown in Fig. 2, it is the result of visualization of Gaussian random projection algorithm, the data set is from a poverty alleviation project of a county. We can vividly see that only one large cluster exists, so it is hard to figure out the differences between points in the graph, each point represents a person in the poverty alleviation project, except for a bunch of points, which we cannot get any details. Then we combine the visualization of Gaussian random projection with radar map, as we choose a small part from the visualization graph, the corresponding radar map will change as well to show a general situation of each attribute, for example, the points we choose in the graph on the right in Fig. 2 has a much higher level of education than the points we pick in the graph on the left.

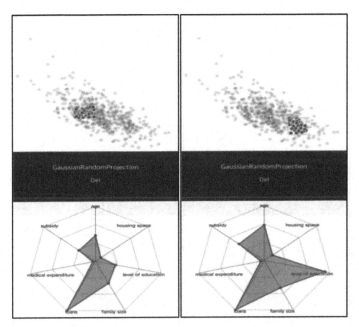

Fig. 2. Gaussian random projection (selected parts are in dark blue) (Color figure online)

The random projection can also be used in conjunction with the expectation-maximization (EM) algorithm easily, which is tested with experiments on synthetic data from a variety of Gaussian mixtures [6], EM algorithm with random projection can save a lot of time in dimension reduction.

2.2 Linear Dimension Reduction Algorithms

According to the relationship between high-dimensional space and low-dimensional space, dimension reduction algorithms can be divided into linear and nonlinear methods. The PCA algorithm and the LDA algorithm are the representative methods for linear dimension reduction algorithms.

Linear Discriminant Analysis Algorithm. LDA belongs to supervised learning, that is, for each given n-dimensional sample S, with a corresponding expected value or category label y. The idea of LDA is pretty simple, which projects or transforms the labeled data into lower dimensional space. In the lower dimensional space, homogeneous samples are as close as possible, while heterogeneous samples are as far as possible, which means that the points projected are grouped by category, clusters by clusters, points in the same cluster will be closer in the projected space. For LDA bi-classification problem, since only two categories exist, all samples will eventually be projected to the one-dimensional space. While for LDA multi-classification problem, for example, original data has C categories in n dimension, then problem comes that how to figure out the optimal method to project the original data to C-1 dimensional space.

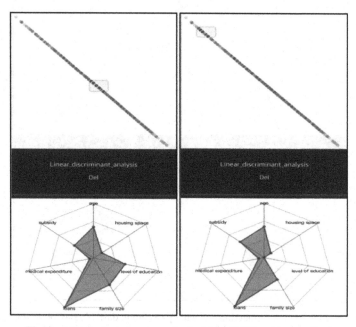

Fig. 3. LDA (selected parts are in dark blue) (Color figure online)

From Fig. 3, we can vividly see that all the points are projected on a straight line, while the selected points change along the line in the visualization graph, the corresponding radar map keep changing as well, then we can figure out the general tendency of different attributes along the line. LDA is well-known for feature extraction and dimension reduction, it is widely used in many areas like image classification [7] and face recognition [8]. Actually, in practical applications, the performance of the LDA algorithm is not that good compared with other algorithms in general, so it often used in conjunction with other algorithms, such as PCA+LDA.

Principle Component Analysis Algorithm. PCA belongs to unsupervised learning, which is probably most widely used dimension reduction algorithm [9] and the most popular multivariable statistical technique [10]. PCA is always used when the data is unlabeled, reduces the dimension of features and meanwhile maintains the features which contribute the most to the variance. Keeping lower-order principle components and ignoring high-order principle components, since lower-order components tend to retain the most important aspects of the data. PCA relies on the original data, the accuracy of the data has a great impact on the analysis results. The main idea of PCA is to get the principal components and their weights by the eigen decomposition of the covariance matrix. The pursuit of PCA is to preserve the internal information of data as much as possible after dimension reduction. The loss of information is minimized after the dimensions are reduced, since PCA does not classify information, while classification becomes more difficult.

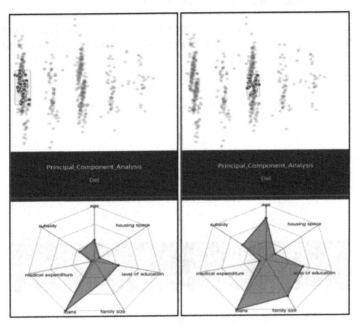

Fig. 4. PCA (selected parts are in dark blue) (Color figure online)

In Fig. 4, clusters can be easily distinguished from the visualization result of PCA, and according to the radar map, we can vividly see the differences between different clusters, and each clusters represent different groups of people. The third group of people are elder than the first group of people with higher subsidy and larger family size, and small housing space, low medical expenditure and high loans are kinds of common characteristics of the poor in this poverty alleviation project.

The LDA algorithm and the PCA algorithm are both linear dimension reduction methods, PCA is an algorithm closely related to LDA. Comparing these two methods, LDA is a supervised learning method, which considers classified information of data set, then the data can be classified in the low dimension space, which cut a lot of computation, while PCA is an unsupervised learning method, and does not take classified information into consideration. LDA pursues to make it easier to distinguish the data points after dimension reduction, and PCA aims to retain the information of data set. The number of dimensions after the LDA method is related to the number of categories, if the original data has n dimensions and c categories, then the dimensions after LDA are 1, 2,... and c−1. While the number of dimensions after the PCA algorithm is related to the data dimensions, if the original data has n dimensions, the dimensions after PCA are 1, 2,... and n dimension. The PCA projections on a coordinate system are orthogonal, while the LDA method does not guarantee that its projections are orthogonal on the coordinate system.

2.3 Nonlinear Dimension Reduction Algorithms

The representative methods of nonlinear dimension reduction methods are mainly kernel-based nonlinear dimension reduction algorithms like kernel PCA and manifold learning algorithms like ISOMAP and LLE.

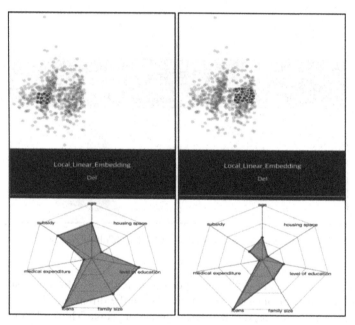

Fig. 5. LLE (selected parts are in dark blue) (Color figure online)

Local Linear Embedding Algorithm. LLE method is one of the Manifold learning algorithms, manifold learning is a kind of framework based on manifolds. Manifolds are abstract in the mathematical sense, but we can regard LLE manifold as an open surface. Dimension reduction algorithm based on manifolds is the process of reducing the dimension of manifolds from high dimension to low dimension, during this process, we hope that some characteristics in the high dimension of manifolds can be preserved. LLE [11] is a very important nonlinear dimensionality reduction method. Compared with traditional dimensionality methods like LDA and PCA, LLE focuses on maintaining local linear features of samples when reducing dimensions, since it, it is widely used in image recognition, data visualization, and other fields. The LLE algorithm is mainly divided into three steps. The first step is the process of finding the nearest neighbor of K, which uses the same method of finding the nearest neighbor as the K-Nearest Neighbor algorithm. The second step is to find the linear relation of K nearest neighbors for each sample and obtain the weight coefficient W of the linear relation. The third step is to use the weight coefficient to reconstruct the sample data in low dimension space.

According to Fig. 5, two clusters are very close to each other, but when we select the dense points of both clusters, the differences in radar maps are easily to tell, the age, subsidy and family size of the left selected points are much higher than them of right selected points.

The LLE algorithm is efficient, but it has some problems. For example, if the number of neighbors k is great than the dimension of input data, the weight matrix is not full rank. To solve such problems, modified locally linear embedding (MLLE) and Hessian-based locally linear embedding (HLLE) come into existence. For HLLE, it maintains the quadratic relationship of the local Hessian matrix instead of the local linear relationship [12]. For MLLE, it considers the distribution of the weight of neighbor while looking for k nearest neighbor, it hopes to find the neighbor weight distribution in the sample in all directions, rather than focusing on one side. LLE is simple to implement with small computational complexity, it can learn local linear low-dimensional manifolds of any dimension. While it has strict requirements in manifold distribution characteristics of data for example, it can not be a closed manifold, sparse data sets, non-uniformly distributed data sets and so on, which limit its application. The algorithm is sensitive to the selection of the nearest neighbor sample number, and different nearest neighbor numbers have a great impact on the final dimension reduction results.

Local Tangent Space Alignment Algorithm. LTSA is a manifold learning algorithm for nonlinear dimension reduction and mainly considers the local tangent space at each point to represent the geometric characteristics of the point [13, 14]. LTSA can be regarded as a kind of variation of LLE, which hopes to maintain local geometric relations of the data set, and meanwhile uses the technique of transition from local geometry to overall properties. The implementation steps for LTSA are as the following, the first step is neighborhood selection, for a sample point, k nearest neighbor points including itself are selected as neighbors. The second step is local linear fitting and the third step is local coordinates integration, the global coordinates are obtained by step by step calculation according to n local projections. Since the LTSA is linear and not implicit, it has a good effect on nonlinear manifolds dimension reduction.

The visualization result of LTSA method is shown in Fig. 6, almost all the points are centered on the bottom left, while only one point is on the bottom right. We select the only one point on the bottom right, and find its housing space is much larger than the average of other people's housing space.

Based on LSTA, linear LTSA(LLTSA), improved LTSA(ILTSA) and generalized ILTSA(GILTSA) are proposed in recent years to deal with the problem of increasing data set, also the new LSTA methods increase the overall accuracy compare to traditional LTSA algorithm.

LLE and LTSA are nonlinear methods that retain local properties, while MDS, ISOMAP, and kernel PCA are the nonlinear algorithms preserving global properties.

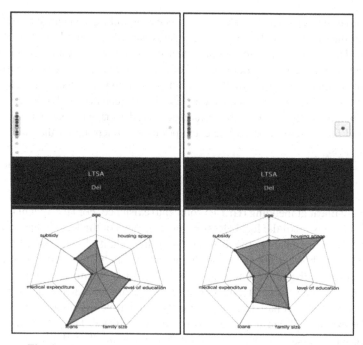

Fig. 6. LTSA (selected parts are in dark blue) (Color figure online)

Multidimensional Scaling Algorithm. MDS is a very traditional method of dimensionality reduction, which takes distance as the standard to project points in high dimensional coordinates to low dimensional coordinates, keeping the relative distance between each other with the minimum change [15–17]. Assuming that the distance matrix of the original high-dimensional data sample is Dh, and the distance matrix of the low-dimensional data sample is Dl, we can select the initial point by using the optimization algorithm, and use the gradient descent method to obtain the best approximation, so that ‖Dh-Dl‖ is the minimum. Meanwhile, we can also use the inner product to obtain the low-dimensional mapping. The former is prone to fall into local optimum when the sample size is large and the latter is stable, but the latter is worse than the former when the sample size is small. According to daily observation or data collection, many data features are not needed, while learning tasks may be limited to a low-dimensional distribution, which is a low-dimensional "embedding" in high-dimensional space. MDS algorithm is an effective low-dimensional embedding algorithm, which means to reduce the dimension of high-dimensional data on the premise that the distance between the original space and low-dimensional space samples is consistent. When applying MDS to data dimension reduction, the basic idea is to ensure that the distance of all data point pairs in low dimensional space is equal to the distance in high dimensional space. MDS uses the similarity between paired samples, aiming to use this information to construct an appropriate low-dimensional space, that is, the distance between samples in this space and the similarity between samples in high-dimensional space are consistent as far as possible. The MDS algorithm calculates the distance matrix for all n k-dimensional data through the distance function, which measures the distance in the original feature space, mainly Euclidean distance [18].

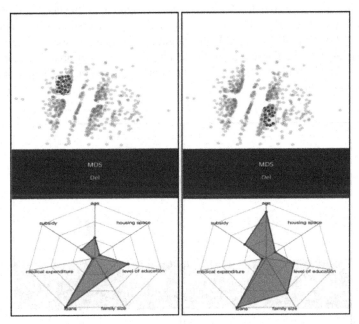

Fig. 7. MDS (selected parts are in dark blue) (Color figure online)

In Fig. 7, we select the top left cluster and the bottom right cluster to see the differences, from the radar map, we can see the housing space, medical expenditure and loan are in common, while the average age of the people in the bottom right cluster is much higher then it in the top left cluster, with relative higher subsidy and family size.

Isometric Feature Mapping Algorithm. ISOMAP is a manifold learning method, and it is used in nonlinear data dimensionality reduction. It is an unsupervised algorithm and its core algorithm is consistent with MDS, but the difference lies in the calculation of the distance matrix in the original space. Many data are nonlinear structure, which is not suitable for direct use of PCA. In a nonlinear data structure, two data points that are far apart on a manifold (geodesic distance) may be very close in a high-dimensional space (Euclidean distance). Only geodesic distance reflects the low-dimensional geometry of manifolds. ISOMAP is based on MDS [19] and retains the essential geometry of nonlinear data, which are geodesic distances between arbitrary point pairs [20]. The process of implementing the ISOMAP method is as the following. First, determining neighborhood for each data point, there are two methods, one is taking the nearest k points as neighbors, and another one is taking all the points in the circle with a selected radius as neighbors. Then we connect these points with edges manifold G build into a weighted flow diagram showing the relationship between adjacent G. Second, calculating the shortest path between all pairs to the geodesic distance matrix on the manifold,

Dijkstra algorithm can be used to calculate the shortest path. Finally, the distance matrix determined according to the shortest path is taken as the input of the MDS algorithm to obtain the data representation that best preserves the essential structure of manifolds in low-dimensional space. When calculating nearest neighbors, if the neighborhood range is specified to be large, then the distant points may be considered as nearest neighbors, causing a "short circuit" problem. If the neighborhood range is specified to be small, then some areas in the figure may not be connected with other areas, resulting in the "circuit breaking" problem. A short circuit or circuit break can mislead later calculations of the shortest path.

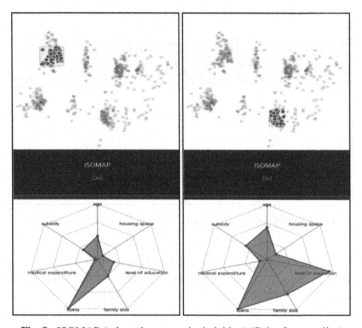

Fig. 8. ISOMAP (selected parts are in dark blue) (Color figure online)

From Fig. 8, the distances between clusters are much larger than the distances between clusters of MDS method. ISOMAP method seems to be more suitable for analyzing this data set than the methods above, since the points in the same cluster are close and the distances between clusters are large, the visualization result performs well.

Comparing ISOMAP with MDS, MDS reduces dimensions and keeps the distance between the samples at the same time, ISOMAP creates a graph by connecting each sample to its nearest neighbors and then tries to preserve the geodesic distance between the samples while lowering the dimension.

Kernel PCA Algorithm. People are able to know the kernel technique if getting to learn support vector machine before, which is to achieve nonlinear classification by using mathematical methods to add features similar to functions. A similar technique can be applied to PCA, allowing complex nonlinear projection dimensionality reduction, which is known as kernel PCA, a method for performing a nonlinear form of PCA [21]. This algorithm is good at maintaining the after-projection of clusters after clustering, and sometimes the expanded data is close to the distorted manifold. By using the kernel technique, we can calculate the similarity of vectors in two high-dimensional eigenspaces in the original eigenspace.

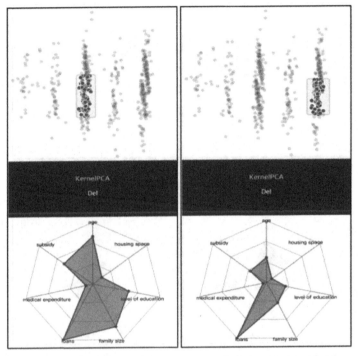

Fig. 9. Kernel PCA (selected parts are in dark blue) (Color figure online)

Kernel PCA is an improved version of PCA, which converts nonlinear, separable data to a new low-dimensional subspace suitable for linear classification of alignment, A kernel PCA can convert data to a high-dimensional space through nonlinear mapping, map it to another low-dimensional space in a high-dimensional space using PCA, and divide samples by a linear classifier. The disadvantage of this algorithm is the high computation cost. The kernel function is an important item in the kernel PCA algorithm, which measures the similarity between vectors by the dot product of two vectors. Common functions include the Gaussian kernel function, polynomial kernel, and hyperbolic tangent kernel.

Kernel PCA is realized in three steps: First, in order to calculate the similarity matrix, the value between any two samples needs to be calculated. Then the kernel matrix is aggregated to make the similarity matrix more clustered. After that, the eigenvalues of the aggregated similarity matrix are arranged in descending order, and the eigenvectors corresponding to the first k eigenvalues are selected, The vectors here are not principal component axes, but the samples are mapped to these axes.

The visualization result of kernel PCA which is shown in Fig. 4, is pretty similar to the result of PCA as shown in Fig. 9, the clusters are easily distinguished, while for the left two clusters, the distances between points in the same cluster are not that close to each other.

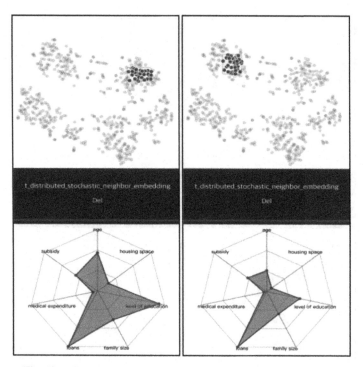

Fig. 10. t-SNE (selected parts are in dark blue) (Color figure online)

t-Distributed Stochastic Neighbor Embedding Algorithm. t-SNE algorithm was proposed by Laurens van der Maaten and Geoffrey Hinton in the year 2008 [22], it can effectively map high-dimensional data to low-dimensional space and maintain the local structure of data in high-dimension space. t-SNE algorithm is an extension of the SNE algorithm, the SNE method utilizes the distribution of adjacent data points of each data point for dimension reduction. When we talk about t-SNE, we should first know the idea of SNE, which is to express the similarity between points through conditional probability with high-dimensional data. t-SNE is an unsupervised dimension reduction method.

The reason for speaking of t-SNE is that in the deep learning test, visualization is needed to analyze the characteristics of the data, so as to know whether the interval between similar categories is small enough and the interval between different categories is large enough in the classification task [23]. t-SNE adopts the method of symmetric SNE for the distribution in high dimensions, while the distribution in low dimensions adopts the more general T distribution, which is also symmetric. The reason for using T distribution is that T distribution has a little bit taller and longer tail than the normal distribution, which helps the data to be distributed more evenly in two dimensions [24–26]. Although t-SNE greatly improves SNE, they have a very common problem, great time and energy consumption [27–30]. It is difficult to build the network and the gradient descent is too slow when the samples are large.

The visualization result of t-SNE algorithm is shown as Fig. 10, which is similar to the result of ISOMAP, shown in Fig. 8, however, the distance between clusters are smaller than them in the visualization result ISOMAP, and the distances between points in the same cluster of t-SNE method are larger than the distances between points in the same cluster of ISOMAP.

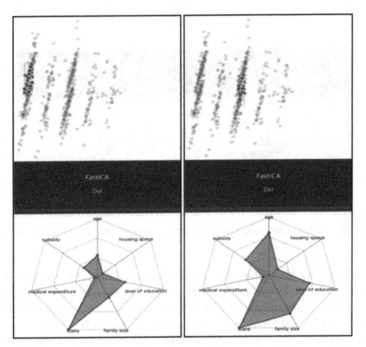

Fig. 11. Fast ICA (selected parts are in dark blue) (Color figure online)

Fast Independent Component Analysis Algorithm. Independent component analysis (ICA) is a linear transformation to calculate using statistical principle. ICA is divided into iterative algorithms based on information theory criteria and algebraic methods based on statistics, such as Fast ICA algorithm, Infomax algorithm, and maximum likelihood estimation algorithm and so on. Fast ICA algorithm, which is also known as a fixed-point algorithm [31], is a fast optimization iterative algorithm, which adopts batch processing, and each iteration involves a large number of sample data. Fast ICA is based on kurtosis, maximum likelihood, maximum negative entropy and so on.

From Fig. 11, the visualization result of Fast ICA is almost the same as the results of PCA and kernel PCA. We can see that the distances between points in the same cluster are much smaller than those in the results of PCA or kernel PCA, since the points in FastICA result only take about two-thirds of canvas, while the points in PCA and kernel PCA results almost spread all over the canvas.

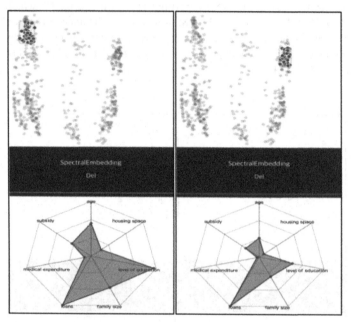

Fig. 12. Spectral Clustering (selected parts are in dark blue) (Color figure online)

Spectral Clustering Algorithm. In spectral clustering, the Laplacian matrix is used for dimension reduction. The general idea of Spectral clustering is that assuming the original matrix is A and infinite relation is 0, the resulting relation matrix is B, then we get diagonal matrix D, the diagonal is the sum of each row of B, and all other elements are 0. Then the Laplacian matrix can be obtained according to the formula, we reduce the dimension of the Laplacian matrix, which is the same as that of PCA, while this time, we are not going to get the eigenvector corresponding to the maximum eigenvalue, the minimum eigenvalue instead. Spectral clustering is simple to implement, but it is not obvious to figure out why it works and what it really does. To solve the problem, different versions of spectral clustering algorithm have been proposed [32, 33]. As one of the most popular modern clustering algorithms, spectral clustering has many applications in machine learning computer vision.

In Fig. 12, the visualization of spectral clustering is similar to the results of MDS, ISOMAP, while the distances between points in the same cluster are too large, so the performance of spectral clustering for analyzing this poverty alleviation data set is not that good as the performance of ISOMAP.

3   Display with the Original Data Set

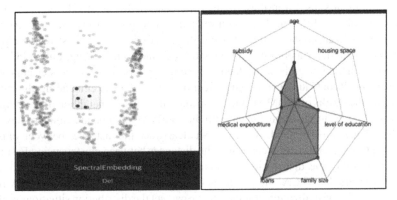

Fig. 13. Points selected

name	age	subsidy	medical expenditure	loans	family size	level of education	housing space
105.0	41	30472.02	10296.87	40000	5	1	75
178.0	55	52569.24	8596.67	40000	10	1	80
195.0	39	8897.77	2990.12	40000	3	1	80
220.0	46	26645.55	89614.8	40000	5	1	83
278.0	59	31037.16	45598.29	40000	10	1	90
296.0	48	10705	9072.87	40000	3	1	90

Fig. 14. Corresponding data of the selected points

We can not only get the general information from radar map, but also can vividly see the original data as we pick any parts of the visualization graph of different algorithms, as shown in Fig. 13 and Fig. 14. The original data set we use has multiple features, such as subsidy, loans, and family size, it is poverty alleviation data set for a county, and since the radar graph is especially suitable for giving a holistic evaluation for multivariable architecture, then we combine the different dimension reduction algorithms with radar map, once we pick an area from the visualization graph after using dimensionality reduction methods, then the radar map will vividly show the general information, and the original data corresponding to the selected area will be given automatically as well, which means that we can learn not only the general information after reducing dimension but also the characteristics of original data at the same time. Combining information before and after reducing dimensions, which makes these high-dimensional data set much easier to understand.

4 Conclusion

In this paper, we introduce and visualize some typical dimension reduction algorithms and make comparisons. From these figures, we can vividly see the differences of performance results of different dimension reduction algorithms using the same data set. From the visualization, the results of using PCA, kernel PCA and Fast ICA are pretty similar. For Gaussian random projection and local linear embedding, unlike PCA and t-distribution neighbor embedding having several clusters, just one cluster appears in each of the results of Gaussian random projection and local linear embedding algorithms. Comparing the results of ISOMAP and t-distribution stochastic neighbor embedding, the distances of nodes in the same cluster with the ISOMAP method are smaller than them with the t-distribution method. Also, we can clearly see the distances between clusters using the PCA algorithm are greater than the distances between clusters using Fast ICA.

We also study the distribution of points. For Fig. 15, we select a part from the visualization graph of PCA, the positions of the same points we pick in PCA will be displayed in other visualization graphs, and we can get the distribution situations of these points in the graph of other algorithms. We pick a small part from the same cluster in the graph of PCA, and we can see that these points are almost in the same cluster in the graph of other algorithms, for LLE, there are not many clear clusters, but we can also see these points distribute closely.

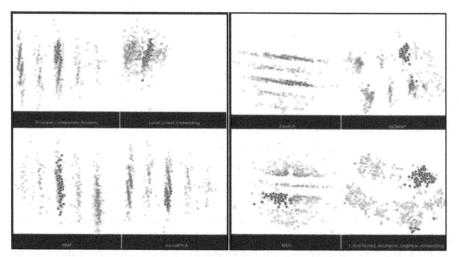

Fig. 15. Distribution of the same points with different algorithms (selected parts are in dark blue) (Color figure online)

In general, we cover 11 dimension reduction algorithms, which are introduced in detail above, while in fact, we actually study more than these, we do not give detailed introduce in this paper, like Modified LLE in Fig. 1. Just comparing the introduced algorithms, we can learn the differences between these methods. For example, although the random projection method sacrifices some accuracy, it greatly reduces the computation.

Table 1. The comparison table of different algorithms

Algorithm	Advantages	Disadvantages	Attributes
Random projection	Greatly reduce computation.	Sacrifice some accuracy	
LDA	Compared with the ambiguity of PCA, its purpose is more clear, and it can reflect the differences between samples better	Limited by types of samples; The maximum number of dimensions of the projection space is C-1 (the original data has C categories)	Supervised learning; Linear
PCA	The concept is simple; Minimum error; The main information is extracted	Calculate co-variance matrix causes large calculation; When gross corruption exists, PCA cannot grasp the real subspace structure of data	Unsupervised learning; Linear
LLE	Can process and analyze nonlinear signals; The selection of parameters is few, so the characteristic parameters can be optimized better	Require dense sampling; Embedding dimension and noise in the signal will affect the performance of dimension reduction in high-dimension space	Unsupervised learning; Nonlinear
LTSA	Reflect the local geometric features of manifolds	Not suitable for processing data sources with high curvature distribution and sparse distribution	Manifold learning; Nonlinear
MDS	Retain the relative relation of original data well	Cannot deal with high-dimensional nonlinear data	Nonlinear; Unsupervised
ISOMAP	Suitable for the internal flat low-dimensional manifold	Not suitable for the manifolds with large intrinsic curvature	Manifold learning; Unsupervised
NMF	Wide range of Applications	The choice of K is ambiguous; NMF training takes time	Nonlinear; Unsupervised
Fast ICA	Fast convergence; Simple and effective	Kurtosis value can only be estimated from the measured sample	Nonlinear; Unsupervised
t-SNE	Very useful for reducing high-dimensional data to 2D or 3D	High computational complexity; The global structure is not explicitly retained	Manifold learning; Unsupervised
Spectral clustering	Effective for sparse data	Rely on similarity matrix, different matrices cause various results	Nonlinear; Unsupervised

t-SNE has high computational complexity, it is very useful for reducing high-dimensional data to 2D or 3D. The following comparison Table 1 is a summary of the advantages and shortages of various typical dimension reduction algorithms. For more details, please visit our Dagoo platform [34]. Dimensional reduction is a typical method that aims to find the features and patterns in the high dimensional space. These methods have wide applications in financial field, medical field e.g. ADR.

Funding Acknowledgement. This paper is support by the Program for Guangdong Introducing Innovative and Enterpreneurial Teams (Grant No.: 2017ZT07X183), the Pearl River Talent Recruitment Program Innovative and Entrepreneurial Teams in 2017 (Grant No.: 2017-ZT07X152), the Shenzhen Fundamental Research Fund (Grants No.: JCYJ20170306141038939, KQJSCX20170728162302784, KQTD2015033114415450 and ZDSYS201707251409055), and Department of Science and Technology of Guangdong Province Fund(2018B030338001), and Shenzhen Science and Technology Innovation Committe, (Basic Research (Free Exploration No.: CYJ20170818104824165).

References

1. Song, L., Ma, H., Wu, M., Zhou, Z., Fu, M.: A brief survey of dimension reduction. In: Peng, Y., Yu, K., Lu, J., Jiang, X. (eds.) IScIDE 2018. LNCS, vol. 11266, pp. 189–200. Springer, Cham (2018). https://doi.org/10.1007/978-3-030-02698-1_17
2. Fodor, I.K.: A Survey of Dimension Reduction Techniques. No. UCRL-ID-148494. Lawrence Livermore National Lab., CA, US (2002)
3. Tsai, C.-W., et al.: Big data analytics: a survey. J. Big Data 2(1), 21 (2015)
4. Engel, D., Hüttenberger, L., Hamann, B.: A survey of dimension reduction methods for high-dimensional data analysis and visualization. In: Visualization of Large and Unstructured Data Sets: Applications in Geospatial Planning, Modeling and Engineering-Proceedings of IRTG 1131 Workshop 2011. Schloss Dagstuhl-Leibniz-Zentrum fuer Informatik (2012)
5. Zhang, T., Yang, B.: Big data dimension reduction using PCA. In: 2016 IEEE International Conference on Smart Cloud (SmartCloud). IEEE (2016)
6. Brigham, E.: Random projection in dimension reduction: applications to image and text data. In: ACM SIGKDD ICKDDM (2001)
7. Ye, F., Shi, Z., Shi, Z.: A comparative study of PCA, LDA and kernel LDA for image classification. In: 2009 International Symposium on Ubiquitous Virtual Reality, Gwangju, pp. 51–54 (2009)
8. Lu, J., Plataniotis, K.N., Venetsanopoulos, A.N.: Face recognition using LDA-based algorithms. IEEE Trans. Neural Networks 14(1), 195–200 (2003)
9. Jolliffe, I.: Principal Component Analysis. Springer, Berlin Heidelberg (2011). https://doi.org/10.1007/b98835
10. Abdi, H., Williams, L.J.: Principal component analysis. Wiley Interdisc. Rev. Comput. Stat. 2(4), 433–459 (2010)
11. Roweis, S.T., Lawrence, K.S.: Nonlinear dimensionality reduction by locally linear embedding. Science 290(5500), 2323–2326 (2000)
12. Dou, J., Qin, Q., Tu, Z.: Robust edit propagation based on Hessian local linear embedding. In: 2017 29th Chinese Control and Decision Conference (CCDC), Chongqing, pp. 3336–3339 (2017)
13. Zhang, Z., Zha, H.: Nonlinear dimension reduction via local tangent space alignment. In: Liu, J., Cheung, Y.-m., Yin, H. (eds.) IDEAL 2003. LNCS, vol. 2690, pp. 477–481. Springer, Heidelberg (2003). https://doi.org/10.1007/978-3-540-45080-1_66

14. Yang, G., Xu, X., Zhang, J.: Manifold alignment via local tangent space alignment. In: 2008 International Conference on Computer Science and Software Engineering, Hubei, pp. 928–931 (2008)
15. Cox, T.F., Cox, M.A.A.: Multidimensional Scaling. Chapman and hall/CRC, Boca Raton (2000)
16. Borg, I., Groenen, P.: Modern multidimensional scaling: theory and applications. J. Educ. Meas. **40**(3), 277–280 (2003)
17. Kruskal, J.B., Wish, M.: Multidimensional Scaling, vol. 11. Sage, London (1978)
18. Li, Y.: Locally multidimensional scaling for nonlinear dimensionality reduction. In: 18th International Conference on Pattern Recognition (ICPR'06), Hong Kong, pp. 202–205 (2006)
19. Bengio, Y., et al.: Out-of-sample extensions for LLE, Isomap, MDS, Eigenmaps, and spectral clustering. In: Advances in Neural Information Processing Systems (2004)
20. Fan, M., et al.: Isometric multi-manifold learning for feature extraction. In: 2012 IEEE 12th International Conference on Data Mining. IEEE (2012)
21. Schölkopf, B., Smola, A., Müller, K.-R.: Kernel principal component analysis. In: Gerstner, W., Germond, A., Hasler, M., Nicoud, J.-D. (eds.) ICANN 1997. LNCS, vol. 1327, pp. 583–588. Springer, Heidelberg (1997). https://doi.org/10.1007/BFb0020217
22. Maaten, L., Hinton, G.: Visualizing data using t-SNE. J. Mach. Learn. Res. **9**, 2579–2605 (2008)
23. Mounce, S.: Visualizing smart water meter dataset clustering with parametric t-distribution stochastic neighbor embedding. In: 2017 13th International Conference on Natural Computation, Fuzzy System and Knowledge Discovery (ICNC FSKD), Guilin, pp. 1940–1945 (2017)
24. Cheng, S., Zhong, W., Isaacs, K.E., Mueller, K.: Visualizing the topology and data traffic of multi-dimensional torus interconnect networks. IEEE Access **6**, 57191–57204 (2018)
25. Cheng, S., Xu, W., Mueller, K.: RadViz Deluxe: a component-aware display for multivariate chemical data. Processes **5**(4), 75 (2017)
26. Cheng, S., Mueller, K.: The data context map: fusing data and attributes into a unified display. IEEE Trans. Visual Comput. Graphics **22**(1), 121–130 (2016)
27. Cheng, S., Mueller, K., Xu, W.: A framework to visualize temporal behavioral relationships in streaming multivariate data. In: New York Scientific Data Summit, pp. 1–10, New York, August 2016
28. Cheng, S., Mueller, K.: Improving the fidelity of contextual data layouts using a generalized Barycentric coordinates framework. In: 2015 IEEE Pacific Visualization Symposium (PacificVis), pp. 295–302 (2015)
29. Cheng, S., De, P., Jiang, S.H., Mueller, K.: TorusVis^ND: unraveling high-dimensional torus networks for network traffic visualizations. In: First Workshop on Visual Performance Analysis, pp. 9–16 (2014)
30. Cheng, S., Xu, W., Mueller, K.: ColorMapND: a data-driven approach and tool for mapping multivariate data to color. IEEE Trans. Visual Comput. Graphics **25**(2), 1361–1377 (2019)
31. Spurek, P., Jacek, T., Śmieja, M.: Fast independent component analysis algorithm with a simple closed-form solution. Knowl.-Based Syst. **161**, 26–34 (2018)
32. Ng, A.Y., Jordan, M.I., Weiss, Y.: On spectral clustering: analysis and an algorithm. In: Advances in Neural Information Processing Systems (2002)
33. Von Luxburg, U.: A tutorial on spectral clustering. Stat. Comput. **17**(4), 395–416 (2007)
34. Cheng, S., et al.: Dagoo – A platform for big data visualization (2018). http://www.dagoovis.com

Quantum Searchable Encryption for Cloud Data Based on Delegating Quantum Computing

Yinsong Xu[1]([⊠]), Wenjie Liu[1,2], Junxiu Chen[1], and Lian Tong[3]

[1] School of Computer and Software, Nanjing University of Information Science
and Technology, Nanjing 210044, People's Republic of China
mugongxys@foxmail.com, wenjiel@163.com, cjxccc981@163.com
[2] Jiangsu Engineering Center of Network Monitoring, Nanjing University of
Information Science and Technology, Nanjing 210044, People's Republic of China
[3] School of Information Engineering, Jiangsu Maritime Institute, Nanjing 211100,
People's Republic of China
dianxin040204nv@126.com

Abstract. Based on delegating quantum computing (DQC), a DQC model that adapts to multi-qubit and composite quantum circuits is given firstly. In this model, the single client with limited quantum ability can give her encrypted data to a powerful but untrusted quantum data server and let the data server computes over the encrypted data without decryption, where the computation is a quantum circuit composed of multiple quantum gates. Then, the client generates the decryption key to decrypt the computing result according to the circuit of computation. However, this model cannot meet the situation of multi-client accessing or computing encrypted cloud data in the cloud environment. To solve this problem, we let the client outsource key generation to a trusted key server, which composes the quantum cloud center with the data server. The clients only perform X and Z operation according to the encryption or decryption key. Then, combined with Grover algorithm, a quantum searchable encryption scheme for cloud data based on delegating quantum computing is proposed in this paper. The data server mainly uses Grover algorithm to perform search computation on the encrypted data. Moreover, a concrete example of our scheme is discussed next, where the data server searches for 2 target items from 8 items of the encrypted data. Finally, security of our proposed scheme is analysed, which can protect the security of the data.

This work was supported by the National Natural Science Foundation of China under Grant 61672290, Grant 71461005, and Grand 61802002, in part by the Natural Science Foundation of Jiangsu Province under Grant BK20171458, in part by the Natural Science Foundation of Jiangsu Higher Education Institutions under Grant 19KJB520028, and in part by the Priority Academic Program Development of Jiangsu Higher Education Institutions (PAPD).

X. Zhang et al. (Eds.): CloudComp 2019/SmartGift 2019, LNICST 322, pp. 396–409, 2020.
https://doi.org/10.1007/978-3-030-48513-9_32

Keywords: Quantum searchable encryption · Delegating quantum computing · Untrusted data server · Trusted key server · Grover algorithm

1   Introduction

In recent years, cloud computing has achieved great development both in academic and industry communities as it provides economic and convenient service, which can recommend to people what they want [1,2], provide energy saving solutions [3,4], and so on. And now more and more clients are planning to upload their data onto the public clouds. However, data stored in the cloud server may suffer from malicious use by cloud service providers. Considering data privacy and security, it is a recommended practice for data owners to encrypt data before uploading onto the cloud [5,6]. Therefore, an efficient search technique for encrypted data is extremely urgent.

A popular way to search over encrypted data is searchable encryption (SE). The first searchable encryption was proposed by Song *et al.* [7]. This scheme uses stream ciphers and pseudo-random functions to implement ciphertext retrieval, but it also has a series of problems, such as low search efficiency and data privacy. Therefore, Goh [8] built a index structure based on the Bloom filter to achieve fast retrieval of ciphertext data. However, the Bloom filter itself has a certain error rate, and the result returned by the cloud server to the data user may not be accurate. Besides, Curtmola *et al.* [9] and Boneh *et al.* [10] use the idea of "keyword-file" to construct a symmetric searchable encryption scheme and a public key search able encryption scheme, respectively. Both schemes have significant improvements in safety and efficiency. Nowadays, many researchers have tried to use kNN algorithm [11], user interest model [12], blockchain technology [13], and so on, to improve the search efficiency and data privacy.

On the other hand, in the field of quantum computation, to protect the privacy of client's data, many researchers have proposed a novel model of quantum computation: blind quantum computation (BQC), where the client with limited quantum resources can perform quantum computation by delegating the computation to an untrusted quantum server, and the privacy of the client can still be guaranteed. BQC can be generally divided into two categories: one is the measurement-based blind quantum computation (MBQC), and the other is the circuit-based blind quantum computation (CBQC). In MBQC, measurement is the main driving force of computation, which follows the principle of "entangle-measure-correct", and a certain number of quantum qubits are entangled to form a standard graph state [14,15]. Different from MBQC, CBQC is based on the quantum circuit that is composed of many kinds of quantum gates [16–19]. Among them, Fisher [18] and Broadbent [19] firstly proposed a representative CBQC model: delegating quantum computation (DQC). In their protocols, an untrusted server can perform arbitrary quantum computations on encrypted quantum bits (qubits) without learning any information about the inputs, where the quantum computations are implemented by a universal set of quantum gates $(X, Z, H, S, T, CNOT)$. And then the client can easily decrypt the results of the computation with the decryption key. However, since Fisher and Broadbent only considered two parties, Kashefi *et al.* [20] proposes a multi-party delegated quantum computing protocol later. But, this protocol is actually under the measurement-based quantum computing framework, which belongs to MBQC and is not DQC.

In order to implement multiclient DQC, i.e., different clients can store or search their data in the quantum cloud center, we propose a quantum search-able encryption scheme for cloud data based on delegating quantum computing. Our scheme has five components: encryption key generation, encryption, search, decryption key generation and decryption. Clients firstly use X and Z gates to encrypt their data with the encryption keys, where the encryption keys are gen-erated by the key server, and then send the encrypted data to the data server. The data server performs search computation (i.e., Grover algorithm) on the encrypted data if other clients need, where the search computation are imple-mented by a universal set of quantum gates $(X, Z, H, S, T, CNOT)$. During the search computation, the data server assists the key server to generate decryption keys. Finally, the clients who need the search result from the data server, also use X and Z gates to decrypt the encrypted search result with the decryption keys from the key server.

The rest of the paper is organized as follows. Section 2 provides some pre-liminary knowledge about quantum computation and how to perform quantum computing on encrypted qubit. Then, a quantum searchable encryption scheme for cloud data based on delegating quantum computing is proposed in Sect. 5. Moreover, we give a concrete example that use Grover algorithm to search on encrypted 2-qubit state in Sect. 4. And security analysis is discussed in Sect. 5. Finally, Sect. 6 gives conclusion of this paper.

2   Preliminaries

2.1   Quantum Computation

As we know, the bit is the fundamental concept of classical information, and has a state, either 0 or 1. Similar to the classical bit, the quantum bit (called qubit) [21] is the basic unit of quantum information and has two possible states $|0\rangle$ and $|1\rangle$, which is often referred to as quantum superposition state,

$$|\varphi\rangle = \alpha |0\rangle + \beta |1\rangle, \tag{1}$$

where α, β are complex numbers, and $|\alpha|^2 + |\beta|^2 = 1$. $|0\rangle$ and $|1\rangle$ can be repre-sented by vectors,

$$|0\rangle = \begin{bmatrix} 1 \\ 0 \end{bmatrix}, \qquad |1\rangle = \begin{bmatrix} 0 \\ 1 \end{bmatrix}. \tag{2}$$

Then, $|\varphi\rangle$ can be expressed in vector form $|\varphi\rangle = \left(\begin{smallmatrix} \alpha \\ \beta \end{smallmatrix}\right)$.

Analogous to the way that a classical computer is built from an electrical circuit containing wires and logic gates, a quantum computer is built from a quantum circuit containing wires and elementary quantum gates to carry around and manipulate the quantum information. Single-qubit gates, such as *Pauli-X*, *Pauli-Z*, H (*Hadamard*), S and T are the simplest form of quantum gates, and they can be described as 2×2 unitary matrices as below,

$$X = \begin{bmatrix} 0 & 1 \\ 1 & 0 \end{bmatrix}, \quad Z = \begin{bmatrix} 1 & 0 \\ 0 & -1 \end{bmatrix}, \quad H = \frac{1}{\sqrt{2}} \begin{bmatrix} 1 & 1 \\ 1 & -1 \end{bmatrix}, \quad S = \begin{bmatrix} 1 & 0 \\ 0 & i \end{bmatrix}, \quad T = \begin{bmatrix} 1 & 0 \\ 0 & e^{i\pi/4} \end{bmatrix}. \tag{3}$$

Multi-qubit gates are also the important units in a quantum circuit. The prototypical multi-qubit quantum logic gate is *controlled-NOT* (i.e., $CNOT$) gate (shown in Fig. 1), which has two input qubits, known as the control qubit and the target qubit, respectively. If the control qubit is set to 0, then the target qubit is left alone. If the control qubit is set to 1, then the target qubit is flipped.

$$CNOT = \begin{bmatrix} 1 & 0 & 0 & 0 \\ 0 & 1 & 0 & 0 \\ 0 & 0 & 0 & 1 \\ 0 & 0 & 1 & 0 \end{bmatrix}$$

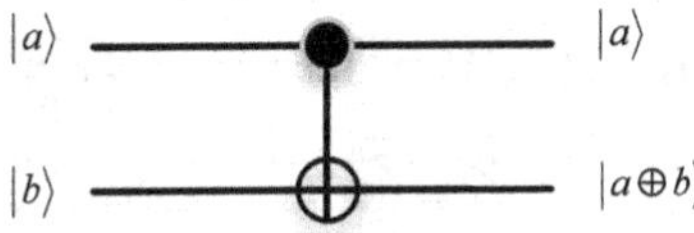

Fig. 1. Matrix representation and quantum circuit of $CNOT$ gate.

2.2 Delegating Quantum Computing

This delegating quantum computing (DQC) scheme was firstly proposed by Fisher [18] and Broadbent [19]. It (see Fig. 2a) starts with a client who has quantum information that needs to be sent to a remote server for processing. The client first encrypts one input qubit $|\psi\rangle$ and sends it to a quantum server, who performs a computation U on the encrypted qubit. The server returns the state which the client decrypts to get $U |\psi\rangle$.

In the scheme, to encrypt a qubit $|\psi\rangle$, a client applies a combination of Pauli X and Z operations to get a encrypted qubit $X^a Z^b |\psi\rangle$, where $a, b \in \{0, 1\}$ (as well as $c, d \in \{0, 1\}$ for the $CNOT$ gate in Fig. 2f). Then, the server perform quantum computing U, which is composed of unitary operations from the Clifford group $\{X, Z, H, S, CNOT\}$ and one additional non-Clifford gate, T gate. As shown in Fig. 2b-f, when $U \in \{X, Z, H, S, CNOT\}$, clifford gates do not require any additional resources, and decryption is straightforward. However, when $U = T$ (see Fig. 2g), the server requires the client to send an auxiliary qubit $Z^d P^y |+\rangle$, where $y, d \in \{0, 1\}$. to control a $CNOT$ gate with the encrypted qubit. The server measures the encrypted qubit and outcome $c \in \{0, 1\}$ is returned to the client, which is used in decryption. The client sends a single classical bit, $x = a \oplus y$, to control a S gate on the auxiliary qubit, which is returned to the client as $X^{a''} Z^{b''} R |\psi\rangle$, where $a'' = a \oplus c$ and $b'' = a(c \oplus y \oplus 1) \oplus b \oplus d \oplus y$.

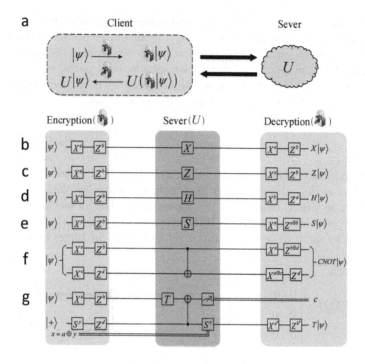

Fig. 2. Protocol for delegating quantum computing

3   Quantum Searchable Encryption for Cloud Data Based on Delegating Quantum Computing

In this section, we firstly give a simple multi-qubit DQC model, which only contains two parties: client and single server.

3.1   A Multi-qubit DQC Model

Suppose the client *Alice* wants the single server *Bob* to search over her encrypted data. The basic process of this model is given as below, and the frequently used variables and notations are listed in Table 1.

1. *Alice* should encrypt the data with Pauli operators $\{X, Z\}$ depending on a classical encryption key $ek = (x_0, z_0)$, and send it to *Bob*.
2. When *Bob* performs search computation on the encrypted data, *Alice* computes the decryption key for the encrypted data, where the search computation is generally composed of a set of unitary gates $\{X, Z, H, S, T, CNOT\}$ in the quantum circuit. For the sake of clarity, the decryption key generation rules for arbitrary unitary transforms $\{X, Z, H, S, T, CNOT\}$ in the circuit are combed in Algorithm 1.

3. *Alice* also only needs to decrypt the search result with X and Z gates depending on the decryption key.

Table 1. Explanations for frequently used variables and notations.

Variables and notations	Explanations
$\mathbb{N}$, $\mathbb{N}^+$	$\mathbb{N} = \{0, 1, 2, \cdots\}$ is a set of non-negative integers, and $\mathbb{N}^+ = \{1, 2, 3, \cdots\}$ is a set of positive integers
M, m, $n(m, n \in \mathbb{N}^+)$	$M = 2^m$ is the number of items to be searched, and each item $data(j)$ contains data of n bits, where $j \in \{0, 1, 2, \cdots, M-1\}$
ek, dk, sk	ek and dk are $2n$-bit encryption and $2n$-bit decryption keys, respectively, for Alice's data. dk is encrypted with sk
$x_r(k)$, $z_r(k)(r \in \mathbb{N}^+, k \in \mathbb{N})$	(x_r, z_r) is the $2n$-bit intermediate key of the rth round in Algorithm 1; $ek = (x_0, z_0)$; $x_r(k)$ is the kth bit of x_r and $z_r(k)$ is the kth bit of z_r
ζ	$\zeta = \{I, X, Z, H, S, T, CNOT\}$
X_i, Z_i, H_i, S_i, T_i, $CNOT_{i,l}$	X_i, Z_i, H_i, S_i, or T_i denotes applying a X, Z, H, S or T gate on the ith qubit of the input state and letting the other qubits unchanged; $CNOT_{i,l}$ denotes performing a $CNOT$ gate on the ith and l^{th} qubits of the input, which act as the control and target qubits, respectively

Algorithm 1. (decryption key generation rules for arbitrary unitary transform in ζ). Suppose $|\psi\rangle$ is an n-qubit quantum state, U is an n-qubit unitary transform composed of gates from the universal gate set ζ, and G represents any one gate of ζ. Let $ek = (x_0, z_0)$ and $U_0 = \otimes_{k=1}^n I$, the encrypted quantum state $(\otimes_{k=1}^n X^{x_0(k)} Z^{z_0(k)}) |\psi\rangle$ is equivalent to $U_0(\otimes_{k=1}^n X^{x_0(k)} Z^{z_0(k)}) |\psi\rangle$; the updated decryption key $dk_{r+1} = (x_{r+1}, z_{r+1})$ for U_{r+1} and ek satisfying Eq. 4

$$G \otimes U_r(\otimes_{k=1}^n X^{x_r(k)} Z^{z_r(k)}) |\psi\rangle = (\otimes_{k=1}^n X^{x_{r+1}(k)} Z^{z_{r+1}(k)}) U_{r+1} |\psi\rangle, \quad (4)$$

where $U_{r+1} = G \otimes U_r$, is calculated as follows:

- If $G = I$, X_i, or Z_i, then
  $dk_{r+1} = dk_r$.
- If $G = H_i$, then
  $(x_{r+1}(i), z_{r+1}(i)) = (z_r(i), x_r(i))$,
  $(x_{r+1}(k), z_{r+1}(k)) = (x_r(k), z_r(k))(k \neq i)$.
- If $G = S_i$, then
  $(x_{r+1}(i), z_{r+1}(i)) = (x_r(i), x_r(i) \oplus z_r(i))$,
  $(x_{r+1}(k), z_{r+1}(k)) = (x_r(k), z_r(k))(k \neq i)$.
- If $G = CNOT_{i,l}$, then
  $(x_{r+1}(i), z_{r+1}(i)) = (x_r(i), z_r(i) \oplus z_r(l))$,
  $(x_{r+1}(l), z_{r+1}(l)) = (x_r(i) \oplus x_r(l), z_r(l))$,
  $(x_{r+}(k), z_{r+1}(k)) = (x_r(k), z_r(k))(k \neq i)$.

- If $G = T_i$ (suppose the secret bits *Alice* chooses for this T gate are y and d, and the related one-bit measurement result from *Bob* is c, which is shown in Fig. 2g), then
$$(x_{r+1}(i), z_{r+1}(i)) = (x_r(i) \oplus c, x_r(i) \cdot (c \oplus y \oplus 1) \oplus z_r(i) \oplus d \oplus y),$$
$$(x_{r+}(k), z_{r+1}(k)) = (x_r(k), z_r(k))(k \neq i).$$

3.2   Outsourcing Key Generation to a Trusted Key Server in the Cloud Environment

As mentioned above, we can see that this DQC model consumes a large amount of computing and communication resources on clients. Let us give a concrete example first. Suppose *Alice* sends the encrypted superposition state to *Bob* and *Bob* use Grover algorithm to search out result state which *Alice* needs. Since Grover's algorithm is composed of a series of unitary transforms, it can be applied directly on an encrypted superposition state and obtained the encrypted search result by the use of DQC. It is known that the Grover's search is made up of a sequence of repeated Grover iterations, and each iteration contains an oracle that has the ability to mark items satisfying a specific search condition. For NP problems, solutions can be recognized in polynomial time; this means each Grover iteration can be constructed with polynomial elementary gates. Suppose the search space has $M = 2^m$, then, there may be $O(\sqrt{M} \cdot ploy(m))$ T gates (when each Grover iteration contains polynomial T gates). So, *Alice* needs to interact with *Bob* frequently to update the decryption key. This will put a huge amount of computing and communication pressure on *Alice*.

Besides, clients only search over their own encrypted data in this model, which is not beneficial to data sharing. To solve these problems, outsourcing key generation to a trusted cloud key server is a good solution. There are rich computing and communication resources in the cloud environment. Moreover, it is also suitable for data sharing and key management. That is, we divide the client into two parties: a thin client (*Alice*) and a trusted cloud key server (*Charlie*). The requirements and constraints on *Charlie* are given in Constraint 1.

Constraint 1. (Requirements and constraints on the key server). The key server *Charlie* obeys the following two constraints:

1. *Charlie* has the ability of performing key update rules and prepares four different states of qubits:

$$|+\rangle = \frac{|0\rangle + |1\rangle}{\sqrt{2}}, |-\rangle = \frac{|0\rangle - |1\rangle}{\sqrt{2}}, |+_y\rangle = \frac{|0\rangle + i|1\rangle}{\sqrt{2}}, |-_y\rangle = \frac{|0\rangle - i|1\rangle}{\sqrt{2}}, \quad (5)$$

which can serve as auxiliary qubits for T gates in the circuit of search as well as the encodings of keys by quantum key distribution (QKD).

2. *Charlie* honestly negotiates with clients about the encryption key, performs decryption key generation rules with *Bob*, then, sends the encrypted decryption key to clients who need it. The key transforming also relies on quantum key distribution.

Thus, our scheme runs among clients ($Alice_1$, $Alice_2$, $\cdots$, $Alice_n$), the key server ($Charlie$) and the data server (Bob) as illustrated in Fig. 3. These clients should firstly negotiate with the key center about the encryption key which is used to encrypt their data, and then send the encrypted data to Bob. Bob can perform search computation on the encrypted data as long as other clients need. Once Bob finishes search, $Charlie$ should generate the decryption key for the encrypted data synchronously. Finally, the clients can decrypt the search result to get the plain data with the decryption key from $Charlie$.

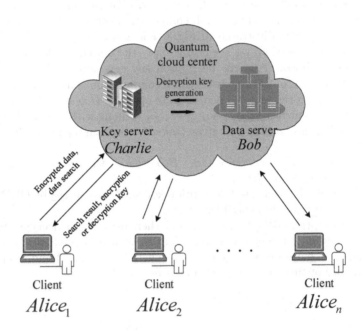

Fig. 3. The situation of quantum searchable encryption for cloud data

3.3 Quantum Searchable Encryption for Cloud Data Based on Delegating Quantum Computing

For the sake of simplicity, we take four parties (the data owner $Alice_1$, the data searcher $Alice_2$, the data server Bob and the key server $Charlie$) as an example to describe our scheme. The specific process of our scheme is as follows and shown in Fig. 5.

1. $Alice_1$ sends a number n (the length of her encrypted state) to $Charlie$.
2. $Charlie$ sends a string of $2n$ random binary bits back to $Alice_1$ by the BB84 protocol [22], where $|+\rangle$, $|+_y\rangle$ stands for 0, and $|-\rangle$, $|-_y\rangle$ stands for 1. The $2n$ bits of the binary string act as ek.

3. $Alice_1$ encrypts her superposition state $|\psi\rangle = \frac{1}{\sqrt{M}} \sum_{j=0}^{M-1} |j, data(j)\rangle$ with $ek = (x_0, z_0)$ and sends encrypted state $E_{ek} |\psi\rangle$ (shown in Eq. 6) to Bob, where the item index j within $|\psi\rangle$ is not encrypted.

$$E_{ek} |\psi\rangle = \frac{1}{\sqrt{M}} (I^{\otimes m} \otimes (\otimes_{k=1}^{n} X^{x_0(k)} Z^{z_0(k)})) \sum_{j=0}^{M-1} |j, data(j)\rangle \tag{6}$$

4. $Alice_2$ wants Bob to search on $E_{ek} |\psi\rangle$, and $Charlie$ generates the decryption key synchronously. The search computation can be composed of Grover algorithm, which is illustrated in Fig. 4. For a search space of $N = 2^n$ elements and one solution, we need only apply the search oracle $O(\sqrt{N})$ times to obtain a solution. And the decryption key generation rules for arbitrary unitary transform in the circuit of search computation is listed in Algorithm 1 as below. During the search, once a T gate appears, Bob asks $Charlie$ to send an auxiliary qubit from $\{|+\rangle, |+_y\rangle, |-\rangle, |-_y\rangle\}$ along with a related key bit w (i.e. x in Fig. 2g) to him and gives $Charlie$ a measurement result (i.e. c in Fig. 2g).

5. When the search is completed, Bob sends the search result state $E_{dk}(Search(|\psi\rangle))$ to $Alice_2$.

6. $Charlie$ sends the encrypted decryption key $sk(dk)$ to $Alice_2$ by QKD, where $sk(dk)$ can only be decrypted by $Alice_2$.

7. $Alice_2$ decrypts $sk(dk)$ to get dk, and then uses dk to decrypt the state $E_{dk}(Search(|\psi\rangle))$ to get the search result $Search(|\psi\rangle)$ (i.e., $Alice_2$ performs X^{x_r} and Z^{z_r} gates on $Search(E_{ek} |\psi\rangle)$, where $dk = (x_r, z_r)$ and r represents the number of times that Algorithm 1 is executed.).

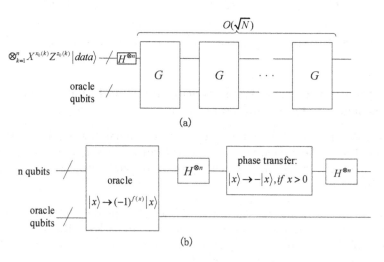

Fig. 4. Schematic circuit for Grover algorithm. (b) is the schematic circuit for G in (a).

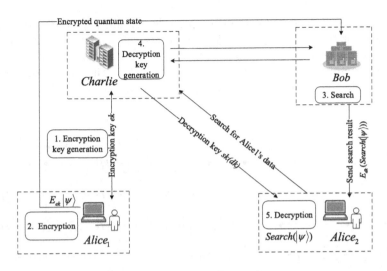

Fig. 5. The process of our scheme

4 An Example of Two-Qubit Quantum Search

Suppose $Alice_1$ has a set 000, 001, 010, 011, 100, 101, 110, 111 and $Alice_2$ wants to find the items of 001 and 011 from this set. *Bob* uses Grover algorithm to find their items, and the circuit of search computation is shown in Fig. 6. Although there are some $T^\dagger$ gates in this circuit, the decryption key update rule is as same as T gate, and the S gates in the Fig. 2 g are replaced with $S^\dagger$ gates. The example proceeds in seven steps provided below.

1. $Alice_1$ sends a number 3 to *Charlie*.
2. *Charlie* sends a string of 6 random binary bits back to $Alice_1$ by BB84 protocol, where $|+\rangle$, $|+_y\rangle$ stands for 0, and $|-\rangle$, $|-_y\rangle$ stands for 1. The 6 bits of the binary string act as $ek = (x_0, z_0)$.
3. $Alice_1$ encrypts her superposition state $|\psi\rangle = |+\rangle_1|+\rangle_2|+\rangle_3|-\rangle_4$ with X and Z gates, and sends encrypted state $E_{ek}|\psi\rangle = (\otimes_{k=1}^{4} X^{x_0(k)} Z^{z_0(k)})(|+\rangle_1|+\rangle_2 |+\rangle_3|-\rangle_4)$ (The fourth qubit does not need to be encrypted, i.e., $x_0(4) = 0$, $z_0(4) = 0$.)
4. $Alice_2$ wants *Bob* to search on $E_{ek}|\psi\rangle$, and *Charlie* compute the decryption key synchronously. During the search, the circuit in Fig. 6 has seven $T^\dagger$ and T gates. *Charlie* needs to randomly generates 14-bit (y_i, d_i) $(y_i, d_i \in \{0, 1\}; 1 \leqslant i \leqslant 7)$ to control S^y (or $S^{\dagger y}$) and Z^d (see in Fig. 2g), which can determine each state of 7 auxiliary qubits from $\{|+\rangle, |+_y\rangle, |-\rangle, |-_y\rangle\}$. *Charlie* sends these 7 auxiliary qubits and 7 related bits $w_i (1 \leqslant i \leqslant 7)$ to *Bob*. For other Clifford gates, *Charlie* performs the same operation as Algorithm 1.
5. When the search is completed, *Bob* sends the search result state $E_{dk}(Search(|\psi\rangle))$ to $Alice_2$.
6. *Charlie* sends the encrypted decryption key $sk(dk)$ to $Alice_2$ by QKD, where $sk(dk)$ can only be decrypted by $Alice_2$.

7. $Alice_2$ uses sk to decrypt the encrypted decryption key $sk(dk)$ and use dk to decrypt the state $E_{dk}(Search(|\psi\rangle))$ to get the search result $Search(|\psi\rangle)$ (i.e., $Alice_2$ performs $X^{x_{26}}$ and $Z^{z_{26}}$ gates on $Search(E_{ek}|\psi\rangle)$. The circuit of search computation in Fig. 6 has 26 gates. Therefore, the number of executing Algorithm 1 is 26 and $dk = (x_{26}, z_{26}).$).

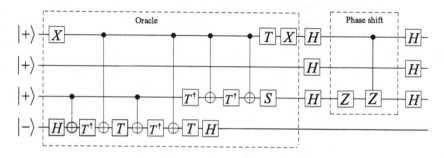

Fig. 6. The circuit of Grover algorithm to search $|001\rangle$ and $|011\rangle$ from $|+\rangle|+\rangle|+\rangle$.

5   Security Analysis

Suppose *Bob* is dishonest and wants to get data information from $E_{ek}|\psi\rangle$. He firstly needs to ek about the encrypted data, when he gets $E_{ek}|\psi\rangle$ sent by $Alice_1$. Since $Alice_1$ only sends the encrypted data to *Bob*, there is no other information interaction between $Alice_1$ and *Bob*, *Bob* cannot get any information about ek from $Alice_1$. Except $Alice_1$, only *Charlie* has information about ek. Especially, there is some information about ek in an auxiliary qubit (i.e., one of $\{|+\rangle, |+_y\rangle, |-\rangle, |-_y\rangle\}$) and a related key bit w (i.e., x in Fig. 2g) when *Charlie* sends them to *Bob*. Since $w = x_0 \oplus y$, *Bob* only needs to know the value of y. However, he is unable to determine the value of y when he uses $\{|+\rangle, |-\rangle\}$ or $\{|+_y\rangle, |-_y\rangle\}$ measurement base to measure this auxiliary qubit. So *Bob* cannot get any information about the encrypted data.

Suppose an eavesdropper *Dave* attempts to decrypt the encrypted data by eavesdropping on the key transforming (including ek and dk). Since the key transforming relies on BB84 protocol, both parties in the communication can detect the presence of the eavesdropper. Therefore, the security of the encrypted can be guaranteed.

As analysed in above, our scheme can protect the privacy of the encrypted data (Fig. 7).

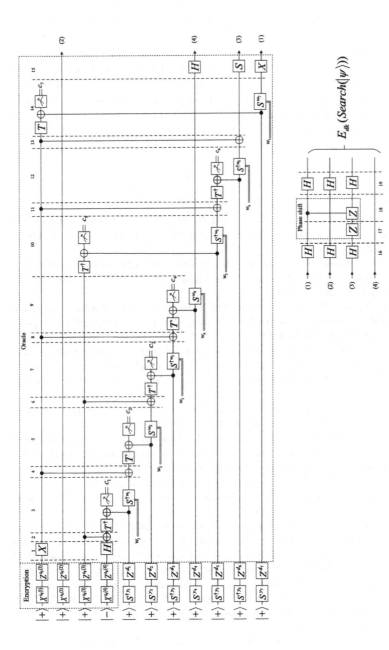

Fig. 7. The quantum search on $E_{ek}|\psi\rangle$. In the circuit, w_i $(1 \leqslant i \leqslant 7)$ represents that the intermediate key (corresponding to this qubit and X gate) XOR y_i. For example, when performing 5th level in the circuit, five gates have been performed before, so the intermediate key for the fourth qubit is $(x_5(4), z_5(4))$. Then, $w_2 = x_5(4) \oplus y_2$

6   Conclusion

In this paper, we propose a quantum searchable encryption scheme for cloud data based on delegating quantum computing. In our scheme, the quantum cloud center, composed of the key server and the data server, can provide storage and search services for key management and encrypted data. The clients only need limited quantum ability to encrypt or decrypt the data. And the decrypted search result is equivalent to the original data, which achieves the purpose of searchable encryption. Moreover, we give an example of our scheme to verify the feasibility of our scheme. Besides, the security of our scheme is analysed in detail, which can protect the privacy of the data. Furthermore, certification of the client's legality will be our next work.

References

1. Cao, Y., Kaiwartya, O., Zhuang, Y., Ahmad, N., Sun, Y., Lloret, J.: A decentralized deadline-driven electric vehicle charging recommendation. IEEE Syst. J. **13**(3), 3410–3421 (2019)
2. Qi, L., et al.: Finding all you need: web APIs recommendation in web of things through keywords search. IEEE Trans. Comput. Soc. Syst. (2019). https://doi.org/10.1109/TCSS.2019.2906925
3. Qie, X., Jin, S., Yue, W.: An energy-efficient strategy for virtual machine allocation over cloud data centers. J. Netw. Syst. Manage. **27**(4), 860–882 (2019). https://doi.org/10.1007/s10922-019-09489-w
4. Qi, L., Chen, Y., Yuan, Y., Fu, S., Zhang, X., Xu, X.: A QoS-aware virtual machine scheduling method for energy conservation in cloud-based cyber-physical systems. World Wide Web **23**(2), 1275–1297 (2019). https://doi.org/10.1007/s11280-019-00684-y
5. Bösch, C., Hartel, P., Jonker, W., Peter, A.: A survey of provably secure searchable encryption. ACM Comput. Surv. **47**(2), 1801–1851 (2014)
6. Xu, X., Liu, Q., Zhang, X., Zhang, J., Qi, L., Dou, W.: A blockchain-powered crowdsourcing method with privacy preservation in mobile environment. IEEE Trans. Comput. Soc. Syst. (2019). https://doi.org/10.1109/TCSS.2019.2909137
7. Song, D.X., Wagner, D., Perrig, A.: Practical techniques for searches on encrypted data. In: Proceeding 2000 IEEE Symposium on Security and Privacy, S&P 2000, Berkeley, CA, USA, pp. 44–55 (2000)
8. Goh, E.: Secure indexes. IACR Cryptol. ePrint Arch. **2003**, 216 (2003)
9. Curtmola, R., Garay, J., Kamara, S. Ostrovsky, R.: Searchable symmetric encryption: improved definitions and efficient constructions. In: Proceedings of 13th ACM Conference on Computer and Communications Security, USA, pp. 79–88 (2006)
10. Boneh, D., Di Crescenzo, G., Ostrovsky, R., Persiano, G.: Public key encryption with keyword search. In: Cachin, C., Camenisch, J.L. (eds.) EUROCRYPT 2004. LNCS, vol. 3027, pp. 506–522. Springer, Heidelberg (2004). https://doi.org/10.1007/978-3-540-24676-3_30
11. Xia, Z., Wang, X., Zhang, L., Qin, Z., Sun, X., Ren, K.: A privacy-preserving and copy-deterrence content-based image retrieval scheme in cloud computing. IEEE Trans. Inf. Forensics Secur. **11**(11), 2594–2608 (2016)

12. Fu, Z., Ren, K., Shu, J., Sun, X., Huang, F.: Enabling personalized search over encrypted outsourced data with efficiency improvement. IEEE Trans. Parallel Distrib. Syst. **27**(9), 2546–2559 (2016)

13. Chen, L., Lee, W.-K., Chang, C.-C., Choo, K.-K.R., Zhang, N.: Blockchain based searchable encryption for electronic health record sharing. Future Gener. Comput. Syst. **95**, 420–429 (2019)

14. Broadbent, A., Fitzsimons, J., Kashefi, E.: Universal blind quantum computation. In: 50th Annual IEEE Symposium on Foundations of Computer Science, Atlanta, GA, pp. 517–526 (2009)

15. Kong, X., Li, Q., Wu, C., Yu, F., He, J., Sun, Z.: Multiple-server flexible blind quantum computation in networks. Int. J. Theor. Phys. **55**(6), 3001–3007 (2016)

16. Arrighi, P., Salvail, L.: Blind quantum computation. Int. J. Quantum Inf. **4**(5), 883–898 (2006)

17. Tan, X., Zhou, X.: Universal half-blind quantum computation. Ann. Telecommun. **72**(9), 589–595 (2017)

18. Fisher, K.A.G., et al.: Quantum computing on encrypted data. Nat. Commun. **5**, 3074 (2014)

19. Broadbent, A.: Delegating private quantum computations. Can. J. Phys. **93**(9), 941–946 (2015)

20. Kashefi, E., Pappa, A.: Multiparty delegated quantum computing. Cryptography **1**(2), 12 (2017)

21. Nielsen, M.A., Chuang, I.: Quantum Computation and Quantum Information, 10th edn. Cambridge University Press, New York (2002)

22. Bennett, C.H., Brassard, G.: Quantum cryptography: public key distribution and coin tossing. In: International Conference on Computers, Systems & Signal Processing, Bangalore, India, pp. 175–179. Springer (1984)

Quantum Solution for the 3-SAT Problem Based on IBM Q

Ying Zhang[1,2], Yu-xiang Bian[2,3], Qiang Fan[2,3], and Junxiu Chen[4(✉)]

[1] NARI Information and Communication Technology Co., Ltd.,
Nanjing 210003, China
zhang_ying2@sgepri.sgcc.com.cn

[2] NARI Group Corporation/State Grid Electric Power Research Institute,
Nanjing 211106, China
bianyuxiang@sgepri.sgcc.com.cn

[3] NRGD Quantum Technology Co., Ltd., Nanjing 211106, China
nrgd_lw@163.com

[4] School of Computer and Software, Nanjing University of Information Science
and Technology, Nanjing 210044, China
cjxccc981@163.com

Abstract. Quantum computing is currently considered to be a new type of computing model that has a subversive impact on the future. Based on its leading information and communication technology advantages, IBM launched IBM Q Experience cloud service platform, and achieved phased research results in the quantum simulator and programming framework. In this paper, we propose a quantum solution for the 3-SAT problem, which includes three steps: constructing the initial state, computing the unitary U_f implementing the black-box function f and performing the inversion about the average. In addition, the corresponding experimental verification for an instance of the Exactly-1 3-SAT problem with QISKit, which can connect to IBM Q remotely, is depicted. The experimental result not only show the feasibility of the quantum solution, but also serve to evaluate the functionality of IBM Q devices.

Keywords: Quantum computing · 3-SAT problem · IBM Q · QISKit · Grover algorithm

1 Introduction

With the continues development of quantum field, quantum computing has become a hot research field. And a key to quantum computing is the study of quantum algorithms. Firstly, Feynman [1] proposed the idea of combining

J. Chen—This work is supported by Science and Technology Project of NRGD Quantum Technology Co., Ltd., "Research on Power Quantum Security Service Platform and Key Technologies of Multi-mode Access".

X. Zhang et al. (Eds.): CloudComp 2019/SmartGift 2019, LNICST 322, pp. 410–423, 2020.
https://doi.org/10.1007/978-3-030-48513-9_33

quantum mechanics with computational problems in 1982. Then, Deutsch and Jozsa proposed Deutsch-Jozsa algorithm [2] which is the first quantum algorithm. Compared with the traditional calculation, the algorithm has obvious acceleration. In 1994, the emergence of Shor algorithm [3] not only accelerates the computing speed, and also affects the running basis of RSA encryption technology. In addition, the search algorithm proposed by Grover [4] in 1996 is also a very classic algorithm. Generally speaking, the search complexity of computers can be depicted as N (N is the size of database). Because of its wide application, Grover algorithm further demonstrates the advantages of quantum computing. The above mentioned quantum algorithms, especially Shor algorithm and Grover algorithm, fully demonstrate the development potential of quantum computing, which can be widely used in data security and commercial development. At present, there are many new quantum algorithms come into being, such as quantum secure sharing (QSS) [5,6], quantum key agreement (QKA) [7,8], quantum secure direct communication (QSDC) [9–11], quantum private comparison (QPC) [12–15], quantum sealed-bid auction (QSBA) [16,17], remote preparation of quantum states [18–21], quantum steganography [22–24], delegating quantum computation [25,26], and quantum machine learning algorithms [27,28]. However, these algorithms also have some shortcomings and can be improved. However, these improvements are theory research, few would give the experimental results show that, after all, from the real it's early, in other words, the advent of quantum computer algorithm to improve the existence of a real error, whether can the real experiment, whether real applications remains to be further investigation Therefore, we need a quantum simulation cloud platform, which can provide us with a good environment to verify and improve quantum algorithms.

At the end of 2017, an open-source quantum computing framework, namely QISKit [29], is released by IBM, which allows the users to implement remote quantum experimental verification of IBM Q [30] through localized python programming. The SAT problem is the oldest and well-known NP-Complete problem. There have been many algorithms and techniques that have been invented to solve it. The best SAT solvers can solve tens of thousands of variables. We know that the NP-Complete problem could be converted in polynomial time, and the SAT solver is very efficient. Then the SAT is naturally very practical. In this paper, we use QISKit to directly program the algorithm for an Exactly-1 3-SAT problem, and connect the remote IBM 5-qubit device (i.e., ibmqx4) to verify the quantum solution in the real quantum computer.

The remaining structure of the paper is as follows: In Sect. 2, preliminaries about quantum computation, IBM Q and Grover's algorithm are briefly introduced. In Sect. 3, the quantum solution based on the Grover's algorithm, which is used to solve the 3-SAT problem, is depicted. In addition, we give an instance of this problem, and then its implementation circuit and QISKit program are presented, respectively. Subsequently, the experimental result of the solution for Exactly-1 3-SAT problem are analyzed in detail in graphical form. Finally, Sect. 4 is dedicated for conclusion.

2   Preliminaries

2.1   Quantum Computation

According to the analysis of the superposition principle, we can find that the change of state of quantum information units can add up with several possible situation. For a quantum state, we can control a quantum bit to get two quantum state. If we can control N qubits at the same time, it represents that we can get 2^N condition for effective control, information storage times to grow exponentially. This is a quantum computer parallel computing ability. We can design different quantum circuits by referring to quantum gate sets, so that we can use quantum states to transmit information and achieve the purpose of quantum communication.

In traditional computer, a bit represents a Boolean variable with a range of $\{0, 1\}$. However, a quantum bit is a vector which is in 2-dimensional complex Hilbert space, which represents the state of a two-state quantum system. $|0\rangle$ and $|1\rangle$ are used to refer to the corresponding "0" and "1" state, where "$|\rangle$" is called Dirac notation. Quantum ratio has two unique properties: superposition and entanglement, which can be used for specific calculations. Specifically, superposition state refers to the state of a single quantum bit that could be described as the superposition of two ground states, just like schrodinger's cat, which is a superposition of life and death. The quantum superposition state $|\varphi\rangle$ is expressed as

$$\begin{bmatrix} \alpha \\ \beta \end{bmatrix} = \alpha \begin{bmatrix} 1 \\ 0 \end{bmatrix} + \beta \begin{bmatrix} 0 \\ 1 \end{bmatrix}. \tag{1}$$

α and β represent the probability amplitude of $|0\rangle$ and $|1\rangle$ respectively, where $|\alpha|^2$ can be understood as the probability of observing the quantum bit is 0, and $|\beta|^2$ could be understood as the probability of observing the quantum bit is 1. The state of quantum bit satisfies normalization, namely: $|\alpha|^2 + |\beta|^2 = 1$. The superposition state of a qubit could be viewed as the linear superposition of states 0 and 1. It is linear and entangled state.

Quantum computers are built from quantum circuits that contain wires and basic quantum gates, which is in order to carry and manipulate some of the quantum bits that carry communication information. Quantum gates can be divided into two types: single qubit gates and multiple qubit gates. Quantum gate can all be represented in the form of a matrix U. The unitary limit ($U^\dagger U = I$, where $U^\dagger$ is a conjugate transpose of U, obtained by U transpose and complex conjugate of U) is the only limitation on quantum gates [31], each valid quantum gate can be represented as a unitary matrix. For visual display, in Table 1 below we list some line symbols and matrix representations used in this paper.

In the actual quantum circuit, we use special line symbol to represent the quantum gate, and a line symbol represents a quantum gate that can manipulate the quantum state.

Table 1. Common quantum gate and line symbols

Quantum gate	Line symbol	Matrix form
Hadamard	—[H]—	$\frac{1}{\sqrt{2}}\begin{bmatrix} 1 & 1 \\ 1 & -1 \end{bmatrix}$
Pauli-X	—[X]—	$\begin{bmatrix} 0 & 1 \\ 1 & 0 \end{bmatrix}$
Pauli-Y	—[Y]—	$\begin{bmatrix} 0 & -i \\ i & 0 \end{bmatrix}$
Pauli-Z	—[Z]—	$\begin{bmatrix} 1 & 0 \\ 0 & -1 \end{bmatrix}$
Controlled-NOT		$\begin{bmatrix} 1 & 0 & 0 & 0 \\ 0 & 1 & 0 & 0 \\ 0 & 0 & 0 & 1 \\ 0 & 0 & 1 & 0 \end{bmatrix}$
Controlled-Z		$\begin{bmatrix} 1 & 0 & 0 & 0 \\ 0 & 1 & 0 & 0 \\ 0 & 0 & 1 & 0 \\ 0 & 0 & 0 & -1 \end{bmatrix}$

$$X \equiv \begin{bmatrix} 0 & 1 \\ 1 & 0 \end{bmatrix}. \tag{2}$$

If X-gate is applied to manipulate the quantum state $|\psi\rangle = \alpha|0\rangle + \beta|1\rangle$, the result of the operation can be obtained by multiplying the vector:

$$X\begin{bmatrix} \alpha \\ \beta \end{bmatrix} = \begin{bmatrix} \beta \\ \alpha \end{bmatrix}. \tag{3}$$

2.2 IBM Q

In 2016, IBM opened the IBM Q experience prototype 5-qubit device to the public. Then, they launched IBM Q [30], which is the first general-purpose quantum computer for commercial and scientific research. In the same year, they proposed two devices with 5 qubits named ibmqx2 and ibmqx4. In 2018, a third public device with 16 qubits (ibmqx5) is added which can be accessed using QISKit. Recently, they have announced that they successfully built and tested a 20-qubit device for their client. Meanwhile, their simulator is up to 32 qubits for more and more people to use and research. The experimental verification of quantum algorithms has become a reality, providing reliable data support for the research and development of quantum algorithms to help us assist in the analysis of the performance of the algorithm.

In IBM Q, all devices provide a lot of elementary gates, such as: X-gate, H-gate, cX-gate (control-NOT gate), cZ-gate (control-Z gate), ccX-gate (control-control-NOT gate, namely Toffoli gate) and so on. The coupling map of ibmqx2 and ibmqx4 are shown in Fig. 1. In general, two qubit gates may act between adjacent qubits, which are connected by a superconducting bus resonator. IBM Q experienced the use of cross-resonance interaction technology as the basis for quantum gate operations. When the qubits with higher frequencies are selected as control qubits and the qubits with lower frequencies are selected as targets, the interaction becomes stronger, so the qubits' frequency determines the gate's steering direction.

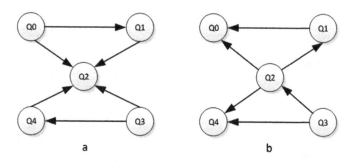

Fig. 1. The coupling map picture: ibmqx2(a) and ibmqx4(b). The arrows point from the qubit with higher frequency to that with lower frequency

Quantum Information Software Kit(QISKit) [29] is a Software Kit for designing short-depth Quantum circuits and building short-term Quantum applications and experiments on Quantum computers. Relevant data are collected after the program compilation is completed. In summary, the QISKit toolkit includes python-based software tools for creating, manipulating, visualizing, and exploring quantum states, tools for describing qubits, scripts for batch processing, and compilers for mapping required experiments to actual hardware. Different from the IBM Q web page experiment mode, this kind of programming call mode can overcome the cumbersomeness of drawing complex circuit diagrams on web pages, and has the advantage of easy expansion of composite quantum gates and easy preservation of experimental data.

2.3   Grover's Algorithm

Grover's algorithm [4] is one of the main algorithms in quantum computing. It is better than the best classical algorithm to do square acceleration when dealing with the problem of searching M target Numbers from unordered D databases.

In other words, the time required for the classical algorithm to complete the task is proportional to, while the quantum algorithm can be implemented within the time scale. If D is a very large number, it saves a lot of time. The power of the Grover algorithm lies in its versatility: its formulas are universal and can be applied to many problems, such as cryptography, matrix and graphics problems, optimization, and quantum machine learning. The detailed implementation steps of the Grover quantum search algorithm could be seen in Fig. 2:

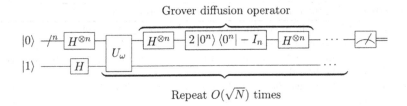

Repeat $O(\sqrt{N})$ times

Fig. 2. Quantum circuit representation of Grover algorithm

The steps of Grover's algorithm are as follows: let $|s\rangle$ represents the uniform superposition of all states.

$$|s\rangle = \frac{1}{\sqrt{N}} \sum_{x=0}^{N-1} |x\rangle. \tag{4}$$

A "quantum oracle" operator U_ω is required in Grover's algorithm, which could identify the target solution to the search problem and turn their magnitude negative. And we apply the operator U_ω on the states. Then the operator $U_s = 2|s\rangle\langle s| - I$ is the grover-diffusion operator. Then the operator U_s is applied on the states after U_ω. Next, we perform the measurement Ω on then quantum state. The result will be eigenvalue λ_ω with probability approaching 100% for $N \gg 1$. From λ_ω, that Ω may be obtained.

3   Quantum Solution for the 3-SAT Problem Based on IBM Q

The SAT problem is well-known as the first NP-Complete problem [32]. The NP-Complete problem could be rotated within polynomial time. And the efficiency of the SAT solver is good. So the SAT problem is naturally very practical. SAT is used for test verification in many fields such as EDA. And it also can be used in AI fields such as automatic theorem proving and so on.

A quantum solution for the 3-SAT problem is proposed in this paper. The problem of 3-SAT can be described as follows: the assignment requires that each clause contain a truth value. For the input data, the formula in conjunctive normal form $\wedge_{k=1}^m C_k$ over n Boolean variables $x_1, \ldots, x_n$, with m literals per clause $C_1, \ldots, C_m$. For the Output data, is there an assignment of $x_1, \ldots, x_n$

such that every clause $C_1, \ldots, C_m$ has exactly one true literal? In order to solve this problem, a quantum solution for the 3-SAT problem based on the Grover's algorithm is proposed, which is to find satisfying assignment.

The quantum solution can be divided into three steps:

(1) constructing the initial state.
(2) computing the unitary U_f with the black-box function f.
(3) performing the inversion about the average.

Program 1: Quantum solution for the 3-SAT problem

> **input** : SAT formula in conjunctive normal form $\wedge_{k=1}^{m} C_k$ over n Boolean variables x_1, x_2, x_3, with 3 literals per clause C_1, C_2, C_3.
>
> **output**: The answer of x_1, x_2, x_3 such that every clause C_1, C_2, C_3 has exactly one true literal.

```
1  #constructing a 3-qubit initial state, the x4 is an auxiliary qubit;
2  circuit.x(x4);
3  for j in 4 do
4      circuit.h(xj);
5  end
6  #computing the unitary Uf implementing the black-box function f;
7  formula=[C1, C2, C3];
8  def Uf(circuit, x1, x2, x3, formula)
9  #performing the inversion about the average
10 for  j in range(3) do
11     circuit.h(x[j]);
12     circuit.x(x[j]);
13 end
14 for  j in range(3) do
15     circuit.ccZ(circuit,[x[j] for j in range(2)], x[2]);
16 end
17 for  j in range(3) do
18     circuit.x(x[j]);
19     circuit.h(x[j]);
20 end
```

Program 1 shows the detailed procedure of the quantum solution for SAT problems.

In our experimental implementation, an Exactly-1 3-SAT instance is specified as a list of clauses, where there are three integers in each clause. In this paper, we agree that a positive integer is an index of positive text and a negative integer is the opposite. For example, the corresponding python list is shown as follows.

$$(x_1 \nabla x_2 \nabla \neg x_3) \wedge (\neg x_1 \nabla \neg x_2 \nabla \neg x_3) \wedge (\neg x_1 \nabla x_2 \nabla x_3) \tag{5}$$

We use the up formula as an example and the symbol ∇ is used to emphasize that this is an Exactly-1 3-SAT formula, rather than the usual $\wedge$. This is like a problem definition that requires each clause to have only one real word. Based on Grover's algorithm, we are going to use three subsections to show the processes of our solution.

3.1   Constructing the Initial State

We take 3 qubits as an example to show how to prepare an initial quantum state. In Grover's algorithm, a function with an n-qubit input and a single-qubit output is applied. We need n qubit and an ancilla qubit to prepare the initial state. The circuit for constructing a 3-qubit initial state can be seen in Fig. 3. And the corresponding program in python using QISKit can be seen in Program 2.

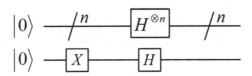

Fig. 3. Circuit for constructing an initial quantum state.

Program 2: Constructing the initial state

```
1 def input_state(n):
2     for j in range (n) do
3         circuit.h(f_in[j]);
4 end
5     circuit.x(f_out);
6     circuit.h(f_out);
```

3.2   Computing Unitary U_f Implementing the Black-Box Function f

The implementation of U_f for an Exactly-1 3-SAT problem is the most complex part of the code, and there are several ways to complete it. To reduce computational complexity and save resources, the problem of computing U_f is decomposed by introducing m ancilla qubits. For each clause, a highly efficient and feasible quantum circuit is constructed in which the phase of the corresponding auxiliary qubit is reversed if and only if there is only one true word in the clause (here, these auxiliary qubits will be initialized in state $|0\rangle$).

Taking $x_1 \wedge (\neg x_2) \wedge x_3 \wedge (x_1 \nabla \neg x_2 \nabla x_3)$ as an example, we show the corresponding circuit in Fig. 4. We apply three H gates to get initial states, and then the next three C-NOT (Control-Not) gates complete the function of $x_1 \wedge (\neg x_2) \wedge x_3$ and store the result in $q[3]$. And the next two CC-NOT (Control-Control-Not) gates complete the function of $(x_1 \nabla \neg x_2 \nabla x_3)$ and the result is stored in $q[3]$ finally.

Then, inspired by the above circuit, we drawn the circuit for $(x_1 \nabla x_2 \nabla \neg x_3) \wedge (\neg x_1 \nabla \neg x_2 \nabla \neg x_3) \wedge (\neg x_1 \nabla x_2 \nabla x_3)$ in Fig. 5. $q[3], q[4]$ and $q[5]$ are auxiliary qubits. And the final result is stored in $q[6]$. The corresponding program in python using QISKit can be seen in Program 3.

Program 3: Computing the unitary U_f implementing the black-box function f

```
1  def black_box_u_f(circuit, f_in, f_out, aux, n, exactly_1_3_sat_formula):
2      num_clauses = len(exactly_1_3_sat_formula);
3      for (k, clause) in enumerate(exactly_1_3_sat_formula) do
4          for literal in clause do
5              if literal > 0 then
6                  circuit.cx(f_in[literal − 1], aux[k]);
7          end
8              else
9                  circuit.x(f_in[−literal − 1]);
10                 circuit.cx(f_in[−literal − 1], aux[k]);
11         end
12     end
13         circuit.ccx(f_in[0], f_in[1], aux[num_clauses]);
14         circuit.ccx(f_in[2], aux[num_clauses], aux[k]);
15         circuit.ccx(f_in[0], f_in[1], aux[num_clauses]);
16         for literal in clause do
17             if literal < 0 then
18                 circuit.x(f_in[−literal − 1]);
19         end
20     end
21         if (num_clauses==1) then
22             circuit.cx(aux[0], f_out[0]);
23     end
24         else if (num_clauses==2) then
25             circuit.ccx(aux[0], aux[1], f_out[0]);
26     end
27         else if (num_clauses==3) then
28             circuit.ccx(aux[0], aux[1], aux[num_clauses]);
29             circuit.ccx(aux[2], aux[num_clauses], f_out[0]);
30             circuit.ccx(aux[0], aux[1], aux[num_clauses]);
31     end
32  end
33      for (k , clause ) in enumerate(exactly_1_3_sat_formula) do
34          for literal in clause do
35              if literal > 0 then
36                  circuit.cx(f_in[literal − 1], aux[k]);
37          end
38              else
39                  circuit.x(f_in[−literal − 1]);
40                 circuit.cx(f_in[−literal − 1], aux[k]);
41         end
42     end
43         circuit.ccx(f_in[0], f_in[1], aux[num_clauses]);
44         circuit.ccx(f_in[2], aux[num_clauses], aux[k]);
45         circuit.ccx(f_in[0], f_in[1], aux[num_clauses]);
46         for literal in clause do
47             if literal < 0 then
48                 circuit.x(f_in[−literal − 1]);
49         end
50     end
51  end
```

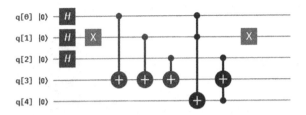

Fig. 4. Circuit for $x_1 \wedge (\neg x_2) \wedge x_3 \wedge (x_1 \nabla \neg x_2 \nabla x_3)$.

3.3 Performing the Inversion About the Average

In order to carry out inversion operation on the average value of all the obtained quantum state amplitudes, we need to perform the following operations:

$$\sum_{j \in \{0,1\}^n} \alpha_j |j\rangle_n \rightarrow \sum_{j \in \{0,1\}^n} \left(2 \left(\sum_{k \in \{0,1\}^n} \frac{\alpha_k}{2^n} \right) - \alpha_{\bar{j}} \right) |j\rangle_n \qquad (6)$$

where $\sum_{k \in \{0,1\}^n} \frac{\alpha_k}{2^n}$ is the average value of all the obtained quantum state amplitudes, and therefore we update the corresponding amplitudes by taking twice the average and subtracting each coefficient from it. This mapping is realized by the matrix as follows.

$$W = \begin{pmatrix} \frac{2}{2^n} - 1 & \frac{2}{2^n} & \cdots & \frac{2}{2^n} \\ \frac{2}{2^n} & \frac{2}{2^n} - 1 & \cdots & \frac{2}{2^n} \\ \vdots & \vdots & \ddots & \vdots \\ \frac{2}{2^n} & \frac{2}{2^n} & \cdots & \frac{2}{2^n} - 1 \end{pmatrix} = \begin{pmatrix} \frac{2}{2^n} & \frac{2}{2^n} & \cdots & \frac{2}{2^n} \\ \frac{2}{2^n} & \frac{2}{2^n} & \cdots & \frac{2}{2^n} \\ \vdots & \vdots & \ddots & \vdots \\ \frac{2}{2^n} & \frac{2}{2^n} & \cdots & \frac{2}{2^n} \end{pmatrix} - I^{\otimes n} \qquad (7)$$

And the corresponding program in python using QISKit can be seen in Program 4.

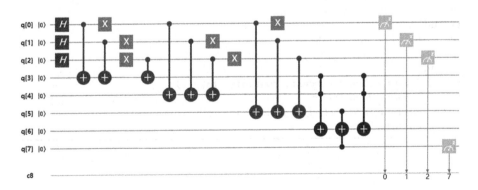

Fig. 5. Circuit for $(x_1 \nabla x_2 \nabla \neg x_3) \wedge (\neg x_1 \nabla \neg x_2 \nabla \neg x_3) \wedge (\neg x_1 \nabla x_2 \nabla x_3)$.

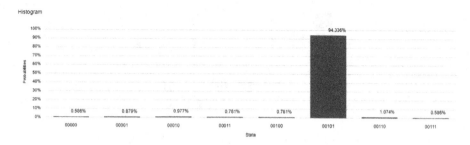

Fig. 6. Result for $(x_1 \triangledown x_2 \triangledown \neg x_3) \wedge (\neg x_1 \triangledown \neg x_2 \triangledown \neg x_3) \wedge (\neg x_1 \triangledown x_2 \triangledown x_3)$.

Together with the above three programs, Program 5 shows the whole program for quantum solution in python using QISKit, which is used to solve the Exactly-1 3-SAT problem.

After executing Program 5, we can get the result for an instance of Exactly-1 3-SAT in Eq. 5, which can be seen in Fig. 6. Obviously, $|101\rangle$ (i.e., $x_1 = 1$, $x_2 = 0$, $x_3 = 1$) is the answer to $(x_1 \triangledown x_2 \triangledown \neg x_3) \wedge (\neg x_1 \triangledown \neg x_2 \triangledown \neg x_3) \wedge (\neg x_1 \triangledown x_2 \triangledown x_3)$. Then, we could get the answer with 94% probability through the quantum solution.

Program 4: Inversion about the average

```
 1 def inversion_about_average(circuit, f_in, n):
 2      for j in range(n) do
 3           circuit.h(f_in[j]);
 4 end
 5      for j in range(n) do
 6           circuit.x(f_in[j]);
 7 end
 8      3_controlled_Z(circuit, [f_in[j] for j in range(n − 1)], f_in[n − 1]);
 9      for j in range(n) do
10           circuit.x(f_in[j]);
11 end
12      for j in range(n) do
13           circuit.h(f_in[j]);
14 end
15 def 3_controlled_Z(circuit, controls, target):
16      circuit.h(target);
17      circuit.ccx(controls[0], controls[1], target);
18      circuit.h(target);
```

Program 5: Quantum solution for Exactly-1 3-SAT problem

```
1    import sys;
2    from qiskit import QuantumRegister, ClassicalRegister;
3    from qiskit import QuantumCircuit;
4    from qiskit import compile, Aer;
5    from qiskit.tools import visualization;
6    n = 3;
7    exactly_1_3_sat_formula = [[1, 2, −3], [−1, −2, −3], [−1, 2, 3]];
8    f_in = QuantumRegister(n);
9    f_out = QuantumRegister(1);
10   aux = QuantumRegister(len(exactly_1_3_sat_formula) + 1);
11   ans = ClassicalRegister(n);
12   qc = QuantumCircuit(f_in, f_out, aux, ans, name =′ grover′);
13   input_state(qc, f_in, f_out, n);
14   black_box_u_f(qc, f_in, f_out, aux, n, exactly_1_3_sat_formula);
15   inversion_about_average(qc, f_in, n);
16   black_box_u_f(qc, f_in, f_out, aux, n, exactly_1_3_sat_formula);
17   inversion_about_average(qc, f_in, n);
18   for j in range (n) do
19       qc.measure(f_in[j], ans[j]);
20   quantum_simulator = Aer.get_backend('qasm_simulator_py');
21   qobj = compile(qc, quantum_simulator, shots = 2048);
22   job = quantum_simulator.run(qobj);
23   result = job.result();
24   counts = result.get_counts('grover');
25   visualization.plot_histogram(counts);
```

4 Conclusion

In this paper, a quantum solution for the 3-SAT problem based on Grover's algorithm is proposed, which includes three steps: constructing the initial state, computing the unitary U_f, implementing the black-box f and performing the inversion of the average amplitude of all quantum states. Next, the corresponding experimental verification for an Exactly-1 3-SAT problem instance with QISKit, which can connect to IBM Q remotely, is depicted. We can get the answer $|101\rangle$ with 94% probability through the quantum solution. The experimental result not only show the feasibility of the quantum solution, but also serve to evaluate the functionality of IBM Q devices. For this kind of localized programming mode based on QISKit, the design of quantum functional circuits can be packaged in the form of functions for reusing and expansion. With the increasing scale of practical problems, we need to consider the design of feasible quantum circuit optimization scheme.

References

1. Feynman, R.P.: Simulating physics with computers. Int. J. Theor. Phys. **21**, 467–488 (1982). https://doi.org/10.1007/BF02650179
2. Deutsch, D., Jozsa, R.: Rapid solution of problems by quantum computation. Proc. R. Soc. Lond. Ser. A (Math. Phys. Sci.) **439**(1907), 553–558 (1992)
3. Shor, P.W.: Polynomial-time algorithms for prime factorization and discrete logarithms on a quantum computer. SIAM Rev. **41**(2), 303–332 (1999)
4. Grover, L.K.: A fast quantum mechanical algorithm for database search. In: Proceedings of ACM Symposium on the Theory of Computing, pp. 212–219 (1996)
5. Liu, Z.-H., Chen, H.-W., Xu, J., Liu, W.-J., Li, Z.-Q.: High-dimensional deterministic multiparty quantum secret sharing without unitary operations. Quantum Inf. Process. **11**(6), 1785–1795 (2011). https://doi.org/10.1007/s11128-011-0333-z
6. Chen, X.B., Tang, X., Xu, G., Dou, Z., Chen, Y.L., Yang, Y.X.: Cryptanalysis of secret sharing with a single d-level quantum system. Quantum Inf. Process. **17**(9), 225 (2018)
7. Huang, W., Su, Q., Liu, B., He, Y.H., Fan, F., Xu, B.J.: Efficient multiparty quantum key agreement with collective detection. Sci. Rep. **7**(1), 15264 (2017)
8. Liu, W.J., Xu, Y., Yang, C.N., Gao, P.P., Yu, W.B.: An efficient and secure arbitrary N-party quantum key agreement protocol using bell states. Int. J. Theor. Phys. **57**(1), 195–207 (2018). https://doi.org/10.1007/s10773-017-3553-x
9. Liu, W.J., Chen, H.W., Li, Z.Q., Liu, Z.H.: Efficient quantum secure direct communication with authentication. Chin. Phys. Lett. **25**(7), 2354–2357 (2008)
10. Liu, W.J., Chen, H.W., Ma, T.H., Li, Z.Q., Liu, Z.H., Hu, W.B.: An efficient deterministic secure quantum communication scheme based on cluster states and identity authentication. Chin. Phys. B **18**(10), 4105–4109 (2009)
11. Xu, G., Chen, X.-B., Li, J., Wang, C., Yang, Y.-X., Li, Z.: Network coding for quantum cooperative multicast. Quantum Inf. Process. **14**(11), 4297–4322 (2015). https://doi.org/10.1007/s11128-015-1098-6
12. Liu, W., Liu, C., Wang, H., Jia, T.: Quantum private comparison: a review. IETE Tech. Rev. **30**(5), 439–445 (2013)
13. Liu, W.J., Liu, C., Liu, Z.H., Liu, J.F., Geng, H.T.: Same initial states attack in Yang et al.'s quantum private comparison protocol and the improvement. Int. J. Theor. Phys. **53**(1), 271–276 (2014)
14. Liu, W.J., Liu, C., Chen, H.W., Li, Z.Q., Liu, Z.H.: Cryptanalysis and improvement of quantum private comparison protocol based on bell entangled states. Commun. Theor. Phys. **62**(2), 210–214 (2014)
15. Liu, W.-J., Liu, C., Wang, H., Liu, J.-F., Wang, F., Yuan, X.-M.: Secure quantum private comparison of equality based on asymmetric W state. Int. J. Theor. Phys. **53**(6), 1804–1813 (2014). https://doi.org/10.1007/s10773-013-1979-3
16. Liu, W.-J., et al.: Multiparty quantum sealed-bid auction using single photons as message carrier. Quantum Inf. Process. **15**(2), 869–879 (2015). https://doi.org/10.1007/s11128-015-1202-y
17. Liu, W.J., Wang, F., Ji, S., Qu, Z.G., Wang, X.J.: Attacks and improvement of quantum sealed-bid auction with EPR pairs. Commun. Theor. Phys. **61**(6), 686–690 (2014)
18. Liu, W.J., Chen, Z.-F., Liu, C., Zheng, Y.: Improved deterministic N-to-one joint remote preparation of an arbitrary qubit via EPR pairs. Int. J. Theor. Phys. **54**(2), 472–483 (2015). https://doi.org/10.1007/s10773-014-2241-3

19. Chen, X.-B., Sun, Y.-R., Xu, G., Jia, H.-Y., Qu, Z., Yang, Y.-X.: Controlled bidirectional remote preparation of three-qubit state. Quantum Inf. Process. **16**(10), 1–29 (2017). https://doi.org/10.1007/s11128-017-1690-z
20. Qu, Z.G., Wu, S.Y., Wang, M.M., Sun, L., Wang, X.J.: Effect of quantum noise on deterministic remote state preparation of an arbitrary two-particle state via various quantum entangled channels. Quantum Inf. Process. **16**(306), 1–25 (2017)
21. Wang, M.M., Yang, C., Mousoli, R.: Controlled cyclic remote state preparation of arbitrary qubit states. CMC-Comput. Mater. Continua **55**(2), 321–329 (2018)
22. Qu, Z., Cheng, Z., Liu, W., Wang, X.: A novel quantum image steganography algorithm based on exploiting modification direction. Multimedia Tools Appl. **78**(7), 7981–8001 (2018). https://doi.org/10.1007/s11042-018-6476-5
23. Qu, Z., Chen, S., Ji, S., Ma, S., Wang, X.: Anti-noise bidirectional quantum steganography protocol with large payload. Int. J. Theor. Phys. **57**(6), 1903–1927 (2018). https://doi.org/10.1007/s10773-018-3716-4
24. Qu, Z.G., Zhu, T.C., Wang, J.W., Wang, X.J.: A novel quantum stegonagraphy based on brown states. CMC-Comput. Mater. Continua **56**(1), 47–59 (2018)
25. Liu, W.-J., Chen, Z.-Y., Ji, S., Wang, H.-B., Zhang, J.: Multi-party semi-quantum key agreement with delegating quantum computation. Int. J. Theor. Phys. **56**(10), 3164–3174 (2017). https://doi.org/10.1007/s10773-017-3484-6
26. Liu, W.J., Chen, Z.Y., Liu, J.S., Su, Z.F., Chi, L.H.: Full-blind delegating private quantum computation. CMC-Comput. Mater. Continua **56**(2), 211–223 (2018)
27. Lloyd, S., Mohseni, M., Rebentrost, P.: Quantum algorithms for supervised and unsupervised machine learning. eprint arXiv (2013)
28. Liu, W.-J., Gao, P.-P., Yu, W.-B., Qu, Z.-G., Yang, C.-N.: Quantum relief algorithm. Quantum Inf. Process. **17**(10), 1–15 (2018). https://doi.org/10.1007/s11128-018-2048-x
29. QISKit: Open Source Quantum Information Science Kit. https://qiskit.org/. Accessed 12 Apr 2018
30. IBM quantum computing platform. https://www.research.ibm.com/ibm-q/. Accessed 11 Apr 2017
31. Nielsen, M.A., Chuang, I.L.: Quantum Computation and Quantum Information, 10 Anniversary edn. Cambridge University Press, Cambridge (2011)
32. Garey, M.R., Johnson, D.S.: Computers and Intractability, vol. 29. W. H. Freeman and Company, New York (1972)

Cloud Grazing Management and Decision System Based on WebGIS

Dong Li[1,2,3], Chuanjian Wang[1,2,3(✉)], Tianying Yan[1], Qilei Wang[1], Ju Wang[1],
and Wanlong Bing[1]

[1] College of Information Science and Technology, Shihezi University, Shihezi 832000, China
wcj_inf@shzu.edu.cn
[2] Geospatial Information Engineering Research Center,
Xinjiang Production and Construction Corps, Shihezi 832000, China
[3] Geospatial Information Engineering Laboratory,
Xinjiang Production and Construction Corps, Shihezi 832000, China

Abstract. In order to improve the information level of animal husbandry and solve the problems of unreasonable utilization of grassland resources, this study was based on 3S technology, making full use of the advantages of GIS information processing and Cloud computing resources. A cloud grazing management and decision system based on WebGIS was developed. The system took the mainstream Web browser as the client platform. The functions of displaying the real-time position of the herd, querying historical trajectory, monitoring grassland growth and estimating situation of grassland utilization were achieved by the system. For the server side, the spatial management technology of spatial data engine ArcSDE and SQL Server 2012 was applied to store data. Tomcat 7.0 was used as the Web server and ArcGIS Server 10.3 was used as GIS Server. The automation of data processing was realized by calling ArcPy package through Python script. The results were published automatically to the ArcGIS Server for client display. The system can provide decision-making basis for ranchers and grassland livestock management departments to manage grazing and grassland. It enables ranchers to make reasonable and effective grazing plans, so as to make balanced utilization of grassland resources and promote the sustainable development of grazing animal husbandry.

Keywords: WebGIS · Grazing management · Monitor · Perception · Cognition

1 Introduction

Grassland is not only an important ecological barrier for the earth, but also the material basis for the livestock production in pastoral areas [1]. China's natural grassland is about $4 \times 10^8 hm^2$. It accounts for 41.7% of the country's land area [2], 90% of which has different extent of degradation [3]. However, overgrazing is one of the important causes of grassland degradation [4–7]. Due to the backwardness of infrastructure construction in pastoral areas and the poor communication conditions, it is difficult for ranchers

X. Zhang et al. (Eds.): CloudComp 2019/SmartGift 2019, LNICST 322, pp. 424–436, 2020.
https://doi.org/10.1007/978-3-030-48513-9_34

and grassland livestock management departments to control effectively herders' grazing behavior and grassland utilization. To a great extent, it has affected the scientific decision-making of grassland construction projects, such as rotational grazing [8, 9], light grazing [10], grassland ecological compensation [11], and fence enclosure [12, 13]. Therefore, it is necessary to develop a cloud grazing management and decision system for rapid and large-scale monitoring of grazing behavior, herd feeding, grassland growth and grassland utilization. The system can provide decision-making basis for ranchers and grassland livestock management departments to manage grazing and grassland. It is of great practical significance to promote the sustainable development of animal husbandry and grassland ecology.

In recent years, domestic and foreign scholars have applied 3S technologies to their studies. In terms of GPS location perception, Pérez et al. and McGranahan et al. used GPS and GPRS technology to monitor the captive animals and provide information such as walking distance and herd behavior in the study area [14, 15]. The daily walking distance of the animal was obtained by the analysis. Liao et al. used the GPS collar to track and monitor the cattle herds in the African grassland. The relationship between the behavior types of cattle and the statistical parameters of the movement was established [16]. They analyzed and predicted the temporal and spatial distribution of the cattle movement behavior and resource selection patterns. Bailey et al. used GPS and accelerometer motion sensing device to monitor the behavioral changes of the cattle and predict the health of the animals [17]. In terms of RS perception, Ali et al. obtained experimental farm grass biomass by using the raw spectral bands of the satellite sensing. ANN(artificial neural network) was found to provide significant improvements in biomass estimation by them [18]. Ancin-Murguzur et al. used remote sensing satellites and a portable spectrometer (ASD FieldSpec 3) to perceive the spectrum of forage crops in high latitudes. The multivariate models were used to predict crop yields in high latitudes [19]. Pérez-Ortiz et al. used super-high spatial resolution UAV images and ground sampling data to perceive ground weed distribution. They used classification techniques to find the optimal machine learning model and developed a weed positioning system [20]. Pavel Propastin used the SPOT-VGT satellite to perceive the spectral information of the study area. The monitoring system was developed to quantify the link between climatic conditions and disaster risk [21]. Punalekar, et al. used optical remote sensing data (proximal hyperspectral and Sentinel 2A) to perceive experimental field spectra. The precision of estimated biomass was increased by the radiative transfer model [22]. In terms of environmental cognition, the relevant scholars mainly use RS and GIS to achieve the environment monitoring [23–27]. However, there are still few mature biomass estimation systems.

The above study work mainly used 3S technology to achieve the trajectory monitoring of the herds and grassland monitoring. These studies have the following limitations:

- Existing grazing management systems have few functions of monitoring feed intake of herds. Therefore, it is unable to meet the higher requirements on pasture monitoring for grassland livestock management departments.
- Although existing grassland monitoring systems have achieved the monitoring function of various grassland resources, there are few systems that achieved the function of grassland utilization estimation.

The purpose of this study is to develop a cloud grazing management and decision system. The specific objectives are to 1) to calculate the situation of feed intake, grassland growth and grassland utilization, and 2) to publish automatically the results to ArcGIS Server.

2 Methods

2.1 System Requirement Analysis

2.1.1 System Functional Requirements

Although the relevant grazing management systems had realized functions such as real-time location monitoring of herds, historical trajectory query and fence alarm, it still couldn't meet the requirements of ranchers and grassland livestock management departments, such as the situation of feed intake, grassland growth and grassland utilization. Therefore, in addition to the basic functions of herd real-time location monitoring and historical trajectory query, the system should also include the functions of feed intake of the herd, grassland biomass and grassland utilization estimation.

2.1.2 System Data Requirements

The trajectory data of the herd was collected by the GPS device. In terms of the number of data, the number of devices would determine the quality of the data. Appropriate increase in the number of devices would result in more trajectory data. It would improve the fault tolerance and representativeness of the data, and it enabled the data to more accurately describe the herd trajectory.

In terms of data quality, high-quality trajectory data was an important data guarantee for monitoring grazing behavior and estimating grassland utilization situation. Akasbi, et al. shows that the shorter the data recording time interval, the closer the recorded trajectory is to the actual grazing trajectory [28]. Therefore, the recording interval of data should be as short as possible.

Remote sensing image data were needed for grassland growth monitoring and grassland utilization estimate. Satellite remote sensing technology can provide large-scale image data with small geographical constraints, but it has low resolution, long acquisition period and poor timeliness. UAV (Unmanned aerial vehicle) remote sensing image has high resolution and high timeliness, but its work is limited by its endurance. It limits the acquisition of image data. Therefore, the system needed to combine two data acquisition methods. According to the requirements of different regions, the appropriate remote sensing image data was selected to accurately monitor the grassland biomass in the corresponding area.

2.1.3 User Requirements

The users had different functional requirements in various application scenarios. In practical applications, after the herdsmen login to the system, the system automatically assigned them to the corresponding ranch. The herdsmen could query the herd information and their working status. They could also view the location of all the current herds in the pasture. For the ranchers and grassland livestock management departments could view the real-time location, the historical trajectory, the feed intake distribution of the herd, and the situation of grassland utilization.

2.2 System Design

2.2.1 System Architecture Design

The architecture of the system was mainly divided into four layers (Fig. 1). They were application layer, presentation layer, business logic layer and data layer.

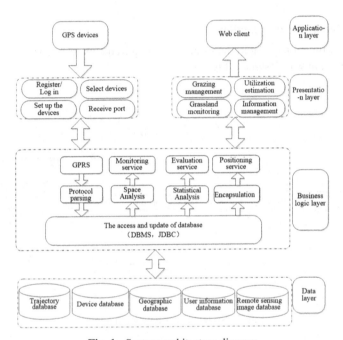

Fig. 1. System architecture diagram

The application layer consisted mainly of GPS devices and Web browsers (client). GPS devices were used to collect the trajectory data of herds. Web browsers were used to provide interface of data visualization to users.

In the presentation layer, we could select or add GPS devices, and set the communication mode, address and port of the GPS devices. According to different types of users, the system provided corresponding functions such as grazing management, grassland monitoring, grassland utilization estimation and information management.

In the business logic layer, GPS devices used GPRS technology to communicate with the GServer of the exlive platform. The GServer parsed the GPS protocol and stored the trajectory data into the database. The data was encapsulated into JSON format data to achieve the location service by calling the interface of GServer. Other functions of the business logic layer used the Python script to read the relevant data from the database and call the API of ArcGIS or ENVI to automatically process the relevant data at a fixed time. The results were published automatically to the ArcGIS Server. The thematic maps need a lot of historical GPS data, traditional servers need too much time to process large-scale data. Therefore, the spatial analysis server of this system was built on the cloud server by Hadoop, which improved the computing power of the traditional server, and the results were provided to users in time.

The data layer included a trajectory database, a device information database, a remote sensing image database, a geographic information database, and a user information database, which were respectively used to store GPS trajectory information, GPS device information, remote sensing images, geographic information, and user information.

2.2.2 Design of Client Function

After related functional requirements and user requirements were analyzed, the client function diagram was designed (Fig. 2).

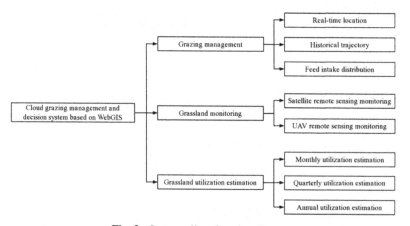

Fig. 2. System client function diagram

2.2.2.1 Grazing Management

Real-time location, historical trajectory, and feed intake distribution functions were included in the grazing management module. The user could set the GPS positioning time interval and the pasture boundary range. The real-time location function could locate the position of herds. The feeding route was displayed by the historical trajectory function according to the retrieval period. The feed intake distribution function could query the distribution of feed intake during the retrieval period, so that the herdsmen and ranchers grasped the feeding situation of the herds in time.

2.2.2.2 Grassland Monitoring

The grassland monitoring function obtained grassland growth situation by satellite remote sensing and UVA remote sensing. It displayed the spatiotemporal distribution map of grassland growth situation on the client side for livestock management.

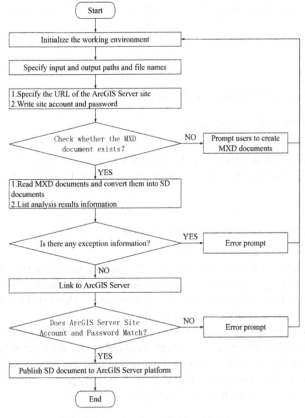

Fig. 3. Automatic publishing flowchart

2.2.2.3 Grassland Utilization estimation

When the client sent a grassland utilization query request to the server, the server found the corresponding estimation result and sent it to the client. The client provided user with a spatiotemporal distribution thematic map and a pie chart of the grassland utilization estimation.

2.2.3 Design of Server Function

The server was in charge of the storage of the trajectory data, the processing of remote sensing images, and the publishing of the results. When the server received the GPS trajectory data, it began data parsing, stored the valid field in the location information database, and used the spatial data engine (SDE) to manage the location information database, which can effectively save time and space.

The server used Python scripts to calculate the feed intake of the herd and grassland biomass, and used two kinds of grassland estimation models to estimate the grassland utilization. The estimation results of feed intake of the herd, grassland biomass and grassland utilization were stored into SQL database by ArcSDE. The processing results would be automatically published to ArcGIS Server in the time (such as 12:00 p.m.) when the system was accessed less frequently. When the server received the client's query request, it called ArcGIS API for JavaScript to respond to the client's request quickly and sent the relevant results to the client.

2.3   Core Function Realization and Testing

2.3.1   Trajectory Data Acquisition

The position information was collected by collars with GPS devices. It was encapsulated according to the data transmission standard and sent to the server through the data communication link. The data information was parsed and stored in the SQL Server database.

2.3.2   Realization of Data Processing Function

2.3.2.1 Feed Intake Distribution Module

The feed intake distribution module called ArcPy package to process the data of the herd trajectory. By creating a grid and using the model of the feed intake distribution of the herds, the feed intake in different regions was calculated. The distribution maps of the feed intake in different regions were obtained.

In terms of the normal grazing, there is no significant difference in the daily feed intake of the herd [28]. The greater the number of GPS points, the greater the feed intake. In this paper, the fishnet tool of ArcGIS was used to grid the study area. According to the proportion of GPS points in each grid to the total GPS points in the study area, the feed intake of the herd in each cell was calculated:

$$\sum I = F \cdot N \cdot \frac{A_i}{\sum A_i} \cdot \frac{1}{S} \tag{1}$$

Where $\sum I$ is the feed intake of the herd for N days (g/m^2), A_i is the number of GPS trajectory points in the i-th cell of the feed N days, $\sum A_i$ is the total GPS trajectory points of the feed N days for herd.

The projection of trajectory data, grid analysis and frequency distribution statistics of trajectory points were the cores of the calculation of feed intake. They were achieved by calling the related functions of ArcPy package, such as Project_management() function, CreateFishnet_management() function, Spatial Join_analysis() function, AddField_management() and CalculateField_management() functions of ArcPy package.

2.3.2.2 Grassland Monitoring Module

• Estimation of Grassland Biomass Based on Satellite Remote Sensing

Zhang et al. used Landsat 8 OLI remote sensing data and ground measured biomass data to build grassland estimation model through statistical analysis [29]. The result showed that the grassland biomass of the sunny slope and shady slope had a good fitting effect with the soil-adjusted vegetation index (SAVI) (sunny slope $R^2 = 0.703$, shady slope $R^2 = 0.712$). The grassland biomass was calculated:

$$f(x) = \begin{cases} 178.71 \cdot x^2 + 97.199 \cdot x + 37.794, & \text{sunny slope} \\ 112.01 \cdot x^2 + 305.36 \cdot x - 59.296, & \text{shady slope} \end{cases} \tag{2}$$

Where x is the value of RVI, and f(x) is grassland biomass.

- Estimation of Grassland Biomass Based on Remote Sensing of UAV

Shize, et al. used the UAV multi-spectral image ground measured biomass data to build grassland estimation model through statistical analysis [30]. The result showed that the grassland biomass of the sunny slope and shady slope had a good fitting effect with the ratio vegetation index (RVI) (sunny slope $R^2 = 0.781$, shady slope $R^2 = 0.813$). The grassland biomass was calculated:

$$f(x) = \begin{cases} 2.659 + 12.583 \cdot x, & \text{sunny slope} \\ 36.951 + 16.589 \cdot x, & \text{shady slope} \end{cases} \tag{3}$$

Where x is the value of RVI, and f(x) is grassland biomass.

The data of the images was processed and analyzed by calling Radiometric Calibration, FLAASH Atmospheric Correction and BandMath module. The distribution map of grassland biomass was obtained.

2.3.2.3 Grassland Utilization Estimation Module

- Grassland Utilization Estimation Using Trajectory and Remote Sensing

The utilization process of natural grassland is a process of continuous interaction between grazing behavior and grass growth. The grass growth and grazing behavior should be considered when estimating the utilization situation of natural grassland. Grassland biomass wouldn't change significantly in a short period of time. If the estimated period was short, the grassland utilization estimation could be based on the compensatory growth principle of the grassland. If the grassland biomass level was the same as the feed intake level, the grassland utilization was moderate utilization. If the grassland biomass level was less than the feed intake level, the grassland was over utilization. If the grassland biomass level was greater than the feed intake level, the grassland was light utilization (Eq. 4):

$$y = F(A, B, T) = \begin{cases} B_T > I_T, & \text{light utilization} \\ B_T = I_T, & \text{moderate utilization} \\ B_T < I_T, & \text{over utilization} \end{cases} \tag{4}$$

Where A is the trajectory data, B is the remote sensing image data, T is the grazing cycle, I_T is the feed intake classification level, and B_T is the biomass classification level.

The function was achieved by calling the relevant functions, such as ExtractMultiValuesToPoints() function, AddField_management(), CalculateField_management() functions of ArcPy package and jenks_breaks() method of Jenkspy package.

- Using Fuzzy Mathematics for Grassland Utilization Estimation.

The grassland biomass has changed significantly over a long period of time, so it is necessary to build a membership function for evaluating the quarterly or annual grassland utilization [31]. The membership function was based on the descending half trapezoid, the rising half trapezoid and the intermediate symmetry in fuzzy mathematics. Taking the feed intake as the domain, the membership functions of the fuzzy comment set V = {good, moderate, poor} are given. The poor utilization of grassland is divided into two different membership functions: one is light utilization (Eq. 5) and the other is over utilization (Eq. 6).

$$\mu_{11}(x) = \begin{cases} 1 & (x < b_1) \\ \frac{b_2 - x}{b_2 - b_1} & (b_1 \le x \le b_2) \\ 0 & (x > b_2) \end{cases} \tag{5}$$

$$\mu_{12}(x) = \begin{cases} 0 & (x < b_4) \\ \frac{-b_4 + x}{b_5 - b_4} & (b_4 \le x \le b_5) \\ 1 & (x > b_5) \end{cases} \tag{6}$$

The intermediate symmetrical distribution function is used to estimate moderate utilization and good utilization of grassland (Eq. 7, Eq. 8, and Eq. 9).

$$\mu_{21}(x) = \begin{cases} \frac{x - b_1}{b_2 - b_1} & (b_1 \le x \le b_2) \\ \frac{b_3 - x}{b_3 - b_2} & (b_2 < x \le b_3) \\ 0 & (x < b_1 \text{ or } x > b_3) \end{cases} \tag{7}$$

$$\mu_{22}(x) = \begin{cases} \frac{x - b_3}{b_4 - b_3} & (b_3 \le x \le b_4) \\ \frac{b_5 - x}{b_5 - b_4} & (b_4 < x \le b_5) \\ 0 & (x < b_3 \text{ or } x > b_5) \end{cases} \tag{8}$$

$$\mu_{3}(x) = \begin{cases} \frac{x - b_2}{b_3 - b_2} & (b_2 \le x \le b_3) \\ \frac{b_4 - x}{b_4 - b_3} & (b_3 < x \le b_4) \\ 0 & (x < b_2 \text{ or } x > b_4) \end{cases} \tag{9}$$

Where b_i is the boundary of different feed intake, i = 1, 2,..., 5; x is the feed intake, g/m^2.

2.3.3   The Achievement of Automatic Publishing Result Function

The results were automatically published to ArcGIS Server platform by Python script. The map documents in folders were automatically published to ArcGIS Server. Automatic publishing process is shown (Fig. 4).

id	VehicleID	UserID	gpstime	recvtime	lng	lat	alt	veo	direct	av	istate
10655	9363485	0	2017-06-13 08:45:04.000	2017-06-13 08:45:06.000	85.777271	44.001484	0	4	72	1	5120
10656	9363485	0	2017-06-13 08:45:09.000	2017-06-13 08:45:11.000	85.777333	44.001462	0	3	123	1	5120
10657	9363485	0	2017-06-13 08:45:14.000	2017-06-13 08:45:16.000	85.777413	44.00144	0	4	120	1	5120
10658	9363485	0	2017-06-13 08:45:19.000	2017-06-13 08:45:21.000	85.777493	44.00144	0	4	109	1	5120
10659	9363485	0	2017-06-13 08:45:24.000	2017-06-13 08:45:26.000	85.777582	44.001453	0	4	94	1	5120
10660	9363485	0	2017-06-13 08:45:29.000	2017-06-13 08:45:31.000	85.777644	44.00148	0	4	78	1	5120
10661	9363485	0	2017-06-13 08:45:34.000	2017-06-13 08:45:36.000	85.777689	44.001516	0	4	42	1	5120
10662	9363485	0	2017-06-13 08:45:39.000	2017-06-13 08:45:41.000	85.777716	44.001569	0	3	32	1	5120
10663	9363485	0	2017-06-13 08:45:44.000	2017-06-13 08:45:47.000	85.777742	44.001604	0	2	18	1	5120
10664	9363485	0	2017-06-13 08:45:49.000	2017-06-13 08:45:51.000	85.77776	44.001604	0	0	18	1	5120
10665	9363485	0	2017-06-13 08:45:54.000	2017-06-13 08:45:57.000	85.77776	44.001604	0	0	18	1	5120
10666	9363485	0	2017-06-13 08:45:59.000	2017-06-13 08:46:02.000	85.77776	44.001604	0	0	18	1	5120
10667	9363485	0	2017-06-13 08:46:04.000	2017-06-13 08:46:06.000	85.77776	44.001604	0	0	18	1	5120
10668	9363485	0	2017-06-13 08:46:09.000	2017-06-13 08:46:12.000	85.77776	44.001604	0	0	18	1	5120
10669	9363485	0	2017-06-13 08:46:14.000	2017-06-13 08:46:16.000	85.77776	44.001604	0	0	18	1	5120
10670	9363485	0	2017-06-13 08:46:19.000	2017-06-13 08:46:21.000	85.77776	44.001604	0	0	18	1	5120
10671	9363485	0	2017-06-13 08:46:24.000	2017-06-13 08:46:26.000	85.77776	44.001604	0	0	18	1	5120
10672	9363485	0	2017-06-13 08:46:29.000	2017-06-13 08:46:31.000	85.77776	44.001604	0	0	18	1	5120
10673	9363485	0	2017-06-13 08:46:34.000	2017-06-13 08:46:36.000	85.77776	44.001604	0	0	18	1	5120

Fig. 4. Data acquisition results

3 Results

In this study, Ziniquan pasture, No. 151st regiment of the 8th division of Xinjiang production and Construction Corps was taken as an example. The experiment was carried out from April to August 2017. This experiment used the GT03C positioning devices produced by Shenzhen Gu Mi Electronics Co., Ltd. to obtain the real-time geographic location of the herd and upload it to the server. The uploaded data included device ID, latitude and longitude, transmission time, etc. (Fig. 3).

The spatial distributed map of the feed intake was obtained when the trajectory points as the input of the feed intake distribution model. The spatial distributed maps of grassland biomass were respectively obtained when satellite remote sensing image and UAV image as the input of the grassland biomass models.

The natural grassland biomass was estimated from April 20, 2016 to May 6, 2016 by satellite remote sensing image (Fig. 5). The area of human activity was in the northwest part of the study. Other areas with high biomass were due to the exuberant growth of grass during this period. At the same time, the weather was so cold that the herd rarely fed in circles. Therefore, the growth speed of grassland was higher than the feeding speed of the herd. The less biomass in the study area was mainly due to the terrain was not suitable for grass to grow.

Grassland utilization in the study area was estimated by fuzzy mathematics evaluation method in 2016. The thematic map of the grassland utilization evaluation was obtained (Fig. 6).

It could be seen from Fig. 6 that the over utilization area was mainly distributed in the southwest of the study area. The main reason for the over utilization was that the terrain of the area was flat, which was conducive to grazing and feeding of herds. And it was the area that herds often pass after they leave the sheepfold.

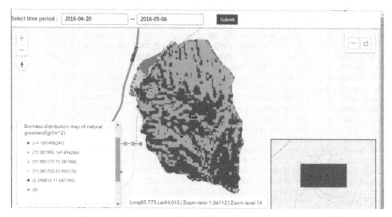

Fig. 5. Distribution of grassland biomass from April 20 to May 6, 2016

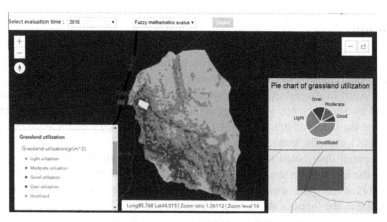

Fig. 6. Distribution of grassland utilization in 2016

4   Conclusions

- The system built the client and server modules. The server was composed of GIS server, Web server, GServer and database. The web browser was used as the client of the system. The GPS terminal uploaded the position information to the GPS server in time. When the client accessed the trajectory information, the web server returned data to the client by requesting GPS server. In addition, the spatial analysis server collected a large amount of GPS data periodically. The data was processed and packed intelligently through the cloud service platform. The result was published automatically to the ArcGIS server by Python. The GPS terminal server and client are combined and coordinated organically in system.

- The system achieved the functions of real-time monitoring of the herd, query of historical trajectory, distribution of feed intake, grassland growth monitoring and grassland utilization estimation. The system can deliver monitoring information and send warning messages to ranchers and animal husbandry management departments in time, so as to guide relevant people to adjust grazing area. In short, it is meaningful to improve grassland productivity and achieve sustainable utilization of grassland. It also can balance grass and livestock, and promote the sustainable development of animal husbandry.

Acknowledgments. We highly appreciate the Yang Yonglin of the Xinjiang Academy of Agricultural Reclamation and the pastoralists of Ziniquan farm, who participated in the GPS trajectory data collection and shared their knowledge on herd. We are thankful to all the professional GIS technicians, graduate students and undergraduates who contributed to the development of this system. We are grateful for the thoughtful and constructive comments of the reviewers that improved this manuscript in major ways.

Funding. This work was supported by the National Key R&D Program of China (Grant No. 2017YFB0504203), the National Natural Science Foundation of China (Grant No. 41461088, and the XJCC XPCC Innovation Team of Geospatial Information Technology (Grant No. 2016AB001).

Conflicts of Interest. The authors declare no conflict of interest.

References

1. Voormansik, K.: Observations of cutting practices in agricultural grasslands using polarimetric sar. IEEE J. Sel. Top. Appl. Earth Obs. Remote Sens. **9**(4), 1382–1396 (2016)
2. Shen, H., Zhu, Y., Zhao, X., et al.: Analysis of current grassland resources in China. Chin. Sci. Bull. **61**(2), 139–154 (2016)
3. Yin, C., Kong, X., Liu, Y., et al.: Spatiotemporal changes in ecologically functional land in China: a quantity-quality coupled perspective. J. Clean. Prod. **238**, 117917 (2019)
4. Marquart, A., Eldridge, D., Travers, S., et al.: Large shrubs partly compensate negative effects of grazing on hydrological function in a semi-arid savanna. Basic Appl. Ecol. **38**, 58–68 (2019)
5. Cavagnaro, R., Pero, E., Dudinszky, N., et al.: Under pressure from above: overgrazing decreases mycorrhizal colonization of both preferred and unpreferred grasses in the Patagonian steppe. Fungal Ecol. **40**, 92–97 (2019)
6. Ren, W., Badgery, W., Ding, Y., et al.: Hepatic transcriptome profile of sheep (Ovis aries) in response to overgrazing: novel genes and pathways revealed. BMC Genet. **20**, 54 (2019)
7. Yu, L., Chen, Y., Sun, W., et al.: Effects of grazing exclusion on soil carbon dynamics in alpine grasslands of the Tibetan Plateau. Geoderma **353**, 133–143 (2019)
8. Dong, L., McCulley, R., Nelson, J., et al.: Time in pasture rotation alters soil microbial community composition and function and increases carbon sequestration potential in a temperate agroecosystem. Sci. Total Environ. **698**, 134233 (2019)
9. Pittarello, M., Probo, M., Perotti, E., et al.: Grazing management Plans improve pasture selection by cattle and forage quality in sub-alpine and alpine grasslands. J. Mt. Sci. **16**(9), 2126–2135 (2019)
10. Yu, H., Li, Y., Odutola, O., et al.: Reintroduction of light grazing reduces soil erosion and soil respiration in a converted grassland on the Loess Plateau, China. Agr. Ecosyst. Environ. **280**, 43–52 (2019)
11. Hu, Y., Huang, J., Hou, H.: Impacts of the grassland ecological compensation policy on household livestock production in China. Ecol. Econ. **161**, 248–256 (2019)
12. Liu, J., Bian, Z., Zhang, K., et al.: Effects of different fencing regimes on community structure of degraded desert grasslands on Mu Us desert. Ecol. Evol. **9**(6), 3367–3377 (2019)

13. Song, Z., Wang, J., Liu, G., et al.: Changes in nitrogen functional genes in soil profiles of grassland under long-term grazing prohibition in a semiarid area. Sci. Total Environ. **673**, 92–101 (2019)

14. Pérez, J., Varga, M., García, J., et al.: Monitoring lidia cattle with GPS-GPRS technology; a study on grazing behaviour and spatial distribution. Vet. Mex. **4**(4), 1–17 (2017)

15. McGranahan, D., Geaumont, B., Spiess, J., et al.: Assessment of a livestock GPS collar based on an open-source datalogger informs best practices for logging intensity. Ecol. Evol. **8**(1), 5649–5660 (2018)

16. Liao, C., Clark, P., Shibia, M., et al.: Spatiotemporal dynamics of cattle behavior and resource selection patterns on East African rangelands: evidence from GPS-tracking. Int. J. Geogr. Inf. Sci. **32**(7), 1523–1540 (2018)

17. Bailey, D., Trotter, M., Knight, C., et al.: Thomas: Use of GPS tracking collars and accelerometers for rangeland livestock production research. Transl. Anim. Sci. **2**(1), 81–88 (2018)

18. Ali, I., Cawkwell, F., Dwyer, E., et al.: Modeling managed grassland biomass estimation by using multitemporal remote sensing data-a machine learning approach. IEEE J. Sel. Top. Appl. Earth Obs. Remote Sens. **10**(7), 3254–3264 (2017)

19. Ancin-Murguzur, F., Taff, G., Davids, C., et al.: Yield estimates by a two-step approach using hyperspectral methods in grasslands at high latitudes. Remote Sens. **11**(4), 400 (2019)

20. Pérez-Ortiz, M., Peña, J.M., Gutiérrez, P.A., et al.: A semi-supervised system for weed mapping in sunflower crops using unmanned aerial vehicles and a crop row detection method. Appl. Soft Comput. **37**, 533–544 (2015)

21. Propastin, P.: Multisensor monitoring system for assessment of locust hazard risk in the lake balkhash drainage basin. Environ. Manag. **50**(6), 1234–1246 (2012)

22. Punalekar, S.M., Verhoef, A., Quaife, T.L., et al.: Application of sentinel-2a data for pasture biomass monitoring using a physically based radiative transfer model. Remote Sens. Environ. **218**, 207–220 (2018)

23. Battude, M., et al.: Estimating maize biomass and yield over large areas using high spatial and temporal resolution Sentinel-2 like remote sensing data. Remote Sens. Environ. **184**, 668–681 (2016)

24. Wang, L., et al.: Comparative analysis of GF-1 WFV, ZY-3 MUX, and HJ-1 CCD sensor data for grassland monitoring applications. Remote Sens. **7**(2), 2089–2108 (2015)

25. Guo, B., et al.: Dynamic monitoring of soil erosion in the upper Minjiang catchment using an improved soil loss equation based on remote sensing and geographic information system. Land Degrad. Dev. **29**(3), 521–533 (2018)

26. Alexandridis, T.K., et al.: Investigation of the temporal relation of remotely sensed coastal water quality with GIS modelled upstream soil erosion. Hydrol. Process. **29**(10), 2373–2384 (2015)

27. Lussem, U., et al.: Using calibrated rgb imagery from low-cost uavs for grassland monitoring: case study at the rengen grassland experiment (rge), Germany. In: ISPRS - International Archives of the Photogrammetry, Remote Sensing and Spatial Information Sciences, vol. XLII-2/W6, pp. 229–233 (**2017**)

28. Akasbi, Z., Oldeland, J., Dengler, J., et al.: Social and ecological constraints on decision making by transhumant pastoralists: a case study from the Moroccan atlas mountains. J. Mt. Sci. **9**(3), 307–321 (2012)

29. Zhang, Y., Yin, X., Wang, X., et al.: Estimation of aboveground biomass of grassland on the northern slope of Tianshan Mountain based on Landsat 8 oli remote sensing image. Remote Sens. Technol. Appl. **32**(6), 1012–1021 (2017)

30. Sun, S., Wang, C., Yin, X., et al.: Estimation of natural grassland biomass based on multi spectral image of UAV. J. Remote Sens. **22**(5), 848–856 (2018)

31. Wang, C., Jiang, H., Lu, W., et al.: Evaluation model of natural grassland utilization based on grazing time and space track. J. Agric. Mach. **49**(8), 181–186 (2018)

Application Design of Provincial Meteorological Service System Based on National Unified Meteorological Data Environment

Qing Chen, Ming Yang[✉], You Zeng, Yefeng Chen, Shucheng Wu, Yun Xiao, and Yueying Hong

Zhejiang Meteorological Information Network Center, Hangzhou 310001, China
zjhzjxlchenqing@163.com

Abstract. A unified data environment is established in China Integrated Meteorological Information Sharing System (CIMISS) or the national meteorological service. The paper discusses the establishment of provincial meteorological service system application flow and scheme based on unified data environment. It creates a seamless integration between local system and China Integrated Meteorological Information Sharing System without changing business processes and system architecture of existing meteorological service system. In the design scheme, the meteorological data is obtained by the multiple services based on unified data environment and data interface. According to different data structures, analytical methods of discrete data, gridded data and raster data are discussed. Finally, efficient and rapid visualization of meteorological data is realized. The result shows that the application flow and scheme that China Integrated Meteorological Information Sharing System used in provincial meteorological service system are effective and feasible. It is hoped that the studies of this paper can provide a reference for accessing unified national meteorological data environment for meteorological service system.

Keywords: Application design of provincial meteorological operational system · Data interface · Analytical methods of data · Visualization methods of data · Application flow and scheme

1 Introduction

The National Integrated Meteorological Information Sharing Platform is a set of integrated meteorological information business platform which integrates data collection, processing, storage management, sharing services and business monitoring [1]. The system stores 14 kinds of meteorological data, including real-time observation data, product generation data and historical compilation data [2]. It provides integrated meteorological observation data and meteorological products sharing services for meteorological services and users of related industries, and meets the needs of modern meteorological business, scientific research and services for meteorological information. The accuracy

© ICST Institute for Computer Sciences, Social Informatics and Telecommunications Engineering 2020
Published by Springer Nature Switzerland AG 2020. All Rights Reserved
X. Zhang et al. (Eds.): CloudComp 2019/SmartGift 2019, LNICST 322, pp. 437–446, 2020.
https://doi.org/10.1007/978-3-030-48513-9_35

of data is difficult to guarantee is difficult to guarantee, for the data entry of each business system is not uniform and the algorithm is different. Some systems have the problem of data redundancy. These factors lead to the inconsistency of product data generated by meteorological operational systems at present [3–6]. The popularization and application of CIMISS system provides a unified meteorological data supporting platform for meteorological business application at provincial, municipal and county levels, realizes data reduction and integrated management, and ensures the accuracy of data [7].

The purpose of this paper is to discuss the effective process and scheme of CIMISS application in provincial meteorological operational system. The seamless connection between localization system and CIMISS system is realized on the basis of maintaining the existing overall business process and system architecture of provincial meteorological operational system. In this way, we can further improve the service ability and access efficiency of meteorological data, and provide some reference for other meteorological operational systems to access CIMISS data environment.

2   Function Design of System

2.1   Architecture of Platform

As shown in in Fig. 1, the system architecture consists of four layers: data access layer, component layer, business logic layer and presentation layer. The data access layer is responsible for the data access scheduling. The component layer is mainly the internal component design of the system. The business layer deals with the business logic of the system. The presentation layer is responsible for the terminal display of the system and provides the user with an interactive interface.

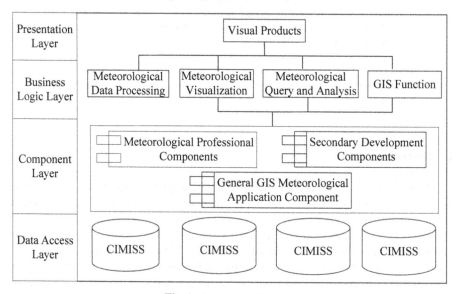

Fig. 1. System architecture

2.2 Functional Design

According to the particularity of meteorological business and function, the platform mainly includes the following parts:

First level, meteorological data processing: Support the analysis of discrete, grid and raster structure type meteorological data, and output meteorological data into various formats, including ShapeFile, Json, Kml, Image, etc. as required. Supported meteorological data products include meteorological station data, grid data, radar products and satellite cloud image products.

Second level, meteorological visualization and caching: Visualization provides the rendering of meteorological data points, lines, surfaces and volumes, and provides users with various forms of visualization effects. It also supports the rapid access of massive meteorological data by using memory database technology and static caching technology.

Third level, meteorological query and analysis: support the retrieval of meteorological elements and download of data files; support the sampling, interpolation, isoline or isosurface generation, smoothing processing of meteorological data and other functions [8].

Fourth level, geographic Information System (GIS) functions: support the management of map layers and the query and operation of geographical data; support the spatial query and analysis based on GIS, including the extraction and analysis of meteorological data, visual analysis; support the production of maps, graphic display and so on.

2.3 Data Access Design

Meteorological data is the core of meteorological operational system. It has many characteristics, such as many kinds of elements, wide coverage and strong timeliness. The meteorological data processed by provincial meteorological operational system are uniformly obtained from CIMISS meteorological data service interface.

At present, most of the meteorological operational system data are obtained from the local meteorological data center by reading the original files, accessing the database, calling the local interface to read the data and so on. At the same time, the meteorological operational system will also write the generated product data back to the local meteorological data center. By developing localized business applications around CIMISS system, the data processing flow is optimized and a unified data service interface is established. After the establishment of CIMISS data environment, business system data is directly obtained through CIMISS data service interface, and the generated product data is transmitted back to CIMISS data environment through CIMISS data service interface. The data access design diagram of meteorological operation system accessing CIMISS data environment is shown in Fig. 2.

3 Research on Technical Method

3.1 Meteorological Data Access Based on CIMISS Environment

Designing Configuration File. XML configuration scheme is designed in this paper by the configuration of XML for meteorological products. By editing the parameters

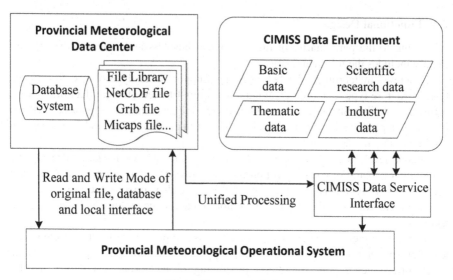

Fig. 2. Data access design

in the XML configuration file, it can add and delete meteorological products, modify the operation, obtain different types of meteorological data, and return the types after acquiring the data. Configuration file makes configuration parameters flexible, makes content and structure independent, and effectively improves the scalability of software [9]. After the system accesses the CIMISS data environment, XML files need to be configured according to the actual requirements of system development.

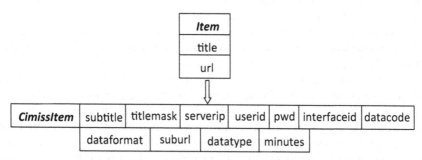

Fig. 3. XML profile diagram of business system accessing CIMISS data environment

The upper part of arrow in Fig. 3 is the configuration of the data product part before the system accesses the CIMISS data environment. The title node represents the product name. The *url* node contains the product's sub-configuration file information, file path, file format and file aging. The lower part of arrow in Fig. 3 is the configuration of the data product part after the system accesses CIMISS data environment. The subtitle represents the product name. The *titlemask* represents the title. The *serverip* represents the IP address of the data obtained through the interface. The userid represents the user name of the access. The *pwd* represents the password of the access. The *interfaceid* represents the interfaceid of the access. The *datacode* represents the data format. The *dataformat* returned after data acquisition. The configuration of *suburl* varies according to the type of data acquired: the configuration of lattice data includes product configuration file, product timeliness, latitude and longitude range, elements to be queried and wildcard of file name, the configuration of site data includes product configuration file, product query condition and wildcard product timeliness of file name. The *datatype* denotes the type of query data (including grid lattice data and station site data). The minute denotes the minute-level timeliness of the product.

Meteorological Data Retrieval Based on CIMISS Interface. CIMISS meteorological data service interface is based on CIMISS data environment, facing meteorological business and scientific research, providing unified, standard, rich data access services and application programming interface (API) [10]. CIMISS establishes a separate access interface for different meteorological data. Each data interface provides multiple functional interfaces and each functional interface has different retrieval parameters. It can retrieve different parameters according to time point, latitude and longitude range, statistical period and so on. Meteorological data and products are obtained by calling the data retrieval interface provided by CIMISS API through input parameters, including station information query, site information query, statistics, grid data retrieval, analysis and tailoring, document products (radar products, satellite clouds, numerical forecast products) retrieval, download and so on. The specific invocation method is shown in Table 1.

Table 1. The methods of the CIMISS interface.

Call method	Call method name	Format of returned data	Applicable information
Call API_to_serializedStr	Gets a serialized string	String (serialized)	Site information, lattice information (point/area), document products (document URL, etc.)
Call API_to_array	Get a two-dimensional string	Array (no descriptive information)	Site data, grid data (point/surface), document products (radar, satellite, numerical prediction)

Structured data are retrieved through API, including site element data, element values of single or multiple points in lattice data, data of a single field in lattice data, station metadata information, attribute information of data field, etc. Retrieving file list information interface and getting picture files encapsulated in Base64 format through API.

The data obtained by the call *API_to_serializedStr* method is returned as a serialized string (xml/json/html/text), and the data obtained by the call *API_to_array* method is returned as a binary array.

3.2   Organization and Analysis of Meteorological Data

According to the difference of data structure, meteorological data can be divided into discrete data, grid data and raster data. Meteorological data need to be analyzed before visualization. At present, most meteorological business systems mainly parse the data of Micaps class format files. The business system directly parses the data acquired in CIMISS after accessing the CIMISS data environment. Data in the form of discrete data include real-time and historical data of various meteorological elements observed automatically (including rainfall, temperature, pressure, relative humidity, visibility, wind, etc.) and site data of external door units such as water conservancy, environmental protection and ocean. The grid products of various meteorological elements (including rainfall, temperature, air pressure, etc.) need to be transformed into grid data first. Satellite cloud map, radar products and numerical model forecasting products need to be converted into raster-type data first.

The process of discrete data processing is to parse text files and assign values to visual sites. Call the CIMISS interface to get the two-dimensional site data and assign the information to the object. Objects include the site area station number, the address of the automatic station, provinces, cities, counties, towns or streets, longitude, latitude, height, numerical value and other attributes.

In the process of Gridding Data processing, CIMISS interface can be invoked to obtain grid field data. According to the latitude and longitude range of grid data and grid size, the latitude and longitude network data covering the research area can be generated. It can also call CIMISS interface to obtain two-dimensional site data, convert the data into grid data, and use interpolation in the process of grid processing of site data. In view of the limited number of meteorological stations and the discreteness of spatial distribution, the data of unknown points are estimated by interpolation based on the data of known samples. The data of discrete points are interpolated into continuous surface data through one or more interpolations, and then the contours or color patches are formed and displayed [11].

In the process of raster data processing, data is pre-mapped and the mapped data is divided into tile data according to a certain scale [12], and these tile data are stored in the file system in the form of picture files. The number of tile data after pre-processing is quite large. These files are organized through a specific file index directory structure, and a large number of tile data are managed and dispatched efficiently to adapt to the rapid transmission of the network and facilitate WebGIS to provide efficient services to the outside world.

3.3   Visualization Method of Meteorological Data

WebGIS Technology based on Silverlight. Data visualization uses Microsoft Silverlight plug-in technology, combined with ArcGIS Server meteorological data service to realize the query, analysis and display of meteorological data based on geospatial discretization, grid, raster and so on. For different data types, different data visualization methods are used. The visualization of discrete data is loaded into map vector layer rendering through the properties of longitude, latitude and numerical value of discrete data. In meteorology, grid data are mainly contours and grid points, which are overlapped on the map. The visualization of grid data is mainly in the form of pictures, which are displayed in the slice layer of the map.

In the process of data visualization, we use Microsoft Silverlight plug-in technology and ArcGIS Server application platform to construct meteorological business system to realize meteorological data visualization and query and analysis of meteorological data based on geographic space. ArcGIS API for Silverlight is used in the meteorological operation system to realize the operation, analysis, simulation and display of meteorological data, cartographic analysis, geographic information processing, spatial analysis, editing and other functions.

WebGIS based on Silverlight plug-in can fuse and render meteorological data including discrete, grid, raster and other data structures, so as to enhance the expressive ability of meteorological data. For the representation of discrete data, the longitude and latitude of each point in the discrete point data set are loaded into the object of geographical graphic layer to display in real time, and different rendering styles are used according to the fields of the data set; for the expression of gridding data, the gridding data obtained after parsing are plotted graphically to generate isoline or isosurface graphics, and the visualization product is generated by superimposing and displaying with geographical information. For the expression of raster data, the Silverlight client obtains the images in jpg, PNG format returned by the server, displays them by slice layer, and then superimposes them on the map base according to coordinate position [13].

Memory Database Technology. Before the meteorological operation system was connected to CIMISS system, the response speed of the system was relatively fast because most of the documents read by the system were localized files. After access to CIMISS system, the response speed of business system becomes slower when displaying meteorological data gridding products. In order to meet the needs of rapid response of the system, the business system introduced memory database technology when displaying meteorological data products after access to CIMISS system. The data in the database is resident in memory, which saves the time of disk I/O and improves the query performance of data [14]. In memory database query processing, cache performance is optimized, data is partitioned into cache to improve cache hit rate, and hash index is used to improve cache performance. In order to reduce the cost of memory access, data is compressed proportionally [15–17].

Static Caching Technology. When the air service system is connected to CIMISS system, the corresponding speed of displaying relatively large data such as raster data (radar, cloud image) is slow. In order to improve the efficiency of interactive response with users, static cache technology is used in the visualization of raster data. The vector data is pre-mapped by the GIS server statically, and the mapped data is divided into slice files, which are organized by a specific file index directory structure for direct invocation by the WebGIS client. Static caching technology effectively improves the product performance, guarantees the efficient browsing of data on the client side and the rapid release of data on the server side.

4 Application Examples

Zhejiang Meteorological Display Platform is one of the successful cases of Zhejiang Meteorological Business System accessing CIMISS system. The data acquired by CIMISS interface greatly meets the requirements of Zhejiang Meteorological Digital Display Platform for wide coverage and high real-time of meteorological data such as station network observation, numerical model and so on. It also provides stable underlying data support for ground, high altitude and numerical model modules in the platform. At the same time, CIMISS interface reduces the maintenance intensity of the platform system, avoids the repeated construction of data sources, and improves the consistency and authority of data. Figure 4 is a comparison of Zhejiang Meteorological Digital Display Platform before and after access to CIMISS data environment.

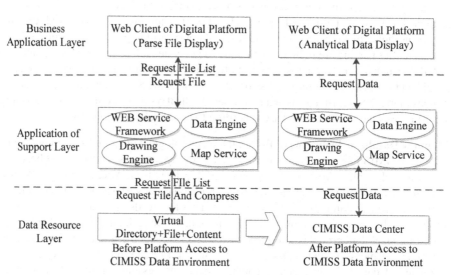

Fig. 4. Contrast chart of Zhejiang Meteorological Digital Display Platform before and after accessing CIMISS data environment

Zhejiang Meteorological Digital Platform based on CIMISS environment only needs to transform the data layer, while the business logic layer and the presentation layer remain basically unchanged. The data source is provided by multiple file servers, instead of the virtual directory on the Web server of the digital platform, it is provided by CIMISS data center, which reduces the construction process of the file server and virtual directory. Data transmission mode changed from file mode to CIMISS data stream mode, which reduced the process of obtaining file list and compressing file decompression. In data parsing mode, the original parsing file content display of the client of the data platform is changed to directly parsing CIMISS data, which reduces the process of parsing files. Figure 5 shows the Zhejiang Meteorological Digital Display Platform after it is connected to CIMISS data environment. Figure 5(a) shows the effect of grid data acquired through CIMISS environment on WebGIS after interpolation. Figure 5(b) shows the effect of raster data acquired through cimiss environment on WebGIS after pre-mapping.

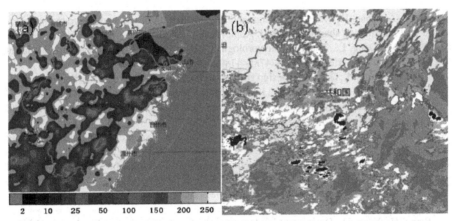

Fig. 5. Effect of Zhejiang Meteorological Digital Display Platform accessing CIMISS data environment (a) Distribution map of precipitation discrete data in Zhejiang province for nearly 24 h at 00:10 on 9 July 2016 (in millimeters) (b) Distribution map of raster data of Fengyun 2E cloud classification (CLC) products at 16:15 on July 12, 2016.

5   Concluding Terminology

In order to meet the needs of meteorological business system, we realize seamless connection between localization system and CIMISS system without changing the business process and system architecture of existing business system. The method proposed in the paper improves the service ability and access efficiency of meteorological data.

(1) In the part of data access business system, the extensibility and portability of the software are improved by designing the structure of XML configuration file. Using CIMISS data interface to obtain meteorological data.

(2) According to the different data structures, the analytical methods of three types of meteorological data, discrete data, grid data and raster data, are discussed respectively.

(3) In the process of meteorological data visualization, Zhejiang meteorological operational system is constructed by using Silverlight plug-in technology and ArcGIS Server application platform to realize meteorological data visualization and meteorological data query and analysis based on geographical space. In order to ensure the rapid release of meteorological data products on the server side and efficient browsing on the client side, memory database technology and static caching technology are adopted.

In summary, the application of CIMISS in Zhejiang Meteorological Operational System is feasible and effective. The application process and scheme provide a good idea for the promotion of CIMISS in National Meteorological services.

References

1. Xiong, A., Zhao, F., Wang, Y.: Design and implementation of national integrated meteorological information sharing system. J. Appl. Meteorol. 4(26), 500–512 (2015)
2. Wang, M., Deng, L., Zhao, F.: Meteorological satellite data storage and service model in CIMISS. Anhui Agric. Sci. 40(8), 4785–4789 (2012)
3. Yang, D., Wang, H., Gong, X.: Design and development of real-time data sharing platform for Yangtze river meteorological center. In: 2011 Annual Meeting of Meteorological Communication and Information Technology Committee of China Meteorological Society, pp. 277–280. China Meteorological Society, Beijing (2011)
4. Li, X., Shan, X., Yue, Y.: Design and implementation of ningxia meteorological data sharing and query system. J. Chongqing Univ. Ind. Commer. 32(3), 55–59 (2015)
5. Li, J., Sheng, W., Wang, G.: Research on meteorological information sharing platform and its key technologies. J. Appl. Meteorol. 17(5), 621–628 (2006)
6. Li, J., Xiong, A.: Summary of research on meteorological science data sharing system. J. Appl. Meteorol. 15(1), 1–9 (2004)
7. Wang, H., Yang, D.: Design and implementation of meteorological and hydrological information sharing system in Yangtze river basin based on CIMSS. Anhui Agric. Sci. 42(32), 11565–11570 (2014)
8. Zhang, X., Wang, W., Wang, P.: Research and implementation of key technologies of 3D meteorological GIS platform. Meteorol. Sci. Technol. 43(2), 226–231 (2015)
9. Guo, R., Wang, B., Ding, J.: XML configuration file parsing and generation technology based on table driven. Comput. Eng. Appl. 42(9), 89–92 (2006)
10. Liu, L., Zhang, Z.: CIMISS Xinjiang meteorological data unified access interface. Desert Oasis Meteorol. 9(1), 116–117 (2015)
11. Wu, H., Luo, B., Wang, W.: Application of GIS technology in the construction of decision-making meteorological service system. J. Appl. Meteorol. 9(3), 380–384 (2008)
12. Shang, X.: Design and Implementation of WebGIS Massive Tile Data Management Engine. Zhejiang Normal University, Jinhua (2012)
13. Wang, T., Wang, E., Guo, H.: Research on web GIS client technology based on silverlight. J. Geo-Inf. Sci. 12(01), 69–75 (2010)
14. Wang, S., Xiao, Y., Liu, D.: Research on key technologies of memory database. Comput. Appl. 27(10), 2353–2357 (2007)
15. Xu, X., Fu, S., Qi, L.: An IoT-Oriented data placement method with privacy preservation in cloud environment. J. Netw. Comput. Appl. 124, 148–157 (2018)
16. Qi, L., Chen, Y., Yuan, Y.: A QoS-Aware virtual machine scheduling method for energy conservation in cloud-based cyber-physical systems. World Wide Web J. (2019). https://doi.org/10.1007/s11280-019-00684-y
17. Qi, L., He, Q., Chen, F.: Finding all you need: web APIs recommendation in web of things through keywords search. IEEE Trans. Comput. Soc. Syst. (2019). https://doi.org/10.1109/TCSS.2019.2906925

Moving Vehicle Detection Based on Optical Flow Method and Shadow Removal

Min Sun[1], Wei Sun[1,2(✉)], Xiaorui Zhang[2,3], Zhengguo Zhu[3], and Mian Li[1]

[1] School of Automation, Nanjing University of Information Science
and Technology, Nanjing 210044, China
sunw0125@163.com
[2] Jiangsu Collaborative Innovation Center of Atmospheric Environment
and Equipment Technology, Nanjing 210044, China
[3] Jiangsu Engineering Center of Network Monitoring, Nanjing University of Information
Science and Technology, Nanjing 210044, China

Abstract. Video-based moving vehicle detection is an important prerequisite for vehicle tracking and vehicle counting. However, in the natural scene, the conventional optical flow method cannot accurately detect the boundary of the moving vehicle due to the generation of the shadow. In order to solve this problem, this paper proposes an improved moving vehicle detection algorithm based on optical flow method and shadow removal. The proposed method firstly uses the optical flow method to roughly detect the moving vehicle, and then uses the shadow detection algorithm based on the HSV color space to mark the shadow position after threshold segmentation, and further combines the region-labeling algorithm to realize the shadow removal and accurately detect the moving vehicle. Experiments are carried out in complex traffic scenes with shadow interference. The experimental results show that the proposed method can well solve the impact of shadow interference on moving vehicle detection and realize real-time and accurate detection of moving vehicles.

Keywords: Moving vehicle detection · Shadow removal · Optical flow method · HSV color space

1 Introduction

In recent years, the popularization of vehicles has caused severe traffic accidents and traffic congestion, and it has become necessary to relieve traffic pressure during peak period. Therefore, in the intelligent transportation system, detecting the moving vehicles and counting them can be used to reasonably regulate the traffic flow of a certain section of the road or quickly arrange traffic policemen to deal with the traffic problems.

In general, there are mainly three kinds of methods to detect moving vehicles, i.e., inter-frame difference method, background subtraction method and optical flow method [1].

The optical flow method has high detection accuracy and can accurately analyze moving targets [2, 3]. At the same time, the optical flow method can also detect moving

X. Zhang et al. (Eds.): CloudComp 2019/SmartGift 2019, LNICST 322, pp. 447–453, 2020.
https://doi.org/10.1007/978-3-030-48513-9_36

targets in the case of background motion. Compared with the inter-frame difference method and the background subtraction method, the optical flow method can obtain more information about moving targets. However, although the optical flow method has high detection accuracy, it cannot obtain an accurate contour of a moving target due to the generation of a shadow.

In this paper, based on traditional optical flow method, the moving vehicle detection algorithm based on optical flow method and shadow removal is proposed. Firstly, the moving vehicle is roughly detected by the optical flow method, and then the shadow detection algorithm based on HSV color space is used to detect the shadow position by threshold segmentation. Then, according to the detected shadow area, accurate moving vehicle detection is realized by removing shadow area. The total detection flow chart is shown in Fig. 1.

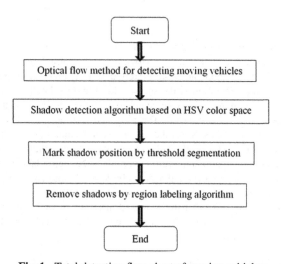

Fig. 1. Total detection flow chart of moving vehicles

2   Moving Vehicle Detection Based on Optical Flow Method

The proposed algorithm is based on the classical Horn-Schunck (HS) algorithm. Based on the four hypotheses of the classic HS algorithm, the optical flow constraint equation can be obtained as follows:

$$f_x u + f_y v + f_t = 0 \tag{1}$$

Then, using the variational calculation [4], the gradient values, f_x, f_y and f_t can be calculated as follows:

$$f_x = \tfrac{1}{4}(f_{i,j+1,k} - f_{i,j,k} + f_{i+1,j+1,k} - f_{i+1,j,k} + f_{i,j+1,k+1} - f_{i,j,k+1} + f_{i+1,j+1,k+1} - f_{i+1,j,k+1}),$$

$$f_y = \tfrac{1}{4}(f_{i+1,j,k} - f_{i,j,k} + f_{i+1,j+1,k} - f_{i,j+1,k} + f_{i+1,j,k+1} - f_{i,j,k+1} + f_{i+1,j+1,k+1} - f_{i,j+1,k+1}),$$

$$f_t = \tfrac{1}{4}(f_{i,j,k+1} - f_{i,j,k} + f_{i,j+1,k+1} - f_{i,j+1,k} + f_{i+1,j,k+1} - f_{i+1,j,k} + f_{i+1,j+1,k+1} - f_{i+1,j+1,k})$$

Thus, we can use the iterative method to solve the optical flow Eq. (1), where n represents the number of iterations.

$$u^{(n+1)} = \bar{u}^{(n)} - \frac{f_x(f_x \bar{u}^{(n)} + f_t + f_y \bar{v}^{(n)})}{\lambda + (f_x^2 + f_y^2)} \qquad (2)$$

$$v^{(n+1)} = \bar{v}^{(n)} - \frac{f_y(f_x \bar{u}^{(n)} + f_t + f_y \bar{v}^{(n)})}{\lambda + (f_x^2 + f_y^2)} \qquad (3)$$

But before solving the Eq. (1), we need to determine two parameters, $\bar{\mu}$ and $\bar{v}$. The two parameters can be calculated by the nine-point difference algorithm [5].

After determining all the parameters, we can solve the velocity field based on the current-frame and previous-frame grayscale images.

3 Moving Vehicle Detection Based on Shadow Removal

The changes of external environments can affect the detection of moving vehicles. How to effectively remove the shadow is an important factor for optical flow detection. A large number of experiments have shown that shadows can be well detected in the HSV color space [6]. Therefore, this paper combines the shadow removal with the optical flow method to eliminate the interference of shadows and make the moving vehicle detection more accurate. The detailed steps are as follows:

i)   Read the video of moving vehicle, determine the shadow areas after converting each frame image in the video two times in the HSV color space, and then convert the obtained image into a grayscale image.
ii) Calculate the optical flow field vector, and add the optical flow field vector to the video frame.
iii) Calculate the average amplitude value of the optical flow vector to obtain the speed threshold; then, extract the moving object according to the speed threshold; finally, remove the noise by the median filter.
iv) Remove the shadow areas on the moving vehicle according to the shadow areas detected by the shadow detection algorithm.
v)   Remove the road area by morphological erosion algorithm, and then fill the "cavity" areas of the vehicle by morphological close operation.

3.1 Shadow Detection Based on HSV Color Space

The pipeline of shadow detection in the HSV color space is: first, input an frame of image and convert the RGB image into a gray image by color space transformation; second, use the Otsu threshold detection method to obtain the threshold of image and binarize the image; third, remove noise by filter; fourth, the shadow area is detected.

HSV Color Model. The HSV color model is similar to an inverted hexagonal pyramid model [7], where V, H and S represent the brightness, color, and saturation, respectively. The transformation from RGB to HSV is shown in Eqs. (4), (5) and (6):

$$S = \begin{cases} \frac{V-\min(R,G,B)}{V}, & V \neq 0 \\ 0, & \text{others} \end{cases} \tag{4}$$

$$V = \max(R, G, B) \tag{5}$$

$$H = \begin{cases} \dfrac{60(G - B)}{V - \min(R, G, B)}, & V = R \\ \dfrac{120 + 60(B - R)}{V - \min(R, G, B)}, & V = G \\ \dfrac{240 + 60(R - G)}{V - \min(R, G, B)}, & V = B \end{cases} \tag{6}$$

Shadow Detection. The HSV color space is closer to human vision and can accurately reflect the information of the target. The shadow of the moving vehicle is detected by the nature of the various parameters on the background by the shadow in the HSV color space. In the detection area, the V component will become smaller and change a lot relative to the background area, and it will be an important parameter for discriminating the shadow. For the S component, the shadow has a lower value and the difference from the background is negative. The H component usually does not change [8]. Based on this feature, the shadow can be detected. The specific algorithm is as follows:

$$SP(i, j) \begin{cases} \text{shadow points,} & \text{if } \alpha \leq T^v_{i,j}/B^v_{i,j} \leq \beta, (I^S_{i,j} - B^S_{i,j}) \leq T^S \\ & \text{and abs}\left(I^H_{i,j} - B^H_{i,j}\right) \leq T^H \\ \text{non-shadow points} & \text{otherwise} \end{cases} \tag{7}$$

where, α and β represent the threshold values of luminance; T^S and T^H represent the threshold values of saturation and color, respectively, and $0 < \alpha < 1, 0 < \beta \leq 1$.

Automatical Threshold Determination Based on Otsu. The Otsu algorithm [8] is used in the HSV color space for shadow detection [8], which is a self-adaptive threshold determination method. The larger the variance between the foreground and the background is, the greater the difference between them is. Assuming t is the set threshold, the gray level of the image is L, then traverse t from 0 to L, if when t is a certain value, for which the variance of foreground and background is the largest, then the t is the required threshold. The variance is calculated as follows:

$$\sigma^2 = A_0 \times (B_0 - B)^2 + A_1 \times (B_1 - B)^2 \tag{8}$$

where, $B = A_0 \times B_0 + A_1 \times B_1$, A_0 is the proportion of the moving target pixels to the total image pixels, B_0 is the average grayscale value of the moving target pixels, A_1 is the proportion of the background pixels to the total image pixels, B_1 is the average grayscale value of the background pixels, and B is the total average grayscale value of the total image.

3.2 Shadow Removal

Remove the shadow of the moving vehicle based on the detected shadows area and obtain accurate vehicle detection. Then use morphology operation [9] to remove the road area. Finally, obtain complete and accurate detection area of the moving vehicle by filling the "cavity" via close operation [9].

4 Experiment

Experiments are implemented on the computer with Intel(R) Core (TM) i5-2410 M CPU 2.30 GHz and 4.00G memory. The image size is 320 × 240 pixels, and the software is programmed by Matlab 2013. The experimental results are as follows.

4.1 Shadow Detection Results

The video of moving vehicles is captured by a camera fixed on an overpass. The video is AVI format with a frame rate of 15 frames/s. The number of moving vehicles is sufficient for the experiments. The following is the experimental results of shadow detection, shown in Fig. 2, where the left column is the original images, and the right column is the detection results of shadow area.

On the right column, the white area indicates the shadow area detected by the shadow detection algorithm based on HSV color space. In order to obtain complete shadow area, the morphological close operation is performed after the image binary based on the threshold segmentation.

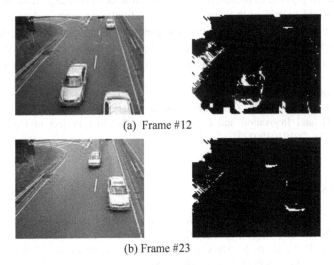

(a) Frame #12

(b) Frame #23

Fig. 2. Shadow detection results based on HSV color space

4.2 Comparison of the Proposed Method and Other Methods

Table 1 shows the performance comparison of the proposed method, background sub-traction method, inter-frame difference method, and traditional optical flow method in terms of average computational time and accuracy. Seen from Table 1, although the back-ground subtraction method, inter-frame difference method, and traditional optical flow method have fast detection speed, they have lower accuracy than the proposed method.

Table 1. Performance comparison of the proposed method and other methods

Methods	Average computational time (millisecond)	Accuracy
Background subtraction method	56	87%
Inter-frame difference method	49	89%
Traditional optical flow method	103	92%
The proposed method	119	95%

5   Conclusion

This paper proposed a moving vehicle detection method based on optical flow method and shadow removal. The proposed method firstly uses the optical flow method to roughly detect the moving vehicle, and then uses the shadow detection algorithm based on the HSV color space to realize the shadow removal, finally accurately detect the moving vehicle. The experiments in complex traffic scenes with shadow interference demonstrate that the proposed method can well solve the impact of shadow interference on moving vehicle detection and realize real-time and accurate detection of moving vehicles.

Acknowledgement. This work is supported in part by the National Nature Science Founda-tion of China (No. 61304205, 61502240), Natural Science Foundation of Jiangsu Province (BK20191401), and Innovation and Entrepreneurship Training Project of College Students (201910300050Z, 201910300222).

References

1. Zhao, X., Su, C., Chen, H.: Research on target detection technology based on video image. Electron. Design Eng. **21**(16), 114–116 (2013)
2. Oh, S., Russell, S., Sastry, S.: Markov Chain Monte Carlo data association for multi-target tracking. IEEE Trans. Autom. Control **54**(3), 481–497 (2004)
3. Yuan, G., Chen, Z., Gong, J.: A moving target detection algorithm combining optical flow method and three-frame difference method. Small Microcomput. Syst. **34**(3), 668–671 (2013)
4. Xia, L., Chen, L., Fu, J., Wu, J.: Symmetries and variational calculation of discrete Hamiltonian systems. Chin. Phys. B **23**(7), 1–7 (2014)

5. Lin, J., Yan, S., Liu, Y.: Application of meshless nine-point difference method in solving marine pollution. J. Dalian Marit. Univ. **30**(1), 78–80 (2004)
6. Gao, W., Dong, H., Lan, L.: Research on moving target shadow detection algorithm in adaptive background. Modern Electron. Technol. **31**(6), 59–61 (2008)
7. Jiang, Y.: Comparative study of three commonly used color models. J. Hunan Univ. Sci. Technol. **28**(4), 37–38 (2007)
8. Gao, X., Li, J., Tian, C.: Modern Image Analysis. Xi'an University of Electronic Science and Technology Press, Xi'an (2011)
9. Yin, Z., Mo, K., Xiong, K.: Defective point data reconstruction based on improved process of morphological operations. Sci. China **54**(12), 3166–3179 (2011)

Refactor Business Process Models for Efficiency Improvement

Fei Dai[1,4], Miao Liu[2], Qi Mo[2,4(✉)], Bi Huang[1], and Tong Li[3,4]

[1] School of Big Data and Intelligent Engineering, Southwest Forestry University,
Kunming, China
[2] School of Software, Yunnan University, Kunming, China
moqiyueyang@163.com
[3] School of Big Data, Yunnan Agricultural University, Kunming, China
[4] Key Laboratory for Software Engineering of Yunnan Province, Kunming, China

Abstract. Since business processes describe the core value chain of enterprises, thousands of business processes are modeled in business process models. A problem is how to improve the efficiency of these models. In this paper, we propose an approach to refactor these models for efficiency improvement. More specifically, we first identify false sequence relations that affect model efficiency based on the sequence relation matrix and the dependency relation matrix. Second, we refactor a business process model by constructing and transforming a dependency graph without altering its output result. After refactoring, the concurrent execution of business tasks in the original models can be maximized such that its efficiency can be improved. Experimental results show the effectiveness of our approach.

Keywords: Business process model · Efficiency improvement · Refactor · Petri net

1 Introduction

Since business processes describe the core value chain of enterprises, many business managers are attracted to build Process-Aware Information System (PAIS). With the board use of PAIS, thousands of business process models [1] are modeled for a variety of purposes, e.g. process analysis and process enactment. Since modeling business process is error-prone [2], the quality of models is difficult to be guaranteed [3]. When modeling a business process model, a question that arises here is that, can we improve its efficiency? For example, two tasks that can be executed concurrently have been modeled as being executed sequentially. Consequentially, the enactment of this process model is inefficient.

Although there is much work on model soundness analysis [4], i.e. proper termination and no dead tasks, this technique cannot be used to improve the model's efficiency. Thus, we focus on refactoring business process models for efficiency improvement.

In our approach, we first identify false sequence relations that affect model efficiency. More specifically, given a business process model, we check whether two business tasks with a sequence relation has a data dependency relation. If the two tasks has no data

X. Zhang et al. (Eds.): CloudComp 2019/SmartGift 2019, LNICST 322, pp. 454–467, 2020.
https://doi.org/10.1007/978-3-030-48513-9_37

dependency relation, the sequence relation among them is false. Second, we refactor a business process model using a dependency graph. After refactoring, tasks in the original business process models can be maximized concurrent execution, so their efficiency can be improved.

In this work, we make the following main contributions:

- We identify false sequence relations based on the sequence relation matrix and the dependency relation matrix.
- We refactor business process models for efficiency improvement by maximizing the task's concurrent execution.

We organize the rest of this article as follows. Section 2 introduces our motivation and related work. Section 3 presents the definitions used throughout this paper. Section 4 presents a refactoring process for efficiency improvement. Section 5 evaluates the effectiveness of our approach. Section 6 concludes our work and points out one future direction.

2 Motivation and Related Work

2.1 Motivation

Figure 1 shows an inefficient online shopping purchase process in [5]. The circles denote places which can have tokens and the rectangles denote tasks. First, goods are bought via the Internet (task A). As a result of task A, the outputs are the buyer's address (variable x) and the money to be paid. Then, goods are shipped (task B). The input of task B is the buyer's address (variable x) and the output is the goods declaration (variable z). Once task C is executed (i.e., the goods are received), the input of task C is the goods declaration (variable z) and the output is the sign for receipt (variable s). Then, the bill is sent to the buyer (task D). The input of task D is the buyer pays the amount (variable y) and the output is the payment request (variable p). After task E is executed (i.e., the bill is paid by the buyer), the input of task E *is* the payment request (variable p) and the output is the completed payment (variable q). Finally, this transaction is archived by the seller (task F), the input of task F is the buyer's signature (variable s) and the completed payment (variable q).

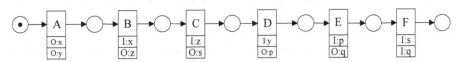

Fig. 1. An inefficient business process model

All the tasks must be executed sequentially in Fig. 1. Since task D can be executed after task C has been completed, there is a sequence relation between them. However, from a data perspective, the sequence relation is false. Since there is no intersection

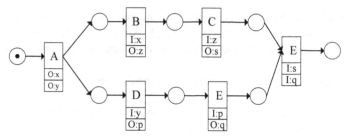

Fig. 2. A refactored business process model with more efficiency

between tasks C and D (i.e., tasks C and D have no data dependency), the two tasks can be executed concurrently.

Based on the analysis, the original model in Fig. 1 is inefficient. After refactoring, Fig. 2 shows the refactored model. Intuitively, the refactored model takes less time to execute, i.e., the refactored model is more efficient than the original model. So this refactoring technique can change the false sequence relation between two tasks in the original process model into a concurrence relation, which maximizes the concurrent execution of the two tasks.

2.2 Related Work

To improve the quality of activity tags, the authors proposed an approach based on corpus's second-order similarity in [6] to automatically annotate activity tags in the business process model. Further, the authors investigated how the activity tag style affects models' comprehensibility in [7]. The authors proposed an automatic refactoring technique for converting the activity tag' style in [8]. These works mentioned above mainly focuses on the quality of the model from the view of activity tags. However, our work focuses on the model's efficiency improvement.

To improve the comprehensibility and maintainability of models, the authors summed up eight process model smells to help process designers identify the process model with low quality in [9]. The authors proposed a refactoring technique based on the measure of activity tag consistency and process overlap, which can automatically identify the opportunity to apply four refactoring operations in [10]. The authors focused on selecting the appropriate business process model operation sets by evaluating the quality of comprehensibility and modifiability in [11]. These works mentioned above mainly focuses on focuses on the comprehensibility and maintainability of the model. However, they also cannot be used to improve the efficiency of models.

The only work on refactoring models for efficiency improvement is in [5]. The authors proposed an approach to refactor business process models for efficiency improvement using process mining technology. Our work is different with Jin's work in that our approach can ensure that the refactored models are structured.

3   Preliminaries

Petri nets are often used to model business process models, due to its formalization foundation and analysis technique.

Definition 1 (*Petri net*): A Petri net is a triple $N = (P, T, F)$ where:

- P is a set of places;
- T is a set of transitions;
- $F \subseteq (P \times T) \cup (T \times P)$ is a flow relation.

State M is the marking of N and can be defined as: $M:P \rightarrow \{0,1,2,3, \ldots\}$. M_0 often refers to the initial state of N.

Denote $X = (P \cup T)$, for a node $u \in X$, ${}^{\bullet}u = \{v \in X \mid (v, u) \in F\}$ is called the preset of u; $u^{\bullet} = \{v \in X \mid (u, v) \in F\}$ is called the postset of u.

Definition 2 (*WF-net*): A Petri net $N = (P, T, F)$ is a WF-net(workflow net), iff:

- $i \in P$ is a source place such that ${}^{\bullet}i = \phi$;
- $o \in P$ is a sink place such that $o^{\bullet} = \phi$; and
- $x \in P \cup T$ is on a path from i to o.

WF-net is a subclass of Petri net. It was first proposed in [12] and was used to model business processes.

Definition 3 (*DWF-net*) [5]: A $DWN = (P, T, F, D, Input, Output)$ is a DWF-net (workflow net with data), where:

- $N = (P, T, F)$ is a WF-net;
- D is the set of data consumed and provided by WF-net;
- *Input*: $T \rightarrow D$ denotes the set of data consumed by tasks,
- *Output*: $T \rightarrow D$ denotes the set of data provided by tasks.

If a DWF-net is unstructured, the work in [13] and [14] discussed how to convert unstructured DWF-nets into structured DWF-nets in detail. Thus we suppose that each DWF-net is structured.

Definition 4 (*Direct sequence relation*): Let $DWN = (P, T, F, D, Input, Output)$ be a workflow net with data, $t_1, t_2 \in T$. We say t_1 and t_2 have a direct sequence relation, denoted as $t_1 > t_2$, if there exists a place $p \in P$, such that $t_1 \in {}^{\bullet}p \wedge t_2 \in p^{\bullet} \wedge |{}^{\bullet}p| = 1 \wedge |p^{\bullet}| = 1$.

Definition 5 (*Transitive sequence relation*): Let $DWN = (P, T, F, D, Input, Output)$ be a workflow net with data, $t_1, t_2, t_3 \in T$. We say t_1 and t_3 have a transitive sequence relation, denoted as $t_1 \gg t_3$, if $t_1 > t_2 \wedge t_2 > t_3$.

In this paper, direct sequence relations and transitive sequence relations are called sequence relations.

Definition 6 (Direct data dependency relation): Let $DWN = (P, T, F, D, Input, Output)$ be a workflow net with data, $t_1, t_2 \in T$, t_1 is executed before t_2, there is a direct data dependency relation denoted as $t_1 \delta^d t_2$, if t_1 and t_2 satisfy one of the following conditions:

- $Output(t_1) \cap Input(t_2) \subseteq D$. That is, there is a true-dependency relation between t_1 and t_2.
- $Output(t_2) \cap Input(t_1) \subseteq D$. That is, there is an anti-dependency relation between t_1 and t_2 t_1 and t_2.
- $Output(t_1) \cap Output(t_2) \subseteq D$. That is, there is an output-dependency relation between t_1 and t_2 t_1 and t_2.

The relation of δ^d can be transitive.

Definition 7 (Transitive data dependency relation): Let $DWN = (P, T, F, D, Input, Output)$ be a workflow net with data, $t_1, t_2, t_3 \in T$, there is a transitive data dependency relation denoted as $t_1 \delta^* t_3$ if $t_1 \delta^d t_2 \wedge t_2 \delta^d t_3$.

Transitive data dependency relations are also transitive. In this paper, direct data dependency relations and transitive data dependency relations are called data dependency relations denoted as δ.

Definition 8 (Control dependency relation): Let $DWN = (P, T, F, D, Input, Output)$ be a workflow net with data, $t_1, t_2 \in T$, t_1 is executed before t_2, there is a control dependency relation between t_1 and t_2, denote as $t_1 \delta^c t_2$, iff $t_1 \in {}^\bullet p \wedge t_2 \in p^\bullet \wedge \neg(|{}^\bullet p| = 1 \wedge |p^\bullet| = 1)$.

4 Our Proposed Approach

Figure 3 shows an overview of our approach, which consists of five steps.

- Step 1: construct a sequence relation matrix from the given business process model.
- Step 2: construct a dependency relation matrix from the given business process model.
- Step 3: identify false sequence relations based on the sequence relation matrix and the dependency relation matrix.
- Step 4: construct a dependency graph.
- Step 5: transform a dependency graph into a DWF-net.

4.1 Construct a Sequence Relation Matrix

According to the α mining algorithm [15], there are three types of task relations, namely sequence relation, selection relation, and concurrency relation. Since only the sequence relation leads to model inefficiency, we try to construct a sequence relation matrix that records the direct sequence relation or the transitive sequence relation between two tasks in a business process model using Algorithm 1.

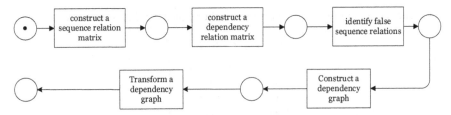

Fig. 3. Overview of our approach

According to definition 4, we obtain all direct sequence relations of $>$ directly by traversing all the places in a business process, which be found in lines 1–9 of Algorithm 1.

According to Definition 5, after direct sequence relations are obtained, the transitive sequence relations of $\gg$ can be computed using the lines 10–18 of Algorithm 1.

Let m and n be separately the number of places and the number of transitions. Algorithm 1's worst time complexity is $O(m*n^2 + n^3)$.

Algorithm 1: construct a sequence relation matrix

Input: $DWN=(P, T, F, D, Input, Output)$
Output: a sequence relation matrix $SM_{|T|*|T|}$
1. **for** $p \in P$ **do**
2.   **if** $(|^\bullet p|{=}{=}1) \wedge (|p^\bullet|{=}{=}1)$ **then**
3.   **for** $t_1 \in {}^\bullet p$ **do**
4.   **for** $t_2 \in p^\bullet$ **do**
5.   set $t_1 > t_2$ in SM;
6.   **end for**
7.   **end for**
8.   **end if**
9. **end for**
10. **for** $t_1 \in T$ **do**
11.   **for** $t_2 \in T$ **do**
12.   **for** $t_3 \in T$
13.   **if**$((t_1{>}t_2 \wedge\ t_2{>}t_3\ \wedge t_1! {\gg} t_3)\ \vee\ (t_1 {\gg} t_2 \wedge\ t_2{>}t_3\ \wedge t_1!{\gg}t_3) \vee (t_1{>}t_2 \wedge\ t_2 {\gg} t_3\ \wedge t_1!{\gg}t_3)$
$\vee (t_1 {\gg} t_2 \wedge t_2 {\gg} t_3 \wedge t_1!{\gg}t_3)$ **then**
14.   set $t_1 {\gg} t_3$ in SM;
15.   **end if**
16.   **end for**
17.   **end for**
18. **end for**
19. **return** SM;

For the model in Fig. 1, we can construct the sequence relation matrix as follows.

$$
\begin{bmatrix}
 & A & B & C & D & E & F \\
A & & > & \gg & \gg & \gg & \gg \\
B & & & > & \gg & \gg & \gg \\
C & & & & > & \gg & \gg \\
D & & & & & > & \gg \\
E & & & & & & > \\
F & & & & & &
\end{bmatrix}
$$

4.2 Construct a Dependency Relation Matrix

For two transitions having a sequence relation, the data dependency relation between them is either δ^d, δ^*, δ^c or null. In this step, we construct a dependency relation matrix using Algorithm 2. The dependency relation matrix records the direct data dependency relation or the transitive data dependency relation between two tasks in a business process model. Besides, the dependency relation matrix records the control dependency relation between two tasks in a business process model.

According to Definition 6, we can obtain all direct data dependency relations of δ^d directly by traversing all the transitions in a business process, which be found in lines 1–7 of Algorithm 2.

According to Definition 7, after direct data dependency relations of δ^d is obtained, the transitive data dependency relations of δ^* can be computed using the lines 8–16 of Algorithm 2 (lines 8–16).

According to Definition 8, we can obtain all control dependency relations of δ^c directly by traversing all the places in a business process, which be found in lines 17–25 of Algorithm 2(lines 17–25).

Let m and n be separately the number of places and the number of transitions. Algorithm 2's worst time complexity is $O(m*n^2 + n^3)$.

Algorithm 2: construct a dependency relation matrix

Input: $DWN=(P, T, F, D, Input, Output)$
Output: a dependency relation matrix $DM_{|T|*|T|}$

---

1 **for** $t_1 \in T$ **do**
2   **for** $t_2 \in T \wedge (t_1 > t_2 \vee t_1 \gg t_2)$ **do**
3   **if** ($(Output(t_2) \cap Input(t_1) \neq \phi) \vee (Output(t_1) \cap Input(t_2) \neq \phi) \vee (Output(t_1) \cap Output(t_2) \neq \phi))$ **then**
4   set $t_1 \delta^d t_2$ in DM;
5   **end if**
6 **end for**
7 **end for**
8 **for** $t_1 \in T$ **do**
9 **for** $t_2 \in T$ **do**
10   **for** $t_3 \in T$
11   **if**$((t_1 \delta^d t_2 \wedge t_2 \delta^d t_3 \wedge t_1! \delta^* t_3) \vee (t_1 \delta^d t_2 \wedge t_2 \delta^* t_3 \wedge t_1! \delta^* t_3) \vee (t_1 \delta^* t_2 \wedge t_2 \delta^* t_3 \wedge t_1! \delta^* t_3) \vee (t_1 \delta^* t_2 \wedge t_2 \delta^d t_3 \wedge t_1!$
  $\delta^* t_3))$ **then**
12   set $t_1 \delta^* t_3$ in DM;
13   **end if**
14   **end for**
15 **end for**
16 **end for**
17. **for** $p \in P$ **do**
18. **if** $((|{}^\bullet p|==1) \wedge (|p^\bullet|>1)) \vee ((|{}^\bullet p|>1) \wedge (|p^\bullet|==1))$ **then**
19.   **for** $t_1 \in {}^\bullet p$ **do**
20.   **for** $t_2 \in p^\bullet$ **do**
21.   set $t_1 \delta t_2$ in DM;
22.   **end for**
23.   **end for**
24. **end if**
25. **end for**
26. **return** DM;

For the model in Fig. 1, we can construct the dependency relation matrix as follows.

$$\begin{bmatrix} & A & B & C & D & E & F \\ A & & \delta^d & \delta^* & \delta^d & \delta^* & \delta^* \\ B & & & \delta^d & & & \delta^* \\ C & & & & & & \delta^d \\ D & & & & & \delta^d & \delta^* \\ E & & & & & & \delta^d \\ F & & & & & & \end{bmatrix}$$

4.3 Identify False Sequence Relations

We identify false sequence relations using Algorithm 3. If the two tasks have a sequence relation in a sequence relation matrix but have no data dependency relation in the corresponding dependency relation matrix, the sequence relation is false. The false sequence relation can be a false adjacent sequence relation (for two adjacent transitions on the same path) or a false transitive sequence relation (for two not adjacent transitions on the same path).

1) a false adjacent sequence relation: If two tasks in a business process model have an adjacent sequence relation in its sequence relation matrix but no direct data dependency relation in its corresponding data dependency relation matrix, the adjacent sequence relation is false.

2) a false transitive sequence relation: If two tasks in a business process model have a transitive sequence relation in its sequence relation matrix but no transitive data dependency relation in its corresponding data dependency relation matrix, the transitive sequence relation is false.

Let n be the number of transitions in a business process model. The worst time complexity of Algorithm 3 is $O(n^2)$.

Algorithm 3: identify false sequence relations

Input: $DWN=(P, T, F, D, Input, Output)$, the related $SM_{|T|*|T|}$, and the $DM_{|T|*|T|}$
Output: the set of false sequence relations FSR
1 **for** $t_1 \in T$ **do**
2   **for** $t_2 \in T$ **do**
3   **if** $((t_1,t_2)$== > in $SRM) \wedge ((t_1,t_2)$== ϕ in $DM)$ **then**
4     $FSR = FSR \cup \{(t_1,t_2)\}$;
5   **end if**
6   **if** $((t_1,t_2)$== $\gg$ in $SRM) \wedge ((t_1,t_2)$== ϕ in $DM)$ **then**
7     $FSR = FSR \cup \{(t_1,t_2)\}$;
8   **end if**
9   **end for**
10 **end for**
11 **return** FSR;

For the model in Fig. 1, we can see that the direct sequence relation between the two tasks C and D is false and that the transitive sequence relations between tasks B and D, C and E, B and E are false.

4.4   Construct a Dependency Graph

We construct a dependency graph using Algorithm 4, which can be used to describe data dependency relations between two tasks intuitively. In the dependency graph, the two tasks with connected arcs must be executed sequentially while the two tasks without arcs can be executed concurrently. In general, the circles denote tasks, the directed edges denote arcs, and the label of each directed edge denotes the type of dependency relations.

Definition 9 (**Dependency graph**): A dependency graph is a triple $DG = (T, A, R)$, where:

- T is the set of tasks $(T \neq \phi)$;
- $A \subseteq T \times T$ is the set of arcs;
- $R: A \rightarrow \{\delta^d, \delta^*, \delta^c\}$ is a labeling function that assigns to each arc x of A a label $R(x)$.

According to Definition 9, we can traverse all the transitions in a business process to obtain a dependency graph directly. The algorithm of constructing a dependency graph can be found in Algorithm 4.

Let n be the number of transitions in a business process model. The worst time complexity of Algorithm 4 is $O(n^2)$.

Algorithm 4: construct a dependency graph

Input: $DWN=(P, T, F, D, Input, Output)$, the related dependency matrix $DM_{|T|*|T|}$
Output: the dependency graph DG
1 $DG.T=DN.T$
2 **for** $t_1 \in T$ **do**
3   **for** $t_2 \in T$ **do**
4   **if** $((t_1,t_2)==\delta^d$ in DM) **then**
5   set $A=A\cup\{(t_1,t_2)\}$; $R=R\cup\{((t_1,t_2), \delta^d)\}$
6   **end if**
7   **if** $((t_1,t_2)==\delta^s$ in DM) **then**
8   set $A=A\cup\{(t_1,t_2)\}$; $R=R\cup\{((t_1,t_2), \delta^s)\}$
9   **end if**
10   **if** $((t_1,t_2)==\delta^f$ in DM) **then**
11   set $A=A\cup\{(t_1,t_2)\}$; $R=R\cup\{((t_1,t_2), \delta^f)\}$
12   **end if**
13   **end for**
14 **end for**
15 **return** DG

For the model in Fig. 1, we construct its dependency graph, which is shown in Fig. 4.

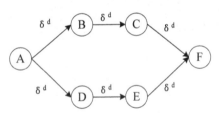

Fig. 4. A dependency graph for the process model in Fig. 1

4.5 Transform a Dependency Graph

Transform a dependency graph means to transform a dependency graph into a DWF-net according to the transforming rules using Algorithm 5. There are four steps:

1) transform node: each node in the dependency graph is transformed into a transition in the Petri net (rule 1);
2) transform sequence structure: each graph segment as shown in Table 1 (rule 2) in the dependency graph is transformed into a sequence structure;
3) transform selection structure:each graph segment as shown in Table 1 (rule 3 and rule 4) in the dependency graph is transformed into a selection structure;
4) add extra places: add the start place and the end place.

Algorithm 5: transform a dependency graph

Input: $DWN=(P, T, F, D, Input, Output)$ and its related simplified dependency graph $SDG = (T, A, R)$

Output: a structured workflow net with data $DN_r=(P_r, T_r, F_r, M_r, D_r, Input_r, Output_r)$

//transform nodes

1. $T_r=T$; $Input_r= Input$; $D_r=D$; $Output_r=Output$;

// transform sequence structures

2. **for** $(t_i, t_j) \in A$ in SDG **do**

3.　$P_r= P_r \cup p_{ij}$; $F_r=F_r \cup \{(t_i, p_{ij})\} \cup \{(p_{ij}, t_j)\}$;

4. **end for**

//) transform selection structures

5. **for** $((t_i, t_j), \mathscr{F}), (t_i, t_k), \mathscr{F}), ..., (t_i, t_s), \mathscr{F})) \in R$ in SDG **do**

6.　$P_r=P_r-\{p_{ik}\}-....-\{p_{is}\}$;　$F_r=F_r-\{(t_i,\ p_{ik})\}-...-\{(t_i,\ p_{is})\}-\{(p_{ik},\ t_k)\}-...-\{(p_{is},t_s)\} \cup (p_{ij},\ t_k)$ $\cup...\cup(p_{ij}, t_s)$;

7. **end for**

8. **for** $((t_i, t_j), \mathscr{F}), (t_k, t_j), \mathscr{F}), ..., (t_s, t_j), \mathscr{F})) \in R$ in SDG **do**

9.　$P_r=P_r-\{p_{kj}\}-....-\{p_{sj}\}$;　$F_r=F_r-\{(t_k,\ p_{kj})\}-...-\{(t_s,\ p_{sj})\}-\{(p_{kj},\ t_j)\}-...-\{(p_{sj},\ t_j)\} \cup (t_k,\ p_{ij})$ $\cup...\cup(t_s, p_{ij})$;

10. **end for**

//add the start place and the end place

11. **for** $t_i \in T_r$ **do**

12.　**if** $^\bullet t_i=\phi$ **then**

13.　$Pr=Pr \cup \{p_{satrti}\}$; $Fr =Fr \cup \{(p_{satrti}, t_i)\}$;

14.　**end if**

15.　**if** $t_i^\bullet=\phi$ **then**

16.　$Pr=Pr \cup \{p_{endi}\}$; $Fr =Fr \cup \{(t_i, p_{endi})\}$;

17.　**end if**

18. **end for**

19. **return** DN_r

Table 1. Transformation rules

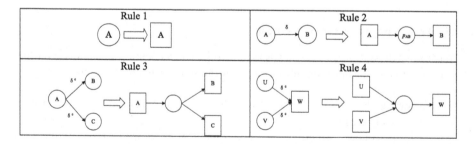

We can transform the dependency graph in Fig. 4 into a DWF-net in Fig. 2 using the above transformation rules.

5   Experiments

We implemented a prototype tool based on PIPE (The Platform Independent Petri Net Editor) [16]. In Fig. 5, the example given in this paper is on the left and the refactored model is on the right.

200 different DWF-nets are generated randomly. All experiments were conducted on the same computer with Inter (R) i5 2.5 GHz and 8 GB RAM, Windows 10 and JDK 7.

To evaluate the effectiveness of our approach, parallelism degree (PD) as Eq. 1 is used to measure the concurrency according to the work in [5, 17]. If the PD of the refactored model is greater than the PD of the original model, it means that our approach can improve the original business process model's efficiency.

$$PD = \sum_{d_{out}(t)>1} (d_{out}(t) - 1) \tag{1}$$

Where $d_{out}(t)$ represents the output degree of task t; $d_{out}(t) > 1$ indicates that the out degree of task t is greater than one. If PD $= -1$, no task in the business process model can execute concurrently.

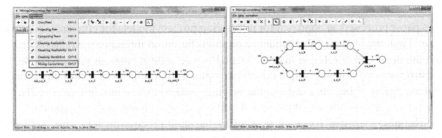

Fig. 5. The screenshot of tool prototype

Table 2 presents some experimental results, including the tasks with $d_{out}(t) > 1$ in the original model (number$_b$), the parallelism degree in the original model (PD$_b$), hit before refactoring($\surd$ indicates the original model is structured and $\times$ indicates the original model is not structured), the tasks with $d_{out}(t) > 1$ in the refactored model (number$_a$), the parallelism degree in the refactored model (PD$_a$), and hit after refactoring ($\surd$ indicates the refactored model is structured and $\times$ indicates the refactored model is not structured) in each example.

From the experimental results, we can see that: 1) In each example, the PD of the refactored model is greater than the PD of the original model. That is, our approach can improve the original business process model's efficiency. 2) All the business process models are structured before and after refactoring. That is, our approach can ensure that the refactored models are structured.

Table 2. Evaluation results

No.	The original model			The refactored model		
	$Number_b$	PD_b	$Structuredness_b$	$Number_a$	PD_a	$Structuredness_a$
1	0	0	✓	1	1	✓
2	0	0	✓	2	4	✓
3	2	2	✓	4	5	✓
4	0	0	✓	1	2	✓
5	0	0	✓	2	2	✓
6	1	2	✓	2	3	✓
7	0	0	✓	2	2	✓
8	1	1	✓	3	3	✓
9	0	0	✓	1	1	✓
10	1	1	✓	1	2	✓

6   Conclusions

This paper proposed an approach for refactoring process models for efficiency improvement. First, we identify false sequence relations based on the sequence relation matrix and the dependency relation matrix. Second, we refactor a business process model by constructing and transforming a dependency graph. In a refactored model, the concurrent execution of business tasks in the original models can be maximized. Finally, we present a prototype implementation and evaluate the effectiveness of our approach.

The next step will focus on refactoring business process models with inefficient process fragments substitution. Inefficient process fragments refer to sequence process fragments with false sequence relations. If we can replace these inefficient process fragments in an original process model with efficient process fragments, its efficiency can be improved.

Acknowledgment. This work was supported by NSFC (No. 61702442 and 61862065), and the Basic Research Project in Yunnan Province (2018FB105).

References

1. Leopold, H., Mendling, J., Reijers, H.A., Rosa, M.L.: Simplifying process model abstraction: techniques for generating model names. Inf. Syst. **39**, 134–151 (2014)
2. Herbst, J., Karagiannis, D.: Workflow mining with InWoLvE. Comput. Ind. **53**, 245–264 (2004)
3. Khlif, W., Ben-Abdallah, H.: Integrating semantics and structural information for BPMN model refactoring. In: Proceedings of the International Conference on Computer and Information Science, pp. 656–660. IEEE (2015)

4. Aalst, W.M.P.: Workflow verification: finding control-flow errors using petri-net-based techniques. In: van der Aalst, W., Desel, J., Oberweis, A. (eds.) Business Process Management. LNCS, vol. 1806, pp. 161–183. Springer, Heidelberg (2000). https://doi.org/10.1007/3-540-45594-9_11

5. Jin, T., Wang, J., Yang, Y., Wen, L., Li, K.: Refactor business process models with maximized parallelism. IEEE Trans. Serv. Comput. **9**, 456–468 (2016)

6. Leopold, H., Meilicke, C., Fellmann, M., Pittke, F., Stuckenschmidt, H., Mendling, J.: Towards the automated annotation of process models. In: Zdravkovic, J., Kirikova, M., Johannesson, P. (eds.) CAiSE 2015. LNCS, vol. 9097, pp. 401–416. Springer, Cham (2015). https://doi.org/10.1007/978-3-319-19069-3_25

7. Mendling, J., Reijers, H.A., Recker, J.: Activity labeling in process modeling: empirical insights and recommendations. Inf. Syst. **35**, 467–482 (2010)

8. Leopold, H., Smirnov, S., Mendling, J.: Refactoring of process model activity labels. In: Hopfe, Christina J., Rezgui, Y., Métais, E., Preece, A., Li, H. (eds.) NLDB 2010. LNCS, vol. 6177, pp. 268–276. Springer, Heidelberg (2010). https://doi.org/10.1007/978-3-642-13881-2_28

9. Weber, B., Reichert, M., Mendling, J., Reijers, H.A.: Refactoring large process model repositories. Comput. Ind. **62**, 467–486 (2011)

10. Dijkman, R., Gfeller, B., Küster, J., Völzer, H.: Identifying refactoring opportunities in process model repositories. Inf. Softw. Technol. **53**, 937–948 (2011)

11. Fernández-Ropero, M., Pérez-Castillo, R., Caballero, I., Piattini, M.: Quality-driven business process refactoring. In: Proceedings of the International Conference on Business Information Systems (ICBIS 2012), pp. 960–966 (2012)

12. Van der Aalst, W.M.P.: The application of Petri nets to workflow management. J. Circuits Syst. Comput. **8**, 21–66 (1998)

13. Polyvyanyy, A., García-Bañuelos, L., Dumas, M.: Structuring acyclic process models. Inf. Syst. **37**, 518–538 (2010)

14. Polyvyanyy, A., García-Bañuelos, L., Fahland, D., Weske, M.: Maximal structuring of acyclic process models. Comput. J. **57**, 12–35 (2014)

15. Van der Aalst, W.M.P., Weijters, T., Maruster, L.: Workflow mining: discovering process models from event logs. IEEE Trans. Knowl. Data Eng. **16**(9), 1128–1142 (2004)

16. Dingle, N.J., Knottenbelt, W.J., Suto, T.: PIPE2: a tool for the performance evaluation of generalised stochastic Petri nets. ACM SIGMETRICS Perform. Eval. Rev. **36**, 34–39 (2009)

17. Mendling, J.: Metrics for Process Models: Empirical Foundations of Verification, Error Prediction, and Guidelines for Correctness. Springer, Heidelberg (2008). https://doi.org/10.1007/978-3-540-89224-3

A New Model of Cotton Yield Estimation Based on AWS

Quan Xu[1], Chuanjian Wang[2,3,4], Jianguo Dai[2,3,4], Peng Guo[1(✉)], Guoshun Zhang[2,3,4], Yan Jiang[5], and Hongwei Shi[1]

[1] College of Science, Shihezi University, Shihezi 832003, XJ, China
xuquan0928@163.com, gp163@163.com
[2] College of Information Science and Technology,
Shihezi University, Shihezi 832003, XJ, China
[3] Geospatial Information Engineering Research Center, Xinjiang Production
and Construction Corps, Shihezi 832003, XJ, China
[4] Geospatial Information Engineering Laboratory, Xinjiang Production
and Construction Corps, Shihezi 832003, XJ, China
[5] Xinjiang Jiangtian Aviation Technology Co. LTD, Shihezi 832003, XJ, China

Abstract. Timely and precise yield estimation is of great significance to agricultural management and macro-policy formulation. In order to improve the accuracy and applicability of cotton yield estimation model, this paper proposes a new method called SENP (Seedling Emergence and Number of Peaches) based on Amazon Web Services (AWS). Firstly, using the high-resolution visible light data obtained by the Unmanned Aerial Vehicle (UAV), the spatial position of each cotton seedling in the region was extracted by U-Net model of deep learning. Secondly, Sentinel-2 data were used in analyzing the correlation between the multi-temporal Normalized Difference Vegetation Index (NDVI) and the actual yield, so as to determine the weighting factor of NDVI in each period in the model. Subsequently, to determine the number of bolls, the growth state of cotton was graded. Finally, combined with cotton boll weight, boll opening rate and other information, the cotton yield in the experimental area was estimated by SENP model, and the precision was verified according to the measured data of yield. The experimental results reveal that the U-Net model can effectively extract the information of cotton seedlings from the background with high accuracy. And the precision rate, recall rate and F_1 value reached 93.88%, 97.87% and 95.83% respectively. NDVI based on time series can accurately reflect the growth state of cotton, so as to obtain the predicted boll number of each cotton, which greatly improves the accuracy and universality of the yield estimation model. The determination coefficient (R^2) of the yield estimation model reached 0.92, indicating that using SENP model for cotton yield estimation is an effective method. This study also proved that the potential and advantage of combining the AWS platform with SENP, due to its powerful cloud computing capacity, especially for deep learning, time-series crop monitoring and large scale yield estimation. This research can provide the reference information for cotton yield estimation and cloud computing platform application.

Keywords: Cotton · Yield estimation · Cloud computing · AWS · NDVI · SENP

© ICST Institute for Computer Sciences, Social Informatics and Telecommunications Engineering 2020
Published by Springer Nature Switzerland AG 2020. All Rights Reserved
X. Zhang et al. (Eds.): CloudComp 2019/SmartGift 2019, LNICST 322, pp. 468–484, 2020.
https://doi.org/10.1007/978-3-030-48513-9_38

1 Introduction

Crop yield estimation exerts a vital part in formulating economic policies, and is an important factor affecting regional economic development, ensuring food security and maintaining sustainable agricultural development [1]. Cotton is one of the main crops in China. It is exceedingly beneficial to farmers and government to cognize cotton's growth and yield, because they can implement corresponding management and formulate policies in advance, so as to obtain better economic and environmental benefits [2].

For a long time, yield estimation has been a research hotspot in agricultural science [3–5]. With the development of science and technology, the research on cotton yield estimation has been developed from traditional ground survey to multi-dimensional and spatio-temporal remote sensing estimation. Yeom proposed an automatic open cotton boll detection algorithm using ultra-fine spatial resolution UAV images [6]. Using NOAA/AVHRR satellite data with high time resolution, Dalezios established NDVI based on time series to estimate cotton yield [7]. By integrating the concept of cotton growing area with similarity analysis of time-series NDVI data, Gao proposed a method of cotton yield estimation [8]. In a word, cotton estimates which based on time series is an effective method, but how to improve the accuracy of the estimated model is a challenging issue, yet to be adequately resolved. Besides, remote sensing image data based on time series requires great computing power and the conventional methods are not conducive to the rapid application and promotion of the estimation model.

Recently, quite a few cloud computation platforms for geospatial data processing have become available with big data-processing tools and high-performance computational power [9], including Google Earth Engine (GEE), Amazon Web Service (AWS) and National Aeronautics and Space Administration (NASA) Earth Exchange (NEX) [10]. They possess plentiful imagery archives and data products, and also can be easily carried out for thematic mapping as well as spatiotemporal analyses, with the support of parallel-processing computation and advanced machine learning algorithms [11]. The advent of cloud computation platforms has altered the way of storing, managing, processing and analyzing of massive amounts of large-scale geospatial data [12]. Zhang investigated the potential and advantages of the freely accessible Landsat 8 Operational Land Imager (OLI) imagery archive and GEE for exact tidal flats mapping [13]. By using GEE, Venkatappa determined the threshold values of vegetation types to classify land use categories in Cambodia through the analysis of phenological behaviors and the development of a robust phenology-based threshold classification (PBTC) method for the mapping and long-term monitoring of land cover changes [14].

The explicit goal of this research is to propose a new cotton yield estimation model with the help of cloud computing platform to accurately draw cotton yield estimation map. The research results can provide technical ideas for more convenient, accurate and widely used cotton yield estimation.

2 Materials and Methods

2.1 Study Area

In this paper, Shihezi reclamation area of the 8th division of Xinjiang production and construction corps in China was selected as the study area. It is located between latitudes

44° 29′ 36″ and 44° 29′ 55″ North and longitudes 86° 01′ 00″ and 86° 01′ 50″ East. The total area of the study area is about 637.08 acres, as shown in the Fig. 1. Xinjiang has unique ecological and climatic conditions, even continuous farmland, and standard farmland construction. The mechanization and scale of cotton planting are relatively high, making it the most suitable area for remote sensing yield estimation and precision agriculture in China [15].

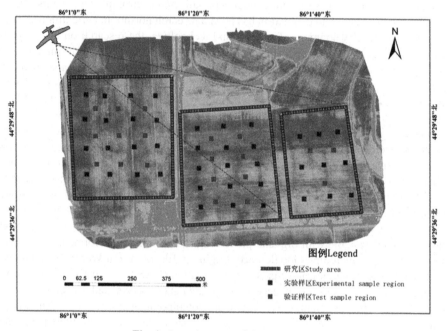

Fig. 1. Location map of the study area

2.2 Datasets

UAV Data. The UAV data are obtained by Dapeng cw-10 UAV equipped with sensors of Canon camera EF-M18-55, which is mainly used for the extraction of cotton seedlings. The data is a visible remote sensing image of the UAV taken at 11 am on May 23, 2018, with a resolution of about 2.5 cm. At the time of data collection, the weather was good and there was no wind. The UAV has a flight height of 150 m with a longitudinal overlap of 80% and a side overlap of 60%. Visible light data obtained by UAV are calibrated and corrected by Pix4D software, and the whole workflow is automatically accomplished by the software.

Sentinel-2 Data. Sentinel-2 data are mainly obtained from AWS, which is used in monitoring the growth of cotton in multi-time. The satellite carries a multispectral imager (MSI), with an altitude of 786 km, covering 13 spectral bands and a width of 290 km. The ground resolution is 10 m, 20 m and 60 m respectively. Sentinel-2 data are the only data that contains three bands in the range of the red edge, which is exceedingly effective for monitoring vegetation health [16].

Ground Measured Data. The measured data on the ground are mainly used in calculating the process data and verify the results. In order to record the position and boundary of ground measured data in detail and precisely match with UAV data, the experiment found a total of 60 evenly distributed sample areas in the research area, including 40 experimental sample areas and 20 verification sample areas. We inserted a rod in the center of each sample area and placed a red disk at the top of the rod. The size of the sample area is 3 × 3 m. Therefore, it is indispensable to find the position of each rod in the image, and extend 1.5 m up, down left and right respectively based on the center of the rod, so as to obtain the position and vector boundary of the sample area. Experiments demonstrate that the accuracy of the ground data collected by this method is higher than that of other positioning methods, such as handheld GPS.

2.3 Yield Estimation

By using UAV data, exact information of cotton seedling emergence can be obtained to grasp the spatial position and quantity of seedlings in the region. Using Sentinel-2 data, the growth state of cotton can be monitored in multi-time to estimate the boll number. Based on the above results, the estimated yield of per cotton can be acquired. Therefore, this study proposed a cotton yield estimation model and method based on SENP (Seedling Emergence and Number of Peaches) with this notion, which provides a technical method for realizing more precise cotton yield estimation (Fig. 2).

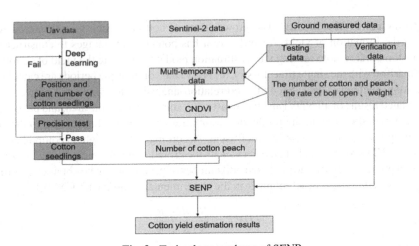

Fig. 2. Technology roadmap of SENP

Cotton Seedling Extraction. Deep learning has the characteristics that can extract the image features automatically to make precise classification and recognition decisions

[17]. Therefore, aiming at the high resolution remote sensing data of UAV, this experiment uses the Fully Convolutional Networks (FCN) to extract the seedlings of cotton. This network is frequently used in processing remote sensing images and has achieved favorable results [18, 19]. We input the remote sensing image of cotton seedlings into the cloud computing platform. Subsequently, we use the U-Net model which was stored in the cloud computing platform and trained in advance to calculate the input image. Finally, the extracted results are converted into point element classes, which are stored in the cloud platform for later loading into the Sentinel-2 data (Fig. 3).

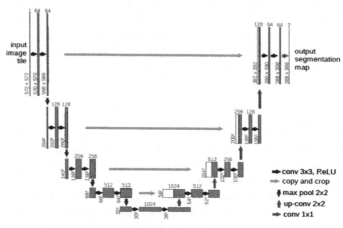

Fig. 3. Structure chart of U-Net

Cotton Growth Monitoring. The growth state of cotton in each growth period will affect the formation of yield. Accordingly it has potential advantages to construct the multi-temporal remote sensing yield estimation model to estimate the yield of cotton by comparison with the single time. Firstly, the NDVI data of multiple periods are calculated by using Sentinel-2 data. Secondly, correlation analysis was conducted between the calculated results of all NDVI and the measured results in the sample area, and the weight of each period of data in the production estimation was obtained according to the size and proportion of the correlation coefficient. According to the weight, a comprehensive NDVI (CNDVI) can be calculated to evaluate the growth state of cotton during the whole growth process. Finally, the predicted boll number of per cotton can be obtained by fitting the measured average peach number in the experimental sample with CNDVI.

$$NDVI = \frac{NIR - R}{NIR + R} \tag{1}$$

$$CNDVI = \sum_{i=1}^{n} a_i NDVI_i \tag{2}$$

Where *NIR* and *R* represent Near Infrared band and Red band respectively and *a* represents the weight of NDVI in different periods.

Cotton Yield Estimation Model. The definition of SENP is formularized as:

$$SENP = \sum_{i=1}^{n} C_i \times Y_i \times T \tag{3}$$

$$Y = N \times W \tag{4}$$

$$T = (\sum_{i=1}^{j} (B_i \div A_i)) \div j \times L \tag{5}$$

In the formula, *SENP* is the predicted total output of cotton in a certain region. And *n* represents the total number of cotton seedlings in the region. *C* represents cotton seedlings of different spatial positions. *Y* represents the predicted yield of per cotton at the corresponding position. *T* represents the rate of boll opening. *N* represents the number of bolls. *W* represents the weight of each boll. And j represents the number of sample areas. *B* represents the number of boll that has opened. *A* represents the total number of bolls in sample area. *L* is a scaling factor (Fig. 4).

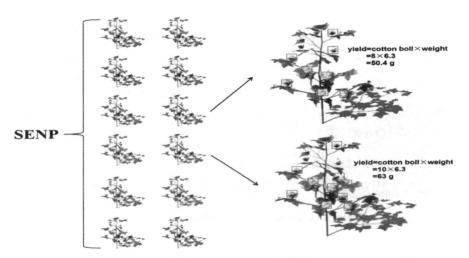

Fig. 4. Concept map of SENP

2.4 Build Cloud Platform Based on AWS and ESE

AWS. Generally, the services provided by cloud computing can be divided into three layers. These three layers are Infrastructure as a Service (IaaS), Platform as a Service (PaaS) and Software as a Service (SaaS) [20]. The first layer is Infrastructure, and the second layer is Platform, and the third layer is Application. Infrastructure services include virtual or physical computers, storage in block, and network infrastructure (such as load balancing, content delivery networks, DNS resolution) [21]. The service of the platform includes object storage, authentication service and access service, runtime of various programs, queue service, database service and so on [22]. The service of application software has many projects, such as mail service, code hosting service and so on. Users can access and use these services through desktop computers, laptops, mobile phones, tablets and other Internet terminal devices. Amazon's cloud service provides dozens of services [23], including IaaS, PaaS and SaaS.

In 2006, AWS began offering IT infrastructure Services to enterprises as Web Services, now commonly referred to as cloud computing. One of the main advantages of cloud computing is the ability to supersede upfront capital infrastructure costs with lower variable costs [24]. Instead of planning and purchasing servers and other IT infrastructure weeks in advance, companies can run hundreds of servers in minutes and get results faster by using cloud computing platform [25]. In 2018, AWS launched 1957 new services and features, delivering innovation at an unmatched pace, especially in new areas such as machine learning and artificial intelligence. At present, Amazon Web Services provide a highly reliable, extensible and low-cost infrastructure platform in the cloud, offering support to hundreds of enterprises in 190 countries and regions, making it the most comprehensive and widely used cloud platform in the world [26] (Fig. 5).

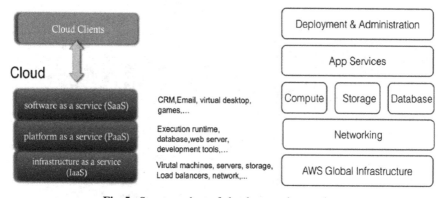

Fig. 5. Structure chart of cloud computing services

ESE. ENVI Services Engine (ESE) is an enterprise server product advanced by Exelis VIS. ESE provides ENVI, IDL, SARscape and other remote sensing image processing capabilities as services to support online, on-demand remote sensing image applications [27]. It breaks down the barrier of professional remote sensing software and high-end hardware for non-professionals and establishes more direct contact between remote sensing experts and prospective end users. ESE can be deployed in a variety of enterprise-level environments, including cluster environment, enterprise-level server or cloud platform [28, 29], etc., making full use of high-performance server hardware conditions to efficiently accomplish the remote sensing image processing of the large amount of data.

ESE is established on top of mainstream REST frameworks and can run in clustered environments, with scalability and load balancing capabilities. ESE gets HTTP and REST requests from the client-side, where ESE performs remote-sensing relevant processing requests, and thereafter passes the results to the application. ESE's image processing function is packaged with JSON standard and can be seamlessly integrated with image data services provided by other middleware (such as ArcGIS Server) (Fig. 6).

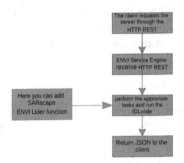

Fig. 6. Workflow of ESE

Cloud Platform Construction. The experiment mainly used AWS and ESE to establish a cloud computing platform for cotton yield estimation. The back-end development of the platform mainly uses Interface Description Language (IDL) to customize applications, such as the calculation of NDVI, the classification of growth monitoring and the calculation of SENP model. While the front-end development of the platform mainly uses JavaScript to create custom Web applications, including the loading of maps, presentation of yield results and so on. The experiments used amazon's Elastic Compute Cloud (EC2) and Simple Storage Service (S3) Cloud services. EC2 is a Web service that provides scalable cloud computing capabilities and is designed to provide developers

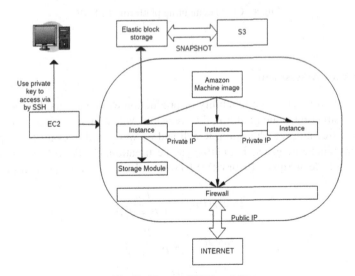

Fig. 7. Usage of EC2 and S3

with easy access to network-scale computing [30]. S3 is an internet-oriented storage service that can store and retrieve data anywhere on the Web at any time (Fig. 7).

At the same time, AWS in the global region and AWS in the Chinese region are used respectively. AWS in the global region is mainly used for downloading Sentinel-2 data, calculating NDVI and storing data, and after that passing the results to AWS in the Chinese region. While AWS in the Chinese region mainly calculates UAV data and multi-temporal NDVI data, and uses SENP model to estimate cotton yield. The final consequence can be viewed in real time via the Web on a computer, tablet or mobile phone (Fig. 8).

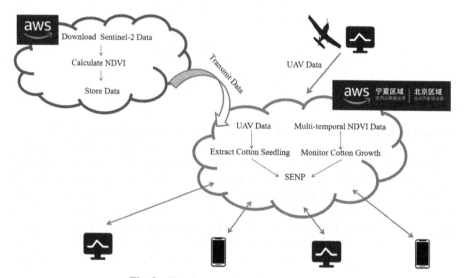

Fig. 8. Cloud computing platform of SENP

2.5 Accuracy Assessment

In order to strictly verify the reliability of production estimation model and the feasibility of constructing cloud platform, the precision evaluation is carried out by rigorous standards. Three indexes, Precision, Recall and F_1 were used to evaluate the precision of cotton seedling emergence. For cotton yield estimation, Coefficient of Determination (R^2) and Root Mean Square Error (RMSE) were selected to evaluate the results.

$$Precision = \frac{TP}{TP + FP} \tag{6}$$

$$Recall = \frac{TP}{TP + FN} \tag{7}$$

$$F_1 = \frac{2 \times Precision \times Recall}{Precision + Recall} \tag{8}$$

$$RMSE = \sqrt{\frac{\sum\limits_{i=1}^{N} (\tilde{Y}_i - Y_i)^2}{N}} \tag{9}$$

$$R^2 = \frac{(\sum\limits_{i=1}^{N} (\tilde{Y}_i - \bar{\tilde{Y}}_i)(Y_i - \bar{Y}_i))^2}{\sum\limits_{i=1}^{N} (\tilde{Y}_i - \bar{\tilde{Y}}_i)^2 (Y_i - \bar{Y}_i)^2} \tag{10}$$

Where *TP* is the number of cotton seedlings correctly extracted. *FP* is the number of cotton seedlings wrongly extracted, and *FN* is the number of cotton seedlings not extracted. N is the number of samples. $\tilde{Y}_i$ and Y_i represent predicted yield and actual yield. $\bar{\tilde{Y}}$ and $\bar{Y}_i$ are the average of predicted and measured yields respectively.

3 Results

3.1 Seedling Emergence and Extraction Results

The emergence of cotton seedlings is a key link in the construction of the SENP model, which will affect the final estimation results to a large extent. Consequently, the methods and results of cotton extraction are crucial. At present, most scholars use spectral information to calculate some vegetation indices of crops for extracting, and most of them have achieved some favorable results [31–33]. But the research on the extraction of cotton seedlings is still infrequent. In this paper, the high-resolution data obtained by UAV were used and the spatial information of each cotton seedling in the region was extracted by deep learning. The study area was about 637.08 mu, and a total of 4,364,255 cotton seedlings were extracted in the end. The density of the cotton was about 6,850 per mu. Verified by the measured data, it can be seen that the accuracy of this method is extremely high. The precision rate is 93.88%, and the recall rate is 97.87%, and the F_1 value is 95.83%. Accordingly, the experimental results manifest that U-Net model can effectively extract emergence information of cotton seedling. It is a valid method, which can not only provide supports for the construction of SENP, but also provide a new idea for extraction of cotton seedling (Fig. 9).

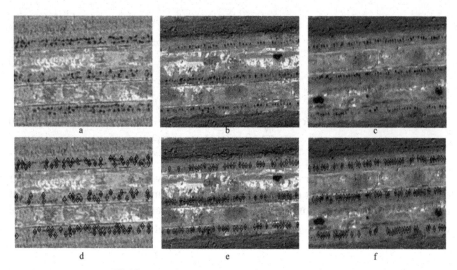

Fig. 9. UAV images and seedling extraction results

3.2 Growth Monitoring Results

The multi-temporal growth monitoring of cotton is also another vital link in the construction of the SENP model and the vegetation growth is an extremely complex process. Since when the conditions of soil, water and chlorophyll change, it may have an impact on the final yield. So it is necessary to monitor the growth of cotton based on time series. By using Sentinel-2 data of cotton in 10 periods, the NDVI values of each period were calculated and analyzed. Furthermore, the correlation between the actual yield and 40 experimental samples was calculated to determine the weight of each period that was selected. By assigning weights to multi-temporal NDVI images, we used an image (CNDVI) to classify the growth state of cotton accurately, objectively and reasonably. According to the results of calculation, the correlation coefficients between NDVI and yield are 0.69, 0.72, 0.75, 0.81, 0.88, 0.87, 0.82, 0.83, 0.75 and 0.72 respectively. The results demonstrate that the correlation between the NDVI and the actual yield in cotton boll period is relatively large, while the correlation between bud stage and boll opening period is relatively small. Therefore, according to the size and proportion of the correlation coefficient, the weights of 0.09, 0.09, 0.10, 0.10, 0.11, 0.11, 0.10, 0.11, 0.10 and 0.09 were assigned to each period's NDVI image to construct CNDVI. The experimental results can show that the estimated results based on multi-period are higher than that based on single period (Fig. 10).

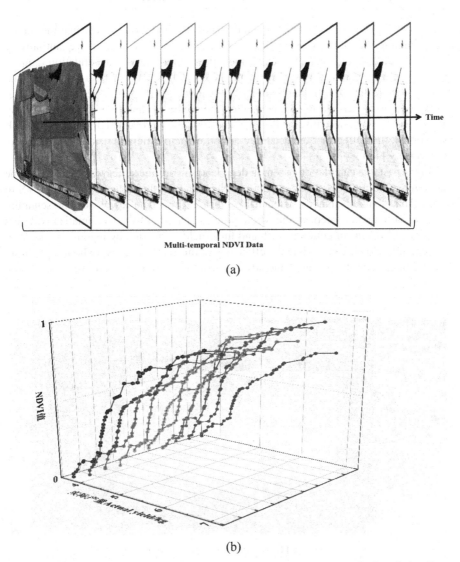

Fig. 10. Cotton data based on time series: (a) Multi-temporal NDVI data; (b) Correlation linear graph of NDVI and actual output in each period

3.3 Output Estimation Results

When the results of cotton seedling extraction and multi-temporal growth monitoring are obtained, the yield estimation model can be constructed. In the experiment, the yield of study area can be estimated with the aid of formula (3). The total area is 637.08 acres and the total output of cotton is 261,200.75 kg. Through the analysis of results, it can be seen that the cotton yield in this region is relatively high. At the same time, there is a positive correlation between the yield and the growth of cotton. Provided that the growth situation is better, the yield is higher, which also accords with the actual situation of production. The experimental results also indirectly reveal that the theory for estimating the yield by using SENP is feasible. In order to further quantitatively verify the accuracy of results, this experiment uses actual yield of 20 validation samples to carry out regression analysis on the predicted results of yield, and selects R^2 and RMSE as indicators to test the reliability of the model. If R^2 gets closer to 1, the better it fits. If R^2 is bigger and RMSE is smaller, the prediction ability will be stronger. By calculation, it can be seen that the R^2 of yield estimation has reached 0.92 and the RMSE is just 6.04, indicating that the accuracy of cotton yield estimation using SENP model is extremely high.

In the past, the calculation based on deep learning or time series was extremely time consuming and requires strong capability. Nevertheless, this experiment uses AWS to give full play to its advantages, so that it takes just 22 s from data download to presentation of yield estimation. Moreover, the whole process is accomplished automatically. Users can view the results of cotton growth and final yield estimation by logging on the Web conveniently. So we can see that the efficiency of this platform is overwhelmingly high, which fully proves the potential and advantages of the combination between SENP and AWS (Fig. 11) (Table 1)

Fig. 11. Results of yield estimation

Table 1. Efficiency of the platform

Tasks	Time
Data download	70 m/s
Cloud computing	12 s
Data transmission	20 m/s
Results show	0.5 s

3.4 Cloud Platform Display

Based on AWS and ESE, this experiment has successfully established an online cloud platform of cotton estimation. The back-end development of the platform is based on IDL, while the front-end development of the platform is mainly based on JavaScript. When users log on the Web through the Internet, they can not only obtain cotton yield estimation, but also realize numerous functions, such as searching and managing information of land, transmitting and viewing sensor information, obtaining meteorological data, generating results report and so on (Fig. 12).

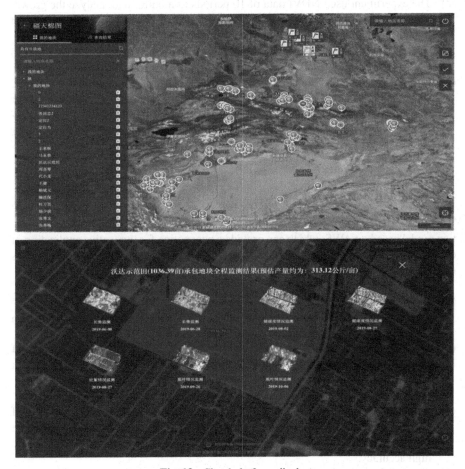

Fig. 12. Cloud platform display

4 Discussion

Prediction of cotton yield is a complicated work, which not only requires considering the practicability and feasibility of the technology, but also requires considering the credibility and accuracy of the prediction results. This paper proposes a new cotton yield estimation model named SENP. The application of this method in accurate yield estimation has certain reference value, but the potential factors that may affect the results of yield estimation still need further exploration and research.

(1) UAV is an effective way to gain high-resolution data with a lot of superiorities. But the capability of data acquisition is relatively influenced by some factors. If search further explores cotton yield estimation methods in larger areas in the future, there may be some limitations on data acquisition.

(2) The experiment used NDVI data of 10 periods to monitor and analyze the growth of cotton, and achieved some favorable results. However, how to choose the best time of cotton monitoring has not been studied systematically. And in the future, we will try to use more data at different times to monitor cotton growth so as to explore the possibility of improving the accuracy of the model.

(3) Cloud computing has many advantages and the platform based on AWS and ESE can efficiently and rapidly calculate the results of yield estimation. In the later stage, it can attempt to further optimize the display of interface and graphics processing algorithm to improve the calculation speed and increase the quality of user experience.

5 Conclusions

Taking full advantage of cloud computing, this paper presents a new cotton yield estimation model based on AWS, which can provide a new notion for innovative application of cloud computing platform and research of cotton yield estimation. The main conclusions of this research are as follows:

(1) For high-resolution data of UAV, U-Net model can effectively extract the information of cotton seeding emergence, accurately obtain the spatial position of each cotton seedling and calculate the total number of cotton in the region.

(2) Exact monitoring results of cotton growth are conducive to the establishment of model. Using NDVI data of cotton in a certain period to evaluate its state is not representative and precise. While using time series data of NDVI is a better way to monitor the growth of cotton.

(3) The experimental results demonstrate that it is feasible to use the information of emergence and growth of cotton to estimate yield. Verified by actual yield, the cotton yield estimation model based on SENP was confirmed to be reliable with high accuracy.

(4) Giving full play to the advantages of cloud computing, an online cotton yield estimation platform based on AWS and ESE was established, which can provide reference information for regional agricultural management and macro decision-making. It has played an active role in boosting the process of precision agriculture in China.

Acknowledgments. This research was supported in part by the national key research and development program of China under grant 2017YFB0504203.

References

1. Maresma, Á., Lloveras, J., Martínez-Casasnovas, J.: Use of multispectral airborne images to improve in-season nitrogen management, predict grain yield and estimate economic return of maize in irrigated high yielding environments. Remote Sens. **10**, 543 (2018)
2. Huang, J., Wang, H., Dai, Q., Han, D.: Analysis of NDVI data for crop identification and yield estimation. IEEE J. Sel. Top. Appl. Earth Obs. Remote Sens. **7**, 4374 (2017)
3. Quarmby, N.A., Milnes, M., Hindle, T.L., Silleos, N.: The use of multi-temporal NDVI measurements from AVHRR data for crop yield estimation and prediction. Int. J. Remote Sens. **14**, 199 (1993)
4. Nuske, S., Wilshusen, K., Achar, S., Yoder, L., Singh, S.: Automated visual yield estimation in vineyards. J. Field Robot. **31**, 837 (2014)
5. Sakamoto, T., Gitelson, A.A., Arkebauer, T.J.: MODIS-based corn grain yield estimation model incorporating crop phenology information. Remote Sens. Environ. **131**, 215 (2013)
6. Yeom, J., Jung, J., Chang, A., Maeda, M., Landivar, J.: Automated open cotton boll detection for yield estimation using unmanned aircraft vehicle (UAV) data. Remote Sens. **10**, 1895 (2018)
7. Dalezios, N.R., Domenikiotis, C., Loukas, A., Tzortzios, S.T., Kalaitzidis, C.: Cotton yield estimation based on NOAA/AVHRR produced NDVI. Phys. Chem. Earth Part B **26**, 247 (2001)
8. Gao, Z., Xu, X., Wang, J., Jin, H., Yang, H.: Cotton yield estimation based on similarity analysis of time-series NDVI. Nongye Gongcheng Xuebao/Trans. Chin. Soc. Agric. Eng. **28**, 148 (2012)
9. Chen, Z., et al.: Integrating OGC web processing service with cloud computing environment for earth observation data. In: International Conference on Agro-Geoinformatics (2017)
10. Dong, J., et al.: Mapping paddy rice planting area in northeastern Asia with Landsat 8 images, phenology based algorithm and Google Earth Engine. Remote Sens. Environ. **185**, 142 (2016)
11. Hird, J.N., Delancey, E.R., Mcdermid, G.J., Kariyeva, J.: Google Earth Engine, open-access satellite data, and machine learning in support of large-area probabilistic wetland mapping. Remote Sens. **9**, 1315 (2017)
12. Gorelick, N., Hancher, M., Dixon, M., Ilyushchenko, S., Moore, R.: Google Earth Engine: planetary-scale geospatial analysis for everyone. Remote Sens. Environ. **202**, 18–27 (2017)
13. Zhang, K., Dong, X., Liu, Z., Gao, W., Hu, Z., Wu, G.: Mapping tidal flats with Landsat 8 images and Google Earth Engine: a case study of the China's eastern coastal zone circa 2015. Remote Sens. **11**, 924 (2019)
14. Venkatappa, M., Sasaki, N., Shrestha, R.P., Tripathi, N.K., Ma, H.: Determination of vegetation thresholds for assessing land use and land use changes in Cambodia using the Google Earth Engine cloud-computing platform. Remote Sens. **11**, 1514 (2019)
15. Wu, C., Chen, X., Tao, Y., Yang, P., Zhang, B., Han, Y.: Research on the application mode of spatial information technology for precision agriculture in Xinjiang. In: IEEE International Geoscience & Remote Sensing Symposium (2005)
16. Delegido, J., Verrelst, J., Alonso, L., Moreno, J.: Evaluation of Sentinel-2 red-edge bands for empirical estimation of green LAI and chlorophyll content. Sensors **11**, 7063 (2011)
17. Deng, L., Yu, D.: Deep learning: methods and applications. Found. Trends Signal Process. **7**, 197 (2014)
18. Lin, H., Shi, Z., Zou, Z.: Fully convolutional network with task partitioning for inshore ship detection in optical remote sensing images. IEEE Geosci. Remote Sens. Lett. **14**, 1665–1669 (2017)

19. Çiçek, Ö., Abdulkadir, A., Lienkamp, S.S., Brox, T., Ronneberger, O.: 3D U-Net: learning dense volumetric segmentation from sparse annotation. In: Ourselin, S., Joskowicz, L., Sabuncu, M.R., Unal, G., Wells, W. (eds.) MICCAI 2016. LNCS, vol. 9901, pp. 424–432. Springer, Cham (2016). https://doi.org/10.1007/978-3-319-46723-8_49

20. Iosup, A., Ostermann, S., Yigitbasi, M.N., Prodan, R., Fahringer, T., Epema, D.H.J.: Performance analysis of cloud computing services for many-tasks scientific computing. IEEE Trans. Parallel Distrib. Syst. **22**, 931 (2011)

21. Bohn R.B., Messina J., Liu F., Tong J., Mao J.: NIST cloud computing reference architecture. In: IEEE World Congress on Services, Washington, DC, USA, 4 July 2011–9 July 2011 (2011)

22. Harnik, D., Pinkas, B., Shulman-Peleg, A.: Side channels in cloud services: deduplication in cloud storage. IEEE Secur. Priv. **8**, 40 (2010)

23. Villamizar M., et al.: Infrastructure cost comparison of running Web applications in the cloud using AWS lambda and monolithic and microservice architectures. In: IEEE/ACM International Symposium on Cluster (2016)

24. Foster, I., Yong, Z., Raicu, I., Lu, S.: Cloud computing and grid computing 360-degree compared. In: Grid Computing Environments Workshop (2009)

25. Al-Dhuraibi, Y., Paraiso, F., Djarallah, N., Merle, P.: Elasticity in cloud computing: state of the art and research challenges. IEEE Trans. Serv. Comput. **11**, 430 (2018)

26. Tihfon, G.M., Park, S., Kim, J., Kim, Y.M.: An efficient multi-task PaaS cloud infrastructure based on docker and AWS ECS for application deployment. Cluster Comput. **19**, 1 (2016)

27. O'Connor, A.S., Lausten, K., Heightley, K., Harris, T.: ENVI Services Engine: Earth and Planetary Image Processing for the Cloud

28. Merv, F., Carl, B.: A review of oil spill remote sensing. Sensors **18**, 91 (2018)

29. Bahr T., Okubo, B.: A New Cloud-based Deployment of Image Analysis Functionality, p. 243 (2013). Verlag Der Österreichischen Akademie Der Wissenschaften

30. Saabith, A.L.S., Sundararajan, E., Bakar, A.A.: Comparative analysis of different versions of association rule mining algorithm on AWS-EC2. In: Badioze Zaman, H., et al. (eds.) IVIC 2015. LNCS, vol. 9429, pp. 64–76. Springer, Cham (2015). https://doi.org/10.1007/978-3-319-25939-0_6

31. Boschetti, M., et al.: PhenoRice: a method for automatic extraction of spatio-temporal information on rice crops using satellite data time series. Remote Sens. Environ. **194**, 347 (2017)

32. Ren, J., Chen, Z., Tang, H.: Regional scale remote sensing-based yield estimation of winter wheat by using MODIS-NDVI data: a case study of Jining City in Shandong province. Chin. J. Appl. Ecol. **17**, 2371 (2006)

33. Unganai, L.S., Kogan, F.N.: Drought monitoring and corn yield estimation in Southern Africa from AVHRR data. Remote Sens. Environ. **63**, 219 (1998)

Cloud Security and Privacy

Intelligent System Security Event Description Method

Jun Hou[1], Qianmu Li[2(✉)], Yini Chen[2], Shunmei Meng[2,5], Huaqiu Long[3], and Zhe Sun[4]

[1] Nanjing Institute of Industry Technology, Nanjing 210023, China
[2] School of Cyber Science and Technology, Nanjing University of Science and Technology, Nanjing 210094, China
qianmu@njust.edu.cn
[3] Intelligent Manufacturing Department, Wuyi University, Jiangmen 529020, China
[4] Jiangsu Zhongtian Technology Co, Ltd., Nantong 226463, China
[5] State Key Laboratory for Novel Software Technology, Nanjing University, Nanjing 210023, China

Abstract. In a cloud environment, the control logic and data forwarding of network devices are separated from each other. The control layer is responsible for the centralized management of network nodes. After it acquires the entire network topology, it can automatically generate a visualized network structure. The security analyst can grasp the connection status of the devices on the entire network in the control domain. The network topology generation method based on the control layer information is directly and efficiently, which can greatly simplify the description of security events in the cloud environment. At the same time, the separate structure also makes the specific details of the underlying network device hidden. Petri-net, as a formal description tool, can be used to describe such a structure. Based on the cloud environment structure, this paper combines the advantages of CORAS modeling and analysis with object-oriented Petri-net theory, and proposes a COP (CORAS-based Object Oriented Petri-net)-based intelligent system security event description method. Model the description of the complexity and dynamics of cloud environment security events.

Keywords: Security event description · CORAS modeling · Petri-net theory

1 CORAS Framework

CORAS is a model-based approach to security risk analysis that maintains and provides the results of the analysis. CORAS is mainly based on some traditional security analysis techniques, such as HazOp, FTA, FMEA, etc., and combines them with system development techniques such as UML to form a modeling analysis description method. CORAS is a graphics and model based approach that give CORAS the following advantages:

(1) CORAS can provide a precise description of the target system. Its syntax and all related security features are easy to use;

© ICST Institute for Computer Sciences, Social Informatics and Telecommunications Engineering 2020
Published by Springer Nature Switzerland AG 2020. All Rights Reserved
X. Zhang et al. (Eds.): CloudComp 2019/SmartGift 2019, LNICST 322, pp. 487–499, 2020.
https://doi.org/10.1007/978-3-030-48513-9_39

(2) The graphical representation of CORAS information enhances the communication and interaction of each participant in the analysis;

(3) CORAS facilitates the documentation of risk assessment assumptions and assessment results.

CORAS can be divided into three different components:

(1) The CORAS Risk Modeling Language: which includes the graphical grammar and textual grammar of the CORAS icon and related semantics;

(2) The CORAS Method: which includes a step-by-step description of the safety analysis process and a guide to constructing a CORAS chart;

(3) The CORAS Tool: This includes tools for documenting, maintaining, and reporting the results of risk analysis.

In addition to including descriptions and analytical methods, the CORAS approach also takes into account international standards for risk management.

1.1 Component-Based CORAS and Petri-Net

In recent years, CORAS has gradually begun to develop toward component-based risk analysis [1]. For complex system analysis tasks, reusable components should be utilized to reduce the amount of work involved, rather than analyzing from scratch. It contains development techniques including syntax, rules, and implementation guidelines for specifying the behavior and system architecture of components. This standardized the incremental analysis of the system. A simple example is given below to illustrate how component-based CORAS describes and analyzes security events. Figure 1 is an example of a modeling analysis of a threat scenario. The circle on the graph represents the threat scene that occurred. Playing files directly is one of the actions.

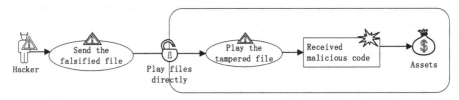

Fig. 1. CORAS modeling analysis of threat scenarios

By sending a tampered music file, the hacker uses the media player buffer overflow vulnerability to threaten the user's related media assets. When the receive file operation is invoked, that is the user plays the file directly, the channel interface calls the tampered music file from the interface of the media player. Once the file is played, it will use a buffer overflow vulnerability to overwrite the pointer address to point to malicious code, threatening the user's assets. In the above threat scenarios, scenarios, risks, and threat assets are defined as individual component objects. The description of the entire security event is done by connecting the calling relationships of the interfaces between the objects. The entire description process is very clear and concise, which is beneficial to the participants involved in the risk analysis and evaluation to understand and communicate the entire risk event. At the same time, related scenes are also very convenient for documenting preservation. If a new threat scenario is created, the entire modeled part is not necessary to make major changes, so the reusability of the model is also guaranteed. However, from the above examples, CORAS can also be found to have shortcomings such as insufficient formal description ability, excessive subjectivity, and insufficient dynamic analysis capability.

Petri-net is a graphical description method based on mathematical theory. It is a special directed graph consisting of the library, transition and flow relationship. And it uses Token to describe the state changes in the graph. The basic Petri-net is defined as following:

Definition 1. Basic Petri-net is a triple:

$$PN = (P, T, F) \tag{1}$$

Where:

(1) P is a finite set of spaces that represent the state of the system; T is a finite set of transitions that represent changes in behavior;
(2) $P \cup T \neq \varnothing$, $P \cap T = \varnothing$;
(3) $F \subseteq (P \times T) \cup (T \times P)$ is a lone set. It is the flow relationship of Petri-net, connecting libraries and transitions;
(4) $Dom(F) \cup Cod(F) = P \cup T$;
    $Dom(F) = \{x | \exists y : (x, y) \in F\}$, $Cod(F) = \{x | \exists y : (y, x) \in F\}$

2 COP Modeling Method

Definition 2. COP is a risk assessment process that defines it as a triple:

$$COOPN = \{SP, OG; OF\} \tag{2}$$

Where,

(1) $SP = \{sp_1, sp_2, \ldots, sp_n\}$ is a sub-process of the COP evaluation process, which can be regarded as a special library;
(2) $OG = \{og_1, og_2, \ldots, og_n\}$ is a collection of Outer Gate Transitions between sub-processes. In order to comply with the description of COP, this paper extends the transition T to G. G can be seen as a special kind of gate transition. This change has the nature of a gate. This paper introduces two different gate transitions, as shown in Fig. 2:

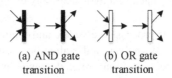

(a) AND gate   (b) OR gate
transition   transition

Fig. 2. Gate transition symbol

(3) $OF = \{of_1, of_2, \ldots, of_n\}$ is a collection of all Outer Flows outside the sub-process, corresponding to the dependencies between the sub-processes.

Definition 3. The COP sub-process sp_i is internally defined as a triple:

$$inner(sp_i) = \{P, IG; IF\} \tag{3}$$

Where,

(1) $P = \{p_1, p_2, \ldots, p_n\}$ is a collection of all the places in the sub-process sp_i;
(2) $IG = \{ig_1, ig_2, \ldots, ig_n\}$ is a collection of all Inner Gate Transitions within sub-process sp_i;
(3) $IF = \{if_1, if_2, \ldots, if_n\}$ is a collection of Inner Flows between all the libraries and transitions in sub-process sp_i.

Definition 4. Sub-process sp_i internal and external communication is defined as a four-tuple, defined as follows:

$$outer(sp_i) = \{IM, OM, OG; OF\} \tag{4}$$

(1) $IM = \{im_1, im_2, \ldots, im_n\}$ is a collection of all In-message queues outside of sub-process sp_i;
(2) $OM = \{om_1, om_2, \ldots, om_n\}$ is a collection of all Out-message queues outside of sub-process sp_i;
(3) The definition of $OG = \{og_1, og_2, \ldots, og_n\}$ and $OF = \{of_1, of_2, \ldots, of_n\}$ is defined in Definition 2;

In the description of modeling using the COP method, the COP model of each object is first given. Secondly, the message input and output interface are defined according to the flow relationship between the objects. Then connect the interfaces according to the flow relationship and initialize the COP model. Finally, a COP analysis was performed.

The COP model initialization algorithm is as follows:

Algorithm: COP model initialization algorithm

Input: Sub-process collection *SP*

Output: COP model initialization result *COP*

1. num← SizeOf(*SP*);   // Get the number of sub-process collections
2. COP ← Φ;   // COP network initialization
3. for i ← 1 to num do{   // Establish sub-processes
      sp_i ← Pop(*SP*, *i*);   // New sub-process sp_i
      AddIM2SP(*IM*, sp_i); // Add sp_i in-message queue *IM*
      AddP2SP(*P*, sp_i); // Add sp_i internal library *P*
      AddIG2SP(*IG*, sp_i); // Add sp_i Inner Gate Transition *IG*
      AddOM2SP(*OM*, sp_i); // Add sp_i Out-message queue *OM*
      IF ← LinkPandIG(*P*, *IG*, *IM*, *OM*); // calculate sp_i Inner Flow *IF*
      AddIF2SP(*IF*, sp_i);   // Add sp_i Inner Flow *IF*
      AddSP2COP(COP, sp_i);   // Add COP sub-process sp_i
   }
4. AddOG2COP(COP, *OG*);   // Add COP Gate Transition *OG*
5. *OF* ← LinkPandIG(*P*, *IG*); // Calculate the COP flow relationship *OF* from the sub-process *SP* and the gate transition relationship.
      AddOF2COP(COP, *OF*);   // Add COP flow relationship *OF*

---

3   Instance Verification

Unified management of the control layer in the cloud environment will introduce new threats. Using network nodes to launch DDoS attacks to controllers is one of them [2]. In order to verify the feasibility and effectiveness of the COP-based cloud environment security event description method, this paper combines the cloud environment structure

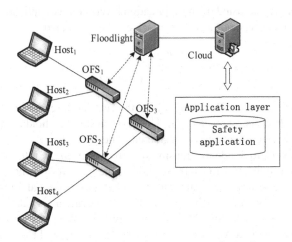

Fig. 3. Experimental environment network topology

proposed in the paper and builds the simulation network environment shown in Fig. 3 by using SDN technology. The paper carried out the DoS attack simulation in the cloud environment and described the security events triggered. The device layer includes multiple hosts, OpenFlow switches, controllers, and application servers. The control layer uses Floodlight as the SDN controller. The application layer runs a security application. The simulation software is mininet [3].

Data packet transmission information is shown in Table 1. After the request is sent, the stream data that is not matched by the OFS flow table will be packaged and delivered to Floodlight. After the Floodlight identifies the packet, it passes the packet to the application layer security application for processing. The security app sends the specified protection policy to Floodlight. Floodlight delivers new flow tables and settings to OFS. Finally, the OFS processes the packet according to the new command. The experiment collects the link bandwidth occupancy rate (*lbor*: link bandwidth occupancy rate), the client packet transmission rate (*psps*: package send per second), and the server-side packet reception rate (*prps*: package received per second) as statistical indicators. The *prps* responses to the attack strength and credibility of the attack. The greater the number of attacks, the more likely the attack is to be a real intrusion.

Table 1. Packet transmission information in the experiment

Number	Send content
p_{51}	Host1 sends ICMP packets to cloud
p_{52}	Host2 sends ICMP packets to cloud
p_{61}	Host3 sends TCP packets to cloud
p_{62}	Host4 sends TCP packets to cloud

A gate threshold value ε can be set as a reference value for the number of alarms, which is dynamically adjusted by the application layer security application, whereby the probability λ of occurrence of a certain attack can be calculated.

$$\lambda_i = \begin{cases} \frac{prps_i}{\varepsilon_i} & if\,(n_i < \varepsilon_i) \\ 1 & otherwise \end{cases} \tag{5}$$

For an attack, when the data is less than the set gate threshold ε_i, the probability value λ_i of the attack is represented by $\frac{prps_i}{\varepsilon_i}$. When the threshold ε_i is exceeded, the probability value λ_i of the attack is considered to be 1.

It is also possible to divide the transmission frequency $prps_i$ into different intervals according to the provisions of GB20984-2007 as the basis for the attack threat assignment. The division between intervals can be divided into non-equal divisions, as shown in Table 2. In this way, the probability λ of an attack occurring is calculated.

The experiment uses the first attack probability calculation method as the evaluation basis. First, Host1 sends ICMP packets at a lower frequency, and Host3 and Host4 send TCP packets at a lower frequency. Host2 sends ICMP packets at increasing frequency

Table 2. Attack probability assignment table

Assignment	Identification	Threat frequency	Frequency range	λ_i
5	Very high	Occur frequently	$> 50\% \cdot lbor$	1
4	High	Very likely to happen	$(20\% \sim 50\%) \cdot lbor$	0.5
3	Medium	Likely to happen	$(10\% \sim 20\%) \cdot lbor$	0.2
2	Low	Less likely to happen	$(5\% \sim 10\%) \cdot lbor$	0.1
1	Very low	Extremely rare	$< 5\% \cdot lbor$	0.01

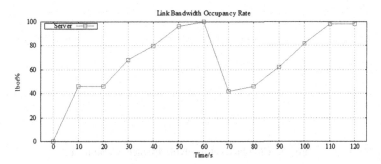

Fig. 4. Cloud link bandwidth occupancy rate

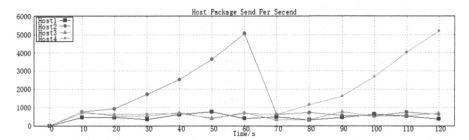

Fig. 5. Host packet transmission frequency

until it occupies all of the link bandwidth and then drops to normal. Host4 then sends TCP packets with increasing frequency until it occupies all of the link bandwidth and then drops to normal. The cloud link bandwidth occupancy, host packet transmission frequency, and cloud packet reception frequency in the experiment are shown in Fig. 4, Fig. 5 and Fig. 6.

It can be seen that as the two DoS attacks progress, the bandwidth is occupied in a large amount, normal traffic cannot be sent, and the connection cannot be established. First, the experimental results were analyzed, and the 27th second of the experiment was selected as the analysis time point, as shown in Fig. 7. In the figure, the red horizontal

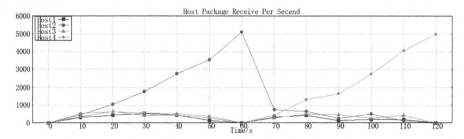

Fig. 6. Cloud packet receiving frequency

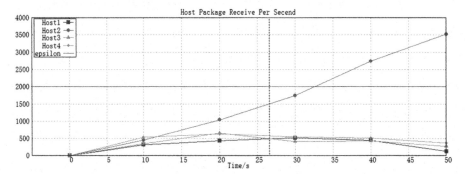

Fig. 7. Cloud packet receiving frequency fragment

Table 3. The possibility of an attack at this moment

Number	Packet acceptance frequency *psps*	Gate threshold value ε	Attack possibility λ
p_{51}	489	2000	0.244
p_{52}	1507	2000	0.753
p_{61}	502	2000	0.251
p_{62}	587	2000	0.294
$p_{51}\ p_{52}$	Total: 1996	Total: 3085	Proportion: 0.647
$p_{61}\ p_{62}$	Total: 1089		Proportion: 0.353

line is the gate threshold value ε, and the red vertical line is the 27th second of the experiment. Assume that both the ICMP gate threshold ε_1 and the ε_2 of TCP are 40% of the bandwidth occupied by the Cloud packet.

Table 3 lists the data on the likelihood of an attack occurring at the red vertical dashed line.

3.1 Attack Scene COP Modeling Definition

The moment is modeled and analyzed according to the COP modeling step:

The moment contains five sub-processes, in which $Host_1 \sim Host_4$ are recorded as potential attack initiators as sub-process $sp_1 \sim sp_4$. Two different potential attack behaviors ICMP and TCP belong to two different sub-processes sp_5 and sp_6. The attacked server is the target Recorded as sub-process sp_7.

(1) Initialize the COP network, assign Φ;

(2) New a sub-process sp_1. sp_1 does not have a library and transitions that need to be described in detail, add sp_1 to the COP network. Similarly, new a sub-process $sp_2 \sim sp_4$. $sp_2 \sim sp_4$ does not have a library and transitions that need to be described in detail. $sp_2 \sim sp_4$ is added to the COP network;

(3) Create a new subprocess sp_5. The behavior im_{51} that initiates the attack within the A sub-process is taken as the input of sp_5. It can be seen from Table 1 that sp_5 includes p_{51}, p_{52} suspected of initiating an ICMP (ig_{51}) attack. Since p_{51}, p_{52} belong to the same ICMP attack ig_{51}, they conform to the "AND" relationship, so add the AND transition ig_{51} to sp_5. Finally, the consequences of the attack are taken as the output om_{51} of sp_5 and added to sp_5. Calculate the internal IF of sp_5. Add the internal stream relationship IF to sp_5. Add sp_5 to the COP network. Similarly, modeling can get sp_6 and add sp_6 to the COP network.

(4) It can be seen from Table 1 that $sp_1 \sim sp_4$. randomly initiates an attack can make a affection of sp_7, so there is a logical OR relationship between the attack behaviors. Add OR gate transitions og_1, og_2 and og_3 to the COP. Calculate OF based on the relationship between the elements and add to the COP.

(5) Improve the COP network;

The modeling results are shown in Fig. 8.

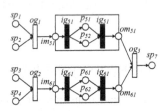   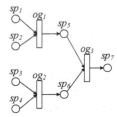

Fig. 8. COP model generated based on attack scenario information

Fig. 9. Dynamically scaled COP model

3.2 COP Method Analysis

(1) **Qualitative description**

In the qualitative description, this way of independent scaling of sub-processes and the describing way of completing the closing and opening of the detail implements

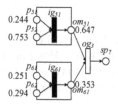

Fig. 10. COP model with attack probability

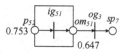

Fig. 11. COP model with an attack gate threshold of 0.6

a description of the different levels of refinement. The sub-processes that have completed the analysis at the same time can be saved independently as the analysis results. Portions of the same analysis content encountered in other analyses can be directly replaced to achieve reuse of the model.

The qualitative results are shown in Fig. 9. It can be clearly seen that $sp_1 \sim sp_4$ initiates two different attacks sp_5 and sp_6 against sp_7. The results of each attack analysis can be saved separately to implement model reuse. The attack process can be scaled independently to achieve a different level of description.

(2) **Quantitative description**

In the quantitative description, the analysis can be performed based on the connection relationship in the COP network. Suppose that the risk of an object being attacked is F. It can be seen from the definition of COP that in the case of the transition of the AND gate, the value of F is determined by the sum of the possibility of initiating the attack precondition. In the case of an OR gate transition, the value of F is determined by the maximum probability of initiating an attack precondition. Bring the possibility of potential attack at this moment in Table 3 to Fig. 8. The possibility of each attack content and attack type is shown in Fig. 10.

According to the definition, the risk value of the possible attack node sp_7 is calculated as follows:

$$F(sp_7) = MAX[0.647 \cdot SUM(0.244, 0.753), 0.3 \cdot SUM(0.251, 0.294)]$$
$$= MAX[0.997, 0.545] \tag{6}$$
$$= 0.997$$

Assuming that the probability of attack to be analyzed exceeds 0.6, the new COP model is shown in Fig. 11.

Among them, ig_{51}, og_3 degenerates into a normal gate transition. At this time, the risk value of sp_7 is:

$$F(sp_7) = MAX[0.647 \cdot SUM(0.753)] = 0.487 \tag{7}$$

(3) **Strategic response**

Once it is detected that the actual risk value of the relevant asset exceeds the acceptable risk value (assumed to be 0.5), the application-level security application performs the flow table update according to the set rules. Then, depending on the magnitude of the risk value, a new forwarding path can be set to offload, limit or block certain stream data. In the experiment, if the gate threshold is exceeded, the forwarding request of the relevant network segment is discarded, and the stream data is discarded. After setting the rules, the Cloud link bandwidth occupancy, Host packet transmission frequency, and Cloud packet reception frequency are shown in Fig. 12, Fig. 13 and Fig. 14. It can be seen that in the case where the transmission packet law is unchanged in the simulation network, the transmission source with the attack intention is blocked, the link occupancy rate of the Cloud end is significantly reduced, and the normal service is guaranteed.

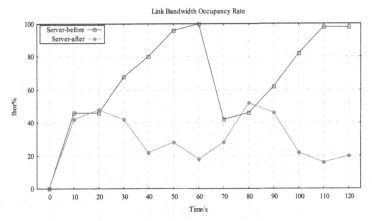

Fig. 12. Cloud link bandwidth usage

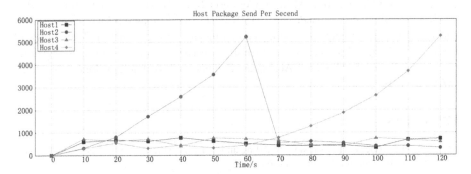

Fig. 13. Host packet transmission frequency

COP inherits CORAS's graphical description, reusability and refined description of the advantages, and uses object-oriented Petri-net to increase the advantages of formal description, scalability and dynamic verification. At the same time, the data source of CORAS quantitative analysis is transformed from subjective expert evaluation into objective scanning analysis, which reduces the human factors in the analysis process and makes the results more reliable.

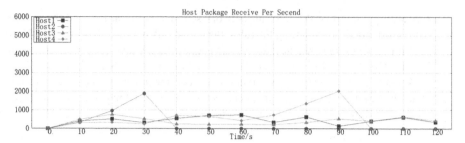

Fig. 14. Cloud packet receiving frequency

4   Conclusion

In this paper, a model-based static security event modeling description method CORAS and object-oriented Petri-net are combined to propose a COP-based security risk modeling method. Compared with the existing model-based methods, the proposed COP model not only inherits the existing model's extensibility, reusability, and refinement description but also enhances the formal description and dynamic analysis capabilities. In the cloud environment structure, the description of the entire network in the control domain can be directly generated based on the control layer information, and the efficiency is far superior to the topology discovery technology in the traditional network. The attack simulation experiment proves that COP can effectively describe the cloud environment security incidents, and can further carry out risk strategy response based on the description results.

This work was supported in part by the Fundamental Research Funds for the Central Universities (30918012204), Military Common Information System Equipment Pre-research Special Technology Project (315075701), 2019 Industrial Internet Innovation and Development Project from Ministry of Industry and Information Technology of China, 2018 Jiangsu Province Major Technical Research Project "Information Security Simulation System", Shanghai Aerospace Science and Technology Innovation Fund (SAST2018-103).

References

1. Hong, J.E., Bae, D.H.: Software modeling and analysis using a hierarchical object-oriented Petri net. Inf. Sci. Int. J. **130**, 131–164 (2000)
2. Brændeland, G., Dahl, H.E.I., Engan, I., Stølen, K.: Using dependent CORAS diagrams to analyse mutual dependency. In: Lopez, J., Hämmerli, B.M. (eds.) CRITIS 2007. LNCS, vol. 5141, pp. 135–148. Springer, Heidelberg (2008). https://doi.org/10.1007/978-3-540-89173-4_12
3. De Oliveira, R.L.S., Shinoda, A.A., Schweitzer, C.M., et al.: Using mininet for emulation and prototyping software-defined networks. In: IEEE Colombian Conference on Communications and Computing, pp. 1–6. IEEE, Bogota (2014)
4. Liu, X., Wang, H., Lai, J., et al.: Multiclass support vector machines theory and its data fusion application in network security situation awareness. In: 2007 International Conference on Wireless Communications, Networking and Mobile Computing, pp. 6349–6352. IEEE, Shanghai (2007)

5. Shin, S., Yegneswaran, V., Porras, P., et al.: AVANT-GUARD: scalable and vigilant switch flow management in software-defined networks. In: ACM SIGSAC Conference on Computer & Communications Security, pp. 413–424. ACM (2013)

6. Xu, X., Liu, Q., Zhang, X., Zhang, J., Qi, L., Dou, W.: A blockchain-powered crowdsourcing method with privacy preservation in mobile environment. IEEE Trans. Comput. Soc. Syst. **6**(6), 1407–1419 (2019)

7. Qi, L., Chen, Y., Yuan, Y., Fu, S., Zhang, X., Xu, X.: A QoS-aware virtual machine scheduling method for energy conservation in cloud-based cyber-physical systems. World Wide Web **23**, 1275–1297 (2020). https://doi.org/10.1007/s11280-019-00684-y

8. Qi, L., et al.: Finding all you need: web APIs recommendation in web of things through keywords search. IEEE Trans. Comput. Soc. Syst. **6**(5), 1063–1072 (2019)

9. Li, Q., Meng, S., Wang, S., Zhang, J., Hou, J.: CAD: command-level anomaly detection for vehicle-road collaborative charging network. IEEE Access **7**, 34910–34924 (2019)

10. Li, Q., Meng, S., Zhang, S., Hou, J., Qi, L.: Complex attack linkage decision-making in edge computing networks. IEEE Access **7**, 12058–12072 (2019)

11. Li, Q., et al.: Safety risk monitoring of cyber-physical power systems based on ensemble learning algorithm. IEEE Access **7**, 24788–24805 (2019)

12. Li, Q., Wang, Y., Pu, Z., Wang, S., Zhang, W.: A time series association state analysis method in smart internet of electric vehicle charging network attack. Transp. Res. Rec. **2673**, 217–228 (2019)

Designing a Bit-Based Model to Accelerate Query Processing Over Encrypted Databases in Cloud

Sultan Almakdi[1,2(✉)] and Brajendra Panda[1]

[1] University of Arkansas, Fayetteville, AR 72701, USA
{saalmakd,bpanda}@uark.edu
[2] Najran University, Najran, Saudi Arabia
smalmukadi@nu.edu.sa

Abstract. Database users have started moving toward the use of cloud computing as a service because it provides computation and storage needs at affordable prices. However, for most of the users, the concern of privacy plays a major role as they cannot control data access once their data are outsourced, especially if the cloud provider is curious about their data. Data encryption is an effective way to solve privacy concerns, but executing queries over encrypted data is a problem that needs attention. In this research, we introduce a bit-based model to execute different relational algebra operators over encrypted databases at the cloud without decrypting the data. To encrypt data, we use the randomized encryption algorithm (AES-CBC) to provide the maximum-security level. The idea is based on classifying attributes as sensitive and non-sensitive, where only sensitive attributes are encrypted. For each sensitive attribute, the table's owner predefines the possible partition domains on which the tuples will be encoded into bit vectors before the encryption. We store the bit vectors in an additional column in the encrypted table in the cloud. We use those bits to retrieve only part of encrypted records that are candidates for a specific query. We implemented and evaluated our model and found that the proposed model is practical and success to minimize the range of the retrieved encrypted records to less than 30% of the whole set of encrypted records in a table.

Keywords: Cloud security · Cloud databases · Encrypted data · Query processing · Searchable encryption · Encrypted databases

1 Introduction

Nowadays, cloud computing is an attractive computation environment for both individuals and organizations since it provides a scalable data storage and high-performance computing unites. These features were not affordable for most individuals and small companies; so previously, only big companies could own such unites. With the presence of cloud computing, this problem has been solved as users can rent storage and computation unites as needed at an affordable price. Moreover, the majority of cloud

X. Zhang et al. (Eds.): CloudComp 2019/SmartGift 2019, LNICST 322, pp. 500–518, 2020.
https://doi.org/10.1007/978-3-030-48513-9_40

providers offer database as a service, in which users and companies outsource their data and can access them anytime, from anywhere. However, people have expressed concern about their privacy when outsourcing sensitive data, as privacy breaches are one of the most common threats in the cloud-computing environment. For example, untrustworthy cloud providers can steal personal customer information such as emails, addresses, and phone numbers and sell them to third parties. Thus, users receive annoying advertisements through emails, the mail, and their phones. Furthermore, if an attack targets a cloud provider, the attackers can gain access to customers' sensitive personal information such as their social security numbers (SSNs). This has serious consequences, as the criminals can impersonate customers in different situations such as financial transactions like phone banking. As a result, sensitive data are restricted from being processed or sold to a third party. Therefore, the cloud-computing environment could become unattractive for consumers if there are no available appropriate solutions for privacy breach and security issues. This issue must be addressed if cloud providers are to gain the trust of users and organizations so that they will outsource their sensitive data without worrying about data leakages.

To solve the problem of privacy breach, data encryption is the only way to ensure that cloud providers cannot learn from the data they store. Different researchers have proposed various models for user-side data encryption, wherein data encryption happens before outsourcing, and decryption happens on the user's side. The problem with this technique is that it conflicts with critical functionalities of cloud environments (e.g., searching for a numeric range of data). Other researchers use what is called onion layer encryption where each data item is encrypted with more than one encryption algorithm to support various query types [24]. However, in case of huge data sets, the penalty is the computational burden, as each data item might have to be decrypted more than once.

In this proposed research, we design a model to execute different relational algebra queries over encrypted data. The proposed model deals with both encrypted numeric data and textual data. We introduce the query manager (QM) component—light software for single users and a trusted server in organizations—which performs the encryption, decryption, and queries translation, leaving a minimal amount of work for users. In addition, in our model, we split the computation into two sides: a cloud provider side and a client side, where we move the majority of the computation to the cloud provider by translating queries into appropriate ways to deal with encrypted data without decrypting them. We design an algorithm for each query category (e.g., select, join, union, intersection, etc.) to enable cloud providers to execute such query categories over encrypted tuples. Further, we encrypt sensitive data in tables with the randomized Advanced Encryption Standard (AES-CBS) encryption algorithm that is neither deterministic (each plaintext always has the same cipher text) nor order preserving in order to provide the highest level of security and privacy.

We classify attributes to sensitive and non-sensitive. Sensitive attributes can be partitioned into partition domains (PDs) by the owner of the table based on possible values for the attribute. The query manager (QM) creates a data structure for the partitions domains (PDs), and then creates a bit vector whose length is equal to the number of PDs and maps each PD to a bit position. The encrypted table in the cloud will have an additional column to store those bits for each tuple. We use those bits to retrieve only candidate encrypted tuples of a query from the cloud. Also, we make our model resistances to different attacks, such as inference attack, that could happen at the cloud site where the attacker could exploit the presence of the bits to infer the possible data distributions. The rest of this paper is structured as follows: in Sect. 2, we discuss related work and previous models. Then, in Sect. 3, we explain the model in detail. We describe how we implemented and evaluated our model in Sect. 4, and we provide the conclusions of this work in Sect. 5.

2 Literature Review

CryptDB is a system proposed by Popa et al. [23] as the first practical system for executing different Standard Query Language (SQL) queries over the encrypted databases. The model was designed to resist two different possible attacks, cloud attacks, and proxy attacks. They introduce onion layers encryption that is encrypting each data item by more than one encryption algorithm to support multiple SQL queries. Moreover, they present new algorithms, including one to handle the join operation. In CryptDB, the primary purpose of the proxy is to perform the crypto processes on behave of the users. One of the downsides of CryptDB is the high computation burden because each data item must be encrypted and decrypted more than once.

Liu et al. in [17] propose the FHOPE system to support complex SQL queries over encrypted data while resisting homomorphic order-preserving attacks. It allows cloud providers to run arithmetic and comparison operators over encrypted data without repeating the encryption. The limitation of this work is that the authors conducted their experiments based on tables with less than 9,000 records. In order to show the efficiency and scalability of the system, using tables with larger numbers of records (e.g., 100,000; 500,000; and 1,000,000) would better in terms of assisting the efficiency and overhead since this requires more decryption processes. A variety of studies related to this system can be found at [7, 8, 16, 18, 19, 24, 30].

Cui et al. propose P-McDb [3], a privacy-preserving search system that enables users to run queries over encrypted data. It uses two clouds to prevent inference attacks, one for data storing and searching and one for database re-randomizing and shuffling. It supports partial searches of encrypted records (as opposed to total searches), a feature referred to as a sub-linear manner. P-McDb can be used by multiple users, and in the case of a user revocation, the data cannot be re-encrypted. In this system, the communication between the two clouds could introduce more delays when compared with other systems, like [23]. Other proposed models in this matter are described in [2, 4–6, 13, 32].

In [10], the authors have created a system that executes relational algebra operators over encrypted data. They add identifiers for attributes to enable service providers to execute queries over data. They split the computation between the end user and the service provider, with the majority of the computation moved to the service provider's side. The limitation of this work is that each tuple is encrypted and stored as a string at the service provider's site. This prevents some of the relational algebra operators (e.g., projection) from being executed on the provider's side, and in some cases, whole encrypted tuples must be returned and decrypted (see [9, 14, 15, 22] for related research).

Osama et al., in [21], propose different approaches for partitioning attributes of tables into multiple domains. They tested their approaches and found that they introduced different delays. Their approaches are based on an order-preserving mapping function, which enables cloud servers to execute different operators as equality operators. The limitation of this work is that they did not consider textual data in their experiments, which would prove that their approaches are practical for relational databases. They should also have considered relational algebra operators.

In [27], the authors proposed SDB that is a model based on dividing data to sensitive and non-sensitive data; only sensitive data are encrypted. The idea is to split the sensitive data into two shares, one share is kept by the data owner (DO) and the second is kept by the service provider (SP) assuming the SP is untrusted. In SDB, the SP cannot reveal anything from the share that it has. Besides, the SDB allows different operators to share the same encryption, providing secure query processing with data interoperability. Similar work can be found in [20, 28, 31].

Bucketization is a method that requires the indexing and partitioning of the encrypted data into more than one bucket. Each bucket has an identification (ID) and holds a set of encrypted records ranging from the minimum to maximum value. The index can be used to execute SQL-style queries over the encrypted data [26]. Various models have been done based on this approach [11, 12, 25, 29].

3   The Model

The main goal of this research is to design a model that protects data in cloud servers from being accessed by curious cloud providers or malicious attackers. Each database table in this model will be encrypted before being outsourced to the cloud, using the randomized encryption algorithm, AES-CBC; concurrently, we enable the cloud server to execute queries over the encrypted data. Unlike traditional database encryption models where the user is the one who encrypts and decrypts the data, as in our previous work [1], our model uses a query manager (QM) as an intermediary between users and the cloud. As shown in Fig. 1, our model features the QM as a light software for single users or a trusted server that resides in the private cloud, for users within organizations. We design the QM to perform the computations, creating minimal work for the user(s). In the following sub-sections, we explain the model in detail.

3.1   The Details of the Proposed Model

We divide the attributes into sensitive and non-sensitive attributes. The sensitive attributes are the only attributes that are encrypted; because if they are not, they would leak private information, whereas non-sensitive attributes do not leak private information. We classified sensitive attributes, where data must be encrypted, into two types: attributes that have limited distinct values, such as student_rank, and attributes that may have too many distinct values (ranges), such as salary. Therefore, each attribute is partitioned into multiple partitions, and the table's owner is the one who predefines these partitions before beginning the encryption process. Then the QM builds a data structure of all partitions for each table, as in Fig. 2. After that, the QM creates a bit vector (BV) for each record where its length equals the total number of partitions for all the sensitive attributes. Then we store those bits in an additional attribute(s) in the encrypted table at the cloud, unlike

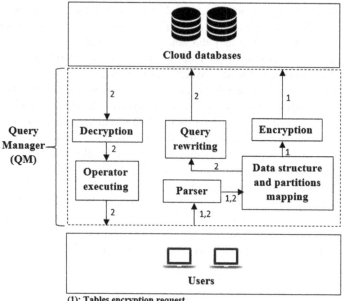

Fig. 1. System architecture

our previous work [1] where we store bit vector(s) in the QM. We use the bits to retrieve only candidate encrypted tuples for a query and element unrelated tuples retrieval. The QM performs the following steps for creating bit vectors (BVs) and encrypting tuples: 1) The table's owner defines partitions domains for each sensitive column and sends a creation request to the QM. 2) According to the PDs, the QM creates a data structure for the table to easily translate queries in the future. 3) The QM takes each record j and creates a bit vector BV_j whose length is equal to the total number of partition domains for all sensitive columns for a table T, map each bit's position to a single domain partition, and initializes all bits with 0's. 4) A bit i in BV_j is set if and only if the data item d under column A equals or belongs to partition domain A_i. 5) The QM shall encrypt sensitive columns' data by AES-CBC and send encrypted data to the cloud database, along with the BV_j from the previous step. 6) The steps above are repeated for all records in Table T. In the cloud, the encrypted table has an additional column (we call it the reference column) to keep a BV for each record. The data type of the reference column that stores BVs is a BIT(n), where n is the number of bits. So, we don't worry about the size growth of the BVs since they are in bits and stored at the cloud. Do the fact that bits attributes can hold up to 64 bits, we could have more than one attribute to store bits. Then when rewriting the query, the QM can take the bits position find the reminder of 64 (e.g. when the bit position is 80, then 80% 64 = 16 which means the bit's position in the second bits attributes is 16). In this way, we can exploit the high computation speed and the massive capacity provided by the cloud to process and store BVs. The longer the BVs are, the less encrypted records are retrieved.

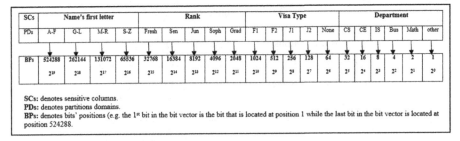

SCs	Name's first letter				Rank					Visa Type					Department					
PDs	A-F	G-L	M-R	S-Z	Fresh	Sen	Jun	Soph	Grad	F1	F2	J1	J2	None	CS	CE	IS	Bus	Math	other
BPs	524288	262144	131072	65536	32768	16384	8192	4096	2048	1024	512	256	128	64	32	16	8	4	2	1
	2^{19}	2^{18}	2^{17}	2^{16}	2^{15}	2^{14}	2^{13}	2^{12}	2^{11}	2^{10}	2^{9}	2^{8}	2^{7}	2^{6}	2^{5}	2^{4}	2^{3}	2^{2}	2^{1}	2^{0}

SCs: denotes sensitive columns.
PDs: denotes partitions domains.
BPs: denotes bits' positions (e.g. the 1st bit in the bit vector is the bit that is located at position 1 while the last bit in the bit vector is located at position 524288).

Fig. 2. Data structure and mapping information at the QM for student table.

Security of Proposed Model. Although it's not an easy process for an adversary (either malicious attacker or curios cloud provider) to learn the distribution of data nor infer the possible values of a column from the BVs, we add another security step to address this vulnerability. The solution is based on encrypting the names of the tables and the sensitive columns by a deterministic encryption algorithm, namely AES-SIV, where the ciphertexts for each plain text are always identical. The reason for that is to maximize the security to the highest level by making it impossible for the adversary to infer or learn from the BVs column the possible values while we enable the cloud provider to execute our queries. For instance, the column "Students-Rank" have limited possible values like grad, senior, junior, etc. Then the adversary could infer those even though they are encrypted with AES-CBC (which always produces different ciphertexts for a plain text). Details and security analysis of AES-SIV can be found in [33]. Note that, having more than ciphertexts share the same prefix is a not concern since the adversary cannot get the plain text unless he obtains the SK (Secrete key), and the SK isn't passed to the cloud in our case. Therefore, by encrypting the names of tables and sensitive columns, we ensure that the adversary can learn nothing from the BVs that we store at the cloud.

Example. Suppose we want to encrypt the students table presented in Table 1: the QM encrypts the table name and the names of sensitive columns by AES-SIV using user's secret key (SK) and create a new table at the cloud. Then the QM takes the first record and parses it to get the values. The name is "Alice," where the first letter is "A," which falls under the range "A–F," so the bit in the position $2^{19} = 524288$ will be set to 1. Then, the rank is "freshman", that will set the bit that mapped to position 2^{15} to 1. Next, the visa type is "F1", so QM sets bit with position 2^{10} to 1; the same process occurs for the department column, which will set position 2^{5} to 1. Now, the bit vector (BV) is "10001000010000100000". The QM will do this for all the records in the table. The encrypted table in the cloud will look like Table 2. To retrieve encrypted data from the encrypted table, when a user submits a query to the QM as

"*select* name from student where department = "computer science"

Table 1. Students table

ID	Name	Rank	Visa type	Department
110	Alice	Freshman	F1	Computer science
111	Sara	Senior	J1	Computer engineering
112	John	Junior	None	Information system
113	Ryan	Sophomore	J2	Math

The QM processes the query as in follow:

1) The QM encrypt the table's name and the sensitive columns' names using the user's SK to obtain the cipher texts as below:

$$CT_1 = E_{AES\text{-}SIV} (\text{"Students"}, SK)$$
$$CT_2 = E_{AES\text{-}SIV} (\text{"Name"}, SK)$$

2) The QM looks up the data structure, finds the bits' representations, then rewrites the query as "*select* CT_2 from CT_1 where reference &32 > 0".
3) The cloud will return only encrypted tuples that have the bit at position 32 $(2^5) = 1$.

3.2 Condition Rewriting

To enable the cloud database server (CDBS) to search over encrypted data, the QM must translate the query conditions in ways that the CDBS can implement them over encrypted tuples. This is a very important step before implementing queries of any query category, such as joins, union, and aggregations. The QM translates queries based on the data structures (DSs) of the table(s) involved in the query. As in [9], we have three kinds of conditions:

1. A condition that has a column and a value, for example,

    Name = "Alice".

2. A condition that has columns only, such as Name = Name.
3. A condition that involves more than one condition, such as Name = "Alice" OR visa type = "F1".

In the first and second kinds, there are five possible operations $\{>, <, =, \geq, \leq \}$. The operation in the third kind is limited to $\{V, \neg, \bigwedge\}$. In the first kind, column and value, the QM parses the query to extract the table's name, columns, and values. Then, for each value v, the QM finds the partition domain PD_i that value v equals or belongs to, and keeps its position. If the operation is "=", then it is straightforward, and the QM substitutes values with its corresponding bit position. We explain this case in detail under selection operation in the next sub-section. If the operation is "> or ≥", then the QM finds the positions of all PDs that are less than v. Therefore, the QM translates the query by substituting value v with the positions separated by OR and "> or ≥" with "=". For instance, suppose we have an employee table, and it has a salary column that is partitioned into three PDs {(1000–5000), (5001–9000), (9001–12000)}. Assume that the bits' positions are 32, 16, and 8, respectively. Suppose that the query is to find "salary > 8000". Now the query condition is translated into "Reference &16>0 OR Reference &8>0". Note that the PD that v is belongs to must be retrieved too with the PDs that must to be retrieved from the cloud, because the PDs are ranges. For the rest of the operation "< or ≤", we treat them in a similar way as "> or ≥", but by taking PDs that are less than or equal to v.

In the second kind, the condition that contains only columns, the QM finds all PDs' positions for every table involved in the condition. If the operation is "=", the QM rewrites the query condition by substituting the columns' names with pairs (PD_i from column A $\bigwedge$ PD_i from column B, where $PD_i = PD_j$) of the DPs' positions separated by the OR operation (pair1 V pair2 V pair3 …). To illustrate this, consider Table 1 (students table) and assume that we have another table (students_info table) and both tables have the same data structure as in Fig. 2. Suppose the condition is "where students.name = students_info.name". Let's say that,

$CT_1 = E_{\text{AES-SIV}}$ ("Students", SK)
$CT_2 = E_{\text{AES-SIV}}$ ("students_info", SK)

We assume that the owner of the two tables is one who owns the *SK*. The translation will look like the following:

"where ((CT_1.Reference&524288>0 AND CT_2.Reference&262144>0) OR

(CT_1.Reference&262144>0 AND CT_2.Reference&131072>0) OR

(CT_1.Reference&131072>0 AND CT_2.Reference &65536>0) OR

(CT_1.Reference&65536>0 AND CT_2.Reference &32768>0))"

We do the same if the columns are numeric, and the operation sign is { >, <, ≥, ≤ }, where we arrange the pairs in a way to satisfy the order condition.

In the third kind, the condition that contains more than one condition, each condition can be one of the above two kinds separated by AND or OR operations. Therefore, once all conditions are translated using the two translation methods, we need to combine the translation result with the AND or OR operation as in the query. For example, consider Table 1. Suppose the condition is (where Name = "Alice" OR Visa type = "J2"). This condition has two conditions with the OR operation, so the translation can be (where reference&524288>0 OR reference&128 >0). We perform the same method with the AND operation.

Table 2. $E_{AES-SIV}$ ("Students", SK), encrypted students table at the cloud. Note that the names of the columns are encrypted too using AES-SIV where $ct_n=$ $E_{AES-SIV}$ ("Name", SK), $ct_r=$ $E_{AES-SIV}$ ("Rank", SK), $ct_{vt}=$ $E_{AES-SIV}$ ("Visa type", SK), $ct_d=$ $E_{AES-SIV}$ ("Department", SK).

ID	ct_n	ct_r	ct_{vt}	ct_d	Reference
110	*&^	*_^%	*/d	^%^H	10001000010000100000
111	%^&	/+$	&^/	&&%$	00010100000100010000
112	)(#	%$/*	+−*&	)*#R	01000010000001001000
113	$#!	!@~K	*/f	@$%*	00100001000010000010

3.3   Relational Algebra Operators

In this subsection, we describe the set of relational algebra operators the proposed model can support. Most previous studies focused on the select operation, and only a few considered other relation algebra operators, like aggregation, union, intersection, difference, sort, and duplicate elimination. This is because it is challenging to facilitate a model that can support all relational algebra over encrypted data. Therefore, to make the proposed model practical, we provide an algorithm to execute each operator, such that as much of the computation as possible is moved to the cloud provider, leaving minimal work for the QM. The proposed algorithms translate the queries in a way that they filter out only unrelated encrypted records.

Select. The easiest way to implement the *select* operation over encrypted data is to retrieve the whole encrypted table from the cloud, decrypt it at the QM, and then execute the select operation on the data after they have been decrypted. However, this method is not practical in the case of huge tables, because it adds more computation burden on the QM. In an alternative method, in the proposed model, we move as much computation as possible to the cloud database server (CDBS) which has efficient computation unites, so we aim to minimize the range of retrieved encrypted records as much as possible. This can be done as follows: The QM gets the user's query and rewrites it according to tables' data structures (DSs), and then sends the translated select query to the CDBS (note that the QM translates the clauses that involve only sensitive columns). Then the CDBS executes the translated query and sends back the result (encrypted tuples for all candidate records). Now, the QM decrypts and applies the selection operation to them to filter unrelated data before returning the result to the user. We illustrated the process in the example in the previous Sub-sect. (3.1). Algorithm 1 demonstrates the steps that are performed by the QM to execute the select operator.

Join. To enable the proposed model to support the *join* operator, we must consider deferent cases for the join condition: 1) The join condition involves only non-sensitive columns, 2) the join condition involves only sensitive columns that have limited distinct values, and 3) the join condition involves sensitive columns that may have too many distinct values. The first case is straightforward, as the QM is required only to forward the query to the cloud database server (CDBS). Then it decrypts the result and removes the duplication.

Algorithm 1: Select operator

1:	Input < Table name, List of all columns, List of all data items $di(s)$ >
2:	**If** none of columns c_i mentioned in the query are sensitive
3:	**Forward** the query to CDBS
4:	**Decrypt** encrypted data
	Send result back to the user
5:	**If** all column(s) c_i mentioned in the query are sensitive
6:	**For** each data item di / value v being searched for under column c_i
7:	**Find** the bit's position that mapped to the partition domain PD that di falls under in the table's data structure DS_T.
8:	**Rewrite** the query and substitute values by bits' positions.
9:	**Send** the translated query to CDBS to retrieve candidate tuples (CTs)
10:	**Decrypt** CTs then **implement** select again to filter out unrelated records.
11:	**Send** result back to the user

In the second case, the QM uses the data structure DSs of the tables mentioned in the *join* condition to match the PDs of the tables. In Table T_1, each PD_j under a sensitive column SC_i is joined with each PD_j under a sensitive column SC_i in Table T_2 if and only if the PD_j from T_1 equals the PD_j from T_2. Note that the QM does this only for columns that are involved only in the join condition.

The third case is based on range PDs. The QM joins the PDs from both tables, and it ensures that each PD_i of the SC from Table T_1 is joined with each PD_i of the SC from Table T_2 if DP_i has at least one element that is common. For example, suppose we have two tables, Table A and Table B. We want to join them by the salary column. Suppose the salary DPs in Table A are [PD_1 (10,000–15,000), PD_2 (15,001–20,000), PD_3 (20,001–25,000), PD_4 (25,001–30,000)], and for Table B are [PD_1 (10,000–20,000), PD_2 (20,001–30,000)]. The QM joins PD_1 from Table B with PD_1, PD_2 from Table A because PD_1 of Table B contains elements from both PD_1 and PD_2 of Table A, and so on. Then the QM rewrites the query and sends it to the cloud. The cloud returns the join result to the QM, which decrypts only the columns involved in the join condition, and checks whether the plain texts satisfy the join condition. Then the QM decrypts the whole tuple only if the two values satisfy the join condition. Otherwise, the QM skips to the next tuple. We do so to eliminate unnecessary decryption processes. The QM eliminates duplicates after finishing decrypting the whole result. Algorithm 2 shows the steps of the *join* operation.

Aggregation. In this operation, we have two cases: First, the condition clause is based on column(s) where its partitions domain PDs values are not ranges. In this case, the CDBS efficiently implements the aggregation operation over encrypted data, and sends back the result to the QM, which needs only to decrypt the result and send it back to the user. Note that the QM may not implement the aggregation operator again over the decrypted data, because the candidate tuples retrieved from the CDBS are the exact query result.

For example, consider Table 1, Table 2, and Fig. 2; a query *select* count(*) from a student department where the department = "Computer science" is translated to "*select* count(*) from $E_{AES-SIV}$("Student", SK) where reference &32 >0", and it returns only the number of tuples that satisfy the condition, because the condition is based on the partition domain "computer science" that is not a range of values. The second case is the condition clause, which is based on column(s) where its partitions domains' values are ranges. In this case, in addition to the first case, the QM implements the aggregation operator again over decrypted candidate tuples. This is because the candidate tuples have tuples unrelated to the query, as the PDs are ranges. In the average operation, we leave the whole calculation to be done at the QM. However, we minimize the range of encrypted records retrieved from the CDBS by only those that satisfy the condition clause of the average query. Algorithm 3 below illustrates the steps.

Algorithm 2: Join operator

1:	Input < Tables names, List of all columns, List of all data items di(s) >
2:	**If** none of columns mentioned in the join condition are sensitive
3:	**Forward** the query to CDBS
4:	**Decrypt** encrypted data and **Remove** duplication
	Send result back to the user
5:	**If** all columns mentioned in the query are sensitive
6:	**If** the SCs have limited distinct values
7:	**Join** the bit's position of each partition domain PD_i of a SC_k from table T_m with the equivalent PD_i of a SC_x from table T_n
8:	**If** the SCs have range values
9:	**Join** the bit's position of each partition domain PD_i of a SC_k from table T_m with each PD_i of a SC_x from table T_n if it has at least 1 common value.
10:	**Rewrite** the query and substitute columns' names by bits' positions separated by OR operation.
11:	**Send** the translated query to CDBS to retrieve candidate tuples (CTs)
12:	**Decrypt** CTs and **Remove** duplication
13:	**Send** result back to the user

Sorting. Executing a sorting operator over encrypted data is not an easy process. However, in the proposed model, we can make the cloud server filter out unrelated records first according to the PDs of the data structure (DS). Then the QM decrypts the returned sorted result from the cloud and executes the sort operator over them again. The sorting computation needed from the QM before returning the final result to the user and after retrieving candidate tuples is significantly small, because the CDBS sends back only candidate records that fall under a certain partition domain(s). However, the CDBS will return a group of records that are not sorted except by partition domain. For example, to retrieve tuples that have income ranging from 50k to 60k, the cloud server returns all records that have income within this range unsorted, because they are encrypted. Therefore, the QM sorts them after the decryption process. Algorithm 4 shows the processes.

Algorithm 3: Aggregation operator

1:	Input < Tables names, List of all columns, List of all data items *di*(s) >
2:	**If** none of columns mentioned in the aggregation query are sensitive
3:	**Forward** the query to CDBS
4:	**Decrypt** encrypted data and **Remove** duplication
	Send result back to the user
5:	**If** all columns mentioned in the query are sensitive
6:	**Reconstruct** the query by substituting data items/ values by the bits' positions that mapped to the PDs that contain data items.
7:	**Send** the query to CDBS
8:	**If** the SCs in the aggregation query are not ranges
9:	**Decrypt** the result
10:	**Send** result back to the user
11:	**If** the SCs in the aggregation query are ranges
12:	**Decrypt** the result
13:	**Execute** aggregation operator again over the result
14:	**Send** result back to the user

Algorithm 4: Sort operator

1:	**Do** steps 1 to 14 from aggregation algorithm

"Note that we need to substitute the term" aggregation" by "sort"

Duplicate Elimination. In our model, to execute the duplicate elimination operator, we make the CDBS execute a selection query over encrypted data without duplication elimination *keyword* by just substituting the columns and values of the condition with the positions of the corresponding bits in the reference column. Then the QM selects *distinct* values before sending the results back to the user. For example, the query: select *distinct* Name from students where department = "Computer science" is translated to: *select* the name from $E_{AES-SIV}$("Student", SK) where reference &32>0. The CDBS returns all encrypted names where the bit position 32 is set to 1 in the reference column. Then the QM implements the DISTINCT or DISTINCTROW keyword over the decrypted records to eliminate the duplication. Algorithm 5 below shows the processes.

Algorithm 5: Duplicate -Elimination operator

1:	**Do** steps 1 to 9 from select algorithm
2:	**Decrypt** encrypted data
3:	**Execute** Duplicate -Elimination operator again over the result
4:	**Send** result back to the user

Project. We can implement the project at the cloud database server (CDBS) by using the select operator. We cannot eliminate the duplication in the cloud; however, we can delay this step until the encrypted tuples arrive at the QM, which will be able to eliminate duplicates after decrypting the cipher texts. Note that we do not retrieve all the encrypted tuples' column values, as each column's value is encrypted separately. In this case, we illuminate unnecessary decryption processes. Algorithm 6 illustrates the processes.

Algorithm 6: Project operator

1:      Input < Tables names, List of all columns, List of all data items di(s) >
2:      **If** none of columns mentioned in the project query are sensitive
3:          **Forward** the query to CDBS
4:          **Send** result back to the user
5:      **If** all columns mentioned in the project query are sensitive

6:          **Forward** the query to CDBS
7:          **Decrypt** the result
8:          **If** the term "DISTINCT" is present in the query

9:              **Implement** *distinct* over decrypted data
10:          **Send** result back to the user

Union. Before explaining how the proposed model performs the union operation over encrypted data, we discuss the two fundamental conditions of the union operation. First, all tables involved in the union operation must have the same number of columns. Second, the domain of the ith column in Table A must be the same as the ith column in Table B. In the proposed model, the QM translates the union query, using the condition translation methods proposed in the previous section, to the CDBS. Then the CDBS implements the union operator, and it returns all tuples of both relations. Note that we cannot eliminate duplication in the cloud, because the PDs could have at least one PD as a range. For example, the first letter column for Name has four PDs {a-f, g-l, m-r, s-z}, and we cannot remove the duplication before the decryption process. Therefore, we defer the removal of duplicates until after the encrypted tuples are decrypted by the QM. We assume that all tables are encrypted with the same encryption key, because if each table were encrypted with a different key, that would result in incorrect decryption. In Algorithm 7, we show the steps.

Algorithm 7: Union operator

1:      Input < Tables names>
2:      **Forward** the query to CDBS
3:      **Decrypt** the result of union query
4:          **Implement** *distinct* over decrypted data

Intersection. The intersection operation has the same two conditions as in the union operation. However, instead of retrieving all encrypted tuples of both tables (Table A and Table B), we retrieve only the tuples that are common to the tables. We must simulate the intersection operation, because it is impossible to apply it over encrypted tuples. To do that, in the CDBS, we use the inner join between the two tables, where the join condition is based on PDs that are not ranges, as range-based PDs return more candidate tuples. Then the CDBS executes a query to choose the tuples from Table A that exist in the join result. After that, the CDBS returns the joining result to the QM, which eliminates duplicates after the decryption process. For example, suppose that Table A and Table B have attributes (Name, Visa type, Rank). Then we perform the inner join operation where the join condition is "visa type = visa type AND Rank = Rank). Note that, in the condition, we substitute the columns' names with the positions of the corresponding bits to enable the CDBS to execute the operation. This filters out too many uncommon tuples in the cloud, which results in fewer decryption operations by the QM. Algorithm 8 below illustrates the processes.

Algorithm 8: Intersection operator

1:	Input < Tables names>
2:	**Find** all common sensitive columns that are not ranges between the tables
3:	**For** each table T_i
4:	**Find** bits' positions of PDs
5:	**Initiates** an inner join query where the joining condition is based on the equivalence of the bits obtained from step 4 for each table.
6:	**Send** the query to CDBS
7:	**Decrypt** the result of join.
8:	**Implement** *distinct* over decrypted data to **Remove** duplication
9:	**Send** result back to the user

---

4   Implementation and Evaluation

In this section, we describe how we implemented the proposed model and how we evaluated it. To implement the functions of the QM, we used Java to simulate each function in a class. The user submits a plain query to the QM, and the QM parses it, and rewrites it using predefined DSs. There is no need to modify the internals of the database, because the rewriting methods translate the users' queries in ways that can be executed by the CDBS. We used the MySQL server on the user's machine, and we used Java Database Connectivity (JDBC) as a connector from Java to MySQL. As a cloud, we created a MySql account at the university's server to serve as the cloud database server (CDBS).

To evaluate the efficiency of the proposed model, we conducted different experiments in which we measure the time from a plain query is submitted until the result is returned to the user. In some experiments, we submit a query and find the percent of retrieved encrypted records. To accurately measure the efficiency, we compared the proposed model with a traditional database system in which the data were in plaintexts.

In each experiment we performed, we ran queries on a table that held a certain number of records (10K and 20K,) where each table has six attributes (two of them are non-sensitive, two are sensitive but not ranges, and two are sensitive but ranges). That helped us to evaluate our model and determine how the number of records affected the delay time. We tried different queries, with each query coming from the following set of queries:

1) Join.
2) Aggregation (count, max, and min).
3) Select where query conditions contain (one, two, and 3 clauses).

Table 3 illustrates how our model dramatically drops the average of retrieved encrypted candidate records for a query. That means we successfully enable the cloud provider to process queries over encrypted data without decrypting them. We can notice that our model is more efficient when the query condition involves more clauses and the operation between the clauses is the AND. If the OR operation is present in the query condition, our model returns more candidate encrypted tuples because of the nature of the OR operation. Moreover, if the condition contains sensitive columns that are ranges, our model will experience more candidate encrypted tuples to decrypt at the QM. That will add more delay because of the decryption processes and filtering out unrelated tuples from the result.

Table 3. Average number of retrieved encrypted candidate tuples for different select query operations and clauses. N.R denotes the number of records in a table.

N.R	Average number of retrieved encrypted candidate tuples from cloud				
	1 clause	2 clauses (AND)	3 clauses (AND)	2 clauses (OR)	3 clauses (OR)
10K	2035	303	44	3408	6227
20K	4758	583	96	7281	12106

In Fig. 3, we compare the delay of our model and the delay of traditional database system TDBS (where data are not encrypted). We ran select queries where condition contains three clauses but with different operations, AND and OR. We can see that the delays when the AND operation is present in the condition is significantly small when compared with the delay when the OR operation is present in the condition.

Figure 4 shows the percent of encrypted records reprocessed at the QM after the decryption in union and intersection operations. In the intersection, we found that our model filters out approximately 83% of uncommon encrypted tuples at the cloud, and only about 17% of the entire result was common. This is because we can't eliminate the duplication at the cloud when we have range attributes, e.g. salary. Similarly, in *join* and *union*, less than 30% of the results were filtered out at the QM. According to this,

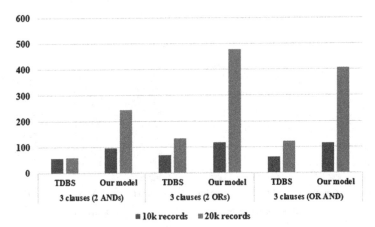

Fig. 3. Delays in our model and how they are affected by the number of clauses and operations in a query condition.

we can say that our model efficiently reduces the delay that results from unnecessary decryption processes.

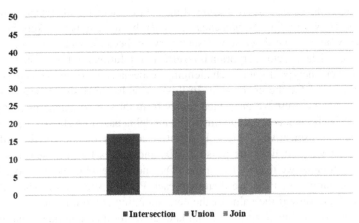

Fig. 4. The % of tuples reprocessed at the QM after decrypting the intersection, union, and join results.

In Fig. 5, we can see that the execution time is neglectable when the aggregation query is based on sensitive columns that are not ranges. In such case, the QM doesn't perform decryption; however, the QM will execute the aggregation query over decrypted data if the query is based on a range column, that is why we see the execution time is higher than the first case (non-range columns).

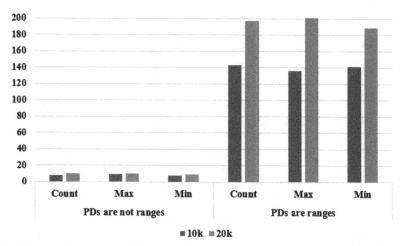

Fig. 5. The execution time in *ms* for aggregation operators (count, max, and min) when the query condition has sensitive columns that are not ranges vs. sensitive columns that are ranges.

5 Conclusion

Cloud computing is an attractive computing environment for all types of users and companies. However, privacy breaches, not only by malicious attackers but also by curious providers, is the downside of such service, because users lose access control over outsourced data. Data encryption is an effective solution for this problem. However, searching over encrypted data is challenging, especially if a randomized encryption algorithm is used for the encryption. In this research, we design a secure model to process queries and retrieve encrypted tuples from encrypted databases that preserve privacy and is efficient at the same time. The model is based on classifying columns as sensitive and non-sensitive, where only sensitive columns are encrypted. Furthermore, the table's owner predefines the possible PDs and ranges for each sensitive column. Then for each table, we make a DS of the PDs, and create a bit vector whose length is equal to the number of PDs. We then map each PD to a specific bit where this bit is set to one if and only if the value of the corresponding column is equal or belongs to this PD. We use the bits to retrieve candidate tuples for a certain query that minimize the range of the retrieved encrypted tuples. The encrypted table in the cloud will have an additional column (the reference column) to store bit vectors. To make the model practical, we facilitate it to support most relational algebra operators. We performed different experiments to test the efficiency of the model and found that it reduces the range of retrieved encrypted tuples to about 30% of the whole encrypted tuples in a table.

References

1. Almakdi, S., Panda, B.: Secure and efficient query processing technique for encrypted databases in cloud. In: 2019 2nd International Conference on Data Intelligence and Security (ICDIS). IEEE (2019)

2. Alsirhani, A., Bodorik, P., Sampalli, S.: Improving database security in cloud computing by fragmentation of data. In: 2017 International Conference on Computer and Applications (ICCA). IEEE (2017)
3. Cui, S., Asghar, M.R., Galbraith, S.D., Russello, G.: P-McDb: privacy-preserving search using multi-cloud encrypted databases. In: 2017 IEEE 10th International Conference on Cloud Computing (CLOUD), pp. 334–341. IEEE, June 2017
4. Cash, D., et al.: Dynamic searchable encryption in very-large databases: data structures and implementation. In: NDSS 2014. The Internet Society (2014)
5. Cash, D., Grubbs, P., Perry, J., Ristenpart, T.: Leakage-abuse attacks against searchable encryption. In: Ray, I., Li, N., Kruegel, C. (eds.) SIGSAC 2015, pp. 668–679. ACM (2015)
6. Stefanov, E., Papamanthou, C., Shi, E.: Practical dynamic searchable encryption with small leakage. In: NDSS 2013, vol. 71, pp. 72–75 (2014)
7. Gentry, C.: Fully homomorphic encryption using ideal lattices. In: STOC, vol. 9, no. 2009, pp. 169–178, May 2009
8. Gentry, C., Halevi, S., Smart, Nigel P.: Fully homomorphic encryption with polylog overhead. In: Pointcheval, D., Johansson, T. (eds.) EUROCRYPT 2012. LNCS, vol. 7237, pp. 465–482. Springer, Heidelberg (2012). https://doi.org/10.1007/978-3-642-29011-4_28
9. Hacigümüş, H., Iyer, B., Li, C., Mehrotra, S.: Executing SQL over encrypted data in the database-service-provider model. In: Proceedings of the 2002 ACM SIGMOD International Conference on Management of Data, pp. 216–227. ACM (2002)
10. Hacigumus, V.H., Raghavendra Iyer, B., Mehrotra, S.: Query optimization in encrypted database systems. U.S. Patent No. 7,685,437, 23 Mar 2010
11. Hore, B., et al.: Secure multidimensional range queries over outsourced data. VLDB J. 21(3), 333–358 (2012)
12. Hore, B., Mehrotra, S., Tsudik, G.: A privacy-preserving index for range queries. In: Proceedings of the Thirtieth International Conference on Very Large Data Bases-Volume 30. VLDB Endowment (2004)
13. Li, K., Zhang, W., Yang, C., Yu, N.: Security analysis on one-to-many order preserving encryption-based cloud data search. IEEE Trans. Inf. Forensics Secur. 10(9), 1918–1926 (2015)
14. Kamara, S., Moataz, T.: SQL on structurally-encrypted databases. In: Peyrin, T., Galbraith, S. (eds.) ASIACRYPT 2018. LNCS, vol. 11272, pp. 149–180. Springer, Cham (2018). https://doi.org/10.1007/978-3-030-03326-2_6
15. Li, J., Liu, Z., Chen, X., Xhafa, F., Tan, X., Wong, D.S.: L-EncDB: a lightweight framework for privacy-preserving data queries in cloud computing. Knowl.-Based Syst. 79, 18–26 (2015)
16. Liu, D., Wang, S.: Nonlinear order preserving index for encrypted database query in service cloud environments. Concurrency Comput. Pract. Exp. 25(13), 1967–1984 (2013)
17. Liu, G., Yang, G., Wang, H., Xiang, Y., Dai, H.: A novel secure scheme for supporting complex SQL queries over encrypted databases in cloud computing. Secur. Commun. Netw. 2018, 15 (2018)
18. Liu, X., Choo, K.K.R., Deng, R.H., Lu, R., Weng, J.: Efficient and privacy-preserving outsourced calculation of rational numbers. IEEE Trans. Dependable Secure Comput. 15(1), 27–39 (2018)
19. Liu, Z., Chen, X., Yang, J., Jia, C., You, I.: New order preserving encryption model for outsourced databases in cloud environments. J. Netw. Comput. Appl. 59, 198–207 (2016)
20. Asghar, M.R., Russello, G., Crispo, B., Ion, M.: Supporting complex queries and access policies for multi-user encrypted databases. In: Juels, A., Parno, B. (eds.) CCSW 2013, pp. 77–88. ACM (2013)
21. Omran, O.M.: Data partitioning methods to process queries on encrypted databases on the cloud. Theses and Dissertations. 1580 (2016)

22. Poddar, R., Boelter, T., Popa, R.A.: Arx: A strongly encrypted database system. IACR Cryptology ePrint Archive **2016**, 591 (2016)
23. Popa, R.A., et al.: CryptDB: processing queries on an encrypted database. Commun. ACM **55**(9), 103–111 (2012)
24. Agrawal, R., Kiernan, J., Srikant, R., Xu, Y.R.: Order preserving encryption for numeric data. In: Proceedings of the ACM SIGMOD International Conference on Management of Data (SIGMOD 2004), Paris, France, June 2004, pp. 563–574. ACM (2004)
25. Raybourn, T., Lee, J.K., Kresman, R.: On privacy preserving encrypted data stores. In: Park, James J.(Jong Hyuk), Ng, J.K.-Y., Jeong, H.Y., Waluyo, B. (eds.) Multimedia and Ubiquitous Engineering. LNEE, vol. 240, pp. 219–226. Springer, Dordrecht (2013). https://doi.org/10.1007/978-94-007-6738-6_28
26. Raybourn, T.: Bucketization techniques for encrypted databases: quantifying the impact of query distributions. Dissertation, Bowling Green State University (2013)
27. Shastri, S., Kresman, R., Lee, J.K.: An improved algorithm for querying encrypted data in the cloud. 2015 Fifth International Conference on Communication Systems and Network Technologies (CSNT). IEEE (2015)
28. Tu, S., et al.: Processing analytical queries over encrypted data. In: Proceedings of the VLDB Endowment. vol. 6. no. 5 (2013)
29. Wang, J., et al.: Bucket-based authentication for outsourced databases. Concurrency Comput. Pract. Exp. **22**(9), 1160–1180 (2010)
30. Wang, W., Hu, Y., Chen, L., Huang, X., Sunar, B.: Exploring the feasibility of fully homomorphic encryption. IEEE Trans. Comput. **64**(3), 698–706 (2015)
31. Wong, W.K., et al.: Secure query processing with data interoperability in a cloud database environment. In: Proceedings of the 2014 ACM SIGMOD international conference on Management of data. ACM (2014)
32. Zhang, Y., Katz, J., Papamanthou, C.: All your queries are belong to us: the power of file-injection attacks on searchable encryption. In: USENIX Security 2016, pp. 707–720. USENIX Association (2016)
33. Harkins, D.: Synthetic initialization vector (siv) authenticated encryption using the advanced encryption standard (aes) (2008)

Review of Research on Network Flow Watermarking Techniques

Hui Chen[1,2], Qianmu Li[1,2(✉)], Shunmei Meng[1,2], Haiyuan Shen[1,2], Kunjin Liu[1,2], and Huaqiu Long[3]

[1] School of Computer Science and Engineering, Nanjing University of Science and Technology, Nanjing 210094, China
qianmu@njust.edu.cn
[2] Jiangsu Zhongtian Technology Co., Ltd., Nantong 226463, China
[3] Intelligent Manufacturing Department, Wuyi University, Jiangmen 529020, China

Abstract. In cloud environment, a framework for cross-domain collaborative tracking could find intruders hidden behind autonomous domains by linking these autonomous domains effectively. The autonomous domain in framework could select the appropriate intrusion tracking technology to implement intra-domain tracking according to its own operating rules and communication characteristics. As an active traffic analysis technology, network flow watermarking technology could accurately locate the real positions of intruders hidden behind intermediate hosts (stepping stones) and anonymous communication systems. Furthermore, it has many advantages such as high precise rate, low false alarm rate, short observation time and so on. For these advantages and its high efficiency of intra-domain tracking, it has become the hot spot in academe research in recent years. Therefore, this paper did the following work: (1) research on network flow watermarking technology; (2) conclude the implementation framework of network flow watermarking technology; (3) analyze the principles and implementation processes of several mainstream network flow watermarking schemes; (4) analyze threats to network flow watermarking.

Keywords: Network flow watermarking technology · Intra-domain tracking · Threats to network flow watermarking

1 Mainstream Network Flow Watermarking Techniques

Network flow [1] is a sequence of unidirectional data packets or frames transmitted between any different nodes in the network for a period of time. It is also known as communication flow or packet flow. A unidirectional network flow could be uniquely represented by a tuple made up of the following eight elements: source IP address, destination IP address, source port number, service type, destination port number, protocol number, input interface and output interface. The network flow association determines the communication relationship by detecting the correlation between network flow of sender and receiver, and then implements intrusion tracing.

© ICST Institute for Computer Sciences, Social Informatics and Telecommunications Engineering 2020
Published by Springer Nature Switzerland AG 2020. All Rights Reserved
X. Zhang et al. (Eds.): CloudComp 2019/SmartGift 2019, LNICST 322, pp. 519–528, 2020.
https://doi.org/10.1007/978-3-030-48513-9_41

The closest watermarking embedder to the attacker is responsible for the generation of original watermark signal, watermark coding and watermark modulation. Its concrete process is: First, the watermarking embedder uses random number generator SNG to generate an original watermark signal with a specified length, and encodes it. Then embedder modulates the passing network flow according to a specified strategy of watermarking implementation. After that the original watermarking signal generated is carried by the network flow. Finally, the identifier of network flow and the original watermark signal are stored in a tracking database. In general, there are two deployment schemes of the watermark embedder. One is embedding a specific watermark into the network flow of response message by using NAT or router near the target server, and another is applying a watermark signal to intra-domain network flow in boundaries of autonomous domains.

The watermarking detector is responsible for demodulation, decoding and watermarking similarity comparison of the received network stream. The work flow of detector is mainly as follows: When the network flow carrying watermark signal is transmitted to the watermark detector located near a victim host by network, intermediate hosts (stepping stones) or anonymous communication systems, the watermarking detector first records the characteristics of the received network flow. And then it demodulates network flow to obtain coded signals of watermark according to the watermark parameters shared with the watermark embedder. After getting the final recovered watermark signals by decoding coded signals, the detector could use comparison functions to obtain the similarity between the final recovered watermark signals and the original watermark, such as cosine similarity or Hamming distance. Finally, the similarity is compared with the preestablished thresholds. If the similarity is greater than the given threshold, it is considered that there is an association between sender and recipient of network flow. In other words, the communication relationship between sender and recipient of the network flow could be confirmed.

There is a set of dynamically changing hidden watermark parameters shared between the watermarking embedder and the watermarking detector when the network flow watermarking scheme is implemented. The watermark detector needs to use the same watermark parameters as the embedder to complete the extraction of watermark signal. Watermark signal won't be extracted if parameters are different, which prevents the watermark information from being acquired and attacked by attackers. It means that the robustness and privacy of watermark information are enhanced.

The generation of original watermark signal, selection of watermark carrier and methods of watermark embedding will all affect the effect of tracking when network flow watermarking techniques are used. This section introduced the principles and implementation steps of several existing mainstream network watermarking techniques.

1.1 Network Flow Watermarking Technique Based on Flow Rate

The core idea of network flow watermarking technique based on flow rate is to embed the watermark signal by adjusting the flow rate in different time periods after selecting different time periods in the target network flow duration. The DSSS scheme proposed by Yu et al. [2] combines direct sequence spread spectrum technology with watermark based on flow rate. It not only improves the capacity of the watermark, but also enhances the ability of tracking multiple attack traffic in parallel. Its implementation framework is shown in Fig. 1:

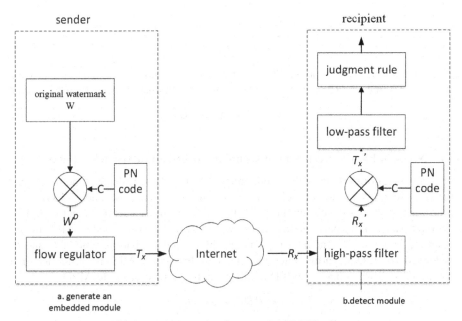

Fig. 1. Implementation framework of DSSS scheme

First, a binary original watermark signal of a specified length $W = \{w_1, w_2, \ldots, w_n\}$, $|W| = n$ is generated, then a watermark information bit W^D could be gotten after spreading W by DSSS. W^D is expressed by formula 1. And spreading W need set PN Code $C = \{c_1, c_2, \ldots, c_m\}$, $|C| = m$ in advance. w_i^D is the corresponding watermark signal of w_i after spreading original watermark W. w_i^D is expressed by formula 2.

$$W^D = W \times C = \begin{pmatrix} w_1 \\ \vdots \\ w_n \end{pmatrix} \times \begin{pmatrix} c_1 \cdots c_m \end{pmatrix} = \begin{pmatrix} w_1^D \\ \vdots \\ w_n^D \end{pmatrix} \tag{1}$$

$$w_i^D = \begin{pmatrix} w_i c_1 \cdots w_i c_m \end{pmatrix} \tag{2}$$

After W^D is obtained, each watermark signal of W^D is embedded in the original network flow according to formula 3. In formula 3, S represents the original flow rate of the network flow, T_x represents the flow rate after the watermark signal is modulated, $w_i c_j$ represents the j-th code element of the i-th spread spectrum watermark signal in W^D. And I_{PN} is the duration of modulating each code element.

$$T_x = w_i c_j A + S \tag{3}$$

Let rate of receiving network flow be R_x, which is shown in formula 4. In this formula, z is noise. The watermarking detector first removes DC component S in R_x through high-pass filter, then obtains R'_x which is shown in formula 5.

$$R_x = w_i c_j A + S + z \tag{4}$$

$$R'_x \approx w_i c_j A + z \tag{5}$$

After that, the receiver dispreads R'_x by formula 6 and obtains T'_x. Finally, the original watermark signal could be recovered after noise zC is eliminated through low-pass filter.

$$T'_x = w_i c_j AC + zC \tag{6}$$

1.2 Network Flow Watermarking Technique Based on Inter-packet Delay

For a unidirectional network flow containing n data packets, t_i denotes the time when the i-th packet P_i in the network flow arrives at the current host, and t'_i denotes the time when P_i leaves the current host. For the i-th and j-th packets in the network flow, the inter-packet delay between the arrival time of P_i and P_j is defined as AIPD (arrive inter-packet delay), and the inter-packet delay between the departure time of P_i and P_j is defined as DIPD (departure inter-packet delay). In general, AIPD is used as a carrier for modulating watermarks. So IPD in this paper refers specifically to AIPD.

$$AIPD_{i,j} = t_i - t_j \tag{7}$$

$$DIPD_{i,j} = t'_i - t'_j \tag{8}$$

The watermarking scheme based on inter-packet delay selects the interval delay of several pairs of data packets in the network flow as the watermark carrier, and embeds a watermark signal by adjusting the size of one or more sets of IPD means. Wang et al. [3] proposed an improved IPD scheme when tracking anonymous VOIP telephony traffic. The schematic diagram of its principle is shown in Fig. 2:

Firstly, $A = \{P_1, \ldots, P_{2r}\}$ are denoted by 2r packets selected from the network flow, and $B = \{P_{1+d}, \ldots, P_{2r+d}\}$ are denoted by 2r packets selected in increments of d. For A and B, P_i is a packet, and $|A| = |B| = 2r$. The packets in A and B are mapped one by one to obtain 2r packet pairs $\langle P_1, P_{1+d} \rangle, \ldots, \langle P_{2r}, P_{2r+d} \rangle$, in which r represents redundancy.

The IPDs between each pair of packets in the 2r packet pairs are calculated, and then they are divided into 2 groups, which are recorded as IPD^1 and $IPD^2 (|IPD^1| = |IPD^2| = r)$. $\overline{Y_{r,d}}$ is the mean difference for IPD^1 and IPD^2. It could be calculated by formula 9, 10.

$$Y_{r,d} = \frac{(ipd_k^1 - ipd_k^2)}{2}, k = 1, 2, \ldots, r \tag{9}$$

$$\overline{Y_{r,d}} = \frac{1}{r} \sum_{k=1}^{r} Y_{r,d} \tag{10}$$

The watermark signal is embedded according to the mean difference $\overline{Y_{r,d}}$. And it is denoted as $w, w \in \{-1, 1\}$. The embedding principle is as follows:

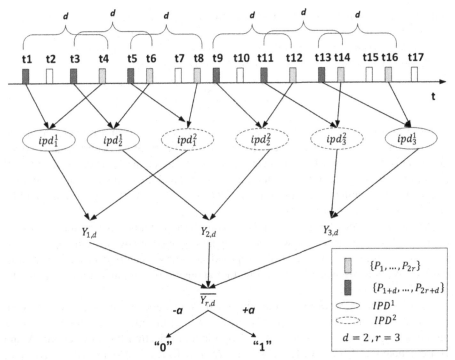

Fig. 2. Example of IPD allocation in network flow watermarking technique based on inter-packet delay

- If $\overline{Y_{r,d}} < 0$, $w = -1$, IPD^1 and IPD^2 don't need to be adjusted.
- If $\overline{Y_{r,d}} < 0$, $w = 1$, the IPD of IPD^1 will be increased and the IPD of IPD^2 will be decreased to ensure $\overline{Y_{r,d}} > 0$. The corresponding operation is to delay packets from group B in IPD^1 and packets from group A in IPD^2.
- If $\overline{Y_{r,d}} \geq 0$, $w = -1$, the IPD of IPD^2 will be increased and the IPD of IPD^1 will be decreased to ensure $\overline{Y_{r,d}} < 0$. The corresponding operation is to delay packets from group A in IPD^1 and packets from group B in IPD^2.
- If $\overline{Y_{r,d}} \geq 0$, $w = 1$, IPD^1 and IPD^2 don't need to be adjusted.

When the watermark detector receives the network flow, IPD^1 and IPD^2 could be obtained by using the same parameters and random strategies as the watermark embedder. And then $\overline{Y_{r,d}}$ is calculated by formula 9, 10. Finally, the watermark signal W' could be recovered according to formula 11.

$$W' = \begin{cases} -1, \overline{Y_{r,d}} < 0 \\ 1, \overline{Y_{r,d}} \geq 0 \end{cases} \qquad (11)$$

1.3 Interval Centroid Based Network Flow Watermarking Technique

Network flow is a sequence of unidirectional data packets or frames transmitted between any different nodes in the network for a period of time. Its duration is divided into n equal time periods in units of T, which are time slots: $I_0, I_1, \ldots, I_{n-1}$. There are m data packet packets $P_1, P_2, \ldots P_m$ in I_i, and $t_i (i = 1, 2, \ldots, m)$ indicates the timestamp of each packet arrival. If t_0 denotes the start time of I_i, $\Delta t_i = (t_i - t_0) mod T$ indicates the offset time of P_i relative to t_0. The centroid of I_i is defined as:

$$C(I_i) = \frac{1}{m} \sum_{i=1}^{m} \Delta t_i \tag{12}$$

Wang et al. [3] proved that if X is used as a divisor to perform a modulo operation on a random variable Y that is much larger than X, the result will approximately obey uniform distribution on [0, X]. It means that if there are enough packets in I_i, Δt_i will approximately obeys uniform distribution on [0, X], and the mathematical expectation of Δt_i will be stabilized at a invariant $T/2$ ($E(\Delta t_i) = T/2$). This invariant could be used as a stable watermark carrier.

Because the watermarking scheme based on centroid of time slot uses the centroid of the network slot as carrier, the watermark signal is embedded by changing the centroid value of the time slot. Wang et al. proposed an interval centroid based watermarking (ICBW) scheme when tracking low-rate anonymous communication systems. Its principle is as follows:

As Fig. 3 shows, according to the predefined parameters, the duration of the network flow is divided into 2n time slots ($I_0, I_1, \ldots, I_{2n-1}$) in units of T. These time slots are equally divided into group A and B by random selection function. Group A and B are denoted as $I_k^A (k = 0, 1, \ldots, n - 1)$, $I_k^B (k = 0, 1, \ldots, n - 1)$, $|A| = |B| = n$. And then an original watermark signal W whose length is l could be generated ($W = \{w_1, w_2, \ldots, w_l\}$, $|W| = l$).

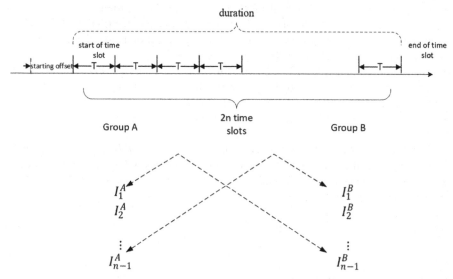

Fig. 3. Example of time slot selection and allocation in ICBW scheme

After that r time slots are randomly extracted from group A and group B to embed the watermark signal w_i. Each time slot is denoted as $I_{i,j}^A (j = 0, 1, \ldots, r - 1)$ or $I_{i,j}^B (j = 0, 1, \ldots, r - 1)$, and r ($r = n/l$) represents redundancy. $I_{i,j}^A$ represents the j-th time slot with w_i in group A, and $I_{i,j}^B$ represents the j-th time slot with w_i in group B. A_i and B_i (the combined slot centroids of $I_{i,j}^A$ and $I_{i,j}^B$) are calculated by formula 13, 14. $N_{i,j}^A$ indicates the number of packets in $I_{i,j}^A$ and $N_{i,j}^B$ indicates the number of packets in $I_{i,j}^B$. $Cent\left(I_{i,j}^A\right)$ is the centroid of $I_{i,j}^A$ and $Cent\left(I_{i,j}^B\right)$ is the centroid of $I_{i,j}^B$. N_i^A and N_i^B indicate the total number of packets with w_i in group A and B respectively.

$$A_i = \frac{\sum_{j=0}^{r-1}\left[N_{i,j}^A Cent\left(I_{i,j}^A\right)\right]}{\sum_{j=0}^{r-1} N_{i,j}^A} = \frac{\sum_{j=0}^{r-1}\left[N_{i,j}^A Cent\left(I_{i,j}^A\right)\right]}{N_i^A} \tag{13}$$

$$B_i = \frac{\sum_{j=0}^{r-1}\left[N_{i,j}^B Cent\left(I_{i,j}^B\right)\right]}{\sum_{j=0}^{r-1} N_{i,j}^B} = \frac{\sum_{j=0}^{r-1}\left[N_{i,j}^B Cent\left(I_{i,j}^B\right)\right]}{N_i^B} \tag{14}$$

$$Y_i = A_i - B_i \tag{15}$$

After Y_i is calculated by formula 15, w_i is embedded by adjusting Y_i. The specific embedding method is as follows:

- If $w_i = 1$, A_i and B_i will be adjusted to ensure $Y_i \approx \alpha/2$ (α is modulation amplitude). The adjustment scheme is to compress the time of packet in $I_{i,j}^A$ according to formula 16, which could increase its slot centroid. In formula 16, $\Delta t_{i,j,k}$ indicates the offset of the k-th packet of $I_{i,j}$ relative to the start time slot, and $\Delta t_{i,j,k}'$ is the calculated offset value. And the corresponding time slots in group B remain unchanged.

$$\Delta t_{i,j,k}' = \alpha + \frac{T - \alpha}{T} \Delta t_{i,j,k} \tag{16}$$

- If $w_i = -1$, A_i and B_i will be adjusted to ensure $Y_i \approx -\alpha/2$ (α is modulation amplitude). The adjustment scheme is to compress the time of packet in $I_{i,j}^B$ according to formula 16, which could increase its slot centroid. And the corresponding time slots in group A remain unchanged.

When the watermark detector receives the network flow carrying watermark signals, $2n$ time slots are obtained according to the same parameters and divided into group A and B by using the same random allocation strategy S. After that, A_i, B_i and Y_i could be calculated by formula 13–15.

2 Threats to Network Flow Watermarking Technologies

Network flow watermarking technology embeds watermark signals in network flow by actively modifying the traffic characteristics of the network flow. So these characteristics also become targets for attackers to detect and decipher watermarks. This section mainly introduces the following attack methods:

(1) Watermark Attack Based on Digital Filtering

In reference [4], an intrusion tracking technology which use flow rate to modulate watermark in anonymous networks was studied. Based on the research, a watermark detection method based on digital filtering was proposed. The method first intercepts the network flow with a watermark online, and add an identifier to it. The method then uses the Bayesian classifier for offline training to analyze frequency domain of its characteristic. Finally, the method can identify whether the network flow carries a watermark. Experiments show that the method can effectively detect network flow watermarking technique based on flow rate and effectively enhance the Wireless Mix Network's ability to resist this technique.

(2) Attack Based on Time Analysis

By analyzing the watermarking scheme based on inter-packet delay, Peng et al. [5] proposed an attack method based on the analysis of IPD between adjacent intermediate hosts(stepping stones). The attack method uses expectation maximization algorithm to estimate the proportion of quantization step to packet delay, and uses the Bayesian classification rule to identify the packet carrying an identifier. Peng et al. gave specific measures for watermark recovery or removal in four cases. These measures allow an attacker to remove a watermark from a chain of stepping stones or to copy a watermark to a chain without stepping stones in some cases. After evaluating the detection rate of watermarking, the false positive rate, and the minimum number of delayed packets, the attack method they proposing can detect the watermark signal by the sequential probability ratio. It can be used to real-timely detect on whether the network flow carries a watermark.

(3) Multi-flow Attack

Kiyavash et al. [6] studied several timing-based flow watermarking schemes (e.g. IBW, ICBW, DSSS). They found that modulating watermark will produce a long empty time segment without any packets arriving because these schemes divide the duration of the network flow into different time slots to embed the watermark signal. The long empty time segment can facilitate attackers to discover the existence of watermark. Attackers often align multiple watermarks carrying network flows and conduct a multi-flow attack (MFA). MFA can be used to detect the watermark signal carried in the network flow, and even recover the watermark parameter to remove the watermark in the network flow. In addition, it can also be used to detect network flows carrying different watermark signals.

(4) Attack Based on MSAC (Mean-Square Autocorrelation)

In the spread spectrum watermarking scheme like DSSS-W, the direct sequence spread spectrum of the watermark signal is often performed by using the pseudo noise code (PN code). The method can significantly reduce the interference of network jittering to the efficiency of watermarking tracking, and enhance the stability of watermark signals. It has been widely adopted. However, the network flow using the same PN code has strong autocorrelation. Jia et al. [7] defined the value of MSAC and determined whether there is a watermark in the network flow by calculating value of MSAC. The scheme that they proposed is called attack based on MSAC. Compared with MFA, attack based on MSAC only needs to compare multiple segments of a data stream to detect the existence of watermark signals, which is simpler and more efficient.

(5) DSSS Watermark Removal Attack Based on TCP Flow Control Mechanism
In the network flow watermarking based on inter-packet delay, embedding watermark signals will cause periodic alternating of high throughput and low throughput. And DSSS makes the periodic alternating more visible. Luo et al. [8] proposed LZPL attack. The attack first detects the abnormal sequence by locating the period of low throughput in the network flow, and removes the watermark signal with spread spectrum modulated in the network stream through the TCP flow control mechanism. It does not require the support of routers and relay nodes. So it is easy for implementation.

3   Conclusion

In cloud environment, a framework for cross-domain collaborative tracking could find intruders hidden behind autonomous domains by linking these autonomous domains effectively. The autonomous domain in framework could select the appropriate intrusion tracking technology to implement intra-domain tracking according to its own operating rules and communication characteristics. As an active traffic analysis technology, network flow watermarking technology could accurately locate the real positions of intruders hidden behind intermediate hosts (stepping stones) and anonymous communication systems. Furthermore, it has many advantages such as high precise rate, low false alarm rate, short observation time and so on.

Acknowledgments. This work was supported in part by the Fundamental Research Funds for the Central Universities (30918012204), Military Common Information System Equipment Pre-research Special Technology Project (315075701), 2019 Industrial Internet Innovation and Development Project from Ministry of Industry and Information Technology of China, 2018 Jiangsu Province Major Technical Research Project "Information Security Simulation System", Shanghai Aerospace Science and Technology Innovation Fund (SAST2018-103).

References

1. Callado, A.: A survey on internet traffic identification. IEEE Commun. Surv. Tutorials **11**(3), 37–52 (2009)
2. Yu, W., Fu, X.: DSSS-based flow marking technique for invisible traceback. In: 2007 IEEE Symposium on Security and Privacy, Berkeley, CA, USA, pp. 18–32. IEEE (2007)
3. Wang, X., Chen, S.: Tracking anonymous peer-to-peer VoIP calls on the internet. In: 12th ACM Conference on Computer and Communications Security, pp. 81–91. ACM, Newyork (2005)
4. Li, Q.: Safety risk monitoring of cyber-physical power systems based on ensemble learning algorithm. IEEE Access **7**, 24788–24805 (2019)

5. Peng, P., Ning, P.: On the secrecy of timing-based active watermarking trace-back techniques. In: 2006 IEEE Symposium on Security and Privacy, Berkeley/Oakland, CA, USA, pp. 315–349. IEEE (2006)
6. Kiyavash, N., Houmansadr, A.: Multi-flow attacks against network flow watermarking schemes. In: 17th USENIX Security Symposium, pp. 307–320. USENIX Association, Berkeley (2008)
7. Jia, W., Tso, F.P.: Blind detection of spread spectrum flow watermarks. In: 28th IEEE International Conference on Computer Communications, Rio de Janeiro, Brazil, pp. 2195–2203. IEEE (2009)
8. Luo, X., Zhang, J.: On the secrecy of spread-spectrum flow watermarks. In: Gritzalis, D., Preneel, B. (eds.) European Conference on Research in Computer Security 2010. LNCS, vol. 6345, pp. 232–248. Springer, Heidelberg (2010)

A Multi-objective Virtual Machine Scheduling Algorithm in Fault Tolerance Aware Cloud Environments

Heyang Xu[1]([⊠]), Pengyue Cheng[1], Yang Liu[1], Wei Wei[1], and Wenjie Zhang[2]

[1] Henan University of Technology, Zhengzhou 450001, Henan, China
xuheyang124@126.com, chengy_cathy@163.com,
liu_yang@haut.edu.cn, nsyncw@126.com
[2] Information Engineering University, Zhengzhou 450001, Henan, China
xy_zwj@sohu.com

Abstract. In modern cloud datacenters, virtual machine (VM) scheduling is a complex problem, especially taking consideration of the factor of service reliability. Failures may occur on physical servers while they are running cloud users' applications. To provide high-reliability service, cloud providers can adopt some fault tolerance techniques, which will influence performance criteria of VM scheduling, such as the actual execution time and users' expenditure. However, only few studies consider fault tolerance and its influence. In this paper, we investigate fault tolerance aware VM scheduling problem and formulate it as a bi-objective optimization model with quality of service (QoS) constraints. The proposed model tries to minimize users' total expenditure and, at the same time maximize the successful execution rate of their VM requests. The both objectives are important concerns for users to improve their satisfactions, which can offer them sufficient incentives to stay and play in the clouds and keep the cloud ecosystem sustainable. Based on a defined cost efficiency factor, a heuristic algorithm is then developed. Experimental results show that, indeed, fault tolerance significantly influences some performance criteria of VM scheduling and the developed algorithm can decrease users' expenditure, improve successful execution rate of their VM requests and thus perform better under fault tolerance aware cloud environments.

Keywords: VM scheduling · Cloud computing · Fault tolerance · QoS · Users' expenditure

1 Introduction

In modern cloud environments, providers can offer their customers the opportunities to configure service requests with specific resource requirements, such as hardware and software resource, and then encapsulate all these resource together into virtual machines (VMs) [1]. By renting VMs from cloud providers and uploading their computing requests to cloud data centers, customers can conveniently access and manage their applications

© ICST Institute for Computer Sciences, Social Informatics and Telecommunications Engineering 2020
Published by Springer Nature Switzerland AG 2020. All Rights Reserved
X. Zhang et al. (Eds.): CloudComp 2019/SmartGift 2019, LNICST 322, pp. 529–543, 2020.
https://doi.org/10.1007/978-3-030-48513-9_42

from anywhere at any time. They no longer need to purchase and maintain the sophisticated hardware and software resources for their peak loads and thus can decrease their total cost of ownership [2, 3]. Thus cloud computing has now become one of the most popular information communications technology paradigms and is widely accessed by nearly all internet users in direct or indirect manners [4].

How to allocate each of the cloud users' VM request to an appropriate cloud resource is the central issue involved in VM scheduling under cloud computing environments. This is a complicated and changeling problem, in which different performance criteria should be optimized and at the same time, users' QoS requirements (e.g. deadline and budget) should be satisfied [5]. For cloud users, they generally want their service request are successfully completed (i.e., their respective deadlines and budgets are fulfilled) with the possible minimal expenditure. Conversely, if their service requests often miss the deadlines, or the incurred expense is high, then users will undergo low level of satisfaction degree and may lose interest in the cloud system and could finally leave it, which will be adverse to the sustainable cloud ecosystem [3]. Therefore, this paper mainly focuses on two major performance criteria of VM scheduling, i.e., successful execution rate of users' VM requests (SERoV) [3, 6] and the total expenditure (TE) that users need to spend on completing users' requests [7–9].

Moreover, another important concern in real-world cloud datacenters is that failures may occur on physical servers (PSs) while executing cloud users' VM requests. This may also depress the level of users' satisfaction degree (LoUSD) [9]. So in order to increase the LoUSD, cloud providers generally adopt some fault tolerance techniques in their data centers to improve the offered service reliability, such as fault recovery. Fault recovery employs check-pointing and roll-back schemes and can enable a failed VM to recover and resume the executing of the VM from an error [10]. However, it will in turn influence the considered performance criteria in VM scheduling, such as SERoV and TE, which is worthy of further research.

Many researches recently have investigated VM scheduling under cloud environments, from which mostly focusing on optimizing different performance criteria of different parties, such cloud providers and users (details are given in Sect. 2). For example, Zhang et al. [8], from users' standpoint, explored the cost-efficient VM scheduling with the endeavor of minimizing the total expenditure for executing their VM requests. For adjusting to the changing resource demands, Meng and Sun [11] mainly considered the situation of workload fluctuations and developed a feedback-aware resource scheduling algorithm based on the resource granularity of containers. In [12], Yu et al. tried to optimize some criteria from cloud providers' aspect and proposed a probability-based guarantee scheme, which can effectively decrease the total migration overhead by avoiding unnecessary VM migrations. In previous work [3], we formulated the VM scheduling problem as a multi-objective optimization model by considering the major concerns of both parties, namely minimizing users' total expenditure and at the same time, guaranteeing the profit fairness among all the cloud providers. Some useful approaches have been proposed to resolve VM scheduling in cloud computing. However, most of these studies are failed to consider the influences of resource failures and their recoveries, which leads to a dilemma that the proposed approaches can't applied to the real-world cloud data centers. Therefore, this paper further studies the VM scheduling problem by taking into account the influences of resources failures and their recoveries, which can be denoted by fault tolerance aware VM scheduling problem.

The rest of the paper is organized as follows. Section 2 reviews the related state-of-the-art studies on VM scheduling. Section 3 describes the fault tolerance aware VM scheduling problem in details. In Sect. 3, we formulate the studied problem as a multi-objective optimization model. The developed algorithm is given in Sect. 4. Section 5 presents the experimental configurations, results and analyses. Finally, Sect. 6 concludes this paper.

2 Related Work

Lots of efforts were focused on the research on VM scheduling in clouds and many partly feasible solutions were also proposed. For example, Wei et al. [13] aimed to improving the resource utilization of cloud data center's physical servers and developed a heterogeneity-based VM scheduling algorithm whose main idea is to guarantee that the workloads on different kinds of resources of a PS are balanced. In [14], Imai et al. adopted continuous air traffic optimization method to optimize VM scheduling and proposed a time-series prediction based VM scheduling algorithm. The proposed algorithm can effectively reduce the total running time of used VMs while achieving similar performance. In [15], Secinti and Ovatman studied energy optimization of cloud data centers by minimizing the number of VM migrations and service level agreement violations under fault tolerance aware cloud environments. Moreover, many other researches [16–18] also explored power consumption aware VM scheduling problem and tried to find the best solutions for cloud datacenters' energy optimization. These researches, from cloud providers' standpoint, explored VM scheduling problem by optimizing different performance criteria.

Some related works studied VM scheduling from cloud users' respective and made endeavors to optimize their major concerns. For example, Wang et al. [19] tried to decrease the response time of users' applications with high performance computing requirements and developed a synchronization aware VM scheduling algorithm by considering both intra-VMs' and inter-VMs' synchronization demands. In [20], Kohne et al. further studied service level agreement (SLA) aware VM scheduling problem by considering two service level objectives, i.e., resource usage and availability. Zeng et al. [21] studied workload-aware VM scheduling problem with the objectives of minimizing the network latency and maximizing the bandwidth utilization. Some other effective execution time aware solutions, such as [22, 23], are also proposed for scheduling VMs in cloud data centers. Nevertheless, in cloud environments, another important concern for users to execute their VM requests is the total expenditure, which is not well resolved in these studies.

For reducing users' execution cost, some researches explored cost-based approaches to address the problem [3, 8, 24–26]. In [24], Li et al. tried to cut down users' expenditures for renting the required computing resources under hybrid cloud environments and developed an online resource scheduling algorithm by adopting Lyapunov optimization framework. A particle swarm optimization (PSO)-based scheduling algorithm is developed in [25] with the aim of minimizing users' total cost for executing their submitted

VM requests. From the perspective of reducing the number of VMs rented from cloud providers, Ran et al. [26] developed a dynamic VM scheduling strategy to determining the number of rented VMs according to users' varied QoS requirements. In [27], Sotiriadis et al. discovered that resource usages of running VMs vary highly among their whole runtime by extensive experiments. Based on this discovery, they developed a performance aware VM scheduling algorithm.

It can be found that although related studies have explored many aspects of performance criteria of VM scheduling, one of the most important factors for both cloud providers and users, i.e. service reliability, is not well addressed. In order to improve service reliability, modern cloud data centers generally adopt fault recovery techniques, which in turn will influence the performance criteria of VM scheduling, i.e., increasing the actual runtimes of users' VM requests and inevitably raising users' expenditures. This influence is worthy of deep research. However, only few of existing studies explored this influence. For example, Sun et al. [28] investigated the tradeoff between performance and energy consumption when reliability factor is considered. Our recent work [29] explored the impact of resource failures and their recoveries and proposed a cost optimization model under fault tolerance aware cloud environments.

From the above review of the related work, it can be noted that existing studies have explored VM scheduling problem from different aspects by optimizing different objectives, however, only few works consider the influence of resource failures and their recoveries, in which the level of users' satisfaction degree, one of the most attractive concerns for cloud users, is not well addressed. On the basis of the existing works, this paper further takes users' satisfactions into consideration and explores fault tolerance aware VM scheduling problem by considering the influences of resource failures and recoveries.

3   Problem Description and Optimization Model

3.1   Problem Description

In cloud environments, users may need to execute their applications by submitting VM requests to cloud providers who own the necessary infrastructure resources in their data centers. Users' VM requests can be submitted at random instants with some specific resource demands (e.g. CPU cores, memory size) and certain QoS requirements [3, 7, 8]. Generally, cloud users always want their applications to be successfully completed as soon as possible and at the same time, at the lowest cost. Thus this paper considers two QoS constraints, i.e., budget and deadline which users are more concerned about. Each VM request may need to execute several tasks and all the tasks contained in the same VM request should be executed concurrently on the same physical server [8, 12, 16, 29]. Suppose that cloud users totally submit $n(n \geq 1)$ VM requests to a cloud data center, denoted by $\mathbf{VM} = \{VM_1, VM_2, ..., VM_n\}$. The i-th VM request $VM_i(1 \leq i \leq n)$ can be characterized by a tuple with six terms, $VM_i = (K_i, WL_i, mem_i, subt_i, B_i, D_i)$ [7, 8, 25]. In the tuple, the term $K_i(K_i \geq 1)$ is the number of tasks contained by VM request VM_i, each of which requires one CPU core to execute. It means that VM_i can be successfully allocated to a PS only if the PS can provide at least K_i CPU cores for it. $WL_i = \{wl_{ik}|1 \leq k \leq K_i\}$ represents the set of workloads of VM_i's K_i tasks, in which wl_{ik} is the workload length that VM_i's k-th task need to complete. The term mem_i denotes the required memory size of VM_i. The term $subt_i$ stands for VM_i's arrival time, which indicates when VM_i arrives at the cloud data center. B_i and D_i are VM_i's budget and deadline constraint respectively. The former indicates that a user's expenditure for executing VM_i must be less than B_i and the latter indicates that the cloud user desires its VM request VM_i to be completed no later than D_i.

In order to satisfy performance requirements of the worldwide users, cloud providers have established some cloud data centers around the world. A cloud data center contains some infrastructure resources, which may consist of thousands of heterogeneous physical servers (PSs). Without loss of generality, we use $\mathbf{PS} = \{PS_1, PS_2, ..., PS_m\}$ to represent the $m (m \geq 1)$ heterogeneous PSs in the cloud data center. The j-th ($1 \leq j \leq m$) physical server, PS_j, can also be characterized by a tuple with six terms, $PS_j = (Core_j, Mem_j, s_j, p_j, \lambda_j, \mu_j)$ [3, 8, 29]. In PS_j, the terms $Core_j$ and Mem_j represent PS_j's CPU and memory capacities, i.e., the number of available CPU cores and memory size respectively. The parameter s_j denotes the processing speed of each of PS_j's CPU cores. p_j represents the price of each of PS_j's CPU cores, which is the cost of renting a single CPU core for a time unit. Suppose that the failures on physical server PS_j follow a Poisson process with the failure rate, denoted by λ_j ($\lambda_j \geq 0$) and the failures on different PSs are independent of one another. That is to say, the interval time series of successive failures on PS_j are independent and obey a negative exponential distribution with the same parameters λ_j, i.e., $F(t) = 1 - e^{-\lambda_j t}$, $t \geq 0$. Once a failure happens on a PS, it will initiate a repair process. Accordingly, we assume that the repair times of failures on physical server PS_j are also independent and follow a negative exponential distribution with the same repair rates, denoted by $\mu_j (\mu_j \geq 0)$, i.e., $G(t) = 1 - e^{-\mu_j t}$, $t \geq 0$ [9, 10].

Thus, the fault tolerance aware VM scheduling problem can be formally described as follows: suppose that there is a cloud data center with m heterogeneous PSs $\mathbf{PS} = \{PS_1, PS_2, ..., PS_m\}$, and all cloud users submit totally n VM requests, $\mathbf{VM} = \{V_1, V_2, ..., V_n\}$, the studied problem is how to map each VM request to a suitable PS, so as to maximize the SERoV and at the same time, minimize users' TE under the cloud environment where fault tolerance techniques are adopted.

3.2 Optimization Model

Definition 1 Scheduling Matrix (SM). Denote by $X = (x_{ij})_{n \times m}$ the scheduling matrix, where the decision variable x_{ij} indicates that whether VM_i is assigned to PS_j. The reasonable range of x_{ij} is 0 or 1: If VM_i is assigned to PS_j, then $x_{ij} = 1$; otherwise, $x_{ij} = 0$.

Denote by τ_{ikj} the *ideal execution time* of the k-th task of VM request VM_i on physical server PS_j, so we have

$$\tau_{ikj} = \frac{wl_{ik}}{s_j}, \tag{1}$$

where wl_{ik}, in terms of millions of instructions (MI), is the workload length of the kth task of VM_i and s_j is the processing speed of PS_j's each CPU core, in terms of million instructions per second (MIPS).

However, in real-life cloud environment, failures may happen on PSs and fault recovery techniques are generally adopted. In this situation, the *actual execution time* of k-th task of VM_i on PS_j, denoted by AT_{ikj}, is different from its ideal execution time. Denote by $N_j(\tau_{ikj})$ the total number of failures that occur on PS_j during the time interval τ_{ikj} and the failure rate of PS_j is λ_j, then the probability of $N_j(\tau_{ikj}) = M$ ($M = 0, 1, 2, \ldots$) can be given by

$$\Pr\{N_j(\tau_{ikj}) = M\} = \frac{(\lambda_j \tau_{ikj})^M}{M!} e^{-\lambda_j \tau_{ikj}}, \quad M = 0, 1, 2, \ldots. \tag{2}$$

It can be seen that $N_j(\tau_{ikj})$ is a stochastic variable whose expectation can be given by

$$E[N_j(\tau_{ikj})] = \lambda_j \tau_{ikj}. \tag{3}$$

Denote by $RT_j^{(M)}$ the recovery time of the M-th ($M = 0, 1, 2, \ldots$) failure occurred on PS_j. By summing up all $N_j(\tau_{ikj})$ failures' recovery times, we can get the total recovery time of PS_j during $(0, \tau_{ikj}]$, denoted by $RT_j(\tau_{ikj})$.

$$RT_j(\tau_{ikj}) = \sum_{M=1}^{N_j(\tau_{ikj})} RT_j^{(M)}. \tag{4}$$

The actual execution time of k-th task of VM_i on PS_j, AT_{ikj}, is the sum of the ideal execution time and the total recovery time on PS_j during executing the task, as shown in Eq. (5).

$$AT_{ikj} = \tau_{ikj} + RT_j(\tau_{ikj}). \tag{5}$$

It can be seen that AT_{ikj} is a random variable whose expectation can be given by

$$E[AT_{ikj}] = \frac{(\mu_j + \lambda_j)\tau_{ikj}}{\mu_j}. \tag{6}$$

Generally, cloud users always hope that their VM requests can be successfully completed at lowest possible expenditure. If users need to spend much expenditures or their VM executions often violate QoS constraints, then they are very likely to lose interest in the data center. Therefore, this paper makes an endeavor to *maximize the successful execution rate of VM requests (SERoV)* and *minimize the total expenditure (TE)* for executing all cloud users' VM requests. Users' total expenditure equals to the sum of the execution costs for all the successfully completed VM requests, as shown in Eq. (7).

$$TE = \sum_{i=1}^{n} \sum_{j=1}^{m} x_{ij} \cdot \left[K_i \cdot \max_{1 \leq k \leq K_i} (AT_{ikj}) \cdot p_j \right], \tag{7}$$

in which x_{ij}, shown in Definition 1, is the decision variable of the studied problem. The term $\max_{1 \leq k \leq K_i} (AT_{ikj})$ is the actual completion time of VM_i on PS_j, which equals to the maximum actual completion time among VM_i's K_i tasks. It can be noted that TE is a random variable whose expectation can be given by

$$E[TE] = \sum_{i=1}^{n} \sum_{j=1}^{m} x_{ij} \cdot \left[K_i \cdot E[\max_{1 \leq k \leq K_i} (AT_{ikj})] \cdot p_j \right]. \tag{8}$$

Denote by θ the SERoV, which can be calculated by the number of successfully completed VM requests divided by n, i.e., the total number of VM requests submitted by all cloud users. Then we have

$$\theta = \frac{1}{n} \sum_{i=1}^{n} \varphi_i, \tag{9}$$

in which the variable φ_i, given by Eq. (10), indicates whether VM request VM_i is successfully assigned to a PS.

$$\varphi_i = \sum_{j=1}^{m} x_{ij}. \tag{10}$$

This paper explores the fault tolerance aware VM scheduling by focusing on optimizing two major performance criteria for cloud users, i.e., *maximizing the SERoV* and *minimizing TE*, under certain budget and deadline requirements. Thus the studied problem can be formulated as a multi-objective optimization model with some constraints.

Objectives:

$$\text{Min} \quad E[TC] = \sum_{i=1}^{n} \sum_{j=1}^{m} x_{ij} \cdot \left[K_i \cdot E[\max_{1 \leq k \leq K_i} (AT_{ikj})] \cdot p_j \right]; \tag{I}$$

$$\text{Max} \quad \theta = \frac{1}{n} \sum_{i=1}^{n} \varphi_i. \tag{II}$$

Subject to:

i). For each $i \in \{1, 2, \ldots, n\}$ and each $j \in \{1, 2, \ldots, m\}$, the value of decision variable x_{ij} is within the range of $\{0, 1\}$;

ii). For each $i \in \{1, 2, \ldots, n\}$, then $\sum_{j=1}^{m} x_{ij} \leq 1$;

iii). For each $j(1 \leq j \leq m)$, then $\sum_{i=1}^{n} x_{ij} K_i \leq Core_j$ and $\sum_{i=1}^{n} x_{ij} mem_i \leq Mem_j$;

iv). For each $i \in \{1, 2, \ldots, n\}$, if the value of decision variable x_{ij} is 1, then physical server PS_j must satisfy Eq. (11) and Eq. (12).

$$wt_i + E[\max_{1 \leq k \leq K_i} (AT_{ikj})] \leq D_i; \tag{11}$$

$$K_i \cdot E[\max_{1 \leq k \leq K_i} (AT_{ikj})] \cdot p_j \leq B_i. \tag{12}$$

The first optimization objective, (I), is to minimize the expectation of total expenditure for executing all cloud users' VM requests. The second one, (II), is to maximize the successful rate of their VM requests. By optimizing the two objectives, cloud providers can offer sufficient incentives for their users to stay and play in the data centers, which cloud help to keep the cloud ecosystem sustainable.

The constraint i) gives the decision variable x_{ij}'s feasible region. The second constraint, ii), guarantees that a VM request must be allocated to exactly one PS. The third constraint, iii), is PS_j's resource capacity restrictions, which means that the total CPU cores and memory size required by VM requests assigned to PS_j must not exceed its CPU and memory capacities respectively. The last one, constraint iv), ensures that if VM_i is allocated to PS_j, then the physical server should satisfy VM_i's deadline and budget requirements. The term wt_i, in Eq. (11), is the waiting time interval that VM request VM_i waits for being executed on PS_j. The term $E[\max_{1 \le k \le K_i}(AT_{ikj})]$ is the expectation of actual execution time of VM_i on PS_j. Equation (11) guarantees that VM request VM_i's waiting time sums up its actual execution time should not exceed the required deadline. Equation (12) guarantees that the expenditure for executing VM_i on PS_j must not exceed the required budget.

From the above descriptions, it can be seen that the proposed multi-objective optimization model belongs to the combinatorial optimization, which is NP-hard problem [30]. Heuristic-based approaches, which can offer an approximately optimal solution in an acceptable time frame proportional to the number of variables, have recently attracted much attention to deal with VM scheduling problem [3, 30]. Therefore, this paper develops a heuristic method, i.e., *greedy-based best fit decreasing scheduling (GBFDS) algorithm*, to solve the fault tolerance aware VM scheduling problem.

4   Proposed Algorithm

Before describing the details of GBFDS algorithm, we first define two concepts used in the developed algorithm.

Definition 2. Cost Efficiency (CE) factor: The cost efficiency of physical server PS_j is mainly influenced by four parameters, i.e., its CPU cores' price (p_j), processing speed (s_j), failure rate (λ_j) and recovery rate (μ_j). If failures frequently occur on PS_j, then VM requests assigned on the server will experience long executing time, which will inevidently increase users' expenditure. Similarly, if the price of PS_j's CPU core is high, it will also increase users' cost for executing their VM requests. On the contrary, the higher its processing speed is, the shorter time that the PS needs to complete a VM request. And similarly the higher its recovery rate is, the shorter time the PS recovers from a failure. Therefore, the CE factor of PS_j, denoted by $CE(PS_j)$, can be defined as the product of its processing speed, recovery rate and the inverse of its failure rate and CPU cores' price, as shown in Eq. (13). The higher a PS's CE factor is, the lower the cost for executing a VM request is.

$$CE(PS_j) = \frac{\mu_j s_j}{\lambda_j p_j}. \tag{13}$$

Definition 3. Candidate Server Set (CSS): For an arbitrary VM request $VM_i \in \mathbf{VM}$, if the available resources (CPU cores and memory size) of a physical server $PS_j \in \mathbf{PS}$ are no less than VM_i's resource requirements and, at the same time, can successfully complete VM_i's tasks before the specified deadline with the expenditure no more than its budget, then PS_j is a candidate server of VM_i. The candidate server set of VM_i, denoted by CSS_i, is composed of all its candidate servers.

If a VM request's CSS contains few candidate servers, it means that the VM request's QoS constraints are tight or its resource demands are very high and few PSs can satisfy its requirements. Granting high priorities to these VM requests can effectively increase their successful execution rate.

Based on above-mentioned definitions and analysis, the proposed algorithm preferentially schedules the VM request whose CSS has fewest candidate physical servers to improve SERoV. In order to decrease could users' total expenditure, GBFDS algorithm allocates the VM request, VM_i, whose CSS contains more than one candidate server to the server whose cost efficiency factor is the smallest among VM_i's candidate servers. The processes of GBFDS algorithm are shown as follows.

Algorithm 1: Greedy-based Best Fit Decreasing Scheduling (GBFDS) algorithm

---

Inputs: $\mathbf{VM} = \{VM_1, VM_2, \ldots, VM_n\}$ and $\mathbf{PS} = \{PS_1, PS_2, \ldots, PS_m\}$.

Outputs: the scheduling matric $\mathbf{X} = (x_{ij})_{n \times m}$.

1 Initialization: mark all VM requests' states as *unscheduled*

                set $\mathbf{X} = 0$ and all VM requests' CSSs as Φ;

2 sort physical servers in descending order by CE factor, such as $PS_1', PS_2', \ldots, PS_m'$;

3 **foreach** *unscheduled* VM request $VM_i \in \mathbf{V}$ **do**

4   **foreach** physical server PS_j' $(1 \leq j \leq m)$ **do**

5   **if** PS_j can satisfy VM_i's resource demands and QoS requirements **then**

6        $CSS_i = CSS_i \cup PS_j'$;

7   **if** $CSS_i = \Phi$ **then**

8   add VM request VM_i to unsuccessful scheduled set U;

9   change VM request VM_i's state to *failed scheduling*;

10   **else if** $|CSS_i| = 1$ **then**

11   assign VM request VM_i to the candidate server (PS_j' might as well) in CSS_i;

12   change available resource capacities (CPU cores and memory size) of PS_j';

13   set $x_{ij} = 1$;

14   change VM request VM_i's state to *scheduled*;

15 **while** there exists *unscheduled* VM request in $\mathbf{V}$ **do**

16   find the candidate server set with fewest candidate servers, CSS_i might as well;

17   assign VM_i to the physical server PS_j' whose subscript is the smallest in CSS_i;

18   change the available resource capacity of PS_j';

19   set $x_{ij} = 1$;

20   change VM request VM_i's state to *scheduled*;

21 **return** $\mathbf{X}$;

Initially, GBFDS algorithm sets all VM requests' states as *unscheduled*, all VM requests' CSSs as empty set and all the elements x_{ij} of $\mathbf{X} = (x_{ij})_{n \times m}$ as 0. After this, all the PSs are sorted in descending order by their values of CE factors. Might as well, the order of PSs after sorting is PS_1', PS_2', ..., PS_m'. Then, the following steps will be iteratively executed by GBFDS algorithm.

For each VM request VM_i $(1 \leq i \leq m)$ in the state of *unscheduled*, GBFDS algorithm firstly find out its candidate server set, CSS_i, by orderly checking PS_1', PS_2', ..., PS_m'. During this process, if one VM request VM_i's candidate server set CSS_i is empty, which means that no existing physical server can satisfy VM_i's resources or QoS requirements, then the VM request, VM_i, can't be successfully scheduled and its state will be changed to *failed*. Otherwise, if the VM request VM_i's candidate server set only contains one candidate server, PS_j', then GBFDS algorithm preferentially schedules VM_i and assigns it to PS_j' and then changes the relevant parameters. Secondly, for the other VM requests with more than one candidate server in their candidate server sets, the proposed algorithm preferentially schedules the VM request VM_i, which contains fewest candidate servers in its candidate server set CNS_i and then assigns VM_i to its candidate server PS_j' whose CE factor value is the smallest among all the PS in CNS_i. The scheduling process will be iteratively invoked until all VM requests are not in *unscheduled* state. Finally, GBFDS algorithm returns the values of the obtained scheduling matric, $\mathbf{X} = (x_{ij})_{n \times m}$.

5 Performance Evaluation

5.1 Simulation Configurations

In the experiments, we simulate a cloud data center, which totally contains one hundred physical servers. The number of CPU cores of each PS is an integer within the range of $\{2, 4, 8, 16\}$, which is randomly generated by a uniform distribution. The memory size of each PS is also randomly generated by a uniform distribution within the range of $\{4\ \text{GB}, 8\ \text{GB}, 16\ \text{GB}, 32\ \text{GB}\}$. For the parameters of processing speed and price of each physical server's CPU cores, we use the similar approach adopted in [3, 9, 10, 19, 29] to generate the values. The former parameter is in the range of 100–200, which is randomly generated by a uniform distribution with the average speed of 150, in terms of million instructions per second (MIPS). The CPU core's price of each PS is within the range of 0.35–1 and roughly linear with its processing speed, which is used to guarantee that a faster PS needs more renting expenditure than a slower one for executing the same VM request. The failure rates and the recovery rates of physical servers are uniformly distributed within the range of [0.01, 0.1] and [0.05, 0.15], respectively [9, 10, 28].

For the parameters of users' VM requests, all the experiments randomly set their arrival times within the range of (0, 100], which means that all VM requests arrive at the data center within a scheduling interval ($T = 100$ s). Their required number of tasks (i.e., CPU cores) and memory sizes are both integers, which randomly generate by uniform distributions within the range of [1, 7] and $\{1\ \text{GB}, 2\ \text{GB}, 3\ \text{GB}, 4\ \text{GB}\}$ respectively. Tasks' workload lengths are uniformly generated within the value set, $\{100000, 120000, 140000, 160000, ..., 500000\}$, in terms of million instructions (MI). The required deadline of each VM request is roughly linear with its average estimated runtime of the largest workload among all its tasks with a 10% variation and the budget requirement is set as its deadline multiplying by the number of task, as well as the average price with a 10% variation. For eliminating the influence of causal factors, all the experiments are repeatedly conducted 100 times and the presented results are the mean value of these repeated experiments.

5.2 Performance Metrics

In order to test and verify the feasibility of the proposed optimization model and algorithm, we compare the developed algorithm with two other related ones, i.e., FCFS [19] and MBFD [29], under four popular performance metrics. The first measured metric is the SERoV, which is one of the optimization objectives of the proposed model and can be calculated by Eq. (9) and Eq. (10). The second one is the *average expenditure* (AE), which can be calculated as the expectation of total expenditure (shown in Eq. (8)) divided by the number of successfully executed VM requests. The third metric is the *average execution time* (AET), which is the average value of all the successfully executed VM requests' actual completion times. The actual completion time of a successfully executed VM request is defined as the time span between its submitted time and completed time. The last measured metric is the *overall user satisfaction* (OUS). Generally, the cloud users want their submitted VM requests can be successfully completed as soon as possible and at the same time, at the lowest possible expenditure. Therefore, the satisfaction of the cloud user who submits VM require VM_i, denoted by us_i, is influenced by three factors, i.e., whether VM request VM_i is successfully executed or not (φ_i), the used time and expenditure for executing VM_i. Denote by $Etime_i$ and $Ecost_i$ the execution time and expenditure of VM request VM_i respectively, so we have

$$us_i = \varphi_i \cdot [\alpha \cdot \frac{d_i - Etime_i}{d_i} + \beta \cdot \frac{b_i - Ecost_i}{b}]. \tag{14}$$

In Eq. (14), α and β are cloud users' preference coefficients for time and cost with the values satisfying $\alpha + \beta = 1$. If a cloud user prefers its VM request to be completed as soon as possible, then we can set $\alpha > \beta$, and vice versa. In this paper, we trade time and expenditure as two factors with equal importance and thus set $\alpha = \beta = 0.5$

Summing up the values of all cloud users' satisfactions, we can get the overall user satisfaction, *OUS* (as shown in Eq. (15)).

$$OUS = \sum_{i=1}^{n} us_i. \tag{15}$$

5.3 Simulation Results

In this section, we conduct two experiments to fully evaluate the performance of the proposed model and developed algorithm.

Experiment 1. In this experiment, we first fixed all physical servers' recovery rate as 0.1 to observe the influence of failure rate under varied values from 0.01 to 0.1. The obtained results are shown in Table 1. It can be seen that, with the increasing of PSs' failure rate, the results of SERoV and OUS smoothly decrease and these of AE and

AET gradually increase, which means that all the measured metrics get worse. This is because, with the increasing of failure rates, the probability that failures happen on a physical server increases, which will evidently increase the execution time of users' VM requests, thus increasing users' expenditures. This will be more likely to violate users' deadline and budget constraints and thus decrease the SERoV.

Table 1. Results obtained by GBFD algorithm with different failure rates when physical servers' recovery rate is fixed as 0.1.

Failure rete	SERoV	AE	AET	OUS
0.01	100%	2.22	0.84	102.11
0.02	100%	2.42	0.91	93.37
0.03	100%	2.63	0.99	84.64
0.04	100%	2.83	1.06	75.90
0.05	100%	3.02	1.11	68.10
0.06	100%	3.24	1.19	59.15
0.07	100%	3.44	1.24	51.86
0.08	100%	3.66	1.33	42.18
0.09	97%	3.90	1.37	33.45
0.1	72%	3.70	1.56	17.08

Second, Table 2 shows the results of measured metrics obtained by GBFDS algorithm with varied recovery rates under the situation that all physical servers' failure rate is fixed as 0.01. It can be found that all the measured metrics get better with recovery rate varying from 0.05 to 0.14. The reason lies in that, with the increasing of physical servers' recovery rates, the recovery time that a failed PS needed to recover from a failure is decreased and thus the average execution cost decreases, which means that the PS will be more likely to successfully complete the served VM requests and thus increase successful execution rate and cloud users' satisfactions.

Thus, we can conclude that, as expected, adopting fault tolerance techniques in cloud data centers does have significant impact on the performance metrics of VM scheduling.

Experiment 2. In this experiment, we evaluate the performance of the developed GBFDS algorithm by comparing with other ones. The results of the four performance criteria obtained by different algorithm are presented in Table 3. From the results, we can the following trends: First, the developed GBFDS algorithm can obtain the highest successful execution rate. Compared with FCFS and MBFD, GBFDS algorithm can successfully execute more VM requests by 12.05% and 4.25%, respectively. This is because GBFDS algorithm preferentially schedules tight-QoS-constrained VM requests whose candidate server sets may have few candidate servers. Granting higher priority to schedule these VM requests can increase their probability of being successfully completed and thus improve SERoV. Second, the developed GBFDS algorithm can achieve

Table 2. Results obtained by GBFD algorithm with different recovery rates when physical servers' failure rate is fixed as 0.05.

Recovery rete	SERoV	AE	AET	OUS
0.05	71.5%	3.70	1.56	17.08
0.06	100%	3.73	1.34	39.42
0.07	100%	3.48	1.26	50.13
0.08	100%	3.29	1.20	57.69
0.09	100%	3.14	1.15	63.62
0.10	100%	3.02	1.11	68.10
0.11	100%	2.94	1.10	70.57
0.12	100%	2.86	1.07	74.44
0.13	100%	2.80	1.05	77.24
0.14	100%	2.74	1.03	79.64

the smallest average expenditure (AE) of all successfully executed VM requests. Specifically, compared with other methods, GBFDS algorithm can cut down the users' AE by about 2.79% and 0.71%, respectively. Third and most important, the developed GBFDS algorithm can obtain the highest degree of user satisfaction. Compared with the other methods, GBFDS algorithm can improve cloud users' satisfaction by about 20.1% and 10.4%, respectively. It can be concluded that, compared with some popular algorithms, the developed GBFDS algorithm can achieve higher successful execution rate, lower execution cost, and most important, higher degree of user satisfaction in most cases. Thus the proposed GBFDS algorithm can meet users' satisfaction better.

Table 3. Results obtained by compared algorithms under fault tolerance-aware environments.

Metrics	FCFS	MBFD	GBFDS
SERoV	82.3%	90.1%	**94.35%**
AE	2.87	2.81	**2.79**
AET	1.23	**1.19**	1.21
OUS	57.69	63.74	**69.26**

6   Conclusions

In this paper, we deal with the problem of fault tolerance aware VM scheduling. By considering the impact of fault tolerance techniques, two stochastic models of actual execution time and cost are deduced. Then the studied problem is formulated as a multi-objective optimization model with multiple QoS constraints. A greedy-based best fit decreasing algorithm is then developed. Finally, the experimental results demonstrate the feasibility of the proposed model and algorithm. As future work, we will consider the situation that not all failures are recoverable and VM requests may fail.

Acknowledgements. This work is partially supported by the National Natural and Science Foundation of China (No. 61472460, 61702162 and U1504607), Natural Science Project of the Education Department of Henan Province (No. 19A520021), Program for Innovative Research Team (in Science and Technology) in University of Henan Province (No. 17IRTSTHN011), Science and Technology Project of Science and Technology Department of Henan Province (No. 172102110013), Plan for Nature Science Fundamental Research of Henan University of Technology (No. 2018QNJH26), Plan For Scientific Innovation Talent of Henan University of Technology (No. 2018RCJH07) and the Research Foundation for Advanced Talents of Henan University of Technology (2017BS016).

References

1. Armbrust, A.M., Fox, A., Griffith, R., et al.: A view of cloud computing. Commun. ACM **53**(4), 50–58 (2010)
2. Liu, L., Qiu, Z.: A survey on virtual machine scheduling in cloud computing. In: Proceedings of 2nd International Conference on Computer and Communications, Chengdu, China, pp. 2717–2721. IEEE (2016)
3. Xu, H., Liu, Y., Wei, W., Zhang, W.: Incentive-aware virtual machine scheduling in cloud computing. J. Supercomput. **74**(7), 3016–3038 (2018)
4. Madni, S.H.H., Latiff, M.S.A., Coulibaly, Y.: Resource scheduling for infrastructure as a service (IaaS) in cloud computing: challenges and opportunities. J. Netw. Comput. Appl. **68**(1), 173–200 (2016)
5. Mann, Z.Á.: Allocation of virtual machines in cloud data centers—a survey of problem models and optimization algorithms. ACM Comput. Surv. **48**(1), 11 (2015)
6. Wang, Z., Hayat, M.M., Ghani, N., et al.: Optimizing cloud-service performance: efficient resource provisioning via optimal workload allocation. IEEE Trans. Parallel Distrib. Syst. **28**(6), 1689–1702 (2017)
7. Singh, S., Chana, I.: QRSF: QoS-aware resource scheduling framework in cloud computing. J. Supercomput. **71**(1), 241–292 (2015)
8. Zhang, R., Wu, K., Li, M., et al.: Online resource scheduling under concave pricing for cloud computing. IEEE Trans. Parallel Distrib. Syst. **27**(4), 1131–1145 (2016)
9. Xu, H., Yang, B., Qi, W., Ahene, E.: A multi-objective optimization approach to workflow scheduling in clouds considering fault recovery. KSII. Trans. Int. Inf. **10**(3), 976–995 (2016)
10. Sun, P., Wu, D., Qiu, X., Luo, L., Li, H.: Performance analysis of cloud service considering reliability. In: Proceedings of IEEE International Conference on Software Quality, Reliability and Security Companion (QRS-C), Vienna, Austria, pp. 339–343. IEEE (2016)
11. Meng, L., Sun, Y.: Context sensitive efficient automatic resource scheduling for cloud applications. In: Proceedings of the 11th International Conference on Cloud Computing, Seattle, USA, pp. 391–397 (2018)
12. Yu, L., Chen, L., et al.: Stochastic load balancing for virtual resource management in datacenters. IEEE Trans. Cloud Comput. (in press online). https://doi.org/10.1109/tcc.2016.2525984
13. Wei, L., Foh, C.H., He, B., et al.: Towards efficient resource allocation for heterogeneous workloads in IaaS clouds. IEEE Trans. Cloud Comput. **6**(1), 264–275 (2018)

14. Imai, S., Patterson, S., Varela, C. A.: Elastic virtual machine scheduling for continuous air traffic optimization. In: Proceedings of 16th International Symposium on Cluster, Cloud and Grid Computing, Cartagena, Colombia, pp. 183–186. IEEE (2016)

15. Secinti, C., Ovatman, T.: Fault tolerant VM consolidation for energy-efficient cloud environments. In: Luo, M., Zhang, L.-J. (eds.) CLOUD 2018. LNCS, vol. 10967, pp. 323–333. Springer, Cham (2018). https://doi.org/10.1007/978-3-319-94295-7_22

16. Xu, H., Yang, B.: Energy-aware resource management in cloud computing considering load balance. J. Inf. Sci. Eng. **33**(1), 1–16 (2017)

17. Mishra, S.K., Puthal, D., Sahoo, B., et al.: An adaptive task allocation technique for green cloud computing. J. Supercomputing **74**(1), 370–385 (2018)

18. Xu, H., Liu, Y., Wei, W., Xue, Y.: Migration cost and energy-aware virtual machine consolidation under cloud environments considering remaining runtime. Int. J. Parallel Prog. **47**(3), 481–501 (2019)

19. Wang, D., Dai, W., Zhang, C., Shi, X., Jin, H.: TPS: an efficient VM scheduling algorithm for HPC applications in cloud. In: Au, M.H.A., Castiglione, A., Choo, K.-K.R., Palmieri, F., Li, K.-C. (eds.) GPC 2017. LNCS, vol. 10232, pp. 152–164. Springer, Cham (2017). https://doi.org/10.1007/978-3-319-57186-7_13

20. Kohne, A., Pasternak, D., Nagel, L., et al.: Evaluation of SLA-based decision strategies for VM scheduling in cloud data centers. In: Proceedings of the 3rd Workshop on Cross Cloud Infrastructures and Platforms, no. 6. ACM, London (2016)

21. Zeng, L., Wang, Y., Fan, X., et al.: Raccoon: a novel network I/O allocation framework for workload-aware VM scheduling in virtual environments. IEEE Trans. Parallel Distrib. Syst. **28**(9), 2651–2662 (2017)

22. Guo, M., Guan, Q., Ke, W.: Optimal scheduling of VMs in queuing cloud computing systems with a heterogeneous workload. IEEE Access **6**, 15178–15191 (2018)

23. Yu, Q., Wan, H., Zhao, X., et al.: Online scheduling for dynamic VM migration in multicast time-sensitive networks. IEEE Trans. Industr. Inf. (online press). https://doi.org/10.1109/tii.2019.2925538

24. Li, S., Zhou, Y., Jiao, L., et al.: Towards operational cost minimization in hybrid clouds for dynamic resource provisioning with delay-aware optimization. IEEE Trans. Serv. Comput. **8**(3), 398–409 (2015)

25. Somasundaram, T.S., Govindarajan, K.: CLOUDRB: a framework for scheduling and managing high-performance computing (HPC) applications in science cloud. Future Gener. Comput. Syst. **34**, 47–65 (2014)

26. Ran, Y., Yang, J., et al.: Dynamic IaaS computing resource provisioning strategy with QoS constraint. IEEE Trans. Serv. Comput. **10**(2), 190–202 (2017)

27. Sotiriadis, S., Bessis, N., Buyya, R.: Self managed virtual machine scheduling in cloud systems. Inf. Sci. **433**, 381–400 (2018)

28. Sun, P., Dai, Y., Qiu, X.: Optimal scheduling and management on correlating reliability, performance, and energy consumption for multi-agent cloud systems. IEEE Trans. Reliab. **66**(2), 547–558 (2017)

29. Xu, H., Cheng, P., Liu, L., Wei, W.: Fault tolerance aware virtual machine scheduling in cloud computing. In: Proceedings of 5th International Symposium on System and Software Reliability, Chengdu, China. IEEE (2019)

30. Kurdi, H., Al-Anazi, A., et al.: A combinatorial optimization algorithm for multiple cloud service composition. Comput. Electr. Eng. **42**, 107–113 (2015)

PSVM: Quantitative Analysis Method of Intelligent System Risk in Independent Host Environment

Shanming Wei[1,2], Haiyuan Shen[1], Qianmu Li[2(✉)], Mahardhika Pratama[3],
Meng Shunmei[2], Huaqiu Long[4], and Yi Xia[5]

[1] Jiangsu Zhongtian Technology Co., Ltd., Nantong 226463, China
[2] School of Computer Science and Engineering, Nanjing University
of Science and Technology, Nanjing 210094, China
qianmu@njust.edu.cn
[3] Nanyang Technological University, Singapore 639798, Singapore
[4] Intelligent Manufacturing Department, Wuyi University, Jiangmen 529020, China
[5] PT. Sinoma Engineering Indonesia, Jakarta Utara 14440, Indonesia

Abstract. Quantitative risk analysis of security incidents is a typical non-linear classification problem under limited samples. Having advantages of strong generalization ability and fast learning speed, the Support Vector Machine (SVM) is able to solve classification problems in limited samples. To solve the problem of multi-classification, Decision Tree Support Vector Machine (DT-SVM) algorithm is used to construct multi-classifier to reduce the number of classifiers and eliminate non-partitionable regions. Particle Swarm Optimization (PSO) algorithm is introduced to cluster training samples to improve the classification accuracy of the constructed multi-classifier. In the ubiquitous network, the cost of information extraction and processing is significantly lower than that of traditional networks. This paper presents a quantitative analysis method of security risk based on Particle Swarm Optimization Support Vector Machine (PSO-SVM), and classifies the flow data by combining the way of obtaining the flow data in ubiquitous networks, so as to realize the quantitative analysis of the security risk in ubiquitous networks.

In the experiment, KDD99 data set is selected to verify the effectiveness of the algorithm. The experimental results show that the proposed PSO-SVM classification method is more accurate than the traditional one. In the ubiquitous network, this paper builds an experimental environment to illustrate the implementation process of security risk analysis method based on PSO-SVM. The risk analysis results show that the analysis value of risk in ubiquitous network fits well with the change trend of actual value. It means quantitative analysis of risk can be achieved.

Keywords: DT-SVM · PSO-SVM · Ubiquitous network

1 Introduction

Risk analysis of security incidents is a typical nonlinear classification problem with finite samples. Support Vector Machine (SVM), widely used in situational awareness of

X. Zhang et al. (Eds.): CloudComp 2019/SmartGift 2019, LNICST 322, pp. 544–552, 2020.
https://doi.org/10.1007/978-3-030-48513-9_43

traditional network, provides a good classification model for this kind of problem. Compared with traditional network node, which can only get the relevant information of the transmitted packets, the application layer in ubiquitous network architecture can obtain all flow data in the control domain through the control layer. The cost of information extraction and processing can be reduced significantly, making the application prospect of security analysis based on stream data much wider.

As a machine learning algorithm, SVM is based on statistics. SVM has the advantages of strong generalization ability and fast learning speed. It can solve the problem of smaller training set error and larger test set error in traditional machine learning algorithm. SVM can use limited sample information by finding a balance between learning ability and learning accuracy to solve the classification problems of limited samples. At the same time, DT-SVM has fewer sub-classifiers and eliminates unclassifiable region. It is a good method of multi-classification SVM construction. However, it may cause accumulation of misclassification, which is mainly due to the error of the upper classifier. To improve the performance of the classifier, we propose in this paper to cluster the training samples, construct an optimal binary tree classification, and construct DT-SVM using the classified samples and tree structure. The traditional clustering algorithm has good applicability to the clustering problem of low-dimensional data, but its ability to process high-dimensional data and massive data is not enough. The clustering method based on the Particle Swarm Optimization (PSO) can deal with clustering problem in high-dimensional data with quick convergence, thus obtain the global optimal solution. This paper presents a quantitative analysis method of security risk based on PSO-SVM, and classifies the flow data by combining the way of obtaining the flow data in ubiquitous networks, so as to realize the quantitative analysis of the security risk in ubiquitous networks.

The paper is organized as follows: Sect. 1 is the introduction of the paper, Sect. 2 introduced multi-classification problems; Sect. 3 is about the Improvement of DT-SVM by PSO algorithm; Sect. 4 tells the process and result of experiment; Sect. 5 is the conclusion of this paper.

2   Multi-classification Problems

Multi-classification problem of SVM is a hots pot in the field of machine learning. Basic SVM only aims at binary-classification problem. Faced with multi-classification problems, there are many solutions:

One-Versus-Rest SVM: 1-v-r SVM trains k binary-classification SVM for k classes. When constructing the SVM of the first class, the training samples belonging to the first class and the rest belong to another class. When test sample x input into the K binary-classification SVM, and x belongs to the SVM class with the maximum value.

One-Versus-one SVM: 1-v-1 SVM constructs $k(k-1)/2$ binary-classification SVM for k classes. The test samples are inputted into the binary-classification SVM, Then the value of each class is accumulated, and X belongs to the class with the highest accumulated value. These two kinds of SVM may exist unclassifiable regions, so they only used in the case of fewer classes.

Multi-class Support Vector Machine: M-SVM solves k SVMs simultaneously for k classes. It belongs to an optimization problem, but because the objective function is too complex and the computational complexity is too high, so the practicability is not high when the accuracy is guaranteed.

Decision directed acyclic graph SVM: The construction method of DAG-SVM is the same as that of 1-v-1 SVM. But in the test phase, each binary classification SVM is used as a node to generate a binary directed acyclic graph. $k(k-1)/2$ internal nodes correspond to $k(k-1)/2$ SVMs and k leaf nodes correspond to k classes. Thus, for a problem with k classes, to estimate the class of a test point, we need to evaluate the output of $k-1$ classifiers. DAG-SVM has faster decision-making speed and fewer classifiers, but root-node classifiers have a greater impact on the classification results. Different root-node classifiers have different results which lead to great uncertainty in the final classification results.

Multi-class Support Vector Machine Based on Decision Binary Tree: DT-SVM constructs $k-1$ binary-classification SVMs for k classes. When constructing the i-th class of SVM, the training samples belonging to the i-th class are divided into the first class. The other class includes $i+1, i+2, \ldots, k$ class.

A decision binary tree is constructed from the root node. DT-SVM constructs fewer binary-classification SVMs and eliminates unclassifiable regions. The nearer the leaf node has the fewer the total training samples of SVM. It is a better method to construct multi-classification SVM. There are also some problems in DT-SVM. The error classification of a root node will lead the error to the next leaf node, which will lead to the accumulation of errors.

3   Improvement of DT-SVM by PSO Algorithm

The error accumulation problem of DT-SVM is mainly caused by the error of upper classifier. In order to improve the performance of classifiers, we should follow the construction principle of "easy before difficult". Firstly, the training samples are clustered and an optimal decision binary tree classification is constructed. On this basis, DT-SVM is constructed. The traditional clustering algorithm has good applicability to the clustering problem of low-dimensional data, but it is not effective when facing high-dimensional data and massive data. PSO: Particle Swarm Optimization can deal with clustering problem in high-dimensional data better. Its converge speed is faster and it can get optimal solution more easily.

3.1   PSO Algorithm

PSO algorithm is a kind of swarm intelligence evolutionary algorithm. Its basic idea is to find the optimal solution through cooperation and information sharing among individuals in a group. The parameters of PSO algorithm is less and it can be realized easily. It is widely used in various optimization problems, such as the optimal classification of samples. In this paper, PSO clustering algorithm is used to find the optimal two-class partition in the sample set. The algorithm is as follows:

3.2 Improved DT-SVM Construction Algorithms

Algorithm: PSO: Particle Swarm Optimization

Input : Training sample

Output : Two Classes of Clustering Results of Samples

---

1. Initialize particle swarm optimization, randomly classify particles in two classes, and calculate cluster centers of different classes as position coding of particles.
2. Calculate particle fitness and initialize particle velocity to 0.
3. Calculate the individual and global optimal positions of each particle based on fitness
4. Update the velocities and positions of all particles
5. Cluster analysis of particles according to the nearest neighbor rule and cluster center coding
6. Calculate the clustering center and update the particle fitness based on the new clustering division,
7. Update individual and global optimal positions of particles
8. If the maximum number of iterations is reached, the run ends with the output of the classification result, otherwise jump 4

Before constructing DT-SVM, PSO clustering algorithm is used to classify training samples, and the optimal binary decision tree structure is generated to maximize the separability of samples. The classified samples and decision tree structure are used to construct the model. The construction algorithm of DT-SVM based on PSO clustering is as follows:

Algorithm: Construction algorithm of DT-SVM based on PSO clustering

---

Input : Training samples
Output : DT-SVM

---

1. Sample the initial training set
2. Use PSO algorithm to divide the sample into two sub-nodes
3. Judge whether sub-node 1 is separable, if it can be separable jump 2
4. Judge whether sub-node 2 is separable, if it can be separable jump 2
5. All nodes can't be separable, then generate decision binary tree
6. Constructing DT-SVM with the Samples and Binary Tree Structure

---

4 Quantitative Analysis Experiment

To verify the effectiveness of the method, this paper uses KD99 data set to test. The KDD99 data set is based on the DARPA data. And Professor Wenke Lee removes a large number of identical connection records and some duplicate data when DoS attacks occur. At the same time, the data set is cleaned and preprocessed. This data set is widely accepted as the standard of attack test data set. The data set contains normal flow data and 39 kinds of attack flow data, which belong to four attack modes: Probe, DoS, R2L and U2R.

4.1 Data Preprocessing

Each connection in the KDD99 dataset contains 41 feature dimensions and one label dimension, the format is as follows:

> 0,icmp,ecr_i,SF,520,0,0,0,0,0,0,0,0,0,0,0,0,0,0,0,0,0,0,0,511,511,0.00,0.00,0.00,0.00,1 .00,0.00,0.00,255,255,1.00,0.00,1.00,0.00,0.00,0.00,0.00,0.00,smurf.

In the 41 feature dimensions, there are four main characteristics: 9 basic characteristics of TCP connection, 13 content characteristics of TCP connection, 9 network traffic time characteristics and 1 host network traffic characteristics. Among these features, there are 9 discrete features and 32 continuous features, and the metrics of continuous features are not exactly the same.

Firstly, is Preprocessing the data. The discrete features should be continuous and coded before we process them. For example, for the second feature, protocol type, it can be mapped to integers so that TCP = 1, UDP = 2, ICMP = 3, and other types = 4. Other discrete features are also mapped in this way. Secondly, data are standardized and normalized to facilitate analysis and processing. Finally, each connection has 41 features. In this paper, PRFAR attribute reduction algorithm proposed in document [74] is used to select attributes, remove irrelevant and redundant features, reduce data dimension and amount, and improve the training speed of classifiers.

4.2 Analysis of Experimental Results

KDD99 dataset contains many attack instances, which can be considered as a breadth test to test the coverage of the system for attack detection. The dataset used in this paper is kddcup. data_10_percent training set and test set.

The experiment implements PSO-SVM algorithm based on Python's Libsvm software package. The constructed multi-classifier is shown in Fig. 1.

The multi-classifier constructed in this paper regards all the traffic that cannot be classified as attack traffic. Although this method may misjudge normal access as attack, it has much less consequences than misjudge attack as normal traffic. The classification results are shown in Table 1.

The experimental results prove that the proposed method is feasible and PSO-SVM method has more advantages in classification accuracy. Although the training time of the proposed method is longer than that of several SVM algorithms, the construction process

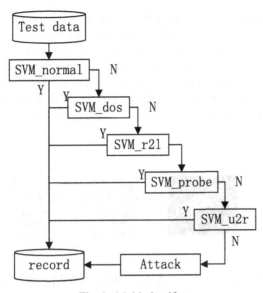

Fig. 1. Multi-classifier

Table 1. Experiment results

Accuracy	Attack categories			
	DoS	R2L	PROBE	U2R
SVM	95.3017	85.8407	98.2906	82.2951
Document[74]	100	91.558	90.3846	88.2353
PSO-SVM	99.2108	97.1722	98.7991	93.274

of DT-SVM is usually prior and will not affect the real-time classification. The controller of Ubiquitous Network Control Layer (Ubiquitous Network Control Layer) can obtain the flow data of all network nodes, and the risk analysis efficiency of Ubiquitous Network is much higher than that of traditional network. This paper uses a simple network structure to illustrate the analysis process of the analysis method proposed in the ubiquitous network environment.

4.3 Risk Calculation

Taking the risk analysis calculation principle proposed by GB20984-2007 as an example, the risk value can be calculated in the following formula:

$$R = R(A, T, V) = R(L(T, V), F(L_a, V_a)) \tag{1}$$

In the formula, R represents the value of security risk; A represents assets; T represents threats and V represents vulnerabilities, and L_a, V_a represent the value of assets and the severity of vulnerabilities affected by security incidents. L represents Indicate the possibility of security incidents and F represents the loss caused by security incidents.

Based on the ubiquitous network structure proposed in this paper, a simple ubiquitous network environment is built to illustrate the security risk analysis process based on PSO-SVM. The experimental environment topology is shown in Fig. 2. The risk application runs on Server. Floodlight in the control layer obtains the flow data in the network, and the attacker sends the flow to Server.

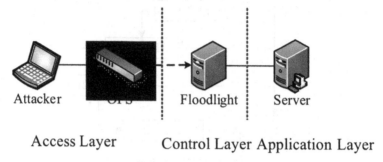

Access Layer   Control Layer Application Layer

Fig. 2. Experimental Network environment topology

36,000 data are extracted from the test set to reduce the percentage of attack traffic to total traffic, adjust the proportional relationship, and randomly scramble it as simulation traffic data. The specific amount of traffic is shown in (Table 2).

Table 2. Flow data table

Label	Kind	Number
0	DoS	7000
1	R2L	4000
2	PROBE	800
3	U2R	200
4	Normal	24000

In the simulation environment, more than 1000 network traffic data are replayed at a speed of about 1000 bars per second. Record the flow data per minute and calculate the security risk in one minute, then calculate the security risk in one hour, and classify the traffic using the trained multi-classifier as the analysis result. Because the test data of DRAPA organization does not give the network topology description, the following settings are made when completing the simulation experiment: 20% of the total traffic is used as the threshold value, the ratio of an attack traffic to the threshold value is used as the probability of the network being threatened by such attack, and the probability of exceeding the threshold value is 1; Vulnerability is 1, that is, all attacks have corresponding vulnerability; asset value is 1, that is, all assets are equally important; the proportion of an attack traffic to the total attack traffic is regarded as the weight of the attack, and because vulnerability is equal to the attack weight and the severity of vulnerability, the calculation formula can be simplified as follows:

$$R = R(T \cdot V_a) \tag{2}$$

At the same time:

$$T(Attack_i) = \begin{cases} \frac{Attack\_traffic_i}{\varepsilon} & if(Attack\_traffic_i < \varepsilon) \\ 1 & otherwise \end{cases}$$

$$V(Attack_i) = \frac{Attack\_traffic_i}{\sum\limits_{i=1}^{l} Attack\_traffic_i} \tag{3}$$

The comparison between quantitative analysis value and actual value of specific attack risk is shown in Fig. 3, Fig. 4. It can be seen that the fitting degree between quantitative analysis value and actual value curve is very good, and the quantitative analysis value is slightly higher than the actual value. Because classifiers tend to classify unknown traffic as attack traffic.

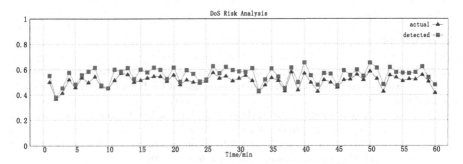

Fig. 3. DoS attack risk analysis

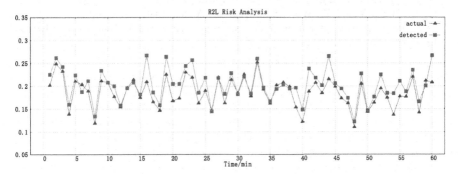

Fig. 4. R2L attack risk analysis

5 Conclusion

Quantitative risk analysis of security incidents is a typical non-linear classification problem under limited samples. Firstly, the related theory of SVM is introduced. SVM has strong generalization ability, fast learning speed, and can solve the classification problem under limited samples very well. To solve the problem of multi-classification, DT-SVM algorithm is used to construct multi-classifier to reduce the number of classifiers and eliminate unclassifiable regions. PSO algorithm is introduced to cluster training samples to improve the classification accuracy of the constructed multi-classifier. In the experiment, KDD99 data set is selected to verify the effectiveness of the algorithm. The experimental results show that the proposed PSO-SVM classification method is more accurate than the traditional one.

This work was supported in part by the Fundamental Research Funds for the Central Universities (30918012204), Military Common Information System Equipment Pre-research Special Technology Project (315075701), 2019 Industrial Internet Innovation and Development Project from Ministry of Industry and Information Technology of China, 2018 Jiangsu Province Major Technical Research Project "Information Security Simulation System", Shanghai Aerospace Science and Technology Innovation Fund (SAST2018-103).

References

1. Xu, X., Liu, Q., Zhang, X., Zhang, J., Qi, L., Dou, W.: A blockchain-powered crowdsourcing method with privacy preservation in mobile environment. IEEE Trans. Comput. Soc. Syst. 1-13 (2019)
2. Qi, L., et al.: A QoS-aware virtual machine scheduling method for energy conservation in cloud-based cyber-physical systems. World Wide Web 5(2019)
3. Qi, L., et al.: Finding all you need: web APIs recommendation in web of things through keywords search. IEEE Trans. Comput. Soc. Syst. **6**, 1–10 (2019)
4. Li, Q., Meng, S., Wang, S., Zhang, J., Hou, J.: CAD: command-level anomaly detection for vehicle-road collaborative charging network. IEEE Access **7**, 34910–34924 (2019)
5. Li, Q., Meng, S., Zhang, S., Hou, J., Qi, L.: Complex attack linkage decision-making in edge computing networks. IEEE Access **7**, 12058–12072 (2019)
6. Li, Q., Wang, Y., Pu, Z., Wang, S., Zhang, W.: A state analysis method in smart internet of electric vehicle charging network time series association attack. Transportation Research Record (2019)

Coordinated Placement of Meteorological Workflows and Data with Privacy Conflict Protection

Tao Huang[1], Shengjun Xue[1,2(✉)], Yumei Hu[3], Qing Yang[1], Yachong Tian[1], and Dan Zeng[4]

[1] School of Computer Science and Technology, Silicon Lake College, Suzhou, China
nuisthuangtao@163.com, sjxue@163.com, whuyq@163.com, 779273334@qq.com
[2] School of Computer and Software, Nanjing University of Information Science and Technology, Nanjing, China
[3] Shanghai Huanan Environmental Management Limited Company, Shanghai, China
shymhu@163.com
[4] Library of Wuhan University of Technology, Wuhan University of Technology, Hubei, China
zengd@whut.edu.cn

Abstract. Cloud computing is cited by various industries for its powerful computing power to solve complex calculations in the industry. The massive data of meteorological department has typical big data characteristics. Therefore, cloud computing has been gradually applied to deal with a large number of meteorological -services. Cloud computing increases the computational speed of meteorological services, but data transmission between nodes also generates additional data transmission time. At the same time, based on cloud computing technology, a large number of computing tasks are cooperatively processed by multiple nodes, so improving the resource utilization of each node is also an important evaluation indicator. In addition, with the increase of data confidentiality, there are some data conflicts between some data, so the conflicting data should be avoided being placed on the same node. To cope with this challenge, the meteorological application is modeled and a collaborative placement method for tasks and data based on Differential Evolution algorithm (CPDE) is proposed. The Non-dominated Sorting Differential Evolution (NSDE) algorithm is used to jointly optimize the average data access time, the average resource utilization of nodes and the data conflict degree. Finally, a large number of experimental evaluations and comparative analyses verify the efficiency of our proposed CPDE method.

Keywords: Meteorological · Coordinated placement · NSDE · Data access time · Resource utilization · Data conflict

© ICST Institute for Computer Sciences, Social Informatics and Telecommunications Engineering 2020
Published by Springer Nature Switzerland AG 2020. All Rights Reserved
X. Zhang et al. (Eds.): CloudComp 2019/SmartGift 2019, LNICST 322, pp. 553–568, 2020.
https://doi.org/10.1007/978-3-030-48513-9_44

1   Introduction

1.1   Background

With the advancement of meteorological data acquisition technology and the improvement of meteorological service requirements [1–3], the number and types of meteorological data continue to grow, and it has gradually become a typical industry big data [4,5]. At the same time, the computational complexity of meteorological applications is increasing [5], so the meteorological department offloads a large number of meteorological applications and data to cluster for execution and storage [6,7]. However, in order to improve the average response time of all meteorological applications, meteorological department analyzes the characteristics of massive meteorological data and rationally distributes meteorological big data to each storage node [8,9]. In addition, based on the overall placement of meteorological big data, meteorological department continues to study how to properly place all tasks and data to each node in cluster [8], thereby reducing the average data access time for all tasks in the application [10,11].

However, as the number of meteorological applications and data offloaded to cluster increases rapidly [12], the resource utilization of nodes in cluster is also being paid more and more attention [13], and it has become an important indicator to measure the performance of placement method [14,15]. In addition, with the improvement of the confidentiality of meteorological data, the placement of conflicting data has also received more and more attention. While improving the resource utilization of nodes, it is also necessary to avoid placing those conflicting data in the same storage node to ensure the security of meteorological data [16–18]. Therefore, the collaborative placement of tasks and data for each meteorological application has become a challenge. In response to this challenge, this paper proposes an optimization method for collaborative placement of tasks and data in the meteorological applications.

1.2   Paper Contributions

In this paper, the main contributions are as follows:

- We model the meteorological application in the meteorological fat-tree network as a workflow, and all operations in the meteorological application are modeled as a series of tasks in workflow.
- The coordinated placement problem of meteorological tasks and data is modeled as a multi-objective optimization problem.
- We propose a optimization method for the coordinated placement of meteorological tasks and data based on NSDE algorithm to optimize the object functions of model.

2   Analysis of Meteorological Scenarios

2.1   Meteorological Fat-Tree Network

Meteorological networks usually use the tree structure, but the bandwidth is layer-by-layer convergence in the traditional network, and the network congestion is likely to occur. Therefore, based on the traditional tree network structure, the Fat-tree topology network structure has been proposed and has been widely adopted by the meteorological department. The Fat-tree network structure is divided into three layers from top to bottom: core layer, aggregation layer and edge layer, the aggregation layer switches and the edge layer switches form a pod. The bandwidth of Fat-tree topology network is not convergent, and there are multiple parallel paths between any two nodes, so that it can provide high throughput transmission service and high fault tolerance for the meteorological data center.

In actual meteorological applications, a public meteorological cloud data center is constructed based on the virtualization technology and the Fat-tree network topology. The switches in each department constitute a Pod, or all the switches of several adjacent departments constitute the same Pod, and each Pod connects to the servers of the department to which it belongs. According to the rules of Fat-tree, if the meteorological cloud data center contains N^{pod} Pods, the number of edge switches and aggregation switches in each pod is $N^{pod}/2$, the number of servers that can be connected in each pod is $(N^{pod}/2)^2$, and the number of core switches is also $(N^{pod}/2)^2$. Figure 1 shows a meteorological Fat-tree network topology with four Pods. In practical applications, the network size of meteorological department is usually much larger than this.

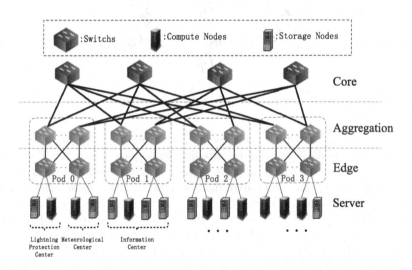

Fig. 1. A meteorological Fat-tree network with 4 pods.

2.2 Meteorological Scene and Workflow Description

In the current meteorological big data cloud processing mode, in order to improve the service efficiency of massive meteorological historical data and reduce the average data access time. The meteorological department analyzes the characteristics of historical data that have been the most important data source for various meteorological applications, and reasonably stores the historical data in certain fixed storage nodes. In addition, user input data that can be dynamically placed during application execution is also an important data source for each application. Therefore, based on the placed meteorological historical data, the coordinated placement of tasks and input data in the meteorological applications is completed, so that the average data access time and the data conflict degree are minimized, the average resource utilization of all used nodes is maximized.

Based on workflow technology, each meteorological application can be modeled as a meteorological workflow, and operations in meteorological application can be modeled as a set of tasks in workflow. Figure 2 shows the workflow of weather forecast production.

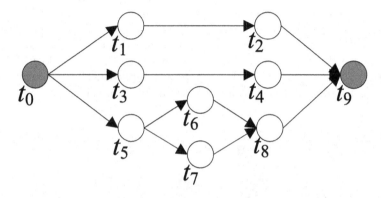

Fig. 2. The workflow of weather forecast production.

As the starting task, task t_0 represents *Data Collection* operation, including: automatic station data, radar data, satellite nephogram and so on. Task t_1 and task t_2 represent *Historical Weather Summary* operation and *Historical Weather Analysis* operation, that summarize the historical weather phenomena and analyze the causes of historical weather formation in the past 48 h, respectively. Task t_3 and task t_4 represent *Real-time Weather Summary* operation and *Real-time Weather Analysis* operation, that summarize the current weather phenomena and analyze the causes of current weather formation, respectively. Task t_5 represents *Forecast Mode Calculation* operation, the future weather is calculated in real time based on *European Centre for Medium-Range Weather Forecasts (ECMWF)* and *Global Forecasting System (GFS)*. Task t_6 and task t_7 represent *Weather Situation Analysis* operation and *Meteorological Elements Analysis* operation, that analyze the future weather situation and the future meteorological elements based on the calculation results of forecast model, respectively. Task t_8 represents *Generation of Forecast Model Conclusions* operation, based on the analysis for weather situation and meteorological elements, the final conclusion of forecast model is formed. As the termination task, task t_9 represents

Generation of Weather Forecast Conclusion operation, based on the analysis of historical weather and real-time weather, combined with the conclusion of forecast model, the final weather forecast conclusion is formed.

3 Problem Modeling and Formulation

3.1 Problem Modeling

In this section, we mainly model the coordinated placement problem of tasks and data, and formulate this model.

Assume that a meteorological workflow consists of M tasks, which can be defined as $TS = \{t_0, t_1, t_2, ..., t_{M-1}\}$. The data source of meteorological workflow mainly includes P input data and Q historical data, so the input data set and the historical data set can be defined as $D^{inp} = \{d_0^{inp}, d_1^{inp}, d_2^{inp}, ..., d_{P-1}^{inp}\}$ and $D^{his} = \{d_0^{his}, d_1^{his}, d_2^{his}, ..., d_{Q-1}^{his}\}$. Therefore, the relationship between tasks and data can be expressed as $\gamma = \{\gamma_0, \gamma_1, \gamma_2, ..., \gamma_{M-1}\}$, where $\gamma_m = \{d_a^{inp}, ..., d_c^{inp}, d_c^{his}, ..., d_e^{his}\}$ represents the data set required for the m-th task t_m. If there are K pairs of conflicting data, the conflicting relationship between these conflicting data can be expressed as $\beta = \{\beta_0, \beta_1, \beta_2, ..., \beta_k, ..., \beta_{K-1}\}$, where $\beta_k = \{d_x, d_y\}, (d_x, d_y \in \{D^{inp}, D^{his}\})$ represents the k-th pair of conflicting data.

3.2 Data Access Time Model

In the meteorological Fat-tree network, it is assumed that the task t_m and its required data are stored in the compute node u_i and the storage node u_j, respectively, and the data amount is d_n. The positional relationship between u_i and u_j can be defined as $\delta_{i,j}$, then:

- If u_i and u_j are the same node, then $\delta_{i,j} = 0$;
- If u_i and u_j belong to the same switch, then $\delta_{i,j} = 1$;
- If u_i and u_j belong to the different switches of the same pod, then $\delta_{i,j} = 2$;
- If u_i and u_j belong to the different pods, then $\delta_{i,j} = 3$;

Therefore, according to the positional relationship $\delta_{i,j}$ between u_i and u_j, the access time T_m^{AC} of the task t_m for the data can be expressed as:

$$T_m^{AC} = \begin{cases} 0; & \delta_{i,j} = 0 \\ 2 * d_n/B_{se}; & \delta_{i,j} = 1 \\ 2 * (d_n/B_{se} + d_n/B_{ea}); & \delta_{i,j} = 2 \\ 2 * (d_n/B_{se} + d_n/B_{ea} + d_n/B_{ac}); & \delta_{i,j} = 3 \end{cases} \tag{1}$$

where B_{se}, B_{ea}, and B_{ac} represent the bandwidth between the server and the edge layer switch, the bandwidth between the edge layer switch and the aggregation layer switch, and the bandwidth between the aggregation layer switch and the core switch, respectively.

Therefore, the data access time of task t_m for its required data set γ_m can be calculated as:

$$T_m^{Total} = \sum_{d_n \in \gamma_m} T_m^{AC} \tag{2}$$

Then, the average data access time for M tasks can be calculated as:

$$T_{avg}^{AC} = \sum_{m=0}^{M-1} T_m^{Total} / M \tag{3}$$

3.3 Resource Utilization Model

Assume that the number of compute nodes and storage nodes are N^{col} and N^{sto}, respectively. And the resource of each compute node and storage node are VM_{MAX}^{col} and VM_{MAX}^{sto}, respectively. The amount of resources required for each task and each data are expressed as $TVM = \{tvm_0^{col}, tvm_1^{col}, ..., tvm_m^{col}, ..., tvm_{M-1}^{col}\}$ and $DVM = \{dvm_0^{sto}, dvm_1^{sto}, ..., dvm_n^{sto}, ..., dvm_{P+Q-1}^{sto}\}$, respectively. tvm_m^{col} and dvm_m^{col} represent the amount of resources required for the m-th task and the n-th data, respectively.

Therefore, the placement of M tasks on the compute nodes can be represented as the two-dimensional array $CT[N^{col}, M]$, and the placement of $P + Q$ data on the storage nodes can be represented as the two-dimensional array $SD[N^{sto}, P + Q]$, then:

$$CT[i, m] = \begin{cases} 1; t_m \text{ is placed on the } i - th \text{ compute node} \\ 0; Otherwise \end{cases} \tag{4}$$

$$SD[j, n] = \begin{cases} 1; d_n \text{ is placed on the } j - th \text{ storage node} \\ 0; Otherwise \end{cases} \tag{5}$$

Then, the resource utilization of the i-th compute node and the j-th storage node can be expressed as U_i^{col} and U_j^{sto}, respectively.

$$U_i^{col} = \sum_{m=0}^{M-1} tvm_m^{col} * CT[i, m] / VM_{MAX}^{col} \tag{6}$$

$$U_j^{sto} = \sum_{n=0}^{P+Q-1} dvm_n^{sto} * SD[j, n] / VM_{MAX}^{sto} \tag{7}$$

If the number of compute nodes and storage nodes that have been used is N_{use}^{col} and N_{use}^{sto}, respectively. The average resource utilization of the currently used compute nodes and storage nodes can be expressed as $\overline{U^{col}}$ and $\overline{U^{sto}}$, respectively.

$$\overline{U^{col}} = \sum_{i=0}^{N^{col}} U_i^{col} / N_{use}^{col} \tag{8}$$

$$\overline{U^{sto}} = \sum_{j=0}^{N^{sto}} U_j^{sto} / N_{use}^{sto} \tag{9}$$

Finally, the average resource utilization of compute nodes and storage nodes is calculated as:

$$\overline{U} = \frac{N^{col}}{N^{col} + N^{sto}} * \overline{U^{col}} + \frac{N^{sto}}{N^{col} + N^{sto}} * \overline{U^{sto}} \tag{10}$$

3.4 Data Conflict Model

Because the closer the conflicting data is placed on network, the greater the possibility of privacy breaches. Therefore, in order to ensure data privacy, conflicting data should be prevented from being placed on the same node or the same pod.

Assume that there are N^{SN} pairs of conflicting data placed on the same node. There are N^{SS} pairs of conflicting data placed on the different nodes of the same edge layer switch. There are N^{SP} pairs of conflicting data placed under different edge layer switches of the same pod. We set the corresponding weights w_0, w_1 and w_2 for these three placement of conflicting data.

Then, the data conflict degree for all conflicting data can be expressed as:

$$C = w_0 * N^{SN} + w_1 * N^{SS} + w_2 * N^{SP} \tag{11}$$

where $w_0 + w_1 + w_2 = 1$, the closer the conflicting data are placed, the larger the corresponding weight. Therefore, in this experiment, the three weights are set to 0.55, 0.3, and 0.15, respectively.

3.5 Objective Functions

In this paper, the coordinated placement of meteorological workflow and data with privacy conflict protection has been modeled as a multi-objective optimization problem. Average data access time, average resource utilization, and data conflict degree are used as the three objective functions of this optimization problem. Therefore, this optimization model can be expressed as:

$$Min(T_{avg}^{AC}, \overline{U}), Max(C) \tag{12}$$

In addition, this optimization problem also needs to meet certain constraints, that is, the used resources of each node cannot exceed the maximum resource amount of node, so the constraint can be expressed as:

$$s.t. \forall U_i^{col} \leq 1, \forall U_j^{sto} \leq 1 | 0 \leq i < N^{col}, 0 \leq j < N^{sto} \tag{13}$$

In addition, he symbols used in this work are summarized uniformly in the following table (Table 1).

Table 1. Symbols and meanings.

Symbols	Meanings
γ	Relationship between tasks and data
β	Conflicting relationship between data
δ	Positional relationship between nodes
T_m^{Total}	Data access time of the task t_m
T_{avg}^{AC}	Average data access time for M tasks
U_i^{col}	Resource utilization of the i-th compute node
U_j^{sto}	Resource utilization of the j-th storage node
$\overline{U}$	Average resource utilization of all nodes
C	Data conflict degree for all conflicting data

4   Problem Optimization

In Sect. 3, the coordinated placement of meteorological workflow and data has been modeled as a multi-objective optimization problem. In this section, based on NSDE algorithm, this multi-objective problem is optimized. Firstly, we encode the multi-objective optimization problem and generate the initial parental population. Secondly, based on the parental population, the mutation operation, crossover operation, and selection operation are continuously performed. In the selection phase, we adopt fast non-dominated sorting and crowding distance calculation to select individuals whose objective functions are relatively good to retain to the next generation. Finally, through comparing the utility values of multiple excellent individuals, the individual with the best utility value are output as the final result.

4.1   Encoding

According to the total number of compute nodes and storage nodes, the placement strategy of each task and data is encoded as a real number between $[0, N^{col} + N^{sto}]$. And each real number represents the location where the corresponding task or data is placed. After the encoding operation is completed, the placement strategies set $X = \{X^T, X^{OD}\}$ is generated, where $X^T = \{x_0^T, x_1^T, x_2^T, ..., x_m^T, ..., x_{M-1}^T\}$ represents the corresponding compute node locations of M tasks. $X^{OD} = \{x_0^{OD}, x_1^{OD}, x_2^{OD}, ..., x_{P-1}^{OD}\}$ represents the corresponding storage node locations of P input data. In addition, the placement position X^{HD} of all historical data is fixed.

4.2   Objective Functions

As the three objective functions of this optimization problem: the average data access time, the average resource utilization, and the data conflict degree, we need to find a suitable placement scheme so that all three objective functions are relatively good, not one or two of them are relatively good. The calculation of average data access time is illustrated in Algorithm 1. Then, the NSDE algorithm optimizes the population and finally obtain the best placement strategy.

Algorithm 1. Calculate the Average Data Access Time

Require: X, D, TS, M, γ
Ensure: T_{avg}
 1: **for** t_m in TS **do**
 2:     **for** d_k in γ_m **do**
 3:         $d = d_k, i = X_m^T, j$ *is position of* d_k
 4:         *calculate* T_m^{AC} *by* (1)
 5:         $T_m^{Total} + = T_m^{AC}$
 6:     **end for**
 7: **end for**
 8: *calculate* T_{avg}^{AC} *by* (3)
 9: **return** T_{avg}^{AC}

4.3 Optimizing Problem Using NSDE

As an efficient population-based global optimization algorithm, NSDE is adopted to optimize this multi-objective optimization problem. Firstly, we need to initialize an initial population as the first parental population.

Initialization. The size of population is NP, so this initial population can be expressed as $X = \{X_0, X_1, ..., X_i, ..., X_{NP-1}\}$, where X_i is the i-th individual of population, and represents a placement strategy for all tasks and data. If this optimization problem has M tasks and P user input data, then X_i can be expressed as $X_i = \{x_0, x_1, x_2, ..., x_M, x_{M+1}, ..., x_{M+P-1}\}$ that represents the placement strategies for M tasks and P user input data.

Evolution. Based on the parental population, the *mutation, crossover,* and *selection* operations are performed recurrently.

In the *mutation* phase, according to the mutation factor F and three randomly selected individuals X_a, X_b and X_c, the mutation individual H_i is calculated as follows:

$$H_i = X_a + F * (X_b - X_c) \tag{14}$$

Finally, the mutation population $H = \{H_0, H_1, ..., H_i, ..., H_{NP-1}\}$ whose size is also NP is generated.

In the *crossover* operation, according to the specified crossover probability CR, the corresponding genes from the parental individual R_i and the mutation individual H_i are selected to form the crossover individual R_i. The specific calculation process is as follows:

$$R_{i,j} = \begin{cases} H_{i,j}, & rand(0,1) \leq CR || j = j_{rand} \\ X_{i,j}, & Otherwise \end{cases} \tag{15}$$

Finally, the crossover population $R = \{R_0, R_1, ..., R_i, ..., R_{NP-1}\}$ is generated.

In the *selection* operation, based on the population $Y = \{Y_0, Y_1, ..., Y_i, ..., Y_{2NP-1}\}$ merged by the parental population X and the crossover population R, the *fast non-dominated sorting* method is performed for all individuals. Then, all individuals in population Y are divided into multiple non-dominated layers to achieve that all individuals in the lower non-dominated layer have better fitness values than individuals in the higher non-dominated layer. And for each individual in the same layer, we continue to calculate the crowding distance. Finally, the individuals in the lower non-dominated layer are preferentially retained into the next generation parental population X, and secondly the individuals with better crowding distances in the same layer are retained into the next generation parental population X until the size of X is NP.

Iteration. The *mutation, crossover*, and *selection* operations are continuously performed based on the parental population X to achieve population evolution, and multiple excellent individuals are obtained finally.

Utility Value Comparison. For the multiple excellent individuals obtained by NSDE, we also need to perform the *utility value comparison* to obtain the optimal individual as the final result. If T_{avg}^i, $\overline{U^i}$ and C^i represent the average data access time, the average resource utilization, and the data conflict degree of X_i, respectively, T_{avg}^{min}, T_{avg}^{max}, $\overline{U^{min}}$, $\overline{U^{max}}$, C^{min} and C^{max} represent the minimum and maximum of the corresponding fitness values, respectively. Therefore, the utility value v_i of X_i can be calculated as following:

$$v_i = \frac{1}{3} * \left(\frac{T_{avg}^{max} - T_{avg}^i}{T_{avg}^{max} - T_{avg}^{min}} + \frac{\overline{U^i} - \overline{U^{min}}}{\overline{U^{max}} - \overline{U^{min}}} + \frac{C^{max} - C^i}{C^{max} - C^{max}} \right) \tag{16}$$

where the larger v_i, the better the individual X_i is.

5   Experiment and Analysis

Aiming at the three optimization goals of the coordinated placement problem, we designed a series of experiments and compared CPDE method with another common coordinated placement method in meteorological department. Firstly, we introduce the settings of parameters and another common coordinated placement method used in this experiment. Then, the performance of the two methods is compared and analyzed.

5.1   Parameters Setting and Comparison Method

In this experiment, we optimized three different scale workflows and compared the performance of several optimization methods. Assume that the sizes of workflows are set to 2, 4 and 6, respectively, and each workflow contains 20 tasks, but the data sets required for each task and the ordering of tasks execution are different. The setting of parameters used are as shown in the following table (Table 2).

Table 2. Parameters setting.

Parameter	Value
Number of compute nodes	19
Number of storage nodes	17
Bandwidth of the edge layer	200 MB/s
Bandwidth of the aggregation layer	500 MB/s
Bandwidth of the core layer	1 GB/s
Forwarding power of the switch	5 W

Besides our proposed CPDE method, we also compare performance with another coordinated placement method commonly used by meteorological department, the Coordinated Placement method based on Greedy algorithm (CPG), which is briefly described as follows:

Compared with data conflict degree, CPG is more concerned with average data access time and average resource utilization. Based on historical data that has been placed, tasks are preferentially placed at the computing node closest to their required historical data to ensure that each task has the shortest average data access time for historical data. Secondly, based on the placement of each task, the input data is preferentially placed on the storage node closest to the task set to which is belongs. And for the storage nodes having the same distance, the input data is preferentially placed on the storage node with highest resource utilization. However, our proposed CPDE method estimates the average data access time, the average resource utilization and the data conflict degree comprehensively, and optimizes the placement strategy using NSDE algorithm.

5.2   Comparison and Analysis of Method Performance

In this section, we will compare and analyze the performance of two methods on the three objective functions to demonstrate the superiority of our proposed CPDE method in terms of overall performance.

Figure 3 and Fig. 4 shows the performance comparison of CPDE method and CPG method on the average data access time indicator and the average resource utilization indicator based on three scale data sets. Overall, the difference between two methods in these two performance indicators is not very

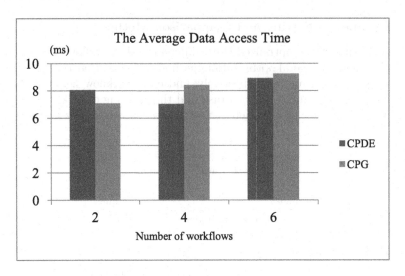

Fig. 3. Comparison analysis of the average data access time.

obvious. Only when the data set is small, for example, the number of workflows is 2, the performance of CPG method on the average data access time indicator is better than CPDE method, but the performance of CPDE method on the average resource utilization indicator is better than CPG method. However, with the size of data set expands, the performance of CPDE method on the average data access time indicator gradually begins to outperform CPG method, but the performance of CPG method on the average resource utilization indicator gradually also begins to outperform CPDE method.

Figure 5 shows the performance comparison of CPDE method and CPG method on the data conflict degree indicator based on three scale data sets. It can be clearly seen that the two methods have a large gap in this performance, and the performance of CPDE method is always significantly better than CPG method.

CPG method prioritizes the average data access time indicator and the average resource utilization indicator, and both of these indicators tend to place all tasks and data centrally to ensure the less data access time and the higher resource utilization. But CPG method does not consider the data conflict degree indicator, because in order to ensure the smaller data conflict degree, it is necessary to disperse the conflicting data, which contradicts the placement principle of CPG method. However, our proposed CPDE method can optimize these three indicators at the same time, so that CPDE method has better comprehensive performance than CPG method.

Finally, it can be determined that our proposed CPDE method is definitely better than CPG method, which has been verified in this experiment.

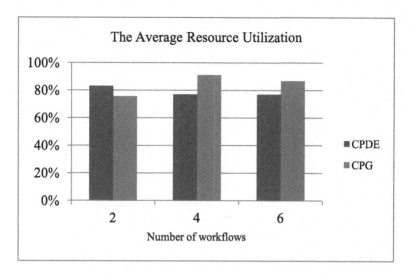

Fig. 4. Comparison analysis of the average resource utilization.

6   Related Work

In order to improve the execution efficiency of applications in the cluster, optimizing the data placement strategy helps to reduce the data access time to the application.

Li et al. proposed a two-stage data placement strategy and adopt the discrete PSO algorithm to optimize the placement of data for reducing data transfer cost [4]. In [7], aiming at the efficient data-intensive applications, an adaptive data placement strategy considering dynamic resource change is proposed, based on the resource availability, this placement strategy can reduce the data movement cost effectively. Ebrahimi et al. proposed a BDAP data placement strategy, which is a population-based distributed data placement optimization strategy [8]. These data placement strategies have a good effect. However, with the rapid increase of applications and data in the cluster, the resource utilization of equipment is also receiving more and more attention. In [10], based on the limited resources, Whaiduzzaman et al. proposed a PEFC method to improve the performance of cloudlet. In [12], Chen et al. proposed a correlation-aware virtual machine placement scheme to enhance resource utilization. In addition, ensuring the stability and security of data in cluster is also receiving increasing attention. In [14], Kang et al. formulated the data placement problem as a linear programming model and developed a heuristic algorithm named SEDuLOUS for solving the Security-aware data placement problem. At the same time, some scholars have conducted comprehensive research on these indicators. In [16], proposes a BPRS big data copy placement strategy, which can reduce the data movement of each data center and improve the load balancing problem.

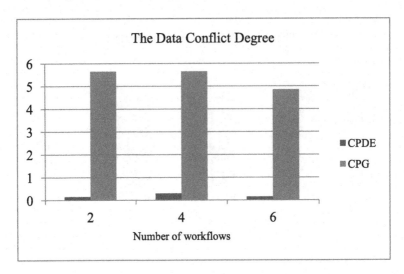

Fig. 5. Comparison analysis of the data conflict degree.

However, to the best of our knowledge, there are still few placement strategies that consider the three important factors of average data access time, average resource utilization and data conflict degree. Therefore, based on these three objectives, this paper proposes to optimize the placement of tasks and data using NSDE algorithm, and achieved remarkable results.

7   Conclusion and Future Work

The meteorological department mainly optimizes the placement of massive meteorological historical data for reducing the average data access time of applications. But it lacks the optimization of the coordinated placement of tasks and input data in each application. Therefore, firstly, the coordinated placement problem of meteorological workflows and data is modeled as a multi-objective optimization problem. And minimizing the average data access time and the data conflict degree, maximizing the resource utilization are used as the three optimization objectives. Secondly, we analyze and construct the models of these three objective functions, respectively. Then, based on NSDE algorithm, we propose a coordinated placement optimization method named CPDE to optimize the multi-objective problem. Finally, by comparing with the commonly used coordinated placement methods of meteorological departments, the availability and superiority of our proposed CPDE method is demonstrated.

However, in the future work, we also need to further consider the energy consumption of the data center and the execution time of each application from the perspective of resource providers and users, respectively. In addition, We consider to appropriately improve our proposed CPDE method to improve the performance of method, such as the optimization speed.

Acknowledgment. This research is supported by the Scientific Research Project of Silicon Lake College under Grant No. 2018KY23.

References

1. Li, X., Li, D., Wan, J., Vasilakos, A.V., Lai, C.-F., Wang, S.: A review of industrial wireless networks in the context of industry 4.0. Wireless Netw. **23**(1), 23–41 (2015). https://doi.org/10.1007/s11276-015-1133-7
2. Lin, B., et al.: A time-driven data placement strategy for a scientific workflow combining edge computing and cloud computing. IEEE Trans. Ind. Inf. **15**(7), 4254–4265 (2019)
3. Tang, J., Tang, X., Yuan, J.: Traffic-optimized data placement for social media. IEEE Trans. Multimedia **20**, 1008–1023 (2017)
4. Li, X., et al.: A novel workflow-level data placement strategy for data-sharing scientific cloud workflows. IEEE Trans. Serv. Comput. **12**, 370–383 (2019)
5. Dong, Y., Yang, Y., Liu, X., Chen, J.: A data placement strategy in scientific cloud workflows. Future Gener. Comput. Syst. **26**(8), 1200–1214 (2010)
6. Deng, K., Kong, L., Song, J., Ren, K., Dong, Y.: A weighted k-means clustering based co-scheduling strategy towards efficient execution of scientific workflows in collaborative cloud environments. In: IEEE Ninth International Conference on Dependable, Autonomic and Secure Computing, DASC 2011, 12–14 December 2011, Sydney, Australia, pp. 547–554 (2011)
7. Kim, H., Kim, Y.: An adaptive data placement strategy in scientific workflows over cloud computing environments. In: NOMS 2018–2018 IEEE/IFIP Network Operations and Management Symposium, pp. 1–5 (2018)
8. Kashlev, A., Lu, S., Ebrahimi, M., Mohan, A.: BDAP: a big data placement strategy for cloud-based scientific workflows. In: 2015 IEEE First International Conference on Big Data Computing Service and Applications, pp. 813–820 (2015)
9. Liao, Z., Yu, B., Liu, K., Wang, J.: Learning-based adaptive data placement for low latency in data center networks. In: IEEE 43rd Conference on Local Computer Networks (2018)
10. Whaiduzzaman, M., Gani, A., Naveed, A. PEFC: performance enhancement framework for cloudlet in mobile cloud computing. In: IEEE-ROMA-2014, pp. 224–229 (2014)
11. Xu, X. et al.: A multi-objective data placement method for IoT applications over big data using NSGA-II. In: IEEE International Conference on Internet of Things (iThings) and IEEE Green Computing and Communications (GreenCom) and IEEE Cyber, Physical and Social Computing (CPSCom) and IEEE Smart Data (SmartData), pp. 503–509 (2018)
12. Chen, T., Zhu, Y., Gao, X., Kong, L., Chen, G., Wang, Y.: Improving resource utilization via virtual machine placement in data center networks. Mobile Netw. Appl. **23**(2), 227–238 (2017). https://doi.org/10.1007/s11036-017-0925-7
13. Cui, L., Zhang, J., Yue, L., Shi, Y., Li, H., Yuan, D.: A genetic algorithm based data replica placement strategy for scientific applications in clouds. IEEE Trans. Serv. Comput. **11**(4), 727–739 (2015)
14. Kang, S., Veeravalli, B., Aung, K.M.M.: A security-aware data placement mechanism for big data cloud storage systems. In: IEEE 2nd International Conference on Big Data Security on Cloud (BigDataSecurity), IEEE International Conference on High Performance and Smart Computing (HPSC) and IEEE International Conference on Intelligent Data and Security (IDS), pp. 327–332 (2016)

15. Wang, R., Yiwen, L., Zhu, K., Hao, J., Wang, P., Cao, Y.: An optimal task placement strategy in geo-distributed data centers involving renewable energy. IEEE Access **6**, 61948–61958 (2018)
16. Liu, L., Song, J., Wang, H.: BRPS: a big data placement strategy for data intensive applications. In: IEEE 16th International Conference on Data Mining Workshops (ICDMW), pp. 813–820 (2016)
17. Shu, J., Liu, X., Jia, X., Yang, K., Deng, R.H.: Anonymous privacy-preserving task matching in crowdsourcing. IEEE Internet Things J. **5**(4), 3068–3078 (2018)
18. Chi, Z., Wang, Y., Huang, Y., Tong, X.: The novel location privacy-preserving CKD for mobile systems. IEEE Access **6**, 5678–5687 (2018)

Method and Application of Homomorphic Subtraction of the Paillier Cryptosystem in Secure Multi-party Computational Geometry

Meng Liu[1]([✉])[iD], Yun Luo[2], Chi Yang[3], Dongliang Xu[1], and Taoran Wu[4]

[1] School of Mechanical, Electrical and Information Engineering,
Shandong University, Weihai, China
{liumeng,xudongliang}@sdu.edu.cn
[2] Faculty of Engineering and Information Technology,
University of Technology Sydney, Ultimo, Australia
yun.luo@student.uts.edu.au
[3] School of Computer Science and Technology, Huazhong University of Science
and Technology, Wuhan, China
chiyangit@gmail.com
[4] College of Professional Studies, Northeastern University, Boston, USA
wu.ta@husky.neu.edu

Abstract. A secure two-party computation protocol for the problem of the distance between two private points is important and can be used as the building block for some secure multi-party computation (SMC) problems in the field of geometry. Li's solution to this problem is inefficient based on OT_m^1 oblivious transfer protocol and some drawbacks still remain while applied to compute the relationship between a private circle and a private point. Two protocols are also proposed based on the Paillier cryptosystem by Luo et al. and more efficient than Li's solution, but there also remain some drawbacks. In this paper, we propose an idea to improve the efficiency of secure protocol by using its homomorphic subtraction based on the Paillier cryptosystem. Then we apply it to solve the secure two-party computation problem for the distance between two private points. Using our solution, the SMC protocol to the relationship between a private point and a private circle area is more efficient and private than Li's solution. In addition, we also find that our solution is also more efficient than the BGN-based solution and much better while the plaintext can be in some large range.

Keywords: Secure multi-party computation · Homomorphic cryptosystem · Computational geometry · Subtraction

Supported by Shandong Provincial Natural Science Foundation under grant ZR2019PF007.

X. Zhang et al. (Eds.): CloudComp 2019/SmartGift 2019, LNICST 322, pp. 569–581, 2020.
https://doi.org/10.1007/978-3-030-48513-9_45

1   Introduction

SMC protocol can be employed for collaboratively computing a function by parties based on multiple private input information, but these private inputs will not be revealed. SMC is a very important research area in cryptographic research problems, and its solutions have been widely used in secure statistical analysis [11], privacy-preserving clustering [16], data mining [1,18], bidding and auction [7,26], cooperative scientific computation [10,28], set intersection [9, 12,27] and secure computational geometry [2,6,19,29,30]. Yao's Millionaires' problem is the first SMC problem that was introduced by Yao [20,31].

The secure calculation of the distance between two private points is a fundamental problem that needs to be solved in the field of geometry and an SMC protocol to it can be used as a building block for some SMC geometry problems [17,20]. Secure multi-party computational geometry problem is a special area of SMC, and we should put forward to some special solutions to these problems that are more effective than general theoretical solutions.

The rest of this paper is organized as follows:

We outline the related work in Sect. 2. In Sect. 3, we introduce and demonstrate a method of homomorphic subtraction of the Paillier cryptosystem. We apply our method to solve the secure two-party computation problem for the distance between two private points in Sect. 4. In Sect. 5, an SMC protocol to the relationship between a private circle area and a private point is proposed by using our protocol in Sect. 4. In Sect. 6, we show efficiency analysis and experiment results between our solution and Li's solution. And we also compare and analyse the computation costs of the solutions based on the Paillier cryptosystem and the BGN cryptosystem. The last section concludes this paper and discusses the future work.

2   Related Work

Some computational geometry problems have been studied [2,17]. However, most of their solutions are based on OT_m^1 oblivious transfer protocol. These solutions need so many oblivious transfer that they are not very efficient. Li et al. [17] researched the secure two-party computation problem for the distance between two private points based on OT_m^1 protocol, but their solution is highly inefficient. While Protocol 2 proposed in [17] is applied to compute the relationship between a private point and a private circle, there are still some drawbacks. Homomorphic Cryptosystem is used more and more in SMC fields, especially Millionaire protocol. The Paillier cryptosystem supports additively homomorphic encryption and has been widely used in some solutions to secure multi-party computation. Luo et al. [22] present a protocol for solving the problem of secure computation for the distance between two private points based on the Paillier cryptosystem. And it is more efficient than Li's solution and has been used to solve the problem of general geometric intersection problem [25]. Luo et al. [22] also present a point-inclusion protocol based on the protocol for the problem of secure computation of the distance between two private points, but some drawbacks also remain. The BGN homomorphic scheme can allow one multiplication and multiple additive operations over the encrypted data and can be used to solve some SMC problems, but its performance is still slow over composite-order group [3,8]. Bilogrevic et al. [5] addressed the privacy-preserving problem in Location-Sharing-Based Service based on the BGN and both the Paillier and ElGamal cryptosystem respectively, and they claimed that the Paillier-based solution would have a better performance than BGN-based one. In 2010, Freeman [13] proposed a conversion solution to improve performance of BGN cryptosystem. In the BGN cryptosystem, the plaintext must be restricted to be in some small range(integers less than some bound L, say $L = 10^8$) and its decryption can be quickly computed in $O(\sqrt{L})$ time by using Pollard's kangaroo algorithm, otherwise the discrete logarithm can be very slowly computed, as is a serious disadvantage in some cases. Huang et al. introduced two SMC protocols to compute the distance between two parties' private vectors, while the first protocol must have a semi-honest third party and the second one was based on randomization technique rather than encryption [15]. Then Huang et al. continued to propose a secure computation protocol for the distance between two private vectors based on privacy homomorphism and scalar product [14], but the performance is not efficient enough for 2-dimensional vector. In 2018, Peng et al. put forward to a quantum protocol to calculate the distance between two private points based on QKD-based effective quantum private query [24]. However, this solution needs $O(n)$ space complexity and $O(N \log(N))$ communication complexity, and the fact performance has not been evaluated.

In this paper, we utilize a novel idea based on the Paillier cryptosystem and it can deal with negative value and be used to efficiently solve some secure two-party computational problems in the field of geometry.

3   Method of Homomorphic Subtraction of the Paillier Cryptosystem

The Paillier cryptosystem is a probabilistic asymmetric algorithm for public key cryptography [23]. The Paillier cryptosystem is a homomorphic cryptosystem that only supports additive homomorphisms. Even given only the public key and the ciphertext of m_1 and m_2, we can still calculate $E(m_1 + m_2) = E(m_1) \cdot E(m_2)$ [21].

Theorem 1. *Let* $((n, g), (\lambda, \mu), E, D, \mathbb{Z}_n)$ *be a Paillier encryption scheme [20],* $f = m_1 \cdot m_2 + m_3 \cdot m_4 + ... + m_{2i+1} \cdot m_{2i+2} + ... + m_{2k+1} \cdot m_{2k+2}$, *where* $|m_j| \in \mathbb{Z}_n$, $0 \le i \le k$, $f \in \mathbb{Z}_n$, *we define that* $m'_j = n + m_j$ *if* $m_j < 0$ *otherwise* $m'_j = m_j$ *and* $f' = m'_1 \cdot m'_2 + m'_3 \cdot m'_4 + ... + m'_{2i+1} \cdot m'_{2i+2} + ... + m'_{2k+1} \cdot m'_{2k+2}$, *then* $D(E(f)) = D(E(f'))$.

Proof. Obviously,

$$f' = m'_1 \cdot m'_2 + m'_3 \cdot m'_4 + ... + m'_{2i+1} \cdot m'_{2i+2} + ... + m'_{2k+1} \cdot m'_{2k+2},$$
$$f = m_1 \cdot m_2 + m_3 \cdot m_4 + ... + m_{2i+1} \cdot m_{2i+2} + ... + m_{2k+1} \cdot m_{2k+2},$$

so $f \equiv f' \mod n$, $f' = f + k \cdot n$.
By binomial theorem,

$$(1+n)^x = \sum_0^x \binom{x}{k} \cdot n^k = 1 + n \cdot x + \binom{x}{2} \cdot n^2 + higher\ power\ of\ n,$$

This indicates that:
$$(1+n)^x \equiv 1 + n \cdot x \mod n^2.$$

Generally, let $g = n + 1$, therefore,

$$g^{k \cdot n} \mod n^2 = (1+n)^{k \cdot n} \mod n^2 = (1 + k \cdot n \cdot n) \mod n^2 = 1.$$

$$E(f') = g^{f'} \cdot r_1^n \mod n^2$$
$$= g^{f+k \cdot n} \cdot r_1^n \mod n^2$$
$$= g^f g^{k \cdot n} \cdot r_1^n \mod n^2$$
$$= g^f \cdot r_1^n \mod n^2$$

$$E(f) = g^f \cdot r_2^n \mod n^2$$

Thus,
$$D(E(f)) = D(E(f')).$$

4   Building Block

An SMC problem for the distance between two private points will be introduced and its protocol will be able to be used as a building block of some other SMC problems in the field of computational geometry. And Protocol 1 will also help to solve other problems in the field of computational geometry.

$$\begin{aligned} |PQ|^2 &= T + D_A(t) \\ &= T + U + 2x_2 \cdot W + 2y_2 \cdot V \\ &= x_1^2 + y_1^2 + x_2^2 + y_2^2 + 2x_2(n - x_1) + 2y_2(n - y_1) \\ &= (x_1 - x_2)^2 + (y_1 - y_2)^2 \end{aligned} \tag{1}$$

Thus, Protocol 1 is correct.

Privacy. In Protocol 1, Alice knows x_1, y_1 and $|PQ|$, but she cannot infer $Q(x_2, y_2)$ from these information. Similarly, Bob only knows $|PQ|$ and cannot infer $P(x_1, y_1)$.

But we notice that Protocol 1 is correct if $(x_1 - x_2)^2 + (y_1 - y_2)^2 \in Z_n$. Let one of the public encryption key parameters of a Paillier cryptosystem be n, Protocol 1 should be correct if $0 \le x_1, y_1, x_2, y_2 < \sqrt{\frac{n}{2}}$ to any two points $P(x_1, y_1)$ and $Q(x_2, y_2)$.

Protocol 1: Distance between two private points

Inputs: Alice's private point $P(x_1, y_1)$ and Bob's private point $Q(x_2, y_2)$.

Output: The distance $|PQ|$ between $P(x_1, y_1)$ and $Q(x_2, y_2)$.

The protocol:

1. Setup:
   Alice generates a key pair for a Paillier cryptosystem and sends the public key to Bob. The corresponding encryption and decryption is denoted as $E_A(\cdot)$ and $D_A(\cdot)$.
2. Alice:
   (a) computes $T = x_1^2 + y_1^2$, $W = n - x_1$ and $V = n - y_1$.
   (b) computes $E_A(W)$, $E_A(V)$ and sends them to Bob.
3. Bob:
   (a) computes $U = x_2^2 + y_2^2$.
   (b) computes $t = E_A(U) \cdot E_A(W)^{2x_2} \cdot E_A(V)^{2y_2}$ and sends it to Alice.
4. Alice:
   (a) computes $|PQ| = (T + D_A(t))^{\frac{1}{2}}$.
   (b) tells the distance $|PQ|$ to Bob.

The SMC problem of distance between two private points have been studied [17]. The solution as a building block has been employed in some solutions to solve secure computational problems in the field of geometry. The existing secure two-party computation solution to the problem is based on OT_m^1 oblivious transfer protocol where m is a security parameter such that $\frac{1}{m}$ should be small enough. This solution needs 4 times OT_m^1 oblivious transfer, so it is highly inefficient. In general, modular multiplication(or exponentiation) operations are the most time-consuming computation, so modular multiplications will be only counted as the cost. In Protocol 1, our solution only takes 3 times public key encryptions and 1 time decryption which needs about $7 \log(n)$ times modular multiplications and Li's solution needs about $4 \cdot (2m + 3) \log(q)$ times modular multiplications, where q is a large modulo prime. So our solution is more efficient.

5 Relationship Between a Private Circle Area and a Private Point

Li et al. have also studied and solved some other SMC problems in the field of geometry based on the relationship between two private points [22]. We can also apply our Protocol 1 as a new building block to these secure computational geometric problems and these new solutions should be more efficient. In order to illustrate the practical applications of Theorem 1, we also will introduce a more efficient and private solution to secure multi-party computation problem of the relationship between a circle area and a private point.

The solution proposed by Li et al. can determine the relationship between a private circle area and a private point is based on whether the distance between the private point and the center of the private circle is greater than the radius of the circle [17,22]. For example, Bob decides to bomb a circle area whose center is $Q(x_2, y_2)$ and radius is r in another country, Alice has an interesting point of $P(x_1, y_1)$. Using Protocol 2 in [17], if Alice knows $|PQ| > r$ and Bob can bomb the circle area, but if $|PQ| \leq r$, Alice can tell her interesting point and Bob cannot bomb the point. If the point $P(x_1, y_1)$ is not within the circle area, no information should be known by Alice and Bob. Li et al. claims that Protocol 2 in [17] is private, but we find two drawbacks. We describe them as follows.

1. After Protocol 2 in [17] is completed, though Alice cannot know $Q(x_2, y_2)$ and r, but she can know that the center point $Q(x_2, y_2)$ of the circle is on the circumference of a circle whose center is $P(x_1, y_1)$ and radius is $|PQ|$. Figure 1 shows the knowledge known by Alice.

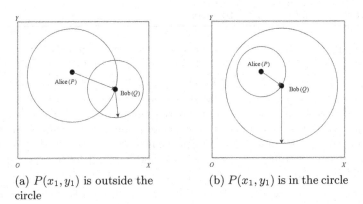

(a) $P(x_1, y_1)$ is outside the circle

(b) $P(x_1, y_1)$ is in the circle

Fig. 1. The knowledge known by Alice after executing Protocol 2 in Li's solution.

2. Suppose that Alice has more than one point of interest, for example two points, $P_0(x_0, y_0)$ and $P_1(x_1, y_1)$. Alice can compute the possible center point $Q(x_2, y_2)$ of the circle area according to the following formulas:

$$\begin{cases} |P_0Q| = \sqrt{(x_0 - x_2)^2 + (y_0 - y_2)^2} \\ |P_1Q| = \sqrt{(x_1 - x_2)^2 + (y_1 - y_2)^2} \end{cases} \tag{2}$$

In Ref. [22], Luo et al. also proposed a point-inclusion protocol (Protocol 2) based on their protocol to the secure two-party computation problem of distance between two private points, but some drawbacks still remain. In Protocol 2 [22],

$$u' = (x_0 - a)^2 + (y_0 - b)^2 + v'$$
$$u'' = v - v' - r^2$$
$$u = u' + u''$$
$$u \overset{?}{\leftrightarrow} v \Leftrightarrow (x_0 - a)^2 + (y_0 - b)^2 \overset{?}{\leftrightarrow} r^2$$

Suppose that,

$$\begin{cases} (x_0 - a)^2 + (y_0 - b)^2 = n - 5 \\ v' = 8 \\ r^2 = 1 \\ v = 20 \end{cases}$$

$$u' = (x_0 - a)^2 + (y_0 - b)^2 + v'$$
$$= n - 5 + 8$$
$$= n + 3$$
$$\equiv 3 \quad \mathrm{mod} \quad n$$
$$u = u' + u''$$
$$= 3 + v - v' - r^2$$
$$= 3 + 20 - 8 - 1$$
$$= 14$$
$$u < v$$

But, because of the large prime n, $(n-5) > 1$, i.e., $(x_0 - a)^2 + (y_0 - b)^2 > r^2$, as is inconsistent with $u < v$.

We introduce a new protocol based on our Protocol 1 to the secure multi-party computation of the relationship between a private point and a circle area. Our protocol can get rid of the above-mentioned drawbacks.

Similarly, we notice that Protocol 2 is correct if $(x_1 - x_2)^2 + (y_1 - y_2)^2 + R \in Z_n$. Protocol 2 must be correct if $0 \leq x_1, y_1, x_2, y_2 < \sqrt{\frac{n}{4}}$ and $0 \leq r < \sqrt{\frac{n}{2}}$ and $0 \leq R < \frac{n}{2}$.

Privacy.

1. Compared with Protocol 2 in Ref. [17], after Protocol 2 is completed, Alice cannot know that the center point $Q(x_2, y_2)$ of the circle is on the circumference of a circle whose center is $P(x_1, y_1)$ and radius is $|PQ|$ due to the random number R.
2. Even if Alice has more than one point of interest, for example two points, $P_0(x_0, y_0)$ and $P_1(x_1, y_1)$, Alice cannot compute the possible center point $Q(x_2, y_2)$ of the circle area according to the following formulas due to the random numbers R_0 and R_1:

$$\begin{cases} u_0 = (x_0 - x_2)^2 + (y_0 - y_2)^2 + R_0 \\ u_1 = (x_1 - x_2)^2 + (y_1 - y_2)^2 + R_1 \end{cases} \tag{3}$$

So Protocol 2 is more private than Protocol 2 in Ref [17].

Protocol 2: Relationship between a private circle area and a private point

Inputs: A private point $P(x_1, y_1)$ and a circle area whose center is $Q(x_2, y_2)$ and radius is r.

Output: Whether or not $P(x_1, y_1)$ is outside the circle area.

The protocol:

1. Setup:
   Alice generates a key pair for a Paillier cryptosystem and sends the public key to Bob. The corresponding encryption and decryption is denoted as $E_A(\cdot)$ and $D_A(\cdot)$.
2. Alice:
   (a) computes $T = x_1^2 + y_1^2$, $W = n - x_1$ and $V = n - y_1$.
   (b) computes $E_A(W)$, $E_A(V)$ and sends them to Bob.
3. Bob:
   (a) computes $U = x_2^2 + y_2^2$ and generates a random number R.
   (b) computes $t = E_A(U + R) \cdot E_A(W)^{2x_2} \cdot E_A(V)^{2y_2}$ and sends it to Alice.
   (c) computes $v = r^2 + R$.
4. Alice computes $u = T + D_A(t)$ and Alice and Bob can decide which of u and v is larger by using Yao's Millionaire protocol. If $u > v$, then $P(x_1, y_1)$ is outside the circle area; and if $u \leq v$, then $P(x_1, y_1)$ is in the circle area, or on the circumference.

---

6 Efficiency Analysis and Experiment Results

In this paper, we introduce a secure two-party computation protocol to distance between two private points based on the Paillier cryptosystem supporting subtraction. Li's solution is based on OT_m^1 Oblivious Transfer protocol, where m is a security parameter such that $\frac{1}{m}$ is small enough. Their solution needs 4 times OT_m^1 oblivious transfer. As we mentioned before, modular exponentiation operation is the most time-consuming computation. OT_m^1 Oblivious Transfer protocol takes $2m + 3$ times modular exponentiations, and one Paillier cryptosystem encryption takes modular exponentiation only once and one decryption also takes modular exponentiation only once [21]. Based on the above discussion, we summarize the results of time-consuming in Table 1 and communication cost in Table 2. Results show that the computational cost of our solution is the same as Luo's, and the communication traffic is less than Luo's. And both of Luo's and our solutions are more efficient than Li's solution.

Table 1. Comparison of computational time-consuming results.

Protocol	Alice	Bob	Total
Li's solution [17]	12	$8m$	$8m + 12$
Luo's solution [22]	2	3	5
Ours (Protocol 1)	2	3	5

Note: computation cost is measured in the number of modular exponentiations.

Table 2. Comparison of communication cost results.

Protocol	Communication traffic	Rounds
Li's solution [17]	$8m + 4$	9[a]
Luo's solution [22]	4	3
Ours (Protocol 1)	3	3[a]

Note: communication cost is measured in the number of large numbers and the number of communication rounds.
[a]The last round in Li's solution and our solution is not in Luo's solution, so it is not counted while comparing.

To better compare the actual computational cost of our solution based on the Paillier homomorphic cryptosystem supporting subtraction and Li's solution based on OT_m^1 Oblivious Transfer protocol, we implement our Protocol 1 and Li's solution [17] based on Charm-Crypto framework in Python 2.7. We builded the Charm-Crypto framework based on GMP 6.0.0 without the side-channel silent mpz_powm_sec function. All experiments were performed on a computer running the Ubuntu subsystem on a Windows 10 system with a 3.50 GHz Intel i5-4690 processor and 8 GB of RAM. The results are summarized in Table 3 and Fig. 2.

Table 3. Experiment results of Li's solution.

Security parameter m	Processing time (ms)
2^1	9
2^5	98
2^8	760
2^{10}	3037
2^{11}	6053
2^{12}	12113
2^{13}	24233
2^{14}	48609
2^{15}	97096

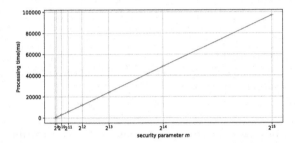

Fig. 2. Processing time vs. security parameter m.

From Table 3 and Fig. 2, we can see that as security parameter m increases linearly the cost of Li's solution is increased linearly. If Bob chooses to guess, his chance of guessing the correct x_1 is $\frac{1}{m^2}$. So the chance that Bob guesses the correct point $P(x_1, y_1)$ is $\frac{1}{m^4}$, which should be small enough. Li's solution should be secure while the probability of a random guess is $\frac{1}{2^{80}}$, and the processing time is about **52** min. Except for the key setup and the decrypting time, the processing time of our Protocol 1 is only **4** ms and the total processing time is about **8** ms while the key length of n is 1024 bits (80-bit AES security level) and encryption operation can be simplified to $(nm+1) \cdot r^n \mod n^2$. In summary, our Protocol 1 is more effective and practical based on the Paillier cryptosystem than Li's one based on OT_m^1 Oblivious Transfer protocol.

In addition, we also compare the fact computation cost of our solution based on the Paillier cryptosystem and the solution based on the BGN cryptosystem. The BGN cryptosystem is also implemented using Python 2.7 based on Charm-Crypto. The reasonable solution can also be easily constructed based on the BGN cryptosystem by multiplication in ciphertext space and omitted in this paper. The discrete logarithm is computed by using Pollard's kangaroo algorithm. In Table 4, the BGN cryptosystem is tested based on composite-order group (Type a1 pairing, Base field size is 1024 bits) and primer-order group (Type f pairing, Base field size is 160 bits) at 80-bit security level, respectively [4,8].

Table 4. Processing time (ms) of two solutions based on BGN ($L = 10^8$) and Paillier at 80-bit security level.

Protocol phase	BGN (composite-order)	BGN (prime-order)	Paillier
Setup	56.6	152.5	2.7
Protocol execution	130.4	140.1	4
Result decryption	430.5	7442	1.3

Overall, Table 4 shows that our solution is also more efficient based on the Paillier cryptosystem than the solutions base on the BGN cryptosystem over composite-order and prime-order group at 80-bit security level. In addition, the plaintext of the BGN-based solution must be restricted to be in some small range L, and its decryption can be quickly computed in $O(\sqrt{L})$ time. It is a serious disadvantage if the plaintext needs to be in some large range. The plaintext of our solution can be in some large range L (for example $L = 2^{1024}$ and $0 \leq x, y < 2^{511}$ at 80-bit security level in Protocol 2. However, the plaintext of the BGN-based solution must be restricted to be in some small range L, for example $L = 10^8$ and $0 \leq x, y < 5000$. So our solution based on Paillier cryptosystem is better while the plaintext can be in some large range.

7   Conclusion and Future Work

We have introduced a method and application of homomorphic subtraction in the Paillier cryptosystem. It is a novel idea and very useful in the fields of secure multi-party computational geometry. We have used it to solve the secure two-party computation problem for the distance between two private points, which can also be used as a building block of some other secure multi-party computational problems in the field of geometry. Our solution is more efficient and private than Li's solution. Morevoer, our protocol is also more efficient than the solution based on the BGN scheme. The plaintext of our solution can be in some large range, but the BGN scheme must be restricted to be in some small range. So our solution based on Paillier cryptosystem is better while the plaintext can be in some large range. We also have addressed some drawbacks in Li's and Luo's solution. There are some interesting secure multi-party computational problems in the field of geometry that can be studied based on our idea. For example, we will study the secure multi-party computational problem for the relationship between a private point and a private polygon area and propose some efficient solutions to them. Moreover, we also think that our method can be used in some other security fields.

References

1. Agrawal, R., Srikant, R.: Privacy-preserving data mining. In: Proceedings of the 2000 ACM SIGMOD International Conference on Management of Data, SIGMOD 2000, pp. 439–450. ACM, New York (2000)
2. Atallah, M.J., Du, W.: Secure multi-party computational geometry. In: Dehne, F., Sack, J.-R., Tamassia, R. (eds.) WADS 2001. LNCS, vol. 2125, pp. 165–179. Springer, Heidelberg (2001). https://doi.org/10.1007/3-540-44634-6_16
3. Au, M.H., Liu, J.K., Fang, J., Jiang, Z.L., Susilo, W., Zhou, J.: A new payment system for enhancing location privacy of electric vehicles. IEEE Trans. Veh. Technol. **63**(1), 3–18 (2014)
4. Barker, E., Barker, W., Burr, W., Polk, W., Smid, M.: NIST SP800-57: recommendation for key management part 1: general (revised). Technical report, NIST (2007)
5. Bilogrevic, I., Jadliwala, M., Joneja, V., Kalkan, K., Hubaux, J.P., Aad, I.: Privacy-preserving optimal meeting location determination on mobile devices. IEEE Trans. Inf. Forensics Secur. **9**(7), 1141–1156 (2014)
6. Yang, B., Yang, C.H., Yu, Y., Xie, D.: A secure scalar product protocol and its applications to computational geometry. J. Comput. **8**(8), 2018–2026 (2013)
7. Bogetoft, P., et al.: Secure multiparty computation goes live. In: Dingledine, R., Golle, P. (eds.) FC 2009. LNCS, vol. 5628, pp. 325–343. Springer, Heidelberg (2009). https://doi.org/10.1007/978-3-642-03549-4_20
8. Boneh, D., Goh, E.-J., Nissim, K.: Evaluating 2-DNF formulas on ciphertexts. In: Kilian, J. (ed.) TCC 2005. LNCS, vol. 3378, pp. 325–341. Springer, Heidelberg (2005). https://doi.org/10.1007/978-3-540-30576-7_18
9. Dachman-Soled, D., Malkin, T., Raykova, M., Yung, M.: Efficient robust private set intersection. Int. J. Appl. Cryptol. **2**(4), 289–303 (2012)
10. Du, W., Atallah, M.J.: Privacy-preserving cooperative scientific computations. In: Proceedings of the 14th IEEE Workshop on Computer Security Foundations, CSFW 2001, Washington, DC, USA, pp. 273–282. IEEE Computer Society (2001)
11. Du, W., Han, Y.S., Chen, S.: Privacy-preserving multivariate statistical analysis: linear regression and classification. In: Proceedings of the 4th SIAM International Conference on Data Mining, Lake Buena Vista, Florida, vol. 233, pp. 222–233 (2004)
12. Freedman, M.J., Nissim, K., Pinkas, B.: Efficient private matching and set intersection. In: Cachin, C., Camenisch, J.L. (eds.) EUROCRYPT 2004. LNCS, vol. 3027, pp. 1–19. Springer, Heidelberg (2004). https://doi.org/10.1007/978-3-540-24676-3_1
13. Freeman, D.M.: Converting pairing-based cryptosystems from composite-order groups to prime-order groups. In: Gilbert, H. (ed.) EUROCRYPT 2010. LNCS, vol. 6110, pp. 44–61. Springer, Heidelberg (2010). https://doi.org/10.1007/978-3-642-13190-5_3
14. Huang, H., Gong, T., Chen, P., Malekian, R., Chen, T.: Secure two-party distance computation protocol based on privacy homomorphism and scalar product in wireless sensor networks. Tsinghua Sci. Technol. **21**(4), 385–396 (2016)
15. Huang, H., Gong, T., Chen, P., Qiu, G., Wang, R.: Secure two-party distance computation protocols with a semihonest third party and randomization for privacy protection in wireless sensor networks. Int. J. Distrib. Sens. Netw. **11**(7), 475150 (2015)

16. Jha, S., Kruger, L., McDaniel, P.: Privacy preserving clustering. In: di Vimercati, S.C., Syverson, P., Gollmann, D. (eds.) ESORICS 2005. LNCS, vol. 3679, pp. 397–417. Springer, Heidelberg (2005). https://doi.org/10.1007/11555827_23
17. Li, S.D., Dai, Y.Q.: Secure two-party computational geometry. J. Comput. Sci. Technol. **20**(2), 258–263 (2005)
18. Lindell, Y., Pinkas, B.: Privacy preserving data mining. In: Bellare, M. (ed.) CRYPTO 2000. LNCS, vol. 1880, pp. 36–54. Springer, Heidelberg (2000). https://doi.org/10.1007/3-540-44598-6_3
19. Liu, L., Wu, C., Li, S.: Two privacy-preserving protocols for point-curve relation. J. Electron. (China) **29**(5), 422–430 (2012)
20. Liu, M., et al.: Privacy-preserving matrix product based static mutual exclusive roles constraints violation detection in interoperable role-based access control. Future Gener. Comput. Syst. (2018)
21. Liu, M., Zhang, X., Yang, C., Pang, S., Puthal, D., Ren, K.: Privacy-preserving detection of statically mutually exclusive roles constraints violation in interoperable role-based access control. In: 2017 IEEE Trustcom/BigDataSE/ICESS, pp. 502–509. IEEE (2017)
22. Luo, Y.L., Huang, L.S., Zhong, H.: Secure two-party point-circle inclusion problem. J. Comput. Sci. Technol. **22**(1), 88–91 (2007)
23. Paillier, P.: Public-key cryptosystems based on composite degree residuosity classes. In: Stern, J. (ed.) EUROCRYPT 1999. LNCS, vol. 1592, pp. 223–238. Springer, Heidelberg (1999). https://doi.org/10.1007/3-540-48910-X_16
24. Peng, Z., Shi, R., Wang, P., Zhang, S.: A novel quantum solution to secure two-party distance computation. Quantum Inf. Process. **17**(6), 1–12 (2018). https://doi.org/10.1007/s11128-018-1911-0
25. Qin, J., Duan, H., Zhao, H., Hu, J.: A new lagrange solution to the privacy-preserving general geometric intersection problem. J. Netw. Comput. Appl. **46**, 94–99 (2014)
26. Shih, D.H., Huang, H.Y., Yen, D.C.: A secure reverse Vickrey auction scheme with bid privacy. Inf. Sci. **176**(5), 550–564 (2006)
27. Xie, Q., Hengartner, U.: Privacy-preserving matchmaking for mobile social networking secure against malicious users. In: Proceedings of the 2011 Ninth Annual International Conference on Privacy, Security and Trust (PST), pp. 252–259. IEEE (2011)
28. Xiong, H., Zhang, E., Chim, T., Yiu, S., Hui, L.C.K.: Weighted average problem revisited under hybrid and malicious model. In: Proceedings of the 2012 8th International Conference on Computing Technology and Information Management, vol. 2, pp. 677–682 (2012)
29. Yang, B., Shao, Z., Zhang, W.: Secure two-party protocols on planar convex hulls. J. Inf. Comput. Sci. **9**(4), 915–929 (2012)
30. Yang, B., Sun, A., Zhang, W.: Secure two-party protocols on planar circles. J. Inf. **8**(1), 29–40 (2011)
31. Yao, A.C.: Protocols for secure computations. In: Proceedings of the 23rd Annual Symposium on Foundations of Computer Science, SFCS 1982, Washington, DC, USA, pp. 160–164. IEEE Computer Society (1982)

A Secure Data Access Control Scheme Without Bilinear Pairing in Edge Computing

Xiaofei Sheng[1], Junhua Wu[1], Guangshun Li[1,2]($\boxtimes$), Qingyan Lin[1], and Yonghui Yao[1]

[1] College of Information Science and Engineering, Qufu Normal University, Rizhao 266700, China
guangshunli@qfnu.edu.cn
[2] Hong Kong Polytechnic University, Hong Kong, China

Abstract. Edge computing, as an extension of cloud computing, subcontracts the personal private data to edge nodes on the edge network of Internet of Things (IoT) to decrease transmission delay and network congestion. So, a major security concern in edge computing is access control issues for shared data. In this paper we introduce a scheme without bilinear pairing encryption (Un-BPE) to provide access control in edge and cloud communication. To achieve confidentiality, verifiability and access control, the secret key is generated by Key Trust Authority (KTA), end users and edge node together, and saved in cloud platform; the operations of verification are performed by the adjacent edge node; and the operations of encryption and decryption are performed by the terminal device. We verify the efficiency of our scheme in terms of the security of the encryption algorithm and the performance of the system. The analysis of the proposed scheme reveals better computational efficiency.

Keywords: Access control · Edge computing · Bilinear pairing · Data encryption

1 Introduction

Cloud computing [1] can provide elastic computing resources to users, meet the requirement of the end users. However, the centralized computing systems are starting to suffer from the unbearable transmission latency and degraded service due to the development of IoT and big data. Edge computing is a burgeoning technology with distributed system, which has the characteristics of location awareness, low latency, mobility support, etc. [2]. It can not only process a large

Supported by organization x.

amount of data and improve our quality of life, but also collect real-time data for data monitoring and analysis [3].

Although edge computing network extends computing resources to the edge of the network, greatly improving the resource transmission efficiency [4,5], but it also has many security issues similar to those in the cloud [6]. Communication security is one of the most important concerns for users when using edge computing to transfer data to the cloud for storage and processing [7]. In the process of communication, edge computing network is threatened by data abnormal change, location privacy disclosure and unauthorized access [8,9]. Moreover, they are more easily compromised and low-trustworthy since fog nodes are deployed at the network edge with much lower cost than cloud servers [10], they are more vulnerable to attacks and less reliable. At the same time, Alrawais et al. pointed out that the research on the security of fog computing in the IoT is still in its infancy, and faces many security access problems [11].

In order to effectively solve the authentication, privacy protection, access control and other important issues [12] in edge computing. [13] researched the authentication and authorization of IoT, and pointed out that the cost of authentication and authorization should be allocated to the edge nodes. It lays a foundation for researching the authentication and authorization technology in edge computing. [14] proposes a fine-grained data access control protocol based on the properties and cipher text updates, In order to ensure the security of data, outsourcing sensitive data to the cloud storage. But it leads to the transmission delay of the data. Outsourcing most of the encryption and decryption operations to the fog node will lead to the decrypted ciphertext in the process of sending to the user is attacked. Yang et al. proposed a concrete construction with lightweight computational overhead for health IoT system, introducing a semi-trusted computing center to perform most of the heavy calculations in the data encryption phase, which reduces the computational energy consumption of user terminals [15], but it cannot guarantee the correctness of the ciphertext. Chen et al. proposed ABS outsourcing protocols, which greatly reduced the computing overhead of the client side by outsourcing intensive computing to untrusted CSP [16], but the signature of this protocol was of high complexity. Our protocol does not completely rely on CSP for key generation, and delegates some operations to edge nodes and users, which guarantees the security of ciphertext and reduces the computation of edge nodes.

Similar to the cloud servers, edge nodes are not fully trusted as well, data security would raise great concerns from users when they store sensitive data on cloud servers through edge nodes [17,18]. To ensure secure communication, Al-Riyami and Paterson put forward the certificateless public key cryptography, in which not only ID-based cryptography (IBC) solved the key escrow problem, but also the users private key is generated by the user and the key generation center (KGC) together [19]. This result in KGC cannot obtain the users complete private key, solving the problem of untrusted third parties. Huang et al. proposed a certificateless multi-recipient encryption (AMCLE) protocol that based on bilinear pairing and mapping to point (MTP) hash functions [20], which are less efficient and time consuming. Li et al. performed a security proof on the certificateless signcryption mechanism proposed by the random oracle model [21], but this protocol requires multiple bilinear mapping operations. Scheme [20,21] uses bilinear mapping for key generation and signcryption calculation, all of which have low computational efficiency. In addition, existing symmetric [22] ciphers cannot meet the security and privacy requirements of data transmission based on edge computing. Inspired by these questions, we proposed a certificateless multi-receiver scheme without bilinear pairing to edge computing, which uses scalar point multiplication to improve computational efficiency. In addition, in order to conduct the security of the key escrow, the edge node and the end users respectively calculate the private key and the public key, thereby ensuring the security of the key and reducing the users computing. This paper main contributions are as follows: (1) A key authentication scheme without bilinear pairing encryption (Un-BPE) in edge computing is proposed to improve the efficient and security of data access control. (2) Outsourcing part of the encryption and decryption operations to the KTA, reducing the amount of computing by the end user; secret key generation is done by the KTA, the end users and the edge nodes together, ensuring its security.

2   Preliminaries

2.1   Secure Data Access Model

The securely system model consists of core cloud platform(CC), edge node(EN), key trust authority(KTA), IoT data owner(DR) and IoT end user(IE), as shown in Fig. 1.

Core cloud platform (CC): It has high computing power and data storage capacity for storing the final key and ciphertext.

Edge node (EN): It is deployed at the edge of the network and provides various services, includes master edge node EN_m and adjacent edge node EN_a. The edge node is mainly responsible for generating the public key; transmitting the public key and ciphertext through the secure channel.

Key trust authority (KTA): It generates the master key and system parameters and publishes for the system. When the end users request data access, it can generate the partial secret key to ensure the security of sensitive data. We assume that the key trust authority is semi-trusted.

Internet of Things end user (IE): It used to generate the private value and the private value parameter of the end users and store it. After receiving the ciphertext and the secret key from the edge node, To fished the decrypted process and verified it.

Internet of Things data owner (DR): It stores some temporary real-time data in the IoT device to capture resources in the cloud. It used to generate ciphertext and transmit it to the edge node.

2.2   Computational Problems

In what follows, the definitions of computational Diffie-Hellman problem, and assumptions are given.

Definition 1. *Computational Diffie-Hellman (CDH) problem. Let P be a generator of the additive cyclic group G of order p. Given $P \in G_p$, $a, b \in Z_p^*$, to meet $Q = aP, R = bP$. Computation of abP is computationally hard by a polynomial time-bounded algorithm. The probability that a polynomial time-bounded algorithm A can solve the CDH problem is defined as:*

$$Adv^{CDH}(A) = Pr[A(P, Q, R) = abP | a, b \in Z_p^*, Q, R \in G_p].$$

Definition 2. *Computational Diffie-Hellman assumption. For any probabilistic polynomial time-bounded algorithm A, $Adv^{CDH}(A)$ is negligible. That is, $Adv^{CDH}(A) \leq \varepsilon$. For some negligible function ε, every $0 < k^c < 1$, there exists k_0 such that $\varepsilon(k) \leq k^c$ for every $k \geq k_0$.*

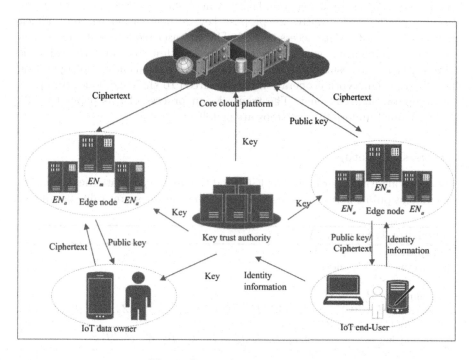

Fig. 1. Secure data access model.

2.3 Security Models

Our scheme can establish secure communication in edge computing network. Therefore, the system should satisfy the following security target.

Message Confidentiality: Users' private data is only provided to legal node. In our proposed system, we use the UN-BPE scheme to ensure the securely communication of the access control.

Message Authentication: Our system should resist the petaggressive, prevents the attacker to change or steal the data information. Therefore, we should introduce a appropriate security mechanisms to ensure the validity of the data. In addition, we have set up message validation steps to enhance key security.

Key escrow security: In our scheme, KTA is adopted for key management and distribution, so as to reduce the risk of user privacy data leakage during data access and ensure the security of data transmission.

3 The Proposed Protocol

In edge computing, reducing complexity is necessary because most devices are resource constrained. Firstly, we propose key authentication without bilinear pairing to guarantee data access control. The end user requests data access, and decrypts the ciphertext with the decryption algorithm. Secondly, the KTA distributes the key to ensure its security; and performs partial encryption operation. Thirdly, the signcryption operation is outsourced to the edge node to improve the computational efficiency. The transmission process of this paper uses the secure channel uniformly. The steps are as follows:

3.1 System Setup

The Setup algorithm is running by KTA and the user to generate the master key, the systems public parameters, users secret value and the secret value parameter.

Algorithm 1. Setup.KTA

1: **Input:** k, p, E
2: Selecting the G_p and P
3: Selecting $S \in Z_p^*$
4: Computing $P_{pub} = SP$
5: Selecting $H_0 : \{0,1\}^* \times Z_p^* \to Z_p^*$, $H_1 : \{0,1\}^* \times Z_p^* \times Z_p^* \to Z_p^*$, $H_2 : \{0,1\}^* \to Z_p^*$, $H_3 : \{0,1\}^* \times G_p \times Z_p^* \times Z_p^* \times \ldots \times Z_p^* \to Z_p^*$.
6: Computing $params = < p, F_p, E, G_p, P_{pub}, E_k, D_k, H_0, H_1, H_2, H_3 >$

The KTA runs the Algorithm 1, and then saves the master key S secretly, and announces the systems public parameter $Params$. Where k is a generates elliptic curve, p is a prime integer, E is an elliptic curve that defined on finite field F_p, G_p is an additive cyclic group on E and its generator P, the master key S is a randomly chosen integer, P_{pub} is the systems public key, E_k is a symmetric encryption function, D_k is the corresponding decryption function, H_0, H_1, H_2, H_3 are the secure hash functions.

The user selects a randomly generated integers $v_i \in Z_p^*$, and then edge nodes through a secure channel send $V_i = v_i P$ and the identity information ID_i to KTA, and saves the v_i secretly, where v_i is the secret value of the ID_i, V_i is the secret value parameter of the ID_i.

3.2   Key Generation

The key generation algorithm is running by the user, the edge node and the KTA, and finally generates the users public and private keys.

Algorithm 2. KeyGen.KTA

1: Selecting $d_i \in Z_p^*$
2: Computing $Pp_i = H_0(ID_i, V_i)P + d_i P$
3: Computing $Ps_i = H_0(ID_i, V_i)P + (s + d_i)(mod p)$

After receiving the ID_i and V_i from the user, the KTA runs the Algorithm 2 to obtain the users partial public key Pp_i and the partial private key Ps_i, and transmits Ps_i and Pp_i to the edge node through the secure channel. Where the d_i is a randomly secret integer.

Then the edge node runs the Algorithm 3 to obtain the user public key PK_i and saves it.

Algorithm 3. KeyGen.edge

1: checking whether the equation $Ps_i P = Pp_i + P_{pub}$
2: If its really, performing the step 4
3: Else rejecting the Ps_i and Pp_i
4: computing $PK_i = Pp_i + H_1(ID_i, V_i, d_i)V_i$

Proof: The establishment of the equation $Ps_i P = Pp_i + P_{pub}$ guarantees the correctness of the partial private key verification of the user. The derivation process can be expressed in Eq. (1).

$$\begin{aligned}
Ps_i &= (H_0(ID_i, V_i) + s + d_i) \\
&= H_0(ID_i, V_i)P + d_i P + sP \\
&= Pp_i + P_{pub}
\end{aligned} \tag{1}$$

Through the above derivation, the equation $Ps_i P = Pp_i + P_{pub}$ is established. The results show that the key extraction algorithm is correct for the partial private key verification.

Then the user computes $SK_i = H_0(ID_i, PK_i)(PS_i, V_i, d_i)v_i)(mod p)$ as the private key, and saves it.

3.3   Data Signcryption

The data signcryption algorithm is running by the data owner r, and finally generates the ciphertext and the verification message.

Algorithm 4. Sign-cryption

1: Computing $Q_i = PK_i + P_p ub$, where $i = 1, 2, \cdots, n$
2: Selecting $w \in Z_p^*$
3: Computing W=wP, $F_i = wH_0(ID_i, PK_i)Q_i$ and $\alpha_i = H_1(ID_i, F_i, W)$, where $i = 1, 2, \cdots, n$
4: Selecting $\zeta \in Z_p^*$
5: Computing $f(x) = \prod_{i=1}^n (x - a_i) + \zeta(mod p) = a_0 + a_1 x + \cdots + a_{n-1}x^{n-1} + x^n, a_i \in Z_p^*$
6: Computing $k = H_2(\zeta)$, $h = H_3(M||ID_r, \zeta, a_0, a_1, \cdots, a_{n-1}, W)$
7: Computing H^{-1} and making ites meet the $hh^{-1} \equiv 1 mod p$, computing $z = h^{-1}(SK_r + w)(mod p)$
8: Computing $T = < ID_r, W, M, z, j, a_0, a_1, \cdots, a_{n-1} >$
9: Computing $B = H_0(ID_r, PK_r,)W$, $J = E_\eta(T)$, $C = (B + J) \bigoplus P_{pub}$
10: Computing $V = < ID_r, C >$

The data owner r runs the Algorithm 4, and sends the ciphertext T to adjacent edge node of the end user through cloud platform, and sends the verification message V to the edge node EN_a adjacent to the master edge node EN_m. Where M is the plaintext.

3.4   Data Verification

The data verification algorithm is running by the adjacent edge node EN_a, and finally computes the T'.

Algorithm 5. Verification

1: Computing $B = H_0(ID_r, PK_r,)W$,
2: Computing $J' = C \bigoplus P_{pub} - B$,
3: Computing $T' = D_\eta(J')$

The adjacent edge node EN_a runs the Algorithm 5, and sends T' to the adjacent edge node of end user through the cloud platform. The adjacent edge nodes verify the $T' = T$ is true. If not, output terminator "$\perp$". Else, the edge node sends the ciphertext T to end user.

3.5   Data Decryption

The data decryption Algorithm 6 is running by the end user to obtain the plaintext M to decryption.

Algorithm 6. De-cryption

1: Computing $F_i = SK_iW$, $\alpha_i = H_1(ID_i, F_i, W)$
2: Computing $f(x) = \prod_{i=1}^{n}(x - a_i) + \zeta(modp) = a_0 + a_1x + \cdots + a_{n-1}x^{n-1} + x^n$ and $\zeta = f(\alpha_i)$
3: Computing $k = H_2(\zeta)$
4: Computing $h' = H_3(M||ID_r, \zeta, a_0, a_1, \cdots, a_{n-1}, W)$
5: Checking the $h' = h$ holds
6: If its really, performing the next step
7: Else rejecting the M and exit the process
8: Obtainable the PK_r and checking $hzP = H_0(ID_r, PK_r)(PK_r + P_{pub}) + W$ holds
9: If its really, then received the plaintext M and exit the process
10: Else rejecting the M and exit the process

Where PK_r is the public key of the data user.

Proof: The correctness of the decryption algorithm is guaranteed by $h' = h$ and $hzP = H_0(ID_r, PK_r)(PK_r + P_{pub}) + W$, and deductions that these two equations hold are shown in the following.

For every receiver r_i, with the ciphertext T, it has $F_i = SK_iW$ and $\alpha_i = H_1(ID_i, F_i, W)$. Then with the α_i, it can compute $\zeta = f(\alpha_i)$, and then obtain $k = H_2(\zeta)$. Finally it has $h' = H_3(M||ID_r, \zeta, a_0, a_1, \cdots, a_{n-1}, W)$. So the equation $h' = h$ holds.

When decrypting the identity ID_r of the data owner, the end user can obtain the data owners public key and has computing the Eq. (2).

$$
\begin{aligned}
hzP &= H_0(ID_r, PK_r)(PK_r + P_{pub}) + W \\
&= SK_rP + W \\
&= H_0(ID_r, PK_r)(Ps_r, +H_1(ID_r, V_r, d_j)v_r)P + W \quad (2) \\
&= H_0(ID_r, PK_r)(Pp_r, +H_1(ID_r, V_r, d_j)V_r + P_{pub}) + W \\
&= H_0(ID_r, PK_r)(PK_r + P_{pub}) + W
\end{aligned}
$$

4   Algorithms Analysis

4.1   System Cryptanalysis

In this section, we analyze the safety strength of our proposed scheme from the aspects of message confidentiality, authentication and unforgeability.

Message Confidentiality. In our scheme, we use the Un-BPE to ensure the safety of the key. Our model provides a model for encryption and decryption data, and Un-BPE provides the key of encryption and decryption. Since the public key is produced jointly by the KTA and the edge nodes, and the secret key is produced jointly by the KTA and the end user and kept privately by the end user. Thus spite nodes cannot gain the public key.

Authentication. Suppose that the cloud could send the key to the DR through the edge node, the DR use the algorithm Sign-cryption to encrypt data, and then disclosure the message. When the edge nodes gain the message, they need the public parameters, which are computed by algorithm Setup.KTA. At the same time, the edge nodes gain the verification message, and then it verify the signature via Sign-cryption. If passed, the edge node send the ciphertext and the end users decrypt the ciphertext to obtain the plaintext M; otherwise, it is termination.

Unforgeability. A malicious node must have the user's private key to product an available signature for a legitimate user, but the malicious node cannot deduce the private key. A malicious node cannot create a new available ciphertext from another user's ciphertext. If the malicious nodes alter the ciphertext, the receiver can use the algorithm to examine that the ciphertext is vicious. Therefore, we said that our proposed scheme is unfalsifiable.

4.2   Efficiency Comparison

Through the simulation experiment, some basic operation consumption time is tested: T_p refers to the time consumed by the table bilinear pair operation; T_e refers to the time consumed by the table modulus power operation; T_{pe} refers to the table bilinear pair exponential operation time; T_a refers to the time consumed by the point addition operation; $T_s m$ refers to the table scalar point multiplication operation Time consuming; T_h refers to the time it takes for the hash function to map to a point (MTP). The experimental environment is Dell notebook (i5-4200U CPU@1.60 GHz 8 GB memory Windows 7 operating system), the time spent on the above basic operations is shown in Table 1. It is worth noting that we only consider the time of these operations as defined in Table 1, and don't consider the time of other operations, because their run time is negligible compared to the operations defined in Table 1.

Table 2 shows the efficiency comparison between our protocol and the encryption and decryption phases of the [20, 24–26] protocol. Where n is the number of data recipients. Since the system setup and key generation phases are primarily performed on the KTA, and the safety of these two phases is more important, which was discussed in Chapter 5, we study the efficiency of the encryption and decryption phases. The protocols of [24] and [20] are based on certificateless encryption with bilinear pairing encryption algorithm, our protocol, [25] and [26] are based on the scalar point multiplication in ECC for encryption and

Table 1. Time consumed by basic operations/ms

Operation	Running time
T_p	12.019
T_e	34.068
T_{pe}	9.045
T_a	0.023
$T_s m$	6.032
T_h	6.720

decryption operations. As can be seen from Table 2, our protocol efficiency is more effective than [20,24], but lower than [25,26]. The reason is that our program decryption process has the steps to verify the source of the message, but the program [25,26] does not.

Table 2. Comparison of algorithm efficiency

Protocol	Encryption	Decryption
[24]	$2(n+1)T_e + (n+1)T_{sm}/2$	$T_{sm}/2 + T_{pe} + 2T_p + T_a$
[20]	$(n+1)T_{sm}/2 + nT_{pe} + nT_p + nT_h$	$T_{sm}/2 + T_p$
[25]	$(n+1)T_{sm}/2 + 2nT_a$	$T_{sm}/2$
[26]	$(3n+1)T_{sm}/2 + nT_a$	T_{sm}
Our protocol	$(n+1)T_{sm}/2 + nT_a$	$T_{sm} + T_a$

When the number of our data receivers is n=1, the comparison between our protocol and [20, 24–26] protocol is shown in Fig. 2. It can be clearly seen from Fig. 2 that our protocol is based on double-based without certificate. Linear encryption protocols are more efficient in the encryption and decryption phases. achieve the anonymity of the data receiver (end user), which means that no other device except the sender knows the identity of receiver. The protocol [24,25] doesn't consider the recipients anonymity, which means that the recipients identity in his ciphertext is directly revealed. Our protocol and [25] have partial private key verifiability, which can effectively prevent the KTA from generating false partial private keys to spoof end users. However, since protocols [20,24] and [26] have no partial private key verifiability, they cannot prevent malicious attacks. Our protocol and [24] implement the signature function to ensure the reliability of the message and prevent the attacker from pretending to send the message as the sender. However, the protocol [20,25,26] does not have this function. In short, our solution has more features, is safer and more suitable for practical applications.

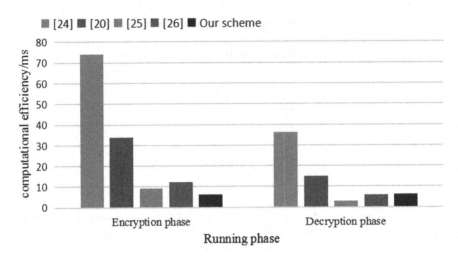

Fig. 2. Efficiency comparison.

5   Conclusion

In this paper, we propose to apply a non-bilinear pairing encryption protocol to edge computing. On the one hand, part of the calculation and storage is outsourced to the central edge node and key trust authority, so as to reduce the computational overhead of the end user, abandon the traditional bilinear pairing algorithm to improve efficiency; on the other hand, based on the Un-BPE algorithm, reduce The number of traditional ECC-encrypted scalar points, using KTA and the user to calculate the key at the same time, enhances the security of data access in edge computing.

References

1. Li, J., Yao, W., et al.: Flexible and fine-grained attribute-based data storage in cloud computing. IEEE Trans. Serv. Comput. **10**(5), 785–796 (2017)
2. Zhu, J.T., Shi, T., et al.: Task scheduling in deadline-aware mobile edge computing systems. IEEE Internet Things J. **6**(3), 4854–4866 (2019)
3. Rathore, M., Paul, A., et al.: IoT-based big data: from smart city towards next generation super city planning. Int. J. Seman. Web Inf. Syst. **13**(1), 28–47 (2017)
4. Li, G., Xi, S., et al.: Resource scheduling based on improved spectral clustering algorithm in edge computing. Sci. Program. **5**, 1–13 (2018)
5. Li, G., Liu, Y., et al.: Methods of resource scheduling based on optimized fuzzy clustering in fog computing. Sensors **19**(9), 2122 (2019)
6. Xi, Y., Qi, Y., et al.: IoT-based big data: from smart city towards next generation super city planning. Complexity, 1–9 (2017)
7. Shiraz, S.: The extended cloud: review and analysis of mobile edge computing and fog from a security and resilience perspective. IEEE J. Sel. Areas Commun. **35**(11), 2586–2595 (2017)

8. Zhang, J., Chen, B., et al.: Data security and privacy-preserving in edge computing paradigm: survey and open issues. IEEE Access **6**, 18209–18237 (2018)

9. Cai, Z., Zheng, X., et al.: A private and efficient mechanism for data uploading in smart cyber-physical systems. IEEE Trans. Netw. Sci. Eng., 1 (2018)

10. Hoe, S.L.: Defining a smart nation: the case of Singapore. J. Inf. Commun. Ethics Soc. **14**(4), 323–333 (2016)

11. Alrawais, A., Alhothaily, A., et al.: Fog computing for the internet of things: security and privacy issues. IEEE Internet Comput. **21**(2), 34–42 (2017)

12. Gai, K., Qiu, M., et al.: Blend arithmetic operations on tensor-based fully homomorphic encryption over real numbers. IEEE Trans. Ind. Inf. **14**(8), 3590–3598 (2018)

13. Kim, H., Lee, E., et al.: Authentication and authorization for the internet of things. IT Prof. **19**(5), 27–33 (2017)

14. Huang, Q., Yang, Y., et al.: Secure data access control with ciphertext update and computation outsourcing in fog computing for internet of things. IEEE Access **5**, 12941–12950 (2017)

15. Yang, Y., Zheng, X., et al.: Lightweight distributed secure data management system for health internet of things. J. Netw. Comput. Appl. **89**, 26–37 (2016)

16. Chen, X., Li, J., et al.: Secure outsourced attribute-based signatures. IEEE Trans. Parallel Distrib. Syst. **25**(12), 3285–3294 (2014)

17. Lee, K., Kim, D., et al.: On security and privacy issues of fog computing supported Internet of Things environment. In: International Conference on the Network of the Future, Montreal, pp. 1–3 (2015)

18. Roman, R., Lopez, J., et al.: Mobile edge computing, Fog et al.: a survey and analysis of security threats and challenges. Fut. Gener. Comput. Syst. **78**(TP.2), 680–698 (2018)

19. Alriyami, S.S., Paterson, K.G., et al.: Certificateless public key cryptography. Asiacrypt **2894**(2), 452–473 (2003)

20. Huang, Y.H., Huang, S.S., et al.: Efficient anonymous multireceiver certificateless encryption. IEEE Syst. J. **11**(4), 2602–2613 (2017)

21. Li, F., Shirase, M., et al.: Certificateless hybrid signcryption. Math. Comput. Model. **57**(3), 324–343 (2013)

22. Lester, C.G., Nachman, B., et al.: Bisection-based asymmetric MT2 computation: a higher precision calculator than existing symmetric methods. J. High Energy Phys. **3**, 1–16 (2015)

23. Yuan, Y., Li, D., Tian, L., Zhu, H.: Certificateless signature scheme without random oracles. In: Park, J.H., Chen, H.-H., Atiquzzaman, M., Lee, C., Kim, T., Yeo, S.-S. (eds.) ISA 2009. LNCS, vol. 5576, pp. 31–40. Springer, Heidelberg (2009). https://doi.org/10.1007/978-3-642-02617-1_4

24. Selvi, S.S.D., Vivek, S.S., Shukla, D., Rangan Chandrasekaran, P.: Efficient and provably secure certificateless multi-receiver signcryption. In: Baek, J., Bao, F., Chen, K., Lai, X. (eds.) ProvSec 2008. LNCS, vol. 5324, pp. 52–67. Springer, Heidelberg (2008). https://doi.org/10.1007/978-3-540-88733-1_4

25. Islam, S.H., Khan, M.K., et al.: Anonymous and provably secure certificateless multireceiver encryption without bilinear pairing. Secur. Commun. Netw. **8**(13), 2214–2231 (2015)

26. He, D., Wang, H., Wang, L., Shen, J., Yang, X.: Efficient certificateless anonymous multi-receiver encryption scheme for mobile devices. Soft Comput. **21**(22), 6801–6810 (2016). https://doi.org/10.1007/s00500-016-2231-x

Simulations on the Energy Consumption of WRF on Meteorological Cloud

Junwen Lu[1], Yongsheng Hao[2,3](✉), and Xianmei Hua[4]

[1] Engineering Research Center for Software Testing and Evaluation of Fujian Province, Xiamen University of Technology, Xiamen 361024, China
[2] School of Mathematics and Statistics, Nanjing University of Information Science & Technology, Nanjing 210044, China
yongshenghao@yahoo.com
[3] Network Centre, Nanjing University of Information Science & Technology, Nanjing 210044, China
[4] Xiamen Lihan Information Technology, Xiamen 361024, China

Abstract. In the paper, we try to evaluate the energy consumption of meteorological applications on meteorological cloud of on different kinds of processors. We take WRF (Weather Research and Forecasting model) model as the typical model. Three major factors are including in the evaluation: the energy consumption, the execution time, and the parallelism. The moldable parallel tasks have a scope of parallelisms. But after the job has an execution state, and the parallelism cannot be changed during the execution. Different to most of past research, our system support slots time and every job needs a few slot times to execute it. We give a detailed analysis of DVFS (Dynamic Voltage and Frequency Scaling) model for WRF and evaluate the different performance of three kinds of CPUs in different aspects, and at last, based the analysis of the attributes of the three CPUs and the nonlinear speedup of WRF under different numbers of resources, simulations result are given to address the energy consumption of WRF under different environments. We hope our research can help us to enhance the scheduling method of parallel tasks.

Keywords: Moldable parallel tasks · Energy consumption · WRF · Simulations · Energy efficiency

1 Introduction

Many methods have been used to the schedule parallel tasks. Most of methods pay attention to the execution time of the parallel tasks [1]. Those methods try to meet the deadline of job and maximize the output of the system. Different to those methods, this paper pays attention to the energy consumption of parallel tasks (ECPT) when the system supports slot time. A detailed example of WRF is given to discuss the energy consumption under different voltages and computing frequency. We do not want to give and compare the scheduling method. Our target is to evaluate some factors when every

© ICST Institute for Computer Sciences, Social Informatics and Telecommunications Engineering 2020
Published by Springer Nature Switzerland AG 2020. All Rights Reserved
X. Zhang et al. (Eds.): CloudComp 2019/SmartGift 2019, LNICST 322, pp. 594–602, 2020.
https://doi.org/10.1007/978-3-030-48513-9_47

jobs needs some slots to execute it. Those factors include: the execution time, energy consumption and CPUs. We hope our study can help us deeply understand the scheduling influence to the job and the system targets. Besides that, because of the importance of the weather forecast, we also hope we can give methods for the scheduling of weather models.

ECPT has been widely evaluated in many platforms. DAG (Directed Acyclic Graph) are widely used to simulate parallel tasks. According to the DAG of paralle tasks, some methods are addressed to save energy consumption, and keep the performance of others aspects, such as execution time, fairness and so on [2, 3]. Different to those methods, this paper tries to consider the two aspects at the same time: the speedup of the parallel tasks and the DVFS of the resources.

In this paper, we will give a example of parallel tasks-WRF, which is widely used in the weather forecast. Based on the speedup of WRF [4] and the DVFS of three CPUs, we will model and evaluate the energy consumption of WRF under different conditions. Last, simulations are given for the energy consumption of WRF.

The contributions of the paper include:

(1) We give the DVFS model for WRF. The model supports wall time (or slot time). In fact, this model can be used for all moldable parallel tasks that which support wall time.
(2) We model consumed resources and the related energy consumption for moldable parallel tasks, which supports wall time, and can be used for all moldable parallel tasks.
(3) We give a detail comparisons of the performance of three kinds of CPUs in the energy efficiency.
(4) We give the energy consumption of WRF on three kinds of CPUs. We hope this can help we to better understand the energy consumption of MPA (moldable parallel tasks) under different QoSs (Quality of services) requirements (such as deadline, execution time).

We organize the paper as follows: The related work is addressed in Sect. 2. We describes the consumed resource model of WRF in Sect. 3. Section 4 gives the DVFS model of the resource. Section 5 illustrates energy consumption model of WRF. Section 6 addresses the simulation results. Section 7 give the sumary of the paper.

2   Related Work

Energy consumption is a hot problem is the scheduling. For the parallel tasks, many methods have been proposed from different aspects, either in the Grid, Cluster, or in the Cloud. Those methods mainly focus on the attribute of DAG, and use DVFS technology to reduce energy consumption. Energy-Aware method [2] are used to save energy for scheduling parallel tasks in Clusters. They take a threshold to make a tradeoff between energy consumption and execution time. I. Manousakis et al. gives a OpenMP-like tool to support energy-aware scheduling task-parallel applications. The tool traces the parallel execution and supports estimating the per-task energy consumption [8]. In order to reduce energy consumption and satisfy the QoS requirement, T. Zhou et al. [9] address a Workflow task scheduling algorithm based on DVFS under the Cloud environment. Through merging the relatively inefficient processors by reclaimings the slack time, which use the slack time after severs are merged. Y. Xia et al. [10] present a novel stochastic framework to enhance energy efficiency. There are four important facts in the scheduling, including tasks (virtual machine requests) arrival rate, and other metrics of datacenter servers. And then using queuing network-based analysis, they address analytic solutions for three targets. Since scientific workflows are widely executed across multiple clouds, and thus enhances energy consumption, X. Xu et al. [11] uses EnReal to hand those changes. They also address a energy-aware scheduling algorithm for virtual machine management to support scientific workflow executions.

Some methods also engage to save the energy consumption by considering the speedup of the parallel tasks [12, 13]. Past work always based upon the Amdahl's law and assumed an ideal system without overheads [13].

Those methods all focus on how to schedule resources to save energy consumption. And in this paper, we address the relation between the performance, the energy consumption, and the execution time. We hope the result can help us further to improve the performance and save energy. We use a WRF model to discuss those relation.

3   Consumed Resources Model of WRF

The speedup in Fig. 1 has a nonlinear speedup. WRF can work under different speedups under different parallelisms, WRF is modeled as:

$$WRF_i = \left\{ <para_{i,j}, et_{i,j}> | max_i \geq j \geq 1 \right\} \tag{1}$$

For the job WRF_i, the parallelism has a scope between 1 and max_i. If $para_{i,j}$ is smaller than max_i, $et_{i,j}$ will be shorter; with the increase of the number of resources (more than max_i) for the job, it lengthens the execution time, because the system consumes more time to get (or send) data between various nodes. $para_{i,j}$ and $et_{i,j}$ are the parallelism and the related execution time. The speedup of the job is [6]:

$$sp_i = \frac{et_{i,1}}{et_{i,j}}$$

In Fig. 1, WRF (for some certain weather parameters) can work under the parallelism in [1, 48]. The X axes are the numbers of the allocated resources and the Y axes are the execution times. When the value of X axes is more than 48, enhancing number of resources cannot save the execution time. So in the scheduling, it is not always right more resource can decrease the execution time. When we consider the energy consumption, the problem becomes more difficult.

There are some reasons to the explain the relation in Fig. 1. Amdahl's Law and Gustafson's Law [14, 15] are always used to explain the relation in Fig. 1.

Amdahl's Law: the maximum parallel execution time percentage is par, the serial execution time percentage is $1-par$, and the parallelism is p. Amdahl's Law gives the

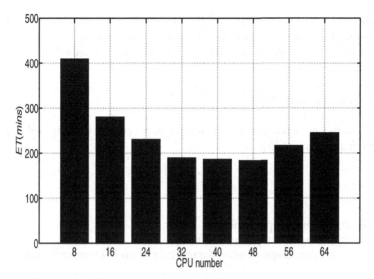

Fig. 1. Execution time vs. number of CPUs

speedup sp of a parallel task when the parallelism is p:

$$sp \leq \frac{1}{(1 - par) + \frac{par}{p}}$$

(2)

Some people criticized this that it dose not consider overheads, including communication, synchronization, and so on. Amdahl's Law has drawback especially with the increasing number of resources, the execution time would be lengthen.

Gustafson's Law is the law for scaled speedup. Scaled speedup is as follows:

$$sp \leq p + (1 - p)s$$

where, p is the parallelism, s is the serial execution time percentage of a parallel task on a given data set size.

Most of time, the speedup of a parallel task has a maximum value and can not be enhanced when it gets the maximum parallelism. Only some of time, the speedup is a constant, called the phenomenon as super-linear speedup. Most of time, the speedup has a range under a certain condition. We can get the maximum speedup by Amdahl's Law and Gustafson's Law. But for the two laws, there is difficulty in estimating the value of *par* and *s*.

We also can get some support for Fig. 1 for the two laws. With the enhancement of parallelisms, WRF reduces in the execution time (while the number of resources is less than 48), then, the value gradually increase with the further increasing of the number of resources (which the number of resources is more than 48). The reason is with the increasing of the resources, the system consumes more cost in exchanging information between resources.

At the same time, WRF supports wall time (wat), which is the maximum of continuous execution time. After a wat, the system stops the parallel tasks and then saves the data to the next wat. This wall time helps the user to find the error in the algorithm and improves the efficiency of the system if the job has an error in it.

In formula (1), we suppose the WRF_i works under the standard CPU, in other words, the resource has a working frequency of 1.

4   DVFS Model of WRF

A DVFS-enable resource has a mapping-set between the working voltage v_n and executing frequencies f_n [5]:

$$RS = \cup_{1 \leq ntemp \leq N}\{v_n, f_n, e_n\} \tag{3}$$

Where

- v_n is the nth resource supply voltage;
- f_n is the nth resource computing frequency;
- e_n is the power consumption when the resource is working under v_n and f_n.

If $n_1 < n_2$, then $f_1 \leq f_2$. Though the resource supplies the dynamic voltage, and here, we suppose that the voltage is a constant during in a time slot (wall time). Because if the voltage of every resources can be changed during the time slot, there is difficulty to keep steps of every parallel tasks.

We model the energy consumption according to CMOS logic circuits model. The dynamic power consumption can be defined as:

$$P_{dy} = \alpha C_l V_s^2 f_c \tag{4}$$

Where,

- α: switch rate;
- C_l: capacitance;
- V_s: working voltage;
- f_c: computing frequency.

Suppose the highest working voltage is V_{hest}, and the maximum dynamic consumed energy is P_{hest}. Then we can get the value of the dynamic consumed energy power consumption P_{sp} under the supply voltage is V_{sp} and the clock frequency is f_{sp}:

$$P_{sp} = P_{hest} \frac{f_{sp} V_{sp}^2}{f_{hest} V_{hest}^2} \tag{5}$$

Even there are no jobs on the resource, the resource also needs consuming energy, called as the idle power consumption P_{idle}. The total power consumption P is:

$$P = P_{sp} + P_{idle} \tag{6}$$

Formula (7) is used to denote energy efficiency:

$$E - F_n = \frac{e_n}{f_n} \tag{7}$$

5 Energy Consumption for WRF

For the parallel task WRF_i, let us suppose it has been assigned $para_{i,temp}$ resources, in other words, the parallelism of the job is $para_{i,temp}$. When the resources are working under $<v_{ntemp}, f_{ntemp}, e_{ntemp}>$ and the wall time of resources is wat. The execution time of WRF_i is:

$$ET(WRF_i) = \left\lfloor \frac{et_{i,temp}}{f_n * wat} \right\rfloor * wat \tag{8}$$

The total number of consumed resources:

$$CR(WRF_i) = \left\lfloor \frac{et_{i,temp}}{f_n * wat} \right\rfloor * wat * para_{i,temp} \tag{9}$$

The total consumed idle energy consumption is:

$$IEC(WRF_i) = \left\lfloor \frac{et_{i,temp}}{f_n * wat} \right\rfloor * wat * para_{i,temp} * P_{idle} \tag{10}$$

The total dynamic energy consumption:

$$DEC(WRF_i) = \frac{et_{i,temp}}{f_n} * para_{i,temp} * P_{dy} \tag{11}$$

According to formula (10) and (11), the total energy is:

$$TCE(WRF_i) = IEC(WRF_i) + DEC(WRF_i) \tag{12}$$

6 Simulations and Comparisons

In this section, first, we will evaluate three kinds of CPUs [5] on the energy efficiency, then we will give a comparison of energy consumption of WRF on the three kinds of CPUs.

In this section, We give a comparison for the energy consumption of WRF on three kinds of CPUs. Evaluate the energy consumption of WRF.

The WRF is modeled as [5], which has a nonlinear speedup. We evaluate the energy consumption of a same task under three kinds of CPUs.

Figures 2, 3 and 4 are the energy consumption of WRF (under a certain kinds of weather parameters) on different kinds of CPUs. In Figs. 2, 3 and 4, the axis has the same meaning. The X axis are the work state of Different kinds of CPUs. Those include the working voltage and the working frequency. The Y axis are the parallelisms of resources, in other words, they are the parallelisms of WRF. The Z axis are the energy consumptions of WRF under different kinds of working states. From Figs. 2, 3 and 4, we find that no matter under which kinds of CPUs, the energy consumption increases with the increasing of parallelisms. The reason is with the increasing of parallelism, the job need consumed more resources. We also find that INTEL540 always has the largest

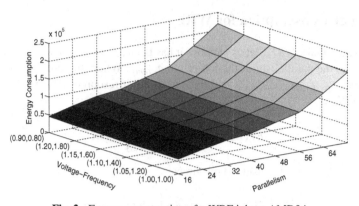

Fig. 2. Energy consumption of a WRF job on AMD34

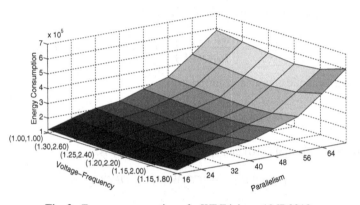

Fig. 3. Energy consumption of a WRF job on AMD2218

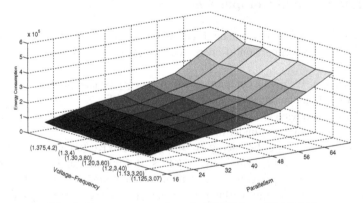

Fig. 4. Energy consumption of a WRF job on INTEL540

value in energy consumption, on the contrary, AMD34 always has the lowest value. For the special CPUs, even under the same parallelism, we also need to assign the suitable voltage and computing frequency to reduce energy consumption. For example, under INTEL540, when the parallelism is 64, (1.125, 3.07) has the lowest energy consumption.

In general, the parallelism has the largest influence to the energy consumption, and then we should select the right kinds of CPUs and decide the right working voltage and frequency to ensure the job satisfy the deadline requirement. Most of time, we can choose the resources with the highest energy efficiency while the job satisfies its deadline. But sometime, if the job can not be completed before its deadline, we should give a priority to the resources that have a higher speed.

7 Conclusions

Here, we analyze the energy consumption of WRF. We give the models for DVFS, resources model and energy consumption model. The performance of three kinds of CPUs is given in the simulation when the system support slot time. And based on the three kinds of processors, we model the energy consumption of WRF. Simulation results show that we should not only select the right processor which has the lowest power consumption, but also reduce energy consumption by selecting the working voltage and frequency. Some methods also have been used to reduce overall *energy according to multiple* aspects [16–18]. Though those methods target to reduce the energy consumption, but none of them consider the attributes of the scheduling target (the attributes of the program) and the resources (the attributes of those resources) at the same time. If we can consider those aspects at the same time, we can find some new methods to minimize the energy consumption of the scheduling. In the future, we hope we can not only evaluate the energy consumption of more meteorological models, but also we will consider different kinds of deadlines (soft and hard deadline) to the job. At the same time, we also hope we can find a scheduling method for those weather models which not only meet the deadline, at the same time, has a relative smaller value in the energy consumption.

Acknowledgment. The work was partly supported by the National Social Science Foundation of China (No. 16ZDA054).

References

1. Meixner, A., Redgrave, J.R., Shacham, O., et al.: Energy efficient processor core architecture for image processor. U.S. Patent Application 10/275,253, 30 April 2019
2. Ziliang, Z., Adam, M., Xiaojun, R., Xiao, Q.: EAD and PEBD: two energy-aware duplication scheduling algorithms for parallel tasks on homogeneous clusters. IEEE Trans. Comput. **60**(3), 360–374 (2011)
3. Singh, V., Gupta, I., Jana, Prasanta K.: An energy efficient algorithm for workflow scheduling in iaas cloud. J. Grid Comput. 1–20 (2019). https://doi.org/10.1007/s10723-019-09490-2
4. Hao, Y., Cao, J., Ma, T., et al.: Adaptive energy-aware scheduling method in a meteorological cloud. Future Gener. Comput. Syst. **101**, 1142–1157 (2019)

5. Liu, W., Wei, D., Chen, J., Wang, W., Zeng, G.: Adaptive energy-efficient scheduling algorithm for parallel tasks on homogeneous clusters. J. Netw. Comput. Appl. **41**, 101–113 (2014). https://doi.org/10.1016/j.jnca.2013.10.009. ISSN 1084-8045

6. Gillespie, M.: Amdahl's law, gustafson's trend, and the performance limits of parallel applications (2008). WWW-sivu: http://software.intel.com/sites/default/files/m/d/4/1/d/8/Gillespie-0053-AAD_Gustafson-Amdahl_v1__2_.rh.final.pdf

7. Li, X., Garraghan, P., Jiang, X., et al.: Holistic virtual machine scheduling in cloud datacenters towards minimizing total energy. IEEE Trans. Parallel Distrib. Syst. **29**(6), 1317–1331 (2018)

8. Manousakis, I., Zakkak, F.S., Pratikakis, P., Nikolopoulos, D.S.: TProf, an energy profiler for task-parallel programs. Sustain. Comput. Inform. Syst. **5**, 1–13 (2015). https://doi.org/10.1016/j.suscom.2014.07.004. ISSN 2210-5379

9. Tang, Z., Qi, L., Cheng, Z., Li, K., Khan, S.U., Li, K.: An energy-efficient task scheduling algorithm in DVFS-enabled cloud environment. J. Grid Comput. **14**(1), 55–74 (2015). https://doi.org/10.1007/s10723-015-9334-y

10. Xia, Y., Zhou, M., Luo, X., Pang, S., Zhu, Q.: A stochastic approach to analysis of energy-aware DVS-enabled cloud datacenters. IEEE Trans. Syst. Man Cybern. Syst. **45**(1), 73–83 (2015)

11. Xu, X., Dou, W., Zhang, X., et al.: EnReal, an energy-aware resource allocation method for scientific workflow executions in cloud environment. IEEE Trans. Cloud Comput. **4**, 166–179 (2015)

12. Lazarescu, M.T., Cohen, A., Lavagno, L., et al.: Energy-aware parallelization toolset and flow for C code (2019)

13. Kavanagh, R., Djemame, K., Ejarque, J., et al.: Energy-aware self-adaptation for application execution on heterogeneous parallel architectures. IEEE Trans. Sustain. Comput. **5**(1), 81–94 (2019)

14. Banerjee, K.B.P.: Approximate algorithms for the partitionable independent task scheduling problem. In: Proceedings of the 1990 International Conference on Parallel Processing, vol. I, pp. 72–75 (1990)

15. Tao, M., Dong, S.: Two-tier policy-based consolidation control for workload with soft deadline constrain in virtualized data center. In: 2013 25th Chinese Control and Decision Conference (CCDC), pp. 2357–2362, 25–27 May 2013

16. Barros, C.A., Silveira, L.F.Q., Valderrama, C.A., Xavier-de-Souza, S.: Optimal processor dynamic-energy reduction for parallel workloads on heterogeneous multi-core architectures. Microprocess. Microsyst. **39**(6), 418–425 (2015). https://doi.org/10.1016/j.micpro.2015.05.009. ISSN 0141-9331

17. Jia, Z., Zhang, Y., Leung, J.Y.T., Li, K.: Bi-criteria ant colony optimization algorithm for minimizing makespan and energy consumption on parallel batch machines. Appl. Softw. Comput. **55**, 226–237 (2017). https://doi.org/10.1016/j.asoc.2017.01.044

18. Jin, X., Zhang, F., Fan, L., Song, Y., Liu, Z.: Scheduling for energy minimization on restricted parallel processors. J. Parallel Distrib. Comput. **81–82**, 36–46 (2015). https://doi.org/10.1016/j.jpdc.2015.04.001. ISSN 0743-7315

A Survey of Information Intelligent System Security Risk Assessment Models, Standards and Methods

Zijian Ying[1,2,4], Qianmu Li[1,2,3,4(✉)], Shunmei Meng[1], Zhen Ni[3], and Zhe Sun[2]

[1] School of Computer Science and Engineering, Nanjing University of Science and Technology, Nanjing 210094, China
qianmu@njust.edu.cn
[2] Jiangsu Zhongtian Technology Co., Ltd., Nantong 226009, China
[3] School of Information Engineering, Nanjing Xiaozhuang University, Nanjing 211171, China
[4] Intelligent Manufacturing Department, Wuyi University, Jiangmen 529020, China

Abstract. This paper describes the theoretical hierarchy of information security risk assessment, which includes the models, standards and methods. Firstly, this paper generalizes and analyzes the security risk assessment models on the macro scale and proposes a common security risk assessment model by reviewing the development history of the models. Secondly, this paper compares different security risk assessment standards and classifies them into information security risk assessment standards, information security risk assessment management standards and information security risk assessment management implementation guidelines on the mesoscale. Then, on the micro scale, this paper generalizes security risk assessment methods and analyzes the security risk assessment implementation standards, which is the specific implementation method of security assessment work. Finally, this paper proposes a cloud security event description and risk assessment analysis framework based on the cloud environment and the common security risk assessment model we proposed.

Keywords: Assessment models · Security risk · Security standard

1 Introduction

As an important part of network security research, security risk assessment area has undergone several decades of development. Risk assessment is the foundation of all other security technology. According to the definition of information system security risk assessment criterion, security risk assessment is the process of evaluating information security attributes with related technology and management standards. Security risk assessment can be divided into macroscale, mesoscale and microscale in structure. On the macroscale, assessment model is the structural foundation of the security risk assessment. On the mesoscale, assessment standard provides reference for security risk assessment. On the microscale, assessment method provides specific ideas for security risk assessment. The structure of the three-scale model is shown in the Fig. 1. Using

X. Zhang et al. (Eds.): CloudComp 2019/SmartGift 2019, LNICST 322, pp. 603–611, 2020.
https://doi.org/10.1007/978-3-030-48513-9_48

model, standard and assessment method to deal with security threats and protect property is the idea of risk assessment in network security area.

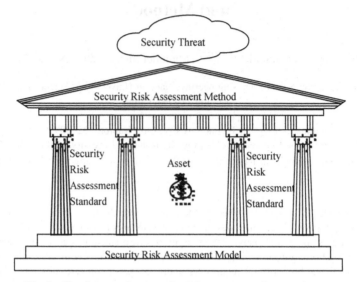

Fig. 1. Cloud computing security risk assessment theory structure.

Some mature technical architectures have been built to address security risk assessment problems in different scales. However, as the rapid development of the information technology, more and more security threats come out, which means security risk assessment technology need to develop either. Meanwhile, the ubiquitous network brings new characters and threats unlike before. This means better methods should be taken to do security risk assessment and protect properties.

This paper sums the models, standards and methods in the theoretical hierarchy of information security risk assessment, proposes a common security risk assessment model, and classifies the different standards and methods.

2 Security Risk Assessment Models

Protection Detection Response (PDR) Model. PDR model, as shown in Fig. 2, is originally proposed by Winn Schwartau. This model considers that protection is the first step, detection is the real-time monitoring of network and reaction is the in-time feedback to the invasion.

Protection Policy Detection Response (P2DR) Model. P^{2}DR model, as shown in Fig. 3, is a dynamic network security system model which is improved from PDR by ISS Company. This model centers on the policy and surrounds with response, protection and detection. Policy contents general policy and specific security policy.

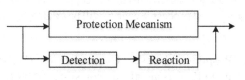

Fig. 2. PDR model.

Fig. 3. P^{2}DR model.

Protection Detection Reaction Restoration (PDR2) Model. PDR^2 model, as shown in Fig. 4, is improved from PDR model. This model is very similar to the P^{2}DR model, and the only different is upgrade the recover segment to the same level with protection, detection and reaction. This model extends the concept of the security from information security to information assurance, and highlight the automatic failure recovery capability.

Policy Assessment Design Implementation Management ER Education (PADIMEE) Model. PADIMEE model, as shown in Fig. 5, is improved from P2DR model by ISS Company and become a more systematic model. Based on analyzing the object, requirements and safety period, this model build a cyclic security model.

Assessment Policy Protection Detection Reaction Restoration (APPDRR) Model. APPDRR model, as shown in Fig. 6, is a passive dynamic defense model for local system

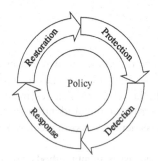

Fig. 4. PDR^2 model.

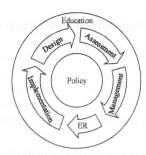

Fig. 5. PADIMEE model.

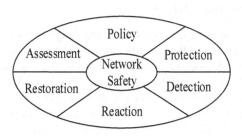

Fig. 6. APPDRR model.

Fig. 7. WPDRRC model.

proposed by Venus which is based on PDR^2 model. This model considers that security is relative and represents a spiral improvement process. Security will be gradually improved in it.

Warning Protection Detection Response Recover Counterattack (WPDRRC) Model. WPDRRC model, as shown in Fig. 7, is an information system security assurance system. It improves by adding Warning and Counterattack before and after PDR^2 model. It centers on staff and uses policy as the basis of the communication technology.

A Security Risk Analysis Model. Figure 8 shows the internal links among the information security models above:

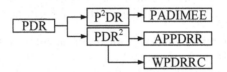

Fig. 8. Information security model evolution.

It has been observed that information security is a cyclic process and the key is protection, detection and the mutual excitation of feedback.

3 Security Risk Assessment Methods

The main components of the security risk assessment method are two aspects, one is risk analysis and the other is risk resolution. The accuracy of risk analysis will have a huge impact on many of following works. Overall, the security risk assessment method consists of the following eight elements: asset description, threat identification, consequence analysis, vulnerability analysis, threat assessment, risk assessment, risk priority and risk management.

With the development of technology, security risk assessment methods have evolved from traditional assessment methods to comprehensive risk assessment management methods.

3.1 Traditional Security Risk Assessment Methods

Attack Trees Analysis (ATA). ATA is an analytical method for exploiting system weaknesses from the perspective of an attacker. It uses the tree structure to describe the possible attacks on the system. Because most risk assessment methods need to make assumptions based on existing information, the accuracy of the assessment will be limited by the accuracy of the hypothesis. To ensure the best results, the conclusions drawn from the attack tree analysis need to be compared to other analysis results or assessed by experts. However building a 100% accurate attack tree model is almost impossible. And this step will greatly increase the complexity of the method. The evaluator needs to grasp the degree of assessment and make the attack tree model good enough. In order to prevent this step from consuming too many resources, the following three conditions need to be considered:

1) Defender's system has vulnerabilities.
2) Attackers need to have enough ability to exploit these vulnerabilities.
3) The expected benefit is the motivation for the attack, and the attacker can gain benefits by attacking.

The main advantage of ATA is that it can be easily rewritten according to the needs and characteristics of the organization. This method also provides the conclusion that which attacks are most likely to occur in terms of the overall system. From a certain perspective, security is not a result, security is a process, and attack tree analysis can form a basic understanding of this process. From a certain perspective, security is not a result but a process, and ATA can form a basic understanding of this process.

Failure Tree Analysis (FTA). FTA is a top-down assessment method. It uses a tree diagram to organically link system security failures to internal failures. In the fault tree, the root node indicates a fault, and the leaf node indicates an event that may cause a fault, which in turn extends. Different layers are linked by logic gate symbols and the upper layer probability is calculated according to the underlying probability. However, the fault tree cannot analyze the hazards and risks caused by the fault time, so it can only be used as a method of some steps in the risk analysis.

Failure Mode Effect and Criticality Analysis (FMECA). FMECA is a single component failure mode analysis and hazard analysis tool. Its purpose is to reduce the possibility of failure and improve the reliability of system operation. FMECA is a bottom-up approach that identifies faults in the form of a discussion and records the results in a table. The disadvantage of this approach is that there are too many limitations in a single unit, ignoring the connections and commonalities between the units.

Hazard and Operability Study (HAZOP). HAZOP is a structured inspection method for potential hazards of the system. It uses structured checks to determine the abnormal operation of the system from normal design. And the purpose of this method is to identify threats. The HAZOP analysis is conducted in the form of a discussion, and the analyst uses a variety of analysis techniques to collect system information into the document as an input to the analysis. In the analysis process, use some system-related questions to form special guidance words to help improve the comprehensiveness of the analysis. This way not only ensures that the analysis results are consistent with the characteristics of the system, but also adds extra information. The results of the analysis are saved in the form of a table.

Petri-net. Petri-net is a graphical modeling tool based on mathematical theory. Petri-net can automatically control the state of the system with the change of the state of the token in the system to describe a dynamic complex system. It is often used in the field of security analysis to analyze security threats that are passed through the system.

Analytic Hierarchy Process (AHP). AHP uses a hierarchical approach to quantify empirical judgments and form quantitative decision values. However, this method is subject to human factors, and there are fluctuations between various indicators and lack of consistency.

The traditional method lacks comprehensive considerations for security risk technology and management, and a single assessment method cannot objectively and accurately reflect the security status of complex information security system engineering.

3.2   Comprehensive Security Risk Assessment Methods

Comprehensive risk assessment methods have a set of implementation steps and theoretical systems, and their solutions for risk assessment are more comprehensive than traditional risk assessment methods. They may contain some traditional analytical methods. However, in addition to these, they generally follow certain security standards and also provide solutions to systemic risks.

CCTA Risk Analysis and Management Method (CRAMM). CRAMM is a security service framework system proposed by the British government. Its purpose is to provide a structured and consistent approach to information security management, as shown in Fig. 9. It is an automated qualitative assessment method, but in order to achieve good results, experts need to participate in the assessment. The purpose of this method is to assess the security of related information systems and networks. To achieve the goal, the method focuses on three aspects:

1) Identify assessment assets
2) Identify threats and vulnerabilities and calculate risks
3) Identify and give countermeasures according to priority

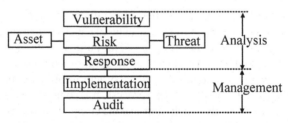

Fig. 9. CRAMM method.

Operationally Critical Treat, Asset, and Vulnerability Evaluation (OCTAVE). OCTAVE is a method developed by Carnegie Mellon University to define the security risks of assessing information within a system organization. This approach provides a new approach to information security for large organizations. OCTAVE enables organizations to view security issues from a risk-based perspective and describe the technology in a commercial perspective. OCTAVE Allegro is a new version that was published in 2007. This version is based on the previous two previous versions of OCTAVE Original (1999) and OCTAVE-S.

OCTAVE Allegro focuses on information assets. One of the advantages of using OCTAVE Allegro is that it can be conducted in the form of a seminar. It provides the required collaborative environment, the necessary guides, work forms and question-naires, and all of the above mentioned content is free. OCTAVE Allegro consists of four stages and eight steps. The results of each step are recorded by the worksheet and used as input for the next step.

Consultative Objective and Bi-functional Risk Analysis (COBRA). COBRA is a risk analysis method created by C&A. COBRA is designed to provide organizations with the means to self-assess their own information technology without the need for additional consultants. COBRA follows the guidance of ISO 17799 and its risk assessment process includes two aspects: One is COBRA Risk Consultant; the other is ISO Compliance.

COBRA Risk Consultant is a questionnaire-based computer program that contains a number of standardized questions to gather information about asset types, vulnerabilities, threats, etc. This approach generates appropriate recommendations and solutions by eval-uating relevant threats. COBRA Risk Consultant is designed based on self-assessment, which can be used without relevant knowledge and without expert involvement. The reports generated by COBRA Risk Consultant are professional business reports that can be read by security professionals or non-professionals. ISO Compliance contains standard questions related to the broad categories specified in the ISO 17799 standard.

Control Objectives for Information and related Technology (COBIT). COBIT is the most internationally recognized and most authoritative standard for security and information technology management and control proposed by ISAKA and has been developed to COBIT 5.

A Platform for Risk Analysis of Security Critical Systems (CORAS). CORAS was formally proposed by Greece, Germany, Norway and the United Kingdom in 2003. It is a qualitative risk assessment method and provides a complete set of graphical language to model threats and risks.

3.3 Security Risk Assessment Methods Comparison

There is no unified evaluation system for security risk assessment methods. This paper presents a simple assessment framework for comparing the various methods described above. The framework evaluates the above methods from the eight aspects: data requirement(DR), tool support(TS), operability(O), application cost(AC), applica-tion range(AR), method type(MT), policy assurance(PA) and support organization(SO). This helps relevant organizations to select appropriate security risk assessment methods based on their needs. Table 1 shows the comparison results.

Table 1. Assessment to the security risk assessment method.

Name	TS	O	AC	AR	MT	PA	SO
ATA	–	Easy	Low	Small	Qualitative	Low	–
FTA	–	Easy	Low	Small	Qualitative	Low	–
FMECA	–	Medium	Medium	Small	Qualitative	Low	–
HAZOP	–	Easy	Medium	Medium	Qualitative	Low	–
Petri-net	–	Difficult	Medium	Medium	Quantitative	Low	–
AHP	–	Easy	Low	Medium	Comprehensive	High	–
CRAMM	–	Difficult	High	Wide	Quantitative	Low	UK
OCTAVE	Y	Difficult	Low	Wide	Comprehensive	High	CMU
COBRA	Y	Medium	Medium	Wide	Qualitative	High	C&A
COBIT	Y	Difficult	Medium	Wide	Qualitative	High	ISAKA
CORAS	Y	Medium	Medium	Wide	Comprehensive	High	EU

4 Cloud Security Event and Risk Analysis Framework

Modeling analysis is one of the important assessment methods and decision-making mechanisms for network security. It can help system designers to clearly understand and identify potential security threats, attacks and vulnerabilities in the system. The basic idea of the model-based attack assessment method is to put the network into operation, and use some threat analysis models of information systems and network security, such as STRIDE, UML, etc., to describe and assess potential threats in the system in advance to prevent problems before they occur. For example, Kkoti et al. combined the STRIDE threat detection model and attack tree technology to implement a threat detection model that can effectively analyze Open Flow security.

Combined with the general security risk assessment models summarized in this paper, a cloud security event description and risk analysis implementation framework is proposed, as shown in Fig. 10. The security event description and risk analysis tools are at the application layer. The network nodes are at the access layer. And the controllers at the control layer are used as bridges to communicate the upper and lower layers. The network node passes the obtained security information to the controller, which aggregates it and passes it to the analysis tool in the application layer. The network node passes the obtained security information to the controller and the controller then aggregates it and passes it to the analysis tool in the application layer. The analysis tool analyzes based on existing model libraries, experience pools, and acquired safety information, and generates analysis reports. The security expert assigns a security policy to the controller based on the analysis report. The controller translates the policy to form a rule command for the network node and passes it to the network node for configuration, thereby forming a closed loop of analysis, protection, and feedback. This model combines the advantages of a ubiquitous network structure with the advantages of a security risk assessment model. It separates and reconstructs the secure data plane from the control plane for modularity, service, and reusability, and decoupling physical and virtual network security devices from their access modes, deployment methods, and implementation functions. At the same time, the model abstracts the underlying layer into resources in the security pool, and intelligently and automatically organizes and manages the business through the top-level unified software programming method, and completes the corresponding security protection functions in a flexible and efficient manner to achieve the purpose of reducing security risks.

5 Conclusion

This paper described the models, standards, and methods involved in the theoretical hierarchy of security risk assessment. Firstly, this paper generalized and analyzed common security risk assessment models on the macroscale. Then, this paper compared and classified different security risk assessment standards on the mesoscale, and divided them into information security risk assessment standards, information security risk management standards, and information security risk management implementation guidelines. What's more, this paper generalized security risk assessment methods and analyzed security risk assessment guidelines on the microscale. This is the implementation method for specific security assessment work. In the end, this paper proposed a cloud security event description and risk analysis implementation framework based on the cloud environment and the security risk assessment model proposed before.

Acknowledgement. This work was supported in part by Military Common Information System Equipment Pre-research Special Technology Project (315075701), the Fundamental Research Funds for the Central Universities (30918012204), 2018 Jiangsu Province Major Technical Research Project "Information Security Simulation System" (electric power and energy), Shanghai Aerospace Science and Technology Innovation Fund (SAST2018-103).

References

1. Xiaolong, X., Liu, Q., Zhang, X., Zhang, J., Qi, L., Dou, W.: A blockchain-powered crowdsourcing method with privacy preservation in mobile environment. IEEE Trans. Comput. Soc. Syst. (2019). https://doi.org/10.1109/TCSS.2019.2909137
2. Qi, L., Chen, Y., Yuan, Y., Shucun, F., Zhang, X., Xu, X.: A QoS-aware virtual machine scheduling method for energy conservation in cloud-based cyber-physical systems. World Wide Web J. (2019). https://doi.org/10.1007/s11280-019-00684-y
3. Qi, L., et al.: Finding all you need: web APIs recommendation in web of things through keywords search. IEEE Trans. Comput. Soc. Syst. (2019). https://doi.org/10.1109/tcss.2019. 2906925
4. Li, Q., Meng, S., Wang, S., Zhang, J., Hou, J.: CAD: command-level anomaly detection for vehicle-road collaborative charging network. IEEE Access **7**, 34910–34924 (2019)
5. Li, Q., Meng, S., Zhang, S., Hou, J., Qi, L.: Complex attack linkage decision-making in edge computing networks. IEEE Access **7**, 12058–12072 (2019)
6. Li, Q., et al.: Safety risk monitoring of cyber-physical power systems based on ensemble learning algorithm. IEEE Access **7**, 24788–24805 (2019)
7. Li, Q., Wang, Y., Pu, Z., Wang, S., Zhang, W.: A time series association state analysis method in smart internet of electric vehicle charging network attack. Transp. Res. Rec. **2673**, 217–228 (2019)

Smart Grid and Innovative Frontiers in Telecommunications

Some Used and Innovative Founders in
Telecommunications

Multiple Time Blocks Energy Harvesting Relay Optimizing with Time-Switching Structure and Decoding Cost

Chenxu Wang[1], Yanxin Yao[1($\boxtimes$)], Zhengwei Ni[2], Rajshekhar V. Bhat[3], and Mehul Motani[4]

[1] Key Laboratory of the Ministry of Education for Optoelectronic Measurement Technology and Instrument, Advanced Equipment Intelligent Perception and Control, Beijing International Cooperation Base for Science and Technology, Beijing Information Science and Technology University, Beijing 100190, China
1125507952@qq.com, yanxin_buaa@126.com
[2] Zhejiang Gongshang University, Hangzhou 310018, Zhejiang, China
nzw_hk@hotmail.com
[3] Indian Institute of Technology Dharwad, Dharwad, India
rajshekhar.bhat@iitdh.ac.in
[4] National University of Singapore, Singapore, Singapore
motani@nus.edu.sg

Abstract. Energy harvesting (EH) is of prime importance for enabling the Internet of Things (IoT) networks. Although, energy harvesting relays have been considered in the literature, most of the studies do not account for the processing costs, such as the decoding cost in a decode-and-forward (DF) relay. However, it is known that the decoding cost amounts to a significant fraction of the circuit power required for receiving a codeword. Hence, in this work, we are motivated to consider an EH-DF relay with the decoding cost and maximize the average number of bits relayed by it with a time-switching architecture. To achieve this, we first propose a *time-switching* frame structure consisting of three phases: (i) an energy harvesting phase, (ii) a reception phase and, (iii) a transmission phase. We obtain optimal length of each of the above phases and communication rates that maximize the average number of bits relayed. We consider the radio frequency (RF) energy to be harvested by the relay is from the dedicated transmitter and the multiple block case when energy is allowed from flow among the blocks, different from the single block case when energy is not allowed to flow among the blocks. By exploiting the convexity of the optimization problem, we derive analytical optimum solutions under the EH scenario. One of the optimal receiving rate for the relay is the same as in single block case. We also provide numerical simulations for verifying our theoretical analysis.

Supported by the Natural Science Foundation of Beijing (4172021), the Importation and Development of High-Caliber Talents Project of Beijing Municipal Institutions (CIT&TCD 201704064), Key research cultivation projects of BISTU (5211910954).

X. Zhang et al. (Eds.): CloudComp 2019/SmartGift 2019, LNICST 322, pp. 615–626, 2020.
https://doi.org/10.1007/978-3-030-48513-9_49

Keywords: Energy harvesting · Time-switching ·
Harvest-transmit-then-receive · Relay

1   Introduction

In recent years, communication technology has developed rapidly, and the resulting energy consumption problem has become more and more serious. Therefore, adding energy harvesting (EH) to the original communication system has
become the preferred solution for researchers. The energy harvesting realizes its
own data transmission and other functions by collecting external energy, which
will effectively improve the energy utilization rate of the current communication system. Energy harvesting is widely used in communication systems. For
example, the application of this technology in wireless sensor networks [4], cognitive radio [5], radio frequency communication [6], and car networking [7] can
improve energy efficiency greatly. In the communication process, the point-to-
point model, the relay model, and the collaboration model are common system
models, and the packet loss rate [8], energy utilization [9], data throughput [10]
and other indicators [1,2]. In [11], the point-to-point data transmission model is
studied. The transmitter is an EH node. The collected energy is used to transmit the data packets transmitted to the transmitter to the receiver. The target
achieves maximum throughput, and the overall process is implemented by the
Q-learning algorithm. The two-hop relay communication model is studied in
[12]. The transmitter and relay nodes are EH nodes, which can exchange causal
knowledge. Therefore, the Markov decision model constructed in [11] is converted into the Markov game model. Construct a local action value function. In
[13], a three-node relay transmission network consisting of a single source node,
a single destination node, and multiple relay nodes using decoding and forwarding is proposed, and the target of minimum energy consumption is realized by
the particle swarm optimization algorithm. Parallel multi-relay model is built in
[14]. The model includes the transmitting node of the primary and secondary
users, the receiving node and the parallel relay node inside the secondary user
model. Both the relay and the secondary user (SU) are provided at the source.
An energy harvesting device in which the relay collects radio frequency energy
emitted from the transmitting source, and the transmitting source collects radio
frequency energy emitted from the secondary re-transmission of the relay. In
[15], the author proposes an energy-saving relay selection method (ESRS) based
on the parallel relay model, which significantly reduces the power consumption.

In this paper, we study the problem of optimizing time fraction and receiving
rate for an EH relay system for multiple block case whose energy comes from the
dedicated transmitter for transferring more information from dedicated transmitter to destination. Both energy and data are allowed to flow among blocks.
The frame structure is determined as three phase: harvesting, receiving information and transmitting information. The time fraction or ratio of these operations
are to determined. The average transmitting rate for the relay is known, while
the receiving rate related to the decoding energy is to be optimized. We have

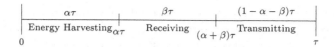

Fig. 1. The communication frame/block structure

the optimal solution in the single block case when energy and data are forbidden to flow among blocks. We consider the energy comes from dedicated receiver. We derive of the optimum time fraction for three operation phases and receiving rate and reach the conclusion that one of the optimal solutions is the same as that in single block case. Finally, numerical results are provided to validate the accuracy of the analysis. The main contributions of the paper are

- We formulate the information transferring and energy usage model for the energy harvesting relay considering the decoding cost.
- We give the solution for multiple block case where both energy and data are allowed to flow among blocks when energy is from dedicated transmitter by assumption and comparison.

2   System Model

We consider an end-to-end communication with an EH relay. The relay extracts the information contained in the signals sent by the transmitter, and then transmits it to the receiver in DF mode. We hope to transmit as most data as possible to the receiver. The energy source of the transmitter and receiver could be seen as infinite, while the energy of the relay is only from energy harvesting. Apparently, the bottle neck of the system is the EH relay which has limited harvested energy from the RF signals of the dedicated transmitter.

For purpose of simplicity and low cost, we design the structure of the relay as simple as possible. We consider a "Harvest-Receive-Transmit" time-switching architecture in this paper. The system consists of energy harvesting unit, decoding unit, transmitting unit, battery and data buffer. The energy harvesting unit harvest energy from RF signals of dedicated transmitter and ambient transmitters, and then store the energy in batteries for later transmitting or receiving freely. In the information receiving period, information is extracted from the received signals in the decoder unit using the energy drawn from the batteries. Then the information is stored in the buffer for later transmitting. In the information transmitting period, the information in the buffer is transmitted using the energy discharged from batteries.

We consider an average transmitting and receiving rate and channel condition when transferring information. So we could represent many parameters for the transmitting and receiving as constants during the block, such as the maximum signal power p_m, channel capacity C, the power gain of channel h, transmitting power p_t. A frame is divided into three parts as shown in Fig. 1. Assume the time length of a frame is τ.

- Over the time duration $[0, \alpha\tau), \alpha \in [0, 1]$, all the signals received are used for harvesting energy. To make the receiver harvest the largest amount of energy, the transmitter should always transmit the symbol with the largest energy. Denote $p_m = \max_x p(x)$ where the maximum is over all possible values of $x \in \mathcal{X}$ and e is the energy harvested outside the bands used for transmission.

- Over the time duration $[\alpha\tau, (\alpha + \beta)\tau), \alpha + \beta \in [0, 1]$, switcher connects to the information extracting circuit. We assume that the decoder is the dominant source of energy consumption at the receiver. Generally, for a fixed channel capacity C [3], we assume the energy consumed for decoding per channel use is a non-decreasing convex function of $\theta = \frac{C}{C-R}$, denoted by $\mathcal{E}_D(\theta)$. All other factors are 'hidden' in this function. $\mathcal{E}_D(0) = 0$. The bits that the relay could be decoded is $I_R = \beta\tau R$.

- Over the time duration $[(\alpha + \beta)\tau, \tau]$, switcher connects to the transmitting circuit and the information decoding is transmitted from the relay to the receiver. For transmission over an additive white Gaussian noise (AWGN) channel with power gain h, and unit received noise power spectral density, we consider the average rate as $W log(1 + hp_t)$ bits per channel symbol during the block.

The may be several specific forms for characterizing the decoding energy consumption. For example, for LDPC codes on the binary erasure channel (BEC), [16] shows that for any $\theta > 0$, there exists a code with code rate of at least R, with complexity per input node per iteration scaling like $log\theta$, to make decoding iterations to converge. The iteration rounds scale like θ. So the total complexity of decoder per channel use scales like $\theta log\theta$ [17].

3   Transmission over a Single Block from Transmitter Only

For a single block transmission, the optimization problem to maximize the amount of information relayed can be formulated as

$$
\begin{aligned}
\text{(P1)} \quad &\max_{\alpha, \beta, \gamma, R} \ I_R, \\
\text{s.t.} \quad &I_R \leq I_T \\
&\beta\mathcal{E}_D\left(\tfrac{C}{C-R}\right) + \gamma p_t + \leq \alpha p_m \\
&0 \leq \alpha \leq 1 \\
&0 \leq \beta \leq 1 \\
&0 \leq \gamma \leq 1 \\
&\alpha + \beta + \gamma = 1 \\
&0 \leq R \leq C.
\end{aligned}
\tag{1}
$$

We assume that the average transmitting rate for the frame is known at the start of the frame, which is representing with a constant channel power gain and a fixed p_t, by optimizing R, α, β, γ. The second constraint follows because γ is time duration for transmission.

Theorem 1. *So there is a single optimal R^*, $\alpha^*, \beta^*, \gamma*$ for Problem of (P1).*

Proof. See Reference [17].

4   Transmission over Multiple Blocks: Energy Harvested from Transmitter Only

We now consider transmission over multiple blocks. We consider an average transmitting and receiving rate as not varying from block to block. So we represent the maximum signal power p_m, channel capacity C and the power gain of channel h as the same constraints for all blocks. The amount of harvested energy from ambient environment is different from block to block. Assume that there are N blocks. We use subscript i to denote the $i - th$ block. We consider the possibility that both energy and data flow to later blocks. The energy harvested from one block could be stored and used in the following blocks. Our goal is maximize the total information delivered to the destination through the relay by choosing proper parameters $\alpha_i\,\beta_i\,\gamma_i$, R_i. Assume p_t is known as the same for all the blocks. The problem could be formulated as (P2).

$$(P2)\ \max_{\alpha,\beta,\gamma,\mathbf{R}} \sum_{i=1}^{N} IR_i = \sum_{i=1}^{N} \beta_i R_i \tau,$$
$$\text{s.t.}\ \sum_{j=1}^{i} IR_j \le \sum_{j=1}^{i} IT_j,$$
$$\sum_{j=1}^{i} IT_j = \sum_{j=1}^{i} log(1 + hp_t)\gamma_j\tau,$$
$$\sum_{j=1}^{i} \alpha_j p_m \ge \sum_{j=1}^{i} \left[p_t\gamma_j + \beta_j \mathcal{E}_{\mathrm{D}}\left(\frac{C}{C-R_j}\right)\right] \tag{2}$$
$$0 \le \alpha_i \le 1, 0 \le \beta_i \le 1, 0 \le \gamma_i \le 1,$$
$$\alpha_i + \beta_i + \gamma_i = 1, 0 \le R_i \le C,$$
$$i = 1,\ldots,N.$$

where $\boldsymbol{\alpha} = \{\alpha_1,\ldots,\alpha_N\}$, $\boldsymbol{\beta} = \{\beta_1,\ldots,\beta_N\}$, $\boldsymbol{\gamma} = \{\gamma_1,\ldots,\gamma_N\}$ and $\mathbf{R} = \{R_1,\ldots,R_N\}$. Notice that Unfortunately, (2) is not a convex optimization problem. We construct another optimization problem (P3).

$$(P4)\ \max_{\alpha,\beta,\gamma,\mathbf{R}} \sum_{i=1}^{N} IR_i = \sum_{i=1}^{N} \beta_i R_i \tau,$$
$$\text{s.t.}\ \sum_{j=1}^{i} IR_j \le \sum_{j=1}^{i} IT_j$$
$$\sum_{j=1}^{i} IT_j = \sum_{j=1}^{i} log(1 + hp_t)\gamma_j\tau$$
$$\sum_{j=1}^{i} \alpha_j p_m \ge \sum_{j=1}^{i} \left[p_t\gamma_j + \beta_j \mathcal{E}_{\mathrm{D}}\left(\frac{C}{C-R_j}\right)\right], \tag{3}$$
$$0 \le \alpha_i \le 1, 0 \le \beta_i \le 1, 0 \le \gamma_i \le 1,$$
$$\alpha_i + \beta_i + \gamma_i = 1, 0 \le R_i \le C, \quad i = 1,\ldots,N.$$
$$\alpha_1 = \alpha_2 = \cdots = \alpha_N,\ \beta_1 = \beta_2 = \cdots = \beta_N,$$
$$\gamma_1 = \gamma_2 = \cdots = \gamma_N,\ R_1 = R_2 = \cdots = R_N.$$

Compared with (2), we see that (3) has more constraints to ensure that the fraction using for EH, receiving and transmission in each block are the same. The following lemma relates the optimization problem (3) with (1).

Lemma 1. *The optimal* α_i, β_i, γ_i, R_i, $i = 1, \ldots, N$, *which maximize the objective function of (3) are* $\alpha_1 = \cdots \alpha_N = \alpha^*$, $\beta_1 = \cdots \beta_N = \beta^*$, $\gamma_1 = \cdots \gamma_N = \gamma^*$, $R_1 = \cdots R_N = R^*$, *where* α^*, β^*, γ^* *and* R^* *are optimal for (1).*

Proof. We argue that $\alpha_1 = \cdots \alpha_N = \alpha^*$, $\beta_1 = \cdots \beta_N = \beta^*$, $\gamma_1 = \cdots \gamma_N = \gamma^*$, $R_1 = \cdots R_N = R^*$ satisfy the first set of constraints in (3), since

$$\alpha^* p_{\mathrm{m}} = \beta^* \mathcal{E}_{\mathrm{D}}\left(\frac{C}{C-R^*}\right) + \gamma^* p_t$$

$$\Leftrightarrow \textstyle\sum_{j=1}^{i} \alpha^* p_{\mathrm{m}} = \sum_{j=1}^{i} \beta^* \mathcal{E}_{\mathrm{D}}\left(\frac{C}{C-R^*}\right) + \gamma^* p_t,$$

$$\Rightarrow \textstyle\sum_{j=1}^{i} \alpha^* p_{\mathrm{m}} \geq \sum_{j=1}^{i} \beta^* \mathcal{E}_{\mathrm{D}}\left(\frac{C}{C-R^*}\right) + \gamma^* p_t,$$

$$\text{for } i = 1, 2, \cdots, N. \tag{4}$$

$$\beta^* R^* \tau = \gamma^* log(1 + hp_t)$$

$$\Leftrightarrow \quad \textstyle\sum_{j=1}^{i} \beta^* R^* \tau = \sum_{j=1}^{i} \gamma^* log(1 + hp_t),$$

$$\Rightarrow \quad \textstyle\sum_{j=1}^{i} \beta^* R^* \tau \geq \sum_{j=1}^{i} \gamma^* log(1 + hp_t),$$

$$\text{for } i = 1, 2, \cdots, N. \tag{5}$$

It is obvious that the last set of constraints are also satisfied. We will prove the optimality via contradiction. Define $\mathcal{O}_N(\alpha_1, \beta_1, \gamma_1, R_1 \ldots, \alpha_N, \beta_N, \gamma_N, R_N) = \sum_{i=1}^{N} \beta_i R_i \tau$. Suppose there exist another $\hat{\alpha}$, $\hat{\beta}$, $\hat{\gamma}$ and $\hat{R}$ such that when $\alpha_1 = \cdots \alpha_N = \hat{\alpha}$, $\beta_1 = \cdots \beta_N = \hat{\beta}$, $\gamma_1 = \cdots \gamma_N = \hat{\gamma}$, $R_1 = \cdots R_N = \hat{R}$ and all the constraints of (3) are satisfied and we have $\mathcal{O}_N(\hat{\alpha}, \hat{\beta}, \hat{\gamma}, \hat{R} \ldots, \hat{\alpha}, \hat{\beta}, \hat{\gamma}, \hat{R}) > \mathcal{O}_N(\alpha^*, \beta^*, \gamma^*, R^* \ldots, \alpha^*, \beta^*, \gamma^*, R^*)$, i.e., $N\hat{\beta}\hat{R}\tau > N\beta^* R^* \tau$. Since it is always optimal to use up all the energy in the end, according to the constraints, we have

$$N\hat{\alpha} p_{\mathrm{m}} = N\hat{\gamma} p_t + N\hat{\beta} \mathcal{E}_{\mathrm{D}}\left(\frac{C}{C - \hat{R}}\right) \tag{6}$$

which means $\hat{\alpha}$, $\hat{\beta}$, $\hat{\gamma}$ and $\hat{R}$ also satisfy the constraints of (1). Since $\hat{\beta}\hat{R}\tau > \beta^* R^* \tau$, the results contradict the truth that α^*, β^*, R^* and γ^* are the optimal values for (1).

The following theorem relates the solution of (3) to the solution of (2).

Theorem 2. *One set of optimal values for* α_i, β_i, γ_i, *and* R_i, $i = 1, \ldots, N$, *which maximize the objective function of (2) are* $\alpha_1 = \cdots \alpha_N = \alpha^*$, $\beta_1 = \cdots \beta_N = \beta^*$, $\gamma_1 = \cdots \gamma_N = \gamma^*$, $R_1 = \cdots R_N = R^*$ *where* α^*, β^*, γ^* *and* R^* *are optimal for (1).*

Proof. Since (3) has four more constraints than (2), assuming one set of optimal values for (2) are given as $\tilde{\alpha}_1, \tilde{\beta}_1, \tilde{\gamma}_1, \tilde{R}_1, \ldots, \tilde{\alpha}_N, \tilde{\beta}_N, \tilde{\gamma}_N, \tilde{R}_N$, it is easy to obtain

$$\mathcal{O}_N(\tilde{\alpha}_1, \tilde{\beta}_1, \tilde{\gamma}_1, \tilde{R}_1, \ldots, \tilde{\alpha}_N, \tilde{\beta}_N, \tilde{\gamma}_N, \tilde{R}_N) \geq$$
$$\mathcal{O}_N(\alpha^*, \beta^*, \gamma^*, R^*, \ldots, \alpha^*, \beta^*, \gamma^*, R^*). \tag{7}$$

Due to property of $\mathcal{E}_D(R)$, by using Jensen's inequality to code rate, we have

$$\sum_{j=1}^{N} \frac{\tilde{\beta}_j}{\Phi} \mathcal{E}_D \left(\frac{1}{1 - \frac{\tilde{R}_j}{C}} \right)$$

$$\geq \mathcal{E}_D \left(\frac{1}{1 - \sum_{j=1}^{N} \frac{\tilde{\beta}_j}{\Phi} \tilde{R}_j / C} \right), \tag{8}$$

where $\Phi = \sum_{k=1}^{N} \tilde{\beta}_k$. Hence, we can derive that

$$\sum_{j=1}^{N} \tilde{\alpha}_j p_{\mathrm{m}} = \sum_{j=1}^{N} \tilde{\beta}_j \mathcal{E}_D \left(\frac{1}{1 - \frac{\tilde{R}_j}{C}} \right) + \sum_{j=1}^{N} \tilde{\gamma}_j p_t^j$$

$$\geq \sum_{j=1}^{N} \tilde{\beta}_j \mathcal{E}_D \left(\frac{1}{1 - \frac{\sum_{k=1}^{N} \tilde{\beta}_k \tilde{R}_k}{\sum_{k=1}^{N} \tilde{\beta}_k C}} \right) + \sum_{j=1}^{N} \tilde{\gamma}_j p_t, \tag{9}$$

So there exists an $R' \geq \frac{\sum_{k=1}^{N} \tilde{\beta}_k \tilde{R}_k}{\sum_{k=1}^{N} \tilde{\beta}_k}$ that makes $\sum_{j=1}^{N} \tilde{\alpha}_j p_{\mathrm{m}} = \sum_{j=1}^{N} \tilde{\beta}_j \mathcal{E}_D \left(\frac{1}{1 - \frac{R'}{C}} \right) + \sum_{j=1}^{N} \tilde{\gamma}_j p_t$. Actually, $R' \geq \frac{\sum_{k=1}^{N} \tilde{\beta}_k \tilde{R}_k}{\sum_{k=1}^{N} \tilde{\beta}_k}$ means

$$\mathcal{O}_N(\tilde{\alpha}_1, \tilde{\beta}_1, \tilde{\gamma}_1, R', \ldots, \tilde{\alpha}_N 1, \tilde{\beta}_N, \tilde{\gamma}_N, R') \geq$$
$$\mathcal{O}_N(\tilde{\alpha}_1, \tilde{\beta}_1, \tilde{\gamma}_1, \tilde{R}_1, \ldots, \tilde{\alpha}_N, \tilde{\beta}_N, \tilde{\gamma}_N, \tilde{R}_N). \tag{10}$$

However, this new R' together with $\tilde{\alpha}_1, \ldots, \tilde{\alpha}_N, \tilde{\beta}_1, \ldots, \tilde{\beta}_N$ and $\tilde{\gamma}_1, \ldots, \tilde{\gamma}_N$, may not satisfy the first group of constraints in (2), so we need to find feasible solutions. To solve it, we let $\beta' = \frac{\sum_{k=1}^{N} \tilde{\beta}_k}{N}$. Then we have

$$N\alpha' p_{\mathrm{m}} = \sum_{j=1}^{N} \tilde{\alpha}_j p_{\mathrm{m}} = \sum_{j=1}^{N} \tilde{\beta}_j \mathcal{E}_D \left(\frac{1}{1 - \frac{R'}{C}} \right) + \tilde{\gamma} p_t$$

$$= N\beta' \mathcal{E}_D \left(\frac{1}{1 - \frac{R'}{C}} \right) + \gamma' p_t, \tag{11}$$

So we can show that the constraints are also satisfied according to the analysis similar to (4) and (5). In addition, we also have

$$\mathcal{O}_N(\alpha', \beta', \gamma', R', \ldots, \alpha', \beta', \gamma', R') =$$
$$\mathcal{O}_N(\tilde{\alpha}_1, \tilde{\beta}_1, \tilde{\gamma}_1, R', \ldots, \tilde{\alpha}_N, \tilde{\beta}_N, \tilde{\gamma}_N, R'). \tag{12}$$

Noticing that $\alpha', \beta', \gamma', R', \ldots, \alpha', \beta', \gamma', R'$ also satisfy all the constraints in optimization problem (3), we can obtain that

$$\mathcal{O}_N(\alpha', \beta', \gamma', R', \ldots, \alpha', \beta', \gamma', R') \leq$$
$$\mathcal{O}_N(\alpha^*, \beta^*, \gamma^*, R^* \ldots, \alpha^*, \beta^*, \gamma^*, R^*). \tag{13}$$

Combining (7), (10), (12) and (13), we can easily obtain the fact that $\mathcal{O}_N(\alpha^*, \beta^*, \gamma^*, R^*, \ldots, \alpha^*, \beta^*, \gamma^*, R^*) = \mathcal{O}_N(\tilde{\alpha}_1, \tilde{\beta}_1, \tilde{\gamma}_1, \tilde{R}_1, \ldots, \tilde{\alpha}_N, \tilde{\beta}_N, \tilde{\gamma}_N, \tilde{R}_N)$.

Comparing Lemma 1 and Theorem 2, we find that the relaxation of constraints that the fraction and code rate in each block are the same can not improve the performance.

Notice that $\{\alpha^*, \beta^*, \gamma^*, R^*\}$ is only one solution for (2). There may be other solutions that have different fractions and R. To be optimal, the code rates in all blocks should be equal due to (9).

5   Numerical Results

Firstly, we focus on the optimization results in single block case. Because the multiple block case solution in each block is the same with the single block case, so the simulation result also reflects multiple block case results. In order to follow the representation in the paper, we adopt energy unit as mW and bit rate unit as Mbits/s.

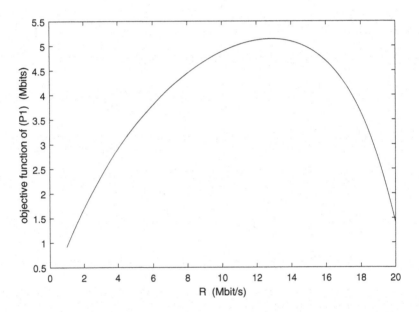

Fig. 2. The objective function value of (P1) versus R

We originally assume that $\mathcal{E}_D(\theta) = 10^{-3} \times \theta log_2\theta$W, $T(p_t) = Blog_2(1 + p_t h')$ bit/s, $B = 10^6$ Hz, $C = 21$ Mbit/s, $N_0 = 10^{-15}$ W/Hz, $\tau = 1s$, $h' = \frac{1}{N_0 W} = 10^9$. As the coefficients at the front in $T(p_t)$ and $\mathcal{E}_D(\theta)$ do not affect the convexity property of the functions, Theorem 1 still holds.

In the following simulation, we adopt energy unit as mW and bit rate unit as Mbit/s. Then we have $\mathcal{E}_D(\theta) = \frac{C}{C-R}log_2\left(\frac{C}{C-R}\right)$ mW, $T(p_t) = log_2(1 + p_t h)$ Mbit/s, where p_t represent x energy unit, $h = 10^6$, C, R and $T(P_t)$ are bit rate with unit Mbit/s.

We assume $C = 21$ Mbit/s, According to $P_1(R^*) = 0$, the numerical result for optimum R^* could be obtained at 18.66 Mbit/s.

In order to verify we plot the objective function of (P1) versus R in Fig. 2. We could easily get the optimum $R^* = 18.66$ Mbit/s. When $p_m = 8$ mW, $p_t = 7$ mW, we could give the optimum $\alpha = 0.6755$, $\beta = 0.2072$ and $\gamma = 0.1173$.

We also give the analysis for α, β and γ which are all varying versus P_t and p_m in Fig. 3, Fig. 4, and Fig. 5. We can observe that when p_m, the average power of the best symbol for EH increases, α decreases, while β and γ increase. It is a correct trend as α, the time duration for EH, could be shorter than before, as a result of the increase of p_m. When the forwarding power p_t increases, γ decreases. It is a correct trend because γ, the time duration for forwarding the same amount of data will decrease, and α, the time duration for EH phase will increase because the forwarding power is less efficient in power as the forwarding data bits I_T is a log function of p_t. For the same reason, β will decrease too, leading to a lower throughput of the relay network.

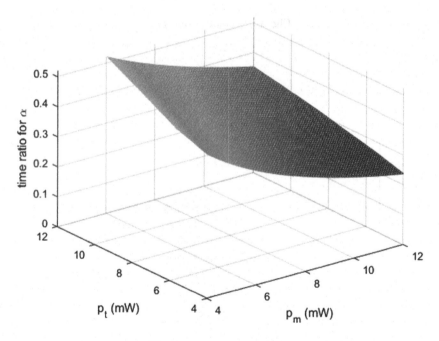

Fig. 3. α versus p_t and p_m

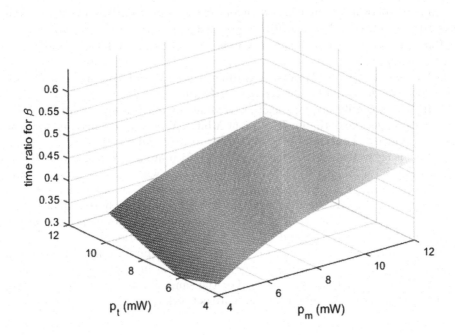

Fig. 4. β versus p_t and p_m

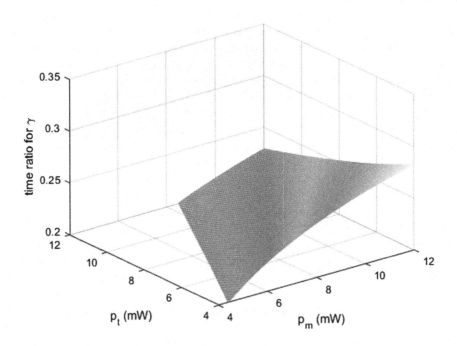

Fig. 5. γ versus p_t and p_m

6   Conclusion

The paper studies maximizing relay information using an energy constrained relay which harvests energy from the dedicated transmitter with a time-switching structure. The energy is allowed to flow among blocks. Given the optimal solution for a single block case, one of the optimal solution for multiple block case is derived. Simulation are done to give the numerical results to verify the correctness of the theoretical analysis.

References

1. Long, H., Xiang, W., Zhang, Y., Liu, Y., Wang, W.: Secrecy capacity enhancement with distributed precoding in multirelay wiretap systems. IEEE Trans. Inf. Forensics Secur. **8**(1), 229–238 (2012)
2. Wang, G., Xiang, W., Yuan, J.: Outage performance for compute-and-forward in generalized multi-way relay channels. IEEE Commun. Lett. **16**(12), 2099–2102 (2012)
3. Xiang, W., Pietrobon, S.S.: On the capacity and normalization of ISI channels. IEEE Trans. Inf. Theory **49**(9), 2263–2268 (2003)
4. Ruan, T.W., Chew, Z.J., Zhu, M.L.: Energy-aware approaches for energy harvesting powered wireless sensor nodes. IEEE Sens. J. **17**(7), 2165–2173 (2017)
5. Long, Y., Zhang, X.Q., He, X.R.: Resource allocation in cognitive radio network with energy harvesting. J. Commun. **39**(9), 67–75 (2018)
6. Jiao, W.G., Li, Y.R., Zhou, W.: Overview of energy harvesting cognitive radio sensor networks. Appl. Electron. Tech. **40**(10), 23–28 (2018)
7. Xie, Y.X.: Performance analysis of dual-hop vehicle networks based on energy Constrained. Lanzhou University of Technology (2018)
8. Wang, L.: Research on packet loss recovery based on network coding in wireless network. Southwest Jiaotong University (2011)
9. Bao, H., Li, M.H., Zhao, W.: Self-interference harvesting analysis for MIMO cognitive radio network with full-duplex relay. J. Huazhong Univ. Sci. Technol. (Nat. Sci. Ed.) **47**(06), 17–22 (2019)
10. Ma, Z.Y.: Power allocation algorithm for multiple relay selection in wireless sensor networks. J. Guilin Univ. Electron. Technol. **39**(03), 202–205 (2019)
11. Blasco, P., Gunduz, D., Dohler, M.: A learning theoretic approach to energy harvesting communication system optimization. IEEE Trans. Wireless Commun. **12**(04), 1872–1882 (2013)
12. Ortiz, A., Al-Shatri, H., Weber, T., Klein, A.: Multi-agent reinforcement learning for energy harvesting two-hop communications with full cooperation (2017)
13. Liu, X.L., Liu, D.N., Li, H.J., Li, Z.: Derivation of the performance of the relay system and simulation analysis of the system under energy cooperation. J. Xidian Univ. **51**(08), 1850–1856 (2018)
14. Wu, H.R., Qiu, R.H.: Throughput analysis of cognitive relay networks with energy harvesting sources. Commun. Technol., 1–8 (2019)
15. Jiang, Z.Y., Xiao, K.: Energy-saving relay selection method in wireless energy harvesting cooperative communication. Comput. Eng., 1–7 (2019)

16. Ni, Z., Motani, M.: Online policies for energy harvesting receivers with time-switching architectures. IEEE Trans. Wireless Commun. **18**, 1233–1246 (2019)
17. Wang, C.X., Ni, Z.W., Bhat, R.V., Yao, Y.X., Motani, M.: Time-swithching energy harvesting relay optimizing considering decoding cost. summited to SmartGIFT 2019–4th EAI International Conference on Smart Grid and Innovative Frontiers in Telecommunications (2019)

Spectrum Sharing in Cognitive Radio Enabled Smart Grid: A Survey

Shuo Chen[(✉)]

Key Laboratory of the Ministry of Education for Optoelectronic Measurement Technology and Instrument, Beijing Information Science and Technology University, Beijing, China
chenshuo@bistu.edu.cn

Abstract. Smart grid is viewed as the next-generation electric power system to meet the demand of communication and power delivery in an intelligent manner. With large scale deployment of electric power systems, smart grid faces the challenge from large volume data and high spectrum needs. To realize efficient spectrum utilization in the fact of spectrum scarcity, cognitive radio (CR) is involved in smart grid and generates the cognitive radio enabled smart grid. Cognitive radio enabled smart grid coexists with primary network by employing CR technologies including spectrum sensing, sharing, access and so on. Spectrum sharing is an important CR technology which realizes network coexistence without harmful interference through radio resource allocation. In this paper, a comprehensive survey is provided to review the state-of-the-art researches on spectrum sharing in cognitive radio enabled smart grid. We identify the network architecture and communication technology issues of cognitive radio enabled smart gird, and illustrate the investigation of spectrum sharing in different radio resource dimensions to highlight the superiority in efficient spectrum utilization.

Keywords: Smart grid · Cognitive radio · Spectrum sharing

1 Introduction

Smart grid has been regarded as the most promising next-generation power grid by overcoming the challenges faced by conventional power grid including increasing power demands, old electric power facilities and decreasing reliability. Through involving a series of advanced information technologies, smart grid supports two-directional communication between utilities and customers, and has the superiorities of self-monitor, self-healing and energy storage [1]. Compared with traditional power grid, smart grid realizes the efficiency, reliability and security of the electrical power grid system [2].

The features and superiorities of smart grid rely on effective communication between utilities and customers to exchange control and consumption information. Therefore,

This work was supported by the National Natural Science Foundation of China under Grant No. 61901043, and by the Research Fund of Beijing Information Science and Technology University No.1925012, 2019.

X. Zhang et al. (Eds.): CloudComp 2019/SmartGift 2019, LNICST 322, pp. 627–635, 2020.
https://doi.org/10.1007/978-3-030-48513-9_50

smart grid communication plays an important role in the design and construction of smart grid [3]. Wired communication and wireless communication are two categories of communication technologies employed in smart grid. For wired communication, power-line communication utilizes the electric power wiring to realize communication function. Compared with wired communication, wireless communication is more flexible and economical for the deployment of an electric power system [4]. Zigbee, WiMAX and cellular communication are common wireless communication manners in smart grid. With large scale deployment of electric power systems, wireless communication technologies in smart grid face the challenge from large volume data and high spectrum needs. The traditional spectrum allocation manner is fixed to licensed users, which is not efficient any more.

Cognitive radio (CR) is a promising technology applied in smart grid to achieve efficient utilization of spectrum resources [5]. There are two types of communication networks: the primary network and secondary network. The primary network is the licensed user of spectrum resources, and the secondary network is unlicensed user and has lower priority than the primary network to access the spectrum resources. Different from fixed spectrum allocation manner, CR allows secondary network to sense the spectrum of primary network, share and access the spectrum of primary network without harmful interference. In CR enabled smart grid, the smart grid communication opportunistically accesses the communication resources of other wireless applications. Through the exploitation of communication resources, the CR enabled smart grid can utilize the spectrum in an efficient manner to support large volume data and high spectrum needs in smart grid.

Spectrum sharing is an essential technology of CR. When spectrum is occupied by primary network, the secondary network applies spectrum sharing technology to share the spectrum with primary network without harmful interference to primary network. In CR enabled smart grid, smart grid communication can access spectrum of other communication systems through spectrum sharing. In the view of resource dimensions, existing researches of spectrum sharing in CR enabled smart grid can be divided into spectrum sharing in time, frequency, space, power and code domains.

- Spectrum sharing in time domain allows smart grid to communicate when spectrum is not occupied by primary network, which is spectrum sensing technology of CR [6].
- Spectrum sharing in frequency domain allocates spectrum resources to avoid harmful interference to primary network [7].
- Spectrum sharing in space domain, also known as spatial spectrum sharing, allows secondary network to access the spectrum of primary network in specific geographic regions [8].
- Spectrum sharing in power domain allocates the transmitted power of secondary network to keep the interference to primary network below interference threshold [9].
- Spectrum sharing in code domain allows secondary network to utilize different code words from primary network to access spectrum [10].

There are several related survey papers about CR enabled smart grid. The survey in [11] briefly illustrates how to apply CR in smart grid communication and realize the operation and control of smart grid. In [1], a comprehensive overview is provided including network architecture of CR enabled smart grid, spectrum sensing mechanism and network protocol progress. An up-to-date review on standards and security issues is offered in [12] for smart grid based on cognitive radio technologies. To the author's knowledge, there are no surveys paying attention to spectrum sharing technology in CR enabled smart grid. In this survey, a comprehensive survey is provided which illustrates the architecture and technologies of CR enabled smart grid and highlights spectrum sharing technology from different resource dimensions.

2   Cognitive Radio Enabled Smart Grid

2.1   Architecture and Paradigm

Architecture. CR enabled smart grid has three communication architectures including cognitive home area network (HAN), cognitive neighborhood area network (NAN) and cognitive wide area network (WAN).

A cognitive HAN is designed to perform commissioning and control functions through adopting cognitive radio technologies in a HAN [13]. By employing cognitive home gateway (HGW), a cognitive HAN contains the ability of self-configuration and self-adaptation. A cognitive HAN performs the function of commission by identifying the appearance and leave of devices, constructing a communication network, and maintaining the network link. Cognitive radio technologies guarantee a HAN not to conflict with the primary communication.

A cognitive NAN is treated as the intermediate node between cognitive HANs and cognitive WANs. By employing a cognitive NAN gateway (NGW) as the center, a cognitive NAN firstly connects a number of HANs to collect consumer information such as power consumption, then transmits the consumer information to the control center through cognitive WAN [14]. With cognitive radio technologies, cognitive NANs can access the spectrum of other communication networks on the premise of communication security.

As the upper tier of the SG communication architecture, a cognitive WAN is constructed by several cognitive NANs and conducts communication between cognitive NANs, smart grid devices and substations. On one hand, a cognitive WAN utilizing cognitive radio technologies communicates with cognitive NANs to collect consumer information and transmit control information. On the other hand, a cognitive WAN is connected to core network through licensed communication fashions such as cellular network and wired network to guarantee communication capacity and security [15].

Figure 1 briefly shows the relationship among three communication architectures. Cognitive HANs are responsible for collecting consumer data and transmitting the data to cognitive NANs through HGWs. Each cognitive NAN is connected with several cognitive HANs and responsible for transmitting the data from cognitive HANs to the control center. A cognitive WAN is constructed by several cognitive NANs, which collects consumer data via cognitive radio technologies and transmits to control center via licensed communication fashions.

Paradigm. According to the spectrum access fashion, there are three kinds of communication paradigms for CR enabled smart grid: underlay, overlay and interweave [16].

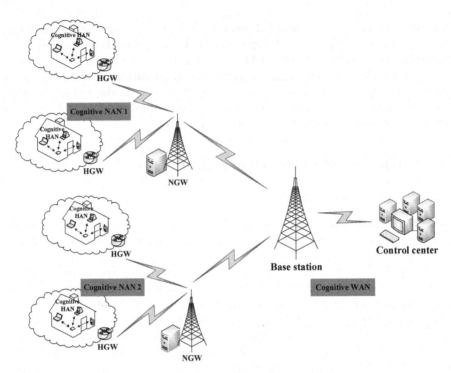

Fig. 1. Architectures of CR enabled smart grid.

The choice of communication paradigms is mainly determined by occupancy of spectrum, interference threshold of primary network, cost efficiency of CR enabled smart grid.

For underlay communication paradigm, CR enabled smart grid shares the spectrum with other communication systems simultaneously. Through adjust transmitting parameters, CR enabled smart grid controls the interference to primary network below a certain interference threshold depending on the performance requirement of primary network. The underlay communication paradigm is suitable for HAN due to the characteristics of low data rates and short ranges [1].

In overlay communication paradigm, CR enabled smart grid has prior information of primary network such as transmit pattern and strategy, mitigates interference from primary network and relays primary data to the receiver in primary network. Through identifying primary network and relaying primary data, CR enabled smart grid cooperates with primary network and thus achieves high security and data rates.

Interweave communication paradigm utilizes spectrum sensing technology to make CR enabled smart gird access spectrum which is not occupied by primary network. When spectrum is occupied by primary network, CR enabled smart grid as the secondary network continues to monitor the spectrum so as to communicate when primary network stops transmitting. Like underlay communication paradigm, interweave communication paradigm is suitable for HAN.

2.2 Standardization

For cognitive radio technologies and smart grids, there have been a lot of efforts to promote the standardization. For instance, IEEE 802.22 is the first standard for cognitive radio communication, which specifies how wireless regional area networks (WRANs) can operate in TV white space (TVWS) [5]. A lot of international organizations are driving the standardization of smart grid such as U.S. National Institute of Standards and Technology and European Union Technology Platform [17].

The standardization of CR enabled smart grid is still on the way. IEEE 802.15.4 g [18] and IEEE 802.15.4e [19] are two standards for CR enabled smart grid on TVWS. As a supplement standard of IEEE 802.15.4, IEEE 802.15.4 g provides the physical layer design of CR enabled smart grid. IEEE 802.15.4e is another supplement standard of IEEE 802.15.4, which specifies the medium access control layer design of CR enabled smart grid.

2.3 Application

CR enabled smart grid is flexible to be employed in licensed or unlicensed spectrum with different architectures and paradigms. Meanwhile, it's feasible to adjust the transmitting parameters of CR enabled smart grid to satisfy different quality of service (QoS) requirements of both CR enabled smart grid and primary network. Based on the advantages above, CR enabled smart grid has various applications [12].

According to QoS requirements of smart grid, the applications are divided into three categories: robust-aware application, real-time application and security-aware application. Table 1 shows the specific applications of CR enabled smart grid.

Table 1. Applications of CR enabled smart grid

Application	QoS requirement	Example
Robust-aware application	High stability and reliability of power grid system	Distributed generation system [20]; Automatic generation control [21]
Real-time application	High transmitting speed	Real-time pricing and demand response management [22]
Security-aware application	Safety, reliability, and security of smart grid	Wide area situation awareness [12]

3 Spectrum Sharing

3.1 Motivation and Classification

Spectrum sharing is an essential technology of CR enabled smart grid. With the large scale deployment of smart grid and increasing demand for spectrum resources, spectrum sharing can support large scale access to spectrum and high spectral efficiency through sharing the spectrum of other communication systems.

As classified by communication paradigms, spectrum sharing is divided into three categories: underlay, overlay and interweave spectrum sharing. Underlay spectrum sharing enables smart grid to transmit secondary signals when primary spectrum is occupied by primary network. In overlay spectrum sharing, secondary network has prior information of primary network, utilizes the prior information to mitigate interference from primary network, and transmits primary signals as a relay to generate cooperation relationship with primary network. For interweave spectrum sharing, smart grid senses the occupation of spectrum, opportunistically shares the spectrum of primary network when the spectrum is not occupied.

When classified by resource dimensions, existing research of spectrum sharing in CR enabled smart grid can be divided into spectrum sharing in time, frequency, space, power and code domains.

3.2   Spectrum Sharing in Resource Dimensions

Spectrum sharing in time domain, that is spectrum sensing technology, allows smart grid to communicate when spectrum is not occupied by primary network. The survey paper [1] provides a comprehensive survey of spectrum sensing technologies employed in smart grid. The commonly used spectrum sensing methods in CR enabled smart grid are energy detection, matched filter and feature detection. The study in [6] employs energy detection method to enable spectrum utilization of smart grid, where the spectrum sensing time of CR enabled smart grid is optimized under the constraint of protection on primary network. [23] also pays attention to the optimization of spectrum sensing time, which researches a cognitive radio based switching procedure to optimize the spectrum sensing time. The research in [24] utilizes spectrum sensing combined with channel switching technologies to realize high reliability and timeliness, where the spectrum sensing time is optimized to reduce the packet loss and delay time. In [25], spectrum sensing method is improved by proposing a multi-objective approach which satisfies the optimization of spectrum sensing time and communication cost.

Spectrum sharing in frequency domain allocates spectrum resources to avoid harmful interference to primary network. The research in [7] allocates spectrum resources to multiple secondary users in CR enabled smart grid with the aid of clustering technology under practical constraints. In [26], the authors consider the requirements difference of secondary users including serving priority and spectrum bandwidth, and employ binary particle swarm optimization method to optimize the spectrum allocation problem. An improved spectrum allocation method of [26] is proposed in [27], which considers the difference of secondary user priority and spectrum idle time, and utilizes hidden Markov model to make the spectrum allocation decision. Markov model is also utilized for spectrum allocation in [28], where a spectrum allocation based spectrum sharing scheme is proposed based on Markov chain model. In [29], a spectrum allocation scheme is proposed to allow hierarchical data transmission in CR enabled smart grid based on clustering technology considering spectrum availability and secondary user priority. The study in [30] concerns the optimization of spectrum allocation strategy in cognitive radio NAN gateway using differential pricing and admission control.

Spectrum sharing in space domain, also known as spatial spectrum sharing, allows secondary network to access the spectrum of primary network in specific geographic regions. In [8], a joint spatial and temporal spectrum sharing scheme is proposed for demand response management in cognitive radio enabled smart grid. The proposed scheme utilizes the geographic distribution difference of secondary users caused by large scale deployment of smart grid in a large geographic area. Traditionally, spectrum sensing and sharing performance of secondary users in different region is regarded as the same. The proposed scheme in [8] exploits the spectrum opportunities in joint spatial and temporal domain to improve the spectrum sharing performance in CR enabled smart grid.

Spectrum sharing in power domain allocates the transmitted power of secondary network to keep the interference to primary network below interference threshold. Several optimization methods can be employed to optimize the power allocation to secondary users [9, 31]. Iterative water filling is a conventional optimization method in power allocation, which utilizes the information of channel noise and interference to calculate the transmit power of each secondary user until convergence. Game theory is a common method used by spectrum sharing in power domain. In game theory, each secondary user is treated as a player in game, and plays with other players with a certain payoff until achieving Nash equilibrium. Genetic algorithm is suitable for the spectrum sharing problem whose optimal solution in closed form is hard to derive. For genetic algorithm based spectrum sharing, each secondary user is regarded as the chromosomes while the possible solutions are the genes inside a chromosome. The weakness of genetic algorithm is that it is difficult to get global optimum, even simulation is not guaranteed to be convergence.

Spectrum sharing in code domain allows secondary network to utilize different code words from primary network to access spectrum. In [4], spectrum sharing in code domain is investigated based on linear precoding technology, which enables the secondary users in CR enabled smart grid to share spectrum with primary network without harmful interference. Through deploying pre-coder and decoder, the interference among multiple secondary users and primary network is avoided when sharing the same spectrum to communicate. In [10], code division multiple access is utilized to realize the coexistence between CR enabled smart grid and primary network. By proposing a specific kind of orthogonal chip sequence allocation in spread spectrum communications, spectrum sharing is realized in code domain to improve the spectral efficiency of CR enabled smart grid.

4 Conclusion

Smart grid is the most promising next-generation electric power system to solve the problems of traditional power grid. Smart grid communication is an important function which is satisfied by wired communication and wireless communication. In the face of large volume data and high spectrum needs, fixed spectrum allocation fashion is not suitable for smart grid. By employing cognitive radio technologies, cognitive radio enabled smart grid can realize efficient spectrum utilization. Through adjusting transmitting parameters of cognitive radio enabled smart grid, spectrum sharing technology enables cognitive smart grid to share the spectrum resource with primary network while avoiding harmful interference to the primary network. In this survey paper, we have surveyed the architecture, paradigm, standardization and application of cognitive radio enabled smart grid. Moreover, we have illustrated the investigation of spectrum sharing in different radio resource dimensions. In conclusion, spectrum sharing is essential to improve network capacity and spectrum utilization in cognitive radio enabled smart grid.

References

1. Khan, A.A., Rehmani, M.H., Reisslein, M.: Cognitive radio for smart grids: survey of architectures, spectrum sensing mechanisms, and networking protocols. IEEE Commun. Surv. Tutor. 18(1), 860–898 (2016)
2. You, M., Liu, Q., Sun, H.: New communication strategy for spectrum sharing enabled smart grid cyber-physical system. IET Cyber-Phys. Syst. Theory Appl. 2(3), 136–142 (2017)
3. Yu, R., Zhang, C., Zhang, X., et al.: Hybrid spectrum access in cognitive-radio-based smart-grid communications systems. IEEE Syst. J. 8(2), 577–587 (2014)
4. Islam, S.N., Mahmud, M.A., Oo, A.T., et al.: Interference management for cognitive radio enabled smart grid communication. In: IEEE Pes Asia-pacific Power & Energy Engineering Conference. IEEE (2018)
5. Ghassemi, A., Bavarian, S., Lampe, L.: Cognitive radio for smart grid communications. In: Proceedings of IEEE SmartGridComm, Gaithersburg, MD, USA, pp. 297–302 (2010)
6. Peng, Y., Wang, P., Xiang, W., Li, Y.: Secret key generation based on estimated channel state information for TDD-OFDM systems over fading channels. IEEE Trans. Wirel. Commun. 16(8), 5176–5186 (2017)
7. Alam, S., Aqdas, N., Qureshi, I.M., et al.: Clustering-based channel allocation scheme for neighborhood area network in a cognitive radio based smart grid communication. IEEE Access 6, 25773–25784 (2018)
8. Long, H., Xiang, W., Zhang, Y., Liu, Y., Wang, W.: Secrecy capacity enhancement with distributed precoding in multirelay wiretap systems. IEEE Trans. Inf. Forensics Secur. 8(1), 229–238 (2012)
9. Hiew, Y.K., Aripin, N.M., Din, N.M.: Asynchronous iterative water filling for cognitive smart grid communications. In: Computer Applications & Industrial Electronics. IEEE (2015)
10. Xiang, W., Barbulescu, S.A., Pietrobon, S.S.: Unequal error protection applied to JPEG image transmission using turbo codes. In: Proceedings 2001 IEEE Information Theory Workshop (Cat. No. 01EX494), pp. 64–66 (2001)
11. Dehalwar, V., Kolhe, M., Kolhe, S.: Cognitive radio application for smart grid. Int. J. Smart Grid Clean Energy 1(1), 79–84 (2012)
12. Le, T.N., Chin, W.L., Chen, H.H.: Standardization and security for smart grid communications based on cognitive radio technologies – a comprehensive survey. IEEE Commun. Surv. Tutor. 19, 423–445 (2016)
13. Yu, R., et al.: Cognitive radio based hierarchical communication infrastructure for smart grid. IEEE Netw. 25(5), 6–14 (2011)
14. Meng, W., Ma, R., Chen, H.-H.: Smart grid neighborhood area networks: a survey. IEEE Netw. 28(1), 24–32 (2014)
15. Liu, F., Wang, J., Han, Y., Han, P.: Cogitive radio networks for smart grid communications. In: Proceedings of 9th Asian Control Conference (ASCC), Istanbul, Turkey, pp. 1–5 (2013)
16. Kouhdaragh, V., Tarchi, D., Coralli, A.V., et al.: Cognitive radio based smart grid networks. In: Tyrrhenian International Workshop on Digital Communications-green ICT. IEEE (2013)

17. Güngör, V.C., et al.: Smart grid technologies: Communication technologies and standards. IEEE Trans. Ind. Informat. **7**(4), 529–539 (2011)
18. IEEE Standard 802.15.4 g, Part 15.4: Low-Rate Wireless Personal Area Networks (LR-WPANs) Amendment 3: Physical Layer (PHY) Specifications for Low-Data-Rate, Wireless, Smart Metering Utility Networks, IEEE Standard 802.15.4 g (2012)
19. IEEE Standard 802.15.4e, Part 15.4: Low-Rate Wireless Personal Area Networks (LR-WPANs) Amendment I: MAC Sublayer, IEEE Standard 802.15.4e (2012)
20. Kabouris, J., Kanellos, F.D.: Impacts of large-scale wind penetration on designing and operation of electric power systems. IEEE Trans. Sustain. Energy **1**(2), 107–114 (2010)
21. Ma, X., Li, H., Djouadi, S.: Networked system state estimation in smart grid over cognitive radio infrastructures. In: Proceedings of 45th Annual Conference on Information Sciences and Systems (CISS), Baltimore, MD, USA (2011)
22. Bu, S., Yu, F.R.: Green cognitive mobile networks with small cells for multimedia communications in the smart grid environment. IEEE Trans. Veh. Technol. **63**(5), 2115–2126 (2014)
23. Cacciapuoti, A.S., Caleffi, M., Marino, F., et al.: Sensing-time optimization in cognitive radio enabling Smart Grid. In: Euro Med Telco Conference. IEEE (2014)
24. Deng, R., Maharjan, S., Cao, X., et al.: Sensing-delay tradeoff for communication in cognitive radio enabled smart grid. In: IEEE International Conference on Smart Grid Communications (SmartGridComm), 2011 (2011)
25. Hsiao, W.L., Chiu, W.Y.: Spectrum sensing control for enabling cognitive radio based smart grid. In: 2016 2nd International Conference on Intelligent Green Building and Smart Grid (IGBSG) (2016)
26. Yang, S., Wang, J., Han, Y., et al.: Dynamic spectrum allocation algorithm based on fairness for smart grid communication networks. In: Control Conference. IEEE (2016)
27. Yang, S., Wang, J., Han, Y., et al.: Dynamic spectrum allocation algorithm based on matching scheme for smart grid communication network. In: IEEE International Conference on Computer & Communications. IEEE (2017)
28. Ma, R., Chen, H.H., Meng, W.: Dynamic spectrum sharing for the coexistence of smart utility networks and WLANs in smart grid communications. IEEE Netw. **31**(1), 88–96 (2017)
29. Aroua, S., El Korbi, I., Ghamri-Doudane, Y., Saidane, L.A.: Hierarchical fair spectrum sharing in CRSNsfor smart grid monitoring. In: 2018 IEEE 87th Vehicular Technology Conference (VTC Spring) (2018)
30. Zhao, X., et al.: Spectrum allocation with differential pricing and admission in cognitive-radio-based neighborhood area network for smart grid. In: 2018 IEEE/IFIP Network Operations and Management Symposium (2018)
31. Jiang, T.: On-demand cognitive radio communications for smart grid. In: 2016 IEEE International Conference on Smart Grid Communications (SmartGridComm) (2016)

Colorization of Characters Based on the Generative Adversarial Network

Changtong Liu, Lin Cao, and Kangning Du[✉]

Beijing Information Science and Technology University, No. 35, North Fourth Ring Road, Beijing, China
kangningdu@outlook.com

Abstract. With the development of economy, global demand for electricity is increasing, and the requirements for the stability of the power grid are correspondingly improved. The intelligence of the power grid is an inevitable choice for the research and development of power systems. Aiming at the security of the smart grid operating environment, this paper proposes a gray-scale image coloring method based on generating anti-network, which is used for intelligent monitoring of network equipment at night, and realizes efficient monitoring of people and environment in different scenarios. Based on the original Generative Adversarial Network, the method uses the Residual Net improved network to improve the integrity of the generated image information, and adds the least squares loss to the generative network to narrow the distance between the sample and the decision boundary. Through the comparison experiments in the self-built CASIA-Plus-Colors high-quality character dataset, it is verified that the proposed method has better performance in colorization of different background images.

Keywords: Image colorization · Intelligent electric grid · Generative Adversarial Network

1 Introduction

The construction of the global smart grid is developing rapidly, and its protection devices are distributed in different areas and play an extremely important role in the safe and stable operation of the power grid [1–5]. However, the protection devices of the current power grid lack intelligent monitoring of the operating environment of the equipment, especially the images taken by optical, infrared and other monitoring devices at night are mostly gray-scale images. Aiming at the above problems, this paper proposes a gray image coloring method based on generating anti-network, which achieves accurate coloring of characters and background in the image and improves the use value of the image. The application model of the colorization system is shown in Fig. 1. Especially at night, the gray-scale image of the device environment is collected in real time by the image sensor and transmitted to the smart grid control center. The collected gray-scale image is judged by the control center, and the gray-scale image with the suspicious problem is selected. Then it is uploaded to the gray-scale image colorization subsystem

X. Zhang et al. (Eds.): CloudComp 2019/SmartGift 2019, LNICST 322, pp. 636–649, 2020.
https://doi.org/10.1007/978-3-030-48513-9_51

to colorize the image with suspicious problems and transmit the colorized image back to the smart grid control center. Relative to the gray-scale image, the color image contains more valuable information, and the control center makes an accurate judgment for the color image. In recent years, in the field of image, the application of digital processing technology and deep learning methods have been gradually deepened [6, 7].

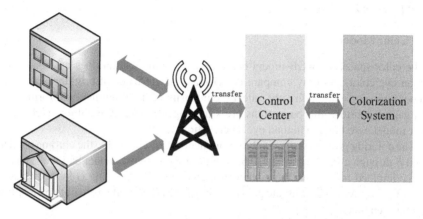

Fig. 1. Color system application model

Traditional image coloring methods mainly include local color expansion of methods [8, 9] and color transfer of methods [10, 11]. The traditional image colorization method requires a large number of artificial work or reference images with similar scenes, so it is greatly influenced by artificial factors and the coloring complexity is high.

In order to reduce the influence of artificial factors in the traditional image coloring method, the method based on deep learning [12–15] has been gradually proposed. Iizuka et al. [12] used a two-channel network to combine the local features of the image with global prior information to achieve automatic coloration of gray-scale images. Larsson et al. [13] used the VGG network [16] to extract image features and predict the color distribution of each pixel. Zhang et al. [14, 15] proposed a gray image coloring method for classifying pixel points and based on user guidance.

In recent years, the Generative Adversarial Network (GAN) [17] has achieved great success in the field of image generation. Compared with the traditional neural network [18], GAN generates higher image quality. However, GAN's training is unstable and prone to mode collapse. Therefore, Zhu et al. [19] proposed a Cycle Generative Adversarial Network (Cycle-GAN) based on Isola [20] to improve the stability of the training network.

In summary, for the security problem of power grid equipment, this paper proposes a method of portrait intelligent coloring, which is mainly used for colorization of grayscale images in nighttime environment, which can enable observers to obtain more information from color images and improve the ability to monitor the environment. The generation network is switched to the U-Net network [21] to improve the image generation details and to add the least squares loss as an optimization target for image coloring to improve the stability of the network. In the discriminant network, the image features are extracted by means of multi-layer feature fusion, so that the extracted features more represent image details. Finally, the model is trained with improved consistency loss. In this paper, experiments are carried out on the self-built CASIA-Plus-Colors dataset. The results verify the effectiveness of the proposed method.

2   Approach

2.1   Color Model

In the color space, the RGB model based on color combination does not adapt to the human eye color, can only compare the visual characteristics of brightness and color temperature, and cannot directly reflect the intensity of the illumination information in the image. Therefore, this paper transforms an image from an RGB color model to a Lab color model based on the human eye's perception of color.

The coloring process is to map the component x of L channel to the chroma channels a and b through a network model. The output of the network model and the L channel are recombined into a new three-channel image, and the resulting colorized image is $\tilde{X} = (X_L, \tilde{X}_a, \tilde{X}_b)$. The ultimate goal of training the color model is to obtain an optimal mapping relationship of $X_L \rightarrow \tilde{X}_{ab}$.

2.2   Network Structure

The traditional GAN is one-way generation, using a single loss function as a global optimization target, which may map multiple samples to the same distribution, resulting in a pattern crash. CycleGAN uses a loop to generate confrontation, effectively avoiding this deficiency of traditional GAN. This paper proposes a colorization model based on CycleGAN, which improves the traditional GAN reverse-transfer optimization network. It uses the consistency loss of reconstructed data to reverse the whole network and strengthens the stability of the original network. At the same time, in order to improve the integrity of the generated image information, the residual network is used to improve the original generation network; and the multi-feature fusion method is introduced into the discriminant network, so that the extracted features more represent the details of the image.

Color Network Model. The colorization model in this paper consists of four subnetworks which are respectively the generation network G: responsible for mapping the L-channel gray-scale image to the ab-channel color component, generating the network F: responsible for mapping the ab-channel color component to the L-channel gray-scale image, discriminating the network: used to discriminate between the L-channel grayscale image and the gray-scale image generated by the generated network, and the discrimination network: used to distinguishing between the real color image and the composite image of the generated ab-channel component and L-channel gray-scale image. The goal of the network is to obtain an optimal correspondence by training the L channel component and the ab channel color component, and mapping the L channel gray-scale image to the ab channel color component. The network structure is shown in Fig. 2.

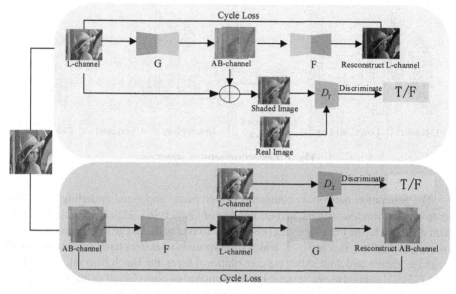

Fig. 2. Generative adversarial network structure

The above sub-networks constitute a pair of cyclic generation networks that respectively map the input samples to the intermediate domain and then reconstruct the data of the intermediate domains back into the original domain. For example, an L-channel gray-scale image is input, which is eventually mapped back to the gray-scale image, and the intermediate domain data is the generated ab-channel color component. Similarly, when the input is an ab-channel color component, it will eventually be reconstructed back into the original domain. The middle domain is the gray-scale image generated by the F network.

In the original CycleGAN, the two cyclic generative networks are independent of each other. When the two cyclic processes are completed, the consistency loss of the cyclic generative network is calculated separately. The colorization model of this paper combines the data reconstructed by two loop generation networks which recombines the output ab-channel color component and L channel gray-scale image to obtain a reconstructed color image. Then, the L1 distance between the reconstructed color image and the real color image is calculated as the cyclic consistency loss of the network, and the reverse transmission optimization of the entire network is realized together.

Generative Network Model. In the traditional GAN, the generative network consists of only a simple convolution layer and a deconvolution layer. When extracting features, it is easy to lose local information of the image and limit the coloring effect of the network. As shown in Fig. 3, in order to avoid the above problem, the generated network uses residual network to connect the features outputted by each layer in the underling layer to the corresponding upper layer through a skip connection. The purpose of adding skip connections is to pass shallow information directly to the deconvolution layer of the same height, forming thicker features and improving image generation details.

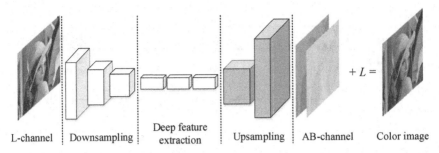

Fig. 3. Generative network structure

The generation network is composed of two parts: upper and underling layer. The underling section has 4 layers, and the number of filters is [64, 128, 256, 512]. As can be seen in Fig. 3, during the underlying process, each layer of the image features is convolved twice, and the filter size is 3 × 3, which of purpose is to extract basic information such as image texture structure. After the convolutional layer, the Batch Normalization (BN) layer [25] is designed to adjust the data distribution after convolution so that the output of the convolution is distributed in the near-origin field of the activation function, reducing the gradient dispersion rate and avoiding the gradient disappearing. The active layer uses a Leaky Rectified Linear Unit (LRELU) instead of the original Rectified Linear Unit (RELU) [19], which aims to reduce the computational complexity and does not lead to negative neurons in the value area are all zero. The purpose of generating the network is to map the input to the distribution of the target domain space, for example, according to the lip shape feature corresponding to the reddish process.

Discriminant Network Model. The traditional discriminant network uses a single layer feature to express the entire image, and it is easy to lose the details of an image. Therefore, this paper introduces the multi-feature fusion method of the discriminant network (see Fig. 4). The use of the fused features enhances the expression of image detail and improves the accuracy of image recognition. At the same time, in order to avoid dimensional disaster, coding network is added behind the fusion layer to reduce dimensions of feature.

The generated component $\tilde{X}_{ab}$ is combined with the L-channel component to form a colored image, and the discriminating network D_Y distinguishes between it and the real color image. Because of the correlation between the two, the discriminator can learn through the convolutional neural network to obtain more effective image features and correctly classify the two types of images. For discriminating the network, first input a three-channel 256 × 256 color image, and then after 6 convolutions with strides, finally output 256 feature maps which of size is 5 × 5. The convolution kernel size of the feature extraction is 5 × 5, the convolution step is 2, and the number of feature maps of each convolution layer respectively are 8, 16, 32, 64, 128, 256. After the convolution, the features are fused, and the fourth layer and the fifth layer are subjected to the average pooling layer of different size to generate 448 feature maps. Then feature map is stretched to a vector of 11264-dimensional length, and the feature's dimension is reduced to

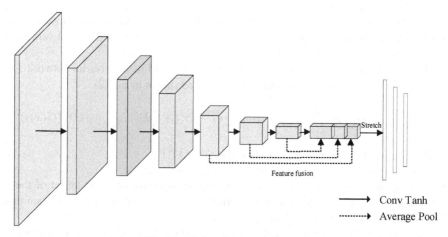

Fig. 4. Adversarial network model

1024 dimensions using a multi-layer full connection. In order to further prevent over-fitting during feature dimension reduction, the Dropout layer is added after the fully connected layer, and the probability value is set to 0.7. Finally, the feature vector is input to the Sigmoid function [26] to determine whether the generated image conforms to the distribution of the real image. For the other discrimination network, the input image is a single-channel gray-scale image, and the model structure is the same as the discrimination network D_Y.

2.3 Loss Function

The traditional GAN only uses the generative adversarial loss function, and there is redundant mapping space. This paper combines the traditional generative adversarial loss and the cyclic consistency loss to supervise the training network jointly, effectively avoiding this problem.

Generative Adversarial Network. The cyclic generation applies a process of mapping the input image to the intermediate domain image against the resistive loss in the network. The original cross entropy loss is as shown in Eq. (1), which makes it impossible for the generator to further optimize the generated image recognized by the discriminator which may result in a low quality of the network generated image. Inspired by Mao [22], the paper uses the least squares loss instead of the traditional generative adversarial loss. Comparing with the original loss function, the least squares loss will process the generated samples away from the decision boundary and the decision is true, and the generated samples far from the decision boundary will be placed near the decision boundary. According to the different distance from the decision boundary, a stable and high-quality network is constructed.

$$L_{GAN}(G, D_Y, X, Y) = E_{y \sim P_{data}(y)}[\log D_Y(y)] + E_{x \sim P_{data}(x)}\{\log\{1 - D_Y[G(x)]\}\}$$

$$(1)$$

Where $x \sim P_{data}(x)$ and $y \sim P_{data}(y)$ are the probability distributions of the samples X and Y respectively. $E_{x \sim Pata(x)}$ and $E_{y \sim Pata(y)}$ are the expected values for the respective sample distributions.

Therefore, for the generative network $G : X \to Y$ and its adversarial network D_Y, the least squares loss function definition herein is as shown in Eq. (2).

$$\min_{D_Y} L_{LSGAN}(D_Y) = \frac{1}{2}E_{y \sim P_{data}(y)}[(D_Y(y) - 1)^2] + \frac{1}{2}E_{x \sim P_{data}(x)}[(D_Y(G(x)))^2]$$

$$\min_{G} L_{LSGAN}(G) = \frac{1}{2}E_{x \sim P_{data}(x)}[(D_Y(G(x)) - 1)^2] \tag{2}$$

The generating network G generates the X domain data to match the target of the Y domain distribution, and discriminant network D distinguishes the real Y domain data $\{y\}$ and the generated sample $\{G(x)\}$.

Training the discriminator, the loss function goal is to make the discriminator distinguish between the real sample and the generated sample, maximizing $D_Y(y)$ and minimizing $D_Y(G(x))$. Training generator, the goal of the loss function is to make the generated data close to the real data, maximizing $D_Y(G(x))$. The target of the loss is shown in Eq. (3).

$$G^* = \arg \min_{G, D_Y} L_{GAN}(G, D_Y, X, Y) \tag{3}$$

For the generation network $F : Y \to X$ and the corresponding discriminant network, the same generative adversarial loss is also introduced, and the loss target is as shown in Eq. (4).

$$F^* = \arg \min_{F, D_X} L_{GAN}(F, D_X, Y, X) \tag{4}$$

Cyclic Consistency Loss. The traditional GAN only uses the adversarial loss training network to learn the relationship of the input image mapping to the target image, but it cannot solve the redundant mapping problem existing in the generated network. The cyclic generation network uses the loop consistency loss to better ensure the stability of the generated data and reduce other redundant mapping relationships.

Based on this idea, this paper proposes to recombine the reconstructed data and calculate its L1 loss with the input color image as the network's cyclic consistency loss.

In Fig. 2, the samples of the L-channel gray-scale image and the ab-channel color component are x_{ab} and x_L.

$x_{ab} \to G(x_{ab}) \to F(G(x_{ab})) \approx \hat{x}_{ab}$ and $x_L \to F(x_L) \to G(F(x_L)) \approx \hat{x}_L$ in the network are respectively two reconstruction processes. This paper separately calculates the consistency loss of reconstruction data. The equation is as follows:

$$L_{cyc}(G, F) = E_{x \sim P_{data}(x)}[||F(G(x) - x||_1] + E_{y \sim P_{data}(y)}[||G(F(y)) - y||_1] \tag{5}$$

The complete objective function includes adversarial loss and cyclic consistency loss, as shown in Eq. (6):

$$L(G, F, D_X, D_Y) = L_{LSGAN}(G, D_Y, X, Y) + L_{LSGAN}(F, D_X, Y, X) + \lambda L_{cyc}(G, F) \tag{6}$$

Among them, the x parameter is used to adjust the weight of the least square loss and the cycle consistency loss.

We aim to solve:

$$G^*, F^* = \underset{G,F,D_X,D_Y}{\arg\min} \; L(G, F, D_X, D_Y) \tag{7}$$

3 Experimental Data

There are many publicly available Face Databases, such as Public Figures Face Database and Celebrity Faces Attributes Database, which are mainly used in face recognition and other fields. The portrait images of these characters are mostly concentrated in the face area of the person, and the image quality is different. The effect of training with these pictures is not good. In order to solve the problem of the database, based on the CASIA-FaceV5 database, the data set is expanded by crawling technology. The final database contains a total of 9,500 color images of various poses and backgrounds, referred to as CASIA-PC (CASIA-Plus-Color).

CASIA-FaceV5 is a database published by the Chinese Academy of Sciences. The database is an open Asian portrait dataset containing 2,500 high-quality color images from 500 people. Through observation, it is found that most of the characters in the database are frontal photos in a monochrome background, lacking scenes in the actual environment.

(1)   (2)   (3)   (4)

Fig. 5. This is an example of the self-built data set in this article. (1) From CASIA (2)–(4) From WEB

In order to solve the problem of lack of the real scene portrait in CASIA-FaceV5 database, based on the database, this paper uses the crawler technology to complete the task of automatically and modularly collecting 7000 colored portraits.

In this paper, the CASIA-PC dataset was used. The size of all the images was adjusted to 225 × 225 pixels, and the database was divided into training set and test set. The training set consisted of 8600 randomly selected images; the remaining images were used as test sets. Examples of the database are shown in Fig. 5, wherein the first column is picked from the CASIA database and portraits of the second to the fourth columns are picked from collected portraits. As can be seen in Fig. 5, the scenes of the self-built dataset are rich and the color is colorful, which increases the difficulty of coloring.

In order to objectively evaluate the quality of the generated image, Structural Similarity Index (SSIM) [24] and Peak Signal to Noise Ratio (PSNR) are used to evaluate the image.

4   Experiment and Analysis

4.1 Experimental Procedure

Experimental Pretreatment. In the pre-processing stage of the experiment, the color model of each image is transferred from RGB to Lab model, and the L-channel and the ab-channel component of the colorful portraits are separated as the input of the network.

Setting Parameters. In the data training process, both the generator and the discriminator use the Adam optimizer with an initial learning rate of 0.0002 and a momentum of 0.5 to update the parameters of the network, and the linear attenuation method is used to reduce the learning rate gradually. After continuous iterative training until the model converges, storing the parameters of the entire network.

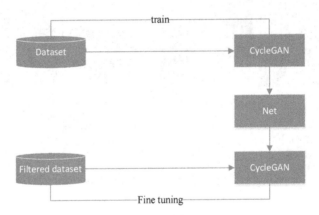

Fig. 6. Model training process

Experiment Procedure. The experimental process is shown in Fig. 6 and can be divided into two phases. In the first stage, 8600 training samples are used to train the entire network to obtain a colorization model. In order to avoid over-fitting of the network, when the network is trained with a large data set, due to the different quality of images, some will have color distortion and image blurring, which will affect the coloring effect of the model. Therefore, in the second stage of the experiment, some training samples with relatively high quality were selected in the larger original data set, and the parameters of the network were fine-tuned. The first stage of the experiment is to make the generative network G learn the correspondence from the gray image mapping to the ab-channel color component, and the second stage is to improve the accuracy of the model coloring.

4.2 Experimental Results and Analysis

The coloring results of different methods are shown in Fig. 7. The first column is the gray image of the L-channel; the second column is the origin color image; the third column is the coloring result of the original CycleGAN; the fourth column is based on the third column method, which of generative structure is changed to the residual network; the last column is the coloring result of the method in this article.

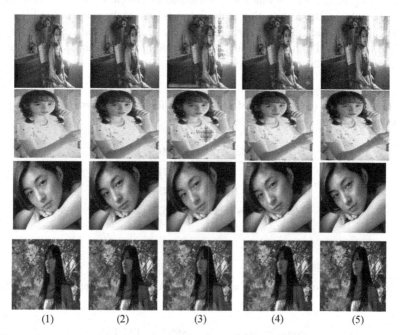

(1)   (2)   (3)   (4)   (5)

Fig. 7. Comparison of different methods of coloring effects. (1) Gray Scale (2) Original image (3) CycleGAN (5) CycleGAN + Residual (5) Method of this paper

According to the results of different colorization model, when using the original CycleGAN model for coloring, the effect is rough, the color saturation and coloring accuracy are low, and problems such as coloring wrong or overflow may occur. For example, in the third line of Fig. 7, the leaves in the original image are mistakenly colored into other colors. And in the fifth line, the color belonging to the face area is beyond its own range and spreads to areas such as trees and sky. The method of generative network using the residual network, the coloring result of the model, as shown in the second line, greatly improves the coloring accuracy of a single image. Although under complex background images, the effect of coloring has been improved. There is still the problem of coloring wrong, which is more obvious in its third line. In contrast, the coloring results of the method of this paper are more accurate and natural, and even in images with complex backgrounds, the true colors of portraits and backgrounds can be more accurately given. And it can correctly distinguish different targets in the image and reduce the phenomenon of color overflow, as shown in lines 3 and 4 of the paper's method. In addition, the coloring result of the first line is worth noting. The change in color of the clothing happened. This is because the database lacks the same style costume, or the similar clothing is mostly gray-black. This shows that the training set has a great influence on the coloring result.

This paper compares the PSNR and SSIM average indicators of the three models in a single color and a complex background. As shown in Tables 1 and 2, under the objective index evaluation, with the enrichment of the network structure of three models, the coloring effect in the monochrome background and the complex background is improved in turn. In addition, the colorization of the monochrome background image is relatively easy, because its structure and texture are relatively simple, and the average index of the image in the monochrome background of the same model is significantly higher than that of the image in the complex background.

Table 1. Comparison of average SSIM and PSNR indicators of different methods in complex background

Network model	SSIM/%	PSNR/dB
CycleGAN	95.4718	30.0658
CycleGAN + Residual	96.7481	34.1508
Method of this paper	97.2621	38.4907

Table 2. Comparison of average SSIM and PSNR indicators of different methods in monochrome background

Network model	SSIM/%	PSNR/dB
CycleGAN	96.5804	35.6529
CycleGAN + Residual	97.3104	38.0507
Method of this paper	98.2316	38.6084

In addition, this paper is compared with other coloring models, and the results are shown in Fig. 8. Iizuka [12] uses a two-channel convolution network, and the colorization results are brighter in color, but the coloring accuracy is low. Larsson [13] uses the VGG network to extract image features. The coloring model solves the problem in coloring wrong, but the partial area of the portrait becomes blurred. Zhang [14] classifies each pixel in the image which has high coloring accuracy and clear characters, but low color saturation. When using the method of the paper, the accuracy of colorization is high, the discrimination of different targets is higher, and the color is more natural. However, when coloring the same target, there are problems such as uneven color distribution and low saturation. This paper compares the SSIM and PSNR indexes of the proposed method in different background with other color models, as shown in Tables 3 and 4, respectively. In different scenarios, the image using the proposed method has a higher SSIM and PSNR values than other methods, indicating that the results of the method are more similar to the original image, and the distortion is smaller.

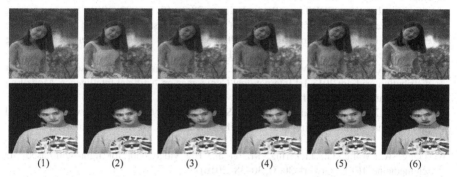

(1)   (2)   (3)   (4)   (5)   (6)

Fig. 8. Comparison of colorization results of different models (1) Gray Scale (2) Original image (3) Larsson (4) Iizuka (5) Zhang (6) Method of this paper

Table 3. Comparison of average SSIM and PSNR indicators of different models in monochrome background

Network model	SSIM/%	PSNR/dB
Iizuka	95.4205	34.6785
Larsson	97.3620	34.6668
Zhang	98.8255	36.9591
Method of this paper	99.0219	38.4917

5 Conclusion

In order to achieve effective monitoring of operation of smart grid on night, this paper proposes a coloring method based on Generative Adversarial Network. The method adopts an improved consistency loss, calculates the L1 loss of the color image and generative image, and achieves the reverse transmission optimization of the entire network.

The generative network uses the Residual Network to extract image features to maintain the stability of the information; the discriminant network extracts image features by means of multi-feature fusion. The experiment proves that compared with the similar methods, the model of this paper is suitable for character coloring in complex scenes, and can complete the task of protecting grid equipment at night effectively.

References

1. Zhang, H.Y., Li, S.D.: Design of adaptive line protection under smart grid. In: 2011 International Conference on Advanced Power System Automation and Protection, vol. 1, pp. 599–603. IEEE (2011)
2. Jing, S., Huang, Q., Wu, J., et al.: A novel whole-view test approach for onsite commissioning in smart substation. IEEE Trans. Power Delivery **28**(3), 1715–1722 (2013)
3. Lin, H., Wang, C., Lei, W.: The design of overvoltage testing system for communication equipment in smart grid. In: 2016 IEEE PES Asia-Pacific Power and Energy Engineering Conference (APPEEC), pp. 1812–1816. IEEE (2016)
4. Halim, H.A., Amirruddin, M., Noorpi, N.S., et al.: An improved protection scheme for smart distribution grid. In: 2013 1st International Conference on Artificial Intelligence, Modelling and Simulation, pp. 337–341. IEEE (2013)
5. Long, H., Xiang, W., Zhang, Y., et al.: Secrecy capacity enhancement with distributed precoding in multirelay wiretap systems. IEEE Trans. Inf. Forensics Secur. **8**(1), 229–238 (2012)
6. Xiang, W., Wang, G., Pickering, M., et al.: Big video data for light-field-based 3D telemedicine. IEEE Network **30**(3), 30–38 (2016)
7. Xiang, W., Barbulescu, S.A., Pietrobon, S.S.: Unequal error protection applied to JPEG image transmission using turbo codes. In: Proceedings 2001 IEEE Information Theory Workshop (Cat. No. 01EX494), pp. 64–66. IEEE (2001)
8. Levin, A., Lischinski, D., Weiss, Y.: Colorization using optimization. ACM Trans. Graph. (TOG) **23**(3), 689–694 (2004)
9. Heo, Y.S., Jung, H.Y.: Probabilistic Gaussian similarity-based local color transfer. Electron. Lett. **52**(13), 1120–1122 (2016)
10. Xiao, Y., Wan, L., Leung, C.S., et al.: Example-based color transfer for gradient meshes. IEEE Trans. Multimedia **15**(3), 549–560 (2012)
11. Qian, Y., Liao, D., Zhou, J.: Manifold alignment based color transfer for multiview image stitching. In: 2013 IEEE International Conference on Image Processing, pp. 1341–1345. IEEE (2013)
12. Iizuka, S., Simo-Serra, E., Ishikawa, H.: Let there be color!: joint end-to-end learning of global and local image priors for automatic image colorization with simultaneous classification. ACM Trans. Graph. (TOG) **35**(4), 110 (2016)
13. Larsson, G., Maire, M., Shakhnarovich, G.: Learning representations for automatic colorization. In: Leibe, B., Matas, J., Sebe, N., Welling, M. (eds.) ECCV 2016. LNCS, vol. 9908, pp. 577–593. Springer, Cham (2016). https://doi.org/10.1007/978-3-319-46493-0_35
14. Zhang, R., Isola, P., Efros, A.A.: Colorful image colorization. In: Leibe, B., Matas, J., Sebe, N., Welling, M. (eds.) ECCV 2016. LNCS, vol. 9907, pp. 649–666. Springer, Cham (2016). https://doi.org/10.1007/978-3-319-46487-9_40
15. Zhang, R., Zhu, J.Y., Isola, P., et al.: Real-time user-guided image colorization with learned deep priors. arXiv preprint arXiv:1705.02999 (2017)
16. Simonyan, K., Zisserman, A.: Very deep convolutional networks for large-scale image recognition. arXiv preprint arXiv:1409.1556 (2014)

17. Goodfellow, I., Pouget-Abadie, J., Mirza, M., et al.: Generative adversarial nets. In: Advances in Neural Information Processing Systems, pp. 2672–2680 (2014)
18. Kingma, D.P., Welling, M.: Auto-encoding variational bayes. arXiv preprint arXiv:1312.6114 (2013)
19. Zhu, J.Y., Park, T., Isola, P., et al.: Unpaired image-to-image translation using cycle-consistent adversarial networks. In: Proceedings of the IEEE International Conference on Computer Vision, pp. 2223–2232 (2017)
20. Isola, P., Zhu, J.Y., Zhou, T., et al.: Image-to-image translation with conditional adversarial networks. In: Proceedings of the IEEE Conference on Computer Vision and Pattern Recognition, pp. 1125–1134 (2017)
21. Ronneberger, O., Fischer, P., Brox, T.: U-net: convolutional networks for biomedical image segmentation. In: Navab, N., Hornegger, J., Wells, W.M., Frangi, A.F. (eds.) MICCAI 2015. LNCS, vol. 9351, pp. 234–241. Springer, Cham (2015). https://doi.org/10.1007/978-3-319-24574-4_28
22. Mao, X., Li, Q., Xie, H., et al.: Least squares generative adversarial networks. In: Proceedings of the IEEE International Conference on Computer Vision, pp. 2794–2802 (2017)
23. Glorot, X., Bordes, A,. Bengio, Y.: Deep sparse rectifier neural networks. In: Proceedings of the Fourteenth International Conference on Artificial Intelligence and Statistics, pp. 315–323 (2011)
24. Wang, Z., Bovik, A.C., Sheikh, H.R., et al.: Image quality assessment: from error visibility to structural similarity. IEEE Trans. Image Process. 13(4), 600–612 (2004)
25. Ioffe, S., Szegedy, C.: Batch normalization: accelerating deep network training by reducing internal covariate shift. arXiv preprint arXiv:1502.03167 (2015)
26. Li, C.H., Lee, C.K.: Minimum cross entropy thresholding. Pattern Recogn. 26(4), 617–625 (1993)

Enhanced LSTM Model for Short-Term Load Forecasting in Smart Grids

Jianing Guo[1(✉)], Yuexing Peng[1], Qingguo Zhou[2], and Qingquan Lv[3]

[1] Beijing University of Posts and Telecommunication, Beijing, China
{guojianing,yxpeng}@bupt.edu.cn
[2] Lanzhou University, Lanzhou, China
zhouqg@lzu.edu.cn
[3] Wind Power Technology Center of Gansu Electric Power Company, Lanzhou, China

Abstract. With the rapid development of smart grids, significant research has been devoted to the methodologies for short-term load forecasting (STLF) due to its significance in forecasting demand on electric power. In this paper an enhanced LSTM model is proposed to upgrade the state-of-the-art LSTM network by exploiting the long periodic information of load, which is missed by the standard LSTM model due to its constraint on input length. In order to distill information from long load sequence and keep the input sequence short enough for LSTM, the long load sequence is reshaped into two-dimension matrix whose dimension accords to the periodicity of load. Accordingly, two LSTM networks are paralleled: one takes the rows as input to extract the temporal pattern of load in short time, while the other one takes the columns as input to distill the periodicity information. A multi-layer perception combines the two outputs for more accurate load forecasting. This model can exploit more information from much longer load sequence with only linear growth in complexity, and the experiment results verify its considerable improvement in accuracy over the standard LSTM model.

Keywords: Long short-term memory · Short term load forecasting · Recurrent neural network

1 Introduction

Load forecasting plays an important role in many departments of electric power system since it is the basis of planning generation, maintain and energy selling. Ranaweera et al. [1] has quantitatively analyzed how prediction error impacts the operation of electric power system. Douglas et al. [2] performed the assessment for system operating risk with known distribution variance of forecasting result. The analyzing of these two articles indicates electric power systems necessarily keep asking for more accurate load forecasting. With the establishment of smart grids, intelligent scheduling has become a new requirement. As the basis of electricity power scheduling, intelligent load forecasting faces new challenges of considering diversified influenced factors and being adaptive to fluctuation. Within all kinds of load forecasting, short term load forecasting (STLF)

X. Zhang et al. (Eds.): CloudComp 2019/SmartGift 2019, LNICST 322, pp. 650–662, 2020.
https://doi.org/10.1007/978-3-030-48513-9_52

forecasts the maximum or average load from one day to one week ahead. It helps the coordination between electric power system departments, the planning of generation and unit commitment scheduling. Accurate STLF is significant to electric grid for saving limited energy and asset. According to the accurate forecast information, it is possible to reasonably regulate the power generation capacity in order to avoid wasting because the power is hard to save. On the contrary, an inaccurate STLF information can lead to excess supply, or underestimation of load, resulting in costlier supplementary service. Therefore, STLF has become an important project in the field of power system and even a small percentage improve is willing to be saw.

2 Literature Study

Many approaches have been developed for STLF, which can be roughly categorized into statistical methods and machine learning methods. Statistical methods include regression methods and gray models. On the basis of known historical data series, a mathematical model is established to describe the relationship between load value and time in time series method. Regression methods are effective for stationary series by building equations to fit the relationship between independent and dependent variables. While for non-stationary series like load series, regression model cannot fit the fluctuation well. And the prediction is not robust with the time period which is highly influenced by factors like weather or holiday [3]. In the work of Cho et al. [4] the ARIMA model and transfer function model are applied to the short-term load forecasting by considering weather-load relationship. By comparing the effectiveness with traditional regression method and single ARIMA method, ARIMA model with transfer function achieves better accuracy. Gray models consider the electric power system as a gray system. It has small amount of computation and good prediction effect in system with uncertain factors. But it is only effective in exponential trend load [5].

Electrical load features typical randomness induced by many external factors such as temperature and special events, which facilitates the deployment of machine learning methods such as neural network and support vector machine. Due to its strong capability of well-fitting nonlinear function, machine learning-based STLF methods account for a high proportion of research. Machine learning-based methods can be classified into shallow network and deep neural network. In a neural network, hidden units at shallower location extract some simple and local information [6], while comes to the deeper layers, they can extract more complicated and global features. So with the simple structure, shallow neural network is not able to extract the complicated pattern in load series while deep neural network can fit them more accuracy.

Haqueau et al. [7] proposed a hybrid approach based on wavelet transform and fuzzy ARTMAP network and has good prediction effect in wind farm power prediction. Ghelardonil et al. [8] broke the load time series into two parts with empirical mode decomposition, respectively describing the trend and the local oscillations of the energy consumption values, and then feed them into support vector machine to train. Experiments results show the method has high prediction accuracy in load prediction. Han et al. [9] utilized the state prediction model and algorithm of weighted least squares, the main approach is to take the voltage characteristic as the basic quantity to describe the state characteristics of the system, and adopt the state estimation method to carry out load prediction, which is advantageous for dynamic load prediction. Zhang et al. [10] used extreme learning machine with ensemble structure to forecast the total load of Australian energy market. The ensemble structure helps decrease the uncertainty of prediction. Kong et al. [11] applied the long short-term memory (LSTM) recurrent neural network based framework into residential households' smart meter data. They compare the difference between the residential load forecasting and substation load and the result shows the LSTM networks achieves the best forecasting performance in residential data among other benchmark algorithm.

As a typical deep neural network for time series, LSTM has strong ability of abstracting features and learning the inner complex patterns of load series, and presents state-of-the-art performance. However, it cannot avoid gradient vanishing and exploding problems so that it has the constraints on the input length. Meanwhile, the computation complexity increases non-linearly as the input length increases, and the forecasting accuracy will not increase with the increase of input length, if not worse. In order to upgrade LSTM by overcoming the input length constraint to distill more significant features of load, in this paper an enhanced LSTM is proposed. By reshaping the long load sequences into two-dimensional matrix whose row size accords to weekly period while column size accords to monthly period, two LSTM networks are paralleled to take rows and columns as input and feed an MLP for better information merging. The model realizes better prediction performance with only linear complexity increase, and experiment result verifies its enhancement over standard LSTM model.

3 Enhanced LSTM Model

3.1 Discovery of Rules in Data

In this section we firstly statistically analyze the feature of load to lay a foundation for the design of the proposed model, and then briefly introduce standard LSTM model to mention its pros and cons. At last, an enhanced LSTM model is detailed to state its main idea to upgrade LSTM network and its structure.

Periodicity. Temporal correlation is the first considerable factor for time series. By analyzing load profiles, it is clear that load is periodic in weeks, months and years. By utilizing the periodicity in the forecasting, the prediction effect can be improved. Figure 1 shows the periodicity in week in the load series (see Fig. 1). Each curve describes the total used load in Toronto in three weeks of May in 2015. It can be shown in the figure that the trends of the three weeks are similar. In other words, load series is periodic on weekly scale. Monthly periodicity is shown in Fig. 2. Three figures respectively corresponding to curves in summer, winter and transitional seasons (spring and autumn) (see Fig. 2). Each curve shows the load through a month. It is clear that load of each season has similar trend. The yearly periodicity in shown in Fig. 3, which shows the load used in 12 months in 2014, 2015 and 2016 in Hangzhou. It is clear that the trend of three curves have highly similarity (see Fig. 3).

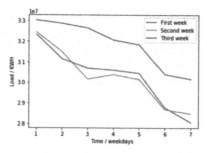

Fig. 1. Curves of load in a week, including three weeks of May 2015 of Toronto

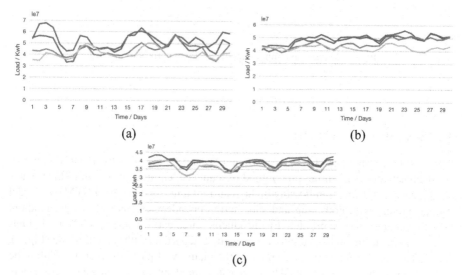

Fig. 2. Curves of a month in *(a)* Summer *(b)* Winter *(c)* Transitional season

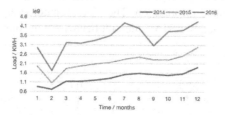

Fig. 3. Curves of total used load in 12 months for 2014, 2015 and 2016 in Hangzhou

Weather. Weather is another well-known key factor to be considered for STLF, especially the temperature factor. Paravan et al. [12] has performed an experiment showed that temperature is high positively correlated to load in summer and negatively correlate in winter. What means when temperature arises in summer, people need to use electrical product like air conditioner to cool themselves, so load arises as well. While in winter if the temperature decreases, electric blanket are used to get warm if the temperature decreases, as load arises. Figure 4 are curves of the maximum temperature and load in 2012 of Toronto in Canada (see Fig. 4). It is clear to show the negative correlation in winter and positive in summer. In spring and autumn, temperature and load are less correlated, so they are regarded as transitional seasons.

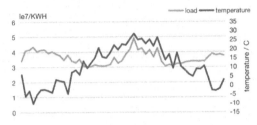

Fig. 4. Maximum temperature versus load in Toronto in 2012

3.2 Long-Short Term Model

Long short-term memory (LSTM), a variant of recurrent neural network (RNN), which is a deep network performing pretty good in sequence learning since it introduces gates to sift previous information flowing in the recurrent unit. As its name, LSTM can model data accurately with both long and short-term dependencies, and relieve the gradient vanishing and exploding problem by introducing three gates. Same as RNN, LSTM has a chain of repeating modules to process each time step's data with same flow (see Fig. 5). But LSTM adds an internal cell to process the memory of past information. Within the cell, past information is controlled by three gates: input gate, forget gate and output gate. The cell permits the network not remembering all past information, instead, the network remembers, stores and transfers only the most related information to the current value and forget the less related information. Therefore, remembering information for long periods of time is practically LSTM's default behavior, not something they struggle to learn.

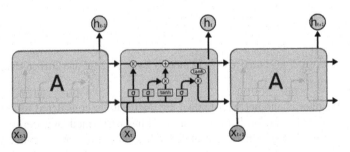

Fig. 5. The repeating module in an LSTM network [13]

3.3 The Enhanced LSTM Model

With the gates, LSTM can remember the most useful temporal information and build a relationship with current circumstance. Because of its good capacity to model sequence with long dependency, LSTM has been applied and achieved state-of-the-art results in many fields of sequence learning, such as speech recognition, machine translation and language generation However, it has not been sufficient maturely applied on time series with long relevance such as STLF which features typical large periodicity. Moreover, the training cost increases non-linearly with the length of input sequence, and the accuracy sometimes decreases when input sequence continue to increase. It is the reason only several days' data are used to predict the following days' load in the existing works [14]. However, from the rule in Sect. 3.1 it is known that load has high weekly and monthly similarity, which means we can upgrade the LSTM if we can use the data months ago instead of just few days. The proposed model utilizes much longer data to improve the prediction performance with a little payload of training complexity. The method performs better by bringing temporal dependency of load profile into full play.

The proposed model consists of two LSTM networks in parallel and a MLP, which is illustrated in Fig. 6 (see Fig. 6). The first one LSTM network of the proposed model takes advantage of daily periodicity of load series which has been shown in Sect. 3.1. Except for the proximity of the curves' trend, temperature values are always closed within several adjacent days, which is well understood. It means that the sequence of load values has high dependency within a few days. Accordingly, the first LSTM network (also termed row LSTM network which takes the rows of the reshaped data matrix as the input) takes the last seven days' load as input and external factors as well such as special event index, month index, and weather factor including maximum, minimum and average temperatures.

Besides the temporal dependency information distilled by the row LSTM network, the weekly and monthly periodicity information is exploited by the second LSTM network (namely, the column LSTM network taking the columns of the reshaped load matrix as the input sequences). In Sect. 3.1, it is proved that there is also dependency in the scale of week and month as well. For example, the load profile of one week in May is similar to the profiles of another week. What is more, the load profile of one particular day is similar to the profiles of another day with the same type of weekday in different weeks. Which means, to forecast a load value in Monday, the other LSTM network takes the data of past weeks' Monday as input, which amount to contain the temporal dependency information through two months. Therefore, the relative information useful for prediction can be extracted from the input without taking the whole months' data in the network. Except for the load value, other four influencing external factors are included as same as the first network. By utilizing the periodicity of load series, the temporal dependency can be extended from a week to two months with a little payload of training complexity.

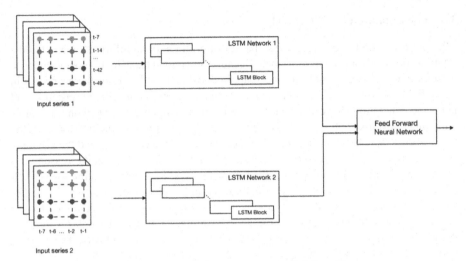

Fig. 6. Structure of the enhanced LSTM model

4   Experiments

4.1   Introduction of the Dataset

The experiments are performed on load and temperature dataset of Hangzhou city in East China. There are eight kinds of factors for each day, including the load in kilowatt-hour (KWH), maximum and minimum temperatures in centigrade, precipitation, holiday, day of week, month and date. Data are collected every day from 1st January 2014 to 3rd March 2017, with a total of 1185 data.

4.2   Data Pre-processing

Pre-processing transformations are applied in following order: (*i*) recognition and removing of abnormal data, (*ii*) trend removing, (*iii*) one-hot encoding (*iv*) standardization. Each operation is successively reversed to evaluate the forecast produced by the model.

Data Cleaning and Missing Values Processing. The practical dataset often contains abnormal values or may be missing. The presence of these data brings significant disturbance to normal data, hence affects the prediction accuracy. If the anomaly data is too large, it even misleads the prediction results. Therefore, the adverse effects caused by abnormal data must be eliminated. For the missing data, we fill the vacancy with the average of data before and after the lost data. As to abnormal data, in Hangzhou dataset, data from 1st January 2016 to 1st March 2017 is shown in (see Fig. 7). It can be seen that there are three obvious valleys in the load profile. The valleys near 1st February in 2016 and 2017 are regular since they are at the Spring Festival of China and people will stay at home and same valleys can be seen every year in the dataset as well. While there is an abnormal valley at 1st September 2016 and it is not a major holiday in China. By collecting news at the day, we found that G20 Financial Summit was hold in Hangzhou from 4th September to 5th September and most enterprises gave holidays for a few days before and after it. Since there is no similar rule with the data in these days in the dataset, no data can be used to fit the trend of it, what means it is unique and independent incident. As a result, there are nearly two weeks' data against the regular rule that need to be removed from the dataset. After the processing, the new dataset consists of 1171 measurements.

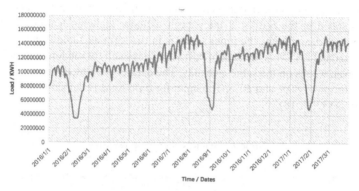

Fig. 7. Data from 1st Jan 2016 to 1st Mar 2017

Processing for the Trend Factor of Load. From the partial load profile of Hangzhou in (see Fig. 8 (a)) it can be figured out that the value of load keeps increasing through years, which is regarded as a trend item of the load dataset. Since there will be a scaling process later, the scaling effect to the proceeding years' data would be stronger than that to the later ones if the trend factor remains. This can bring change to the natural rule of the load and then reduce the forecasting accuracy. Therefore, the trend is filtered out by applying a daily differentiating. The load profile after differentiated can be seen in Fig. 8 (b). It tells the trend factor is removed from the load that can improve the forecasting accuracy of models in neural networks.

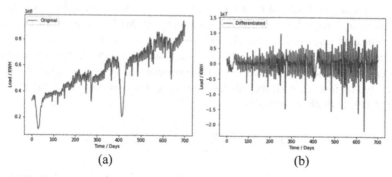

(a)   (b)

Fig. 8. *(a)* The original load profile. *(b)* The load profile after differentiated

One-Hot Encoding. Some affecting factors are category variables, which are one-hot encoded for easy processing of LSTM model. One-hot encoding codes n- class value into n-tuple binary vector.

4.3   Experiments Set-up

The experiment is implemented in Keras library with Tensorflow as backend. After pre-processed stated in the Sect. 4.2, the dataset includes eighteen features, as shown in Table 1. For each weekday, the input series is in the form as Table 2 shows. The input for the horizontal LSTM is the data in past seven days and for the longitudinal LSTM is the past seven weeks on the same weekday. The dataset is divided into train set and test set in proportion of 80% and 20%. The input for train set is reshaped in $(127, 7, 18)$ and for test set is $(32, 7, 18)$.

Table 1. Features after pre-processing

m_1	m_2	m_3	m_4	m_5–m_{17}	m_{18}
Max temperature	Min temperature	Rain	Holiday	Month	Power

Table 2. The form of inputs

Horizontal LSTM	$\{m_1(t-7), m_2(t-7), \ldots, m_1(t-6), m_2(t-6), \ldots, m_{17}(t-1), m_{18}(t-1)\}$
Longitudinal LSTM	$\{m_1(t-49), m_2(t-49), \ldots, m_1(t-42), m_2(t-42), \ldots, m_{17}(t-1), m_{18}(t-1)\}$

In the model, both LSTM networks use two layers' structure, and the two networks are merged by Merge layer in Keras. After merging, MLP composed of two-layered fully connected layer is added to the network to adjust the weights slightly and then output a predicted value. To decide the best configuration for the model, different values of hyper parameters are evaluated. For each combination, the performance of the model is evaluated on test set, with the forecasting error defined as mean absolute percentage error (MAPE), which is defined by

$$MAPE = \frac{1}{N} + \sum_{n=1}^{N} \frac{\left[\widehat{y_n} - y_n\right]}{y_n} * 100\% \tag{1}$$

where y_n and $\hat{y}_n$ are the real and the forecast load value at the n_{th} day and N is the length of the load sequence. Several hyper-parameters need to be specified and the value of each hyper-parameter is uniformly sampled from a given interval. The process of hyper-parameters is as followed: Adam is used as gradient descent strategy, whose hyper-parameters are kept to the default value in Keras. The default step size $\varepsilon = 0.001$, the rate of exponential decay in first-order and second-order moment estimation $\rho_1 = 0.9$ and $\rho_2 = 0.999$, $\delta = 10^{-6}$. The setting of other hyper-parameters is shown in Table 3 according to repeating experiments. The simulation is performed for data with seven different weekdays (Monday, ..., Sunday). To evaluate the performance of the system, the prediction is also realized in other benchmark algorithms, including single LSTM and ARIMA.

4.4 Results

After using different combination of hyper parameters to train the model, the best model for each type of weekday is obtained. The best configuration for the ensemble LSTM model and the comparison of mean absolute percentage error (MAPE) between ensemble LSTM and single LSTM of forecasting the load after seven days is shown in the Table 3.

Table 3. Configuration for ensemble LSTM and the accuracy comparison between ensemble and single model

Day	Configuration						MAPE	
	Hidden units	Epoch	L_1	L_2	Dropout	Dense neuron	Merged LSTM	Single LSTM
Mon.	20	48	0	0.01	0.1	20	2.605%	3.426%
Tue.	20	52	0	0.0018	0.2	20	2.631%	3.312%
Wed.	10	49	0	0.01	0.2	20	2.352%	3.287%
Thu.	20	42	0.01	0.01	0.2	20	2.434%	3.335%
Fri.	20	68	0	0	0.1	20	2.509%	3.435%
Sat.	20	110	0	0.001	0.2	10	2.314%	3.185%
Sun.	20	43	0.01	0.01	0.2	10	2.625%	3.298%

From the results we can observe that the enhanced LSTM model achieves an MAPE performance of 2.495% for all weekdays and outperforms standard LSTM model whose MAPE is 3.325%. Except for the average accuracy, it can also be seen from the last two columns that the accuracy for weekday are all improved. The predicted and real load are shown in Fig. 9. It is clear that the enhanced LSTM's profiles are much closer to the real data, especially in the case of sharp fluctuation of the real load.

Classic ARIMA model is also evaluated, and it achieves MAPE of 3.386%, which is a little worse than standard LSTM model. The real and predicted loads are shown in Fig. 10 for the last 85 days of the test set (see Fig. 10). It can be seen that ARIMA behaves badly when a sharp fluctuation comes up, verifying ARIMA not suitable for time series with high randomness.

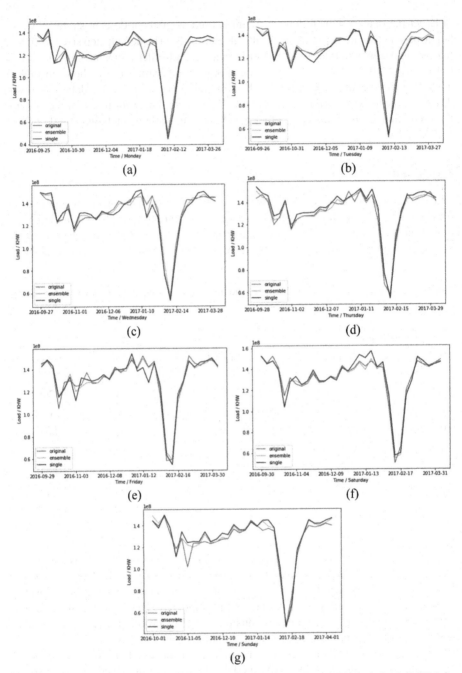

Fig. 9. Comparison between real value and predicted value in ensemble and single LSTM for *(a)* Mondays *(b)* Tuesdays *(c)* Wednesdays *(d)* Thursdays *(e)* Fridays *(f)* Saturdays *(g)* Sundays

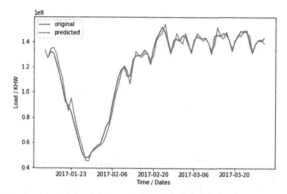

Fig. 10. Comparison between real value and predicted value in AIMA for the last 85 samples

5 Conclusion

Based on the characteristic analysis of load and the shortcoming of mainstream STLF models, an enhanced LSTM model is developed. Classic LSTM holds excellent learning capability to model the temporal inner pattern of short time sequences so that it presents the state-of-the-art performance, but it cannot avoid gradient disappear problem and thus has limit on the length of the input sequence. Since electrical load features typical weekly and monthly periodicity, the fully utility of the large time-span periodicity will upgrade the STLF performance. In this sense, the proposed model is designed by integrates two LSTM networks and an MLP. The first LSTM network takes the rows of load matrix, which is constructed by reshaping a long load sequence with row size being weekly periodicity, to exploit the similarity of the load in adjacent days, while the other LSTM network takes the columns of the load matrix as input to exploit the weekly and monthly periodicity of the load. The MLP merges the distilled information from two LSTM networks. The proposed model extends the temporal dependency from one week to two months but increases the training complexity in a linear mode. The proposed model is evaluated and compared with ARIMA and standard LSTM network. The simulation results verify its advantage over the reference models, i.e., MAPE performance is decreased from 3.736% of ARIMA and 3.325% of standard LSTM to 2.495% for seven days forecasting.

Acknowledgment. The work of Q. Zhou and Q. Lv is partly supported by project with Grant No. SGGSKY00FJJS1900241.

References

1. Ranaweera, D., Karady, G., Farmer, R.: Economic impact analysis of load forecasting. IEEE Trans. Power Syst. **2**(3), 1288–1392 (1997)
2. Douglas, A.P., Breipohl, A.M., Lee, F.N.: Risk due to load forecast uncertainty in short term power system planning. IEEE Trans. Power Syst. **13**(4), 1493–1499 (1998)

3. Cho, M.Y., Hwang, J.C., Chen, C.S.: Customer short term load forecasting by using ARIMA transfer function model. In: Proceedings 1995 International Conference on Energy Management and Power Delivery, EMPD 1995. IEEE (2002)
4. Ye, G., Luo, Y., Liu, Y., Zhang, J.: Research on method of power system load forecasting based on ARMA model. Inf. Technol. **6**, 74–76 (2002)
5. Liu, B.: Research on household electricity load control strategy based on demand response. Harbin University of Science and Technology (2014)
6. Wang, G., Xiang, W., Pickering, M., Chen, C.W.: Light field multi-view video coding with two-directional parallel inter-view prediction. IEEE Trans. Image Process. **25**(11), 5104–5117 (2016)
7. Haque, A., Mandal, P., Meng, J.: A novel hybrid approach based on wavelet transform and fuzzy ARTMAP network for predicting wind farm power production. In: IEEE Industry Applications Society Annual Meeting (IAS), Las Vegas, NV, USA (2012)
8. Ghelardoni, L., Ghio, A., Anguita, D.: Energy load forecasting using empirical mode decomposition and support vector Regression. IEEE Trans. Smart Grid **4**(1), 549–556 (2013)
9. Han, L., Han, X., Lei, M.: Method for state forecasting and estimation based on nodal load forecasting and generation control. Autom. Electr. Systems **33**(4), 16–20 (2009)
10. Zhang, R., Dong, Z., Xu, Y., Meng, K.: Short-term load forecasting of Australian National Electricity Market by an ensemble model of extreme learning machine. IET Gener. Transm. Distrib. **7**, 391–397 (2013)
11. Kong, W., Dong, Z., Jia, Y., et al.: Short-term residential load forecasting based on LSTM recurrent neural network. IEEE Trans. Smart Grid **10**(1), 841–851 (2017)
12. Xiang, W., Wang, G., Pickering, M., Zhang, Y.: Big video data for light-field-based 3D telemedicine. IEEE Netw. **30**(3), 30–38 (2016)
13. Paravan, D., Debs, A., Hansen C., Becker, D., Hirsch P., Golob, R.: Influence of temperature on short-term load forecasting using the EPRI-ANNSTLF (2003)
14. Understanding LSTM Networks. http://colah.github.io/posts/2015–08-Understanding-LSTMs
15. Bianchi, F.M., Maiorino, E., Kampffmeyer, M.C.: An overview and comparative analysis of recurrent neural networks for short term load forecasting, 11 May 2017
16. Xiang, W., Barbulescu, S.A., Pietrobon, S.S.: Unequal error protection applied to JPEG image transmission using turbo codes. In: Proceedings 2001 IEEE Information Theory Workshop (Cat. No. 01EX494), pp. 64–66 (2001)

Time-Switching Energy Harvesting Relay Optimizing Considering Decoding Cost

Wanqiu Hu[1], Yanxin Yao[1], Zhengwei Ni[2(✉)], Rajshekhar V. Bhat[3], and Mehul Motani[4]

[1] Key Laboratory of the Ministry of Education for Optoelectronic Measurement Technology and Instrument, Advanced Equipment Intelligent Perception and Control, Beijing International Cooperation Base for Science and Technology, Beijing Information Science and Technology University, Beijing 100190, China
1302566503@qq.com, yanxin_buaa@126.com
[2] Zhejiang Gongshang University, Zhejiang 310018, China
nzw_hk@hotmail.com
[3] Indian Institute of Technology Dharwad, Dharwad, India
rajshekhar.bhat@iitdh.ac.in
[4] National University of Singapore, Singapore, Singapore
motani@nus.edu.sg

Abstract. Energy harvesting (EH) from natural and man-made sources is of prime importance for enabling the Internet of Things (IoT) networks. Although, energy harvesting relays in a relay network, which form building blocks of an IoT network, have been considered in the literature, most of the studies do not account for the processing costs, such as the decoding cost in a decode-and-forward (DF) relay. However, it is known that the decoding cost amounts to a significant fraction of the circuit power required for receiving a codeword. Hence, in this work, we are motivated to consider an EH-DF relay with the decoding cost and maximize the average number of bits relayed by it with a time-switching architecture. To achieve this, we first propose a *time-switching* frame structure consisting of three phases: (i) an energy harvesting phase, (ii) a reception phase and, (iii) a transmission phase. We obtain optimal length of each of the above phases and communication rates that maximize the average number of bits relayed. We consider two EH scenarios, (a) when the radio frequency (RF) energy, to be harvested by the relay, is transmitted from a dedicated transmitter, and (ii) when the energy is harvested at the rely from the ambient environment. By exploiting the convexity of the optimization problem, we derive analytical optimum solutions under the above two scenarios and provide numerical simulations for verifying our theoretical analysis.

Supported by the Natural Science Foundation of Beijing (4172021), the Importation and Development of High-Caliber Talents Project of Beijing Municipal Institutions (CIT&TCD 201704064), Key research cultivation projects of BISTU (5211910954).

X. Zhang et al. (Eds.): CloudComp 2019/SmartGift 2019, LNICST 322, pp. 663–673, 2020.
https://doi.org/10.1007/978-3-030-48513-9_53

Keywords: Energy harvesting · Time-switching ·
Harvest-transmit-then-receive · Relay

1   Introduction

Recent days, communication systems with energy harvesting (EH) functions become more and more popular with the rapid development of Internet of things. The harvested energy could complement the scarce energy in mobile situation or out of cable line area. The study on energy harvesting system optimization is very important to improve the energy utilization efficiency or their performance indices of communicate systems.

There are energy harvesting optimization for various communication network such as Wireless sensor network [4], cellular network, internet of things [5] and cognitive network [6]. There are energy harvesting optimization for different scenarios such as point to point system, relay system [1], cooperative system [7], cognitive radio system [8] and multiple antenna system [9]. And also there are energy harvesting optimization for various communication objectives such as outrage probability [2,10], packet drop rate [11], energy efficiency and secure communication [12] and so on.

For relay systems, [7] studies the scenario when both source node (SN) and relay node (RN) have limited energy storage, and SN harvests energy form RF signals of the SN. For different harvesting efficiency and channel conditions, closed-form optimal solutions for the joint SN and RN power allocation are derived to maximize the overall throughput. [13] uses a generalized iterative directional water-filling algorithm to solve the sum-rate maximization problem under half-duplex and full-duplex channels with energy harvesting nodes under any relaying strategy, namely amplify-and-forward, decode-and-forward, compress-and-forward and compute-and-forward. [14] propose two schemes: (1) jointly optimal power and time fraction (TF) allocation, (2) optimal power allocation with fixed TF for a three-node DF half-duplex relaying system. [15] drives the delay-limited and delay-tolerant throughput for a DF single-way and two-way relaying networks with time switching relaying protocol.

Most literature for the energy harvesting relay mainly consider the transmission and receiving energy, such as in [7], but rarely discuss the information decoding energy which is the main energy cost for DF scheme [16]. Our paper mainly focuses on this novel aspect when the information decoding energy is taken into account. The papers [17] considers the decoding cost and the effect of decoding model on energy harvesting receiver. There has not been a study on their effect on the relay system.

In this paper, we study the problem of optimizing time fraction and receiving rate for an EH relay system whose energy comes from the dedicated transmitter and ambient environment for transferring more information from dedicated transmitter to destination. The frame structure is determined as three phase: harvesting, receiving information and transmitting information. The time fraction or ratio of these operations are to determined. The average transmitting rate for the relay is known, while the receiving rate related to the decoding energy is to be optimized. We discuss the single block case when energy is forbidden to flow among blocks. We consider the energy comes from dedicated receiver only and could come both from dedicated transmitter and ambient environment. For all the cases, we give the optimum time fraction for three operation phases and receiving rate. Finally, numerical results are provided to validate the accuracy of the analysis. The main contributions of the paper are

- We formulate the information transferring and energy usage model for the energy harvesting relay considering the decoding cost.
- We give the solutions for single block case when energy is from dedicated transmitter and from both dedicated transmitter and ambient environment, and analyze the solution difference between them.

2   System Model

We consider an end-to-end communication with an EH relay as shown in Fig. 1. The relay extracts the information contained in the signals sent by the transmitter, and then transmits it to the receiver in DF mode. We hope to transmit as most data as possible to the receiver. The energy source of the transmitter and receiver could be seen as infinite, while the energy of the relay is only from energy harvesting. Apparently, the bottle neck of the system is the EH relay which has limited harvested energy from the RF signals of both the dedicated transmitter and ambient RF sources. Both extracting information (decoding) and transmitting information (forward) need energy to run the corresponding circuits.

Solar energy is generally from $1\,uW$ to $100\,mW$ in a small-sized solar cell across day (approximate area of $10\,cm^2$). There are many models to be used for the system. Because the energy harvesting equipment is generally used in small energy scale applications, for purpose of simplicity and low cost, we design the structure of the relay as simple as possible. There is only one antenna shared by the energy harvesting, transmitting and receiving functions or periods with a time-switching on-off controlling the antenna to receive or transmit signals. We consider a "Harvest-Receive-Transmit" time-switching architecture in this paper. The harvested energy which is generally from $1\,uW$ to $100\,mW$ in a small-sized device needs to be stored in storage elements for later operation use. We assume the battery cannot be charged and discharged simultaneously. This assumption is both practical and without loss of generality.

The system consists of energy harvesting unit, decoding unit, transmitting unit, battery and data buffer. The energy harvesting unit harvest energy from RF signals of dedicated transmitter and ambient transmitters, and then store the energy in batteries for later transmitting or receiving freely. In the information receiving period, information is extracted from the received signals in the decoder unit using the energy drawn from the batteries. Then the information is stored in the buffer for later transmitting. In the information transmitting

Fig. 1. The communication block structure at the relay

period, the information in the buffer is transmitted using the energy discharged
from batteries or supercapacities.

Generally, the information is organized in a block or frame to process. In order
to simplify model, we consider an average transmitting and receiving rate and
channel condition when transferring information. So we could represent many
parameters for the transmitting and receiving as constants during the block,
such as the maximum signal power p_m, channel capacity C, the power gain of
channel h, transmitting power p_t. A frame is divided into three parts as shown
in Fig. 1. Assume the time length of a frame is τ.

- Over the time duration $[0, \alpha\tau), \alpha \in [0, 1]$, switcher connects to the EH circuit and all the signals received are used for harvesting energy. To make the
receiver harvest the largest amount of energy, the transmitter should always
transmit the symbol with the largest energy. Denote $p_{\mathrm{m}} = \max_x p(x)$ where
the maximum is over all possible values of $x \in \mathcal{X}$ and e is the energy harvested
outside the bands used for transmission.
- Over the time duration $[\alpha\tau, (\alpha + \beta)\tau), \alpha + \beta \in [0, 1]$, switcher connects
to the information extracting circuit. From [19], we adopt the following
model: for a fixed channel capacity C [3], the energy consumed for decoding a codeword with rate R per channel is a non-decreasing convex func-
tion of R, i.e., $h(R) = \mathcal{E}_{\mathrm{D}}(\frac{C}{C-R})$, where $\mathcal{E}_{\mathrm{D}}(0) = 0$ [19]. $\frac{C}{C-R} \log(\frac{C}{C-R})$ and
$(\frac{C}{C-R})^2 \log^3(\frac{C}{C-R})$ are two common seen instances for $\mathcal{E}_{\mathrm{D}}(\frac{C}{C-R})$ [19]. All the
other factors are 'hidden' in this function. The total number of bits decoded
by the relay in this phase are $I_R = \beta\tau R$ and stored in the buffer for later
transmission. In this phase, no energy is harvested. The total number of bits
decoded by the relay in this phase are $I_R = \beta\tau R$ and stored in the buffer for
later transmission. In this phase, no energy is harvested.
- Over the time duration $[(\alpha + \beta)\tau, \tau]$, switcher connects to the transmitting
circuit and the information decoding is transmitted from the relay to the
receiver. For transmission over an additive white Gaussian noise (AWGN)
channel with power gain h, and unit received noise power spectral density, we
consider the average rate as $W\log(1 + hp_t)$ bits per channel symbol during
the block.

The may be several specific forms for characterizing the decoding energy
consumption. For example, for LDPC codes on the binary erasure channel
(BEC), [18] shows that for any $\theta > 0$, there exists a code with code rate of
at least R, with complexity per input node per iteration scaling like $\log\theta$, to
make decoding iterations to converge. The iteration rounds scale like θ. So
the total complexity of decoder per channel use scales like $\theta\log\theta$ [19].

3   Transmission Over a Single Block from Transmitter Only

For a single block transmission, the optimization problem to maximize the amount of information relayed can be formulated as

$$(\text{P1}) \quad \max_{\alpha,\,\beta,\,\gamma,\,R} I_R,$$
$$\text{s.t.} \quad I_R \le I_T$$
$$\beta \mathcal{E}_D\left(\tfrac{C}{C-R}\right) + \gamma p_t \le \alpha p_m \qquad (1)$$
$$0 \le \alpha \le 1$$
$$0 \le \beta \le 1$$
$$0 \le \gamma \le 1$$
$$\alpha + \beta + \gamma = 1$$
$$0 \le R \le C.$$

We assume that the average transmitting rate for the frame is known at the start of the frame, which is representing with a constant channel power gain and a fixed p_t, by optimizing R, α, β, γ. The second constraint follows because γ is time duration for transmission. To solve (P1), we first give two useful lemmas.

Lemma 1. *To be optimal, the first constraint in (1) must hold with equality, i.e.,*

$$\beta \tau R = log(1 + hp_t)(1 - \alpha - \beta)\tau. \qquad (2)$$

Proof. If the equality in (2) does not hold, we can increase β to make the equality hold. When α, R, p_t are fixed, increasing β means increase the value of the objective function.

Lemma 2. *To be optimal, the third sub-equation in (1) must hold with equality. i.e.,*

$$\beta \mathcal{E}_D\left(\frac{C}{C-R}\right) + (1 - \alpha - \beta)p_t = \alpha p_m. \qquad (3)$$

Proof. If the equality in (3) does not hold, we can increase R to make the equality hold since $\mathcal{E}_D(R)$ is a non-decreasing function of R. When α, β, p_t are fixed, increasing R means increasing the value of the objective function.

Based on Lemma 1 and Lemma 2, we can express α and β in terms of R and p_t.

$$\alpha = 1 - \beta - \frac{\beta R}{log(1 + hp_t)} \qquad (4)$$

$$\beta = \frac{p_m log(1 + hp_t)}{R(p_m + p_t) + (p_m + \mathcal{E}_D)log(1 + hp_t)} \qquad (5)$$

Express β and the objective function in (1) in terms of R and p_t, we can rewrite the objective function of problem (P1) as $\mathcal{O}_1(R) = \beta R \tau$.

Take the derivative of $\mathcal{O}_1(R)$ with respect to R, we have $\frac{\partial \mathcal{O}_1}{\partial R} = p_m \tau log(1 + hp_t)\mathcal{P}_1(R)$, where $\mathcal{P}_1(R) = \frac{R}{R(p_m+p_t)+(\mathcal{E}_D+p_m)log(1+hp_t)}$. For the decoding instances $\theta \log \theta$ common seen in literature, we could further derive following theorem.

Theorem 1. $\frac{\partial \mathcal{P}_1(R)}{\partial R}|_{R\to 0} > 0.$ $\frac{\partial \mathcal{P}_1(R)}{\partial R}|_{R\to C} \to -\infty.$ $\frac{\partial^2 \mathcal{O}_1(R)}{\partial R^2} \leq 0.$

Proof. Assume $T(x) = log(1 + hx)$. $\frac{\partial \mathcal{O}_1}{\partial R} = p_m log(1 + hp_t)\mathcal{P}_1(R)$, where

$$\mathcal{P}_1(R) = \frac{R}{R(p_m+p_t)+(\mathcal{E}_D+p_m)T(p_t)}.$$

We could derive $\frac{\partial \mathcal{P}_1(R)}{\partial R} = \frac{T(p_t-p_c)(\mathcal{E}_D(\theta)+p_m)-T(p_t)\frac{\partial \mathcal{E}(\theta)}{\partial\theta}\frac{R}{(C-R)^2}}{[R(p_m+p_t)+(\mathcal{E}_D+p_m)T(p_t)]^2}$, and $\frac{\partial^2 \mathcal{P}_1(R)}{\partial R^2} =$

$-RT(p_t)\frac{\frac{\partial^2 \mathcal{E}(\theta)}{\partial\theta^2}\frac{1}{(C-R)^4}+2\frac{\partial\mathcal{E}(\theta)}{\partial\theta}\frac{1}{(C-R)^3}}{[R(p_m+p_t)+(\mathcal{E}_D+p_m)T(p_t)]^4}.$

When $\mathcal{E}_D(\theta) = \theta \log \theta$, we could derive $\frac{\partial \mathcal{E}_D(\theta)}{\partial \theta} = log\theta + \frac{1}{ln2}$, and $\frac{\partial^2 \mathcal{E}_D(\theta)}{\partial \theta^2} = \frac{1}{ln2\theta}.$

For $\mathcal{E}_D(\theta) = \theta \log \theta$, when $R \to 0$ and $\theta \to 1$, we could see the numerator of $\frac{\partial \mathcal{P}_1(R)}{\partial R}$ is positive finite while the denominator is positive finite.

So $\frac{\partial \mathcal{P}_1(R)}{\partial R}|_{R\to 0} > 0.$ When $R \to C$ and $\theta \to +\infty$, $\frac{\partial \mathcal{P}_1(R)}{\partial R} \to$ $B\frac{\theta log\theta - (log\theta+\frac{1}{ln2})(\frac{\theta}{C})^2C(1-\frac{1}{\theta})}{\theta^2 log^2\theta} \to -A\frac{1}{log\theta} \to -\infty$, where A, B are positive parameters. $\frac{\partial^2 \mathcal{P}_1(R)}{\partial R^2}$ could easily be seen as non-positive for $R \in [0, C]$.

So there is a single R^* maximizing $\mathcal{O}_1(R)$. We will get the optimum $\alpha^*, \beta^*, \gamma^*$ according to

$$\gamma^* = \frac{R^*(p_m\tau + e)}{(p_m + p_t)R^*\tau + T(p_t)\tau(p_m + \mathcal{E}_D(\frac{C}{C-R^*}))}, \tag{6}$$

$$\beta^* = \frac{T(p_t)(p_m\tau + e)}{(p_m + p_t)R^*\tau + T(p_t)\tau(p_m + \mathcal{E}_D(\frac{C}{C-R^*}))}, \tag{7}$$

$$\alpha^* = 1 - \beta^* - \gamma^*. \tag{8}$$

We could easily find that when e increases, both β and γ will increase, and α will decrease. When α decreases to zero, the energy harvested from ambient environment is enough for the relay, whose value is $\tilde{e}$,

$$\tilde{e} = \frac{\tau\left(p_t R^* + T(p_t)\mathcal{E}_D(\frac{C}{C-R^*})\right)}{T(p_t) + R^*} \tag{9}$$

which is derived from $\beta + \gamma = 1$. Then we have the lemma.

Lemma 3. *The optimal solution for (P2) is $\frac{\partial \mathcal{P}_1(R)}{\partial R} = 0$, α^*, β^* and γ^* could be obtained with (6), (7) and (8) when $e \leq \tilde{e}$; otherwise, α^*, β^* and γ^* could be obtained with (6), (7) and (8) with $e = \tilde{e}$, when $e > \tilde{e}$.*

Remark 1. Intuitively, the energy harvesting period becomes smaller due to the increase of e to allow for more time for receiving and transmitting. When α becomes zero, the energy harvested from ambient environment is enough and β and γ are constant values given by (6) and (7) with $e = \tilde{e}$.

4   Transmission over Single Block: Energy Harvested from Transmitter and Ambient RF Sources

In this section, we consider the case when the receiver harvests energy from both the transmitter and other RF sources. Then the energy harvested are not merely controlled by energy extraction from transmitter. We then maximized the information to destination by jointly choosing optimal α, β, γ, R. p_t is known in assumption. The corresponding optimization problem is given by (P2).

$$
\begin{aligned}
\text{(P2)} \quad & \max_{\alpha, \beta, \gamma, R} I_R, \\
\text{s.t.} \quad & I_R \leq I_T, \\
& \beta \mathcal{E}_D\left(\frac{C}{C-R}\right) + \gamma p_t \leq \alpha p_m + e \\
& 0 \leq \alpha \leq 1 \\
& 0 \leq \beta \leq 1 \\
& 0 \leq \gamma \leq 1 \\
& \alpha + \beta + \gamma = 1 \\
& 0 \leq R \leq C.
\end{aligned}
\tag{10}
$$

We could derive

$$
\alpha = 1 - \beta - \frac{\beta R}{log(1 + hp_t)}.
\tag{11}
$$

$$
\beta = \frac{(p_m \tau + e)log(1 + hp_t)}{R(p_m + p_t)\tau + (p_m + \mathcal{E}_D)log(1 + hp_t)\tau}.
\tag{12}
$$

Express α, β and the objective function in (10) in terms of R and p_t, we can rewrite the objective of problem (P2) as $\mathcal{O}_2(R) = \beta R\tau$. Take the derivative of $\mathcal{O}_2(R)$ with respect to R, we have $\frac{\partial \mathcal{O}_2}{\partial R} = (p_m \tau + e)log(1 + hp_t)\mathcal{P}_2(R)$, where $\mathcal{P}_2(R) = \mathcal{P}_1(R)$. According to Theorem 1, we could derive $\frac{\partial \mathcal{P}_2(R)}{\partial R}|_{R\to 0} > 0$. $\frac{\partial \mathcal{P}_2(R)}{\partial R}|_{R\to C} \to -\infty$. $\frac{\partial^2 \mathcal{O}_2(R)}{\partial R^2} \leq 0$. So there is a single R^* maximizing $\mathcal{O}_2(R)$. We will get the optimum α, β, γ according to (11), (12), (10).

We could easily find that when e increases, both β and γ will increase, and α will decrease. This indicates that the energy harvesting period become smaller due to e to allow for more time for receiving and transmitting.

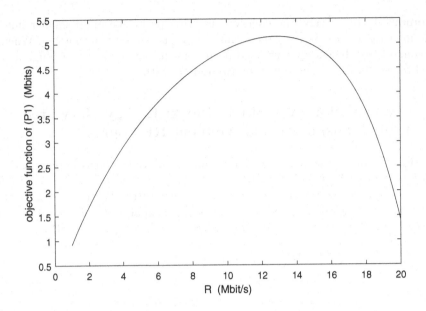

Fig. 2. The objective function value of (P1) versus R

5   Numerical Results

5.1   Energy from Dedicated Transmitter only

Firstly, we focus on the optimization results when energy is from dedicated transmitter only.

We originally assume that $\mathcal{E}_D(\theta) = 10^{-3} \times \theta log_2 \theta \, \text{W}$, $T(p_t) = B log_2(1 + p_t h')$ bit/s, $B = 10^6 \, \text{Hz}$, $C = 21 \, \text{Mbit/s}$, $N_0 = 10^{-15} \, \text{W/Hz}$, $\tau = 1 \, \text{s}$, $h' = \frac{1}{N_0 W} = 10^9$. As the coefficients at the front in $T(p_t)$ and $\mathcal{E}_D(\theta)$ do not affect the convexity property of the functions, Theorem 1 still holds.

In the following simulation, we adopt energy unit as mW and bit rate unit as Mbit/s. Then we have $\mathcal{E}_D(\theta) = \frac{C}{C-R} log_2(\frac{C}{C-R}) \, \text{mW}$, $T(p_t) = log_2(1 + p_t h) \, \text{Mbit/s}$, where p_t represent x energy unit, $h = 10^6$, C, R and $T(P_t)$ are bit rate with unit Mbit/s.

We assume $C = 21 \, \text{Mbit/s}$, According to $P_1(R^*) = 0$, the numerical result for optimum R^* could be obtained at $12.88 \, \text{Mbit/s}$.

In order to verify we plot the objective function of (P1) versus R in Fig. 2. We could easily get the optimum $R^* = 12.88 \, \text{Mbit/s}$. When $p_m = 8 \, \text{mW}$, $p_t = 7 \, \text{mW}$, we could give the optimum α, β and γ in Fig. 3 at $e = 0$.

5.2   Energy from Dedicated Transmitter and Ambient Environment

Now we consider the case when the energy comes from the dedicated transmitter and ambient environment both.

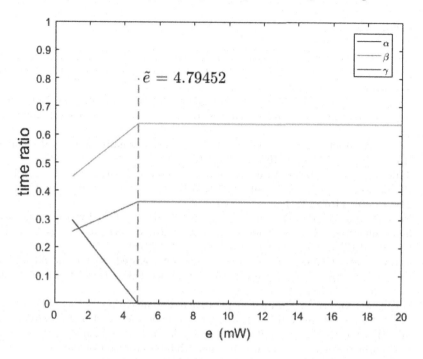

Fig. 3. The value of α, β, γ versus e

When $p_m = 8\,\mathrm{mW}$, $p_t = 7\,\mathrm{mW}$, with $R^* = 12.88\,\mathrm{Mbit/s}$, We present the variation of optimum α, β and γ versus e in Fig. 3. $\tilde{e}$ is computed to be 4.79 mW in this case. We can see that β and γ increase with e, but α decreases with e over $e \leq \tilde{e}$; for $e > \tilde{e}$, both α and β no longer vary, but remain the same as when $e = \tilde{e}$. The numerical results are given by solving (P2).

From these figures, we see the numerical results coincide with the theoretical analysis.

From these figures, we could see the numerical results coincide well with the theoretical analysis for the single block case.

6   Conclusion

This paper formulates the information transferring and energy usage model for the energy harvesting relay considering the decoding cost and give the unique solution for single block case when energy is from dedicated transmitter. When energy is harvested from both dedicated transmitter and ambient environment, energy saturation will occur when harvested energy from ambient environment is large enough. There is a threshold for it when α become zero all the time. Simulations verify the theoretical analysis and give the performance of the system.

References

1. Long, H., Xiang, W., Zhang, Y., Liu, Y., Wang, W.: Secrecy capacity enhancement with distributed precoding in multirelay wiretap systems. IEEE Trans. Inf. Forensics Secur. **8**(1), 229–238 (2012)
2. Wang, G., Xiang, W., Yuan, J.: Outage performance for compute-and-forward in generalized multi-way relay channels. IEEE Commun. Lett. **16**(12), 2099–2102 (2012)
3. Xiang, W., Pietrobon, S.S.: On the capacity and normalization of ISI channels. IEEE Trans. Inf. Theory **49**(9), 2263–2268 (2003)
4. Tang, S., Tan, L.: Reward rate maximization and optimal transmission policy of EH device with temporal death in EH-WSNs. IEEE Trans. Wireless Commun. **16**(2), 1157–1167 (2017)
5. Yang, Z., Xu, W., Pan, Y., Pan, C., Chen, M.: Energy efficient resource allocation in machine-to-machine communications with multiple access and energy harvesting for IoT. IEEE Internet Things J. **5**(1), 229–245 (2018)
6. Verma, D.K., Chang, R.Y., Chien, F.: Energy-assisted decode-and-forward for energy harvesting cooperative cognitive networks. IEEE Trans. Cogn. Commun. Netw. **3**(3), 328–342 (2017)
7. Huang, X., Ansari, N.: Optimal cooperative power allocation for energy-harvesting-enabled relay networks. IEEE Trans. Veh. Technol. **65**(4), 2424–2434 (2016)
8. Wu, H., Qiu, R.: Throughput of cognitive relay networks with energy-harvesting based primary user's interference. In: 2017 4th International Conference on Systems and Informatics (ICSAI), pp. 900–905. IEEE, Hangzhou (2017)
9. Benkhelifa, F., Salem, A.S., Alouini, M.: Sum-rate enhancement in multiuser MIMO decode-and-forward relay broadcasting channel with energy harvesting relays. IEEE J. Sel. Areas Commun. **34**(12), 3675–3684 (2016)
10. Blagojevic, V.M., Cvetkovic, A.M.: Outage probability of energy harvesting DF relay systems in generalized-K fading. In: 2017 13th International Conference on Advanced Technologies, Systems and Services in Telecommunications (TELSIKS), pp. 240–243. IEEE, Nis (2017)
11. Sharma, M.K., Murthy, C.R.: Packet drop probability analysis of dual energy harvesting links with retransmission. IEEE J. Sel. Areas Commun. **34**(12), 3646–3660 (2016)
12. Jindal, P., Sinha, R.: Energy efficiency and secure communication with power splitting energy harvesting technique for single relay network. In: 2017 International Conference on Computer and Applications (ICCA), pp. 215–219. IEEE, Doha (2017)
13. Tutuncuoglu, K., Varan, B., Yener, A.: Throughput maximization for two-way relay channels with energy harvesting nodes: the impact of relaying strategies. IEEE Trans. Commun. **63**(6), 2081–2093 (2015)
14. Hadzi-Velkov, Z., Zlatanov, N., Duong, T.Q., Schober, R.: Rate maximization of decode-and-forward relaying systems with RF energy harvesting. IEEE Commun. Lett. **19**(12), 2290–2293 (2015)
15. Rao, Y.S., Sirigina, R.P., Madhukumar, A.S.: On the DMT of RF energy harvesting-based dynamic decode-and-forward relaying. IEEE Commun. Lett. **21**(1), 200–203 (2017)
16. Grover, P., Woyach, K., Sahai, A.: Towards a communication-theoretic understanding of system-level power consumption. IEEE J. Sel. Areas Commun. **29**(8), 1744–1755 (2011)

17. Ni, Z., Bhat, R.V., Motani, M.: On dual-path energy-harvesting receivers for IoT with batteries having internal resistance. IEEE Internet Things J. **5**(4), 2741–2752 (2018)
18. Luby, M.G.: Practical loss-resilient codes. In: 29th Annual ACM Symposium on Theory of Computing, El Paso, Texas, USA (1997)
19. Richardson, T., Urbanke, R.: The renaissance of Gallager's low-density parity-check codes. IEEE Commun. Mag. **41**(8), 126–131 (2003)

A Resource Allocation Scheme for 5G C-RAN Based on Improved Adaptive Genetic Algorithm

Xinyan Ma[1], Yingteng Ma[2], and Dongtang Ma[2(✉)]

[1] School of Information Science and Technology,
University of Science and Technology of China, Hefei, People's Republic of China
maxinyan@mail.ustc.edu.cn
[2] College of Electronic Science and Technology, National University of Defense Technology,
Changsha, People's Republic of China
{mayingteng11,dongtangma}@nudt.edu.cn

Abstract. Cloud-Radio Access Networks (C-RAN) is a novel mobile network architecture where baseband resources are pooled, which is helpful for the operators to deal with the challenges caused by the non-uniform traffic and the fast growing user demands. The main idea of C-RAN is to divide the base stations into the baseband unit (BBU) and the remote radio head (RRH), and then centralize the BBUs to form a BBU pool. The BBU pool is virtualized and shared between the RRHs, improving statistical multiplexing gains by allocating baseband and radio resources dynamically. In this paper, aiming at the problem of resource dynamic allocation and optimization of 5G C-RAN, a resource allocation strategy based on improved adaptive genetic algorithm (IAGA) is proposed. The crossover rate and mutation rate of the genetic algorithm are optimized. Simulation results show that the performance of the proposed resource allocation strategy is better than the common frequency reuse algorithm and the traditional genetic algorithm (GA).

Keywords: Cloud-Radio Access Network · Resource allocation · Improved adaptive genetic algorithm · Baseband unit · Remote radio head

1 Introduction

With the rapid development of fifth-generation mobile communications (5G), there is an increasing demand for higher-speed services and richer applications, such as enhanced mobile broadband services with higher speed and lower latency (Enhanced Mobile Broadband, eMBB), Massive Machine-Type Communication (mMTC) supporting massive user connections, and Ultra Reliable & Low Latency Communication (URLLC) for ultra-reliable and ultra-low latency. In response to the challenges from diverse application scenarios, rapidly growing business demands and uneven business distribution, major operators and their research organizations are looking for a new low-cost, high-efficiency method to achieve higher income. Among them, Cloud-Radio Access Network (C-RAN) has been introduced into 5G networks due to its high capacity, low latency,

X. Zhang et al. (Eds.): CloudComp 2019/SmartGift 2019, LNICST 322, pp. 674–684, 2020.
https://doi.org/10.1007/978-3-030-48513-9_54

high energy efficiency and flexible deployment, and it is expected to become one of the most effective technical ways to face the above challenges [1].

How to realize C-RAN resource on-demand allocation and dynamic deployment is a key issue that needs to be solved urgently. Zhang et al. used the pure binary integer programming method for LTE uplink to search for the optimal resource allocation solution [2], which has lower complexity than the exhaustive search algorithm. Noh et al. used the Hungarian algorithm for multi-site OFDMA systems to match the balance between users and resource blocks [3], which has lower complexity too. In [4], Sahu et al. used the graph segmentation method to allocate base-band processing resources for the 5G cloud radio access network, which improved the system energy efficiency. In [5], the authors used heuristic search ant colony algorithm to the QoS-based spectrum resource allocation strategy. Genetic Algorithm (GA) is a kind of randomized search method that learns from the evolutionary laws of the biological world. It was first proposed by Professor J. Holland in the United States in 1975. It has inherent hidden parallelism and better global optimization ability than other methods. In [6], the authors conducted a preliminary study on the resource allocation algorithm based on GA for LTE systems.

In this paper, genetic algorithm is introduced into the resource allocation of 5G cloud radio access network. An improved adaptive genetic algorithm (IAGA) is proposed in the dynamic allocation and optimization strategy. The main contributions of this paper are as follows.

(1) Considering the 5G C-RAN architecture, genetic algorithm is introduced into the resource allocation of the C-RAN network, so that better dynamic resource allocation and optimization strategies can be obtained faster.
(2) An improved adaptive genetic algorithm is proposed to optimize the crossover rate and mutation rate. It has faster convergence and better stability than the traditional GA and frequency reuse algorithm.

This remainder of the paper is as follows. Section 2 presents the 5G C-RAN architecture and cell distribution model. Section 3 explains the resource allocation strategy based on GA and the improved adaptive genetic algorithm. Section 4 presents simulation results. Section 5 concludes the paper.

2 System Model

2.1 5G C-RAN Architecture

The concept of C-RAN was first proposed by IBM [7], which was named Wireless Network Cloud (WNC), and then it was derived from the concept of distributed wireless communication system [8], it is also known as "Centralized radio access network." The basic architecture is shown in Fig. 1.

The C-RAN architecture is characterized in that it geographically separates the base-band processing unit and the front-end wireless transmitting unit in the traditional base station. The two parts are connected by a low-latency, high-bandwidth preamble link to form a distributed radio head (RRH) combined with a centralized baseband processing unit (BBU) pool architecture. The core modules include:

(1) Radio frequency remote head (RRH), which mainly includes RF module, related amplifier/filter and antenna. It also includes digital signal processing, digital/analog conversion and other modules.

(2) The baseband processing unit (BBU) pool is shared and virtualized by all RRHs to implement baseband processing functions in the radio access network, such as modulation, coding, filtering and resource allocation.

(3) The pre-transmission link is used to ensure communication between RRH and BBU. Usually, it adopts the optical fiber link, and sometimes the Free Space Optical communication (FSO) or the microwave link may be used. The transmission distance is usually 20 km to 40 km.

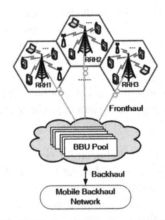

Fig. 1. Basic architecture of C-RAN

In addition, the BBU pool is connected to the mobile backhaul network through a backhaul link.

2.2 Advantages and Technical Challenges of the C-RAN Architecture

Compared with the traditional radio access network (RAN) architecture, the C-RAN architecture has many advantages as follows.

(1) Adapt to non-uniform services and different sized networks. The BBU resources in the C-RAN can be flexibly allocated and can be adaptively adjusted as the overall load in the system changes.

(2) It saves energy and cost. Research shows that C-RAN can save about 71% power consumption, 15% construction cost and 50% operating cost compared with traditional wireless access network [9, 10].

(3) Improve throughput and reduce latency. Signal processing for multiple cells can be finished in the BBU pool, which is easy to implement and reduces the latency in processing and transmission process.

(4) Easy network upgrade and maintenance. Virtualized BBU pools make software and hardware upgrades and maintenance more convenient, and software radio and other technologies can be used to software-configure new frequency bands and new standards.

The C-RAN architecture also brings some new technical challenges as follows.

(1) In the BBU pool, efficient BBU interconnection technology is required to support efficient baseband resource scheduling. The computing, communication, and storage resources for the BBU pool need to be virtualized to accommodate dynamic network load and achieve more flexible resource configuration.
(2) In terms of BBU pool and RRH connection, it is necessary to establish a transmission network that is fast, low-cost, and meets transmission delay and flutter delay.
(3) At the RRH end, the centralized processing architecture enables large-scale interference coordination and RRH cooperation, and thus it is necessary to solve problems such as efficient multi-antenna cooperation and joint radio resources scheduling.

2.3 5G C-RAN Cell Distribution Model

This paper conducts a radio access network consisting of 7-cell clusters (actual cells number in the cluster may not be 7). The cell distribution model is shown in Fig. 2.

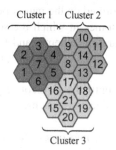

Fig. 2. C-RAN layout with a cluster of seven cells

Each cell (taking the cell No. 7 as an example) has two kinds of neighbors: a neighboring cell (cell No. 1–6) and a remote cell (such as cells No. 8, 9, 16 and 17). This paper only studies interference from neighboring cells.

In order to simplify the issue, this paper allocates resource block (RB) as the basic unit, and each RB contains all the related resources needed to provide services for one user. The system can flexibly adjust the bandwidth and allocate different numbers of RBs to different sizes of bandwidth resources. Assume that the actual available bandwidths are 3 MHz, 5 MHz, 10 MHz, 15 MHz and 20 MHz respectively, and the corresponding RBs are 6, 10, 20, 30, and 40 respectively. The goal is to find the optimal resource allocation strategy to minimize interference and optimize network performance.

3 Resource Allocation Strategy Based on IAGA

3.1 C-RAN RB Allocation Steps

Assume that each mobile user owns one RB, and the number of RBs is N_{RB}. The RB allocation consists of the following three steps:

(1) In each cluster shown in Fig. 2, the BBU pool collects user traffic and channel state information in the area covered by all RRHs. In order to simplify the issue, assuming there are no differences in user service requirements, and each user needs the same RB bandwidth and processing resources.
(2) The BBU pool uses GA to optimize the RBs allocation based on the user information fed back by each RRH, thereby improving the performance of the C-RAN system.
(3) The BBU pool sends a new optimal RB allocation decision to RRHs in each cluster to efficiently configure the mobile network.
(4) Periodically monitor the user information fed back by the RRHs and repeat steps (2) and (3) when the reallocation condition is satisfied.

3.2 GA-Based RB Allocation Algorithm

According to the principle of GA, the RB resource allocation algorithm includes the following steps:

(1) Establishing a chromosomal expression on the RB allocation problem.
(2) Genetic operations are performed on the parent population (The initial population can select a set of chromosomes in which the solution may be concentrated) to generate a new RB configuration scheme, and the next generation population is generated according to the fitness evaluation function on the new configuration scheme.
(3) Repeat the operation in 2 until the GA convergence condition is met, and an approximately optimal RB allocation scheme is obtained.

Chromosome Expression. The chromosomes represent the correspondence between RBs (numbered 1 to N_{RB}) and 7 cell users in each cluster. The RB allocation in each cluster is represented by a single chromosome, which can be represented by Ch, which is a matrix of $7 \times N_{RB}$. The row number of each chromosome matrix indicates the cell number N_C in the corresponding cluster, and the column number of the matrix indicates the user serial number N_U. The matrix item indicates the k-th RB for the i-th user in the j-th cell. Figure 3 shows an example of a chromosome expression with an N_{RB} of 6. In the figure, $Ch(3, 5) = 4$, which means that the fifth user of the third cell is assigned the RB number of 4. Assume that the initial population contains N_I chromosomes.

Genetic Manipulation. Genetic manipulation involves three operations: selection, crossover, and mutation. The first step is to choose, the BBU pool selects N_k chromosomes in the parent population according to the individual evaluation function to remain in the next generation. Followed by crossover, the goal is to generate new chromosomes based on the retained chromosomes. The crossover operation is shown in Fig. 4.

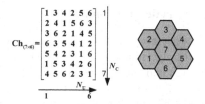

Fig. 3. Illustration of chromosome representation

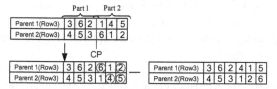

Fig. 4. Crossover operation

The new chromosomes are generated line by line. As shown in Fig. 4, the parental chromosomes are divided into two parts with the third line as the example from the parental 1 and 2 chromosomes, randomly selecting the crossover point (CP). The first step in the intersection is to connect the first part of the parent 1 and the second part of the parent 2 to form the child 1, and the first part of the parent 2 and the second part of the parent 1 are connected to the child 2. Then we find that the RB numbers 6 and 2 in the child 1 are repeated, and the RB numbers 4 and 5 in the child 2 are also repeated. On the other hand, RB numbers 4 and 5 do not appear in child 1, and RB numbers 2 and 6 do not appear in child 2. In order to obtain the final chromosomal expressions in progeny 1 and progeny 2, in step 2, namely the crossover operation, the repeated numbering is replaced with the number that does not appear.

Finally, the mutation, the BBU pool randomly selects two positions on the same line of the chromosome and exchanges their values, according to the mutation probability, and the goal is to add a certain change in the next generation population.

Evaluation Function. The evaluation function, also named the fitness function, it is the basis for the selection operation. This paper defines the evaluation function for a single cluster as

$$
C_{BW} = \frac{\sum\limits_{p=1}^{7} \sum\limits_{i} BW_{RB} \log_2\left(1 + 10^{SINR_i^p/10}\right)}{BW_{N_{RB}}}
\tag{1}
$$

Where BW_{RB} is the bandwidth of each RB (taken as 500 kHz), $BW_{N_{RB}}$ is the total bandwidth of the system (3 MHz, 5 MHz, 10 MHz, 15 MHz or 20 MHz), and $SINR_i^p$ is the signal to noise ratio when the i-th RB is allocated in the cell numbered p. The evaluation function represents the total user capacity in the cluster divided by the total bandwidth that is the spectral efficiency in the cluster.

3.3   Improved Adaptive Genetic Algorithm

To improve the convergence accuracy of the GA and accelerates the convergence speed, an improved adaptive genetic algorithm is designed by adjusting the genetic parameters adaptively. Nowadays, a large number of improved algorithms simulate the biological evolution more vividly according to the characteristics of biological evolution, so that the algorithm can converge to the optimal solution with a large probability. GA crossover and mutation are the key steps to affect the GA operation and performance.

The crossover probability is adjusted with the evolutionary process adaptively. At the beginning of evolution, the crossover probability is chosen to be larger. Such a rough search process is conducive to maintaining the population. Diversity, and in the later stages, detailed search is needed to prevent the optimal solution from breaking down and speed up the convergence.

Adaptive mutation is the process by which the probability of variation varies according to the evolutionary characteristics of the population. The general mutation probability is selected within 0.01, the mutation probability is too large, and the destructiveness to the solution is relatively large. It is easy to make the optimal solution to be lost, the mutation probability is too small, and it is prone to premature phenomenon. Therefore, the adaptive mutation probability generally takes a large to small change. In this way, extensive search at the beginning can maintain the diversity of the population, and careful search at the end will prevent the optimal solution from being destroyed. In addition, in the optimization process, the operation from extensive search to detailed search is performed multiple times. This method can make the algorithm not only ensure the comprehensiveness and accuracy of the search, but also quickly jump out of the local optimum. Quick convergence to the global optimal, experimentally proved that this mutation method has a great improvement in convergence speed and convergence precision compared with the previous adaptive algorithm, especially for multi-peak functions.

Therefore, a nonlinear adjustment to the adaptive crossover rate and mutation rate was made. First, compare the individual fitness function with the average value of the present population, and then calculate the individual's crossover rate and mutation rate by combining the best and the worst individuals. In the evolution of population, the model of excellent individuals is effectively preserved, and the ability of variation of poor individuals is enhanced, so that the algorithm can jump out of the local optimal solution and overcome the premature point. Compared with GA, the new algorithm is simpler and memorizes less. The old individual can adaptively adjust its crossover rate and mutation rate according to the adaptability of surrounding individuals. Experiments show that the new algorithm converges faster and has better stability.

The adaptive crossover rate and mutation rate are shown in formula (2) and (3).

$$
P_c = \begin{cases} \dfrac{P_c\max - P_c\min}{1+\exp(A(\frac{2(f'-f_{avg})}{f\max - f_{avg}}-1))} + P_c\min & f' \geq f_{avg} \\ P_c\min & f' < f_{avg} \end{cases}
\tag{2}
$$

$$
P_m = \begin{cases} \dfrac{P_m\max - P_m\min}{1+\exp(A(\frac{2(f'-f_{avg})}{f\max - f_{avg}}-1))} + P_m\min & f' \geq f_{avg} \\ P_m\min & f' < f_{avg} \end{cases}
\tag{3}
$$

Where f' is the fitness function of a single individual in a population, f_{avg} is the average fitness function of the population under the present iteration, f_{max} is the best fitness function for the population under the present iteration, the maximum value of the crossover rate $P_{cmax} = 1.0$, the minimum value of the crossover rate $P_{cmin} = 0.75$, the maximum value of the mutation rate $P_{mmax} = 0.25$, the minimum value of the mutation rate $P_{mmin} = 0.05$, and $A = 9.903438$.

Based on the above analysis, a GA/IAGA-based C-RAN resource allocation flowchart as shown in Fig. 5 can be obtained. Where g represents the number of iterations, and G represents the maximum number of iterations to ensure GA convergence, which is also known as GA convergence parameters. The initial population construction is randomly selected in a possible solution set.

4   Simulation Results

The simulation parameters settings are shown in Table 1.

Table 1. Simulation parameters for RAWGA in C-RAN

Parameter	Value
Bandwidth of each RB	500 kHz
Total bandwidth in the system	5 MHz
Number of cells in per cluster	7-cell
User distribution	Random uniform distribution
Number of RBs for per user	1

Figure 6 shows the curve indicating the evaluation function C_{BW} as a function of the iterations number g. In the figure, a 7-cell cluster model (Fig. 2) is used, and each cell has 20 users. The initial population has a chromosome number N_I of 30, the number of available RBs is 30, and the maximum number of iterations is $G = 80$. The crossover probability and mutation probability are respectively 0.75 and 0.05. It can be seen from the figure that as the g increases, the evaluation function increases and quickly converges to a stable value.

With the same parameters, based on IAGA, the curve of evaluation function C_{BW} as a function of the iterations number g is shown in Fig. 7. Obviously, it can be seen that the GA originally oscillates the optimal value around 50 generations. Now in Fig. 7 after only 20 generations can converge to the sub-optimal value and 30 generations can get the optimal value.

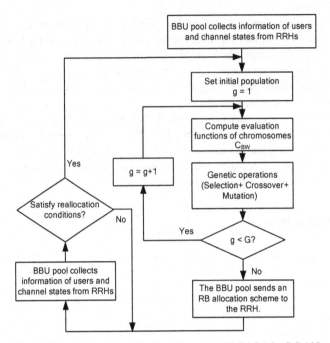

Fig. 5. Flowchart of the RB allocation with GA/IAGA in C-RAN

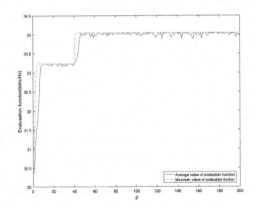

Fig. 6. Evaluation function C_{BW} change with g (GA)

Figure 8 gives the final optimization results based on IAGA, GA and the Universal Frequency Reuse (UFR) rules. It shows that the spectral efficiency of the RB allocation algorithm based on IAGA/GA has been improved evidently. And the closer the spectrum resource is to the number of users, the more advantage the optimization result of the IAGA/GA algorithm is. And the IAGA algorithm is greatly improved compared with the GA algorithm, except for the case of cell users equals 30. The reason why the IAGA is slightly worse than the GA when the number of cell users is equal to 30 is that the IAGA

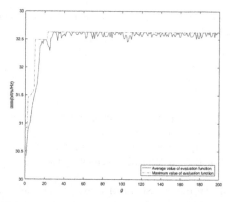

Fig. 7. Evaluation function C_{BW} change with g (IAGA)

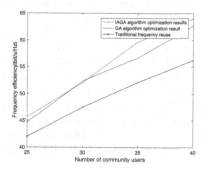

Fig. 8. Comparison between IAGA, GA and UFR

converges to an acceptable suboptimal solution at this point, and the GA converges to the optimal solution. This is inevitable in the course of the algorithm work, but it is acceptable under the condition that the overall performance of the algorithm is better than GA.

5 Conclusion

Resource allocation strategies based on GA and IAGA for 5G C-RAN are investigated. Firstly, collect the user information and CSI from the RRHs. Secondly, the BBU pool uses the IAGA/GA to obtain the optimal resource allocation scheme based on the collected user information. Then, send the obtained optimal resource allocation decision result to the RRHs for each cluster. Finally, it periodically monitors the RRH user and channel state information, and reallocates resources as the network changes. The performance of the proposed scheme is superior to the UFR algorithm, especially IAGA. In the future, we will optimize the resource allocation for the cloud radio access network and further improve the network performance by combining the differences in user service requirements, the virtualization implementation of the BBU pool, the intelligent network environment awareness, and the limitations on the preamble links.

Acknowledgement. This research was supported in part by the China Natural Science Foundation under Grant 61601480 and 61372099.

References

1. Saxena, N., Roy, A., Kim, H.: Traffic-aware cloud RAN: a key for green 5G networks. IEEE J. Sel. Areas Commun. **34**(4), 1010–1021 (2016)
2. Zhang, T., Tao, X., Cui, Q.: Joint multi-cell resource allocation using pure binary-integer programming for LTE uplink. In: Vehicular Technology Conference, Seoul, Korea, May 2014 (2014)
3. Noh, J.-H., Oh, S.-J.: Distributed SC-FDMA resource allocation algorithm based on the Hungarian method. In: IEEE Vehicular Technology Conference Fall, USA, September 2009 (2009)
4. Sahu, B.J.R., Dash, S., Saxena, N., Roy, A.: Energy-efficient BBU allocation for green C-RAN. IEEE Commun. Lett. **21**(7), 1637–1640 (2017)
5. Si-bo, Z.: Spectrum allocation strategy for cloud radio access network based on QoS requirements. Comput. Eng. Softw. **39**(5), 79–83 (2018)
6. Essassi, S., Hamila, R., et al.: RB allocation based on genetic algorithm in cloud radio access networks. In: 2016 International Wireless Communications and Mobile Computing Conference (IWCMC), Cyprus, September 2016, pp. 1002–1005 (2016)
7. Lin, Y., Shao, L., Zhu, Z., Wang, Q., Sabhikhi, R.K.: Wireless network cloud: architecture and system requirements. IBM J. Res. Dev. **54**(1), 4:1–4:12 (2010)
8. Zhou, S., Zhao, M., Xu, X., Wang, J., Yao, Y.: Distributed wireless communication system: a new architecture for future public wireless access. IEEE Commun. Mag. **41**(3), 108–113 (2003)
9. Chen, C.: C-RAN: the road towards green radio access network. Presentation, August 2012
10. Zhang, J., Hu, X., et al.: Energy-latency tradeoff for energy-aware offloading in mobile edge computing networks. IEEE Internet Things J. **5**(4), 2633–2645 (2018)

A Novel Adaptive Multiple-Access Scheme for Wireless Chip Area Network in the Smart Grid System

Xin-Yue Luo, Hao Gao, and Xue-Hua Li[✉]

School of Information and Communication Engineering,
Beijing Information Science and Technology University, Beijing, China
lixuehua@bistu.edu.com.cn

Abstract. The design and construction of the smart grid system in 5G ultra-dense network needs to be effectively integrated with the mobile communication technology. Wireless chip area network (WCAN), as an application of the smart grid, has promising research potential. Focusing on the issue of multi-user network communication, this paper proposes an adaptive time-hopping pulse position modulation (TH-PPM) multiple access scheme that is applicable to WCAN. Combined with the specific applications of WCAN, the wireless channel characteristics of intra/inter chip communication are investigated, the bit error rate (BER) performance of the THPPM multiple-access system is analyzed; then, based on the aforementioned results, an adaptive TH-PPM multiple-access distribution mechanism is proposed and an intelligent transmission mechanism is designed to appropriately select the monopulse signal-to-noise ratio of the intra/inter chip, BER, and transmission rate in WCAN. Finally, the performance is analyzed through simulation and is also compared with the fixed multiple-access technology. The results show that on the premise of ensuring wireless interconnection quality of service of the intra/inter chip, this scheme can allocate system rate and power resource properly, strengthen transmission performance, and address the limitations of fixed multiple-access technology. The findings presented in this paper provide a reference for multi-user multiple-access communication with large capacity.

Keywords: Smart grid · 5G technology · Chip wireless interconnection · Wireless chip area network · Adaptive TH-PPM

1 Introduction

With the increasing demand for electricity, the load on the power grid construction has also increased. The traditional grid operation mode has become increasingly incapable [1]. Therefore, the demand for smart grids with high speed, high integration and good real-time performance is on the rise. In the smart grid,

© ICST Institute for Computer Sciences, Social Informatics and Telecommunications Engineering 2020
Published by Springer Nature Switzerland AG 2020. All Rights Reserved
X. Zhang et al. (Eds.): CloudComp 2019/SmartGift 2019, LNICST 322, pp. 685–698, 2020.
https://doi.org/10.1007/978-3-030-48513-9_55

mobile communication technologies are needed to assist the completion in order to acquire, analyze and process the grid data better, providing reliable power protection for the stable development of society [2].

In the future, mobile communication will occur not only between persons, but will also develop into intelligent interconnections between persons and things, among sensor devices, among intelligent chips, from machine to machine (M2M), and from device to device (D2D), all of which will account for more than 70% of mobile data service. The research on 5G technologies currently focuses on dense networks, device-to-device technology, new-type network architecture, high-band communication, new-type multiple antenna multiple distribution transmission technologies, for the purpose of increasing 4G transmission rate 101000 times, decreasing network delay 510 times and realizing wireless communication with low power consumption and high spectral efficiency [3]. In recent years, the remarkable development of intra/inter-chip wireless intercommunication technology based on high-band UWB and 60 GHz millimeter waves [4–9] has provided technical support to achieve the aforementioned goal as well as to provide a new application situation for 5G super-dense network, namely, wireless chip area network (WCAN). This development can achieve high-speed interconnection and efficient network organization [7–12] of inner integrated circuits, intra/inter chips in PCB, multiprocessor cores in system-on-chip (SoC) circuits, intelligent appliances, and mobile terminals. However, most current research on-chip wireless interconnection technology focuses on point-to-point wireless communication of single users and the transmission data are relatively limited. The application of WCAN is definitely the mode of communication with a large amount of data in the context of multiple users; multi-user interference and inter-symbol interference are the problems that must be considered. Simple modulation schemes such as OOK [4] and BPSK [5–7] cannot meet the requirements of actual application while the OFDM scheme [8] increases the design complexity. Although multiple-access technologies such as TDMA, CDMA, DSBPSK, and TH-PPM are adopted to achieve multiple Intra/inter-chip wireless interconnection [13–17], all of these are at the level of circuit design and BER performance is not analyzed. Meanwhile, the fixed multiple-access distribution scheme adopted wastes the resources when users are few and cannot meet the requirements of system performance when users are many. As a result, a more effective multiple-access technology is needed to raise the transmission performance of the system. An adaptive multiple-access scheme applicable to specific applications of WCAN should be investigated.

This paper is organized as follows. The research background is introduced in Sect. 1. TH-PPM multiple-access performance in WCAN is analyzed in Sect. 2. An adaptive multiple-address design scheme based on TH-PPM is proposed in Sect. 3. The advantages of the proposed scheme compared with those of the traditional fixed multiple-access mechanism are presented in Sect. 4. The research findings are summarized in Sect. 5.

2   Performance Analysis of TH-PPM Multiple-Access in WCAN

In the multiple-access technology based on high-band IR-UWB and 60 GHz pulse radio, TH-PPM technology is comparatively mature. TH-PPM separates pulse repetition period into several time slots by taking advantage of the feature of the minimum duty cycle of UWB pulse signal and combining it with TDMA and CDMA technologies. TH-PPM distinguishes users by different pseudo-random time-hopping codes, and controls pulse position by using data symbols. Compared with DS-BPSK [15], TH-PPM does not need to control the pulse amplitude and polarity requires lower sensitivity with regard to near-far effect and reduces the difficulty of power control, which easily achieves high-speed communication of multiple I/O devices or multiple chips by lower complexity in a shorter distance. In the multichannel context, problems related to crosstalk and resource allocation can be solved by setting the matched multiple-access methods in the layer of MAC. In terms of reducing system complexity and power consumption, the TH-PPM multiple-access modulation technology is suitable for intra/inter-chip wireless interconnection systems. The TH-PPM multiple access technology is adopted in references [16] and [17] to achieve multi-user data-parallel transmission in intra/inter-chip wireless interconnection systems; the circuit design scheme is proposed, but the BER performance is not analyzed. In this section of the current paper, the intra/inter-chip physical channel characteristics, multi-user interference characteristics of intra/inter-chip adopting TH-PPM, noise source, and BER performance are analyzed.

2.1   Intra/Inter-chip Physical Channel Characteristics

The characteristics of a channel, as an indispensable part of the system, has a significant effect on the system performance and design. In the current WCAN networking schemes, intra/inter-chip closely adopts multi-hop self-organizing communications. Electromagnetic signals are line-of-sight transmissions in adjacent processor cores or chips. A simple intra-chip wireless interconnection model and an inter-chip wireless interconnection model are separately shown in Figs. 1(a) and 1(b) [18]. The transmission distance of the intra/inter-chip wireless channel is usually at the level of cm or even mm, and the energy of surface wave accounts for more than 80% of the total energy. The multipath delay is negligible, so the channel can be considered as a Rice channel. Under the ideal medium, the advantage of the surface wave becomes highly obvious, and the Rice factor K value tends to infinity at that moment, so that the intra/inter-chip the channel can be approximately considered as a Gaussian channel. For the sake of theoretical analysis, the Gaussian channel is taken as a channel in this research model and the WCAN composed of chip wireless interconnection in the PCB is the research subject.

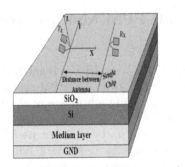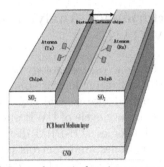

(a) Intra-chip wireless interconnec-(b) Inter-chip wireless interconnection model   tion model

Fig. 1. wireless interconnection model

2.2   Analysis of Multi-user Interference Characteristics in System

In WCAN, the TH-PPM signal of user can be expressed as [16,17,19]:

$$s^{(k)}(t) = \sum_{j=-\infty}^{\infty} \sqrt{E_w} p_{tr} \left(t - jT_f - c_j^{(k)} T_c - \delta d_{[j/N_s]}^{(k)} \right) \tag{1}$$

$p_{tr}(t)$ is an energy normalized monocycle pulse waveform, that is, $\int_{-\infty}^{\infty} |p_{tr}|^2 \, dt = 1$. Its pulse width is T_p, its chip duration is T_c, and $T_p \leq T_c$. $N_h = T_f/T_c$ is the upper limit of maximum value of time-hopping code, T_f is the frame length, $0 \leq c_j^{(k)} < N_h$ is the pseudo-random time-hopping code sequence of user K(user address code), $\lfloor x \rfloor$ represents rounding to x. $d_j^{(k)} \in [0,1]$ is a binary value of the jth pulse transmission of user K. N_s is pulse number of per bit; average pulse repetition period of per bit can be expressed as $T_s = N_s T_f$, so the information bit rate is $R_b = (N_s T_f)^{-1} = (N_s N_h T_c)^{-1}$. δ represents PPM deviation, E_w indicates normalized monocycle pulse waveform energy, and $E_b = N_s E_w$ is information energy per bit. The mentioned relationship is shown by Gaussian pulse waveform in Fig. 2.

To analyze the transmission performance of users in WCAN, the following hypotheses are set:

1. users conduct wireless communications in the system; 0 and 1 with equal probability occurrence and independent identical distribution in the data sequence are produced by all users.
2. Pseudo-noise (PN) code adopted by each user is a gold code, which occurs at random and is mutually independent and equiprobable.
3. For the purpose of improved system flexibility, the antenna gain of receiver and transmitter is 0 dBi.
4. Each user adopts coherent reception, and its specific PN code is known when reception occurs and the soft decision is implemented after detection.

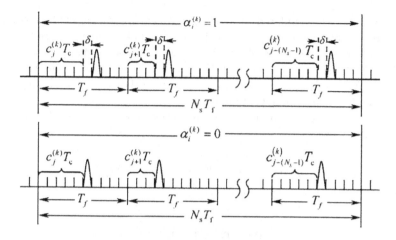

Fig. 2. TH-PPM modulation waveform

5. The system is an asynchronous self-organizing network, but it is based on the assumption that adopting coherent detection, reference receiver, and the corresponding transmitter is totally synchronous.
6. All users can spread ideally and freely without multi-path influence.

Channel impulsion response without multi-path of kth user and its reference receiver is the function of path loss A_k and transmission time delay τ_k. Transmission time delay is mutually independent and it obeys uniform distribution in $[0, T_c)$. Then, in the same environment condition when k users implement transmitting, the total signal received by the reference receiver is

$$
r(t) = \sum_{k=0}^{N_u-1} A_k s_{rec}^{(k)}(t - \tau_k) + n(t)
$$

$$
= A_0 s_{rec}^{(0)}(t - \tau_0) + \sum_{k=1}^{N_u-1} A_k s_{rec}^{(k)}(t - \tau_k) + n(t)
$$

(2)

In decision, because of coherent detection, the signals from the other users are considered as multi-user inference. Let user 0 be the main receiving signal, and then $S_{rec}^{(0)}(t - \tau_0)$ in Eq. (2) is a useful signal; $\sum_{k=1}^{N_u-1} A_k s_{rec}^{(k)}(t - \tau_k)$ is the multi-user inference signal, where $s_{rec}^{(k)}(t)$ is the receiving signal of user k, and as a result of transient characteristics of high-frequency pulse signal, the waveform of should be the second-order differential of transmitting signal $p^{(k)}(t)$. $n(t)$ indicates two types of noise, namely, thermal and switching, that mainly occur in the intra/inter-chip wireless interconnection system [7]. The value of switching noise is usually 10 dB less than that of thermal noise, and its bilateral power spectrum density is $N_0/2$. According to the calculation method of noise power spectrum in [7], the regulated receiving antenna temperature of the intra/inter-chip wireless interconnection system is $T_{ant} = 330K$ and the regulated noise index of the receiver is $F_r = 10\,dB$; thus, thermal noise power spectrum density can be calculated as $-163.92\,dBm/Hz$. Now, the total noise power spectrum density is $N_0 = N_{thermal} + N_{switting} = -163.504\,dBm/Hz$, and this value is used in the following simulation analysis.

When user 0 receiver performs the detection, correlation masks need to be provided as follows:

$$m^{(0)}(t) = \sum_{j=0}^{N_s-1} v^{(0)}\left(t - jT_f - c_j^{(0)}T_c\right) \tag{3}$$

$$v^{(0)}(t) = p_{rec}^{(0)}(t) - p_{rec}^{(0)}(t - \delta) \tag{4}$$

Receiving signal $r(t)$ is multiplied by $m^{(0)}(t - \tau_0)$ and the calculating output is

$$Z^{(0)} = \int_0^{T_b} r(t)m^{(0)}(t - \tau_0)\,dt \tag{5}$$

Place Eqs. (1) (2) (3) (4) in Eq. (5) as follows:

$$Z^{(0)} = Z_0 + Z_{mui} + Z_n \tag{6}$$

In the equation, Z_0 is useful user correlation detection output, Z_{mui} is multi-user interference, and Z_n is Gaussian noise correlation output. According to reference [20]

$$Z_0 = N_s \int_{-\infty}^{\infty} A_0\sqrt{E_w}s_{rec}^{(0)}(t - \tau_0)m^{(0)}(t - \tau_0)dt$$

$$= \begin{cases} +A_0 N_s \sqrt{E_w}[1 - r(\delta)] & d_j^{(0)} = 0 \\ -A_0 N_s \sqrt{E_w}[1 - r(\delta)] & d_j^{(0)} = 1 \end{cases} \tag{7}$$

$$Z_n = \sum_{k=1}^{N_u}\sum_{j=0}^{N_s-1}\int_{\tau_0+jT_f}^{\tau_0+(j+1)T_f} n(t)[p_{rec}^{(0)}(t - jT_f - c_j^{(0)}T - \tau_0)$$
$$- p_{rec}^{(0)}(t - jT_f - c_j^{(0)}T - \delta - \tau_0)]dt \tag{8}$$

$$Z_{mui} = \sum_{k=1}^{N_u}\sum_{j=1}^{N_s-1}\int_{\tau_0+jT_f}^{\tau_0+(j+1)T_f} A_k s_{rec}^{(k)}(t - \tau_k)[p_{rec}^{(0)}(t - jT_f - c_j^{(0)}T - \tau_0)$$
$$- p_{rec}^{(0)}(t - jT_f - c_j^{(0)}T - \delta - \tau_0)]dt \tag{9}$$

2.3   Performance Analysis of System Signal-to-Interference and Noise Ratio and BER

Since each user suffers the same degree of interference in WCAN, the transmission performance of the entire network can be measured according to the BER performance of signals received by each user. BER is the function of signal-to-interference and noise ratio (SINR), and determining the value of SINR in WCAN is extremely important. SINR and BER are analyzed when each chip conducts wireless communication in WCAN. Based on the correlation detection equations illustrated in Sect. 2.2, the sum of useful energy of N_s pulses that compose a 1 bit output in the receiver is

$$E_b = E\left(Z_0^2\right) = E_w^{(0)} A_0^2 N_s^2 [1 - r(\delta)]^2 \tag{10}$$

For system flexibility, let the antenna gain of receiver and transmitter G_{tx} and G_{rx} be 0 dBi. If the distance between the transmitting antenna and the receiving antenna is d, then the wavelength of the antenna is λ, and path loss A_0^2 can be obtained according to the transmission loss model of space free wave as follows:

$$A_o^2 = G_{tx} G_{rx} \left(\frac{\lambda}{4\pi d}\right)^2 \tag{11}$$

The variance of output noise of the receiver is

$$\sigma_n^2 = E\left(Z_n^2\right) = N_s N_0 [1 - r(\delta)] \tag{12}$$

Reference [21] uses probability statistics to get multi-user interference variance, and combining with Eq. (9), multi-user interference variance in 1 bit is

$$\sigma_{mii}^2 = E\left(Z_{mi}^2\right) = \frac{T_p}{T_f} N_s [1 - r(\delta)]^2 \sum_{k=1}^{N_i-1} A_k^2 E_w^{(k)} \tag{13}$$

Since Z_{mui} and Z_n obey Gaussian distribution with the mean value being 0 and the variances being σ_{mui}^2 and σ_n^2 separately, the SINR of the system is

$$\begin{aligned}
SMR &= \frac{E_b}{\sigma_{mi}^2 + \sigma_n^2} \\
&= \frac{E_w^{(0)} \hat{f}^2 N_s^2 [1 - r(\delta)]}{\frac{T_p}{T_f} N_s [1 - r(\delta)]^2 \sum_{k=1}^{N-1} A^2 E_w^{(k)} + N_s N_0 [1 - r(\delta)]}
\end{aligned} \tag{14}$$

To decrease intersymbol interference and maintain good transmission performance, quadrature PPM modulation is used in WCAN-PCB. When $T_c \geq 2T_p$, let $T_c = \beta T_p$, then $1/\beta$ expresses the duty cycle of pulse and $\beta \geq 2$, and now the coherent coefficient is $r(\delta) = 0$. Meanwhile, to facilitate analysis, we suppose that path loss A_k is the same in the transmission of each link among chips, and if $SNR = \frac{E_w A_o^2}{N_0}$ expresses the SNR of unit pulse, then Eq. (14) is simplified as

$$SINR = \frac{N_s}{\frac{T_p(N_u-1)}{T_c N_h} + \frac{N_0}{E_w A_0^2}} = \frac{N_s}{\frac{N_u-1}{\beta N_h} + \frac{1}{SNR}} \tag{15}$$

According to the relationship between SINR and BER, and based on TH-PPM multiple-access modulation technology, the BER formula of a multiple inter-chip wireless interconnection system is expressed as

$$BER = \frac{1}{2}\,\text{erfc}\left(\sqrt{\frac{SINR}{2}}\right) = \frac{1}{2}\,\text{erfc}\left(\sqrt{\frac{N_s}{\frac{2(N_u-1)}{\beta N_h} + \frac{2}{SNR}}}\right) \tag{16}$$

From Eqs. (15) and (16), we find that the values of multi-user SINR and BER in WCAN-PCB are correlated with β (reciprocal value of pulse duty cycle, which depends on the values of T_p and T_c, generally fixed value), N_u (number of users), N_s (number of pulses of each bit), N_h (upper limit of maximum value of time-hopping code), SNR (signal-to-noise ratio of unit pulse), among which the values of N_s and N_h decide the bit transmission rate R_b of users, and SNR and N_s decide the transmitting power of the system.

3   Design of Adaptive TH-PPM Multiple-Access Distribution Scheme in WCAN

In WCAN, because of random access of chips to a certain extent, the network topology structure shows dynamic change, and in the system, noise interference and channel characteristics change randomly. In the wireless communication system, link adaptive technology is used to solve the problems of signal loss and transmission quality decrease caused by a random chance of the channel with multiple users, in which adaptive modulation coding technology and adaptive multiple-access resource distribution technology are used widely. However, adaptive modulation coding technology requires various types of modulation and coding circuits in chips, which is unacceptable to the chip wireless interconnection system because the complex system has strict cost and design requirements. Comparatively, adaptive multiple-access resource distribution technology does not need an additional modulation coding circuit, and automatic distribution of system resources is achieved by real-time adjustment of rate and power, and in this way, this technology is superior to the former in terms of design complexity and cost. For example, a scheme of self-adaptive adjusting code length dynamically proposed in references [22] and [23] can guarantee a higher transmission rate of nodes regardless of power limitation. The TH-PPM multiple-access scheme specific to the WCAN system proposed in [16] and [17] solves multi-user interference to a certain extent, but the scheme adopts a fixed multiple-access mechanism (FMAM) that cannot meet the requirements of changeable

QoS, that is, FMAM may waste considerable system resources when the channel environment is good while communication may not be guaranteed when the channel environment is bad. In this section, an adaptive multiple-access mechanism (AMAM) based on TH-PPM is proposed, which can alter the transmission rate or transmitting power in real-time and select the best resource distribution scheme automatically according to the channel environment; under the demand of QoS, the mechanism can enable the entire system to maintain high communication capacity and low power. Weighing quality, rate, and power of communication is the core of an adaptive algorithm. The adaptive multiple-access distribution scheme in WCAN is shown in Fig. 3.

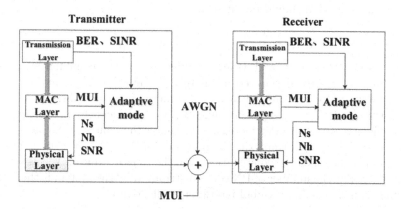

Fig. 3. Adaptive multiple-access distribution scheme in WCAN

In Fig. 3, because N_u and β are known, the BER performance of the system is related to the selection of N_s, N_h, and SNR, and as a result, according to MUI and thermal noise interference originating from various N_u, the adaptive mode chooses the best multiple-access distribution scheme, allowing the entire system to remain relatively stable. The selection process is shown as follows:

1) To guarantee the stability of the system, the value of BER cannot exceed the regulated threshold of QoS, as shown in Table 1, so N_s, N_h, and SNR must meet Eq. (17). From the perspective of elevating resource utilization in maximum, the SINR value of the best multiple-access distribution scheme should be a threshold that meets the regulation of QoS. At this point, if N_s and N_h are confirmed, then the corresponding SNR is obtained.

Table 1. BER upper limit and corresponding SINR threshold required by QoS.

BER level	10^{-4}	10^{-5}	10^{-6}	10^{-7}	10^{-8}	10^{-9}
Required SINR	13.8311	18.1893	22.5950	27.0331	31.4946	35.9737

$$SINR = \frac{N_s}{\frac{N_u - 1}{\beta N_h} + \frac{1}{SNR}} \geq SINR_{\text{trashdd}} \tag{17}$$

2) When the system meets the requirements of QoS, to enable the system to maintain lower power consumption, the SNR threshold of each user should be defined as follows:

$$SNR = \frac{1}{\frac{N_s}{SINR_{\text{treshold}}} - \frac{N_u - 1}{N_h \beta}} \leq SNR_{\text{threshold}} \tag{18}$$

3) To guarantee high-speed transmission for each user in the system, when steps 1) and 2) are finished, the smaller value of $N_s \times N_h$ needs to be selected. The following equation should be satisfied:

$$MIN\,[N_s \times N_h] \leq N_s \times N_h \leq MIN\,[N_s \times N_h] + 3 \tag{19}$$

4) After step 1), steps 2) and 3) are completed, and the combination value of N_s and N_h has to be selected ultimately. If the value of N_s is significantly larger, the pulse transmitted by each bit increases, which then increases the total transmitting power; if the value of N_h is significantly larger, the design complexity of the encoder increases. To weigh the values of N_s and N_h and decrease the design complexity, if the values of $N_s \times N_h$ in several combinations are close, then the combination with the largest value of $N_h^{N_s}$ is selected; at this point, the number of PN codes distributed by the system is the largest, which can reduce intersymbol interference effectively.

The combination of N_s, N_h and SNR selected through the aforementioned algorithm is the best multiple-access distribution scheme, and furthermore, the corresponding bit rate R_b of the signal user and the average power P_{ave} are obtained from the following equations:

$$R_b = \frac{1}{N_s N_h T_c} \tag{20}$$

$$P_{\text{ave}} = \frac{N_s \times SNR \times N_0}{T_c} \tag{21}$$

4   Performance Simulation and Analysis

Based on the adaptive multiple-access distribution scheme proposed in the previous section, the change tendency of information rate R_b and average power P_{ave} of each user in the system following the number of access users N_u is comparatively analyzed through simulation under the AMAM and FMAM schemes separately.

The simulation parameters are set as follows: $N_0 = -163.504\,\text{dBm/Hz}$, $SNR_{\text{threshold}} = 15\,\text{dB}$, $f_c = 10\,\text{GHz}$, $\beta = 8$, $BER = 10^{-4}$. FMAM adopts a fixed parameter setting, while AMAM selects the optimal multiple-access distribution scheme that matches the number of access users Nu in real time according to the change of number.

4.1 Relationship Between Number of Users N_u and Information Rate R_b

The value of R_b reflects the speed of data transmission of the intra/inter chip. Figure 4 shows the relationship between N_u and R_b under the AMAM and FMAM schemes. R_{bi} expresses the rate value of ith FMAM for a single user, and the simulation results show that as long as the values of N_{si} and N_{hi} are defined, the value of R_{bi} is invariable and is inversely proportional to the value of $N_{si} \times N_{ki}$ and unrelated to the value of N_u. Meanwhile, each FMAM corresponds to one $Nu_{\max i}$ that means the maximum number of users supported by the communication system with reliable quality. Once the number of user access has exceeded the maximum, the communication quality of the system is lost. For example, FMAM with [SNR = 15 dB, NsNh (3,4)], although $R_{\aleph 1} = 833$ Mbps has a higher transmission rate, only when the number of users is fewer than six can the communication quality be guaranteed; thus, this FMAM does not apply to the system with many users. However, FMAM with [SNR = 15 dB, NsNh (4,20)], although transmission quality can be guaranteed even if N_u exceeds 40, its transmission rate only reaches 125 Mbps. In this situation, if the number of users is fewer, the rate resource is wasted. Comparatively, according to N_u, AMAM can choose the best resource distribution scheme adaptively and adjust the value of R_b. In this way, on the premise of a reliable communication system, resources can be fully utilized. The disadvantage of uneven resource distribution of FMAM is overcome and the transmission rate is higher than that of FMAM.

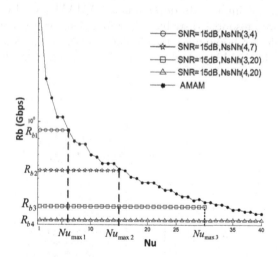

Fig. 4. Relationship between N_u and R_b under AMAM and FMAM

4.2   Relationship Between N_u and P_{ave} Average Power

The value of average power P_{ave} reflects the power consumption level of an intra/inter-chip wireless interconnection system. Figure 5 shows the relationship between N_u and P_{ave} under the schemes of AMAM and FMAM separately. In Fig. 5, each FMAM corresponds to a fixed P_{ave} and when the SNR of each pulse is certain, the value of P_{ave} is proportional to the number of pulse N_s. For example, for FMAM with the same rate, such as [SNR = 15 dB, NsNh(3,8)] and [SNR = 15 dB, NsNh(8,3)], the P_{ave} that the former corresponds to is smaller than the P_{ave} that the latter corresponds to. In addition, as described in Sect. 4.1, each FMAM also corresponds to one $Nu_{max\,i}$, which indicates the maximum number of users supported by the communication system with reliable quality. For example, when SNR = 15 dB, the schemes of NsNh(3,8), NsNh(8,3), NsNh(12,3), and NsNh(20,3) that correspond to the values of $Nu_{max\,i}$ are 12, 14, 21, and 35 separately. However, the disadvantages of FMAM are that only if $N_u = N_{u\,max\,i}$ can the system resource be fully used; if $N_u < N_{u\,max\,i}$, then a large amount of system resource is wasted; if $N_u > N_{u\,max\,i}$, system reliability is not guaranteed. In the AMAM scheme, the power P can be adjusted timely according to the number of users in the system, that is, the reduction of N_u decreases the power while the increment of N_u properly raises the power to resist MUI. AMAM keeps the system relatively stable and, compared with FMAM, it has a higher utilization rate of energy.

Although the AMAM scheme raises the complexity of chip design to a certain extent, with the constant increase of hardware design level, its relatively higher complexity does not impede its development. AMAM has obvious advantages in rate and power resource distribution, and it can utilize maximum system resource and relieve random noise interference caused by random change of user access. As a result, AMAM is highly applicable and indispensable to WCAN.

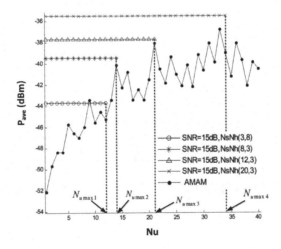

Fig. 5. Relationship between N_u and P_{ave} under AMAM and FMAM

5 Conclusion

Intra/inter-chip wireless interconnection technology complements the smart grid system to compensate for the shortcomings of traditional grid operation modes. With the promotion of 5G technologies, WCAN is becoming one of the applications of the 5G ultra dense network. To solve the problem of multi-user network communication in WCAN, the multi-user interference characteristics of WCAN under TH-PPM multiple-access modulation are analyzed, and the system BER performance analytical model is proposed. Based on this model and by weighing communication quality, rate, and power consumption, the adaptive multiple-access scheme applicable to WCAN is designed. Performance simulation and analysis show that this scheme can guarantee the reliability of intra/inter-chip interconnection, allocate system resources appropriately, and elevate system capacity and transmission performance effectively. At the same time, this scheme reduces realization complexity and power consumption. The results provide a reference for multi-user communication and large capacity in the smart grid system.

Acknowledgment. This study was supported by the Beijing Natural Science Foundation - Foundation of Municipal Commission of Education (KZ201911232046), the Beijing Natural Science Foundation - Haidian Original Innovation Joint Fund Focused on Special Projects (L182039), and the Beijing Natural Science Foundation - Haidian Primitive Innovation Joint Fund Frontier Project (L182032). The authors declare no conflict of interest.

References

1. Dragičević, T., Siano, P., Prabaharan, S.R.: Future generation 5G wireless networks for smart grid: a comprehensive review. Energies **12**(11), 2140 (2019)
2. Ma, K., Liu, X., Liu, Z., et al.: Cooperative relaying strategies for smart grid communications: bargaining models and solutions. IEEE Internet Things J. **4**(6), 2315–2325 (2017)
3. Akpakwu, G.A., Silva, B.J., Hancke, G.P., et al.: A survey on 5G networks for the Internet of Things: communication technologies and challenges. IEEE Access **6**, 3619–3647 (2017)
4. Foulon, S., Pruvost, S., Loyez, C., et al.: A 10GBits/s 2.1pJ/bit OOK demodulator at 60GHz for chip-to-chip wireless communication. In: 2012 IEEE Radio and Wireless Symposium (RWS), Santa Clara, CA, pp. 291–294 (2012)
5. Afroz, S., Amir, M.F., Saha, A., et al.: A 10Gbps UWB transmitter for wireless inter-chip and intra-chip communication. In: 2010 International Conference on Electrical and Computer Engineering (ICECE), pp. 104–107 (2010)
6. Kubota, S., Toya, A., Sugitani, T., et al.: 5-Gb/s and 10-GHz center-frequency Gaussian monocycle pulse transmission using 65-nm logic CMOS with on-chip dipole antenna and high-κ interposer. IEEE Trans. Compon. Packag. Manuf. Technol. **4**(7), 1193–1200 (2014)
7. Wang, G., Xiang, W., Yuan, J.: Outage performance for compute-and-forward in generalized multi-way relay channels. IEEE Commun. Lett. **16**(12), 2099–2102 (2012)

8. Peng, Y., et al.: Secret key generation based on estimated channel state information for TDD-OFDM systems over fading channels. IEEE Trans. Wirel. Commun. **16**(8), 5176–5186 (2017)

9. Yeh, H.H.: Developments of 60 GHZ antenna and wireless interconnect inside multichip module for parallel processor system. University of Arizona, Tucson, AZ (2013)

10. Karim, M.R., Yang, X., Shafique, M.F.: On chip antenna measurement: a survey of challenges and recent trends. IEEE Access **6**, 20320–20333 (2018)

11. Gimeno, C., Flandre, D., Bol, D.: Analysis and specification of an IR-UWB transceiver for high-speed chip-to-chip communication in a server chassis. IEEE Trans. Circuits Syst. I Regul. Pap. **65**(6), 2015–2023 (2017)

12. Catania, V., Mineo, A., Monteleone, S., et al.: Improving energy efficiency in wireless network-on-chip architectures[J]. ACM Journal on Emerging Technologies in Computing Systems (JETC) **14**(1) (2018). Article No. 9

13. Bidwai, S.S., Bidwai, S.S., Mandrupkar, S.G.: Wireless NoC-a revolutionary alternative as interconnection fabric. In: 2018 3rd International Conference for Convergence in Technology (I2CT), pp. 1–4. IEEE (2018)

14. Vijayakumaran, V., Yuvaraj, M.P., Mansoor, N., et al.: CDMA enabled wireless network-on-chip. ACM J. Emerg. Technol. Comput. Syst. (JETC) **10**(4) (2014). Article No. 28

15. Raju, S., Salahuddin, S.M., Islam, M.S., et al.: DSSS IR UWB transceiver for intra/inter chip wireless interconnect in future ULSI using reconfigurable monocycle pulse. In: 2008 International Conference on Computer and Communication Engineering, ICCCE 2008, pp. 306–309. IEEE (2008)

16. Saha, P.K., Sasaki, N., Kikkawa, T.: A CMOS UWB transmitter for intra/interchip wireless communication. In: 2004 IEEE Eighth International Symposium on Spread Spectrum Techniques & Applications, Australia, pp. 962–966 (2004)

17. He, J., Zhang, Y.P.: A CMOS ultra-wideband impulse radio transceiver for interchip wireless communications. In: 2007 IEEE International Conference on Ultra-Wideband, Singapore, pp. 626–631 (2007)

18. Kim, K.: Design and characterization of RF components for inter and intra-chip wireless communications. Ph.D dissertation, Gainesville, University of Florida, FL (2000)

19. Scholtz, R.A.: Multiple access with time-hopping impulse modulation. In: Military Communications Conference, Boston, MA, pp. 447–450 (1993)

20. Long, H., et al.: Secrecy capacity enhancement with distributed precoding in multirelay wiretap systems. IEEE Trans. Inf. Forensics Secur. **8**(1), 229–238 (2012)

21. Qiu, H.B., Zheng, L.: New method of BER calculate for impulse-UWB TH-PPM multiple-access communications. J. Commun. **10**, 133–137 (2005)

22. Le Boudec, J.Y., Merz, R., Radunovic, B., et al.: A MAC protocol for UWB very low power mobile ad-hoc networks based on dynamic channel coding with interference mitigation (2004)

23. Biradar, G.S., Merchant, S.N., Desai, U.B.: An adaptive frequency and time hopping PPM UWB for multiple access communication. In: 2007 6th International Conference on Information, Communications & Signal Processing, pp. 1–5. IEEE (2007)

Author Index

Printed in the United States
By Bookmasters